Professional Web Services Security

Ben Galbraith
Whitney Hankison
Andre Hiotis
Murali Janakiraman
Prasad D. V.
Ravi Trivedi
David Whitney

with
Vamsi Motukuru

Wrox Press Ltd. ®

Professional Web Services Security

First Printed in December 2002

Published by Wrox Press Ltd,
Arden House, 1102 Warwick Road, Acocks Green,
Birmingham, B27 6BH, UK
Printed in the United States
ISBN 1-86100-765-5

Trademark Acknowledgements

Wrox has endeavored to provide trademark information about all the companies and products mentioned in this book by the appropriate use of capitals. However, Wrox cannot guarantee the accuracy of this information.

Credits

Authors
Ben Galbraith
Whitney Hankison
Andre Hiotis
Murali Janakiraman
Prasad D. V.
Ravi Trivedi
David Whitney

Contributing Author
Vamsi Motukuru

Technical Reviewers
Hemant Adarkar
Francis Botto
Christopher Browne
Margarita Isayeva
Romin Irani
Eric Lippert
Ramesh Mani
Nardone Massimo
Thomas Paul
Ravi Trivedi
Abdul Wahid
Paul Wilt

Author Agent
Safiulla Shakir

Project Manager
Abbas Saifuddin Rangwala

Managing Editor
Paul Cooper

Commissioning Editor
Ranjeet Wadhwani

Technical Editors
Dipali Chittar
Anand Devsharma
Kedar Kamat

Production Coordinator
Rachel Taylor

Production and Layout
Santosh Haware
Manjiri Karande

Index
Vinod Shenoy

Proof Reader
Jennifer Williams

Editorial Thanks
Andrew Polshaw
Arunkumar Nair

Special Thanks
Abhishek Gupta

About the Authors

Ben Galbraith

Before graduating from high school, Ben Galbraith was hired by a major Silicon Valley computer manufacturer to develop Windows-based client-server applications with international deployments and hundreds of users. In 1995, he began developing for the Web and fell in love with Unix, vi, and Perl. After building countless web applications with Perl, Ben discovered server-side Java in 1999 and his relationship with Perl has since become somewhat estranged.

Mr. Galbraith is presently a consultant in Provo, Utah. He regularly lectures, evangelizes and gives classes on Java technology. Ben has no college degree but if he had the time he would study both ancient and modern history.

Whitney Hankison

Whitney is a Systems Analyst with the County of Santa Barbara in Santa Barbara, California, USA. She has authored on Professional Windows DNA, and Professional VB.Net 1st and 2nd editions for Wrox Press. Her articles are featured on the webservicesarchitect.com site and are contained is featured in the book *Web Services Business Strategies and Architectures* by Expert Press. She can be reached at whankison@earthlink.net.

Andre Hiotis

Andre Hiotis is an independent Technical Architect who enjoys working with leading edge technologies and using them to solve practical problems that benefit individuals, organizations, and society. Andre enjoyed his stay in Silicon Valley, during the dotcom era, working on wireless, security, and web services initiatives. Currently he is using his experience in developing a P2P network for the fight against terrorism that makes practical use of the Semantic Web, Security, P2P, and Wireless technologies in solving an information integration problem.

Andre currently lives with his family in Ottawa, Canada, and can be reached at ahiotis@mobile.rogers.com.

Andre would like to thank his family and friends for their support.

Murali Janakiraman

Murali Janakiraman has been with Rogue Wave for seven years, and is currently a Software Architect for the XML Products team in Corvallis, Oregon. During his tenure at Rogue Wave, Murali has been a developer, senior developer, and technical lead on almost all of Rogue Wave's database products and XML products. Murali has a Bachelor's degree in Mechanical Engineering from Anna University at Chennai, India, and a Masters degree in Computer Science from Portland State University. He has spoken in various XML conferences such as XML-Europe, web services Edge, Software Development, and in various Web seminars. Murali is currently focussed on Web Services and related XML technologies. His other areas of interest include databases, distributed transactions, and object-relational mapping. Murali is a member of the W3C XML Protocol working group.

"I would like to dedicate this book to my mother who passed away in 2002. Thanks mom for the all the courage and the confidence you have given me. I would like to thank my dear wife Lush and my two loving, adorable sons Vignesh and Arul who bring laughter and meaning to my life. You guys make me whole. I love you."

Prasad D. V.

Besides being an author on .NET technologies, Prasad is a Senior Accounting and Audit professional (a qualified Chartered Accountant in India) with twenty three years of experience in the field of Financial Consulting and over six years of progressively responsible experience in the design and development of business applications software.

He has expertise in the use of Internet technologies and client-server applications with excellent command over Java 2.0, ASP, Visual Interdev 6.0, COM, ADO, VB 6.0/5.0, RDO, IIS 5.0, MS SQL Server 2000, JavaScript, VBScript and .NET Technologies. He has put in place a clutch of ASP.NET web services, which have been listed in XMethods.Com and are being widely used by developers and research scholars to test their real world applications. He was also actively involved in the development of a commercial collaborative computing product called vTrack for Vapor Solutions, an Austin Texas based company.

At ASPToday.com and CSharpToday.com he regularly contributes articles on ASP.NET, security in .NET and component development.

Prasad is presently preparing to qualify himself as an IS Auditor.

Ravi Trivedi

Ravi Trivedi is a Software Analyst for Hewlett Packard (HP), Bangalore. He holds a Masters degree in Computer Science from the Indian Institute of Science (IISc). He is a committer for the open source UDDI4j at www.uddi4j.org and is an expert group member for HP in JAXR (JSR 93). He has been a team lead for UDDI4j and UDDI Team at HP. Ravi has been involved in developing web services infrastructure (UDDI and e-speak) and implemented some of the very first solutions in production using web services.

Ravi can be reached at ravi_trivedi@yahoo.com.

David Whitney

David Whitney is a developer with a major aerospace subsidiary located in Oklahoma City and has been responsible for design, development, and support for numerous projects ranging from engineering analysis, system security, and e-commerce, using languages as old as the "original" FoxBase, and as contemporary as Java, with efforts in C++, Visual Basic, Active Server Pages, Uniface, SQL Server, and others along the way.

He's been involved with computers and software development since he first tripped over his desk chair to volunteer for an after-hours computer program offered in the 10th grade, which was way back in 1980. When he's not reviewing or writing for Wrox, or toiling away at his regular job, he's busy serving as helpdesk, systems analyst, and network guru for his own mini home network of Linux, XP, and NT boxes, and a larger "real" network at his church; all of which fall after his most important jobs as Daddy to his two fabulous kids, Matthew and Lane, and husband to wife Katherine.

David graduated from the University of Oklahoma with a Bachelor of Science in Computer Science from the Engineering College in 1986.

Vamsi Motukuru

Vamsi is currently the VP Engineering and CTO for Phaos Technology Corp, where he is responsible for product engineering, strategic product initiatives and security consulting services. He has extensive industry experience in building components and toolkits that enable other developers and software vendors to build security into their products. At Phaos, he led the development of the world's first commercial hardware accelerated XML Signature and Encryption product.

Vamsi has a cross platform background in design, development and integration of security middleware covering security protocols, security architectures, public-key infrastructure technologies, data communications and distributed systems. He is currently focussed on building a plug gable componentized framework for securing web services and implementing Java security solutions for wireless devices.

Vamsi currently lives in New York, USA. He would like to thank his family, friends, and colleagues at Phaos for their support and encouragement.

Table of Contents

Table of Contents

Table of Contents

Table of Contents

Table of Contents

Table of Contents

Table of Contents

Table of Contents

Table of Contents

Table of Contents

Table of Contents

Introduction

Today the advantages of web services are attracting many businesses to incorporate the technology. Web services offer certain benefits over other technologies, one of them being integration, making it suitable for e-business. Web services are faster and cheaper to develop, easier to deploy and be discovered, and offer more flexibility and interoperability. However, these advantages come along with some security risks, which is the primary concern for most managers today. The security architecture designed for the Web is limited when used for the web services architecture, and the need for new standards is apparent. The solutions to these problems are emerging, creating standards that will enable the Internet world to quickly adapt to the new security architecture.

In this book, we will focus on the emerging security standards that promise to solve most of these security threats. We will pinpoint the security loopholes in the current system, particularly as they relate to the arena of web services. Finally, we present a series of use cases that describe the problem areas and explain the various techniques, standards, and toolkits available to address the problems. All of this will help developers understand, develop, and deploy a secured web service.

What Does This Book Cover?

This book is divided into three parts:

1. Concepts
   The *Concepts* section is a general introduction to web services, including the business motivators that drive them, and the need for security in them.

2. Principles
   The *Principles* section is the crux of this book. It introduces the concepts involved in security, the evolution of web service-specific security standards, and a detailed discussion of each.

3. Applications
   Finally, in the *Applications* section we deal with two detailed case studies, one each for J2EE and .NET.

Who is this Book For?

This book is for web services developers who have a good understanding of the web services architecture – those who have worked on developing and possibly deploying web services on any platform available. Readers familiar with the J2EE or .NET platforms will benefit the most since this book gives a practical case study on each of these platforms. Those who are not familiar with these platforms can still benefit from learning the architecture and principles of security in web services.

This book designed for readers who are seeking real-world, practical information on how to make their web services fully secure. It is also useful for security analysts who are responsible for system integrity.

What You Need To Use This Book

To run the samples in this book you need to have the following, depending on the platform you work on:

❑ JDK 1.4.1 or Visual Studio .NET Framework

❑ Apache Jakarta Tomcat 4.0.6 (as of this writing, Tomcat 4.1.2 has some glitches with Axis) or the Internet Information Server (IIS)

❑ Apache Axis 1.0

❑ Apache XML Security 1.0.4

❑ Verisign TSIK 1.5

The complete source code for the samples is available for download from our web site at http://www.wrox.com/.

Conventions

To help you get the most from the text and keep track of what's happening, we've used a number of conventions throughout the book.

> **These boxes hold important, not-to-be-forgotten information, which is directly relevant to the surrounding text.**

The background style illustrated by this sentence is used for asides to the current discussion.

Keep in mind the following points regarding styles in the text:

❑ We **highlight** important words when we introduce them.

❑ We show keyboard strokes like this: *Ctrl-K*.

❑ We show filenames and code within the text in the following font: `persistance.properties`.

❑ Text regarding user interfaces and URLs is shown in the following font: Menu.

We present code in two different ways:

```
In our code examples, the code foreground style shows new, important, pertinent
code.
Code background shows code that's less important in the present context, or has
been seen before.
```

Customer Support

We always value hearing from our readers, and we want to know what you think about this book: what you liked, what you didn't like, and what you think we can do better next time. You can send us your comments, either by returning the reply card in the back of the book, or by e-mail to feedback@wrox.com. Please be sure to mention the book title in your message.

How to Download the Sample Code for the Book

When you visit the Wrox site, http://www.wrox.com/, simply locate the title through our Search facility or by using one of the title lists. Click on Download in the Code column, or on Download Code on the book's detail page.

The files that are available for download from our site have been archived using WinZip. When you have saved the attachments to a folder on your hard-drive, you need to extract the files using a de-compression program such as WinZip. When you extract the files, the code is usually extracted into chapter folders. When you start the extraction process, ensure that your software (WinZip) is set to use folder names.

Errata

We've made every effort to ensure that there are no errors in the text or in the code. However, no one is perfect and mistakes do occur. If you find an error in one of our books, like a spelling mistake or a faulty piece of code, we would be very grateful for your feedback. By reporting errata you may save another reader hours of frustration, and of course, you will be helping us provide even higher quality information. Simply e-mail the information to support@wrox.com; your information will be checked and if it is correct, it will be posted to the errata page for that title, or used in subsequent editions of the book.

To find errata on the web site, go to http://www.wrox.com/ and simply locate the title through our Advanced Search or title list. Click on the Book Errata link, which is below the cover graphic on the book's detail page.

E-Mail Support

If you wish to directly query a problem in the book with an expert who knows the book in detail, then e-mail support@wrox.com, with the title of the book and the last four numbers of the ISBN in the subject field of the e-mail. A typical e-mail should include the following things:

❑ The **title of the book, last four digits of the ISBN**, and **page number** of the problem in the Subject field.

❑ Your **name, contact information**, and the **problem** in the body of the message.

We *won't* send you junk mail. We need the details to save your time and ours. When you send an e-mail message, it will go through the following chain of support:

- ❑ Customer Support – Your message is delivered to our customer support staff who are the first people to read it. They have files on the most frequently asked questions and will answer anything general about the book or the web site immediately.

- ❑ Editorial – Deeper queries are forwarded to the technical editor responsible for that book. The editor has experience with the programming language or particular product, and is able to answer detailed technical questions on the subject.

- ❑ The Authors – Finally, in the unlikely event that the editor cannot answer your problem, he or she will forward the request to the author. We do try to protect the authors from any distractions to their writing; however, we are quite happy to forward specific requests to them. All Wrox authors help with the support on their books. They will e-mail the customer and the editor with their response, and again all readers should benefit.

The Wrox Support process can only offer support to issues directly pertinent to the content of our published title. Support for questions that fall outside the scope of normal book support is provided via the community lists of our http://p2p.wrox.com/ forum.

p2p.wrox.com

For author and peer discussion, join the P2P mailing lists. Our unique system provides **programmer to programmer**™ contact on mailing lists, forums, and newsgroups, in addition to our one-to-one e-mail support system. If you post a query to P2P, you can be confident that it is being examined by the many Wrox authors and other industry experts on our mailing lists. At p2p.wrox.com you will find a number of different lists to help you, not only while you read this book, but also as you develop your applications.

To subscribe to a mailing list just follow these steps:

1. Go to http://p2p.wrox.com/.

2. Choose the appropriate category from the left menu bar.

3. Click on the mailing list you wish to join.

4. Follow the instructions to subscribe and fill in your e-mail address and password.

5. Reply to the confirmation e-mail you receive.

6. Use the subscription manager to join more lists and set your e-mail preferences.

Why this System Offers the Best Support

You can choose to join the mailing lists or you can receive them as a weekly digest. If you don't have the time, or facility, to receive the mailing list, then you can search our archives. Junk and spam mails are deleted, and your own e-mail address is protected by the unique Lyris system. Queries about joining or leaving lists, and any other general queries about lists, should be sent to listsupport@wrox.com.

1

Web Services

Web services technology is now gaining greater awareness in the IT world. There are some W3C workshops on the subject, and big players such as IBM, Microsoft, and Sun are working on their web services strategies. The idea of linking services together through a network for merging business applications is emerging in leading companies to fight the battle for marketing and competition.

Overall, companies are gearing up and asking difficult questions about interoperability, architectural issues, and security for web services. According to survey reports, security for web services has become the biggest concern for most companies, and some of the issues cannot be completely resolved for years to come.

In this book, we will start by discussing each of the major issues existing in web services security, the available solutions, and some implementations of each. In this chapter, we will have a brief introduction to web services and introduce the concepts that surround them. We will look at what they are, their history and evolution, and why we need them. Later, a discussion on the business motivators, the advancements, and the future projections of web services will give you an understanding of how this technology has progressed and driven the industry in the realm of security.

Let's begin with a discussion of what web services are and what is included in their base components.

A Recap of Web Services

Web services, in general, are services that are offered via the Web. In a web services scenario, a web application sends a request message to a service at some URI using the SOAP protocol over communication protocols like HTTP, SMTP, or FTP. The service receives the request message, processes it, and returns a response message. The URI of the service might be known or might be discovered using the UDDI.

On the other hand, a web service is a software application that interacts with other applications using XML-based messages on Internet-based protocols. It is a program that is published in order to be integrated into business applications over the Web. Web service is not bound to a single business model; instead it provides cross-business compatibility by allowing programmers to integrate commonly used, well-tested code bases. Code that can be used across various platforms and programming languages also brings generalization and interoperability.

Interestingly enough, web services neither are traditional programs for distribution nor are they standard web-based applications.

Hosted and Subscribable

Web services are the first in the shared code concept to have been widely and easily made available. They are available via being hosted and registered in web services directories. Programmers who want to access and use the web service have to make a business transaction with the publisher before using it. Whether the web service usage comes for a price or not, publishers like to track business statistics and information regarding a web service's use. To allow one to use a web service brings the concept of security into the picture, which we will discuss here.

The concept of subscribing to a service allows the customer to buy the processed result functionality of a web service as opposed to a piece of software. The concept of software subscription has flowed throughout the software marketplace, and certainly has not left out the web services industry. Many traditional software companies have begun to sell their software as a renewable yearly license, requiring maintenance to be integrated into the purchase. This causes the consumer to be integrated into the company more tightly than before since it becomes more like a subscription rather than since one-time purchase.

In the web services industry these concepts are carried forward, as the company wishing to utilize the web service is allowed to do so for a predetermined amount of time and for predetermined fees. For instance, the fee for a service could be based on the number of informational inquiries submitted by the subscriber.

The concepts of hosting and subscribability give a company the ability to cut costs while integrating standard web features like weather information or airline ticket sales into their web site. Let's look more closely at the integration of a web service.

Web Service Integration

During the various phases of development of web sites, companies determine if they want to integrate some standard or special features into their sites. Weather information and airline ticket sales are popular examples of web services that integrate well and bring a positive response.

The idea of developing code that integrates well into web sites has been fostered by many programming language compiler manufacturers such as Borland and Microsoft. These vendors also have presented ideas such as web portals, executive portals, and enhancements to their products for mobile support. Portals provide a user with a presentation of vital groups of information on a single screen. The executive portal idea has been evolving for many years, and gained prominence with software that has been designed for cross-platform integration of data. These portals can include popular web services that provide consistent information such as weather updates, or airline travel. The use of WAP-enabled devices also has blossomed, since users wish to access the Internet with them.

Now that we've looked at some of the unique features that have popularized web services, let's look at the evolution that led up to web services and the associated standards.

The Revolution of Web Programming

Web programming has truly had an revolution. Programming languages have been adapted and entire languages have been developed purely to support web site development. Software packages have been developed with the goal common computer users are able to do web programming with "drag-and-drop" ease. While these tools are available, serious web programming is still not for the common user. The development of web services simultaneously reflect both the complexity and ease of the web programming model. Web services combine the complexity of the original programming behind the service with the ease of integration into web sites.

An early attempt at such integration was reflected in the N-Tier approach to programming. This approach was a strong beginning to a distributed computing platform. However, it had topology limitations that have been overcome by utilizing the Internet and the associated protocols. As web-based programming languages have developed, the concepts of shared code, subscription-based sales, and integration came together to provide the ability to publish good, dependable products.

As the programming community and language vendors rose to the challenge to provide the tools, the standards community rose to the challenge to provide associated standards, which made business usages available. Some of the early standards that emerged were XML, SOAP, and WDSL. Let's take a look at some of these standards.

Associated Web Service Standards

Various techniques were developed to solve the problems faced in web services regarding how to make it interoperable, distributable, integratable, and so on. Some of these techniques were proposed by industry giants and became standards over time. We will look at a few of these standards.

XML

One of the emerging concerns of web-based programmers was how to transmit data across HTTP networks in an interoperable manner. XML emerged as an interoperable format. XML typically is stored as easily as readable text files. XML documents have a structure that can be parsed to quickly turn data into other formats, for example for database storage. The XML family of specifications has been and is still being further defined by many initiatives such as the security initiatives we will discuss in this book. Many vendors of storage products, such as database storage products, have enhanced their products to easily handle the XML formats. Standards have been developed for the structure of XML for messaging use. XML has enjoyed widespread adoption and adaptation, which quickly has made it the messaging standard.

RPC, XML-RPC, and SOAP

Remote object accessing technology began with the standard RPC calls, in which a method could be invoked from one application to another remote one. The limitation of the RPC was that it worked on connection-oriented, communication protocols, which cannot be used with the connectionless protocols used in the Internet.

Firewalls were another fundamental problem in the RPC systems. To use the RPC system one required protocol-specific filters with additional software, configuration, and additional management. The XML-RPC evolved in the process of solving these problems.

Another standard that emerged immediately after the XML-RPC was the SOAP. This defines the structure of a message to be communicated across the Internet between a web service client and a host. SOAP emerged due to the problem of firewalls being primarily configured to access objects via HTTP. SOAP does not replace RPC, as it includes the SOAP-RPC and SOAP-Document styles, which is why it is the preferred HTTP-based message protocol.

WSDL

A web service is published for others to discover it and then use it. To be able to use it one needs to describe it, provide details for using it, and place it under the right category, similar to the Yellow Pages. The WSDL standards were developed to fulfil this requirement by creating a standard way of capturing the service description. In this, a service is described in terms of the operations (that is, input/output messages) and a set of interactions between a service provider and a service requestor. It describes the interface or how to interact with the service. The name of the service and a list of operations and their bindings make up the XML-based WSDL file.

From a security point of view, one should keep in mind that this is a plaintext file in ASCII, UTF-8, or some base64-encoded format.

UDDI

Web services needed a way to present a company's information in a manner that compared their features equally. Using search engines for this purpose was not the most efficient means of allowing businesses to interoperate with each other at a web services level, and as a result the UDDI directory of web services emerged.

The UDDI is a registry service project that provides a means for businesses hosting a web service to register with the worldwide registries. The project is focused on assisting businesses in finding each other by allowing the registration of a web service and the searching of registries to locate specific web services based on a number of criteria. The UDDI is not linked directly to any other standards initiatives or standards groups. However, it does take advantage of groups that provide standards and initiatives within the web services industry. The official UDDI web page can be accessed at http://www.uddi.org/.

The Need for Web Services

As we discussed in the last section, web services came about as a natural evolution to web site programming and the problems it presented. As with all computer technologies, this evolution increased creativity and enhanced to the types of interactions customers had with Internet commerce sites. Beyond the code sharing, hosting, and integration aspects we outlined in the prior section, web services evolved due to expanded commerce needs and the need for standardization of existing commerce interactions.

The desire for increased types of business interaction also drove the need for expanding the original basis of interaction that SOAP and XML provided. With these needs becoming more important, the concept of web services established itself not only as a feature to be taken advantage of, but also as an e-commerce need. We'll look in detail in the areas of:

- ❑ Subscription to "known good" services
- ❑ Benefits of transactions and transactional services
- ❑ Standardization of web and consumer interaction
- ❑ Standards acceptance for Internet commerce
- ❑ Code stability

Dependability and Integrity for Internet Commerce

Early in the development of popularity of Internet commerce, mistakes were made regarding security and Internet commerce that shook consumer confidence. Sites began working on improving security and began displaying what their security practices were in an effort to regain consumer confidence. The concept behind regaining user confidence through a site's improved security and integrity flows over to the subscription of web services.

Providing integrity in the web-based product is important, and the perception of any Internet-based product is crucial. With this in mind, the concentration of commerce based on a standard way of exchanging data, such as airline web sites that use a standard airline purchasing web service, caused consumer confidence to rise. This is where the subscription to "known good" services comes into play. If a web service has a good reputation for integrity, it will be used more and thus will cause the subscribing sites to gain consumer confidence.

The standardization of common elements through the shared code concept of a web service assists in the area of the vital need of integrity in commerce web sites. Along with the growing acceptance of such commerce web sites there comes a desire for more and different business services to be available, and thus the benefits of transactions and transactional services come into play.

Let's now discuss how transactions and transactional services are needed in the web commerce industry today.

Benefits of Transactions and Transactional Components

As business opportunities on the Internet have expanded, industries whose interaction with consumers is based on transactions have entered into the picture. Businesses such as financial, stocks and bonds, real estate, and reservation services are a few examples. The initial commerce web sites were generally retail or informational in nature, therefore repeat business was not a huge factor. The businesses listed above depend heavily on repeat business and also on the access they have to the consumer group for which they wish to provide services.

Suddenly, with transactional business available via the Internet, many of these businesses have a greater access than they ever could have dreamed of and they also face a whole new group of competition. Again, integrity comes into play because there is a greater potential for fraud in these areas and therefore trust is of utmost importance. Transactional components have emerged as an important way of doing business. Let's look at some of the available benefits to this type of business.

Online Contracts and Verifiable Transactions

One of the most interesting concepts regarding transactional business being available is the use of the Internet web service for online contract purposes. Some of the hassles in day-to-day life deal with the signature of contracts. Contracts have to be signed by multiple parties, and the verification of contract information is oftentimes required to be certified by multiple other parties in order to be reliable, binding, and dependable. Getting parties in one place is sometimes difficult, and you are guaranteed to have to go out of your way to do so, perhaps missing work or having to make arrangements after hours in order to complete the transaction.

As contrasted with the "hand-shake" contracts of days gone by, the above-mentioned contractual obligation occurs even when the parties are known to each other, due to the growth of lawsuits in our culture today. Many times, a real-time delay can impede this process when parties are many miles apart, perhaps even across the country or on another continent. E-mail and the Internet are two technologies that in many other areas have broken time barriers, so why not use them for our contractual obligations as well? Online contracts can vary from simple things such as school permission forms and standard work-related forms to reservation systems or purchase contracts for stocks, bonds, or real estate.

Any of the above-mentioned items can become online transactions within a web service environment. The element all these items have in common is that they need to be verifiable in order to carry the authority they were designed to carry. For instance, when you manually sign a school permission form, the school keeps it on file so that they can verify the fact that you signed it and can present that evidence to any party requiring it. Examples of parties who might want to know this type of information could be official organizations such as insurance companies or persons such as teachers or guardians.

In any case, the form is on file as verifiable proof that it was completed. An intermediary step to eliminate the storage of paper has been to scan the papers into an electronic storage system for later retrieval. This was presented as a more permanent way to store such information, allowing for easy access at a later time. To take the storage concept a step further, if these transactions are completed online, they are stored electronically and can be pulled up and verified in a timely manner.

One of the topics we'll discuss in the next chapter is integrity. Online transactional systems must have integrity to be able to state that their transactions are verifiable. Officials who access records must agree that online transactional systems are a viable resource for contractual information; therefore the integrity of the system is very important. The system must be able to prove that it has information such as unique signature, date, and time, as well as sufficient security to guard against accidental or purposeful modification, in addition to the previous systems it replaced.

Another factor in making web services available is that services that previously were only available in person are now available online. Let's explore some of the benefits of this.

Availability of Services

In the past, permission forms, financial transactions, and real estate transactions were only available in person before the advent of web services. These are very important transactions that are legally binding, so as we mentioned they must be verifiable. The trust level of all parties has to be equal if the transaction is to be accepted as equivalently valid compared to a paper-based transaction. The fact that these are available via the web is a huge convenience in today's busy lifestyles. Let's discover some of the benefits of each type of transaction.

We'll start with one of the most common type of transactions, reservation systems. Reservation systems include airline, hotel, and vacation systems that have been made available by airlines, local and national agencies, and even from agencies that act as a "middle man," such as automobile clubs that offer an entire list of services from one business. We used to have to go to a reservations business in person, fill out the multiple forms, give them all sorts of ID and credit information and take a lot of time out of our day to make a reasonably simple transaction take place. Now with online systems, we can check out our own pricing information, pick our own routes to, and discover the "best deals" right from our own computer. Once we are in the system our next transaction is even easier and takes less time.

Financial transactions also can take a lot of time to complete in person. Brokers, banks, and other financial institutions making their services accessible online has incresed consumers' knowledge and has enabled them to make more educated financial decisions. Where previously we had to depend on the financial advice of the experts, financial information is abundant on the Internet and we can use that information to form an educated opinion about our financial decisions. Once we have a financial plan, the easiest part should be making the transactions to invest our money into the places we want. With the advent of online services, the transactional part of investment is greatly simplified. The online availability of the complex paper forms that we used to have to fill out makes it easier to complete the transaction without having to spend hours of time in an office completing both the analysis, decision making, and transactional components all at once. We can now do our research, come to our conclusions, and fill out the forms in our own timeframe, which makes it much more convenient and interesting to take part in these financial transactions.

The other type of transaction that is simplified online is the real estate transaction. In person, a client is presented with a dizzying array of documents and forms in duplicate or in triplicate. It becomes time-consuming and confusing to keep track of them all. Also, purchasing or selling real estate takes up a lot of time both in the research and decision-making areas. Much like reservation systems, real estate has put much of the marketplace information online for people to browse through at their leisure, so people can be more focused on what they want, taking less time to eliminate what they don't want to see.

After the research and decision-making part is completed and the transactional phase begins, online transactions can take much less time and energy from both parties. Let's go a step further with our real estate example and talk about some of the benefits we'll receive both from the marketplace information being online and the from transactional part being available as a web service. The following flow chart gives an idea of the processes involved in an online real estate purchase transaction:

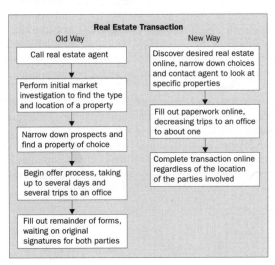

As you can see in the diagram above, online availability of both the research information and the transactional components saves the consumer a lot of time and energy. We can dictate our own time frames in the research area, and we don't have to wait on other people to see property when it is online. Thus we can do better and quicker preliminary decision-making.

As illustrated in the diagram, as in-person real estate transaction entails multiple trips to various offices to fill out forms in a real estate transaction. Under the online web service methodology, the businesses involved in the real estate transaction would allow the consumer to complete those forms online, saving delivery costs, time and money. The web service would have the integrity needed to make the contracts just as legally binding as those which occur on paper.

Digging a little deeper into web service technology and how it has enhanced the standard web-based transaction, the transactional component of the above-described contracts requires authorization on not just the entire contract, but on pieces of the contract. This is similar to a regular real estate transaction in which you must sign in several places, even on the same page. In the past, web-based transactions have been oriented around the "bottom line" signature portion of a transaction, basically verifying that an entire transaction was acceptable.

Web services use the technologies such as digital signatures to allow a detailed level of authorization to take place within a contract. This allows us to sign details within the contract as well as to sign the entire contract itself. The greater the level of detailed authorization that becomes available, the more diverse the transactions over the web will become. Along with this diversity comes the need for standardization, which we examine next.

Standardization of Web/Consumer Interaction

As the abilities available through web services become more diverse, the need for standardization increases. In order to maintain the higher level of integrity required for the transactional web services environment, there needed to be some standardization of how the web and consumer interaction occurred. Some standards have evolved based on consumer expectations of privacy protection and also based on the expectation that their interaction with consumer web sites is secure.

When consumers use a commercial web site, they expect that their information will be kept private so others don't see personal information such as social security numbers or credit card information. They also expect that the web site with which they are interacting has taken sufficient precautions to prevent information theft at any time after their transaction is complete. We have heard stories of banks and financial institutions having information stolen from their computer systems, resulting in stolen identities. Consumer protection is a very big issue in web site interaction.

Consumer protection has driven many companies to review security practices and implementations within their software systems. The industry committees, which we examine further in the next section, have also come up with some standards to assist in this area. In the next chapters, we will be going into detail about as the types of detailed authorization we used in our examples in this chapter. These details have resulted from the intesive care and time committees and companies have put in to establishing recommendations that programmers follow in designing and implementing web services. These standards are meant to maximize the protection provided to consumers.

Standards Acceptance for Internet Commerce

Many times in the technology industry we have seen companies come out with standards that they wish people to follow. Sometimes the standards are accepted, and sometimes other companies come up with competing standards that they feel are better than the original. The competition in regards to setting standards often results in proprietary software that does not interoperate with all operating systems or platforms. These barriers have been rather effectively broken within the web service community, as the largest competing companies have come together to form the standards that are being established for Internet commerce. This will create a positive, win-win situation for the companies and consumers because the standards will be more readily accepted and put into practice.

As programmers, web service designers, and web service host companies enact these standards, it will create a safer environment for Internet commerce, raising consumer confidence and causing more consumers to elect to take part in Internet commerce. As more consumers place their confidence in this technology there will be more types of business willing to invest in the technology necessary to be involved in Internet commerce. As the types of businesses diversify, our lives will be easier and we will be able to accomplish formerly tedious tasks with greater ease. Also, as the standards are put into place, the Internet environment will become more stable. We will discuss this next.

Code Stability

Code stability in the Internet environment is a very important factor. Repeated consumer interaction with a web site is partially based on their comfort level with the basic functionality on the web site. As we discussed earlier in this chapter, code stability is one of the basic concepts provided by web services. Web services provide an approach to code stability through the fact they are shared code and the stiff competition in the web services arena ensure high standards for providers to gain and keep subscribers.

Now that we've looked at the benefits of web services and why we need them, let's take a look at the history behind them and discuss some of the committees driving the standards we're writing about in this book.

The Driving Committees

There is a wide diversification in the businesses and committees that are driving standards for web service based Internet commerce. The biggest difference between the web services standards marketplace and prior standardization efforts is that businesses are working together on the web services standards efforts, as opposed to turning the efforts into competition. Businesses participating in the standardizations efforts are seeing that it will benefit the industry as a whole, and will allow the growth of Internet-based commerce to become exponential.

First, committees have been formed to make recommendations based upon discussions of submissions to the committee. The industry is relying on the decisions of these committees to drive standardization practices. There are also organizations formed to organize and centralize the input and feedback regarding web services so questions can be quickly answered, and information quickly disbursed. In addition, governmental agencies have become involved in the standardization efforts by passing legislation that makes the use of web services a viable alternative and just as legally binding as our manually signed contracts of today. International organizations as well are getting involved to make recommendations regarding global e-commerce. Let's look in detail at some of these organizations and committees.

W3C

The first committee we'll talk about is the W3C committee. This is the World Wide Web Consortium, and their basic function is to develop web standards. Their web site is located at http://www.w3c.org/, and outlines the basic structure and goals of the organization. The main goals as outlined on the web site are to provide standards that keep the Internet accessible, easy to use, secure, innovative, able to be built upon, non-proprietary, and to encourage the expansion and increase of creativity in web site development.

These are lofty and somewhat generalized goals, but the W3C has shown initiative by digging into the details in each of these areas to provide real solutions. They are supervising security standards that we will discuss in this book such as digital signatures, which are enabling contractual businesses to reach a greater level of detail in their transactions with consumers. This committee works hand-in-hand with other committees to provide the detail behind the recommendations that will form the standards for design and development of web services. The committee publishes their results as specifications which are used to guide developers and companies in their design and development goals.

IETF

Another committee-type organization is the IETF, the **Internet Engineering Task Force**. It is a group of technically-oriented individuals and businesses that participate in working groups, which address existing issues and other issues as presented to them. They work in working groups and address many topics that relate to both Internet and web services standards. They were responsible for such notable standards as HTTP, TCP, and UDP. Some of the standards they are addressing in relation to web services including the following:

- ❑ IP over cable data network
- ❑ IP over InfiniBand
- ❑ IP over resilient packet rings
- ❑ IP version 6
- ❑ IP routing for wireless/mobile hosts
- ❑ Protocol for carrying authentication for network access
- ❑ IP security protocol
- ❑ IP security policy
- ❑ Transport layer security
- ❑ XML digital signatures

The IETF web site can be found at http://www.ietf.org/.

OASIS-Open.org

OASIS has been a leader in standards development and support. They are a non-profit, global consortium dedicated to web standards. They have been working on such notable topics as ebXML, WS-Security, and UDDI.

WebServices.org

Along with the committees we've discussed are organizations that have been formed to gather and disburse information regarding web services, WebServices.org, and others like it, is dedicated to providing information in an organized, unbiased manner. You can visit this site at http://www.webservices.org/. This site provides hardware, software, and vendor information specific to web services.

Web Services Architect

This is another web site run by an organization dedicated to gathering and disbursing information about web services. The site has many articles which give technical information specifically regarding the architecture that supports web services. In addition to articles, it provides information regarding current activities in the industry related to web services. The site can be accessed at http://www.webservicesarchitect.com/.

Governmental and International Influence

Governments and international agencies have had influence in the web services arena from multiple perspectives. Government has become involved to facilitate the adoption of web services by passing legislature that makes digital signatures carry the same authority and be as binding as manual signatures are in contractual situations.

One example of international influence in the web service arena is the ebXML initiative. It is sponsored by the United Nations Center for Trade Facilitation and Electronic Business (UN/CEFACT) and the Organization for the Advancement of Structured Information Standards (OASIS). In a nutshell, the ebXML initiative is what is called "next generation EDI," or a new evolving standard for conducting business in a secure and electronic manner.

Traditionally, EDI was a standard that was implemented in proprietary ways to exchange standard business documents such as invoices and purchase orders. ebXML is an emerging standard in its implemention of web services technologies to create global standards.

The presentation of concepts such as ebXML is a good transition into our next topic. We will look at the business motivating factors that drive the need for web services implementations.

Business Motivating Factors for Web Services

Throughout this chapter we've alluded to many business motivating factors that currently exist for web services. However, we need to go into more depth for the reader to understand some of the avenues used by web services and the challenges they present. We'll look at factors such as:

- ❑ Reliability of data
- ❑ Customer access
- ❑ International commerce
- ❑ Streamlining transaction completion

❑ Business side motivating factors – return on investment and revenue base expansion

❑ Service requestor motivating factors – simplicity, availability, and convenience

❑ Internal business motivating factors – developers advantages, integration, and web-based management

Let's begin our look at motivating factors with a discussion of reliability of data.

Reliability of Data

The reliability of data is an issue that concerns both companies and consumers. When looking at data storage from a business point of view, storing data in more than one location can cause integrity problems. Having two information stores can cause data to get out of sync, even if the data sources are managed similarly. Automatic synchronization of the data sources can help, but does not carry an absolute guarantee. We need to ensure the source of the data is as reliable as possible to avoid confusion and misinterpretation.

This concept, as applied to web services, can be seen as a benefit to using a web service. Web service data drives from a centralized location, the web service host. No matter how many web sites have integrated the web service, the host location will still provide the data, and it should be unaltered by the integrating web sites. As we've stated before, reliability of data is an issue that comes up when analyzing the integrity of a web service. Since the competition is stiff among web services providers, data integrity and reliability will play an important role in the selection of a web service by a web site wishing to integrate that type of service.

Customer Access

There are two factors with regard to customer access that should be considered while implementing a web service solution. These factors are a benefit to both the web service host company and the consumer. Firstly, a host will gain access to customers that were unavailable before implementing web services, as contacts need not be personalized as before. From the customer access perspective, real estate companies would be able to benefit from both our customer access benefits mentioned by implementing a web service.

Historically, real estate transactions were primarily taken care of in a personal manner due to the manual nature both the research and contracts. Now potential customers can research information remotely, determine which company they want to deal with and then complete the contact.

However, the burden is on the real estate companies is higher, as they now need to provide good, timely information to potential cross-country customers so that the customers will consider them to be best qualified to assist in the process. This can be a very heavy burden, and sometimes companies choose to remain local because of the cost associated. However the company's access locally is broadened due to the online information provided that was missing before.

The time consumed by the contractual process itself has also decreased as we illustrated before. This is a benefit that enables the company to reach more and distant customers as well.

Local Commerce vs. International Commerce

One of the things that the Web accomplished even in the early stages of e-commerce was to open businesses up to global opportunities. The scope of operations is definitely a business choice that has to be made early on in any e-commerce operation.

Let's again look at the example of the local real estate office. Should it choose, the real-estate office could become integrated with nationwide or even international organizations, which could list the properties it has for sale. On the other hand, its local web site could subscribe to a nationwide or international web service that provides listings. This single business decision could widen the scope of the local office beyond local commerce into the international commerce realm.

All of this extra business that can be generated by the subscription to a web service creates the need for discussion of our next topic – the speed of completing transactions. Another consideration for the international level is that rules and regulations vary in each country; therefore gathering the information for or from foreign lands can be a challenge.

Streamlining Transaction Completion

Web services improve the speed with which we complete our transactions. It accomplishes this by cutting down on the personal interaction time needed, providing avenues to gain document signature faster than ever, and providing a quickly verifiable way to complete the necessary documents. In real-estate transactions, there are many persons and businesses involved. If all parties can access the necessary documents at any time, the delivery and handling time is minimized and the transaction can be completed in the quickest time possible. This is a benefit both to the consumer and businesses involved.

Motivating Factors Particular to a Business

Cost/benefit analysis and business expansion are the two motivators that we want to discuss in this section. As compared to other means of expanding business and cost implications involved, the web services approach pays off the best. In any business, cost justification is a big issue because of budgets and good fiscal management. When you look at cost justification in relation to web services you need to examine all the factors going into the development and maintenance of the web service and weigh that against the other factors that we've mentioned. From the perspective of a business considering whether to become the host of a web service, let's look at a table of costs and benefits to consider in a return on investment analysis:

Costs	Benefits
Hardware – Additional network security, infrastructure, and hardware purchased for project	Reduced customer support costs
Programming – initial and ongoing costs	Opportunity for business expansion
Staff dedicated to daily maintenance and support	Greater business access
Maintenance – hardware and software ongoing costs	Global Availability
Training – staff turnover, hardware and software upgrades, and changes	Opportunity for business expansion

Let's talk again about a real estate business that wants to implement their web site as a web service. It could have a web site detailing its listings, but also include a web service that is available to other real estate agents for subscription. The contracts part would also be integrated within that web service so that remote buyers could complete the transactions online.

Now, with that in mind, let's look at our cost/benefit analysis table. The costs and investments on the left will include hardware, programming, staffing, maintenance, and training. Many of these items are ongoing, so the agency will have to plan for these costs over the long haul, as well as determining the cost of the initial investment. The benefit items on the right are a little more ambiguous, but they can be weighed by determining the overall difference that the web service will make in the level of business offered and taken advantage of.

Through web services, the customer support costs are decreased due to the higher level of clientele that takes advantage of web services as opposed to web sites. As we've mentioned before, there is greater opportunity for business expansion, access, and global availability. These factors carry a lot of weight because they otherwise are either unavailable or can become a cost factor instead of a benefit. The conventional means to gain expansion and access has been through advertising. Advertising is limited in its results, whereas the web service is available all day, and when global agencies integrate it into their sites the growth becomes exponential.

Let's move on to our next area of specific motivators. We'll look next at the motivators for web services from a customer perspective.

Web Service Requestors

When we talk about web service customers in the light of the motivating factors for web services use, we are really talking about two groups of people. There are the customers or subscribers to the web service that has integrated the web service into their site, and the customers of web sites that have integrated web services. Both of these groups benefit from the web service simplicity of use, availability, and convenience.

From the subscriber's perspective it is a lot simpler to integrate a web service into a web site than to try to develop the feature for yourself. From a web site customer perspective, it is easy to use a standardized component of a web site because it is not all "new," but familiar.

From a subscriber's perspective, the availability of services that were not available before should be exciting. New tools available to integrate into a web site makes that web site receive more hits and usage, which should be the goal of the web site host. Also the ability of a business to integrate a web service that gives its business wider access should be exciting as well. From a customer point of view, the availability of business that was only available in person before will be well taken advantage of. The fact that we can complete business in a faster and easier manner is a huge customer benefit.

Finally, there is a convenience generated for both the subscriber and customer that causes web services to be well received. It is definitely more convenient and less costly for a web site host to integrate a web service into their site. It is also more convenient for customers to have information available on the Web so they can discover that information from their home computer.

One other area that we'd like to dig into a little is the motivator that occurs in the internal business environment. Web services benefit the business that chooses to become a web service host in interesting ways, so let's take a look at that.

Motivating Factors Internal to Business

The business that chooses to host a web service has committed to programming standards. This affects how its internal programmers function and how its internal applications and databases are developed and accessed as well. Using web services benefits an organization internally through the shared code base all the developers use, the application integration, the fact that the applications are web-based, and the ability to access internal data outside the organization. Let's take a deeper look at each of these factors.

Shared Code Base for Developers

Web service development reinforces the concept of shared code within the development group of a company. The same benefit we described before for the web site development community crosses over to the internal developers of an organization. For instance, using shared code for authentication to internal web sites is one example of a web service that could be implemented in a government agency that has departmental web sites.

Eliminate Duplicate Development

It costs companies millions each year for developers to "reinvent the wheel" by redeveloping similar coding strategies. Shared code is an efficient factor internal to an organization. Even internal applications should take advantage of this concept. If you think of how many ways the accounting data of a company is accessed, a web service that accesses and encapsulates that data would be beneficial.

The accountants, management, sales, and marketing groups of an organization all access the accounting data for different reasons. One use of an internal web service would be to make that data available in an easy-to-use manner that can be integrated into special reports or other applications. Even just updating contact information within the customer database of an organization would be a beneficial web service, because not everyone in an organization that uses that information should necessarily have direct access to the original source of the information. This usually is the Accounts Receivable module in the accounting system.

If pieces of information such as these were available as a web service, they would easily integrate into departmental applications, and the shared code base concept would pay off because of the consistent outcome derived from the web service.

The next area we want to discuss is internal program maintenance and installation.

Simplified Installation Issues

Web service and web site-based programs are on the rise, and users are gaining familiarity with the data entry and menu structures used in common web sites. One of the biggest maintenance items internal to an organization is managing program revisions on the local computer desktops. While there are many approaches to this, many companies have Windows-based computers and install the applications locally. Managing internal application revision on each desktop can be a hassle if the program is executable-based. If the program is a web-based application there are substantially fever problems and maintenance issues because there are no local components to troubleshoot or maintain.

The last topic we'll discuss for the internal business benefits is the availability of internal data to external users.

External Access to Internal Data

One topic that has been growing over the last few years is the popularity of accessing internal data from external to the company. This is also termed data warehousing. When this trend began, it was mainly focused on traveling personnel within a company, especially the ability to access e-mail when traveling. It has grown to the point that people want to access e-mail, submit expense reports, and even work from remote locations on a regular basis. These issues have a lot to do with security, which is our main topic of this book. The goal is to be able to expose internal resources to the Internet without compromising the integrity of our data. We'll examine the specific approaches to this problem in upcoming chapters, but for this chapter suffice it to say that external access to internal data is a derived benefit from the web services architecture.

Now that we've covered what web services are, their history and benefits, our final major section for this chapter will take a look at the future of web services, some of the goals of industry leaders, and predictions for how they will be used.

The Development, Support, and Future of Web Services

This section will examine the aresa of web services standards that are of interest in this book, the ways in which businesses can take advantage of web services, industry support for web services, and a few predictions for their future capabilities.

Web Services Standards

As web services have evolved, there has been much concern over developing standards for their usage. It was recognized by the industry that this was an evolutionary idea, and so early in their adoption phase industry leaders attempted to keep them from becoming another proprietary competition to enhance proprietary web solutions. The industry has attempted to keep web services as a cross-platform, industry-wide solution to the lightweight messaging need. So far, they have mainly succeeded and continue to succeed by enhancing the original specifications to address emerging needs. Let's begin by mentioning the standards we will specifically discuss in this book.

Message Standards

The message standards that have emerged have led in the exponential use in acceptance of web services. Standards like SOAP, XML, and the messaging standards have emerged to solve industry-wide problems. The capability of the schemas to include digital signature authorization within a message or a section of a document is an example of the evolving standards and the difference they are making.

Now let's look at some areas of business that can take advantage of web services.

Business Areas for Web Services

We have seen some examples in this chapter of areas in which businesses could take advantage of web services. Some other examples could be either internal to the organization, new businesses utilizing web services, or old standards converting to web services.

Within the organization, web services could be integrated into any internal application to make it accessible to external users. Standard processes such as employee time, accounting, or expense reports could be automated in this fashion as well. As we have seen in the financial and real estate examples, just about any business in these areas can gain much efficiency by the use of web services.

We also mentioned the ebXML initiative, where older electronic business standards related to EDI are starting to convert to web service standards. These older business standards can reap security, tracking, and transactional benefits that are cumbersome or don't even exist in the older standards.

Industry Leader Involvement

It is interesting and encouraging to finally see many industry leaders come to mutual agreement on one goal within the industry. The current overwhelming goal that comes from the industry leaders' involvement is to make the Internet a safe, easy, and worldwide source for business opportunity. Let's take a look at some of the major companies involved in that initiative and what they are currently doing.

IBM

IBM is doing a great deal for further development in the web services arena. The company is taking a very diverse approach to web services issues by submitting specifications to the W3C, sponsoring good web sites that provide useful information, providing its WebSphere line of products, and even hosting a UDDI-compliant web services registry. IBM's web-services-specific web site can be found at http://www-106.ibm.com/developerworks/webservices/.

SUN

In an effort to promote web services in an open, non-platform-specific manner, Sun has demonstrated great interest and effort toward development of web services. As the developer and lead influencer in the Java market, Sun has developed the various versions of Java, right up to the current J2EE product. It has labeled vision Sun-ONE (Open Net Environment) and is committed to the web services initiative in the industry. Sun is also involved in the current WS-Security initiative.

BEA

BEA has been primarily involved with the Java movement in the web industry. It has provided tools and specifications in conjunction with development of web services. In addition, BEA has provided specifications and the J2EE toolkits for web services development. Its application server is called WebLogic.

Microsoft

Microsoft have always been very integrated into the standards, tools, and platform areas of web services. It made some of the first early offerings for the development of web services with its line of servers that supported its Visual Studio development suite. Microsoft has been involved with or proposed many standards with relationship to SOAP, XML, and related message standards. In addition, its development platforms have evolved from its initial Windows DNA platform to its current .NET platform.

This discussion makes it clear that the major industry players are involved in the development of registries, tools, and standards for web services development.

Future of Web Services

As was stated before, with the industry involvement and wide acceptance of web services today, it is not too hard to see where they are going. Web services seek to form the basis for many areas of business and to enable many new areas of business to take advantage of Internet exposure. Their use and continued acceptance will be primarily seen in the return on investment and cost advantage, small business expansion, continued acceptance, and global Internet commerce areas.

Cost/Benefit Analysis

The returns on investment and cost factors of a web service are driving its acceptance due to the overall benefits of the web service in comparison to past approaches. We should see a faster acceptance and implementation within the industry due to these factors. We should also see startup businesses turning to web services as a business medium, not dissimilar to the ".COM" companies of the past. Part of the problem with the ".COM" companies of the past was lack of financial analysis due to the ease of web site development and the lack of a relationship between the quality of a web site and the quality of the company it represented.

Web service development takes a lot of analysis and thought from a business perspective, so we should see more concrete companies emerging as a result.

Global Internet Commerce

As we see in our local communities, large chain businesses are very common. These large distribution chains are succeeding in providing consumers with convenience, discount pricing, and the availability of these familiar stores in varied communities. The factors causing success for these stores are also factors that we've mentioned relative to web services. These factors will cause web site hosts to integrate web services in order to provide these benifits to their customers. On a global scale, the web service causes global exposure to a core set of services and makes e-commerce a reality. With the emergence of initiatives such as ebXML, we will see further development of global business exchange and the ability for companies to cost-effectively operate global companies.

Summary

In this chapter we have looked at web services in great detail. We also have discussed the product standards on which web services are based.

In addition, we also discussed why we need web services and some examples of how they have evolved. We looked at financial and real estate examples and discussed their transactional nature and how they have benefited from web service technology. We then looked at the history of web services from perspectives of Internet commerce and the driving need for next-generation tools to conduct the e-commerce business.

We also talked about committees and organizations involved in web services initiatives and how their influence will bring about continued innovation and change. We proceeded to discuss business motivators for the development and use of web services. We looked at motivators for businesses, consumers, and motivators internal to a business organization. Finally, we wrapped up the chapter by looking at the future of web services.

Web Services is a huge topic, and the objective of this book is to bring the reader an understanding of what web services are, and to introduce factors that should be considered in web service development to ensure compliance with industry intiatives. The industry goal is to produce web services that increase global commerce over the Internet, and this goal is highly reflective of the quality of products the Internet brings to the marketplace. Security put in place by the hosting company will play a role in the success of a web service. This book will endeavor to clearly put into perspective the role of security in the development and deployment of the web service.

2
Security

In this chapter, we will be looking at security in relation to web services design and implementation. Security is an issue of changing implications and wide importance. It is difficult to keep up with this ever-changing topic; however, it is important to keep security in mind and to implement it appropriately in each application we develop. In choosing the development tools we use, it is also important to keep in mind that they have security integrated into them, and the use of the security features within our development tools will assist us in adequately addressing the security issue.

Our chapter begins with a discussion of what security represents in a business environment and why we need to be aware of it. Implications of security, as related to web services, and some methods of addressing the issues from both a network physical approach as well as a programmatic approach, will be the focus of our discussion. The items that we will be discussing will address security from a standpoint of authentication, authorization, data transmission and storage, networking, and the application level. We'll discuss the methods of transport layer security for the authentication and authorization, transmission, and storage. We'll discuss items such as IPSec and firewalls, for our networking levels. We'll also discuss today's evolving security standards such as digital security for our application levels.

Let us first begin with our discussion of what security represents to us and what factors we need to acknowledge and deal with in relationship to our web services projects.

Introduction to Security

In this section, we will introduce security in four aspects:

- ❑ What security represents to us as developers and business people
- ❑ Why we need to implement security in our web services
- ❑ What are the implementation considerations
- ❑ What are the factors to consider when implementing security

Let us begin with the considerations involved in what security represents to us.

What Security Represents

Security represents six main factors when it comes to the quality of our web service. It represents the following aspects of the development of a web service:

- ❑ Integrity
- ❑ Assurance
- ❑ Verification
- ❑ Confidentiality
- ❑ Availability

In today's Internet-based businesses, we need to keep these factors in mind so that we can provide our customers with a service they can trust. In addition, we also need to ensure security for our product so that the result of any transaction is in an unaltered state. This is a great challenge with the amount of attacks taking place on the Internet, and we need to be ready for these attacks and thus consider these factors.

Integrity

The word integrity literally means "Rigid adherence to a code of values". Integrity in business is essential for assuring people will use it. When people deal with a product that represents us, such as our web service, we want that product to have every aspect of the above definition of integrity. If we cannot guarantee complete transactions, soundness in the results of those transactions, and consistency with the outcome of their experience to those people who use our web service, then we cannot truly say our web service contains a solid implementation of the standards in the industry.

When examining to security within the web service, we need to apply security to the areas that represent the integrity of the experience the customer receives when utilizing our product. The user should feel assured that his or her transaction was complete, private, and secure. Theirfore, we need to guard against incomplete transactions and insecure access to our web service. For this, we implement means of giving the users feedback confirming what they believe has transpired.

Assurance

Customers need to be assured of the integrity of their transactions. This is done by utilizing industry standard mechanisms recognized by the user, such as authentication mechanisms, and by providing the user with a smooth operating site with which to interact. A web site that is error-prone and insecure attracts disrepute, and causes damage to customer confidence in the product. With the fierce competition in the market today, assurance plays a major role in the sites with which the users choose to interact on a frequent basis.

Verification

The verification of any Internet-based transaction is imperative to any customer who might be using our web site. We need to provide the ability to verify what the transaction was, guard against unauthorized changes, and be able to track any changes to the transaction from any source. Tracking mechanisms within our web site or data sources must be in place, and the ability to recreate transactions from scratch is important to guard against any possible fraudulent attacks. Another term for this could be accountability. Again, we want our web service to be accountable for complete and correct transactions.

Confidentiality

The customers need to be sure that the service they are using ensures confidentiality. As in the example of integrity, we need to maintain high standards of confidentiality to obtain and hold our customers' confidence.

Availability

We need to design our web service security infrastructure so that we can maintain a high availability of our web service. Security plays an important role in our web service's availability because it protects it from internal and external hackers that can cause our web service to become unavailable. Some of the attacks that people use through the Internet to cause web services to become unavailable are **denial of service**, scans and probes, and attacks by viruses. Denial of service attacks send a large quantity of requests to the web server, drowning it in business so it can't respond to normal user requests. Any such attacks are well documented, and have remedial measures that are illustrated in this book.

A web site that deals with these attacks is http://www.cert.org. In addition, many network hardware vendors have information; for example, http://www.cisco.com/warp/public/707/newsflash.html provides information specifically on denial of service attacks. There also exist internal hackers who are people within an organization who use methods to gain access to classified information, or cause the web service to provide misleading information.

All of the above factors represent how security integrates into our daily business. Let us now look at why we need security from a business perspective and how it will affect the life of our business.

Why We Need Security

From a basic business perspective we need security to safeguard our assets, to build customer confidence, and to avoid the liability involved in being the publisher of a web service. Every day web sites are attacked, new viruses are derived, and security loopholes in programs are exposed. It is evident that implementing security safeguards into our web services is important. However, it should be understood that this would invariably be time consuming, and would require a fairly broad knowledge of the architecture behind the web service implementation. As we outlined above, security represents the forefront of the user experience and can affect our success and vitality as a business. In this section we will look at our need for security in the areas for:

- ❑ Safeguarding assets
- ❑ Representation of ourselves to customers
- ❑ Avoiding liability

Let us look in more detail at how security affects our business in the areas outlined here.

Safeguarding Assets

In any business, insurance is purchased for the safeguarding of assets. One of the most important assets of a company that publishes a web service is the web service itself. If we are willing to buy insurance to safeguard our physical assets, we should make the investment in good security to safeguard our web service asset. In the physical realm, a stolen asset causes the business to deplete in value for a period until insurance restores what was lost. Some web services control goods, others information, and others transactions. Compromise of the web service security deals a blow to the assets that the web service controls. As we will see later in this chapter, there are physical security requirements and authentication requirements that will both contribute to the safeguarding of our web service asset.

Representation of Ourselves to Customers

On a web site, the users' experiences usually dictate whether the site becomes a frequently or infrequently used resource. As already outlined in the section on what security represents, what we offer our customers has a great impact on our business. Customers must be able to trust the web service. Security should not be sacrificed in the face of cost or any other cause, as would adversely affect the perception of the service on offer.

Avoiding Liability

Should our product include sales, or any financial transactional component, security must be implemented to avoid liability. The highest liability of any business is the monetary transactional component. It has taken many security measures to erable the Internet to become a viable source for the purchase of commodities. Many still do not trust Internet services providers with their financial information. The reasons for this are mainly that the earlier web sites did not take the security precautions necessary to protect the consumer from interference and fraud. There is now great liability in an Internet-based business and hence security assumes a crucial responsibility.

Let's now move on and look at the five factors of security that we need to consider in our web service implementations.

Implementation Considerations

As we design and implement our web service, we have a lot to think about in terms of security. Considerations that we must make include the following:

- ❑ Type and amount of data we are going to host
- ❑ Type of customers who will access the web service
- ❑ The transaction requirements
- ❑ Response times we want to achieve
- ❑ The resources we will need to expose

Each of these considerations has security implications based on the decisions made. Cost should not limit what we want to achieve, nor should security be ignored due to cost. Let's now look in detail at each of the considerations mentioned above.

Type and Amount of Data

When we design our web service, we need to look at the type and amount of data we need to host, and the different levels of data our customers will want to access. The main types of data we will be dealing with are commercial information, financial transactions, and individual private information. Some web services host non-secure public data, such as weather information. Others host secure non-public data, such as company sales or pricing figures. There might be even one web service providing a blend of both. The type of data we host and the level at which we wish to guard that data will play a part in the way we choose to let users begin using our web service. The amount of data will also affect where that data is hosted and how we design our infrastructure to achieve the best results.

Type of Customers

The earlier we can identify our customer base in the design of our web service, the easier it will be to make critical security decisions. For instance, if we are only designing our web service for users internal to our business, we can rely on existing network credentials to represent who we view as customers. If we have specific customers from known locations, we can employ different security mechanisms to ensure that we know who our customers are. It is hardest to secure ourselves if we allow anyone on the Internet to access our web service or if our customer base is not identifiable, as is the case with anonymous user access. It is easier to determine success level by tracking customers and determining satisfaction levels. In addition, it is easier to make future growth decisions and design modifications with known customers.

Transaction Requirements

Transaction requirements stem from financial transaction or transaction tracking needs. If financial transactions need to take place using the web service, transaction tracking, audit, and identity verification are essential. So are customer identification, knowledge of data accessed by them, and the ability to answer to a number of authorities regarding the transaction. This is important and will require physical, architectural, and programmatic security implementations.

Response Times

Security implementation does not come without overhead. Decisions in the arena of response time include those regarding the level of interaction that will be required when the web service is accessed for the first time, subsequent times, and the response time of the web service while the customer is online with us. To track customers, we need to gather data from them. This is typically done on their first visit. It is assumed that customers would be fairly used to this, and would not take offence from our web site use. At this point, a security certificate could be used, or an authentication mechanism implemented. Subsequent visits should be made minimally intrusive, keeping in mind that we want to keep our web service as secure as possible. Re-verification of data for security purposes has a place in subsequent visits. Our ongoing response times should of course be maximized, but not at the expense of security. Lastly, security implementation should be analyzed and optimized for the best response time.

Resource Exposure

A picture of the architecture behind our web service would include web servers, data servers, security servers and perhaps even a double layer of these servers depending on how expanded our security infrastructure becomes. When designing the security infrastructure for the system, the level of exposure suiting our corporate resources has to be determined. The term resources here means the corporate server assets and data assets. Corporate assets should be exposed only to authorized personnel. Data integrity must be ensured, through backup and recovery mechanisms in the security design.

All of these implementation considerations play important roles in our next topic – factors of security. The factors of security we will explore team up with the topics we've just discussed to help formulate the decisions needed in designing our web service security infrastructure.

Factors of Security

There are six primary factors of security we want to review that should be considered in the scope of any web services implementation. They are identification, authentication, authorization, integrity, confidentiality, and non-repudiation. Each of these factors plays an important role in the representation and implementation that we outlined above in this section. We will be looking at each of these factors and how they play important roles in providing our customers with the experience they are looking for.

Identification

Identifying the users of a web service forms a critical piece of the web services puzzle. It gives us the ability to track the customers and customize our services to them. Also, it helps to identify someone who might be trying to damage our corporate assets by using our web service as a portal to our resources.

During the design phase of a web service we want to identify our users and get some information about them. Once this is determined, we have the ability to find out who the users are, where they are, when they connect to us, and to verify this information against the prior information gathered. Through the use of the means outlined later in this chapter we can verify customer's identities, and ensure that we have the knowledge we need so that we don't sacrifice the integrity of our web service.

Authentication

Once we know the types of users we are dealing with, we can use appropriate security measures to verify his or her identity. Authentication is the verification of the identity of the entity accessing our web service. On completion of verification, the entity is called the **principal** and the information regarding the entity is termed **credentials**. The means of authentication will be dependent on the level at which we need to verify someone's identity. There are many means of authentication, and those that will be included and explained in detail in Chapter 3 are:

❑   Basic

❑   Basic over SSL

❑   Digest

❑   NTLM

❑   Certificates

Users who access very sensitive areas or critical information will need a greater level of authentication than those accessing non-sensitive areas. Certain users will be easier to authenticate, typically based on their location and proximity to our business. For instance, users internal to our business are easy to authenticate based on their already existing user credentials on our internal network.

External users present more of a challenge because they normally are untraceable within our internal business structure. We then need to rely on an external source for verification, such as a certifying or authenticating authority. The consideration of proximity in authentication is critical because integration into an internal security framework can cause exposure to internal resources that need to be guarded. This creates a need to develop architecture that secures and supports authentication mechanisms independent of the level of users we are dealing with.

Authorization

On verifying the identity of whomever we are dealing with, the level of information they get to see is determined. We use the principal and credential information to authorize the users to see certain data, options, and privileges. Their access rights are maintained throughout their session with our web service. We want to limit what users can do because some users may try to exploit any security hole they find in the system. Limiting what users see and can do also helps to ensure the integrity of our system.

Authorization is done on an architectural level, and at a programmatic level, to protect system resources exposed through our web service.

Integrity

For the user to access our information, we need to ensure that what the user sees is accurate, timely, and unmodified. The goals are to ensure completeness of transactions, non-interference of the transactions, accuracy of the information, and verification of transactions and information presented.

Completeness of a transaction involves developing a web service that tracks the individual processes surrounding the transaction. Methods for ensuring completeness of the transaction have to be supplemented by mechanisms for rollback, essential in case of any failures in processing.

Confidentiality

Confidentiality is one of the largest concerns in the industry today in consumer confidence. We have to be able to assure our users that their data confidentiality is of top priority and that they have isolation when engaging in transactions within our web service. Ensuring that authorization of the user is required before allowing him or her to access customer data boosts confidentiality. Any form of intrusion, interference, or modification of data must be guarded against. Fraudulent entries and the changing of data would sacrifice both privacy and the integrity of an entire system.

Customers may also want assurance that their names are not being sold to agencies as part of their participation in the web service, and that information is not being derived from the types of transactions they are engaging in. This topic should be approached in the development cycle when considering resource exposure as mentioned in our previous section. The architecture used to guarantee against resources being exposed and subjected to improper access will also help assure confidentiality.

Non-Repudiation

We must guard against any allegations from customers regarding their experiences with our web service. We can do that only by providing complete tracking of users, transactions, and access to the web service. Without mechanisms in place that allow us in recreating the occurrences of any period of time, allegations could be brought up that a transaction was changed and interfered with. Multiple levels of authorization and mechanisms that can aid in recreating any transaction from scratch will help. The stability of a service is reflected from the management of the perceived response time of the web service to the user. Detailed logging of any changes to customer information requested will be the most effective method in case any questions should arise.

The above sections have discussed factors that will influence the decision on how security will be implemented. We have deliberated on how these factors cause security to be a driving force in all of the planning, development, and implementation phases of a web service, as opposed to being an afterthought. Integration of security principles into all phases of a project is less costly and will cause fewer delays in the project timeline.

Web Services Security Implications

At this point, we want to continue with our discussion of why security is important, particularly to a web service. We will now discuss security issues that arise due to Internet access, security holes particular to web services, and areas within the web service where security is a must.

Let us begin with the security issues that arise due to Internet access.

Web Security Issues

As the Internet has developed into an internationally accessed basis for commerce, it has seen an evolution of security practices and challenges. This accounts for the exponential growth of hackers, virus manufacturers, and other industry enemies that have accompanied the spread of the Internet. In this section, we will investigate the three main concerns related to web commerce, and the two major steps that have been taken to mitigate the concerns.

Hackers and Transaction Interception

When you talk to average people you will get mixed results as to how much they trust web-based commerce. Some people pay their bills, make purchases, and do their banking online, while others refuse to transact online at all. A certain level of mistrust exists because of the disturbing presence of hackers and other people on the Internet. They have broken into web sites, retrieved confidential data and stolen information like credit card details to fraudulently charge merchandise, usually before or without getting caught. In the worse case scenario, hackers have been able to get social security information as well as credit information; therefore we see an increase in stolen identities.

The fact that people can gain this information means that there are ways they can intercept the transactions and gain access to the data within the transaction. These concerns have raised the awareness of the companies that run web sites, and they have built extra security measures to try to regain and raise consumer confidence. The extra security comes at a price, usually reflected in the perceived speed of a site. While this is a concern for the web site companies, it hasn't overridden the need for the extra security.

Let us look at a diagram of how these interceptions can happen. Below, on the left is the customer computer accessing the web site on the right. If the pipe between the two ends is not protected, someone with hacking expertise can intercept the information flowing between them. During a purchase, this information could be credit card, address, or other private information:

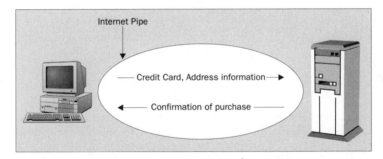

Next, we will discuss some of the early steps that can be taken to resolve these issues.

Certificates, Transport Layer Security, and Encryption

On a web site level, some companies have employed certificate security, transport layer security, and encryption to mitigate their security issues. Each of these mechanisms provides for the integrity, non-repudiation, and confidentiality components that we need in addition to concentrating on authentication and authorization issues. Each of these mechanisms addresses specific security problems. Certificates work in two ways. Server certificates provide verification of the identity of a web site. Client certificates provide authentication and authorization security by offering a secure mechanism to verify the identity of the customer attempting the transaction. Transport layer security includes infrastructure security that protects the assets of the web site company from being compromised.

Encryption provides a way to scramble the data going through the Internet pipe so that if someone attempts to look at the data, it would not be readily readable. Although no level of security is completely secure, these methods slow intruders down, as do locks on a door. If organizations providing we service do not employ the appropriate levels of security, they are inviting intruders to intercept their data. We will cover each of the above-mentioned security mechanisms in detail in the following sections.

Web Services-Specific Security Exploits

Web services use web technologies, with the result that many of the potential attacks against web sites are of concern for web services. The much more focused problem web services face is that the XML messages contain, in plain text form, a concentrated set of data that is likely to be interesting to an adversary. The fact that SOAP messages concentrate a lot of transaction data makes their security over transmission all the more important.

XML Transactional and Identification Concerns

Let us look at our XML transactional concerns by contrasting a purchase from a web site with a contractual transaction with a web service. You will notice that in the table below we cover the login, transaction, and confirmation phases of a web site transaction.

Web Site – Purchase of Product:

Element	Web Site	Security Element
Log onto Web Site	Authentication	Certificate
Put product in basket	Insecure	
Proceed to check out	Insecure	
Send credit card info	Secure	Encryption
Receive receipt	Secure	Encryption
Receive confirmation e-mail	Via e-Mail	None

In the table below, you will see similar elements in a simplified contract transaction. However each part of the interaction with the web service is approached with the level of security needed over that particular part of the transaction. We mention the use of digital certificates that will be explained in detail in following sections.

Web Service – Contract Transaction:

Element	Web Service	Security Element
Log onto web site	Authentication	Certificate
Initiate contract request	Secure	XML encryption
Contract request answered	Secure	Digital certificate on message level
Contract filled out and returned	Secure	Digital certificate and encryption
Receive confirmation message	Secure	Encryption

Later in the chapter, we will introduce XML security-related issues that cover transaction-based solutions, and outline which parts of a web service could be worked upon to make it more secure.

Web Service Security Applications

As we have mentioned above, web services must integrate basic web site security at the identification and authentication levels, with additional levels of security blended into the interaction between the web service and the customer. With that in mind, we will outline three areas of the web service where security should be applied. These areas will be Authentication/Authorization, Transport Layer, and Application layer security.

Authentication/Authorization

Just as with a regular web site, it is necessary for a web service to begin processing by identifying the user via some authentication scheme. That determines what methods the user will be permitted to access. Authentication information potentially may be reused with later transactions. It may be useful to track identity information even for non-sensitive services that require no special authentication, as statistics may be useful to guide future system enhancements.

Transport Layer

Transport layer security is crucial to web services when sensitive information is being transported across the insecure Internet. As we mentioned at the beginning of the chapter, determining the level at which transport layer security will be needed is dependent on identifying the customer base that will access the web service. The transport layer security that will come into play in ensuring the identification process will include the need for end-to-end security, securing corporate assets, and providing secure ways for specific customers to access the data needed.

The goal in transport layer security is to secure the transactions independent of the programming of the web service, and to guard against tools and methods hackers use to access the data, since it is in the Internet pipe between the web service host and the customer. We can use a variety of methods, including IPSec, firewalls, and restricting access to known IP to accomplish transport layer security at the endpoints of our pipe. We can use SSL and other means to cover the transport layer as the data comes through our pipe. Each of these will be discussed in detail in the security terms and concepts section.

Application Layer

Application layer security plays a pivotal role in web service authentication, and verification of the individual parts of XML transactions. Since web services are inherently transactional, it is more than likely that you would want to procure the identification of users, and perform re-validations and re-identifications throughout the transactional process. We will examine approaches to using public key cryptography standards that can verify portions of our message against digital certificates and signatures.

We will now delve into the security terms and concepts that we outlined above, which pertain particularly to web services.

Security Terms and Concepts

In this section, we will explore the security terms and concepts that we outlined in the previous section to provide the reader with a more detailed understanding of what web services security will entail. The objective should be to protect the web service both at an infrastructure level and at a programmatic level. We will describe both the levels in the following sections, and take a detailed look at transport layer security, authentication layer security, and application layer security. Let's begin by looking at a concept that applies to all the security concepts we listed and how it will protect our overall corporate network. This concept is called a DMZ (Demilitarized Zone). Let's now look at this in detail.

DMZ – Demilitarized Zone

A demilitarized zone in the computer world is similar to the one in the military. It is an unprotected zone where all parties have access to everything. In the case of security in our typical network, this demilitarized zone is an area where we place assets such as our web server that hosts our web service site. We place such assets in this area to make it easier for Internet users to access the resource, and add a layer of security that protects the rest of our corporate computing assets. This zone works in conjunction with the transport layer security that we will be detailing shortly. To give you an idea of how a demilitarized zone works into the network infrastructure, let us look at the diagram of a simple DMZ below:

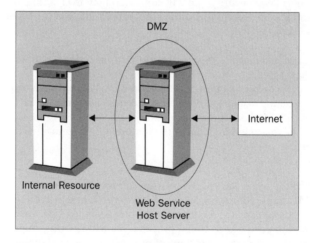

On the left of the diagram, we have an internal resource, such as a database server that feeds our web service. We don't place our primary resources in the DMZ because, as the diagram illustrates, it is exposed directly to Internet users, which may not be safe for our assets. In the internal resources, we would have primary data, program source, and other resources and just feed information the resources in the DMZ so that if the DMZ computers are compromised they can be rebuilt quickly without losing valuable corporate assets and information. We'll enhance our diagram with our other transport layer concepts shortly to give you an entire picture of where the DMZ fits in. Let's now move onto our transport layer security concepts.

Transport Layer Security

Transport layer security, as we've described before, is the infrastructure security that we utilize while creating the infrastructure that surrounds our web site, the communication with customers over the Internet, as well as the protection of our corporate assets. Hackers target these three areas most often. The transport layer security guards against people impersonating other users and hackers trying to steal data off the network.

We will now discuss three main areas for the transport layer security – IPSec, Firewalls, and restriction to known IP.

IPSec

IPSec introduces a few concepts to our infrastructure arena that we want to look in more at detail. IPSec takes advantage of IP – which is the protocol suite that the Internet is based on. IPSec builds a security layer on top of the standard IP protocol using encryption techniques. IPSec uses the HTTPS layer to utilize the encryption techniques. The positive aspects of IPSec are that it secures all of the transmissions on a given network, it guards against the most used hacking techniques, and it is done independent of the application running. The negative aspects are that it adds overhead, thus being slower than plain IP, is complicated, and is complex to integrate with a firewall.

When IPSec is used, the secure tunnel created is called a VPN, or virtual private network. If there are subscribers to a web service that are connected frequently to your server, or if there are vendors that work with the corporation but are located off site, it is wise to invest in VPN technology to enhance the security of the communications between such clients. The diagram below illustrates this concept:

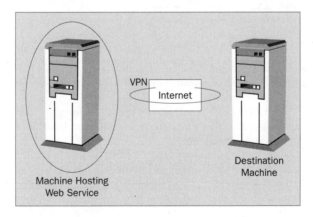

There are a few prerequisites to using IPSec and VPN technology. First, the customer accessing the web service must have a fixed IP Address for the VPN configuration. This can be limiting, especially if we need to offer our web service to anonymous users. Secondly, our other levels of security must accommodate a VPN and IPSec. As we mentioned before, not all firewalls are VPN friendly and oftentimes the client machine must have certain revisions of software on them as well.

Now that we have explored the IPSec approach to our infrastructure, let's look at blocking incoming users and unwanted information with a firewall.

Firewalls

A firewall's main goal is to filter and read the type and destination of any information coming in or going out from the organization. One of its main uses is to have filters that deny intruders access to the internal network. We want to keep in mind that getting through multiple layers of security is always more challenging to a potential intruder than getting through just one layer. Another goal is for the firewall to prevent some common ways of discabling a web site's ability to respond to user requests. Such attempts by hackers to accomplish this are, as has been briefly been touched on earlier, are denial of service attacks.

The web server that contains the web service site usually lives in the DMZ, or demilitarized zone. Remember the DMZ area is open to the Internet and has less security than an internal portion of a network usually would. Between the DMZ area and the internal corporate network there is a firewall mechanism protecting the system from users who might try to gain access to internal network resources. The firewall usually directs the traffic coming from the web site machine directly to any internal resources, such as data servers, and prevents any other resources from being accessed by traffic coming from the web site machine. The concept of the DMZ and firewall working together is illustrated in the diagram below:

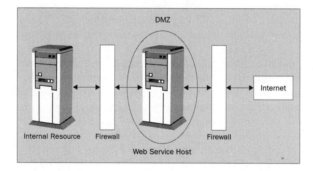

The solution we showed in the diagram above incorporates a firewall mechanism between our web site server and our internal server, as well as another firewall between our web site server and the Internet.

The firewall mechanism filters the traffic coming from the web site to a specific IP address within our internal structure, routing it through different ports. A firewall may limit the traffic from specific data requests, and even refuse to respond to some.

It is most important to remember that incorporating firewalls and DMZ concepts into the network infrastructure is a critical step in protecting the enterprise data. Without these the corporation is literally open to attack as soon as a web server is installed and linked up to the Internet within the corporate network.

Security by Specific IP

Network components called routers route network traffic, called packets, from one destination to another. Routers can read information regarding the content, source, and destination and filter out packets that should not be going into the network. Firewalls often serve a routing function within the DMZ area. Leaving network router devices too open can be dangerous should a program get through the VPN or firewall security surrounding our web servers. Using routers and firewalls to filter network traffic allows us to use them to identify specific IP addres we want to let in and route that traffic to specific places. This routing is illustrated in the diagram on the following page:

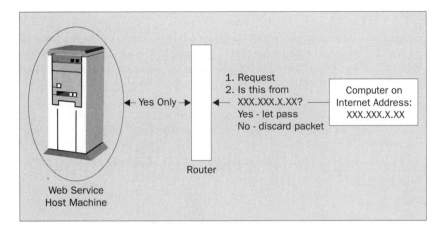

Even at a more complex level, the basic function of the router in this situation is to either let packets pass or to discard them. If we use the routers as filters, it can assist our firewall in decreasing their workload. Let us now move from our transport layer to the authentication layer where security needs to be addressed.

Authentication Layer Security

We will look at four major approaches to authentication. We will look at scenarios where we want to authenticate users programmatically, by using an authentication service and through use of certificates. Let us begin with programmatic authentication.

Programmatic Authentication

Programmers often like to control what their users see and can access by authenticating them once they have reached their destination web service. They track the users' information based on data collected in a registration process. Once the registration process is complete, the users receive their user identification and password information, and can they access the web service. The user is prompted for the user id and password every time he or she tries to access the web service.

Localized Authentication

Localized authentication comes into play when our internal corporate users access resources. There is a network level of security that we take advantage of in localized authentication, as provided by the workstation instead of the user.

The web service can then take advantage of the network credentials to determine the authentication level of the user. This is a seamless method because it does not need any additional information provided by the user for authentication.

Often, localized authentication is used for administrative functions such as database and web site maintenance because the users who perform these functions are usually from within the organization.

Authentication Services

Authentication services are popping up on the Internet to support web services and to assist in solving the centralized web authentication problems. Services such as Microsoft Passport and Verisign Personal Trust Agent accounts allow authentication with web sites that use their services. The diagram below illustrates how a web site would authenticate a user who registered with these types of services:

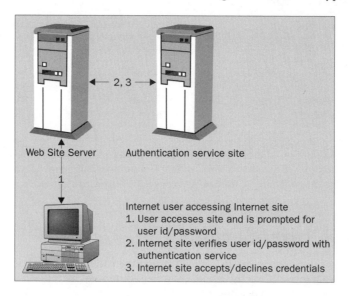

Thanks to authentication services, web sites no longer will have to track independent databases of users, passwords, and associated information. However, each web site has to trust the integrity of such a service provider's system, and believe that the user ids and passwords are protected.

Certificates and Authentication

Certificates work in conjunction with message encryption to prevent hackers from examining the contents of the data flowing in the Internet from the site to customer computers. Certificates are based on a standard called Public Key Cryptography, which is explained in detail in the next section, and are used by implementing SSL (Secure Sockets Layer) for a web site. You can tell a web site is using SSL because the address will be preceded with https:// instead of http://. A notification box similar to the one below will appear and inform you the site is using SSL:

On Internet Explorer, a lock will appear in the right part of the status bar on the bottom of the screen. The SSL implementation ensures that all data going between the web site and the user's computer is encrypted and secure. In the screenshot of expedia.com shown below, note the https:// in the address line:

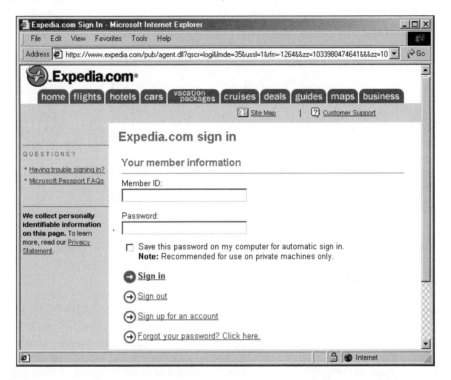

Certificates are issued by very few companies and are issued uniquely on a site-by-site basis. The publisher signs a certificate so that the certificate can be verified. When a certificate is issued by the web site to a client who is signing up for the web site's service, provides the certificate comes across with Public Key Cryptography information attached. In Internet Explorer, you can see the certificate attached to a web site by selecting File, Properties from the menu bar. You will then see the screenshot that follows:

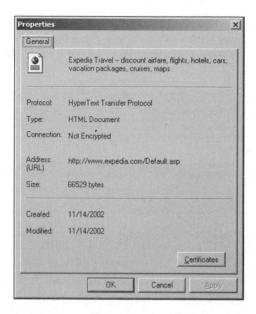

For a document with a security certificate with **Details and Certification Path** tabs, would appear. If you then click the **Certificates** button on the **Properties** window you will see the certificate information screen. For more coverage on this topic, refer chapter 5.

Application Layer Security

Coupled with transport layer and authentication layer security is application layer security. This is an additional layer of security that enhances the other two layers by adding a means to verify the users' authentication through extensions to the programming architecture. This can secure message transmissions down to each part of the message. Standards are still emerging for the XML messaging extensions, and are quite complex.

We will now examine the crucial concepts: Public Key Cryptography, SOAP extensions, Digital Security, and XML Digital Signatures.

Public Key Cryptography

Public Key Cryptography is widely used for web-based authentication and data encryption. Public Key Cryptography is an approach that allows a secure exchange of information between agents without the stringent key exchange regimens of private key systems.

With private key systems, there is one secret key used to encrypt and decrypt messages, and it must be available to both the sender and receiver of the message. Public Key Cryptography involves the use of two keys, a private one that is never exchanged, and a public one that might be collected into some sort of public directory. Secure communications may then be initiated without any exchange of the secret key. PKC algorithms tend to be rather slow, so in practice they normally are used to exchange a key for a much more efficient private key block cipher.

PKC is also used to generate and exchange digital signatures, where the identity is verified based on the fact that only one agent has access to the PKC private key. For instance, if we were to buy a ticket on Expedia, we would need to transmit our credit card information across the Internet to guarantee the purchase. Let's look at a diagram of how the transaction would go. On the right is our computer, on the left the web server at Expedia. First we send message 1, would which involves making a request and providing the public key. The server would use the private key to verify that our certificate identity is valid, and then send a message back asking us for our credit card information. We would use our private key to ensure that we received the request from the appropriate computer, and then we could reply with our information. Communication would continue in this manner until the purchase was complete as shown below:

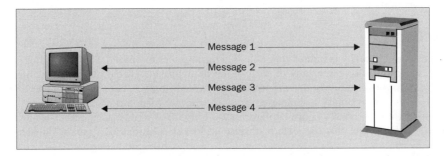

Public Key Cryptography meets the goals of ensuring data integrity, user authentication, and data confidentiality. It has long been a standard in the web industry for issuing validation codes called **certificates**, which are the storage medium for the signature information used in the exchange of information as we illustrated above.

PKC systems generally include secure hashing algorithms such as MD5, SHA1, and RIPEMD160 that are used to generate values that, once encrypted using the PK algorithm, become digital signatures.

SOAP Security Extensions

SOAP security extensions are headers that can be included in the SOAP message in an XML document. They trigger authentication from a client, transmit authentication to a server, or communicate back to a client a new authentication challenge or acceptance. These headers are not read by SOAP engine implementations, and so their use might come at a cost of interoperability. There are two types of the authentication protocols available in the SOAP extensions: basic and digest.

Basic authentication is based on credentials that the client can supply and transmit back to the server. The exchange of information is illustrated in the diagram below:

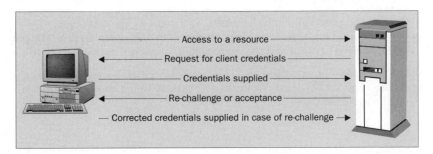

If we look at our last diagram page, the Internet client on the left requests access to the resource on the right. The resource server then requests the client to send the credentials. Upon receipt of the credentials, the resource either refuses the client if the credentials are incorrect or accepts them.

Digest authentication is based on individualized authentications for each SOAP message exchange; therefore the client must re-authenticate upon the request of each SOAP message. This is a step up from basic authentication as it more comprehensively handles responses from resources, using MD5 checksums to resist attacks that might have resulted in intercepted passwords.

SOAP security extensions consist of a very basic form of security, and so should be considered only when security is not a major concern, such as in an intranet-based web service that only will be accessed by internal corporate users.

Digital Security

Digital security is a security standard that allows programmers to embed digital signatures within their documents, programs, drivers, or any other programmatically generated object. It ensures the integrity of operating system components, drivers, and programmed objects. The end user of a computer can now tell if a driver or an object downloaded from an Internet page has a signature or not, and the more recent levels of Internet browsers are configured to notify users of unsigned objects. Below, we have an outline of standards topics that digital signature providers should include in their toolsets.

Digital Signature Provider Standards

When choosing to implement Digital Signatures the tools should provide:

❑ A Digital Signature based on Public Key Cryptography standards
It is important that the utility relies on Public Key Cryptography standards and not a proprietary standard. The main reason for this of course is compatibility across platforms and a standard by which the receiver of the message can communicate. We have seen with the Internet browser world that much overhead can be involved in determining browser compatibility, so sticking to a single standard will be beneficial for everyone.

❑ Ability to support multiple signatures
The ability to support multiple signatures suits documents that would be processed by many users. An example for a corporation would be workflow documents such as approval documents for bills of materials in a manufacturing organization. Internet business mortgage companies often require multiple signatures for documents where the signer is located remotely.

❑ Ability to provide signature cancellation
The tracking mechanisms should provide for a way of tracking the application and for the cancellation of signatures on individual messages, according to the tracking needs of contractual documents.

❑ Ability to provide encryption mechanisms
Security is the most important issue when it comes to document signing. The parties involved should feel assured of document authenticity and business security from third parties.

❑ Ability to provide a timestamp
One requirement for any legal document is the stamp of the date and time at which the document was signed on.

❑ Ability to provide logging and archival
The ability to trace the sequence of signatures and also be able to retrieve that information after a long period of time is important when incorporating Digital Signatures into a document. Many companies that require signed documents must archive them for many years and need to retrieve them for evidence in legal matters. An electronic document is not excluded in legal matters, so archival and retrieval mechanisms are very important.

We will now move onto some of the standards of digital security.

XML Security/XML Extensions

Organizations have taken different approaches to securing XML. XML is a structured text document, and is easily readable and accessible, which contributes to the lack of security in XML documents. We will look at some basic methods for securing XML.

XML Signature Tags

Regarding the elements within XML that relate to the digital signature, there are a few required elements. Below is the structure for the elements and a brief description of each:

❑ The beginning tag is a signature tag, which indicates a digital signature block.

❑ The second tag is a `SignedInfo` tag, which begins a block to encapsulate and describe the signed elements of the XML.

❑ The third and fourth tags, namely the `CanonicalizationMethod` and the `SignatureMethod` tags, determine the algorithms used in processing the Digital Signatures.

❑ The next set of tags, from `Reference` tags to `DigestMethod` and `DigestValue` tags, refer to the digest methods and the signed resource used.

❑ At this point, the `SignedInfo` tag is closed and the actual `SignatureValue` tag follows. Next are the `KeyInfo` tags that describe the sender's certificate information.

❑ At this point the `KeyInfo` and `Signature` tags are closed.

Below is a sample document that illustrates the use of the abovementioned tags:

```xml
<?xml version="1.0" encoding="UTF-8"?>
<Signature xmlns="HTTP://www.w3.org/2000/09/xmldsig#">
  <SignedInfo ID="Sample">
    <CanonicalizationMethod Algorithm="Http://www.w3.org/TR/2001/Rec-xml-cl4n-
20010315"/>
    <SignatureMethod Algorithm="Http://www.w3.org/2000/09/xmldsig#dsa-sha1"/>
    <Reference URI="Http://www.sample.com/sample">
      <DigestMethod Algorithm="Http://www.w3.org/2000/09/xmldsig#sha1"/>
      <DigestValue>1jkl3klj5kljkl5jkl2</DigestValue>
    </Reference>
  </SignedInfo>
<SignatureValue>RDSEF</SignatureValue>
<KeyInfo>
  <X509Data>
  <X509SubjectName>CN=SampleName,O=Sample
Company,ST=Someplace,C=Somewhere</X509SubjectName>
```

```
    <X509Certificate>
       MIJKLJKE308593
    </X509Certificate>
  </X509Data>
</KeyInfo>
</Signature>
```

The tags are included in the XML document to indicate that signature information is present. These tags should be based on current W3C approved signature, certificate, and algorithm references.

Let us now move on to the definition of XML Extensions and how they are used.

XML Extensions

XML Extensions, from a document perspective, represent additional customisable components that extend the existing XML schema, adding security elements to the document. XML databases also provide extensions to store this sort of information. There has been considerable debate over how to best store XML data. Databases have proven most popular, database vendors providing extensions for convenient ways of storing and retrieving XML documents.

From here, let us look at the XML Signature standards.

XML Digital Signature Standards

In this section we will be discussing emerging XML standards in relation to digital signatures. We will look at the building blocks that have evolved regarding digital signatures to include **XKMS (XML Key Management Specification)**, **XKISS (XML Key Information Service Specification)**, **XKRSS (XML Key Registration Service)**, and **XTASS (XML Trust Assertion Service Specification)**. We will also look at the roles of the markup languages **XACML (eXtensible Access Control Markup Language)**, **SAML (Security Assertion Markup Language)**, and **XTAML (XML Trust Axiom Markup Language)**. Each of these utilizes XKMS framework and builds upon it to provide specific solutions to problems in web services business transactions. Here is a diagram of how the specifications build upon each other:

WS-Security		
XKMS		
XKISS	XKRSS	XTASS
XACML	SAML	XTAML

Looking at our diagram we can see how XKISS, XKRSS, and XTASS are extensions to the base XKMS specification, and the associated markup languages help define the schema for the specifications. WS-Security comes into play to further define security specification standards in the industry. Let's begin with our more in-depth discussion on XKMS, which couples with the XKISS and XKRSS specifications.

XKMS

XML Key Management Specification is a standard submitted to the W3C to outline how to manage XML-based digital signatures in the web services environment. It is built on WSDL and SOAP, and is meant to provide tools to integrate elements needed for checking for digital signature-related data. It defines the protocol necessary for distributing and registering public keys used in the XML-DSig specification we will discuss next. The XKMS specification deals with the information found in the KeyInfo tags that we mentioned earlier in the *XML Signature Tags* section.

The XKMS specification is made up of two parts – XKISS and XKRSS. The XKISS specification outlines support for delegating the function of the processing of key information to a service. The service provides the ability to locate, describe, and bind the identification information of a given key. The XKRSS specification supports the key pair registration by a key pair holder and provides support for key pair generation and registration by a key pair service provider.

XACML, SAML, and XTAML

XACML, and SAML XTAML are the primary markup languages for use with XML to provide the syntax for utilizing XKMS specifications. XACML is used for establishing access control for authorization policies in XML, for an XML defined object.

SAML is used for establishing key tracking information as provided for in the XKISS and XKRSS specifications. It defines specifications to exchange security information within the markup language. It utilizes XML digital signatures and encryption. XTAML outlines the syntax for use in tracking information of the established trust credentials.

XTASS

The XTASS specification builds on the XKMS specification to provide a means by which a trust assertion can be processed. In a trust assertion, an authenticating party verifies the identity of an asserter, and provides authentication information to the service requesting it. It essentially is provided by a third party, and makes a statement about the validity of identities or regarding statements made about previously asserted messages. It utilizes public keys and digital signatures in responding to requests. The third party is typically a service credential assertion provider.

Any web service provider which participates in a trust service provided by a third party basically agrees to specific terms which govern the use of that trust service. Currently trust services mainly are being used for high end finance-based transactions. Some examples of these financial transactions could be real estate contracts investment transactions, and accounting documents such as invoices and purchase orders. With the advent of XTASS standards, financial transactions are made available for very low startup costs, and no proprietary standards are required.

WS-Security

WS-Security is a security initiative sponsored by IBM, Microsoft, and Verisign. It is designed to build upon SOAP security extensions and to provide handling of multiple sources of security credentials, sources for those credentials, encryption schemes, and incorporation of all of these factors to produce one overall solution to the scope of security needs. The WS-Security initiative defines a security element that encapsulates the security information to be provided. In particular, this specification is meant not to redefine key management, but as the means to define security schema within XML documents.

Web services security language supports a variety of security models:

- ❑ Multiple security tokens for authentication or authorization
- ❑ Multiple trust domains
- ❑ Multiple encryption technologies
- ❑ End-to-end message-level security

Security Standards Examples

In this section our goal is to provide visual examples of the security mechanisms we've outlined in this chapter. We'll look in detail at examples using IPSec and Firewalls, trust and certificate authentication, and also at SOAP extensions and XML Signature examples. We will wrap up with an extensive example incorporating various security mechanisms, providing an integrated overview of how they all work together.

Transport Layer Security

Transport layer security incorporates a hardware level of security that protects all requests traveling across our network. In this section, we will look at an example with a diagram illustrating how firewall and IPSec integrate into our web services scenario.

Firewall and IPSec Diagram

The diagram below defines the typical traffic pattern generated from a web service client. It goes to a web service, offered from a server behind firewalls. IPSec is used to communicate with the web service client. In our scenario, the web service host has determined he wants only specific PCs to be able to access the web service due to the sensitive nature of the data he is hosting. Only specified clients can take advantage of his web service, based on an agreed set of terms. The web service client establishes the IPSec communication using VPN software. Let us outline the logic behind the communication:

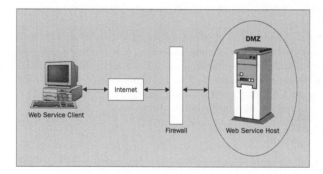

The web service client has the Internet browser opened and the URL typed in for our web service. For this example our web service will be //http:xxx.xxx.xx.x /WebServiceExample and our client address will be yy.y.y.yy.

The client request goes across the Internet to reach the firewall that guards the web service server from Internet intruders. The firewall then finds out whether yy.y.y.yy has access to any resources it guards. If so, it then prompts the client for the security code before it establishes an IPSec connection. Once the client returns the correct credentials to the firewall, it establishes the VPN IPSec-based connection with the client computer and lets the client request pass to the web service.

VPN and firewall connections are programmable to limit the time a client is on, so when the connection expires, authentication would again be required.

The firewall has the ability to pass the credential information supplied by the client upon the establishment of the VPN session, for example pass to the web service the credential information. The web service may use the credentials already established for firewall and/or VPN connections to authenticate the user's request, and return the value of the request without requiring any additional authentication step. Let's utilize what we know by illustrating the next step in the security layers, authentication security.

VPN will henceforth be indicated by encircling the machine hosting the web service.

Authentication Layer Security

At our authentication layer we will want to look in more detail at two types of authentication: the use of an authentication service and the use of standard certificate authentication. Let us begin with the use of an authentication service.

Authentication Service

Authentication service is the utilization of a third party repository of security credentials to authenticate a web service. In our scenario a client makes a request to a web service host. The web service host uses an authentication service to validate client credentials, so there will be interaction with that service as shown in the diagram below:

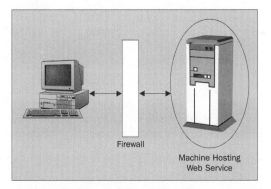

The client PC in the illustration, having been allowed through the firewall, talks with the web service host, which presents the client with an authentication screen:

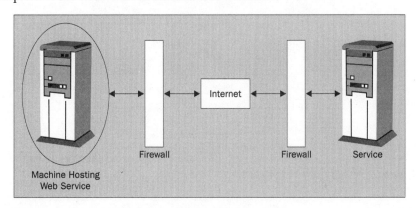

From this point the web service will pass the credentials to the third party authentication service for verification. The authentication service can be an internal resource, though it was an external one in the previous illustration. The authentication service then responds with an acceptance or denial, and the web service completes the client interaction by denying or granting access to the client.

Certificates

The use of certificates is a little more complex than the use of an authentication service, because of the required installation of the certificate in the browser keystore on the web service client. We will illustrate the whole process in the following diagrams.

At the client request point, the client will interact with the web service to use certificates for authentication. The web service requests a client certificate. When the client does not have one, it is redirected to a site where the client can get one installed:

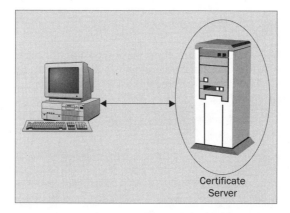

Certificate
Server

The client is referred to a certificate server, which can appropriate and install a certificate for use in interacting with the web service. Certificates expire, and so need to be renewed at predetermined intervals:

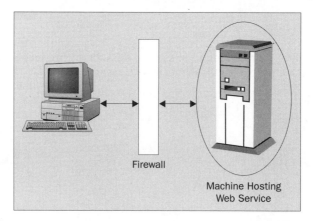

Firewall

Machine Hosting
Web Service

Once the client certificate is installed, the web service can read the credentials from the certificate and determine the access level that the client gets.

Application Layer Security

After the transport layer and authentication layers, the application layer takes over. It may assume that the other security layers did their job, and can interact directly with the web services client. Alternatively, it may implement further security measures to protect the client and web service interaction from intrusion. In the following examples we will illustrate how we would further protect the client interaction by the use of SOAP Extensions and XML digital signature usage.

SOAP Extensions

To review what we learned previously in this chapter, SOAP extensions are SOAP headers that provide security information and protect the individual SOAP messages that are transmitted. In our diagram below, we will illustrate how these messages are packaged:

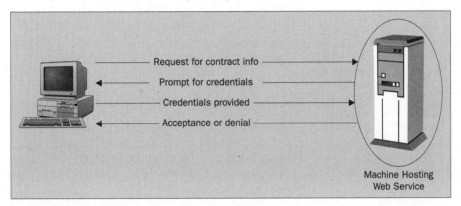

The client computer here is assumed to have been authenticated to the web service at all other levels, and is engaged in a transaction. As it has requested a contractual transaction, the web service requires authentication in order to respond with the correct information:

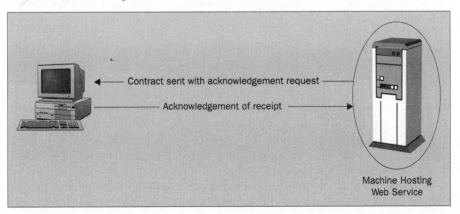

Once the credentials pass, the web service packages the contract information inside SOAP header information. Usually, a receipt acknowledgement is requested. When this is sent and acknowledged, the contract is complete, and is returned with another round of SOAP message level verification of proper credentials to complete the contract.

As seen our illustration, the additionalelements are added to the `<SOAP-ENV:Envelope>` element. This does not include options to protect pieces of our SOAP message.

XML Digital Signature

The XML digital signature transaction can be taken to a deeper level than what we illustrated previously because it is designed to verify multiple pieces of information with a SOAP message. In our earlier example, the transaction would have been complete when the contract was completed and returned with another round of authentication, thus verifying the entire transaction. In more complicated contract scenarios, such as real estate or stock purchase contracts, there are elements within the contract that need authorization as well. As represented by our examples in this section, the signature on the form can be taken care of by a SOAP message envelope, but the individual initials would require XML digital signature technology to accommodate the level of detail required:

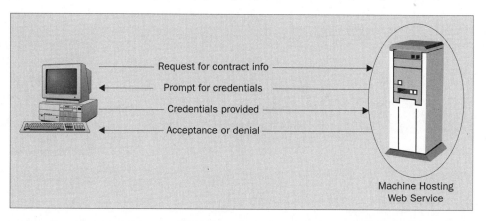

The first part of our scenario is not much different between the two technologies. However the difference in XML digital signatures is that they use the Public Key Cryptography standards. Therefor, the exchange of credentials is really an exchange of the Public Key Pairs instead of SOAP header contained information. Encryption by default is with XML Digital Signatures as opposed to the SOAP extensions, where it is optional:

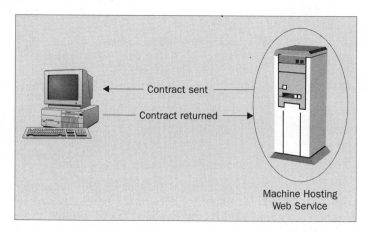

The interaction between the client and the web service is still at the macro level as illustrated on the previous page, but at the internal level of the contract, the authorization is different. Therefore, once the credentials are validated, the contract would be sent. At this point in our scenario, the contract would be a web page with embedded capabilities allowing the receiver to attach the digital signature information this digital signature information is required at a detail level to supply the proper credentials within the contract to then approve or disapprove the various levels of detail that required them. As we illustrated in our prior explanation and XML examples, the digital signatures are embedded into the XML so that when the contract is returned, the digital signatures are at the proper locations for the web service to obtain the tracking information from the signatures.

To summarize all of our illustrations we will now look at an entire transaction through all of the levels of security.

Authentication Integration Example

We are going to look at a web service that utilizes many of the methods illustrated above. Our example will be a school web site that is integrated with a web site with the facility for guardians to obtain permission forms allowing their wards to use school transportation to go on a field trip. When the guardians download the form, they authorize their student both to be on school transportation and to attend the field trip. We will use certificate security and XML digital signatures to complete the permission form.

Part One – Guardian Interaction with School web server

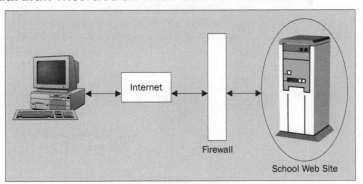

The school web site is being protected by a firewall. At the transport layer the guardian accesses the site through the Internet.

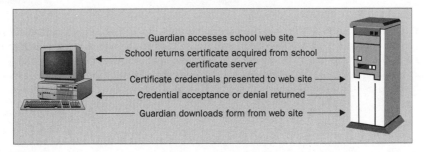

At the authentication layer, the guardian is being requested to provide a certificate in order to use the web site. Once authenticated, the Guardian can access the documents page on the web site.

Part two – Interaction Between all Parties with Regard to the Document

At this point, the school server mediates between the Internet client, who is analogous to the guardian, and the web service host at the district level. The document certainly could be distributed from the school web site, but the authorization information is part of the web service. The web service therefore, will request information with regard to digital signatures at the application level to complete the transaction. Let's go through our XML transaction from a security perspective now.

Transport Layer

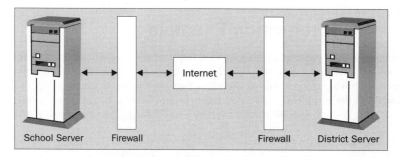

At the transport layer, the school server offers information regarding the document submitted by the client to the school. The firewalls that protect the servers from Internet intruders exchange information regarding source and destination IP Address, and credentials to determine the level of authentication.

Authentication Layer

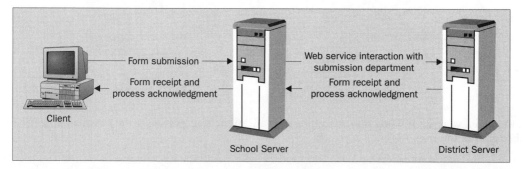

At the point of the document submission, the parent has embedded XML digital signatures into the document. The school server passes the document information to the web service, which that in turn processes the document and the XML digital signature information. After processing, the web service will return an acknowledgement, so the school may then notify the parent of the processing. As the web service processes the document, it logs information such as Digital ID, time, date, and the nature of the signature.

We will look at a process flow diagram that will help integrate the initial analysis and decision making with our detail decisions of what authentication mechanisms we want to implement.

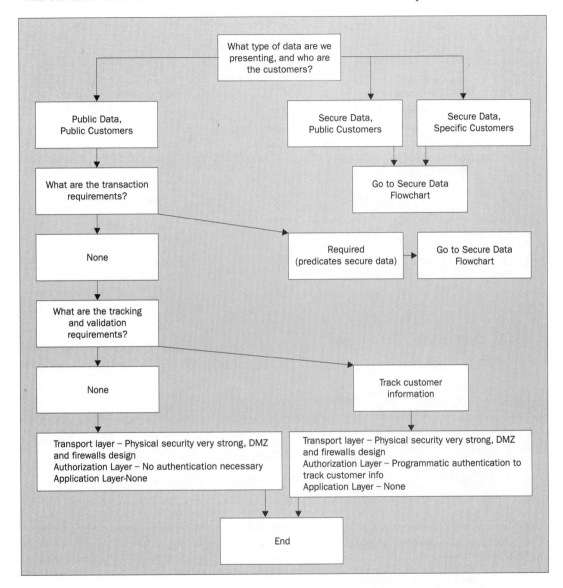

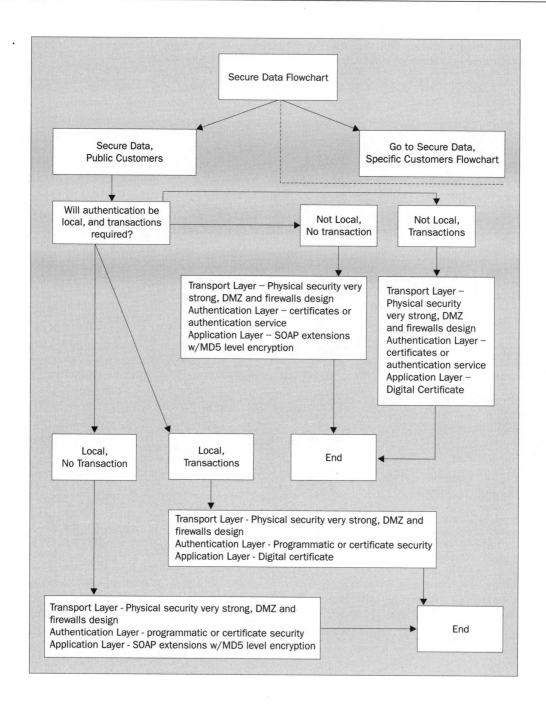

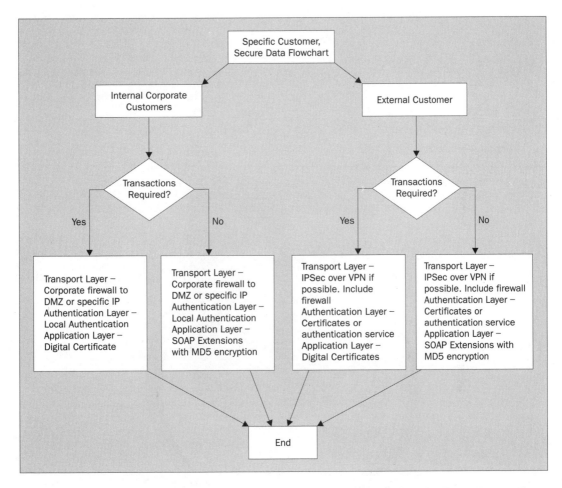

As we see in our diagrams above, the basic decisions outlined in the beginning of the chapter play a very important role in our security implementation.

Summary

In this chapter, we have had a detailed overview of the layers of security involved in a web service. We laid the groundwork for programming and architecture in the upcoming chapters. The most important thing to remember is that there are many critical aspects of security, and many layers to be addressed in regard to web service implementation.

3

Authentication Mechanisms

As we've said earlier, once a user is authenticated the program or infrastructure can then make decisions on what the user can access. The authentication mechanisms we will discuss in this chapter are the first level of authentication to be performed at the time anyone tries to begin the authentication necessary to access our web service.

We will see in future chapters that depending on the need, there would be techniques employed that were necessary for further security checks within the web service. This chapter covers the authentication mechanisms employed when someone first accesses our Web Service. Therefore, these mechanisms work at the server level, and not within the Web Service itself. The authentication mechanisms that we want to discuss in this chapter include:

❑   Basic

❑   Basic over Secure Sockets Layer (SSL)

❑   Digest

❑   NT LAN Manager (NTLM)

❑   Client Certificate authentication

We will begin by looking at an overview of how the mechanisms fit into our web services scenarios. We then move on to each authentication mechanism, giving its architecture, advantages, and disadvantages. Finally, we'll see a detailed example scenario and look at how these techniques work together to form the best security given complex situations.

In the last section we'll take a close look at the Liberty Alliance project. We will start by looking at the objectives, specifications, and areas to which this project applies. The implementation and the available toolkits are covered later.

Let's begin our discussion by determining what we want in our authentication mechanisms and the situations we should keep in mind while picking one.

Authentication Mechanisms Overview

Authentication is a process whereby the user, computer, or application presents valid information that can be verified by the authorizing agent involved in what they are accessing. At the point that the information is verified, the authorizing agent can then decide what is allowed for the user, computer, or application to access. When we are looking at authentication mechanisms, we have quite a few things to keep in mind. We want to choose the features based on the users and situations surrounding our web service. We would probably use a different authentication mechanism for a web service providing free weather information than one selling shoes online, or one selling up-to-the-second stock quotes.

We also will want to pick an authentication mechanism based on how wide of support we want to grant to the base of browsers that are available on the Internet. For example, if our web service has an end-user audience as well as a subscription-based audience, we will have to build in a wider variety of browser support. This would be important if the security mechanisms mentioned in this chapter were used to allow users to access a web service, which was integrated into a standard web page.

If we have a well-known user base, such as an internal corporate environment, we would know that our support base is from a fixed configuration, and would be predictable. Keeping this in mind, let's begin our discussion with a list of desired features within our selected authentication mechanisms.

Desired Features List

Our desired features list will be either specific or broad depending on the audience that we anticipate using our service. Establishing who our users will be provides the information with which we need to begin in any decision we make or in anticipating the requirements they will have when accessing our web service. As we answer these questions, we can move on to the specific questions regarding authentication mechanisms that we'll outline in this section. Let's look now at some of the decisions we will need to make regarding our authentication method.

Support Multiple Versions of Browser

Many of the authentication methods we will discuss are meant to support only current browser releases. As we'll discuss in our next section, depending on the audience, there might need to be a requirement for back-level browser support. The farther back the level of browser that needs to be supported, the lower the level of security that can be used in conjunction with authentication. It is best to check the individual browser specifications with the manufacturers to determine what browsers you really want to support. The browser levels are reviewed in the table to follow in this section.

Level of Integration with Operating System for User Tracking

Many of the authentication mechanisms integrate into the operating system. For example, if a web service client is accessing a host (web server) from a Windows-based machine, the user ID and password information is automatically passed within the HTTP packet. If that user ID and password pair matches a logon name and password on the host machine, then the authentication can be seamless. If authentication is done in this manner, the host machine would then track such information as last login time and date, and would be able to provide such information automatically. For instance, on a Windows machine, NTLM can automatically authenticate a user to a web page hosting a web service on an IIS server. From there, the IIS server can pass on the user ID and password pair to other resources the user need to access, such as a database server.

Firewalls and Proxy Server Integration

As the user base and the required infrastructure are identified, the traffic to our web service passing through either firewalls or proxy servers has to be taken into account. Firewalls and proxy servers can disturb authentication methods due to IP address conflict because of hashing methods. We will see more on hashing methods later in the book.

Level of Encryption Required

Different authentication mechanisms use different levels of encryption. The level of encryption chosen will eliminate some authentication mechanisms from consideration. For instance, basic authentication has virtually no encryption, whereas SSL has a much higher level. The methods graduate from limited to extensive encryption. Whenever critical information, especially when it contains data like user ID and passwords, flows over the Internet, encryption should be considered.

Level of Client Interaction Needed

Many of our authentication mechanisms provide a relatively seamless appearance, while the others that involve certificates require a good deal of user interaction during the initial setup phase of accessing the web service. Many web services want the user to enjoy a seamless experience, and want to avoid too many levels of authentication. The actual need for security, however, should never be compromised for the sake of user experience.

Level of Programmatic Authentication within the Web Service

Lastly, the purpose of looking at the authentication mechanisms is to determine what mechanism to use in light of the level of programmatic authentication that is integrated into the web service code itself. The authentication mechanisms we are talking about in this chapter are taken advantage of purely at an infrastructure level before the code of the web service is executed by the client.

Let's do a quick comparison between the mechanisms that we will be evaluating to highlight them in light of our desired features list. To explain a few of the terms used in the table, upper level browsers are those that support certificates, which include the latest versions of Netscape and IE. Also, under the O/S integration section, "Prompt" indicates that the user will be prompted for user credential information and, "high" means that it is integrated with the O/S so that the user does not have to supply extra information. The "mapping" term refers to the fact that the client certificate is mapped to an existing set of O/S credentials so that the user will not have to supply additional information. Under the programmatic authentication column, "suggested" indicates that additional security within the application would be desired. "Optional" indicates that the infrastructure security has been deemed sufficient and does not need additional security within the application:

Mechanism	Browser	O/S Integration Integration	Firewall	Encryption Friendly	Client Required	Programmatic Interaction
Basic All	Prompt	Yes	Minimal	Minimal	Suggested	None
Basic w/SSL	Upper Level	Prompt	Yes	High	Minimal	Suggested
Digest	Upper Level	High	Yes	High	Minimal	Suggested
NTLM	Any Internet Explorer	High	No	Medium	Minimal	Suggested
Client Certificates	Upper Level	Mapping	Yes	High	High	Optional

As you can see in the table, the higher encryption requires browsers that support the higher encryption levels. Firewalls don't come into play much unless you are using the NTLM method. With these questions in mind, let's look at some scenarios that also will help determine our decisions regarding authentication mechanisms.

Situations Overview

Although we are looking at three scenarios here - corporate internal, remote access, and Internet-based users, a straightforward approach to implementing authentication in XML Web Services is to leverage the authentication features of the protocol used to exchange messages. For most XML Web Services, this means leveraging the authentication features available for HTTP. In this section, we want to present three major categories of users who would influence our selection of an authentication mechanism. The three – corporate internal, remote access, and Internet-based users – each have separate authentication requirements and are truly separate in the scheme of authentication. This section will outline the differences and how they will affect our choice of the authentication mechanism used. Let's begin by looking at a corporate internal web service user and his authentication requirements.

Corporate Internal

Let's look at a specific scenario to help us decide what level of authentication our internal user might need. In our scenario, an internal corporate web site developer wants to take advantage of a time tracking web service. The time tracking web service allows the corporate web service customer to track his time. The time is then used by personnel and payroll to calculate pay. The developer wishes to integrate the web service into his site, which will be accessed by the employees of the corporation. From an architectural viewpoint, the network configuration is illustrated in the diagram below. In short, internal corporate users are accessing the web site server, which is in turn subscribing to the web service being hosted on a separate server. For the sake of completeness, we have also included in the drawing the location of the firewall and Internet access points for the network. The internal users are not routed through the firewall and proxy server, as is depicted below:

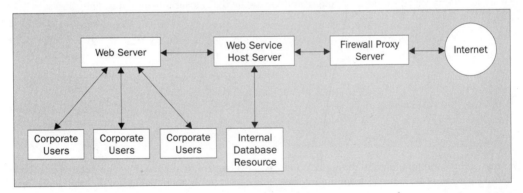

Our internal corporate structure is based on Windows 2000, and uses the IE6 browser. A predictable, standardized environment gives us much help in making our authentication decisions. We have all of the users who will access our web service in the Windows 2000 user list. We also know that our web service controls access to the portions of the program via menu selections; however we want the authentication mechanism to also be able to be used for authentication to a database resource that has been integrated into our web service. Now that our requirements have been analysed, let's review our authentication mechanism needs based on our desires list we outlined earlier:

- ❑ We only need to support IE6 as the browser
- ❑ We want to integrate the credentials with the operating system to pass through to the database resource
- ❑ We don't have to worry about a firewall or proxy server

❑ We want to provide encryption so that the passwords are not easily crackable on the network

❑ We don't want each client to have to interact heavily with the web service to set up the authentication

❑ We know the web service does further programmatic authentication, so we don't need the highest levels of authentication

Now, we can see that we could use NTLM security to meet our needs. We will get into the details of NTLM security later in the chapter.

Remote Access

Let's look again at a specific scenario to help us decide what level of authentication our remote user might need. In our scenario, our user is a corporate marketing manager who wishes to access the web site that is taking advantage of the time tracking web service. The user simply wishes to access the web site that integrates our service. The architectural diagram of the network configuration is illustrated below. In short, remote corporate users accessing the web site server that lives in the corporate Demilitarised Zone (DMZ) that subscribes to the web service. This zone is also known as the Perimeter Network.

The web service is being hosted on a separate server. External user requests are routed through the firewall and proxy server to get to the internal resources that the time tracking service uses. In addition, some networks would also have another server in the DMZ hosting the web service so that the only internal resource being used would be the data server. In high volume-request situations, you would also want to locate a replicated data server in the DMZ for added security and speed. This would provide additional security for the data against intrusion and would locate the data closer to where it is being accessed.

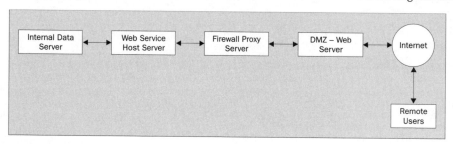

The rest of the configuration and setting is as before. Since we are dealing with a well-defined user base accessing our internal resources from the Internet, it is necessary to keep maximum security. Now, let's analyse our authentication mechanism needs here, based on our requirements outlined:

❑ We only need to support IE6 as the browser

❑ We want to integrate the credentials with the operating system to pass through to the database resource

❑ We do have to worry about a firewall or proxy server

❑ We want to provide maximum encryption so that the passwords are not easily crackable on the network

❑ Since each user is a corporate employee, it is not too much to ask for him or her to go through extra steps to establish a certificate.

❑ We still want the user to provide Windows 2000 credentials for use with our internal data resource

Now, based on comparing our list of analyzed needs, we see that we could use certificate security to meet our needs, coupled with programmatic security that prompts for the Windows 2000 credentials for use with accessing our internal resources. We will be getting into detail on certificate security in our section dedicated to explaining it.

We now move onto our next situation, an Internet user gaining access to our web service.

Internet User

We will look again at a specific scenario to help us decide what level of authentication our remote user might need. In our scenario, a remote company wishes to integrate our web service into its web site to take advantage of our time tracking web service for its employees and then wishes to make a subcontract with our company.

Let's say that this company wishes to access our web service directly. Remote corporate clients would be accessing our web service server that lives in the corporate DMZ. Only the Web Service itself would be able to access internal resources, and would be routed through the firewall and proxy server to get to the internal resources that the time tracking service uses. As with the last scenario, in high volume situations you would also want to locate a replicated data server in the DMZ for added security and speed. This is illustrated in the diagram below:

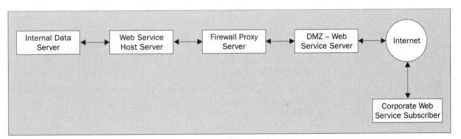

Our corporate structure for subscribers to our Web Service access is based on Windows 2000 accounts being created and is not dependent on a browser, since the subscriber will be developing a web front end for his or her users. However, we would require any subscriber to support the strictest levels of encryption. We would have a well-identified and limited subscriber base. We have all of the subscribers who will access our Web Service in the Windows 2000 user list. Let's analyse our authentication mechanism needs based on our requirements outlined here:

- ❑ We will only support browser/authentication that is based on upper level browser (refer to Mechanism Comparison Table above) support

- ❑ We want to integrate the credentials with the operating system to pass through to the database resource

- ❑ We do have to worry about a firewall or proxy server due to the web service servicing Internet clients from the DMZ area

- ❑ We want to provide maximum encryption so that the passwords are not easy to crack on the network wire

- ❑ Since each user is a corporate employee, it is not too much to ask for him or her to go through extra steps to establish a certificate.

- ❑ We still want the user to provide Windows 2000 credentials for use with our internal data resource

Now, based on comparing our lists of analyzed needs, we could use certificate security, coupled with programmatic security that prompts for the Windows 2000 credentials, for accessing internal resources. We would probably integrate a VPN scenario with the clients so that the data passing through the Internet has maximum security. We'll be getting into detail about certificate security in our section dedicated to explaining it.

Now that we've looked at some of the desired features of our authentication mechanisms and some of how each fits into our features, we will move on to explaining each in detail.

Basic Authentication

Basic authentication is the simplest authentication scheme outside of anonymous access. Although very useful before other mechanisms were developed, Basic Authentication no longer is a recommended authentication method. This section simply lays a foundation for understanding the more complex authentication schemes. Let's look at a diagram to see how this mechanism works:

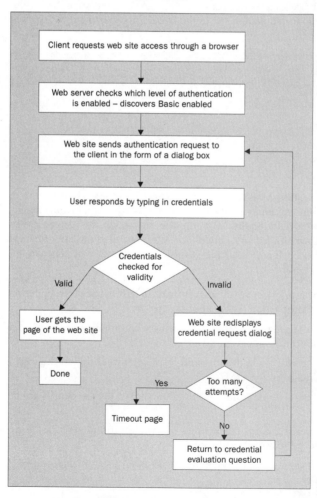

From the flowchart above, the web site has a setting that determines the level of authentication it is willing to accept. Once this is determined, the user request is evaluated based on information the requester supplies. Let's now examine the architecture behind Basic Authentication.

Architecture

In this section, we will look at how the architecture will vary with differences in the users of our web services.

Internal User

The architecture of an internal user is simple. There is no firewall or proxy server interaction necessary, so the request freely interacts with the web server. The requests flow back and forth until either valid credentials are supplied or the requester ends the conversation:

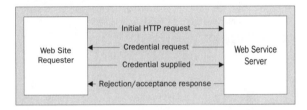

External User

The external user's scenario only changes architecturally due to the firewall/proxy mechanism being in place. The firewall/proxy mechanism would choose to pass on or discard packets coming from the Internet user based on rules that had been set up for the user. Other than that, the requests and responses would take place as normal.

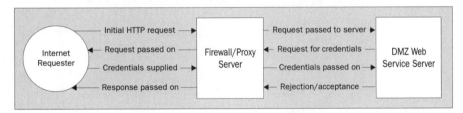

Pros

This method removes many problems that may be encountered when trying to initially troubleshoot client authentication to a Web Service. It is easy to support and has a wide base of support due to its simplicity. This makes it possible to track individual access to a web site because of integration with the O/S. It enables access to network resources and security delegation because of integration with the O/S.

Cons

This method currently is only recommended for test situations due to its inherently insecure nature. The credentials that are supplied by the user are transmitted in clear text, enabling the easiest mechanisms for hacking. Lastly, it depends on network accounts created to pass credentials and to access to other resources.

Basic over SSL

As we said in the above section, Basic authentication is the simplest authentication scheme outside of anonymous access. Basic over SSL is the same authentication scheme, but it uses SSL encryption to enhance the security of the credential transport. It is used when the Basic authentication is an acceptable means of retrieving user information, yet encryption is desired. This would be an acceptable means of getting information requiring little security to users. Let's now look at diagram of how this mechanism works.

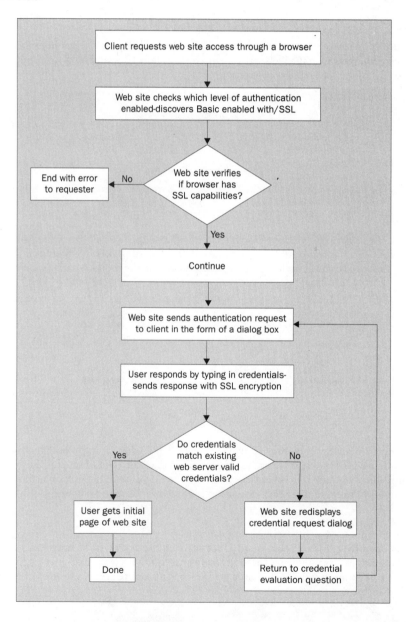

As you can see from the diagram above, it is very similar to the Basic Mechanism diagram with a few additions. When the client request comes in, it can either be preceded by https:// or be redirected to a secure web default page. Upon the redirection, the requesting browser must support SSL or the interaction will fail. Once the SSL interaction is established, all traffic is secure going between the requester and the web site. The remainder of the transaction remains the same, with the web site requesting credentials and either permitting access or the client finally terminating the request.

Internal User Architecture

Not much changes on the architectural diagrams between Basic and Basic over SSL. As you can see in the diagram below, the architecture of an internal user is still simple. There is no firewall or proxy server interaction necessary, so the request freely interacts with the web server. The main difference is that the web server would have a certificate installed and it would be configured such that SSL traffic was mandatory for web site access. At the point of SSL communication being established, the requests flow back and forth until either valid credentials are supplied or the requester ends the conversation.

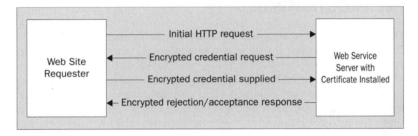

External User Architecture

In Basic Authentication with SSL, the external user's scenario still only changes architecturally due to the firewall/proxy mechanism being in place. The firewall/proxy mechanism would choose to pass on or discard packets coming from the Internet user based on rules that had been set up for the user. Other than that, the requests and responses would take place just as in the Basic over SSL diagram illustrated for the internal user.

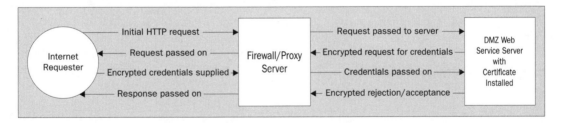

Pros & Cons for Mechanism

The pros and cons for Basic over SSL reflect greatly the same information as with the Basic authentication mechanism. The addition reflected below is the fact that SSL causes overhead on each interaction with the requester, causing a perceived performance decrease for the web site being accessed.

Pros

This method removes many problems that may be encountered when trying to initially troubleshoot client authentication to a Web Service. It is also easy to support and has a wide base of support. Using SSL for Web Services is very much like using SSL for web applications. Encrypting the SOAP messages with SSL protects them from hackers. It makes it possible to track individual access to a web site, which is helpful for Internet users. Lastly, it enables access to network resources and security delegation

Cons

This method currently is only recommended for test situations due to its inherently insecure nature. Although the SSL causes the traffic to be encrypted, the contents are still not encrypted. It depends on network accounts being created in order to pass on credentials and access to other resources. The response time degrades due to SSL supplying encryption for the entire transmission.

The Digest Mechanism

Digest authentication uses a hashing algorithm and a negotiation method with the client to verify credential information. The concept of using an algorithm is to provide a way to securely share the secret, or password. It allows information to pass over the wire that determines if the secret has been shared without revealing the actual secret information. It solves the basic problem that Basic Authentication poses because it does not pass the credential information in clear text. It is used when the basic transportation of data is not a security concern, just the credential information. It is an acceptable means of retrieving user information when encryption is desired so the information to be kept secret stays secret. It would be an acceptable means of getting information that requires little security to users. Because the client credentials are typed in from the requester's end, there is a higher chance of security being compromised at that end and so unique identity cannot be verified, just as we reflected in Basic and Basic over SSL. Let's now look at a diagram of how this mechanism works:

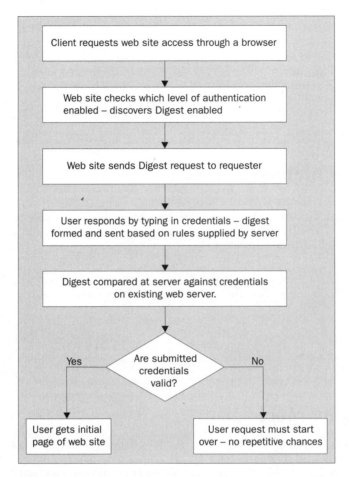

Our main difference in the diagram above is that the server requests a digest of the user credentials to be sent. The digest combines the user credentials with a shared piece of information that determines its unique response to the server. Once the server receives the information, it uses the same rules it gave the client to develop a digest of the shared piece of the information and the user credentials held on the server. If the two digests match, the requester is granted access to the site.

Internal User Architecture

The digest authentication diagram of an internal user is depicted in the diagram below. The architecture for an internal user is still simple. There is no firewall or proxy server interaction necessary, so the request freely interacts with the web server. The main difference is that the web server would request a digest hash of the client credentials for web site access. At the point of the hash being generated and decrypted by the server, the server would compare it to existing credentials at the server and determine the appropriate response to the requester. The acceptance/rejection response is final and the user does not get a chance to respond again.

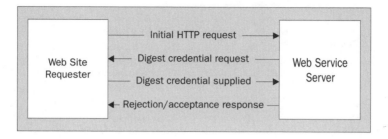

External User Architecture

Again, the external user scenario is different because the firewall/proxy mechanism in place. As usual, the firewall/proxy mechanism would choose to pass on or discard packets coming from the Internet user based on rules that had been set up for the user. Other than that, the requests and responses would take place just as in the Digest diagram illustrated for the internal user.

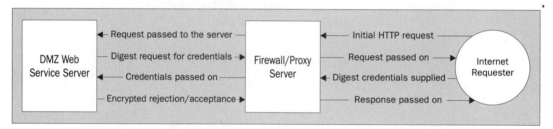

Pros & Cons for Mechanism

The pros and cons for Digest reflect that it provides additional encryption and protects the password information differently from prior reviewed methods. On the cons side, it is not necessarily supported by all developer tools, and is also still relying on some of the same information as the Basic and Basic over SSL scenarios.

Pros

This method protects client credentials well on its own. It provides encryption for keeping credentials secret. In addition, it provides better protection than Basic, and Basic over SSL.

Cons

It may not be widely supported by developer tools for building XML Web Services Clients. Moreover, only current versions of browsers are compatible with digest authentication. In addition, certain hacking mechanisms can exploit this authentication procedure unless it is used in combination with SSL. Lastly, it depends on the network accounts being created to pass on credentials and access to other resources.

NTLM Authentication Mechanism

NTLM is also known as integrated security, and is primarily used in computers capable of using the NT LAN Manager security interactions. This authentication mechanism primarily assists in simplifying the web site access for Windows-based PCs against IIS web sites. It has been available longer than client certificates, but not as long as Basic authentication. It provides a good level of encryption, but many hacking tools have been developed to break into Microsoft's built-in security mechanisms. It is a favored method for internal corporate access because it automatically uses encryption without the overhead of digest or SSL. It is primarily for use with Internet Explorer browsers and so is limited in the browser support area. This also is the only mechanism in our evaluation that will not work over a firewall or proxy server. NTLM gets information as supplied from the browser regarding who is logged into the workstation. If this information matches a Windows account no information is requested from the user.

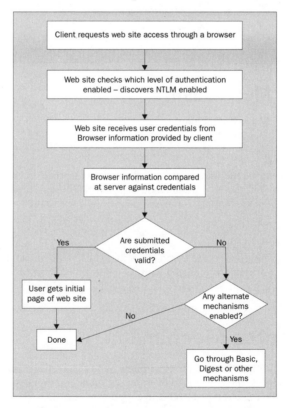

Our main difference in the diagram above is that the server uses the user credentials sent from the browser. Once the server receives the information, it uses the windows security system to determine if the user transmitted a valid user ID/password combination. If so, the user is allowed into the web site. If not, then other authentication methods are used, or the user is denied access. This is the only mechanism that can pass the authentication chore on to another mechanism if it fails.

Looking at our architectural diagrams, you will notice that there will be no diagram for an external user. Since NTLM does not work through firewalls, and a firewall is mandatory when exposing corporate resources directly to the Internet, NTLM is for internal use only.

Internal User Architecture

The digest authentication diagram of an internal user is very similar to the basic diagram. In the diagram below, the architecture of an internal user is still simple. There is no firewall or proxy server interaction necessary. The web server would request a set of the client credentials based on NTLM for web site access. At the point of the hash being generated and decrypted by the server, the server would compare it to existing credentials at the server and determine the appropriate response to the requester.

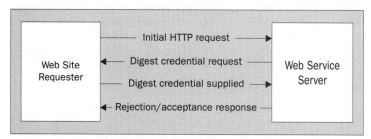

Pros & Cons for Mechanism

The pros and cons for NTLM are listed below.

Pros

This method provides the easiest methodology for authentication internal to an organization, when it is Windows-based. It also can delegate to other methods, should NTLM fail. It requires the least user interaction, and protects client credentials well based on its own encryption.

Cons

Only Internet Explorer-based browsers are compliant with NTLM authentication. It depends on existing network accounts, and on workstations affiliated with the same network, or on any network affiliated as the server to be accessed. Lastly, it cannot be used with a firewall or proxy server.

Client Certificates Mechanism

The maximum level of security within our list of authentication mechanisms is provided by client certificates. It is limited to browser support, and needs a good amount of configuration and user interaction. It requires storage of a certificate on the requester's machine, to support the identity of the user when the web site is accessed. It also requires a certificate on the server to provide the public key and private key information when interacting with the user who has the client certificate.

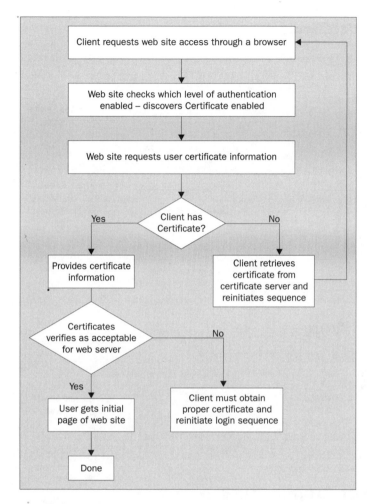

In the diagram above, a certificate is configured on the server so that all interactions with the requester are done via SSL. If the client does not have a certificate, the web site can redirect the client to a valid site to obtain one. This can be from either a corporate internal certificate server or from a valid certifying authority server. Once the client has obtained a certificate, the client then can issue a valid request to the web site. When a client accesses the web site, the web server verifies the client certificate and either accepts it or denies the user access.

Internal User Architecture

The certificate authentication diagram of an internal user incorporates the client certificate scheme into the internal corporate infrastructure. There is no firewall or proxy server interaction necessary. The web server will either accept a client certificate or the client must obtain a valid certificate

We will break down our diagram into ones featuring the client with and without a valid certificate. The acceptance/rejection response is final and the user does not get a chance to respond again.

Client without Certificate

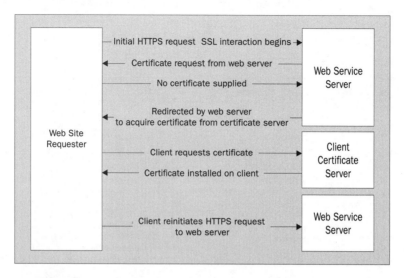

Client with Certificate

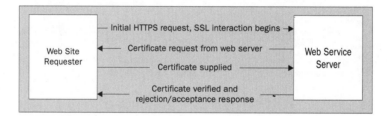

External User Architecture

The external user has the difference of the firewall/proxy mechanism being in place. Normally the web site would be accepting certificates as issued from an Internet-based certificate issuer in this scenario. The scenario is otherwise much the same as an internal user. We will again show the acquisition of the client certificate process separately as we did for the internal user.

Client without Certificate

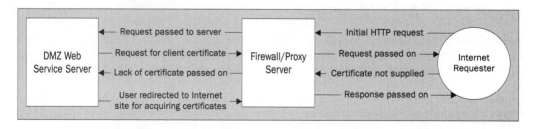

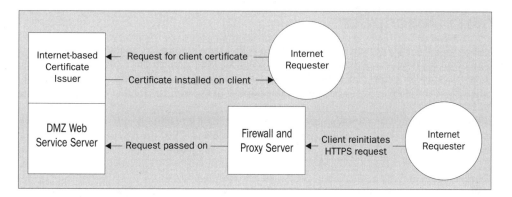

Client with Certificate

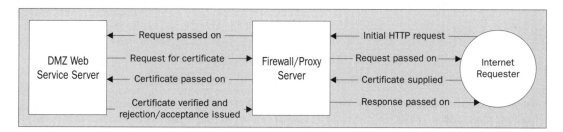

One thing to note: another option that is available now is to use the Internet-based certifying authority as the authentication authority entirely. This option would cause interaction between the web service server and the Internet-based authority for user credential verification as opposed to having internal corporate verification resources.

Pros

This method protects client credentials best. It is the preferred method for authentication external to an organization. It provides a high level of security, and can be mapped to existing user credentials.

Cons

It requires the most user interaction. Not all browsers support certificates, and they need to in order for the certificate to be accepted when first accessing a certificate-based service. SSL usage is detrimental to performance. Digital certificates are not widely accepted yet. Lastly, it may not be widely supported by developer tools for web services.

Situational Case Example

In this section, we present a case study that blends a complex number of users and types of users. We will use all three types illustrated at the beginning of the chapter: corporate internal users, remote access users, and Internet-based users. We will first describe our scenario, look at the logical flow and architectural diagrams related to the scenario, and then describe the authentication mechanism that fits the best.

Scenario Description

Let's say we have a set of products and a web service that handles them for marketing, inventory, and management reporting perspectives. Now, in our scenario, management has designated some of the marketers for travelling only. These marketers are assumed to be out of the office premises for a majority of the time. However, they need to access a secured portion of the web service that deals with inventories.

In addition, we assume that our company has a network built for marketing and ordering companies who have incorporated our web service into their marketing web site. They need to access our web service inventory functionality when one of their customers wishes to place an order for one of our products.

The internal users and the management personnel are assumed to require access to our web service for keeping track of the performance of the marketing employees and for keeping a watch on the inventory levels for manufacturing floor control.

To summarize the situation, our users will be:

❑   Internal management users

❑   On-field marketing employees

❑   External marketing companies' representatives placing an order

What we want to achieve is for all of these users be able to access our web service. Nevertheless, we want to have the best security available on each platform that is accessing our data.

Since we have a well-defined set of users, we can control how they access our web service, and choose the browser to support this. We aren't overly concerned about the amount of client interaction required to set up the secure relationship.

Architecture

Our setup contains Windows 2000 servers and Windows 2000 client workstations with IE6. Our travelling marketers have Windows 2000 laptops with IE6. Our internal corporate environment consists of the marketing web service, which interfaces with a database holding the inventory and customer information needed by our users. This database is hosted on a separate server from our Web Service.

In anticipation of the growth of the number of marketing agencies that need information from us, we have replicated the data onto a data server in our DMZ where the Web Service server is located. The data is synchronized internal and external to the DMZ for consistency.

To minimize the user interaction necessary for management to interact with the Web Service and get their reports, we arrange for a management portal web site internal to our corporation's environment, which interacts with our web service server located in the DMZ.

The application server hosting the web site that the marketing personnel uses hosts a variety of other accounting-related applications, and is hosted internal to our corporate network. The application server interacts with the Web Service server located in the DMZ.

Let's look at a diagram of the infrastructure we just described:

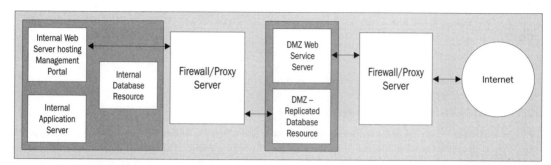

In the diagram above, on the left hand side we have our internal resources including a web server for hosting the management portal, an internal database resource, and an internal application server. These servers would interact with the servers living in the DMZ or the perimeter network, through a firewall and proxy server. In the DMZ, there is a web service server and a replicated database resource. The DMZ machines would interact with requests external to the corporation through a firewall proxy server.

User Request Flow Diagrams

Now, let's discuss the flow of the user requests coming into our web service. We need to look at each user group and analyze how they are getting to the web service and what mechanisms we can use to get them there with the least hassle, without compromising on security. We'll look first at the management users, then at our remote access users, and finally at our external users.

Internal Management Users

Our internal management users will request information from their web site portal. The web site portal then has to communicate with the web service and other machines to fulfill the portal request for a report. We said earlier that we want to limit the amount of interaction management users should undergo in order to set up their interaction, yet we want them to have secure interaction for client authentication. The logical flow of a management users request would look like the following:

1. Client requests web site access through browser

2. Web site sets up secure interaction with client

3. Web site interacts with Web Service on DMZ for information

4. Web Site returns report to user

Remote Marketing Travelers

Our remote marketing travelers will access our data from the Internet. They have a local web-based application that interacts with the Web Service to tell them what they need. As they come into our DMZ, the Web Service has all the resources it needs located in the DMZ to answer any questions. The logical flow of a management users request would look like this:

1. Client interacts with the web-based application using a laptop with Internet access

2. Client web application sets up interaction with Web Service

3. Web Service interacts with database in DMZ for information

4. Web Service returns information to requesting client web application

External Marketing Companies

Assume that the external marketing companies have developed a web site that interacts with our Web Service to provide their customers with the information they need, and that they use their own web site to allow their customers to access our data. The logical flow of the marketing companies request would look like:

1. Marketing company web server sets up interaction with web service

2. Web Service interacts with Database in DMZ for information

3. Web Service returns information to requesting client web application

Now that we have established our criteria and have looked at the logical flow of information for each set of users, we can use this information to analyze each situation and come up with a plan for choosing and implementing the authentication mechanisms related to our web service.

Final Analysis and Decision

As we look at our scenario, we can see that it is truly complex. There really are two ways to approach the final analysis and decision in this case. First, we can select an overall solution that might not be tailored to each set of users, but does provide the minimum requirements for the entire user population. Second, we could tailor the solution to each user group and blend the mechanisms we choose in order to come up with the optimum for each group. Let's start by looking at an overall solution for all three groups.

Overall Decision

If we try to match a single authentication mechanism that would take care of all of our groups above, we would have to choose client certificates because of the requirements of the remote access users. We would choose certificates in that case, because they satisfy the following criteria, crucial to the operations supported by our organization:

❑ They provide the maximum security

❑ We have to interact through a firewall

❑ We aren't concerned about the ease in setup

Almost all of the mechanisms we reviewed have security or firewall issues, with the exception of client certificates. The client certificate choice works well for our external marketing companies because it is a very secure, well-identified form of authentication which we would want for any external organization access our resources. The client certificate is not optimal for the other two groups mainly because it adds a level of complexity they otherwise would not have to go through, as we will see in our next analysis.

Group by Group Decision

No single authentication mechanism fits the overall picture without compromise. It is therefore perfectly acceptable to use multiple authentication mechanisms, each chosen according to scenario. Let's look again at the requirements and make our decisions based on each group.

The internal management group would not be operating through a firewall since they are accessing an internal web server. We want to minimize the hassle they need to undergo to set up the access. Since they are internal to the corporate network, the security is important, but standard encryption will be effective enough. With these criteria in mind, we can choose the NTLM mechanism. Our NTLM mechanism allows the users who are logged in to a network already to pass their credentials through and authenticate a site without additional login information being supplied, and yet will still send those credentials with encryption. Architecturally this would look like:

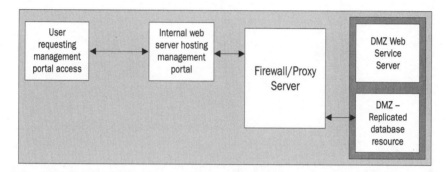

Since the user requesting the portal access is interacting with a server on the corporate network side of the firewall, the NTLM authentication to the web site will work fine. The NTLM authentication would also make it easy to authenticate any additional internal resources the web site may use.

For the travelling marketing user group, we have a choice between digest and client certificates. Client certificates are more secure; however for diversity in our scenario we will say that digest authentication will be sufficient for these users. Remember, digest authentication provides encryption of the credentials only between the remote users and our DMZ Web Service. The encryption gets established by a negotiation that occurs between the server being accessed and the remote user's machine, then a connection is established and processing occurs normally. Architecturally the digest authentication would look like this:

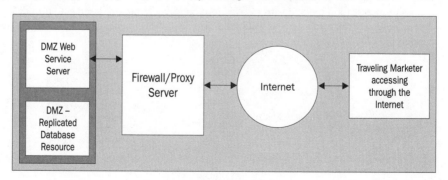

As the diagram above shows, our travelling marketer would access the DMZ Web Service from the Internet through the firewall. Any company resources that the Web Service would access would use the credentials as provided by the marketer at time of login. The conversation between the servers and the client application on the marketer's laptop would be encrypted.

Our final group decision is for our marketing companies who have the web server that needs to communicate with our DMZ-based Web Service. Since we want to maximize security, and are not concerned as much with the amount of setup the company goes through as compared to the security we gain, we would choose client certificates. Architecturally, below is an illustration of a company that has to acquire the certificate and then begin communications with our web server. We have chosen an Internet-based certificate disbursement methodology.

Certificate Acquisition Diagram

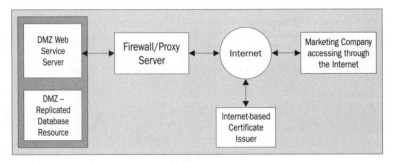

In our diagram above, the marketing company would initiate contact with our Web Service and when a certificate was not found, the company would have to acquire a certificate. This would be done completely through the Internet, as shown on the right side of the diagram. Once a certificate is acquired, the interaction with our Web Service would be reflected as shown below.

After Certificate Acquisition

There is very little difference architecturally between our digest and client certificate diagrams. The manner that they use to negotiate the connection is different however, since there is an extra certificate identity verification step that gets performed when using a certificate.

In this section, we have shown process diagrams and architectural diagrams of the approach that can be taken in determining the authentication mechanisms needed in a complex situation. Each situation differs and the architecture available to a project will vary as well. All of the factors we have reviewed are important and should be included in each decision to be made.

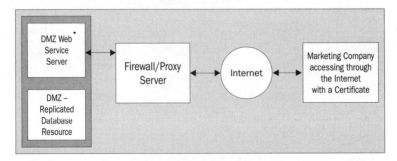

Project Liberty

One major hurdle holding back the widespread deployment of web services has been the lack of a standard security model for authenticating users and establishing network identities.

Existing security models are based on the hierarchical organization of people found in the workplace. All the applications, services, and data that are required for the operation of a business function like human resources and sales tend to be located in a single place, usually on the same network. Under such circumstances, security involves controlling access to the network or domain.

On the other hand, web services expose your application and your data to the Web. Experience shows that the Internet is a minefield of security risks. The primary benefits of web services is the increased flexibility and reduced costs, which are brought about by using XML technologies based on the loose coupling between the data and application/service. The basic idea here is that web services are a disconnected collection of pieces that communicate over the Internet. But this communication over the Internet is vulnerable to hackers and malware. The consequence of this is the disruption of the data/application/service itself, or exposure of the data/application/service to hijacking. Existing security models are designed around tightly-integrated applications/services and are not capable of handling the new model for web services that involves loose coupling between data and application/service.

Several technological initiatives currently are underway to define a security model for XML-based web services, the project Liberty Alliance and the Web Services Interoperability organization (http://www.ws-i.org/) being the most prominent.

Security for Web Services

Like the communications or electric power systems, web services require a security infrastructure that offers uniformity and consistency to all applications/services. This makes security readily available to applications, makes the application security mechanisms transparent to the end user, and offers comprehensive security.

A security infrastructure offers the following core services:

- ❑ **Authentication** – Assurance that the user is who he or she claims to be
- ❑ **Integrity** – Assurance that data has not been altered in transit
- ❑ **Confidentiality** – Assurance that the data cannot be read by anyone but the intended recipient

Integrity and confidentiality are made possible through the use of cryptographic mechanisms. SSL/TLS is the primarily technology used on the Internet to provide integrity and confidentiality and is supported by all Internet-enabled applications.

Authentication on the Internet presents a problem from security and user experience perspective. Typically, a user may have several user IDs and passwords for various systems, each governed by different security and authentication technologies. This situation results in increased password management and system administration costs, loss of user productivity, and increased security risks from unsafe workarounds employed by the user.

For users, it would be much more convenient to log in once and have all further authentication handled in the background, no matter which application the user is working with or where the application is hosted, either inside and outside corporate firewalls.

To meet this utopian goal of universal single sign-on, several industry technological initiatives currently are underway, with the *Project Liberty* being the most mature.

What is a Network Identity?

When users interact with services on a corporate network or on the Internet, they often personalize the services. This personalization is done in order for the users to control the content and presentation of the services. To enable personalization, the services have to be able to uniquely identify (in other words, authenticate) the user. The most widely-used means of authenticating or identifying a user is with a username and password. More secure means of authenticating a user through the use of a smart card or biometrics are employed in the corporate and military world.

The network identity of users is the collection of these authentication attributes (Social Security Number, username/password, PKI certificate, smartcard/token, biometric attributes, PIN) comprising the various services that they can access. Today, users have to create a new identity every time they sign up for an Internet service or access applications hosted on an external network. As a result, it currently is not possible for a user to have a cohesive and tangible network identity.

What is a Federated Network Identity?

When a user authenticates to a particular service, the provider supplies the user with an assertion of the authentication event (SAML Assertion). An identity federation is said to exist between the provider and other service providers when the service providers accept authentication assertion regarding the user from the provider. The authentication assertion that is used to link user identity across business boundaries is referred to as the user's **federated network identity**.

The benefit of identity federation to the user is the need to authenticate once (single sign-on) and access services across business boundaries. Although the user does not have to authenticate more than once in an identity federation, under-the-hood authentication occurs between the authentication assertion provider and the service providers.

The Liberty Alliance specifications provide protocols for establishment of federation of user identity across providers as well as its termination.

What is Liberty Alliance?

The Liberty Alliance Project (http://www.projectliberty.org/) is a business and technology consortium of more than 130 global organizations that was formed in October 2001. The sponsoring members of this alliance include American Express, AOL, Bank of America, Cisco Systems, Citigroup, EDS, Fidelity Investments, France Telecom, General Motors, Hewlett Packard, Intuit, i2 Technologies, MasterCard International, NTT, Nokia, SAP, Sony Corporation, Sun Microsystems, United Airlines, Visa International, Vodafone and just about every other Fortune 500 company except for Microsoft and IBM.

Its mission is to provide the means by which individuals and businesses can engage in business transactions without compromising the privacy and security of the parties involved. To accomplish this mission, the Liberty Alliance will establish open technical specifications that support a broad range of network identity-based interactions and provide businesses with a framework for delivery of services.

The key objectives of the Liberty Alliance are to:

❑ Enable consumers to protect the privacy and security of their network identity information

❑ Enable businesses to maintain and manage their customer relationships without third-party participation

❑ Provide an open single sign-on standard that includes decentralized authentication and authorization from multiple providers

❑ Create a network identity infrastructure that supports all current and emerging network access devices

On July 11, 2002, the Liberty Alliance released version 1.0 of the specification.

Services Provided by the Liberty Specification

Let us look at the services provided by the Liberty specification.

Opt-in Account Linking

Users can choose to link accounts they have with different service providers within circles of trust (such as companies with business agreements or affinity programs).

For example, users might want to get a comprehensive view of their financial assets by linking their checking accounts, stock trading accounts, and retirement accounts. Another example would be to link all their utility bills to see the amount due.

Simplified Sign-On for Linked Account

Once a user's accounts are linked, he or she can log in and authenticate at one linked account and navigate to another linked account, without having to log in again.

For example, if your bank accounts have been linked, you can log in once at any bank and move between any of the linked banks without having to log in again.

Global Logout

Once a user logs out of a linked service provider, the user can automatically be logged out of all other sites to which the user linked at the same time.

For example, if you log out at any one of your linked bank accounts, you will be transparently logged out of every linked bank account.

Authentication Context

Service providers can communicate the type of authentication and identity levels that should be used when the user logs in.

For example, if each bank requires a different username/password for authentication, you can log in securely without having to remember and manage the numerous username/password combinations. Also, since authentication information is transmitted very securely between the banks, you can reuse the same password, but make it much stronger, since you now have to remember just one password. This also allows banks to have support to different authentication technologies while improving the user experience.

Liberty Alliance Client Feature

This facilitates fixed and wireless devices-based client applications to use the Liberty version 1.0 specifications.

The first step in achieving a federated network identity is the establishment of circles of trust as shown in the figure below. These circles of trust are groupings of businesses that have established trust relationships based on an operational agreement and use of Liberty-enabled technology. Users can federate isolated accounts they have with these businesses to transact in a secure and seamless manner. The principal entities from a Liberty perspective are the users, service providers, and identity providers.

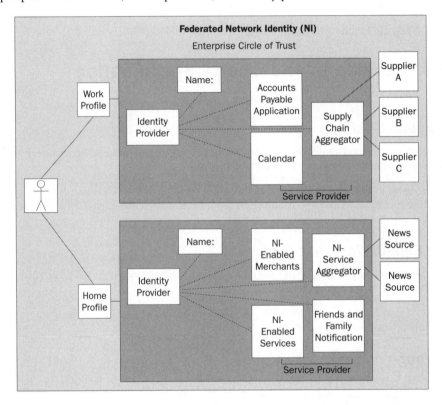

Service providers are organizations offering web-based services, which can include just about any business with an online presence.

Identity providers are service providers offering incentives so that other service providers may affiliate with them. These relationships comprise the formation of circles of trust.

Specifications

The Liberty version 1.0 specifications are designed to enable federated opt-in account linking, simplified single sign on, and single logout for users and businesses on the Internet.

The specification is composed of the following documents:

- ❏ Overview
  Summarizes the engineering requirements and security framework, and discusses the version 1.0 architecture

- ❏ Protocols & Schemas
  Defines a set of protocols that collectively provide a solution for identity federation and single sign-on. Also, defines the XML schemas that providers can use to exchange authentication information

- ❏ Bindings & Profiles
  Defines the HTTP and SOAP-based transport of Liberty protocol messages over communication networks as well as the security considerations associated with Liberty protocols

- ❏ Authentication Context
  Describes the authentication status of a user and defines the associated XML schema

- ❏ Implementation Guidelines
  Defines the minimum set of features that should be implemented in a user agent, identity provider, and service provider

Architecture

The overall Liberty architecture is composed of three orthogonal components:

- ❏ Web redirection
- ❏ Web Services
- ❏ Metadata and schemas

The overall Liberty architecture is shown in the diagram below:

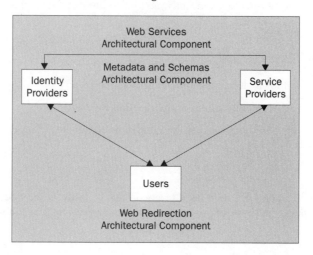

Web Redirection

The web redirection component allows the Liberty-enabled entities to provide services to today's user-agent base that primarily consists of web browsers. Two profiles are defined: **HTTP-redirect** and **form-POST** based redirection. Both the profiles are based on information exchange between the service and identity provider rooted in the user agent as shown below. The relevant information is embedded in the redirect URI in HTTP redirect-based redirection, while a HTTP form contains the relevant information in a form-POST-based redirection.

These components are shown in the figure below:

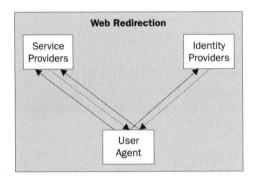

Web Services

This component allows Liberty-enabled entities to communicate directly using SOAP over HTTP or HTTPS. Currently, profiles are defined for interaction between the identity provider and the service provider only.

Metadata and Schemas

This refers to a mutually agreed-upon set of formats that are used by Liberty-enabled entities to communicate provider-specific and other information. Currently, no profiles are defined for this architectural component.

The Liberty architecture is designed to:

- ❑ Be compatible with the user agents that are not Liberty-enabled
- ❑ Obviate the need for a global account/identity namespace
- ❑ Support legacy, current, and future authentication mechanisms
- ❑ Provide a flexible and dynamic distributed system architecture that can meet current as well as future needs

Liberty Protocols

The Project Liberty specification defines a set of protocols that collectively provide a solution for **identity management, cross-domain authentication**, and **session management**. The following are the Liberty protocols:

❑ **Single Sign-on and Federation**
The protocol for identity federation that enables single sign-on

❑ **Name Registration**
The protocol by which a service provider can register an alternate opaque handle (or name identifier) for a user

❑ **Federation Termination Notification (Defederation)**
The protocol by which a provider can notify another provider that a particular identity federation has been terminated

❑ **Single Logout**
The protocol by which providers notify each other of logout events for a single user logout event

Liberty specifications are based on the SAML specification. In SAML terminology, the identity provider acts as an *asserting party* and an *authentication authority* while a service provider acts as a *relying party*. See Chapter 9 for further details on SAML.

Single Sign-on/Federation Protocol

The single sign-on protocol:

❑ Enables a service provider to acquire an authentication assertion from an identity provider to facilitate single sign-on

❑ Enables a service provider to initiate federation of a user identity

Identity federation and single sign-on occurs via a request and response protocol that works as follows:

❑ The service provider issues a SAML `<AuthnRequest>` request to an identity provider, instructing the identity provider to provide an authentication assertion to the service provider.

❑ The identity provider responds with a SAML `<AuthnResponse>` containing authentication assertions to the service provider or a SAML artifact. The response must be signed and should be considered valid only if message signature validation is successful.

Name Registration

At the time of federation, the identity provider generates an opaque handle that serves as the identifier used by the service and identity provider when referring to the user. Subsequently, however, the service provider may register a different opaque handle with the identity provider.

The opaque handle is the `SPProvidedNameIdentifier` that is a SAML `<NameIdentifier>` element. Name registration occurs via a request and response protocol that works as follows:

❑ The service provider sends a `<RegisterNameIdentifierRequest>` message to the identity provider.

❑ The identity provider responds with a `<RegisterNameIdentifierResponse>` message, which is a SAML `<StatusType>` element. The response must be signed and should be considered valid only if message signature validation is successful.

Federation Termination Notification (Defederation)

A service provider sends a message to an identity provider when a user terminates an identity federation between a service provider and an identity provider.

The <FederationTerminationNotification> message is a *one-way* asynchronous signed message sent by the service provider to the identity provider.

The identity provider sends **no** response message.

Single Logout

When a user executes a global logout at a service provider, the service provider sends the <LogoutNotification> message to the identity provider, which in turn sends the <LogoutNotification> message to each service provider to which it provided authentication assertions.

The <LogoutNotification> message is a *one-way* asynchronous signed message sent by the service provider to identity provider.

Here again, the identity provider sends **no** response message.

The following general requirements are applicable to all the protocols:

❑ **XML Signature**
All signed protocol messages should adhere to the W3C XML Signature and the XML Signature constraints in the SAML specifications.

❑ **Protocol and Assertion Versioning**
Version information appears in protocol messages and assertion. This specification defines version 1.0 for the protocol messages and assertion.

❑ **Provider ID**
All providers have a URI-based identifier that must be unique and must not exceed 1024 characters.

❑ **Name Identifiers**
Users are assigned name identifiers (opaque handles) that are limited to 256 characters by identity providers and potentially by service providers. It is important that this be constructed using a pseudorandom value to prevent any correspondence with a user's identity.

❑ **Signature Verification**
Verification of the signature on the signed message must be performed in accordance with the best practices for the certificate path technology in use. For X.509 v3 certificates, use of the path validation algorithm specified in the IETF RFC 2459 or real-time validation using OCSP/XKMS is recommended.

Identity Federation Termination (Defederation) Protocol

Service providers and identity providers wanting to terminate an identity federation use this protocol. Defederation can be initiated by the identity provider or by the service provider. Two channels are used to send the notification message:

❏ **Front Channel** or HTTP-Redirect to communicate between the identity provider and the service provider

❏ **Back Channel** or SOAP/HTTP to communicate between the identity provider and the service provider

Global Logout Protocol

This is used to ensure termination of all sessions that were authenticated by a particular identity provider. This can be initiated by the identity provider or by the service provider. Three channels are used to send the logout notification message:

❏ HTTP/Redirect to communicate between the identity provider and the service provider

❏ HTTP/GET to communicate between the identity provider and service provider

❏ SOAP/HTTP to communicate between the identity provider and the service provider

Profiles and Bindings

A Liberty profile is a combination of message content specification and message transport for a single user-agent type. Profiles are defined for each Liberty protocol and are based on SAML profiles.

A Liberty binding specifies the mechanism of transporting Liberty protocol messages over HTTP-based communication networks. Currently, bindings are defined for SOAP.

The Liberty specification defines four single sign-on profiles, all of which can be described by the interaction diagram shown in the figure below:

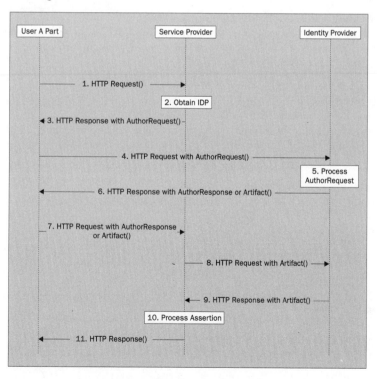

Each of the steps shown above is described below:

1. Send HTTP request
The user agent accesses the service provider requesting access to a desired target service.

2. Obtain identity provider
The service provider obtains information about the appropriate identity provider to redirect the user agent to in Step 3, and the means by which the identity provider is determined is implementation dependent.

3. HTTP response with `<AuthnRequest>`
The service provider redirects the user agent to the identity provider's single sign-on service URL using an HTTP 302 redirect message.

4. HTTP request with `<AuthnRequest>`
User agent accesses the identity provider's single sign-on service URL with the `<AuthnRequest>` information attached to the redirect URL.

5. Process `<AuthnRequest>`
The identity provider processes the `<AuthnRequest>` per the Liberty processing rules. If the user is not authenticated, authentication might occur depending on the contents of the `<AuthnRequest>` message.

6. HTTP response with `<AuthnResponse>` or artifact
The identity provider responds with a `<AuthnResponse>`, a SAML artifact, or an error.

7. HTTP request with `<AuthnResponse>` or artifact
The user agent then accesses the assertion service URL at the service provider with a `<AuthnResponse>`, a SAML artifact, or an error. The form and contents of the response in this step are profile dependent.

8. HTTP request with artifact
This step is required only if the identity provider returns a SAML artifact.

The service provider de-references the assertion using the artifact by sending a `<samlp:Request>` SOAP message to the identity provider to retrieve the assertion corresponding to the artifact.

9. HTTP response with assertion
The identity provider locates the assertion and sends the response in a `<samlp:Response>` SOAP message.

10. Process assertion
The service provider processes the response.

11. Send HTTP response
The user agent is sent a response that either allows or denies access to the originally-requested service.

We move on to define each of the four profiles next.

Liberty Browser Artifact Single Sign-on Protocol Profile

This profile relies on a reference returned by the identity provider, which the service provider must dereference to determine whether the user is authenticated.

This profile consists of a single interaction between the user agent, an identity provider, and a service provider, with a nested sub-interaction between the identity provider and the service provider.

Liberty Browser POST Single Sign-on Protocol Profile

This profile allows authentication information to be supplied without the use of an artifact. It consists of two interactions, the first between the user agent and the identity provider, and the second between the user agent and the service provider. The <AuthnResponse> in step 6 is sent to the user agent embedded in an HTML form that the user agent transfers to the service provider by an HTTP POST.

Liberty WML POST Profile

This profile is similar to the *Browser POST* profile except that it is optimized for the resource constrained to wireless environments.

Liberty Enabled Client and Proxy (LECP) Single Sign-on Protocol Profile

This profile is similar to the *Browser POST* profile in interaction. In addition, an LECP has the ability to discover identity providers and send Liberty messages in the body of the HTTP messages, thereby allowing messages of any size. A Liberty proxy is an HTTP proxy emulating a Liberty-enabled client.

Authentication Context Mechanisms

Authentication context is the additional information that a service provider requires in addition to the authentication assertion from an identity provider in order to make a decision regarding the services that the subject of the authentication assertion is entitled to. The Liberty specification defines a list of authentication contexts that are representative of current technologies and practices in order to simplify the task of assessing and comparing authentication assertions.

The following authentication contexts are defined in the version 1.0 specifications:

- **MobileContract**
  Identifies the case when a mobile user has an identity for which the identity provider has vouched.

- **MobileDigitalID**
  Identifies the case when a mobile user has an identity that is issued after detailed and verified registration procedures, users' consent to sign and authorize transactions, and DigitalID-based authentication.

- **MobileUnregistered**
  Identifies the case when the real identity of a mobile user has not been strongly verified.

- **Password**
  Identifies the case when the user authenticates to an identity provided by presenting a password over an unprotected HTTP session.

- **Password – Protected Transport**
  Identifies the case when the user authenticates to an identity provided by presenting a password over an SSL/TLS-protected session.

95

❏ **Previous-Session**
   Identifies the case when the user has authenticated to an identity provider at some point in the past.

❏ **Smartcard**
   Identifies the case when the user authenticates to an identity provider using a smartcard.

❏ **Smartcard-PKI**
   Identifies the case when the user authenticates to an identity provider through a two-factor authentication mechanism using a smartcard with enclosed private key and a PIN.

❏ **Software-PKI**
   Identifies the case when the user authenticates to an identity provider using an X.509 certificate stored in software.

❏ **Time-Sync-Token**
   Identifies the case when the user authenticates to an identity provider using a time synchronization token.

Implementation Guidelines

Liberty version 1.0 does not specify any formal compliance requirements but only recommendations. The recommended implementation profiles for the different Liberty entities are listed below:

Identity Provider

Feature	Recommendations
Single Sign-on	Must support the browser artifact/POST profiles and should support the WML POST and LECP profiles
Identity Federation	Must support stateless single sign-on association
Defederation	Must support front channel (HTTP-redirect-based) and should support back channel (SOAP-based)
Name Registration	Should implement to support service providers that are back channel (SOAP communication) enabled
Single Logout	Must support front channel (HTTP-redirect-based) and should support back channel (SOAP-based)
Identity Provider Introduction	Must support if simultaneous support for multiple circles of trust is required

Service Provider

Feature	Recommendations
Single Sign-on	Must support the Browser Artifact/POST profiles and should support the WML Post and LECP profiles
Identity Federation	Must support stateless single sign-on association

Feature	Recommendations
Defederation	Must support Front Channel (HTTP-redirect-based) and may support Back Channel (SOAP-based)
Name Registration	Must support this protocol if back channel (SOAP) communication is supported
Single Logout	Must support Front Channel (HTTP-redirect-based) and should support Back Channel (SOAP-based)
Identity Provider Introduction	Must support if simultaneous support for multiple circles of trust is required

User Agent

Feature	Recommendations
Single Sign-on	Must support the LECP profile

Security Requirements

The security mechanisms incorporated into the Liberty specifications, and by extension in Liberty implementations, are listed below:

Security Mechanisms	Channel Security	Message Security
Confidentiality	Required	Optional
Per message data integrity	Required	Required
Transaction Integrity	–	Required
Peer-entity authentication	Identity Provider – Required Service Provider – Optional	–
Data origin authentication	–	Required
Non-repudiation	–	Required

Channel security addresses how communication between the identity providers, service providers, and user agents is protected. The specifications require that SSL 3.0 or TLS 1.0 be used for channel security with X.509 certificate-based peer entity authentication.

Message security addresses the protection of discrete protocol messages passed between the identity providers, service providers, and user agents. The specifications require that XML Signature and XML Encryption be used for message security.

Liberty Toolkits

There currently are two publicly-available Liberty toolkits that enable developers to integrate Liberty functionality into their existing business applications as well as build Liberty-based solutions. They are:

❑ Phaos Liberty 1.0

A commercial Java toolkit from Phaos Technology, this toolkit implements the Liberty protocols and includes integrated security and privacy options. It is targeted at business developers with an easy-to-use API. It includes XML Signature and Encryption, SSL/TLS, and full-strength cryptography libraries. It optionally includes support for smartcards, hardware security modules, and real-time identity validation using XKMS and OCSP. It requires a JAXP 1.1-compliant XML Parser and JDK 1.2 to run.

❑ Sun IPL 0.2

This is an open source Java toolkit from Sun Microsystems. It includes an implementation of a Liberty Identity Provider and Service Provider. It is targeted at Liberty developers who are interested in Liberty protocols and is intended by Sun Microsystems to foster interoperability testing purposes. It requires a JAXP 1.1-compliant XML Parser, JDK 1.3, and the Apache XML Security Toolkit 1.0.3 to run.

If you are interested in hosting Liberty-enabled services, you will have to wait until late 2002 or early 2003, when a variety of products are expected to hit the market. One such product is the **Liberty Identity Server 6.0** from Sun Microsystems.

Resources

Resource	Subject	Link
Liberty Alliance	Project Liberty	http://www.projectliberty.org/
	Version 1.0 Specifications	http://www.projectliberty.org/specs/index.html
Phaos Technology	Liberty Tools	http://www.phaos.com/products/Liberty/Liberty.html
	XML Tools	http://www.phaos.com/products/category/xml.html
	Smart Cards	http://www.phaos.com/products/cryptoki/cryptoki.html
Sun IPL	IPL	http://developer.java.sun.com/developer/codesamples/Liberty.html
	Apache XML Security 1.0.3	http://xml.apache.org/security/index.html
JAXP Compliant XML Parsers	Apache Xerces	http://xml.apache.org/xerces2-j/index.html
	IBM XML 4J	http://www.alphaworks.ibm.com/tech/xml4j/
	Oracle XML Parser for Java	http://technet.oracle.com/tech/xml/parser_java2/content.html

Building Liberty Applications

This section will describe the process of installing and creating Liberty protocol messages and services using the Phaos Liberty toolkit from Phaos Technology.

Phaos Liberty is a pure Java software toolkit that allows Java developers to design and develop single sign-on and federated identity solutions. Phaos Liberty provides tools, information, and samples to help you develop solutions that conform to the Liberty Alliance 1.0 specifications.

Getting Started

Please make sure that you have the following before you start:

- ❑ Java Development environment
  JDK 1.2 or higher is required.

- ❑ XML Parser
  A JAXP 1.1-compliant Java XML parser is required.

- ❑ Phaos Security Libraries
  `Phaos_Security_Engine.jar` (Core Cryptographic Services)
  `Phaos_XML.jar` (XML Signature & Encryption)
  `Phaos_SAML.jar` (SAML)
  `Phaos_Liberty.jar` (Liberty)

- ❑ CLASSPATH environment variable
  Please update the classpath environment variable to include the XML Parser and Phaos Security Libraries. Verify the installation of the XML Parser and Phaos Liberty toolkit by running the sample programs in the `examples/` folder of the Phaos Liberty distribution.

- ❑ Creating Liberty Protocol Messages
  Phaos Liberty contains the following packages:

  - ❑ `com.phaos.xml.liberty`
    Liberty protocols and provider metadata classes

  - ❑ `com.phaos.xml.liberty.ac`
    Liberty authentication context classes

To create a new `<AuthnRequest>` element of the Liberty protocol schema and append it to a document, you can use the following code:

```
Document doc = <Instance of org.w3c.dom.Document>;
com.phaos.xml.liberty.AuthnRequest authnRequest =
        new com.phaos.xml.liberty.AuthnRequest(doc);
doc.getDocumentElement().appendChild(authnRequest);
```

To obtain `<AuthnRequest>` elements an XML document, you can use the following code:

```
Document doc = <Instance of org.w3c.dom.Document>;
NodeList arList = doc.getElementsByTagNameNS(LibertyURI.ns_liberty,
"AuthnRequest");
    if (arList.getLength() == 0)
       System.err.println("No AuthnRequest elements found.");
    // Convert org.w3c.dom.Node object to a com.phaos.xml.liberty.AuthnRequest
    // object and process
    for (int s = 0, n = arList.getLength(); s < n; ++s)
```

99

```
    {
        com.phaos.xml.liberty.AuthnRequest authnRequest =
            new com.phaos.xml.liberty.AuthnRequest((Element)arList.item(s));
        // Process AuthnRequest element
        ...
    }
```

To create a new `<AuthnResponse>` element of the Liberty protocol schema and append it to a document, you can use the following code:

```
    Document doc = <Instance of org.w3c.dom.Document>;
    com.phaos.xml.liberty.AuthnResponse authnResponse =
            new com.phaos.xml.liberty.AuthnResponse(doc);
    doc.getDocumentElement().appendChild(authnResponse);
```

To obtain `<AuthnResponse>` elements from an XML document, you can use the following code:

```
    Document doc = <Instance of org.w3c.dom.Document>;
    // Get list of all AuthnResponse elements in the document.
    NodeList arList = doc.getElementsByTagNameNS(LibertyURI.ns_liberty,
"AuthnResponse");
    if (arList.getLength() == 0)
        System.err.println("No AuthnResponse elements found.");
    // Convert each org.w3c.dom.Node object to a
com.phaos.xml.liberty.AuthnResponse
    // object and process
    for (int s = 0, n = arList.getLength(); s < n; ++s)
    {
        com.phaos.xml.liberty.AuthnResponse authnResponse =
            new com.phaos.xml.liberty.AuthnResponse((Element)arList.item(s));
        // Process AuthnResponse element
        ...
    }
```

To create a new `<FederationTerminationNotification>` element of the Liberty protocol schema and append it to a document, you can use the following code:

```
    Document doc = <Instance of org.w3c.dom.Document>;
    com.phaos.xml.liberty.FederationTerminationNotification ftn =
            new com.phaos.xml.liberty.FederationTerminationNotification(doc);
    doc.getDocumentElement().appendChild(ftn);
```

To obtain `<FederationTerminationNotification>` elements from an XML document, you can use the following code:

```
    Document doc = <Instance of org.w3c.dom.Document>;
    // Get list of all FederationTerminationNotification elements in the document.
    NodeList ftnList =
        doc.getElementsByTagNameNS(LibertyURI.ns_liberty,
"FederationTerminationNotification");
    if (ftnList.getLength() == 0)
        System.err.println("No FederationTerminationNotification elements
found.");

    // Convert each org.w3c.dom.Node object to a
    // com.phaos.xml.liberty.FederationTerminationNotification
    // object and process
```

```
for (int s = 0, n = ftnList.getLength(); s < n; ++s)
{
    com.phaos.xml.liberty.FederationTerminationNotification ftn =
        new com.phaos.xml.liberty.FederationTerminationNotification(
                    (Element)ftnList.item(s));
    // Process FederationTerminationNotification element
    ...
}
```

To create a new <LogoutNotification> element of the Liberty protocol schema and append it to a document, you can use the following code:

```
Document doc = <Instance of org.w3c.dom.Document>;
com.phaos.xml.liberty.LogoutNotification ln =
    new com.phaos.xml.liberty.LogoutNotification(doc);
doc.getDocumentElement().appendChild(ln);
```

To obtain <LogoutNotification> elements from an XML document, you can use the following code:

```
Document doc = <Instance of org.w3c.dom.Document>;
// Get list of all LogoutNotification elements in the document.
NodeList lnList = doc.getElementsByTagNameNS(LibertyURI.ns_liberty,
"LogoutNotification");
if (lnList.getLength() == 0)
    System.err.println("No LogoutNotification elements found.");

// Convert each org.w3c.dom.Node object to a
com.phaos.xml.liberty.LogoutNotification
// object and process
for (int s = 0, n = lnList.getLength(); s < n; ++s)
{
    com.phaos.xml.liberty.LogoutNotification ln = new
      com.phaos.xml.liberty.LogoutNotification((Element)lnList.item(s));
    // Process LogoutNotification element
    ...
}
```

To create a new <RegisterNameIdentifierRequest> element of the Liberty protocol schema and append it to a document, you can use the following code:

```
Document doc = <Instance of org.w3c.dom.Document>;
    com.phaos.xml.liberty.RegisterNameIdentifierRequest
RegisterNameIdentifierRequest rnir =
    new com.phaos.xml.liberty.RegisterNameIdentifierRequest
RegisterNameIdentifierRequest(doc);
    doc.getDocumentElement().appendChild(rnir);
```

To obtain <RegisterNameIdentifierRequest> elements from an XML document, you can use the following code:

```
Document doc = <Instance of org.w3c.dom.Document>;
// Get list of all RegisterNameIdentifierRequest elements in the document.
NodeList rnirList = doc.getElementsByTagNameNS(
        LibertyURI.ns_liberty, "RegisterNameIdentifierRequest");
if (rnirList.getLength() == 0)
    System.err.println("No RegisterNameIdentifierRequest elements found.");
// Convert each org.w3c.dom.Node object to a
```

```
// com.phaos.xml.liberty.RegisterNameIdentifierRequest
// object and process
for (int s = 0, n = rnirList.getLength(); s < n; ++s)
{
    com.phaos.xml.liberty.RegisterNameIdentifierRequest
        RegisterNameIdentifierRequest rnir = new
            com.phaos.xml.liberty.RegisterNameIdentifierRequest
                RegisterNameIdentifierRequest((Element)rnirList.item(s));

    // Process RegisterNameIdentifierRequest element
    ...
}
```

To create a new <RegisterNameIdentifierResponse> element of the Liberty protocol schema and append it to a document, you can use the following code:

```
Document doc = <Instance of org.w3c.dom.Document>;
com.phaos.xml.liberty.RegisterNameIdentifierResponse rnir =
new com.phaos.xml.liberty.RegisterNameIdentifierResponse(doc);
doc.getDocumentElement().appendChild(rnir);
```

To obtain <RegisterNameIdentifierResponse> elements from an XML document, you can use the following code:

```
Document doc = <Instance of org.w3c.dom.Document>;
// Get list of all RegisterNameIdentifierResponse elements in the document.
NodeList rnirList = doc.getElementsByTagNameNS(
    LibertyURI.ns_liberty, "RegisterNameIdentifierResponse");
if (rnirList.getLength() == 0)
    System.err.println("No RegisterNameIdentifierResponse elements found.");

// Convert each org.w3c.dom.Node object to a
// com.phaos.xml.liberty.RegisterNameIdentifierResponse
// object and process
for (int s = 0, n = rnirList.getLength(); s < n; ++s)
{
    com.phaos.xml.liberty.RegisterNameIdentifierResponse rnir = new
com.phaos.xml.liberty.RegisterNameIdentifierResponse((Element)rnirList.item(s));
    // Process RegisterNameIdentifierResponse element
    ...
}
```

Creating Liberty Services

The above section described the construction of Liberty protocol messages using the Phaos Liberty toolkit. This section describes the implementation of various Liberty services.

A Liberty service is a sequence of protocol messages exchanged between the various Liberty entities. For each Liberty service, multiple profiles may be defined.

To implement a Liberty service, you will need to implement the relevant service functionality in the user agent, service provider, and identity provider. For example, to implement the Liberty Browser Artifact profile, please refer to the *single sign-on interaction* diagram. More detailed information about the various Liberty services is available in the version 1.0 specifications.

Other Federated Identity Initiatives

IBM and Microsoft recently proposed an XML-and SOAP-based message security model for web services called WS-Security. IBM and Microsoft plan to come out with a specification for federated identity in the WS-Security world called **WS-Federation**, which will describe how to manage and broker trust relationships in a federated environment.

Future Directions

The Liberty Alliance is set to launch its version 2.0 specifications in early 2003 in which it will tackle permissions-based attribute sharing. Other issues that will be addressed in version 2.0 are:

❑ Permissions-based attribute sharing

❑ Federation of authentication domains

❑ Delegation of authority

❑ Schema/protocols for core identity profile service

A federated network identity is not just a *technical* problem – it's a *business* issue, with policy implications and technology challenges. With members of the Alliance coming from practically every region in the world, there is little doubt that we must consider a wide variety of policy regulations and implications in our daily work. This is a complex task, as the variety of security and privacy protection laws throughout the world is as varied as the Liberty Alliance membership. The Liberty Alliance is working on a set of recommendations designed to assist implementers in complying with privacy and security standards, including components of the Liberty architecture.

To date, more than 50 companies have publicly announced their plans to offer Liberty-enabled products for services in the near future. The coming months should see increased deployment of Liberty-enabled products that should aid the deployment of web services by:

❑ Providing customers with single sign-on convenience and digital identity that is secure and privacy-protected

❑ Providing business with an authentication framework that reduces fraud, improves user experience, and leverages existing technology and business relationships

Summary

In this chapter, we reviewed the details of the following authentication mechanisms:

❑ Basic

❑ Basic over SSL

❑ Digest

❑ NTLM

❑ Client Certificates

We went over in detail the description, architecture, pros and cons of each mechanism. We also went into detail about how they fit into standard situations and how they worked together in complex situations. We hope that this chapter has given you an insight into the tradeoffs that exist between security and stability, and that you have learned that it is worthwhile to apply the best solution that suits the nature of the web service at hand.

It is important to remember that authentication mechanisms form the first security challenge prior to users gaining access to a web service. Therefore, it is important to stress that security must be weighted heavily when compared to user convenience. We never want to sacrifice security just because it will impact our performance speed or our ease of use, because security can prevent our web service from being compromised. As we've stated in this book before, security will be what keeps the Web Service integrity in high regard, and therefore the companies and users will want to use it. Our ultimate goal is to protect the investment we make in the Web Services product we want people to access.

The Liberty project hopes to provide the means by which entities can engage in business transactions without compromising their privacy and security. It defines a way to manage customer relationships without third-party involvement. It wants to create a decentralized authentication authorization mechanism and a network identity infrastructure.

PKI

It goes without saying that the topic of computing security has evolved well beyond the common sense of not keeping your ATM PIN in your wallet, and not using the same password for everything that requires one. Realizing that passwords and good intentions aren't enough to provide sufficient security in contemporary computing environments, we must turn to a distributed technology to build a structure that, at a minimum, establishes a framework for secure computing. That's what **Public Key Infrastructure**, or PKI, and this chapter, are all about.

In a broad sense PKI is a system of policies, servers, and technologies that provide support for cryptographic solutions to critical security issues related to enterprise computing. Such issues relate specifically to the secure exchange of data, the positive identity of entities participating in such exchanges, and the control of systems and data that perform such exchanges. Technologies we will discuss include such things as digital certificates encryption algorithms, as well as private and public encryption keys.

As we delve into the branched topics that descend from PKI, we'll try to remain focused on some essential points that will lead us to realize that PKI is not a single entity, but part of a broader process that provides for a secured computing environment. We will use this guidepost of topics as a benchmark for our progress:

- ❑ What is PKI?
- ❑ The evolution of PKI
- ❑ Cryptography
- ❑ Cryptanalysis
- ❑ Digital certificates
- ❑ Digital signatures
- ❑ How can web services use these components?

Initially, this may seem like a brief list, but we'll discover additional layers of important topics as we proceed through our investigation.

What is PKI?

The term PKI is made up of two parts: **Public Key** and **Infrastructure**. Let's tackle each part separately, and then link them together.

Public Key refers to the class of algorithms used to obscure data from third parties poking around our data and/or our personal and business communications. It should be obvious before we dive into the deep end of the security pool that the basic operation of security involves obscuring data to the point of casual incomprehensibility, but on-demand reconstruction. That's a ridiculously verbose way of saying **encryption**. The specifics of *Public Key* will become apparent in a moment, but for the time being, think of the term literally – publicly available *keys* used to lock something (in this case, data).

In a technical realm, an infrastructure can refer to the fundamental elements used to construct some important corporate resource, such as telecommunications, paging, or general networking. Such a term might imply not merely routers, switches, cables, and hubs in a network, but also the administrative expertise necessary to operate and maintain it efficiently. All the cables and hubs don't do much good if there's no process in place to create accounts, establish access control policies, and regulate day-to-day operation. If the cables et al represent the **hardware**, and the code within them represents software and/or **firmware**, perhaps that administrative element can be called **peopleware**. Whatever it's called, the combination of those elements (hardware, people, and processes) to provide a "living" asset to any organization can be referred to as an infrastructure. We'll find this loose definition to be the most appropriate in our discussion.

If we take the two parts of our definition equation and replace them with our definitions above, we have an interim definition something like this: *The hardware, people, and processes necessary to provide publicly available keys to lock something*. What we know for our purposes is a piece or stream of data that conveys some type of information that needs to be conveyed only to the individuals we designate. This implies some additional layers, not just security, but recipient and sender **identity** as well; and, beyond that, the guarantee that the data that was sent securely was received exactly as it was transmitted. This is what we call **message integrity**.

So this system isn't just about keeping secrets. It's about keeping secrets, getting them to the proper recipient, and making sure the secrets are intact by the time they reach the recipient. We'll find that many of the same types of algorithms used for security are in the same family of algorithms that provide identity and integrity as well. This means we have a firmer working concept of what PKI is all about: *The hardware, people, and processes necessary to provide publicly available encryption keys used for the secure, positive conveyance of confidential data to designated parties.*

The point of all this extra narrative for what may seem an intuitive concept is to highlight the fact that PKI, no matter what you may have read or heard about it, can't properly be said to exist just because one server in a network issues keys, or a particular program supports encryption. If a comprehensive system isn't in place to guide the implementation and use of such resources, it's a piecemeal approach. Security, as many have said before, is part of a process. Just as a home is only as secure as its one unlocked door, computing security is only as tight as the least-secured piece of data traversing the wire. PKI provides a means to mitigate the unrestricted exchange of clear, sensitive data across a networked entity – be it a corporate intranet, or the Internet itself.

Let's dive into this in more detail.

Cryptography

The process of taking some piece of arbitrary data and keeping it secret is known as **cryptography**. Taken in parts, *crypto* means "secret," and the suffix *–graphy* refers quite literally to "writing." Thus, the term *cryptography* maps neatly to its own definition of *secret writing*.

If we have an idea about the process of encryption, then we also should be able to gauge the three critical attributes a sound cryptographic system should possess, which are as follows:

❑ **Secrecy**
Only intended parties can interpret the message we send

❑ **Integrity**
What the recipient receives depends only on what the sender sent

❑ **Authenticity**
The message did, in fact, originate from its claimed author (also termed **non-repudiation**)

Conceptually, these three points can be thought of as a three-legged stool; the absence of any one of these attributes makes the occupant of such a stool crash unceremoniously. Without secrecy, anyone can read our message, which is the whole point of cryptography in the first place. If what our recipient receives isn't exactly what we sent, then the encryption is unreliable and thus useless. Lastly, if authenticity can't be verified, anyone could send a fraudulent message on behalf of the sender.

With our arms comfortably around the notion of securing data and how such a security system must operate at a foundation level, we can now move on to the more concrete aspects of cryptography.

Cryptalgorithms

If cryptography refers to secret writing, and writing software is often a repetitive process of algorithm development, it follows then that a defined process for converting a message into a secret form can be described as a **cryptalgorithm**. If we take a look at this from a mathematical perspective, we could think of cryptography as a function that transforms our original message m, called the *clear text,* into an encrypted message m', known as the *cipher text*:

```
f(m) = m'
```

Reconstructing that message might just be the reverse:

```
f(m') = m
```

We'll see shortly that this mathematical definition of a cryptalgorithm is a bit naïve, but it suffices for the moment. In general, the specific function *f* that performs the encryption could be identified as the implementation of any given cryptalgorithm. Just as there are myriad different cars at the showroom, there are numerous classes of cryptalgorithms, and – in keeping with the automotive metaphor – some are good, and some aren't. Let's take a look at each.

Secret Ciphers

If we can fathom the notion that there literally are infinite possible functions that can produce such an encrypted result, we might be persuaded to believe that coming up with a sufficiently complicated and obscure function would provide ideal security; all that would be necessary is to keep the formula under wraps. Keep that function complicated and secret, so it goes, and nobody will figure out the message. In the security/cryptography world, this technique is termed **security through obscurity**.

While intriguing, this concept doesn't work very well in practice. No matter how complex the function seems to be, it usually proves entirely too breakable for practical use. In many cases, ciphertext derived from secret algorithms falls prey to fairly fundamental cryptanalysis techniques, such as the observation of simple symbol patterns or distributions that allow for ready reconstruction of the cleartext.

What the above ultimately tells us in practical terms is that encryption solutions based on "secret" algorithms are almost as bad as no encryption at all. As we glance at the history of encryption, we discover that even some of the oldest encryption methods did not try to conceal the mechanism of encryption, but rather the key on which the encryption was based. If we look at the mechanism of the **Caesar cipher**, we find that its algorithm is quite public, and that its key is secret. In a nutshell, the Caesar algorithm amounted to the following:

> **For each letter, count n letters down the alphabet from the current letter.**

As there were no supercomputers, seventh order polynomials, or smoldering texts on quantum physics in that era, the process had to be a very simple one that could be accomplished in one's head. The number of letters to count, or *offset*, is now known as the *key* to the algorithm that translates our cleartext into ciphertext. If the key is, say, 4, and the original message is the incredibly non-original HELLO WORLD, the resultant message is revealed in this simple diagram:

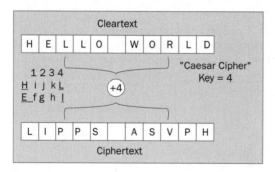

This type of monoalphabetic substitution actually is a weaker form of encryption than that found in the cryptogram. Since the entire message is merely shifted down the alphabet by a constant amount, the cleartext can be derived from the cipher text merely by testing each possible offset value – and only 26 such values exist. So, what does this tell us?

Initially, we can see that the simple shift used by the Caesar cipher isn't very practical. Any form of monoalphabetic substitution will suffer from this same problem. Considering the cryptogram comparison above, an algorithm that *randomly* maps each cleartext letter to a ciphertext equivalent is better, but still weak. Simple letter and word frequency analysis allows for such messages to be broken fairly simply.

If monoalphabetic ciphers in general are too weak for real-world use, we obviously have to find a stronger alternative. Fortunately for us, around the year 1565 a wise French cryptographer by the name of Blaise de Vignere apparently drew a similar conclusion. He constructed what could be termed a more generalized version of the Caesar cipher in which a much stronger key value produced a much stronger ciphertext. The result of Vignere's work is known as the **Vignere cipher**.

Where a Caesar cipher is one in which a single, constant value is used to offset each symbol in the cleartext, a Vignere cipher is one in which the original text is mixed with a string of letters (the key) to create the ciphertext. In contrast to Caesar's **monoalphabetic** cipher, a Vignere cipher is a **polyalphabetic** substitution, because a given letter in the cleartext might map to one of several possible symbols in the ciphertext's symbol space. The letters in the key define each cleartext letter's specific mapping into the ciphertext's symbol space.

In this case, each letter in the cleartext is offset by the numerical value associated with the corresponding letter in the key string. For our example, assume that the letters of the alphabet are simply numbered 1 to 26, and the cipher letter at each position was the result of adding the numbers for each character in the cleartext to the number of the corresponding character in the key. If the result is greater than 26, merely wrap it back to the beginning of the alphabet by subtracting 26. (Another mathematical representation of this would be to say *modulo 26*.)

If, for example, our cleartext string is again HELLO WORLD and the key string is BANANA, the encryption would take "H" and offset it by "B" to give a cipher letter of "J"; "E" plus "A" gives "F"; and so on. Note, also, that if the key string is shorter than the cleartext, we merely repeat it as necessary. The process is illustrated in the following diagram:

Vignere Cipher

Key = "BANANA"

Cleartext	H	E	L	L	O		W	O	R	L	D
Offset	B	A	N	A	N	A	B	A	N	A	N
Cipher	J	F	Z	M	C	A	Y	P	F	M	R

Key text results in different 'KEY' for each symbol in cleartext eg H(8) + B(2) = J (10)

It is apparent that this type of algorithm is much stronger than the simple Caesar cipher we saw earlier. Also it illustrates the importance of a strong key; the word BANANA provides much better encryption than, for example, AAAAAAAA, which would merely offset each character in the cleartext by one. In fact, that would merely reduce the cipher to the Caesar cipher, because the offset of each character is the same. It should follow, then, that the longer the key the better; a short key in this kind of cipher might allow an attacker to see patterns in the ciphertext that could allow educated guesses about the possible length of the key.

With all this in mind, having seen two kinds of key-based ciphers, what can we conclude?

First, the strength of the key is essential. Even a strong algorithm can be hampered by poor key selection. Further, various keys in the Vignere cipher provide *varying* levels of encryption, where all keys for the Caesar cipher gave the *same* level of encryption. Put in another way, no matter what choice we make for the key under Caesar, we find that no one key is any stronger (that is, can produce a stronger ciphertext) than another.

Second, but much more important, is that we can analyze separately the strength of the encryption algorithm and the keys fed to it. If we conclude that stronger keys provide stronger encryption, and know that our encryption function provides no way to obtain our original message *m* from the ciphertext *m'* without the encryption key *k*, then the algorithm itself can be publicly disseminated. The strong *key*, not the algorithm, is the linchpin to protect our secret.

This allows us to draw an important conclusion. Given the use of public algorithms and strong keys drawn from a large pool of possible keys, **key-based** algorithms are the tools of choice for data encryption. Further, public algorithms can be submitted to the cryptographic community for study and analysis, either demonstrating their strength or weakness. This forms an open process by which newer and stronger algorithms are introduced into the encryption community.

Key-based Encryption Algorithms

Algorithms that employ a key, such as the Caesar and Vignere ciphers, have shown us a type of algorithm that fundamentally is more sound than a simple one-way transformation of text – one that accepts not just the cleartext, but also a key. As we will see, key-based algorithms are the foundation of contemporary cryptography. Such algorithms are split into two distinct categories – symmetric (secret key) and asymmetric (public key). Let's take a detailed look at each.

Symmetric Key Algorithms

Mathematically, a cipher such as the Caesar cipher adjusts our original equation representing the process of encryption to one such as this:

$$f(m,k) = m'$$

In this example m, as always, is our cleartext, and m' our ciphertext, but k represents an *encryption key* that is fed to the algorithm with the message to produce the ciphertext. In the case of our Caesar cipher above, the same key that encrypts the message can decrypt the ciphertext, meaning that the following mathematical relationship holds:

$$f'(m',k) = m$$

This equation contains several interesting possibilities. One, if no key is provided, then it can be defined that:

$$f(m,null) = m$$

This says that, with no key, what comes out is what goes in. In our Caesar cipher example above, a key of zero, or a **null key**, produces the original text for the subject cleartext. Second, because it is by definition a function, and a function's value is unique over its range of defined values, a given message plus a given key produces exactly one ciphertext. Conversely, the function when given the ciphertext produces the cleartext in only one circumstance: when the same original key is provided.

Let's look at how well, within this construct, we have technically accommodated our three principles of cryptography. The message is kept secret from anyone provided both parties hold in secret the key used to construct it. The integrity of the message, however, is not guaranteed, because no mechanism exists to compare the cleartext decrypted by the recipient with the cleartext encrypted by the sender. Lastly, neither the authenticity of the sender nor the recipient is established except by the presumed virtue of the process that allows each party to hold the key used to encrypt the message.

There are obvious potential areas of weakness in this structure, such as the secure mutual communication of the single encryption key, or **session key**, between the parties, and ensuring that the key is of sufficient strength such that a third party likely would not be able to synthesize it. Those concerns aside, this particular class of encryption functions represents an important body of functions known as **symmetric key algorithms**. A symmetric algorithm is one in which the same key is used to encrypt the cleartext and to decrypt the ciphertext back into the cleartext. Such routines also are known as *secret key* algorithms, because it is necessary to keep the key secret from any parties other than the originator and the intended recipient.

Symmetric ciphers generally are grouped into two categories. One group is **stream ciphers**, in which a "flow" of data is encrypted one bit at a time. Conversely, the other group of symmetric ciphers is known as **block ciphers**, in which data is encrypted in discrete blocks. Each algorithm type will produce the same ciphertext given the same cleartext and encryption key, yet stream ciphers are generally better performers. RC2, RC4, and the Data Encryption Standard (DES) are all examples of symmetric algorithms.

Symmetric key algorithms are used extensively in cryptographic applications, such as encrypted file systems. One of the most notable applications is the Secure Sockets Layer (SSL) protocol used to secure communications between a web browser and a web server (SSL uses asymmetric encryption for session setup, but symmetric encryption for data exchange). SSL is covered in more detail in Chapter 5.

Asymmetric Key Algorithms

While symmetric key algorithms have their place, we observed in the last section that there are some weaknesses. First, the symmetric nature of the algorithm means that a single key encrypts and decrypts the data being transmitted. If someone grabs that key, a third party theoretically could intercept our transmission and decode it, or interpose fraudulent messages in an existing communication. While the mechanism for exchanging keys should be such that security is preserved, the possibility of compromise remains.

The extension to the symmetric key notion from a mathematical view would then be one in which a *different* key was used to encrypt a given set of data, while a another key decrypted it. *Either* key could be used for encryption, and only the *other* key could reverse it. Put another way, the encrypting key could not decrypt (which should be intuitive, as it would reduce the algorithm to merely another instance of symmetric algorithm).

We could describe such a relationship in this way:

$$f(m, k_1) = m'$$

Where k_1 represents the encrypting key, followed by:

$$f'(m', k_2) = m$$

Where k_2 represents the decrypting key.

This would imply that there must exist a relationship between k_1 and k_2, and more than a passing one. What's implied here is the functional equivalent of a padlock locked by one key, and once locked, the lock's mechanism is adjusted such that only one other key can unlock it. Such a class of algorithm is termed an **asymmetric algorithm**.

Asymmetric, or **public key**, algorithms rely on the notion that the recipient of a secure message will possess what's known as a *key pair*, consisting of a *public key* that is made generally available through some pre-determined mechanism (such as a key or certificate repository, or perhaps via a directory service), and a *private key* that is retained exclusively by the owner. The individual wishing to transmit a secured message to an individual with such a key pair would first take the message and encrypt it with the recipient's *public* key, then send it. The recipient would then decrypt the message with his *private* key, which theoretically is the only key capable of doing so.

This sequence is illustrated in the following diagram:

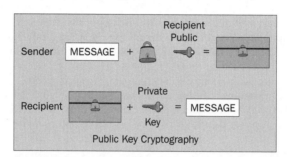

The immediate observations in this scenario are of the vital importance of the private key, and its relationship to its corresponding public key. If the private key is compromised, messages to that individual could be intercepted and decrypted. In such a situation, the key pair must be revoked or invalidated such that the public key associated with that individual is no longer distributed. Unfortunately, if the private key is compromised, there is nothing that can be done to prevent the unauthorized decryption of messages encrypted by its corresponding public key prior to its revocation.

How is it possible that key pairs can be constructed such that one encrypts, and the other decrypts? The earliest algorithms relied on general number theory to accomplish the task. The root lies in a specific area of mathematics known **prime number theory**. A prime number, you will recall, has the characteristic of having no divisors other than itself and one. The problem of creating a public/private key pair is likened to a problem relating to the product of two prime numbers. Assigning a good key for the purposes of public key encryption amounts to picking a *very* large, *probably* prime number.

Notice the italics in the last sentence and two questions arise: "Why *very* large, and why *probably* prime?" Demonstrating that a key possibly is weak in this case amounts to proving that a given number isn't prime. Mathematically, the larger the prospective prime, the harder it is to *factor* that number to prove it isn't prime. Does that mean we just throw out huge random numbers? Surely not – we know that all even numbers aren't prime, and all multiples of 5 aren't prime, so we must be judicious about our selection of "candidate" prime numbers. If we know that large numbers are hard to factor, then we need only select a number that has a high probability of being prime. We have at our disposal several mathematical tests to give us just such a probability, but those tests are beyond the scope of this book. Suffice it to say that we can use one of several algorithms to generate large, *probably* prime numbers that are perfectly suitable for our purposes of public-key encryption.

Asymmetric encryption, also known as public key encryption, is used extensively for secured, identity-specific encryption. Examples of well-known public key encryption algorithms include RSA, DSA, and ElGamal.

Hybrid Encryption

In a situation where a recipient wants to allow anyone to send large amounts of data in a secure manner, using a symmetric algorithm may not be the best solution. Yes, it has a fast implementation, but it has no public key. Neither is an asymmetric algorithm the best solution since it has a public key, but is very slow.

This gives rise to a third type of encryption, which combines symmetric and asymmetric models, known as **hybrid** encryption. One such example of hybrid encryption is the **jumpdog** protocol. In such a scenario, the sender generates a random key for a symmetric algorithm, encrypts it with the recipient's public key, and sends it. The sender then encrypts the large volume of data using the jumpdog protocol, along with this randomly generated key, and sends the ciphertext to the recipient. The recipient can decrypt the encrypted jumpdog key using the private RSA key and then easily decrypt the large ciphertext that he received. The key used for the jumpdog encryption step is then discarded and never reused.

There are myriad other examples in which hybrid encryption could be used. Another potential use might be the direct encryption of data across Ethernet networks. For implementation, examples of other hybrid algorithms include RSA-KEM, RSA-KEM+DEM1, and RSA-REACT.

Drawbacks

Whether symmetric or asymmetric, these key-based algorithms in and of themselves have a couple of simple drawbacks. Whether those drawbacks are relevant to a given implementation is up to the requirements of the subject application.

First, secret key encryption has the problem of creating securely and/or exchanging the session key used for encryption. If the mechanism for swapping the key between the two sides isn't secure, and our third party can intercept that key, our session communications are at risk for interception and/or fraudulent participation.

Second, neither form of key-based encryption provides information about the identity of the sender. Anyone presumably can obtain our public encryption key and send.us a message like "Help National Security – Send $100 to me ASAP," and claim it was authored by a judge; we have absolutely no way of validating it. All we know is that someone said they were a judge, got our encryption key, and sent us a message they wanted us to read.

Public key encryption relies on a mechanism for the distribution of public keys. Remember that to send an encrypted message to someone requires that the recipient's public key be retrieved, so a highly available mechanism for delivering public keys must be in place. We also know, however, that there is a risk associated with compromised private keys, so we recognize that such a key delivery mechanism must also allow for the *revocation* of public keys if the holder of the corresponding private key believes that key has become compromised. If that delivery or revocation mechanism is unreliable, or continues to release revoked public keys, the whole process is compromised.

Most importantly for public key encryption is that the security of the process is only as strong as the security used to protect a given private key. The irony is that the one element that must be left secure is left in the hands of the weakest link in the chain – the human participant. Try as we might to establish policies and procedures to govern how that private key is stored and protected, it will ultimately rest in the hands of the owner to protect it.

The risk is not limited merely to message compromise, but includes the failure to recognize when a key is compromised. If a private key is stored carelessly and a third party captures that key, he will likely do so in such a way that avoids detection. The latency between the time a key is compromised and the corresponding public key is revoked represents a significant window of opportunity for fraudulent use of both.

Another consideration to keep in mind is one of performance. Public key algorithms can take *significantly* longer to operate to encrypt a given chunk of data compared to their secret key counterparts. The tradeoff in performance for security (speed versus key integrity) has to be weighed against the environment in which the conveyed data will be used. Some systems use a hybrid involving both forms of encryption. Refer to Chapter 5 for a discussion on the Secure Sockets Layer for a refresher on how that protocol uses public key encryption to create a *symmetric* session key for secured communication between a web server and a web browser.

Cryptanalysis

The second important topic in encryption is cryptanalysis. If we know that cryptography literally is secret writing, as we discussed earlier, then we should be able to infer that cryptanalysis is the *study* of secret writing. Where **cryptographers** are the hearty souls who *develop* algorithms to encode our messages, **cryptanalysts** are the equally hearty souls doing their level best to *crack* them.

What is the purpose of a cryptanalyst? Such a person objectively assesses the innermost details of a cryptographic algorithm and makes judgments about the relative quality of the encryption the algorithm can perform. Contemporary cryptanalysis requires extensive, detailed study, and knowledge of mathematics.

The value of a cryptanalyst is derived directly from the idea that the strength of our keys, not the secrecy of the algorithms, is essential to reliable, secure encryption services. The algorithms, under the microscope of the cryptanalyst, can be examined to determine if weaknesses exist that might be exploited in one of several ways, including some of the following:

❑ Identifying certain patterns within keys that generate repeatable patterns in ciphertext

❑ Identifying characteristics that suggest multiple keys generate the same ciphertext for different cleartexts

❑ Establishing mathematical foundations for predicting the long-term reliability of an algorithm

❑ Determining key generation algorithms that are at risk for non-uniqueness

❑ Identifying theoretical exploits that, while not necessarily guaranteed to *break* an algorithm, are *more likely* to compromise an algorithm than a similar exploit attempted against another algorithm

Cryptanalysts use numerous techniques to assess various algorithms. In most cases, a designer's intent is to create an algorithm that theoretically is either *unbreakable,* or *computationally infeasible* to break, typically only breakable by what is known as a **brute force** attack. Such an attack is a deliberate attempt to use every possible key within the defined key length until a ciphertext code is broken. The reason such a goal is valuable is that mounting a brute force attack on a system using even marginally long keys will take so long that discovering a key will take an impractical amount of time to accomplish. In some instances, it can be shown that even though a brute force attack is mathematically possible, such an attack using the fastest possible computers would have to run for a time beyond the expected life of our sun.

Public key algorithms may be subject to what is known as a **chosen plaintext** attack, in which a known public key encrypts an arbitrarily selected text, and then a specific group of potential private keys are used to attempt decryption. Success is known at the moment a key is attempted that returns the original plaintext. Cryptanalysts might identify a particular public key algorithm that uses a specific key length to be vulnerable to such an attack, due to certain mathematical patterns found in the generation of ciphertext from different kinds of cleartext.

When cryptanalysts discover genuine weakness in algorithms, or even **break** an algorithm, the publication of such a discovery can allow system designers to determine if the nature of the break renders the algorithm unsuitable for real-world use. In some cases, the demonstration of a break is illustrative only – accomplished by a deliberate organization of multiple, specially designed computers orchestrated to run in concert over a particular period of time. Such a break cautions potential users of the algorithm that the system isn't foolproof, but the only practical way known to leverage its weakness is too complex, impractical, or unrealistic to be implemented by an attacker in a real-world scenario.

The latter environment has become an increasingly important analysis route, given the extraordinary expansion of computing power over the last decade. Algorithms that were deemed practically impossible to break, even with a computer, as recently as the 70's and 80's are now broken and deemed unreliable due to the ability of a greater number of faster computers to perform designated attacks.

Basic cryptanalysis needn't put the mind in the midst of a stack of algebra, calculus, and other higher-order math books. If you've ever worked a **cryptogram** in the newspaper, you've employed your own form of cryptanalysis to a ciphertext message. The analysis of such a message applied the knowledge of letter frequency and word patterns, and it didn't take more than the recognition of a few key words to allow you to solve the entire message. Cryptograms are a simple alphabetic substitution, and the ease with which you can solve them illustrates just how unsuitable such a system is for serious security applications.

Cryptanalysis and its corresponding experts provide an invaluable service to the public key encryption community. Without them, we'd be running systems of unknown strength with keys of unknown quality to produce ciphertext of unreliable content.

Identity

Cryptography and Cryptanalysis together complete the science of **Cryptology**. We've covered a great deal of information about the fundamentals of encryption, various encryption algorithms, and even the techniques used to analyze such algorithms. But they represent only a portion of the public key infrastructure puzzle.

We already know that some of the critical aspects of encryption include secrecy, message integrity, and authenticity. The key-based algorithms above provide all of those characteristics to a degree, but there are certain limitations to the quality of those elements that they provide. That is, if security restricts messages to just the sender and receiver, we assume the recipient is guaranteed since they are the holder of the only key that can decrypt the message encrypted with their public key. That could be termed **passive** authentication. An **active** way of looking at authenticity is termed **non-repudiation**, in which the identity of a participant in a secured conversation cannot be denied.

This concept, which cannot be guaranteed by the public key algorithms we just discussed, can be extended beyond just the participant in a conversation, and involves the use of elements known as **digital certificates** and **digital signatures**.

Digital Certificates

Digital certificates, as you will later see in Chapter 5, consist of a mathematical representation of certain uniquely identifying information about a party. These certificates, when incorporated into an electronic transaction, assert that the owner's identity positively has been used in that transaction. The identity being asserted can be that of an individual, a corporation, or even a server – as in the case of a web server employing SSL. Another use for certificates is for **code signing**, in which code downloaded from Internet contents can be conveyed to have originated from an asserted identity, and arrived unchanged from its origin.

An example of code signing is one in which a Java applet is downloaded from a payment broker service to collect credit card data. The signature on the applet itself can offer the consumer or user of the application a guarantee that the code that was received and installed matched that signed by the original author.

A digital certificate is issued by an organization known as a **Certifying Authority (CA)**. Such an authority is one that goes through the process of confirming the identifying information, and digitally *signing* the certificate such that the CA's *weight* is attached to the accuracy and authenticity of the information provided. It's an odd situation, because the best one can hope to achieve is increasing levels of trust – the question of whether a certificate is trustworthy depends primarily on how much trust is reposed in the certifying authority that issued it. If that particular CA has a sloppy history regarding certificate management, or if third-parties have discovered some peculiar type of compromise for that CA's certificates (allowing for possible certificate forgery), trusting certificates issued by that CA might be a tough proposition to sell.

A digital certificate is known as an **X509** format certificate. The certificate is conveyed in a standard format described next, and we'll explore this format in more detail:

```
                    X509 CERT

(Current :V3)    VERSION

                 ISSUER
                 SERIAL

                 SIGNING
                 ALGORITHM

                 ISSUING
                 AGENCY        (AKA "CA")

                 CERTIFICATE
                 VALIDITY
                 DATES

                 ENTITY
                 IDENTIFIED    (AKA "SUBJECT")

                 "SUBJECT"
                 PUBLIC KEY

(BY "CA")        SIGNATURE
```

The certificate's first field is the *version number*, which is then followed by the *serial number* of the certificate assigned by the CA. The CA signs the certificate using the algorithm specified in the *algorithm* field (along with any algorithm-specific information). The *name* of the CA issuing the certificate is offered next, followed by the *date range* over which the certificate is defined to be valid (in the form of start date, end date). The name of the identified entity is provided in the *subject* field, followed by the sender's *public key* and its corresponding *algorithm*. Lastly, the *signature* of the certificate created by the CA is added to the certificate's final field.

The mathematics behind digital certificates is fairly simple. After combining various, personally identifying information about an entity, a certifying authority will verify the information, attach the entity's public key to it, and then sign the certificate. Once the recipient of the certificate validates the CA's signature, the decision to trust the certificate then depends indirectly on the trust imputed to the CA that issued it.

Often, a *trust* relationship such as this involves a tree of certificates. At the base of the tree is the certificate of the CA, or the *root* CA. That CA may delegate other certificate validation processes to subordinate entities (such as in the case of distributed key management systems), each with its own certificates issued by the root CA; that structure may repeat at each level, thus creating the hierarchical structure of certificates.

Trusting a certificate issued by a CA at **any level** in the tree requires traversing the certificate to its root, and then walking the trust back to the subject certificate. If the root is trusted, and the certificates it issues are trusted, a path from a trusted root authority to the subject certificate is established. Such a traversal is often referred to as a **certificate chain**.

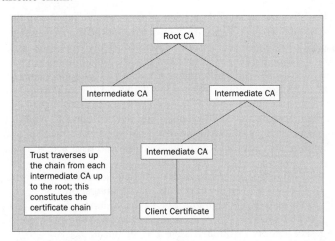

As noted, some key management systems are *distributed*. This means that a central CA may delegate the role of certificate issuance to other servers in an enterprise. For enterprises making heavy use of certificates across a widely dispersed and heavily used network, such distributed management may prove a practical alternative to reposing such a function in a single entity or server. However, distributed mechanisms can increase the complexity of certificate resolution if an increasing number of intermediaries are introduced. Conversely, allowing certificate management to be the task of a single server exposes its own risk because it represents a potential single point of failure in a secured communication network. The need to obtain or validate a certificate may be impaired by the failure of a single server.

In most cases, an explicit traversal of certificates between a principal, its intermediaries, and the root is not necessary and only rarely occurs. This is because most client systems, such as web browsers, already have the root certificates for various popular certifying authorities configured – that means the traversal step across intermediate authorities to get to that root isn't necessary. It's already present.

Chapter 5 includes a lengthy discussion about the ability to positively assert an identity, versus the ability to assert the *user* of an identity. While we won't have the discussion here, suffice it to say that it is important for developers to understand that the presence of a digital certificate doesn't guarantee the *user* of that certificate; it merely guarantees that such an identity was used – fraudulently or otherwise.

A critical point must be made at this juncture of our discussion. The process of creating a digital certificate does nothing to ensure that the asserted identity is *accurate;* it merely says that some third party *asserts* it to be that of a particular individual. Put another way, the CA says that Certificate X positively represents Entity A. On receipt of that certificate, one may choose to trust that CA, and any certificates issued by it. The cement holding this relationship together is the degree to which the trusting party can rely on the assertion made by the CA.

Such a trust relationship is, itself, not free of risk. Consider a conventional retail scenario in which a merchant chooses to accept a check from a customer. In many instances, a retailer will require significant external evidence to establish a positive connection between the identity shown on the check and the person offering the check. Some passerby that says, "Yes, that's John Doe, I promise!" doesn't offer the merchant the same confidence that a photographic form of identification would. But even photographic identification can be faked. The same risks, perhaps even greater, are faced with acceptance of digital certificates. Even if the CA absolutely is trustworthy, that trust can only be relied upon to guarantee the association of a certificate with a particular identity. The CA cannot vouch for the user of that identity.

If a certificate has been co-opted by a third party by some unknown means, all the trusts and assertions in the world will not indicate it. The certificate itself must be revoked, but revocation can be attempted only if its owner is aware of the compromise. Consider a real-world analogy in the latency between the time a credit card is lost, and the time the loss is reported so that the card number can be revoked – that window of time is one in which the card is subject to unauthorized use. This opportunity for the abuse of revoked certificates represents a significant vulnerability in the digital certificate system.

Does this mean that digital certificates are fundamentally flawed? Hardly. What it does mean is that any enterprise opting to engage in a system that requires the use of digital certificates must establish a solid understanding of what they provide, and weigh the tradeoffs and risks accordingly.

If the risks of fraudulent certificate use are deemed to be manageably low, a strong process for management of revoked keys established, and a suitable risk mitigation strategy developed, then a digital certificate-based solution is entirely appropriate. The key is understanding the fact that *just* using digital certificates doesn't guarantee security – a *comprehensive* enterprise approach must be undertaken that encompasses all aspects of security – administrative and technical.

As noted above, the certificate management process is not exclusively one of issuing and storing certificates. When a key expires, it must be removed from the repository system. The potential complexity of removing expired certificates increases as the complexity of any distributed certificate network hosting them may increase. Additionally, revoked keys must be *retained* separately so when such certificates are validated, they can be expressly identified as revoked. Such revocations are maintained on **Certificate Revocation Lists (CRLs)**.

Applications of Digital Certificates in Web Services

The application of digital certificates in web services can be seen in providing identity for user authorization either through a web browser – assuming the browser supports delivery of certificates – or incorporated into client proxies for conventional client-side applications. Let's explore the latter a bit further.

Where a web service can be incorporated into a variety of scenarios, one possible scenario is incorporation into a conventional desktop application such that source code appears to reference locally created objects, where the objects themselves are actually provided by the web service itself. The mechanism that allows for the illusion of local objects accessing a remote object service is the **client proxy**. Most tools used to build web services automatically allow for the creation of the client proxies, but if such proxies are designed to operate on an arbitrary client, and the remote server will require certificates for authentication, the proxies must be built such that the proper client certificates can be identified and sent *at runtime*.

This creates a significant potential problem for the web services developer. Since web services by their nature are platform independent, developing proxies that deliver client certificates may impose a certain degree of client configuration, or differing proxies must be built to allow for any platform-specific mechanisms that may exist for the security of the delivered certificates. Put another way, platform X may store digital certificates in one way, but platform Y may store digital certificates in an entirely dissimilar way – and each may govern how they're used accordingly. This can make the creation of client proxies that cover all the potential bases a non-trivial task.

In some platforms, certificates are stored in a secured portion of the system configuration file, and copied out to the local user's directory structure only at login time. They're otherwise unavailable. Conversely, other systems may store all certificates locally, but control their use with a **passphrase** (as you'll see in Chapter 5, a *passphrase* really means a very, very long password). Neither of these local certificate configurations is exclusive nor exhaustive, and as a result it becomes obvious that client proxies that must deliver such certificates have significant possible obstacles to overcome.

Digital certificates can play an important role in any public-key cryptosystem, but careful consideration must be made for their deployment. Any deployment that does not thoroughly consider certificate revocation and expiration will rapidly prove inadequate. A comprehensive security approach must include not merely servers that deploy and manage certificates, but risk mitigation as well. What are some of the factors that a risk mitigation strategy should include? There's no complete list, but here are a few essentials to consider:

❑ Potential loss associated with unauthorized use of an identity

❑ Potential loss associated with use of an expired identity

❑ Potential loss associated with use of a revoked identity

❑ Risks associated with latency between revocation requests and forwarding of revocations to all servers in a distributed network

❑ Probability that an identity may be compromised

These factors can help assess the quality and comprehensive nature of any certificate-based solution. Another piece of the authentication and validation puzzle is on hand for our next discussion topic, digital signatures.

Digital Signatures

We've discussed how digital certificates can be used for identity purposes, but now let's take a look at another part of the cryptography puzzle. Digital signatures are used to provide information that validates the integrity of the content conveyed to a recipient, and also to provide positive identity of the sender. Where certificates are a **static** entity, signatures could be thought of as a **living** process that changes with each piece of data provided to it. The fundamental goal of digital signatures is to ensure to the recipient of a message that the contents he or she receives are exactly those sent by the sender, and that those bits were, in fact, sent by a specific individual.

Let's take a more detailed look at how digital signatures and non-repudiation work.

First, a sender takes a message and applies a mathematical reduction of that message known as a **hash**. The hashing process produces a *fixed-length* representation of the original information, and that fixed length depends upon the particular hashing algorithm used. Two primary types of hash functions exist: **one-way** functions, and **two-way** functions. The former represents one in which the cleartext cannot be retrieved from the ciphertext; the latter represents just the opposite. For the purposes of hashing within the context of digital signatures, one-way functions are usually sufficient.

After hashing the target message, the sender encrypts the result with his own private key, and combines the original message with the encrypted hash or **signature** and sends the result to the recipient.

> If the data itself is sensitive, the sender may choose to encrypt the combined result with the recipient's public key prior to transmission.

Once the recipient has the message, he/she decrypts it with his/her private key (if necessary). This yields the combined original message plus its signed equivalent. Now, the recipient takes the signed hash, and applies the sender's public key to decrypt it, thus yielding the original hash value. Finally, the recipient performs the hash function on the document – and if the resulting hash matches the hash from the decrypted hash value accompanying it, then two conclusions can be drawn:

❏   The message received by the recipient is the same that was sent by the sender

❏   Someone using the private key of a specific entity's public-private key pair sent the message

This process is illustrated in the following diagram:

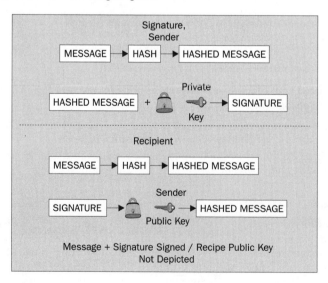

These two conclusions provide two important pieces of the security puzzle. The first provides message integrity – it has not been damaged in transit. Even if a third party intercepted the message, and altered no more than a single bit of the message, the recipient's half of the decryption process would cause the hash validation step to yield mismatches positively indicating message corruption. The second conclusion provides *non-repudiation* – the successful decryption of the signature with the sender's public key verifies that the sender's private key was used to sign the hash of the original document. Note that it does **not** guarantee that the *owner* of the identity performed the signature process – it guarantees only that keys associated with a specific identity were positively used.

Digital Signature Considerations

There are important considerations involving the use of digital signatures in electronic transactions that affect developers and those who digitally sign documents – especially as the use of such signatures is being expanded in the scope of business transactions as the legal equivalent of a conventional handwritten signature. We've covered this ground in more detail in Chapter 5, but we'll summarize that information here for its relevance.

Digital signatures indicate that a particular identity was used. They do not indicate **how** that signature was used. Put another way, if an individual's private key were compromised, anyone discovering that key could begin to perform bogus digital document signatures, and the recipients would have no way of detecting it. The rightful owner of that key would not necessarily become aware of its compromise, either. Where risk mitigation was discussed earlier, a real-world example of such risk could be the financial loss associated with the use of a key to authorize the expenditure or transfer of funds between institutions.

Considerable work has been accomplished to translate digital signatures into elements carrying the same legal weight as a conventional signature, but with a twist. In some states, the use of a digital signature is assumed to have been accomplished by its rightful owner – and thus any such use of a digital signature **is deemed the responsibility of its owner**.

Why does this present a problem for the developer? As of this writing, there is no legal precedent (to the author's knowledge) to establish the actual weight of a digital signature. That means there is no established path of responsibility should such signatures *not* be deemed equivalent to a handwritten signature. If a digital signature is used in a transaction, but the owner of that signature successfully challenges the authenticity of its use, the liability for loss arising from such use may extend in ways only a lawyer could untangle. It is not impossible to consider that such liability might extend to the developer or development organization relying on such a transaction to confirm, for example, the payment for a transaction on an e-commerce web site. Passwords and biometric techniques (such as fingerprints or voiceprints) are tools to secure the process of signing, but even these are not foolproof.

Quick Review

As we move out of this part of our discussion, let's look at a brief recap of what we've studied. We've found that secret algorithms provide poor security, and that publicly disseminated algorithms reviewed by the cryptographic community provide for the best security. We've also found that, in general, the degree of security provided by an algorithm is related directly to the length of the encryption key it requires.

We've also covered three types of encryption algorithms: symmetric, in which a single key encrypts and decrypts our secured data; asymmetric or public-key encryption, in which a public/private key pair is used – one key to encrypt, and the other to decrypt; and hybrid encryption, which combines symmetric and asymmetric encryption protocols.

Web Services and PKI

How can web services take advantage of the services provided by a Public Key Infrastructure? There are a few angles that can be explored. Let's take a look at them.

Client Certificates

Most current web services provide the ability to require or at least accept client-side certificates for user authentication. As you'll see in Chapter 5, server certificates are already required for systems hosting a secure connection via SSL.

An example of the use of a client certificate in a web service could be to control access to an application that provides banking information. Consider a web service that provides numerous functions for account management, including a balance inquiry. Although security for such a service could be provided via a conventional username/password combination, the service could be configured to require a client certificate to establish the user's identity. This could have advantages over a traditional username/password combination in that such certificates expire, requiring certificate holders to maintain or update their certificates regularly to maintain access to their accounts. Contrast this against a username/password combination that may never be updated after it is used initially.

In this scenario, the PKI must be available to issue, maintain, and revoke user certificates. If the server hosting the service uses SSL, then that PKI must also be able to maintain server certificates as well.

PKI-Integrated Applications

SSL is broadly termed within this discussion as an **external** resource – web services are essentially unaware of SSL, and can benefit from it merely by the addition of a server certificate. PKI provides the potential for an **integrated** security infrastructure within a web services application via the combined use of digital certificates and digital signatures, which then provide authentication, identity, and message integrity.

As an example, a web service may be designed to accept digitally signed payloads. The client-side proxies for that application may be configured to use the digital signature algorithm of choice, provided that the required libraries can be installed along with the proxies. Updates to such applications might allow for the replacement of algorithms used by the proxies, although increasing the complexity of client-side deployments is one of the endeavors web services hope to mitigate.

Digital signatures, as we've already discussed, offer important elements of message integrity, non-repudiation, and authenticity, but the extent of their validity, as legal experts review their use, is uncertain, meaning that while the technology exists and can be implemented, caution about downside risks must be managed.

Internal vs. Delegated PKI

An enterprise may choose one of two paths for the creation of a Public Key Infrastructure. One option is an entirely internal one, in which certificates are managed solely within the organization. Another is to delegate the function to existing *external* PKI providers for the purposes of key and certificate management. Each has benefits and drawbacks; the costs of the latter will probably be lower, because it will be reposed in the hands of companies already performing it, and thus already possessing of the servers, structure, and process necessary to handle it.

The potential downsides to an outsourced PKI solution include possible problems with key revocation and expiration, and the risk that any one company may get caught up amidst similar requests from other customers of the same organization. Further, considerations must be made that will determine whether the keys and certificates provided by the company are to be restricted to just company purposes, or should generally be available by the owners of such identities for extra-company purposes, thus increasing the possible risk associated with the compromise of public-private key pairs or latent revocation of certificates.

An internally-hosted PKI solution typically would not have those latter considerations. The scope of such a solution almost certainly would be limited to specific, in-house applications, as most enterprises would have no interest in becoming a repository for truly publicly-available identities. Within that context, *public* would be defined to be the logical boundaries of the organization.

Alternative Security Options

In the midst of the security and identity capabilities with the fundamental PKI, there are also alternatives available that may weigh in against the development of a complete PKI within an enterprise. The Internet has largely been built without a great deal of consideration for secure communications, and web services find themselves in the same boat. The initial implementations of web services have been successful in demonstrating the concept, and first-generation services are proving to be increasingly successful implementations and refinements of the web services paradigm. However, an ongoing sore spot in the increasing implementation of web services has been one of security. What are some other alternatives?

Application-Level Encryption

One overarching theme of security in the web services realm can be the mere use of point-to-point encryption via SSL, or the selective incorporation of encryption at specific points within the application itself via the use of various encryption libraries. Encryption alone doesn't provide authentication or non-repudiation, but it affords at least a basic attempt to thwart third-party interception of data.

Opting for a custom solution that requires a point-per-point assessment of data traversing various application boundaries almost certainly implies a much more complex development effort. On the downside, the type of encryption selected at each point may be different for application-specific reasons, and thus may require the availability of multiple types of encryption libraries, increasing development and deployment complexity. On the upside, however, a precise tailoring of encryption needs can be accommodated – very narrow for specific needs, and more broadly for end-to-end needs.

An additional complication for any encryption-based security component is one of performance. Whether data is encrypted in a point-to-point fashion at the browser-to-server level, or at internal points within the application, an overhead penalty is performed at each end – once to perform encryption, and another to perform the decryption.

The PKI described in this chapter can address many of the security concerns within web applications, but many vendors responsible for the standards under which web services are evolving are establishing protocol-specific security standards that address specified pieces of the communication process. If the security demands of a given web service suggest that one area of security is of greater primary concern than another, one of these specific protocol types might be a more appropriate security solution than the creation of an entire PKI; the cafeteria style selection of various elements could greatly simplify the integration of XML security and the broader issue of PKI. Here are some of those other standards, which will be expanded in more detail in later chapters.

XML Security

IETF RFC 3275 specifies the XML-Signature Syntax and Processing standard, which offers to provide a mechanism and syntax for XML digital signatures. However, this document is only a Request for Comments (RFC), and only sketchy work has been accomplished pursuant to it as of this writing. SUN is reportedly working on a set of APIs for XML-based digital signatures and XML-based digital encryption.

SOAP Security Extensions

The original SOAP specification made no provision for the signature of payload data. This specification attempts to overcome that oversight.

XPKI

The XML PKI directly endeavors to simplify the integration of existing PKI architectures for XML-based solutions.

SAML

The Security Assertions Markup Language (SAML) is a comprehensive attempt to incorporate security in a declarative format using XML. This is a departure from the broad integration of existing PKI-based solutions in a combination of internal and external mechanisms – it creates a baseline for an XML-integrated authentication and encoding framework in which specific security attributes are defined and passed to SAML-aware solution architectures.

SAML represents important emerging work in the field of web services security, and as such merits very careful consideration by developers of web services and applications that use them. If we already know that web services are an XML-based beast, then it should follow as a logical extension of that concept that security elements are simply another manifestation of XML.

In the course of our discussion, we've stressed the importance of having a comprehensive security policy as part of any effort to integrate security, encryption, certificates, or other elements of PKI in an enterprise. A critical design feature of SAML is the notion of "policy points," at which security assertion data is provided in such a manner that a policy point defines the application's response to a given assertion. This represents a model in which a policy can be integrated directly into an application's behavior, not merely grafted on via selective incorporation of disparate products.

Systems designers and developers are well advised to follow the developments of the SAML community closely, as work in this area evolves in the coming months and years. SAML is discussed in depth in Chapter 9.

The Problems

As other standards begin to emerge, each presents its own set of problems along with its own promises. First, many of the "standards" described in the previous section are not IETF standards, and as such almost inevitably carry with them the subtle influence of corporate predispositions. Such predispositions may carry the biases of the desire to sell other types of security products, each of which may or may not tie a customer to an ultimately proprietary solution that suffers from scalability and interoperability issues. Does this mean that security development must be beholden only to IETF standards? Certainly it does not, and not merely for the altruistic reasons of avoiding possible corporate encumbrances.

The rapid growth of the Internet, and increasing popularity of web services, represents a rapid, expansive use of a technology whose standards are governed, regulated, and ultimately controlled by an organization that, through no fault of its own, is necessarily a slow mover. If certain elements of ratified IETF standards are lacking in some way, the IETF is not prone to the rapid modification of those standards to address such failings in what might be termed a "knee-jerk" fashion. As a contemplative body, the IETF has a responsibility to meld the best technical opinion and review of its standards into a deliberate, contemplative process. The result is that certain issues associated with those standards aren't always addressed as quickly as the market may drive, or as individual companies may prefer.

This leaves the developer in the frustrating situation of being the filling in the proverbial Oreo cookie. On the one hand, standards governing web security are lacking, and the IETF will move only in a deliberate manner to amend existing standards to incorporate new elements to deal with the deficiencies. On the other hand, customers demand improved security along with their new products, and waiting for industry standards often implies delays in the development of commercial products. Even if one vendor opts to delay a product pending the development of a more mature standard, it is virtually certain that competitors in the same market will *not* wait, meaning that waiting for IETF action may be a business impossibility. The downside is that incorporating "company specific" or "non-standard" standards gets a product out the door, but perhaps in incompatible or propriety ways that may limit its future market. Truly, the service-standards paradox is one of the problems at the heart of web services security.

Unfortunately, there is no one best answer to this difficult paradox. The fact that there is no best answer points out the fact that the problem of web services security is real and has not yet been sufficiently addressed. For a standards-based solution, the SAML work is one that is receiving considerable attention in terms of integration as a ubiquitous security infrastructure element – not merely for web services – but SAML itself is not an IETF standard. Other work, such as point-to-point encryption and digital certificates, represents individual incorporation of existing PKI technology, but one that does not address the fundamental question of the security of web services themselves.

Recent history tends to demonstrate that the market drives most products to implement some hybrid of commercial and public standards. Netscape, for example, published the SSL specification in 1996, and it was widely adopted in most commercial web browsers. However, that standard was turned over to the IETF, but has never formally been released as a standard (and has been superceded by Transport Layer Security – see Chapter 5). Other vendors, such as Microsoft, take existing published standards and implement them in non-standard ways, most recently with their implementation of the Kerberos authentication protocol in Windows 2000.

Microsoft's implementation of Kerberos is not absolutely consistent with the *pure* Kerberos embraced by the non-Microsoft computing community. Absent the very gory details, it is adequate to describe the differences as ways in which certain data fields are supposed to be managed, as well as other changes that make the implementation incompatible with prior versions of Kerberos. The result is, as we noted earlier, a non-standard implementation of a standard. Some technology observers claim that vendors with sufficient market leverage that engage in a way standards manipulation are guilty of co-opting a standard to make it proprietary – and making their own implementations ubiquitous in a way that makes the *authentic* implementation largely irrelevant, and the ability for it to be controlled in a standards-oriented environment nearly impossible.

This wedge between high-velocity hybrid "corporatized" standards and purely IETF standards opens the door to a third possible option – open source implementations. Open source implementations of existing standards offer the potential of at least some compromise between the opposite extremes we've identified. On the one hand, such implementations often are distributed through the GNU public license, with full source code available for review and possible modification.

Open source products often are developed and maintained by an enthusiastic core of developers that have particular interest in the area of computing embodied by the particular tools they develop. As a result, such tools theoretically could be more readily pushed in a direction that their consumers might desire. On the downside, specialized implementations will require specialized support, and perhaps hamstring a product into earlier versions that the broader Open Source community chooses not to pursue. Other companies are attempting to circumvent the incorporation of open source products into their systems by incorporating license agreement language that claims them to be a "security risk," the veracity of which can only be assessed by the people using them – not the companies producing products in competition with them.

Deploying a PKI

All the discussion to this point has been about the details, algorithms, and history of public key infrastructures. Now, with that understanding in mind, let's talk about deploying a PKI in an organization, and the decidedly non-technical considerations that go into its development. We'll frame two scenarios under which a PKI can be deployed – ways that we've discussed during the earlier portion of the narrative.

We'll then view the notion of deploying a PKI from two perspectives – the technical view and the enterprise view. Let's first have a look at the scenarios.

Full Internal PKI

The first scenario is one in which an enterprise opts to deploy a complete Public Key Infrastructure housed entirely within its own enterprise. This implies a comprehensive network that encompasses essentially all aspects of the enterprise, or at least the entities most likely to require the security services implied by a PKI. The complexity of an enterprise hosting a PKI expands as the complexity of an organization's network increases.

From a macro perspective in either a large or small company circumstance, an internal PKI may offer the potential time expense savings associated with short certificate trust chains. If an enterprise issues its own certificates, each trusting candidate in the enterprise would surely already have the enterprise's root certificate, or have only the shortest of chains to traverse to find the root certificate. This is in contrast to a situation in which a client may have to traverse an *external* certificate chain to find the root CA's certificate, across network links of varying speed and reliability.

Internally-hosted PKI solutions offer complete control over the creation of identity certificates, as well as control over revocation procedures and configuration of certificate replication databases in the presence of a distributed PKI. This is in contrast to a third-party certificate provider who may or may not be able to provide revocation services within a time frame consistent with enterprise policy.

Small Enterprise

On one hand, a small company with a few marginally dispersed physical sites will not need as complex a network as one that crosses international boundaries. The PKI for such a company can be interconnected such that key and certificate management can be accomplished in even a centralized fashion, simplifying maintenance and implementation. Certificate revocation in a centralized PKI should be accomplished with minimal latency, minimizing the risk from compromised certificates. Understand, too, that the risk from such certificates comes not only from possible user identities, but from server identities involved in SSL communication as well.

In the small enterprise scenario, a centralized PKI mitigates the risk associated with revocation latency, and the corresponding problems with failed certificate replication. On the other hand, however, a shutdown of the PKI element that, for example, validates a certificate, would shut down any application services requiring validated certificate access.

Large Enterprise

Larger organizations that do, in fact, span geographically diverse areas – even spanning oceans – undertake a much larger network presence and a correspondingly more complex PKI deployment. For such organizations, which may employ thousands or tens of thousands, a federated or distributed certificate management system is virtually a necessity. A centralized key management system in a large organization represents a critical point of failure risk that is much higher than that posed for a smaller organization.

If a distributed PKI is in place, then tight controls and monitoring must be in place to ensure up-to-date replication of distributed certificate databases. Distributed databases automatically introduce latency problems that their centralized counterparts don't face. If we conversationally view the points at which a PKI is distributed as nodes, and revoke a certificate at that node, any disruption in the connection between that node and the other distributed databases implies a latency window in which certificate revocation has not been communicated throughout the enterprise, thus opening a window in which a revoked certificate could be used at a different point in the enterprise.

A practical real-world example of such a problem could be in a human resources scenario. Consider a situation in which an employee has been terminated, for whatever reason. Certificates that grant that employee access to certificate-controlled resources must be revoked immediately, lest a possibility remain that such an identity could be used after the employee leaves the company. If the HR organization authorized to perform certificate revocation is in the United States, but the employee works in a British subsidiary, the revocation may take place immediately in the organization's US PKI databases, but may occur only after some additional time in the corresponding British databases. Minimizing that latency is a critical element in the integrity of client certificates across the enterprise.

An even worse scenario arises if something compromises the link between subsidiaries. In our above example, we are concerned with the latency between the time a certificate is revoked in the US databases and the time that revocation hits the corresponding distributed databases in Britain. This problem is exacerbated if the physical link between the sites fails – a certificate revoked in the US won't be revoked in Britain until the link is restored and the certificate revocation information flows again, or until someone in the British subsidiary is told to perform the revocation explicitly from their end as well.

Policies

This also illustrates the vital importance of tying a PKI to actual company security policies. In this context, an enterprise can define a **Certificate Practice Statement** (CPS) that defines the practices used by a certifying authority in carrying out its functions. These could tie to company policies in several ways; for example, a policy could state, "client identity certificates of terminated employees must be revoked by a duly authorized individual within X hours of their termination date." Also, company policy could recognize the very real possibility of a link failure between remote sites, and establish a process for certificate revocation to be accomplished directly at the remote site.

The next critical areas that comprehensive policies can address are those in which revocation cannot, for whatever reason, be accomplished immediately. If policies establish a requirement for current documentation about services for which a particular certificate is given access, then application-specific processes can be established to prevent or limit internal application access even if a client certificate otherwise grants access. Such an operation mode could be nothing more than a telephone call to a remote database administrator informing him or her that access to a particular user should be disabled.

Delegated PKI

An enterprise, large or small, may choose to assign all or part of its PKI to an external organization such as a dedicated security services provider. This may have cost benefits for smaller organizations that cannot retain the staff or other resources necessary to provide a complete PKI solution, or can only provide a portion of one. However, the possible complexities of a part-internal, part-delegated PKI may introduce practical difficulties.

Small Enterprise

Small organizations may benefit most from a delegated PKI. **Service-Level Agreements** (SLA) between the enterprise and the security vendor can map policy-defined requirements into performance benchmarks that the vendor must be able to support, for such things as certificate issuance or revocation.

Large Enterprise

Larger enterprises may benefit less from a delegated PKI approach. Many security vendors are relatively small organizations, and may not be able to support the needs of a large-scale organization encompassing thousands of employees.

Where large organizations likely already have a complex network in place, a delegated PKI implies the requirement of *highly reliable* connections to the security provider between all points in the enterprise. Further, a delegated PKI can begin to resemble a centralized implementation if reposed entirely in a service provider, thus creating a significant single point of failure. If the risk associated with that single point of failure exceeds the risk established by enterprise policy, a delegated PKI approach likely is not suitable.

Lastly, a delegated PKI implies some mechanism for individuals to reach out of a corporate network or *intranet* to an external host, and return information from that host to a location within the corporate network. The presence of a path from the internal network to an external entity may be deemed a generic security risk. Accomplishing the necessary communications may require the opening of specific ports on *firewalls*, or the admission of certain external IP addresses into the network that would otherwise not be so permitted.

Policies

In the delegated scenario, policies are equally essential. Where policies can define performance characteristics for an internal PKI, they can map to performance requirements in a Service Level Agreement between an enterprise and the provider. For any enterprise defining a delegated PKI, some sort of SLA that specifically defines as many tangible performance elements as possible is critical to successful implementation. For different levels of performance assurance, specific capabilities and practices can be defined in the CA's CPS.

Technical View

Any technical person can vouch for the relative difficulty of explaining the technical importance of an issue to a non-technical person. The value of a PKI deployment certainly is no exception. As in most cases, many people view the technical issues associated with computing too naively, not giving sufficient weight to the importance of the issues associated with them.

Lack of Understanding

Even technically savvy individuals may not have a comprehensive understanding of what PKI is, and not give it all it is due. They often view it as "something to do with security," and assume that it merits little more attention than your typical password expiration problem.

Developers and analysts in any organization contemplating or having accomplished a PKI deployment should be well-versed in its operation and consequent opportunity to integrate the services it offers into line-of-business applications. This includes all applications an enterprise might develop, not just web services (although web services arguably stands to gain the most). If the analysts charged with implementing *real* applications can convey the value of the PKI into *other* applications as well, the value of the investment has been increased.

Confidence Structure for Key Management

Perhaps the most fundamental aspect of PKI is to understand that it provides a framework or *confidence structure* for key management. If we have an understanding of the value of public-key cryptography, and the potential for identity assertion, non-repudiation, and data security it provides, then we also realize that at the base of that PKI must be a reliable system of key management. Key management involves three basic elements:

- **Key issuance**
  Algorithms to generate public/private keys
- **Public trustable authority**
  For certificate issuance and validation
- **Certificate/key repository**
  For storage of current and expired keys

As you read this, you might opt to slice-and-dice these basic provisions in different ways, and that's fine, but the fundamental elements remain essentially the same. If we have a sound PKI, then we have a means to generate keys for encryption, a means to generate and validate identities via certificates, and a means to track valid and invalid certificates. The absence of any one of these elements compromises the other two.

Vendor Product Partitioning

Security providers are increasing, it seems, by the day. As new and different types of security solutions are needed, such vendors are offering corresponding solutions. Some offer end-to-end PKI support for a completely delegated approach, while others provide selective services to accommodate the requirements of a given customer in an á la carte fashion. For web services, virtually every aspect of a PKI can be used, so a strong definition of the services we need can help us guide the policies used to select the vendors and the elements of any external PKI solution, or define the way an internal PKI is constructed.

A brief summary of some of the higher-profile security vendors illustrates the diversity of product and technology offerings. Some offer tailored PKI solutions, while others offer purely outsourced solutions. Only the implementers of such a solution can assess which best suits their enterprise's requirements.

RSA

RSA Security is one of the better-known names in the security industry. It provides support for all elements of a PKI deployment, from consulting and design to implementation, and offers products for certificate management and user identification within its **Keon** software. RSA is also among the most aggressive security vendors integrating SAML into its product offerings (http://www.rsasecurity.com/).

Entrust

Entrust aggressively targets the web services sector with its product suite. Among its newest offerings is the **Entrust Secure Transaction Platform (ESTP)**. Additionally, Entrust offers certificate services as well as a variety of security solutions, including secure web portals, secure messaging, and secure e-forms. The Entrust Verification Service includes digital signature and time stamping services, and is integrated into the ESTP (http://www.entrust.com/).

Baltimore

Baltimore provides support for the XML Key Management Specification as a means to streamline PKI integration into web services. The Baltimore **UniCERT** 5.0 product is the company's primary PKI offering, and is centered on the XKMS concept to streamline registration and receipt of client certificates. Lastly, they offer customized deployment options that can be tailored to a given organization, even one that is in the process of migrating from or to an outsourced PKI solution (http://www.baltimore.com/).

Verisign

Verisign provides a fully outsourced PKI solution to an enterprise, including certificate management and user identity. Their **Access Management Service** aims to provide the ability to define centralized policies for access control, enabling flexible extension of secured access to users and networks on an as-needed basis (http://www.verisign.com/).

With a view of vendors, let's shift to a view of deployment perspectives.

Enterprise View

We've taken a look at PKI deployment from a technical view, and even provided a very brief insight into how various PKI vendors package their products. Let's view it from the other perspective – at the enterprise level.

Comprehensive Security

From a broad view at the enterprise level, a PKI cannot exist as a standalone entity. It must exist as an integral part of a comprehensive security policy that already exists for the protection of what are already numerous computing–related assets – including hardware and software.

If an increasing number of business processes are finding their way into web services, and the results of those processes are considered proprietary and/or competition sensitive, then the processes that mandate protection of simple word processor documents must be extended to cover web services as well. This means access control, storage control, and a series of other elements. A PKI is part of the puzzle that makes security of web services a reality by providing client certificates for an individual identity, and server certificates for services hosted on SSL-based web servers.

Security for Prospective Customers

If an enterprise is responsible for hosting the data of multiple customers, perhaps hidden under controlled-access web services, such customers may begin to demand a more comprehensive approach to security. The ability to demonstrate a comprehensive security policy in conjunction with a deployed PKI can give prospective customers an understanding of how their data is protected.

Expense Component

Like all good things, ultimately someone has to pay the bills. When the time comes to divide the cost of a PKI deployment among resources, some broad assessments and some tough decisions must be made. Most of the decision process will orbit around these three queries:

- ❑ What do we really need?
- ❑ What's really available?
- ❑ How much does it all cost?

Let's focus on each of these in detail.

What We Really Need

In the ideal world, we'd like to have client certificates that are valid for a brief amount of time, reissued automatically, encryption algorithms that provide perfect security, hashes that are guaranteed to perfectly distinct all bit lengths, and uncorruptible/unhackable security constructs. Unfortunately, we know that none of these things exist. In practical terms, there must be an honest assessment of what an enterprise PKI *needs* to provide. Will we need multiple types of certificates, not merely for identification, but for tasks such as code signing, or secure servers using SSL? Do we need 200-bit hashing algorithms, or will a 168-bit algorithm work just as well? Do we need an option to select from numerous public-key algorithms, or merely one or two?

Again, the importance of an enterprise security policy rears its ugly head. Such a policy, developed in concert with business elements as well as developers and network administrators, can answer many of these questions in advance, and not leave the decisions to an abrupt, ad-hoc decision made on the fly. Defining and prioritizing the needs helps match up what's available (our next point) with cost.

What's Really Available

Our security policy may call for billion-bit encryption, but if it doesn't exist, it's not a very useful requirement. We can match up the prioritized requirements from the first step against the technical realities evident in this step, giving us an honest, real-world perspective on what our security policy in general will provide, and how the PKI in particular can help provide it.

How much it All Costs

The last catch is the cost, and here is where the tradeoffs between performance, necessity, and cost are finally made. Is it cheaper to host an enterprise-wide PKI, or is it better to outsource it? Will outsourcing introduce maintenance problems that may increase process costs not identified in the dollars-and-cents proposal the vendor provides?

Varying performance levels defined in a Service Level Agreement will also impact costs. If an SLA demands specific turnaround on certificate revocation, provided at one cost, a lower threshold of revocation performance may be available at a lower cost. If the cheaper guaranteed performance level is consistent with policy, it may allow monies to be transferred to other elements of the PKI deployment that might not otherwise have been affordable.

The bottom line is that a reconciliation of requirements, availability, performance, and cost must be made to create a successful PKI deployment – not merely for the benefit of web services, but for the enterprise in general.

PKI and Web Services: The Big Picture

To this point, we've covered a broad spectrum of security issues related to web services and possible solutions available through the use of technologies available through PKI. Let's try to combine these pieces to develop a consolidated view of how these two elements can work together.

Understand that public-key cryptography and the PKI solutions that implement them precede web services. Further, web services themselves were not designed with security as a fundamental consideration. This means that security for web services must be provided by taking advantage of programming resources that allow for the integration of PKI capabilities into web service applications, as opposed to taking advantage of resources that implement them naively.

Consider the following diagram that illustrates the various elements of web services, PKI, and how they interrelate:

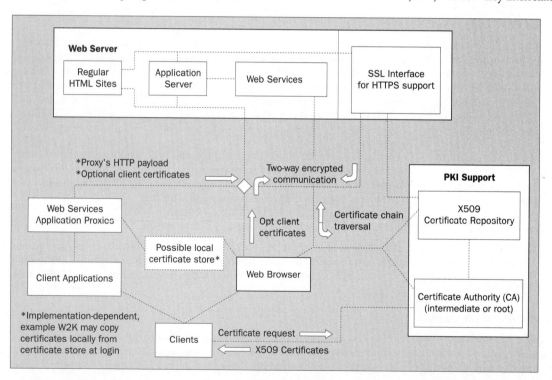

In this illustration, we see the three critical elements of web service applications: a client represented in a web server or conventional client application, an application server, a web browser, and the PKI infrastructure. Because a PKI could be implemented in numerous ways, it is represented as a general service entity in this diagram. Keep in mind that PKI support could involve a lengthy certificate chain or one more certificate repositories, any one of which could be hosted on one or more internal or external servers.

Let's look at these elements individually.

The Client

The client, as noted in the diagram, can be either a web browser or a client application. Let's look at each separately.

Client Applications

A client application implies the installation of a binary executable on a client, essentially in the same way any traditional executable would be installed. In addition to the binary executable are a series of what are termed **web service application proxies** that convert calls within the application into calls to the XML format across HTTP as typically required by the web service.

> *Technically, protocols other than HTTP can be used to transport the payload, but HTTP is the predominate one suitable for this discussion.*

If the web service requires authentication, a conventional username/password scenario within the application that bypasses a PKI solution can provide it. Conversely, the web service may choose to require explicit user authentication via the use of an X509 client certificate, possibly retrieved from a local certificate store on the client where the application is installed. If the client has no certificate to offer, a request for such a certificate can be made to a certifying authority trusted by the web service. Such certificates can be generated locally by an internal root CA, or purchased from a third party provider such as Verisign, Thawte, or Entrust (to name only a few).

Certificates, if required, and the proxied web service payload are then transmitted to the web server – possibly via SSL if a server certificate has been installed. This would require that the appropriate encryption libraries accompany the client application installation.

Web Browsers

A web browser accessed web service implies a simpler client configuration than a conventional application installation. First, a web browser will require no application-specific installation (excepting particular client side elements such as Java applets or ActiveX controls). Second, if the application is hosted via SSL, most browsers automatically are able to support the encryption required to support it. Finally, because the communication between the web browser and the web server already is natively in HTTP, there is no need for application proxies to be installed on the client; the calls to the specific web services likely will be integrated in the server-side code.

Browser-based client identification can be accomplished via X509 client certificates in a manner consistent with client applications via provision of a client certificate possibly stored in a local certificate store. Access to this store may be provided through the web browser itself.

Web Servers

Obviously, the web server is the linchpin of the web services scenario. A web server is client-agnostic; it knows only incoming requests offered through HTTP, and generally is unaware that the request originates from a web browser or a client application proxy. The server may be hosting applications unrelated to web services, and may host a server certificate to support SSL-based incoming connections. If the server is to provide SSL support, a *server certificate* must be requested from the internal CA, or purchased from a third party provider, and installed accordingly.

In most cases, a web server hosting web services will also host an *application server* dedicated to intercepting requests for web service functionality and passing them to the corresponding handler. It should be noted that while an application server is typical, it is not *required;* in fact, it is possible to implement a web service with only a basic web server that supports some type of programmatic interface.

The application server handles incoming service requests, routes them to the appropriate handler, which then may require downstream access to other servers, such as database servers or perhaps even other web servers. Additionally, a web service may need to traverse a certificate chain to determine the validity of a submitted client certificate, thus requiring access to potentially multiple certificate stores, depending upon the length of the certification chain.

Once a request is completed, it is packaged into the proper response format and is sent back to the client via HTTP.

PKI Support

The required PKI support in our broad diagram implies a wide realm of possible secure services support. For our discussion, PKI support primarily involves the ability to accomplish the following:

- ❑ Support requests for X509 certificates
    - ❑ To servers for SSL support
    - ❑ To individuals for identity validation
- ❑ Validate certificates
    - ❑ Ensure provided certificates have not expired
    - ❑ Ensure CA's issuing certificate is not expired
    - ❑ Traverse certificate trust chain until trusted root is found

This generally corresponds to the availability of a certificate store, and to the various relevant certifying authorities that represent either an intermediary or root authority.

It should be stressed that the availability of these elements is critical to the performance of the web service. If something impairs the ability of a web server to validate a certificate supplied by a user, the user may not be able to access the application in a timely manner. For mission critical applications that might involve financial transactions, the inability to perform a funds transfer due to the inability to validate the client could be catastrophic to an organization dependent upon such transactions.

Additionally, web service implementations should provide specific detail back to the client explaining failures in any certificate validation process, including but not limited to the inability to contact the relevant certifying authority, the expiration of the certificate, or the inability to validate the certificate provided.

Summary

In general, we've taken a look at these topics in our discussion of PKIs:

- ❑   What is PKI?
- ❑   The evolution of PKI
- ❑   Cryptography
- ❑   Cryptanalysis
- ❑   Digital certificates
- ❑   Digital signatures

We've seen how published algorithms with strong keys provide superior security to that of secret algorithms, and have discussed the evolution of encryption in general and PKI in particular. We've taken a look at various technical, enterprise, and vendor aspects of PKI as well. We've also tried to stress that deploying a PKI does not mean that a comprehensive security infrastructure is in place in an enterprise. In particular, a truly comprehensive solution implies a series of policies that identify risks, establish plans to mitigate risks, and respond to situations where technology alone will prove inadequate.

The topic of security could, and has, occupied hundreds of pages and spanned entire volumes over the relatively short lifespan of contemporary computing. Here we tried to present a brief view of the PKI capabilities to give you a framework on which to make decisions about security capabilities for your own web services.

5

SSL

When it comes to the use of the World Wide Web, it is assumed that users would be ready to trust web sites with any information they are asked to provide. This might be a legitimate assumption if web servers were inherently safe, so visitors had no need to worry about the safety of their data. However, as security and privacy issues dominate the ever-increasing presence of the web in daily life, the prominence of how those elements are provided is coming under increasing scrutiny. Common questions include: "Is our information secure?" "Can someone intercept our credit card numbers?" and so on.

In this chapter, we'll take a close look at the **SSL (Secure Sockets Layer)** protocol, which is one of the original cornerstones of web security. We'll be looking at several aspects of SSL, but the following topics in particular will guide our discussion:

- ❑ An overview of SSL
- ❑ The need for SSL
- ❑ The working of SSL
- ❑ The two sides of SSL
- ❑ The limitations, caveats, and successors of SSL
- ❑ The role of SSL in web services development

What is SSL?

Internet-connected computers (as well as those on a corporate Intranet) communicate via a protocol known as TCP/IP (Transmission Control Protocol/Internet Protocol). Conceptually, two computers on the network communicate via a "socket" model. Each participant "plugs into" a socket, and once both endpoints are connected, the communication commences. Unfortunately, the basic socket model represents the exchange of data, subject to third-party inspection. The need to secure that data within the socket paradigm thus became apparent.

The Secure Sockets Layer Protocol (SSL) version 1.0 was introduced by the Netscape corporation in 1994 as a mechanism to secure communications between a client and a server. Simply put, SSL defines a mechanism by which two endpoints exchange data in an encrypted format, such that the data exchange offers the following characteristics:

❑ **Security**
A third party, or an eavesdropper, cannot interpret the data being conveyed

❑ **Integrity**
The data received by the recipient matches that sent by the sender

❑ **Identity**
The server receiving the data is always positively identified; optionally, an identity can be asserted for the client as well

SSL operates in a layered fashion – in two components that we'll discuss in detail shortly. At the topmost level is the **handshake** protocol, which operates atop a **record** protocol. Both of these ride the TCP transport. This relationship is illustrated in the following diagram:

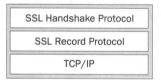

Origins

The idea of securing socket communications involves the use of key-based cryptography. Key-based cryptography refers to taking any original data, known as cleartext, and a particular value known as a key to encode the cleartext into ciphertext via the use of an appropriate algorithm. A more detailed discussion on cryptography was seen in the last chapter. Symmetric encryption uses a single key to encode and decode the cleartext and ciphertext, respectively, while asymmetric or public-key encryption uses a public/private key pair to encode and decode. SSL incorporates both of these techniques.

Although SSL is widely treated as a standard, it is interesting to realize that SSL has never actually gained the formal status of an Internet Standard as published by the **IETF (Internet Engineering Task Force)**. Obviously, this didn't prevent various companies (primarily web browser vendors) from integrating the non-standards into their products, thus giving it the honor of becoming the de-facto standard for web browser-to-web server security, implemented over the Hypertext Transfer Protocol.

Netscape standardized the name **socket** as a reference to the programming model that defines communications across a computer network. The Berkeley Sockets model remains a cornerstone of network programming, abstracting the communication interface between two computers as one in which a **server** process listens on a **port** for inbound connections from interested clients. It likened the connection across the port to the notion of connecting a cable into a socket at both ends of the connection, and passing data across it.

Netscape turned the SSL standard over to the IETF, and subsequent work on SSL led to the development of a draft SSL v3.0 specification in November 1996 (the latest version of this specification can be reviewed at http://wp.netscape.com/eng/ssl3/draft302.txt). IETF drafts expire after six months, and no formalization of the standard was produced. Despite that, implementations of SSL 3.0 found their way into newer versions of popular web browsers, and SSL 3.0 reaffirmed its position as the default for browser-to-server security.

The IETF future for SSL has migrated to a broader scope, known as **TLS (Transport Layer Security)**, and work now revolves around this emerging standard (which can be found at ftp://ftp.rfc-editor.org/in-notes/rfc2246.txt). Although the name has changed, the concept remains substantially the same.

If we know that SSL was built in the shadow of Berkeley Sockets nomenclature, it could be argued that the scope of such a specification is implicitly narrowed to just socket-based communication. TLS broadens the conceptual scope of secure communication beyond any one type of computer-to-computer interchange and abstracts it to the application-to-application level. As the technical concepts are substantially the same, and are merely broadened in scope, TLS is deemed the heir apparent to the SSL environs, although it is likely that SSL 2.0 and 3.0 implementations will be available in browser products for some time to come.

Adding the ability to secure data in the channel between the client and the server opened up the Web to an entirely different breed of application, well beyond the simple, primarily static text and reference sites that were the order of the day. Companies opened web sites that allowed for direct order of merchandise, with customers supplying credit card and shipping information. Banks began offering online financial services, such as account transfers and bill payment. Business-to-business resolution of purchase contracts, shipping, invoicing, and payment were also possible now. As this model has been refined, web services finds itself next in line to serve as a beneficiary of this founding technical work.

What Does SSL Provide?

As mentioned earlier, SSL is intended to provide an encrypted means of data exchange between a client and a server; most typically, a web browser and a web server. Although SSL is applicable to other server protocols, such as Telnet wherein users might connect to Linux servers or update CVS archives, and FTP, its application as a protocol in the vein of web communication is the central theme of our discussion.

As part of the handshake sequence, the server is required to identify itself via a server certificate. The inability of the server to offer such an identity causes the session setup to fail. During the handshake, protocol preferences are exchanged, and a single secret session key is used via a symmetric key algorithm to encrypt and decrypt data sent across the wire. Session keys are discarded at the session's conclusion.

We'll defer a more detailed discussion of the handshake protocol for now.

What Doesn't SSL Provide?

By definition, SSL offers server authentication as well as optional client authentication via use of certificates. What follows in this discussion, however, will be an assertion that may go against the conventional wisdom of how digital identities are supposed to be used. The other area, dealing with the scope of security, is fairly simple. Let's take a look at both.

Client and Server Certificates

Here is an assertion that may seem to go against conventional wisdom:

❑ SSL cannot guarantee the identity of the user at the client end of a connection, even if client certificates are used.

❑ Having said that, SSL does guarantee the identity used at the other end of the connection (only when client certificates are used).

Let's try to make sense of the subtle difference between these two statements.

One aspect of SSL that makes it so attractive is the provision of positive identification of the server, which is required, and optional identification of the client. In both instances, identification is provided via the use of an identity certificate, which holds a numerical representation of certain data that uniquely identifies the certificate's holder as well as its public encryption key.

Ideally, the identities provided by the client and server certificates would be inviolable. If a certificate identifying an individual were used, it was incontrovertible proof that the owner of that certificate was the one using it. Unfortunately, this is not the case. Herein lies one of the emerging problem areas of the web – the legal reliability of digital certificates. Even as developers, we must be keenly aware of the critical technical differences between what digital certificates actually provide versus what vendors assert they provide.

The mathematics and theory behind cryptography and identity work under various assumptions, among which are the security of private keys and trustworthy use of digital certificates. This allows cryptographic texts to make positive assertions that the use of a certificate guarantees the use of that certificate by its assumed owner. But we all know that in the real world few white rooms exist in which the purity of mathematical assumptions are always valid. Identity assertion is one of these very areas.

Earlier in the book, we discussed the fundamental security concept of non-repudiation. As a review, non-repudiation refers to the notion that individuals cannot disaffirm their participation in an electronic transaction. Cryptography tells us that the use of a digital certificate is sufficient to provide non-repudiation. In theory, that's correct, because only the owner of the certificate should know, say, the passphrase necessary to validate use of the client certificate. In practice, however, the use of a digital certificate proves that a particular identity was used. It does not say anything about who or what used that identity.

Let's state this once again to make sure the subtle distinction is understood. The presence of a digital certificate in a transaction proves only that a given certificate was used. It does not say how, or who, used that identity, whether it was it the rightful owner or a malicious third party who, through some unknown means, compromised that certificate and is using it to his own benefit, or to the detriment of its rightful owner.

Consider a real-world analogy. Suppose you awoke one morning to discover that your car had been stolen. After a time, the police contacted you and gave you the good news that your car, undamaged, had been found; the down side, however, was that your car had been used in the commission of a bank robbery. The police (able to discover you as the owner of the vehicle by virtue of its license plate) now identify you as the prime suspect in the crime – only because you were irrefutably identified as the owner of the vehicle, and presumably only you have the key necessary to start the car.

This is perhaps ludicrous but the extreme elements of the example demonstrate the point. An element of a transaction provides information that ties an identity to an act, but that tie is erroneously used to make a positive conclusion about the actor. In theory, the only person who should be able to use a digital certificate is its rightful owner. But the fact that such certificates are not, themselves, completely secure means that such a conclusion is fundamentally unsound. The use of a digital certificate doesn't guarantee the identity of the actor – it provides only the information that a particular identity was used.

The legal problem that becomes an issue for developers is that the use of digital identities is being codified into law. In some states in the US, the use of a digital signature implies use by its owner. It then becomes incumbent upon the owner of that certificate to prove fraudulent use. How might downstream liability fall on the shoulders of a developer when a product employing a digital identity technology works on precisely this assumption, if in court it could be proved that such an assumption were wrong?

There is presently no one-size-fits-all answer to the question of validating the use of such identities, but as developers integrate identity solutions into their products, they must be aware of the difference between what digital identity actually proves versus what it is asserted to prove. These two, as illustrated, are critically dissimilar.

For the remainder of this chapter, we'll make a special point to say that digital certificates assert an identity, but not the user of that identity.

Front-to-Back (or End-to-End) Security

Where the discussion of participant identities became a complex review of coupling identity versus intent, the notion of security scope is relatively simple in contrast.

SSL is declared to be a point-to-point protocol. This means that the security SSL provides is limited to the two immediate endpoints involved in the exchange of data; for the sake of our discussion, that means the web browser and the web server. The presence of security beyond the destination web server cannot be asserted. There exists the potential for a security problem at any point downstream of the server, since the data it receives could be in clear text, and possibly could be re-transmitted to other servers that may or may not have a public Internet presence. The ability to assert secure communications across the span of the entire application is termed "end-to-end" security, and clearly SSL was never designed to provide this type of security guarantee.

The notion of point-to-point security provided by SSL is illustrated in the following diagram:

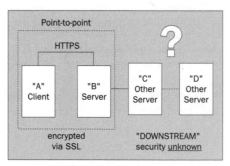

What is meant by downstream servers? It's admittedly an umbrella term to describe any server that might forward any portion of data fed to the destination web server to any other server on the network, or on the Internet. A downstream server could be a simple redirection of a request from a front-end server to a remote server, which is a common configuration in setups that employ reverse proxy.

Reverse proxy is a technique that allows external users to access an otherwise secured internal network. A typical reverse-proxy setup involves a server with two NICs (Network Interface Cards) – one with a public Internet presence, the other with an internal network presence. An external user accesses the server via its public IP address, and provides authentication information that is then proxied back to the internal network through its private network address. Once authentication is complete, the proxy server acts as a wrapper site that merely forwards and returns information between the user and the internal web server hosting the target application.

Normally, reverse proxy access points employ SSL via https, meaning that the authentication information and application data exchanged between the user and the proxy server is encrypted. However, there is no guarantee about the type of encryption (if any) that is employed as the proxy server forwards that data to the actual host server located on the company's private network. Similarly, no information about the security of the data on-the-wire between the host server and any other servers is available, either. The following diagram illustrates this prospective reverse-proxy setup, and how SSL provides only limited security:

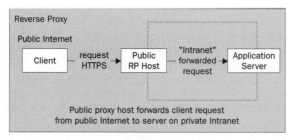

Situations like this require close interaction between the developer and any downstream hosts in order that the type of security provided might be documented and corresponding risks may be evaluated. In most cases, the primary type of downstream server will be a database server hosting application data. If that database is hosted on a server separate from the web server, that server-to-database link represents a separate point-to-point sequence that must be secured in accordance with the requirements of the application, and must be done so independently of any SSL presence between the user and the web server.

Why Do We Need SSL?

We've already covered a significant amount of data about the nature and capability of SSL, but we've not yet addressed a basic question – why is SSL actually necessary? Let's try to view this question from different perspectives.

HTTP

The HTTP or Hypertext Transfer Protocol is the centerpiece of our current web technology. If data flows across the Internet to accomplish anything of interest, it finds its way through HTTP. This is a simple protocol capable of transmitting lots of data in a short time but with one slight drawback. Everything across HTTP is transmitted in plaintext; even the contents of a SOAP transaction uses HTTP as its transport.

Plaintext communication of data across the web is fine for web sites holding the news, sports information, or perhaps your favorite cookie recipe. When dealing with sensitive information such as social security numbers, credit card numbers, cryptographic keys, bank account numbers, or personally identifying information, cleartext transmission rapidly becomes unacceptable. Third parties need only use a network-sniffer or some other simple tool to eavesdrop on the data and use it for whatever self-serving means they choose.

The cleartext transmission of data over HTTP renders it fundamentally insecure for at least the reasons detailed below.

Data is Open to Inspection

Cleartext data flowing between browser and web server is ripe for third-party inspection for a variety of possible uses, not limited to the compromise of user-sensitive data. Other mechanisms available to a third-party eavesdropper on cleartext HTTP transmissions include the ability to make inferences about the structure of a site, and use that information as a basis on which to construct spoofing, redirection, or malformed URL attacks.

A corollary to open data inspection is one of data persistence. If a web site implements persistence of data on the browser, that data may be retransmitted to the server during each browser-server round trip. This means that potentially sensitive data, such as personally identifying information, or sensitive personal data, is exposed across the wire during every page access.

SSL eliminates the possibility of third-party examination of cleartext data by using a single shared secret key, with a symmetric key algorithm to encrypt and decrypt data on both ends of the data transaction during a session. The user's view of SSL incorporation into a web communication is via modification of the URL to use https as the protocol, rather than http.

Inability to Establish Participant Identities

As we've already discussed, participant identities is a potentially vexing problem. There are two distinct sides to the identification coin: asserting an identity for the client, and asserting an identity for the server. Plain HTTP is inadequate for both of these tasks, as we will discuss next.

Server Destination

HTTP provides no mechanism to validate that the server for which data is intended is actually the server to which the data is delivered. Redirection attacks, that cause data or web sites to be spoofed or simulated on other servers without the user's knowledge, provide a great opportunity for the capture of passwords, credit card numbers, or other security-related identity compromises.

SSL attempts to overcome this problem by mandating the use of **server-side certificates** to assert a specific identity for a given server. The server certificate contains information about the common name of the server, which the browser can use to compare with the server requested in the client-supplied URL. If they don't match, the user can be warned and then be allowed to determine if the submission should proceed.

Unfortunately, server certificates aren't foolproof. They are useful only to the extent that they can provide data on the asserted identity of the server, and on whether that matches the intended identity. Notably, mock web sites are built simulating those of more popular vendors, and are registered with a legitimate server certificate. If the terminology used in the description details, used to make the identity of the website, has sufficient likeness to the server certificate of a legitimate vendor, the user may be easily persuaded to accept its legitimacy without question. The bottom line is that the ability of a server certificate to offer protection is limited ultimately to the awareness of the user accessing the site, of possible mismatches between his intended destination and the identity asserted by his actual destination.

Client Identity via Passwords

For clients, HTTP does support a primary type of authentication protocol, known as basic authentication. In this scenario, a protected page causes the server to pass an "authenticate" header to the client, which causes a username/password dialog to appear. The user then supplies appropriate credentials before being granted access to the protected resource.

The basic authentication protocol employed in HTTP does not truly encrypt the supplied password. The browser applies a simple Base64 encoding algorithm to obscure the password in transit, which maps chunks of four eight-bit characters into chunks of three six-bit characters, and provides a character assignment for each mapped character according to a specific alphabet. This means that the cleartext can be readily retrieved from the encoding, and as such renders any password as an immediate target for compromise. With this limitation, it can be suggested that basic authentication provides only the thinnest notion of security.

Some browsers, most notably Microsoft's Internet Explorer, integrate other identification methods. Internet Explorer's Windows Integrated Authentication performs a "cryptographic challenge" sequence to convey an identity to the server. However, this authentication is limited to Windows platforms. For small companies hosting Intranet-based servers and applications, such arrangement may be adequate, but for large deployments, platform-specific solutions are impractical as they are quite limiting.

SSL offers two alternatives to overcome this problem. First, if basic authentication simply cannot be avoided, SSL can still encrypt it through a simple technique known as "Basic over HTTP." This protects the base64 representation of the client credentials that go across the wire to the authenticating server. Alternatively, SSL supports the notion of client-side certificates.

In summary, client certificates serve to tie a particular mathematical representation to a particular user, and bind that representation via the owner's public encryption key. Use of the certificate is intended to be restricted only to its owner, through an implementation-dependent mechanism. So, a specific identity can be established by submitting the certificate to the server. However, as it has already been discussed, client certificates assert only an identity's use, without necessarily revealing by whom. Relying on such certificates as a positive indicator of user identity is thus at one's own risk.

No Guarantee of Data Integrity

HTTP is analogous to a pipe, in that data flows freely in both directions. HTTP does not pay much attention to the size, nature, structure, or type of data being transferred. As a result, there's no way to validate that the data sent by the browser made it to the server, or if the data sent in response made it back to the browser. In more concrete terms, if a server download of a page fails prematurely, HTTP has no way of detecting it or correcting it. Anyone who has seen a web page load only partially, or even has seen an image file scrambled in transit can infer that HTTP can't detect a problem on the server end.

SSL addresses this problem by automatically incorporating what's called a Message Authentication Code (MAC) in each encrypted message. A MAC is constructed by performing a specific mathematical operation known as a hash on the source data. The MAC value is added to the message structure that holds the data, which is then encrypted and sent to its destination. Upon receipt and decryption by the recipient, the message data and MAC are extracted, and the same hash function is performed on the data block. The result of the recipient's hash is compared against the MAC, and if the two values match, the recipient may conclude that the message was undisturbed in transit, and has been received in its entirety.

The SSL Solution

We've described above specific ways where SSL addresses the problems introduced by HTTP. From a broader perspective, here's why SSL can provide these solutions:

❑ SSL is a point-to-point protocol. It defines a distinct communication link between two points, and asserts that link to be secure via a symmetric key encryption algorithm.

❑ The protocol requires the server endpoint to be associated with a trusted assertion of identity via a server certificate.

❑ The protocol allows, but does not mandate, the client endpoint to assert an identity via a client certificate.

❑ SSL guarantees the integrity of the message sent between across the link.

How Does SSL Work?

We've taken a reasonably in-depth look at the particulars of the solutions SSL offers to security problems associated with unencrypted, cleartext HTTP-based transmissions. We'll now move on to a more detailed review of how SSL functions. Note that this will not presume to recite the technical details of the entire SSL 2.0 or 3.0 draft specifications in particular, but at least the technical spirit to convey the operational detail relevant to our discussion.

Overview

Taken broadly, SSL is a basket of encryption and identification technologies bundled together in a single protocol. Public-key algorithms are used to establish a secure mechanism for validation and key exchange, while a symmetric algorithm encrypts data via a shared, secret session key. Hashing functions provide a mechanism for message integrity. The exchange of this data is covered in two layers, known as the **SSL handshake protocol** and the **SSL record protocol**. Initial protocol parameters are established at the server connection time, during the handshake protocol.

The diagram below shows the SSL transaction between client and server:

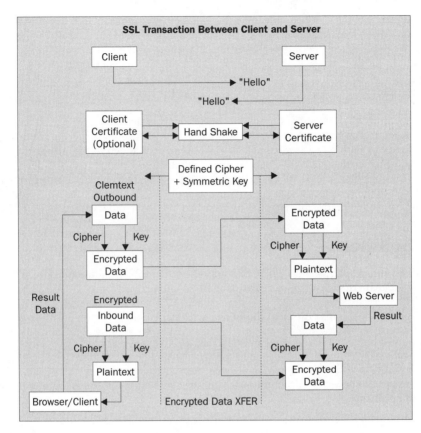

The SSL Handshake Protocol

The SSL handshake protocol operates on top of the SSL record layer, which serves as the basic communication unit within the SSL protocol itself, as seen in an earlier diagram in this chapter.

Handshake is the metaphor given to the mechanism by which a formal sequence of message exchanges is accomplished. SSL, like many other Internet protocols, is implemented as a finite state machine (FSM). A finite state machine is one that always exists in one of a specifically defined set of operating modes or states, and the input into the machine drives the machine from one state to another. This means that, for a given session, two SSL state machines are in complementary operation. The mutual exchange of messages from each state machine drives the other side's state machine throughout the communication process.

Each message in the process consists of a well-defined name and, depending upon the particular message, may contain additional message-specific content, as noted in each message step described below. As we progress through the chapter, we'll refer to this list and explore some relevant aspects of it in more detail.

Following is a diagram of the SSL handshake:

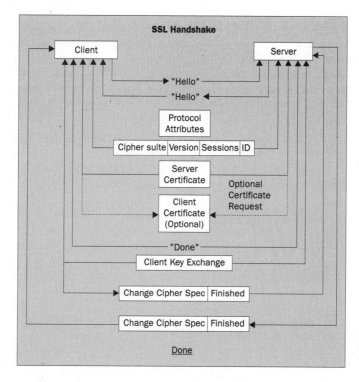

The handshake sequence starts with the polite HELLO message.

1. From the client, a CLIENT HELLO message is sent.

With this initial message, the client sends its own preliminary information, including the protocol version, a list of cipher suites (encryption protocols), such as RSA-MD5, DH-DSS, or FORTEZZA, supported in decreasing order of preference, and compression methods that can be implemented. The details on how this information is ultimately used are expanded in the server response.

2. In response, the server sends a SERVER HELLO message.

Within the context of the HELLO exchange, several basic elements of the protocol implementation are established that will govern the data exchange throughout the life of the session. The primary elements exchanged and established include the following:

❑ Protocol version

❑ Session identifier – Unique for a new communication session, or reused from a previous session

❑ Cipher suite – Encryption protocol

❑ Compression method

Among the protocol versions, the server selects the lower of those reported by the client and that it supports on its own. The server opts for the cipher suite listed highest on the client's list of suites, and exchanges keys accordingly.

Additionally, both the server and the client construct random blocks of information are identified structurally as `ClientHello.random` and `ServerHello.random`. These values, in combination with the selected encryption protocol, will be used to construct an essential session element known as the master secret. The master secret will ultimately be used to construct the secret symmetric (shared) session key used to perform the encryption essential to our security effort.

Individually, the client's HELLO provides a list of available algorithms for each aspect of the communications session (such as encryption and compression). In response, the server selects one of the server-specified encryption algorithms and incorporates the selection into its own HELLO response message.

After the HELLO exchange concludes, the server will transmit its certificate to the client. At that point, the handshake continues.

3. The server optionally sends a SERVER KEY EXCHANGE message.

4. The server optionally sends a CERTIFICATE REQUEST message for client identification.

5. The client responds with one of the following messages:

❑ CERTIFICATE – transmitting the relevant client certificate

❑ NO CERTIFICATE – indicating no certificate is available

6. Then the client then sends a CLIENT KEY EXCHANGE message.

7. The particular contents of this message vary depending upon the type of public key algorithm selected during the HELLO negotiation sequence described in steps 1 and 2.

8. If the client has sent a signing certificate, it will then send a CERTIFICATE VERIFY message to the server to perform certificate validation.

9. The client now sends a CHANGE CIPHER SPEC message, indicating that the selected or pending cipher is ready to be used for subsequent communication.

10. The client then sends FINISHED within the now-current cipher algorithm, and indicates its completion of the handshake protocol.

11. The server, in response, sends its own corresponding CHANGE CIPHER SPEC and now-encrypted FINISHED messages to the client, concluding the handshake sequence.

12. Secured communication commences.

The handshake protocol also allows for the resumption of a previously-established secure session. The client may send a CLIENT HELLO message with a session ID corresponding to the desired previous session. If the server has cached its previous secure session IDs, and finds the client-specified ID therein, the balance of the handshake is skipped, and both sides move to transmit their FINISHED message as described in step 9. If the server can't find the matching ID in its session cache, a full handshake is performed to establish a new communication session with entirely new protocol parameters.

The possible persistence of session identifiers and setups presents an obvious potential security problem. If a third party were to intercept session identifier values, it could spoof a previously secured session. However, such a spoof is computationally infeasible and thus is not a practical source of security concern. At a minimum, a prospective "spoofer" would need to know a great deal more about the session than just the session identifier.

Once secured communication begins, the server and the client persist the selected cipher suite (encryption protocol) until one or the other sides attempts to initiate a CHANGE CIPHER SPEC.

The SSL Record Protocol

Once the SSL handshake is completed, the record protocol steps in to mediate the flow of encrypted data across the connection. The protocol takes the session key established during the handshake, and begins encrypting the outbound data or decrypting the inbound data, as appropriate.

The SSL record protocol establishes the framework under which handshake and data messages are exchanged between the participants in an SSL communication. Each SSL record consists of not more than 2^{14} bytes of data known as an **SSLPlaintext** record.

The SSLPlaintext record incorporates a structure defining the version of the protocol in use, the content of the data in the record, the length of the data, and the data itself. This record structure is then used throughout the SSL communication sequence merely by providing one of the following four content types:

Content Type	Meaning
CHANGE_CIPHER_SPEC	Changing the cipher used for encryption
ALERT	Indication of an error condition
HANDSHAKE	Negotiation of an SSL session
APPLICATION_DATA	Data in an existing SSL session

It is the responsibility of the "higher-level" protocol, such as the handshake protocol, to construct and transmit the record layer blocks appropriate during the corresponding communication phase. In this way, the record layer could be said to encapsulate the higher-level protocols. It maintains no cognizance of the type of data being conveyed but merely defines the format in which the data is presented. In essence, the SSL record protocol provides the "wrapper" around the SSL session data.

Additionally, the abstraction is carried further such that data boundaries are not implied within SSLPlaintext records. This means the intelligence of the beginning and end of a record sequence is reposed to the higher-level protocols preparing the data. This means that multiple SSLPlaintext records (of a common Content Type) could be merged into a larger single record.

When conveying data, the selected cipher is used to convert a single SSLPlaintext record into an SSLCiphertext record. Inbound SSLCiphertext records are decrypted into SSLPlaintext, and SSLPlaintext records are converted into SSLCiphertext records.

Keeping Data Secure and Sound

As we've noted in the discussion, two of the primary features of SSL are data security and integrity, meaning that third parties are excluded from our secured conversations, and what each side sends to the other is exactly what the other side receives. How does SSL accomplish session security and ensure message integrity? Let's look at these issues next.

Session Security

At the simplest level, the session setup provides for the selection of an encryption protocol and a mechanism for the exchange of keys to encrypt and communicate a mutual secret. The mutual secret is then used to develop the secret session key used to encrypt data on the sending end, and to decrypt on the receiving end. Keeping the session key secret is essential because the encryption used is symmetric.

This process involves both public-key and secret-key cryptography. Public-key cryptography facilitates identification and exchange of keys, while the data itself is sent using secret-key algorithms.

The general process of mutual client-server encryption is illustrated below. Following the diagram, we'll take a top-level overview of various symmetric and asymmetric encryption algorithms:

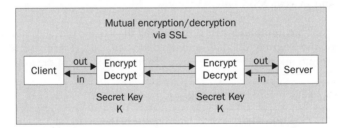

Symmetric Key Algorithms

As mentioned earlier, part of the handshake sequence involves a secure key exchange step that uses an asymmetric algorithm to allow communication of the private session key to both parties. A more comprehensive discussion on encryption algorithms and the broader topic of cryptography will follow in Chapter 6.

Let's now look at examples of some popular symmetric encryption algorithms.

Data Encryption Standard (DES)

DES was released in 1977 under the title of FIPS Publication 46, by the National Bureau of Standards of the United States government. The standards body, now known as the National Institute of Standards and Technology (NIST), released the work as a derivative of prior work accomplished by IBM. DES was deemed suitable for encryption of all non-classified data residing on government computing systems, and was adopted by ANSI in 1981 as a standard suitable for private sector encryption. It has undergone periodic review for the purposes of re-certification, most recently in 1998.

DES has been the target of some controversy over its lifetime. Some cryptography experts contend that the 56-bit key used for DES is too weak to endure the long-term challenges to be imposed by increasingly powerful computing hardware. Not surprisingly, NBS/NIST refuted those claims. More critically, some analysts believe that the National Security Agency imposed deliberate weaknesses if not actual back doors into DES to allow for the discernment of keys and data used in conjunction with communications between individuals or groups involved in criminal activity. Such allegations have been denied, but the debate continues in the security community.

Using hardware and software specifically targeted at the problem of breaking DES, a team of researchers broke DES in July 1998, using hardware costing about $250,000. The growth of higher-speed technology since that time leads some to believe that DES is significantly more vulnerable today than at its inception. The Advanced Encryption Standard (AES) has since succeeded DES.

Triple DES

In response to criticism about potential weaknesses in DES, a subsequent revision to DES was released that amounted to tripling the size of the key and adding more specific rounds to the encryption process.

RC4

RC4 is an encryption protocol allowing for variable-length keys developed by Ron Rivest of RSA Data Security, Inc.

As a trademarked solution, its code was intended to be available only to licensed users of RSA, but word of the availability authentic source leaked to the Internet in late 1994.

IDEA

Xuejia Lia and James Massey created the International Data Encryption Algorithm (IDEA) in 1992. Although it is intended to serve as the successor to DES, and is generally considered the strongest encryption algorithm presently available, it is still not widely implemented.

Asymmetric Key Algorithms for Authentication

Where symmetric key algorithms use a single key to perform encryption and decryption, asymmetric algorithms use one key to encrypt, and another to decrypt. SSL does not use asymmetric algorithms for encryption, but does employ them for the purposes of identification and key exchange.

RSA

Rivest-Shamir-Adleman (RSA) is arguably the best known and one of the strongest public-key encryption algorithms available. It has withstood years of cryptanalysis without significant compromise, and derives strength from its origins in prime number theory. Although it is not proven, the contention is that the only practical way to compromise RSA is to find a cheap way to factor large numbers – a notoriously difficult and expensive problem.

Message Integrity

We discussed earlier that a fundamental shortcoming of HTTP was the fact that it had no mechanisms on either end (web server or web browser) to detect partial and/or corrupted data transfers. SSL attempts to address this problem by incorporating a message authentication code to the message record.

The integrity requirement implies the requirement will verify that what the recipient receives matches what the sender sent. This is accomplished via a mechanism known as hashing.

Secure Message Hashing

If encryption keeps the messages safe, then hashing keeps the messages sound.

Fundamental to this message integrity component is a process known as a hash. A hash is a well-defined operation that takes a sequence of data and reduces it to a string of a given length. The properties of a hash are fairly simple:

❑ Given a message M, computing the hash of M is easy.

❑ Finding two arbitrary messages m_1 and m_2 that compute to the same hash value is difficult.

A picture roughly illustrating this "reduction" process is shown here:

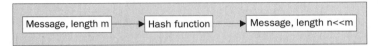

Algorithms that do the hashing are actually fairly simple to implement. What is difficult is finding two messages that hash to the same value. Let's think about that for a moment.

If we take a message of arbitrary length, and we shrink it to a fixed-length value, it is intuitive that we're taking something from an infinitely large range of values and mapping it to a finite range of narrow values. That means that more than one of the large ranges must map to a given value in the narrow range. That seems counter to our integrity goal – if multiple messages map to the same hash value, what good is it? That's where the difficult part comes in.

For a hash of a given length, say 128 bits, that means that there are at most 2^{128} hash values. If we assume, for the moment, that any one hash value is as likely as any other value – meaning that we don't really gain much, if any, information merely by looking at the hash value and comparing it to its original, then the chance of one person picking a message that leads to a hash that's the same as that for a message of another is absolutely insignificant. It means even though a hash reduces data to a fixed length, the likelihood that two messages hash to the same fixed value is very small.

Cryptanalysts examine hashing functions for odd patterns that might give clues about their construction. If such clues can be found, such as unusually frequent patterns of 1s in certain positions, it could be possible to design algorithms that build messages that exploit such a weakness. If the process of finding matching messages proves successful, and thus becomes simple enough to reduce to an algorithm, the hash is considered compromised and unreliable.

As an aside, hashes have long been a tool used in computing applications, for file indexing, database lookups, and similar operations. One-way hashes are used for password security where it is essential that an original message cannot be constructed from the hashed result. Two-way hashes allow for recovery of the cleartext – a common implementation of two-way hashes is in file compression incorporated in some file systems (NTFS in Windows) and in retail compression products such as WinZIP.

There are numerous hashing functions, but two of the primary algorithms are SHA and MD5.

Hashing Algorithms

Hashing is simply a matter of taking a cleartext and reducing it to a mathematically unique, and typically much smaller, representation. One-way hashes do not allow for recovery of the cleartext from the hashed version, while two-way hashes (as you might guess), do. Some examples of popular hashing algorithms follow:

- ❏ **MD5**

  Ron Rivest authored the MD5 protocol as an update to the MD4 hash protocol. MD5 produces a 128-bit hash value for its input text, and is widely used in cryptographic applications.

- ❏ **SHA**

  The Secure Hash Algorithm was published by the National Institute for Standards in conjunction with the Digital Signature Algorithm. It produces a 160-bit digest value for an input message, and has no known attacks or vulnerabilities. NIST asserts that SHA is based heavily on MD-4, the predecessor to Ron Rivest's MD-5 algorithm.

Operational Review

The operation of SSL is conceptually simple at a top level, but has subtleties at the detail level. As we have successfully migrated this field, let's move on from the operational side of the coin to implementation.

SSL – Two Views

Turning SSL from a nice conceptual architecture into a real-world security mechanism requires distinct capability on both sides of the communication pipe. Although the server and client sides perform generally the same function, their specific implementations differ. Let's take a look at each in a bit more detail.

The Server

Setting up an SSL web server isn't just a matter of flipping a check-box on a configuration page. Most web servers have support for SSL built in, but enabling requires the installation of a server certificate. The server certificate contains the public encryption key of the server, and is communicated down to the client as part of the SSL handshake protocol when a secure session commences.

Since the creation of a sever certificate is, by definition, a server-specific process, doing so must be accomplished after the basic web server is already up and running. Once the certificate is created, SSL is turned on only after the certificate is installed.

Individual implementations for accomplishing the details will differ from web server to web server. But here are the general steps necessary for creation of a server certificate:

1. Create a certificate request by providing at least:

   - ❏ Organization name

   - ❏ Organizational Unit (OU), if applicable

   - ❏ Common name for web site (full URL associated with server for this certificate)

2. Forward the request to a Certifying Authority such as Thawte or Verisign:

   - ❏ Certifying authority takes request and validates information

   - ❏ Upon validation, CA issues X509 v3 certificate back to requestor with expiration date

3. Install the Certificate in the web server:

❏ Copy the certificate to a secure location for safekeeping

❏ Install root CA certificate and any intermediaries, if needed

Once the server certificate has been installed, the web server is ready for secure communications. By default, most web servers listen for secure communication requests on Port 443, just as they listen for standard HTTP communications over Port 80. If your application or requirements dictate that a port other than 443 be used, the port number must be specified within the configuration of the particular web server. Also clients must be aware of any non-standard port usage, because the URLs needed to access the site through its secured interface will attempt to use the standard default port.

Example – Creating a Server Certificate Request

With so many different web servers, it is impossible to define all the steps for all possible combinations of server certificate requests. What follows here is an example of using the Internet Information Services 5.0 Management Console snap-in to create a server certificate request. Some web servers provide automated tools to produce this request; others require that the webmaster or other administrative individual prepare the request file manually.

1. Using the IIS management console snap-in, right-click on the **Default Web Site** in the IIS services, and select **Properties**. The IIS site properties dialog box will appear as shown below:

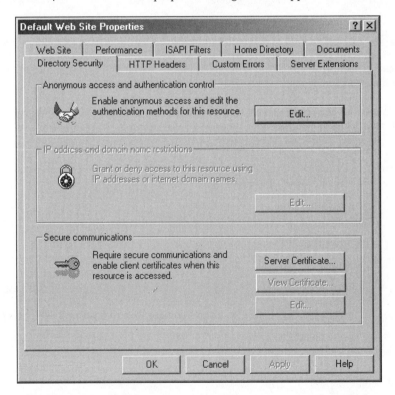

2. Within the Secure Communications block, click the Server Certificate button. This will bring up the splash screen for the Web Server Certificate Wizard:

3. Click Next to bring up the page in which you specify the request type:

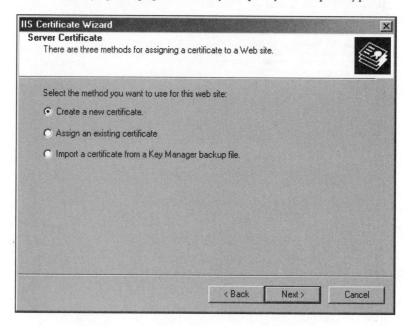

4. This dialog box allows us to map an existing certificate for use on this web server, or to recover a corrupted certificate from a backup file. For the purpose of this example, click on Create a new certificate, and then click Next to bring up the following dialog box:

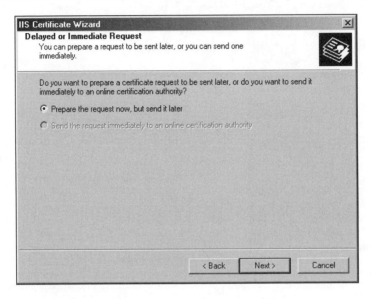

5. This dialog box allows you to transmit the request to the certification authority manually, or to prepare it online. Click the Prepare the request now, but send it later option and click Next to get the following dialog box:

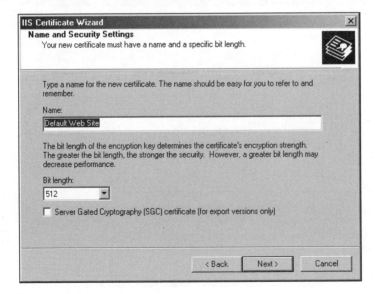

6. This dialog allows you to specify the name for the certificate, which defaults to the site name, and the length of the encryption key desired for the certificate. Be cautious in selecting a bit length; longer keys provide greater security, but at the expense of poorer performance for secured sites. **Server Gated Cryptography** need only be checked if the server is equipped with 128-bit security, but is intended to accommodate clients that support only 40-bit encryption. If it is known that the server will not need to support such clients, this option can remain unchecked. Click **Next** to bring up the **Information** dialog:

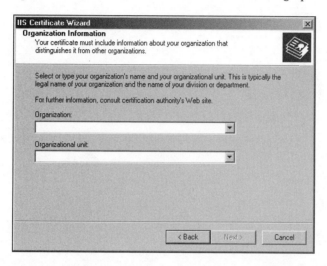

7. This dialog asks for the legal name of the organization requesting the certificate. It is critical that this name match any formal and/or legal registration that might be used by the certifying authority to verify its accuracy. The slightest deviation can prevent the certificate request from completing. The organizational unit can represent the department or group within the organization requesting the certificate. Click **Next** to bring up the **Common Name Specification** dialog:

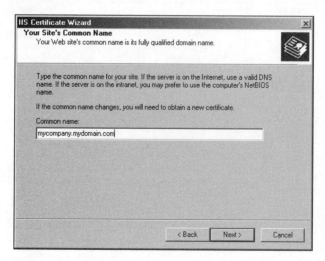

8. This dialog allows the specification for the specific common name to be associated with this server certificate. When browsers connecting to this site validate the server certificate, they will compare the requested server name against that provided in this certificate; if they do not match, the browser can either fail the connection automatically, or issue a warning message notifying the user that the name referenced doesn't match the name of the server specified in the server certificate. Click Next to bring up the Geographical Information dialog:

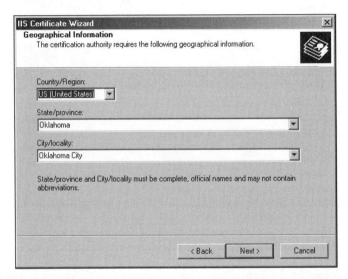

9. This information is incorporated into the information sent into the certificate request, but is not involved in the validation request. Specify as indicated, and click Next to specify a location for the certificate request:

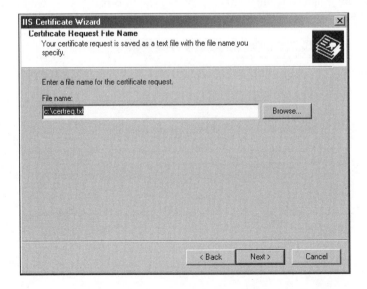

10. Specify the name of the file and its location, and click Next to bring up the request summary validation page:

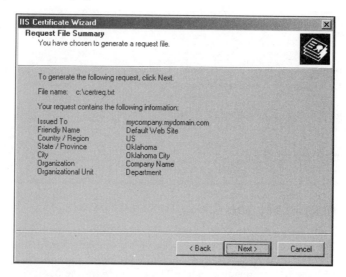

11. Verify that the information provided is correct, and click Next to complete the wizard:

12. This indicates the successful completion of the certificate request wizard. Click Finish to close the dialog box.

The end result of these steps is the creation of the certificate request file, which is a plain text file with innocuous-looking content that appears as follows:

Forwarding the Request to the CA

When the request is complete, it may then be forwarded to a Certificate Authority for fulfillment. Most companies that provide such certificates charge a fee for such a certificate based on a variety of factors, varying with each vendor. For the purposes of research and testing, it is possible to obtain "trial" or "limited duration" server certificates from companies such as Thawte (www.thawte.com) and Comodo (www.instantssl.com). The former issues certificates that are not validated (the submitted information is not verified by Thawte), and are valid for 21 days. The latter issues certificates that are validated, and are valid for 30 days (the screenshots reproduced here are from the Thawte trial certificate registration web site).

1. The first page describes the trial/evaluation nature of the test certificate:

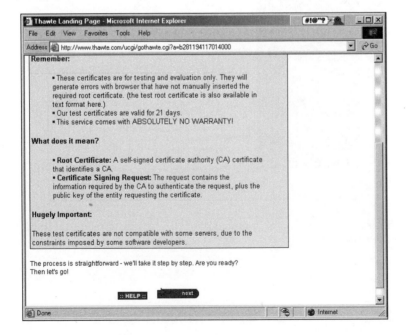

2. Next, the site prompts you to select the type of certificate to construct. In this case, the v3 certificate is selected:

3. The following page prompts the user to select the certificate type to select. For this example, the "standard" format is selected:

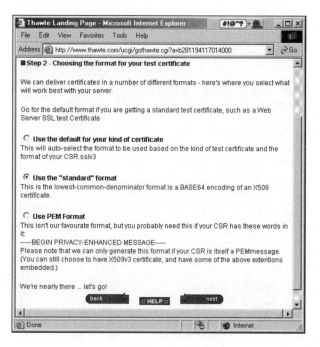

4. The next step illustrated in this screenshot is arguably the most critical. Open your original certificate request and copy the text of the request onto the clipboard. Next, paste it into the CSR box displayed on the page (if any part of the original certificate request is omitted, the certificate generation request will fail):

5. Finally, the site responds with the full temporary certificate. The entirety of the text, from BEGIN CERTIFICATE to END CERTIFICATE must be copied from the web page, and must be pasted into a text editor (such as Notepad) and saved into a plain text file. This certificate file will then be installed into the web server:

Installation of the Certificate

The final step is to enable SSL on your web server by installing the certificate. The following screenshots depict installation of the above certificate into an IIS 5 server.

1. Open the Properties page for the default web site, and click the Directory Security tab. From that tab, in the Secure Communications section, click the Server Certificate button:

2. This opens the first page of the Web Server Certificate Wizard. Click Next to proceed through the wizard steps, during which the server certificate will be imported into the web server:

3. After clicking the Next button, the first page of the wizard appears, asking if a pending certificate request should be completed, or if a new request should be started. Click the radio button beside Process the pending request and install the certificate, and click Next:

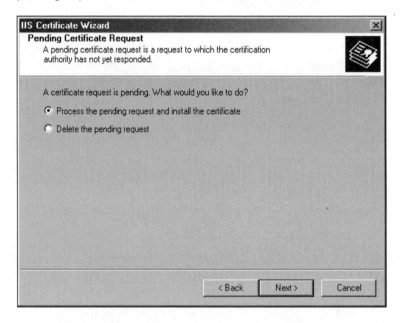

4. The next page asks for the location of the server certificate file. You may type the full path to the filename in the box provided, or browse to the certificate location by pressing the Browse button. In this case, the certificate file is stored in the root of the C: drive:

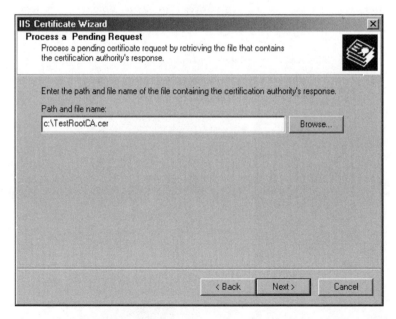

5. With the certificate now in place, the next page of the wizard indicates the details of the certificate it is ready to install. Clicking Next installs the certificate:

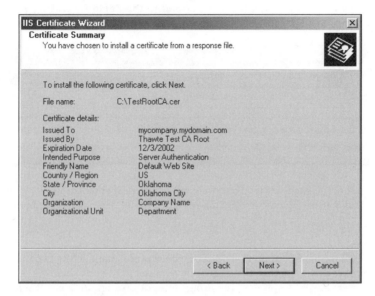

6. Before opening the file, IIS warns you that installing the certificate is a security risk if the source of the certificate is not, itself, trusted. Clicking Yes closes the dialog and completes certificate installation.

7. The completion page shows successful certificate installation. Clicking Finish closes the dialog box:

8. The certificate can now be tested by opening a browser, and accessing the web server by using an HTTPS protocol designation in the URL. For this sample, an ISS virtual directory named SampleSSL has been added to the default web site, and a simple HTML page with the text This is the default page for the Sample SSL site:

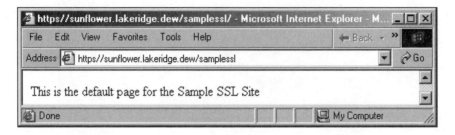

9. The content of the site is correct, and we can further verify that communication between the browser and the server is secured by the presence of the padlock icon in the IE status bar.

The Client

Server configuration for SSL operation is, by far, the more problematic of the two participating entities. Primarily, this stems from the fact that clients are not required to identify themselves to the server as part of the protocol. Servers have the option of requiring, accepting, or ignoring client-side certificates. Clients, predominantly web browsers, have support for non-authenticated client interaction in an SSL communication built in, and have facilities for the installation of client certificates.

Most Internet browsers already support 40-bit encryption as a basic feature, meaning that encryption keys used are 40 bits in length. However, 40-bit encryption is not particularly strong. Conversely, stronger 128-bit encryption is more problematic, because it is permitted for US domestic encryption purposes only. Products employing 128-bit encryption cannot, as of this writing, legally be exported from the United States.

Example – Installing a Client Certificate

A client certificate is used to provide authentication for a user identity, perhaps from a client application designed to accept certificates, or through a web browser. Client certificates are available from a variety of vendors for varying fees, but temporary or trial certificates are available at no cost from some vendors, among which is Verisign (https://digitalid.mysecuresign.com/ct/digitalidCenter.htm). Its temporary Class 2 client certificates are valid for 60 days, which makes them ideal for test purposes.

The following example steps through the process of installing a client certificate into Microsoft Internet Explorer 6.0:

1. From the Tools menu, select Internet Options. This brings up the IE options dialog; click the Content tab:

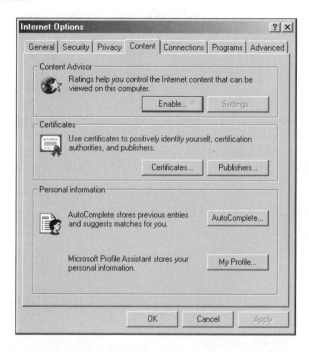

2. Click the Certificates button:

3. By default, this dialog will display with the Personal tab selected. Click the Import button:

4. Click Next:

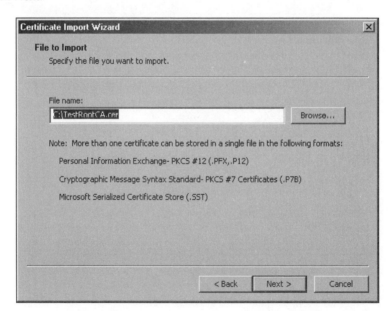

5. Specify the name of the certificate file in the File Name box or browse to the desired location, and click Next:

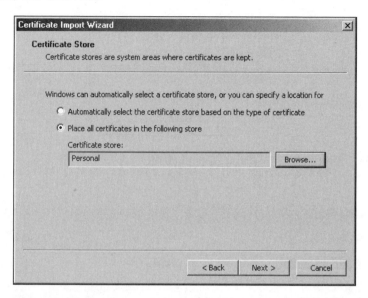

6. This dialog allows you to specify the store under which you wish to place the imported certificate. IE can place the certificate in a store based on the certificate type, or by default can place certificates in a store of your choosing. In this example, leave the defaults as-is and click Next:

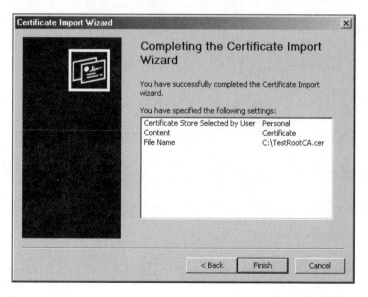

7. After verifying the information, click Finish to complete the certificate import wizard and the following dialog box will appear:

The following steps illustrate the certificate import procedure for Netscape 7.0:

1. From the Edit menu, select the Preferences option:

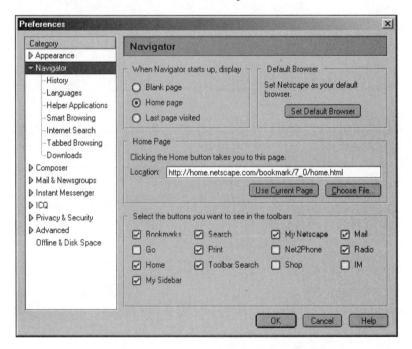

2. Next, click on the Privacy & Security node of the options tree in the left-hand portion of the dialog box:

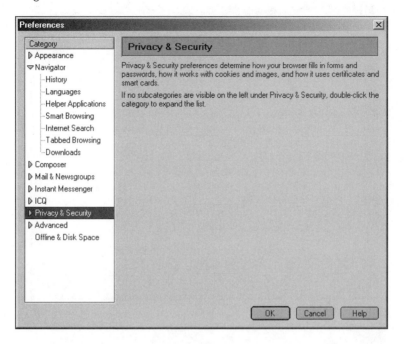

3. Now, click on the Certificates node within the Privacy & Security element:

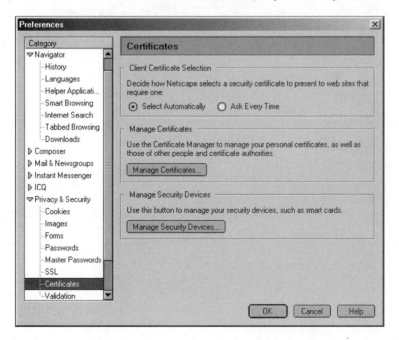

4. From the Manage Certificates section, click the Manage Certificates... button:

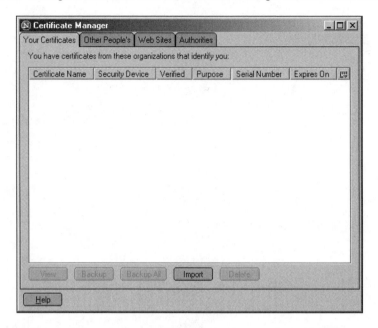

5. Next, with the Your Certificates tab selected, click the Import button:

6. From the above screen, browse to the location of the certificate file, and click Open to import it.

SSL – Limits, Caveats, and Successors

Like all good things, nothing lasts forever, and nothing is perfect. SSL is no exception. As we tread down the last two sections of this chapter, we're going to start with an overview of the practical limits of SSL, its future, and similar topics. Following this, we will discuss the limits and caveats of SSL.

Security

SSL, like any other technology, is only a part of the broader security issue for any enterprise. Such an enterprise encompasses all aspects of security, including risk management, policies for data protection, encryption policies, and the like. Pointing to one entity, such as SSL, and claiming security, is a dangerous and incomplete solution. The point is that security is a chain of interoperating elements, which is only as strong as its weakest link.

Negatives

Way back in mid-1990, SSL was "broken" when an individual with 120 workstations broke Netscape's export version of SSL. Still, SSL is the pervasive security standard as (though it has been broken) this has been in a way that compromises its practical use. Part and parcel of this downside is that even though the server provides positive identification for the session to be established, it is not impossible to fake identities such that the connection to the server is, indeed, secure, but not necessarily to the server the user might intend. Further, there is no security of the data prior to encryption, nor is there any after it is decrypted at the opposite end.

Another problem with SSL is that we know it's only good from point A to point B, and not useful at all for sites beyond point B (refer to the earlier diagram) unless those sites purposely employ it. Yet, we still use it. Let us now see why.

Positives

SSL still works for the intended purposes. Although it has been broken, this does not engender any mechanisms that may be conveniently reproduced to prove threatening to secure communications. SSL still scrambles up your data, and the chances of a third party actually eavesdropping on your data and stealing the secret session encryption key is very remote.

This does not mean that SSL is secure forever. There is every opportunity for some brazen cryptographer to stun the world and release an exploit for SSL. Eventually, SSL might be broken in a severe way, or a new form of security that's better, cheaper, faster, and stronger would come along and offer compelling reasons for us all to mass-download new versions of Internet Explorer and Netscape to get it. Nevertheless, SSL is and remains a perfectly legitimate solution for our current security needs. The point is that it is still good enough to do what it is supposed to do.

The Reality

The simple reality is that nothing is perfect. No matter what may come along to strengthen or replace SSL, someday that will be bettered too.

If you have a strong password policy at the enterprise level, but find out that a user writes down his password in his diary, no security in the world will be enough to solve the problems that a simple breach can construct. The social engineering exploits that allow cryptanalysts to gain passwords merely by asking users casual questions in the midst of casual conversation also show us that the human element will always be the weakest link in any security chain.

Caveats

One of the biggest drawbacks of the SSL implementation in any application is that of performance. Where HTTP simply routes data from point-to-point, limited only by the slower of those two points, SSL over HTTP (HTTPS) imposes three computationally-intensive requirements on both ends. Each side must encrypt its outbound data, and decrypt its inbound data. Furthermore, each side performs message authentication by performing a hash on its outbound data to create a MAC, and by performing a hash on the decrypted inbound data to recompute the MAC for comparison.

Anything that increases the latency introduced by SSL will have a downstream effect that would be felt even more keenly by most web services. By their nature, web services usually are implemented in what could be described informally as a layered manner; layers abstracting the client from the back-end data and structures as much as possible. As a result, web services with no security overhead may not perform as well as counterparts not designed in the same manner.

Let's restate this in a slightly different manner. If a more conventional web application can return x amount of data in y seconds, chances are an identically-tasked web service would take y + n seconds, where $n>0$. Adding SSL's encryption overhead to the equation will almost certainly magnify the problem; as with so many other issues, a tradeoff of application performance and security must be assessed on a per-instance basis to determine if performance impacts are worth the security they provide.

Successors

Given that SSL is the ubiquitous browser-to-server security mechanism, it's hard to conceive of a literal successor to it. SSL's protocol revisions and later submission to the IETF, and between-time incorporation into virtually every browser and security device this side of your right eyeball, ensure that SSL as a protocol name stands to persist for some time to come.

As we noted earlier, the last protocol work with SSL was associated with development of the 3.0 specification in 1996. Since that time, the IETF has taken over work on SSL and has renamed it Transport Layer Security, or TLS. If there were to be a true successor to SSL, TLS would probably be the first choice – not because it represents some wholesale departure from SSL, but because it represents a natural progression from SSL.

An earlier work, known as Private Communications Technology, included aspects of security, but has been superseded by SSL 3.0 and TLS.

How can Web Services take Advantage of SSL?

We're coming down to the home stretch of our discussion about SSL, and we're going to try and attack a fundamental question: Where and how do SSL and web services intersect?

Clearly, web services present a different type of problem than conventional, static web sites. Role identities may need to be verified. A broader, bigger chunk of data typically crosses the wire given the significantly chattier nature of web service transports. Moreover, such services almost certainly are going to be used to wrap enterprise and/or corporate process on the server-side and to provide new problems, such as application proxies, on interested clients.

Let's start our discussion from an architectural perspective.

SSL is Architecturally External

Web services provide an extraordinary extension to the concept of a web server, extending the traditional notion of a remote procedure call server. Such services are wrapped within the existing framework of web servers and web browsers – conceptually, you don't necessarily need any special new tools or special types of web servers to host simple web services.

SSL, on the other hand, has its arms around the process of browser-to-server communication. It doesn't know or care what's going across the wire; it just knows it's supposed to turn what's going across the pipe into an indecipherable code, and rebuild it on the other end. SSL support is incorporated into most browsers by default, which is of benefit to the user.

This is to say, then, that SSL is architecturally external to web services. SSL provides essentially the same service for web services that is does for conventional web sites, because the encryption, hashing, and handshaking mechanisms are employed outside the realm of the application itself. That's in contrast to inter-application security objectives, such as encryption of particular data elements for persistent storage. The former is out of the application's control; the latter is entirely developer-controlled (library selection, encryption algorithms, etc). To do this, a variety of client Java libraries are available, such as SSLRef, SSLPlus, SSLava, and SSLeay.

Identity Validation

We already know that SSL supports optional client-side identity assertion using client certificates. Web services can be configured to require and/or accept client-side certificates. Requiring certificates may impose a maintenance burden on users accessing an application through a web site, with certificates having to be installed on multiple client machines, not to mention the implicit existence of a sufficiently robust PKI in an organization to support the creation of such certificates.

Although web browsers are increasingly the interface of choice for most large-scale applications, web services clearly provide an opportunity to change the way client applications are deployed. If the objects of a given web service are to be consumed by more conventional client applications in addition to or instead of a web browser, application proxies will be exported that must become part of the client installation. If those services require client certificates, those proxies must be written in such a way to be cognizant of client certificates and deliver them to the web service.

An abstract mechanism for delivering certificates can be seen theorized by the creation of a protected web service object, and an access proxy object. The access proxy object constructs identification information from the client certificate resident on the machine, and is then attached to or passed as a parameter of an authentication method of the protected web service.

Delivery of client identities in this manner creates some logistical and security-related problems. If a client proxy must deliver a certificate on an ad-hoc basis (that is, at any time), then that certificate must be available on the client at all times, or requested by and delivered to the client on-the-fly. Such certificates may need to be installed on multiple machines, such as in the case of a traveling user with a laptop. If the certificate is persisted locally, security mechanisms must be in place to protect the certificate, and such protections are inevitably going to be operating system dependent.

Windows, for example, controls the availability of client certificates by use of the user's Windows logon. Other implementations require the submission of a passphrase before the certificate can be used. In either case, multiple, disparate mechanisms for client certificate protection imply an additional level of complexity for the enterprise PKI, and the security structure surrounding it.

Communication Security and Integrity

It stands that the most important part of SSL is the first S – Secure. Web services are the beneficiary of this merely for the presence of the protocol.

Another valuable element SSL provides to web services is data integrity. As part of the SSL specification, we already know that message authentication codes are added to each outbound message, and are recomputed upon receipt for comparison. HTTP, as noted, provides no such guarantee.

The Cost of Security and Integrity

Tradeoffs between application performance and security must be made for configuration management. Each of these tradeoffs must be made against hard, honest assessments of the importance of each component within the architecture of the given system. The toughest part of the assessment is to realize there are no easy, one-size-fits-all answers. Again, security is not about selecting one element or protocol and deeming it "secure," but is actually in the development of a broader security plan for the enterprise.

Following here is a list of the kinds of considerations as the tradeoffs between the costs and benefits of security and integrity:

❑ What are the real risks of application data exposure to third parties? More specifically, are we protecting data that is truly sensitive, such as customer credit card numbers, social security numbers, or bank account information? Or are we protecting something less sensitive, where the risk of damage from compromise is smaller? Even more narrowly, are we protecting data merely to discourage the casual snooper who may not have a malevolent intent? The latter two scenarios might suggest that a less intense security solution be considered.

❑ What are the administrative complications associated with certificate management? Part of the cost of any security solution will have an administrative component. Clients that access web services through application proxies may make for a good architecture, but part of the corresponding administrative cost will be in the complexity in the distribution and installation of those proxies on each client machine that will require them. Further, if an individual will roam from machine to machine, an additional administrative concern will be the security of user certificates on potentially multiple-client machines. If an application will be distributed across diverse geographical sites, a complex implementation such as this may prove administratively costly.

❑ How much performance impact will be imposed? SSL imposes a substantial performance impact between the communicating parties due to the inherent mathematical intensity of encryption and decryption.

❑ Is the cost of performance worth the security tradeoff? If we think of the criticality of our secured data as existing on a sliding scale, and the volume of users accessing the corresponding application on a similar scale, we'd discover that marginally critical data accessed in a prospectively high-volume environment might suffer from the overhead imposed by SSL. Conversely, critical data might require encryption regardless of the volume.

❑ Is the type of security imposing too great a performance risk? Key lengths and algorithm types can have an impact on the performance of SSL. Longer keys do, in fact, provide better security (in general), but they also slow transaction performance. If performance in an SSL-secured application is poor, a change of algorithm types might affect performance positively. The inherent difficulty in predicting performance at this level is due to the variability of network performance, volume of traffic at any given time, and the reproducibility of performance patterns over a relevant length of time.

Summary

In this chapter, we've taken both top-level and detail-level views of SSL and tried to tie them to real-world practical impacts for the development of web services.

6

XML Signature

Chapter 4 provided a basic introduction to digital signatures. By ensuring support for data integrity, authenticity, and non-repudiation, digital signatures provide the key functionality needed to promote the trusted exchange of data among web services. Realizing the growing need for digital signatures in the XML environment, in June 1999 W3C teamed up with IETF to work on a specification to support digital signing of documents using XML syntax. Combining the XML expertise of W3C and the cryptographic expertise of IETF in February 2002 this group released a set of specifications to support creation and representation of digital signatures in XML syntax.

In this chapter, we take a detailed look at the XML digital signature specification published by the combined W3C-IETF XML Signature working group. We hope to provide enough perspective so that you understand all the details related to XML Signature and start using it in your applications. While we do provide an in-depth coverage of the XML Signature specification, this chapter is not intended to be a reference document for the specification.

We will be covering the following topics in this chapter:

- ❑ The motivation behind XML Signature and the problem space XML Signature tries to address
- ❑ Detailed overview of XML Signature grammar with examples
- ❑ Creating and validating digital signatures using XML Signature rules
- ❑ XML Signature algorithms
- ❑ Discussion of XML Signature implementations
- ❑ Security considerations and other limitations of the XML Signature specification

Why XML Signature?

Digital signature, or the ability to digitally sign a document, is not a new concept. An XML document, like any other document, can be signed using existing technologies such as Public Key Cryptography Standards from RSA laboratories (PKCS) or Privacy-Enhanced Mail services (PEM) [RFC 1421]. So, is XML Signature just another addition to the existing list of standards or does it address a new problem space?

While the existing methodologies can be used to apply digital signatures to a whole XML document, there is no standard mechanism to sign specific portions of an XML document.

If a document can be signed only in its entirety, it eliminates the possibility of making any further changes to the document. The flexibility to sign only specific portions of a document is essential where one may want to leave open the possibility of further changes and additions to the same signed document. For example, a signed document may be sent to a reviewer for comments and he or she may not wish to make those comments a part of the signature. If the signature only can be applied to the full document, any additions made by the reviewer would invalidate the original signature.

The ability to sign specific portions of a document is an essential feature for any document that could be authored at different times by different parties. Imagine a patient's record being maintained for a long period of time. This record may have entries from various doctors, recording their analysis and recommendations. Every doctor making changes to the document would take responsibility only for his or her entries and would wish to sign only that portion of the patient's record. We would not be able to make this possible without the ability to sign specific portions of the patient's record.

Imagine a workflow environment in which a document is passed from one department to another. It is critical that each department signs and takes responsibility only for the specific portion it modifies. Workflow in a web services environment may involve many third parties with the documents crossing organizational boundaries. It is important in such cases to sign and capture the changes made by each organization. The following diagram shows the patient visit workflow:

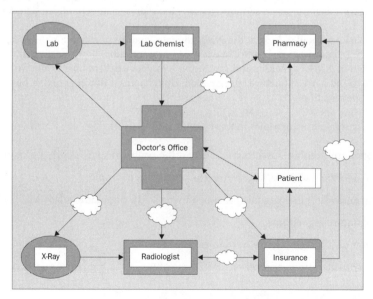

The interaction starts with the patient visiting the clinic. Assume that the patient's records are maintained in XML and all communications happen electronically. Some of the interactions are remote and cross organizational boundaries. The clouds in the above diagram represent remote interactions, and the communication across organizational boundaries occurs through web services hosted by the different parties involved. Let's see the interactions that take place during the visit.

Assume that the initial patient's record appears as shown below:

```
<Patient name="John Gartner" id="548-61-3456">
  <Address>...</Address>
  <PreviousVisits >...</PreviousVisits>
</Patient>
```

The following sections show the progression of the patient's record at each stage. The messages generated at each stage get added to the patient's record, identified by the <patient> root element.

The doctor examines the patient and records his initial observations for further lab and x-ray analysis:

```
<Patient name="John Gartner" id="548-61-3456">
...
  <Visit date="10/10/2002" id="TenthOctoberPhysical">
    <DoctorCheckUp>
      <Observations DoctorName="Arul Murali" id="TenthOctoberObservation">
        <BloodPressure>...</BloodPressure>
        <PatientComplaint>Right Knee pain</PatientComplaint>
        <Comments>
          Seems normal. Recommend Blood test and Kneecap x-ray
        </Comments>
      </Observations>
    </DoctorCheckUp>
  </Visit>
</Patient>
```

The lab records its findings, adds the lab chemist's expert comments, and forwards it to the doctor's office:

```
<Visit date="10/10/2002" id="TenthOctoberPhysical">
...
<Lab  date="12/10/2002" id="TenthOctoberLabResult">
  <LabTechnician name="" id="789-675-234"/>
  <Blood LDL="132" HDL="45" Triglycerides="195" Total="217"/>
  <UricAcid level="8.5"/>
</Lab>
</Visit>
```

The x-ray lab attaches the image to the patient's record and passes the x-ray details to a radiologist for expert observations:

```
<Visit date="10/10/2002" Id="TenthOctoberPhysical">
...
  <Xray date="12/10/2002" TechnicianName="Robert Weldon"
        Id="TenthOctoberKneeXRay">
    <Image type="RightKneeCapFront"
           ref="http://www.xlab.com/jgartner/12/10/2002/kneefront.jpeg"/>
    <Image type="RightKneecapBack"
           ref="http://www.xlab.com/jgartner/12/10/2002/kneeback.jpeg"/>
  </Xray>
</Visit>
```

The radiologist adds her observations and sends it to the doctor's office for further processing:

```
<Xray date="12/10/2002" TechnicianName="Robert Weldon"
     Id="TenthOctoberKneeXRay">
  <Image type="RightKneeCapFront"
          ref="http://www.xlab.com/jgartner/12/10/2002/kneefront.jpeg"/>
  <Image type="RightKneecapBack"
          ref="http://www.xlab.com/jgartner/12/10/2002/kneeback.jpeg"/>
  <Radiologist name="Lush Murali" id="768-940-234">
    <Comments>Nothing abnormal noticed</Comments>
  </Radiologist>
</Xray>
```

The doctor makes his final recommendations based on lab and x-ray results and adds those comments to the patient's record:

```
<Visit date="10/10/2002" Id="TenthOctoberPhysical">
<Recommendations DoctorName="Arul Murali">
  <Comments>
    Uric acid level high. High risk for Gout. Recommend purine restricted
    diet and medication. Cholesterol on the increase and slightly high.
    Recommend watch diet and exercise.
  </Comments>
  <Prescription>
  <Tablet qty="30" dose="once daily">Colchicine</Tablet>
</Prescription>
</Recommendations>
```

The doctor's office sends a prescription to the online pharmacy:

```
<Prescription>
  <From>...</From>
    <For>...</For>
    <Details>...</Details>
</Prescription>
```

The accounts department of the doctor's office sends a bill for the services to the patient's insurance company:

```
<BillTo insurer="Cigna HealthCare" plan="35678">
<ProcessedBy name="Juci Hontz"/>
<Patient name=John Gartner" id="">
<Services Doctor="Arul Murali">...</Services>
<Charges>...</Charges>
```

Finally, the radiologist office and the pharmacy bill the insurance company for services rendered. The insurance company settles the claims and sends a summary of expenses to the patient (these two interactions are not shown here for the sake of brevity).

From the above interactions it is easy to see the need to sign specific portions of a document. Neither would the radiologist want to sign for the doctor's recommendations, nor would the doctor like to vouch for the radiologist's analysis.

Multiple Signatures

As you already may have reasoned from the above example, if the respective individual signs each interaction and subsequent addition of data to the patient's record, we will not end up just with one signature in the `<Patient>` document, but with multiple signatures from various parties.

The "extensible" aspect of XML makes it entirely natural to add supplementary elements to the same document. The ability to support multiple signatures in the same document is an important and critical feature in a web service environment where many web services run by different corporations may collaborate to achieve a single work order represented by a single XML document. In our example, the doctor would not make recommendations unless the information provided by the lab and x-ray were signed.

The XML Signature specification provides the ability to attach multiple signatures that apply to different portions of the document.

Persistent Signatures

Digital signatures are not a requirement only when transporting documents from one party to another. The interactions shown in the patient workflow example typically are preserved for long periods of time. It is critical that any digital signature solution provide a reasonable and simple mechanism to preserve such signatures.

Existing digital signature solutions are more focused on message communication and transportation of documents. For instance, with SSL and IPsec, in order to provide assurance that the document has been signed, additional information must somehow be attached alongside the document. SSL or IPSec signatures would have to be attached outside the document, but this becomes unwieldy to manage.

Furthermore, these signatures would apply to the entire document. As seen in our example, if a document passes through some form of a "workflow" process involving multiple processing steps, maintaining signatures would require preserving every single document, verbatim, which again will quickly grow unwieldy and inefficient.

By making it possible to represent the signatures inline as part of the original document, the XML Signature specification avoids any ad-hoc methods needed to manage and persist digital signatures and provides a flexible, standardized framework for multiple agents to sign and persist multiple portions of the documents.

Web Services and Signatures

Web services impose their own set of requirements that cannot be addressed efficiently by the existing digital signature solutions.

XML

First and foremost, web services that are based on standard protocols such as SOAP and WSDL are characterized by their use of XML as a standard data representation format and message format. It is not unreasonable to imagine web services implementations where only XML tools exist.

If digital signatures are to exist as part of the message being communicated, it is essential and convenient to represent these signatures in a standard XML-based format. We would not want to tie web services implementations that are based on open and standard protocols to any proprietary format for processing signatures. In our example, the online pharmacy may receive many prescriptions from various doctors. Imagine the complexities the pharmacy implementation may have to go through if each doctor's signature is based on different formats.

The existing digital signature technologies do not provide a standard mechanism to represent the signature in XML. By making it a goal to use XML syntax for representing the digital signatures, the XML Signature initiative fully integrates digital signatures with the XML environment, forming a strong foundation for the development of secured web services.

Remote Referencing

Going back to our patient workflow example, the message from the radiologist to the doctor's office does not include the actual x-ray image but just a reference to the same. The doctor probably is more interested in the analysis than the image, and if needed the image is always available for access. Though the image is not part of the signed message sent by the radiologist, her signature must encompass the image in order to protect the integrity of her analysis.

Such situations are common in web services environments where the ability to sign referenced data is as critical as the ability to sign enclosed data for both performance and security reasons. Such references may not just include references to same type of data but may encompass data in various formats. For instance, if the patient has undergone the ultrasound scanning, the references may include some video clips of the scan.

The references need not always be external and may include internal references. For example, the doctor's office sends messages to the pharmacy using SOAP as shown below:

```
<SOAP:Envelope xmlns:SOAP=http://www.w3.org/2000/09/>
  <SOAP:Header>
   <Signature ref="OriginalData">...</Signature>
  <SOAP:Header>

  <SOAP:Body>
    <Prescription id="OriginalData" xmlns="http:\\www.arulclinic.com">
      <From>...</From>
      <For>...</For>
      <Details>...</Details>
    </Prescription>
  <SOAP:Body>
<SOAP:Envelope>
```

Assuming the `<Signature>` represents the signature, the reference to the data being signed contains an internal reference.

The XML Signature specification makes it possible to include both internal and external references to various formats and types of data under the same signature.

Multiple Parties

One of the motivations behind web services is to realize the dream of loosely coupled plug-and-play applications where services hosted by different parties may collaborate to execute a single work order. We saw this on a smaller scale with our patient workflow example. It is quite reasonable to expand those interactions and add more complex interactions, such as the pharmacy web service interacting with the patient insurance company to check on whether "brand name" drugs are permitted or "generic drugs" should only be used, insurance limits, co-pay information, etc. The doctor's office web service may be enhanced to consult a web service such as .NET service to include the patient's details and preferences such as pharmacy preferred, labs preferred, and insurance used. This offers a better quality of service to patients.

In summary, applications crossing organizational boundaries and multi-party involvement are more commonplace in web services. This makes it all the more important to support the various features discussed earlier such as the ability to sign portions of a document, multiple signatures in the same document, and ability to persist those signatures without ad-hoc mechanisms.

XML Signature Overview

Now that we have seen how XML Signature specification stands out from the existing digital signing technologies, let us dive into the specification and take a closer look. In this section, we provide a high-level overview of the basic syntax and the core features supported by the specification.

XML Signature specification supports digital signing of any arbitrary digital content including XML documents. As seen earlier, one of the fundamental features of XML Signature is its ability to support signing of specific portions of an XML document.

You can use XML Signature to sign more than one type of resource. For example, data objects as varied as an XML document, an XML fragment, binary data such as a JPEG image, and character data such as an HTML page could be signed together as part of a single signature.

In XML Signature, the signatures are applied to the digital content via an indirection. Here, the signature is not applied directly to the original or the digest form of the data. Instead, the digital content or contents to be signed are first digested and placed in an XML element. This element is then digested and cryptographically signed. The XML Signature represents the signed form of the XML element rather than the original data. Digesting is a process of applying an algorithm such as a SHA-1 message digest algorithm to calculate a digest or a hash value of the data. The signature is applied to this digest or hash value. Since digests usually occupy a fraction of the original data size, taking digests reduces the time needed to encrypt and sign data, and the reduced size results in efficient transmission and storage.

In XML Signature, the digital signature is represented in XML and is identified by the root `<Signature>` element. Information about the original data object that is signed is represented in the `<Signature>` element via URIs. There are four different ways of relating the data objects and their XML Signature represented by the `<Signature>` element as follows:

- ❑ The data object can be embedded within the XML Signature. This is called an **enveloping signature** and the `<Signature>` element becomes the parent of the local data object.

- ❑ The data object can embed the XML Signature within itself. This is called an **enveloped signature** and the `<Signature>` element becomes the child of the original data object.

❏ The data object resides within the same XML document containing the XML Signature. This is called **detached signature** and the `<Signature>` element is a sibling of the original data object.

❏ The data object resides external to the document containing the XML Signature. This is also called **detached signature** and the `<Signature>` element carries a reference to the external data object.

Basic XML Signature Structure

The structure of the `<Signature>` element enables one to carry additional information along with the digest value. The key needed to validate the signature also can be carried as part of the `<Signature>` element. The following is the basic structure of the `<Signature>` element (? denotes zero or one occurrence, * denotes zero or more occurrences, and + denotes one or more occurrences):

```
<Signature ID?>

  <SignedInfo>

    <CanonicalizationMethod/>
    <SignatureMethod/>

    (<Reference URI? >

        (<Transforms/>)?
        <DigestMethod/>
        <DigestValue/>

    </Reference> ) +

  </SignedInfo>

  <SignatureValue/>
  (<KeyInfo/>)?
  (<Object ID? />)*

</Signature>
```

The `<SignedInfo>` element contains the information about the data objects that are actually signed. The `<SignatureValue>` contains the digital signature value that is the encrypted digest of the `<SignedInfo>` element. The `<CanonicalizationMethod>` specifies the algorithm used to canonicalize the `<SignedInfo>` element before it is digested, and the `<SignatureMethod>` specifies the cryptographic algorithm used to convert the canonicalized `<SignedInfo>` into `<SignatureValue>`.

The `<Reference>` element identifies the data object via its URI attribute and carries the digest value of the data object. The `<Transforms>` element, which is the child of the `<Reference>` element, lists the processing steps applied to the data object before it was digested. The transformation operations could include operations such as canonicalization, encoding/decoding, compression/inflation, XSLT, XPath, XML Schema validation, or XInclude.

The `<DigestMethod>` specifies the digest algorithm applied to the data object to yield the digest value contained under the `<DigestValue>` element. The `<DigestMethod>` algorithms are applied after the application of `<Transforms>`. Though the URI attribute of the `<Reference>` element is optional, it can be omitted only once in case there are multiple `<Reference>` elements within a `<Signature>` element. This condition is made to ensure the unambiguous matching of the data objects. Note that signature validation requires access to the original data object and if it is not specified through the URI attribute of the `<Reference>` element, then the recipient must be provided with the data object through some other means.

The optional `<KeyInfo>` element indicates the key to be used to validate the signature. The `<KeyInfo>` is left optional because the signer may not wish to reveal the key information to all parties. Also, it is possible that the key information is known within the application's context and need not be represented explicitly.

The `<Object>` element, which is also optional, can occur any number times and can contain any data that the application may wish to include.

Example: Detached Signature

Let us now use the XML Signature syntax to sign one of the interactions seen in the patient visit workflow example. In this example, we sign the initial observation made by the doctor, which is indicated by the `<Observations>` element.

The doctor's office uses detached signature where the original data and the signature exist together as sibling elements. We use the following XML Signature procedure to create the signature:

- ❑ We create the `<Reference>` element, setting its URI attribute to the `<Observations>` element.

- ❑ The `<Observations>` element is canonicalized and then the digest of the `<Observations>` element is calculated and collected under the `<DigestValue>` element of `<DigestMethod>`. The details of canonicalization are captured under the `<Transforms>` element.

- ❑ The `<Reference>` element is then collected under `<SignedInfo>` and necessary `<CanonicalizationMethod>` and `<SignatureMethod>` elements are added.

- ❑ The `<SignedInfo>` element is canonicalized using the specified canonicalization algorithm and the digest of `<SignedInfo>` is calculated. This digest value is then signed and the signed value is captured under the `<SignatureValue>` element.

- ❑ Finally, we create the `<Signature>` element capturing the `<SignedInfo>` and `<SignatureValue>` elements.

In this example, we do not represent the key information as part of the `<Signature>` element. The patient's record now appears as:

```
<Patient name="John Gartner" id="548-61-3456">
...
  <Visit date="10/10/2002" id="TenthOctoberPhysical">
   <DoctorCheckUp>
    <Observations DoctorName="Arul Murali" id="TenthOctoberObservation">
      <BloodPressure>...</BloodPressure>
      <PatientComplaint>Right Knee pain</PatientComplaint>
      <Comments>
        Seems normal. Recommend Blood test and Kneecap x-ray
```

```
      </Comments>
    </Observations>
    <Signature Id="TenthOctoberDoctorobservation"
             xmlns="http://www.w3.org/2000/09/xmldsig#">
      <SignedInfo>
        <CanonicalizationMethod
                Algorithm="http://www.w3.org/TR/2001/REC-xml-c14n-
                20010315"/>
        <SignatureMethod
                Algorithm="http://www.w3.org/2000/09/xmldsig#dsa-sha1"/>
        <Reference URI="#TenthOctoberObservation">
          <Transforms>
            <Transform
                Algorithm="http://www.w3.org/TR/2001/REC-xml-c14n-
                20010315"/>
          </Transform>
          </Transforms>
          <DigestMethod Algorithm="http://www.w3.org/2000/09/xmldsig#sha1"/>
            <DigestValue>j6lwx3rvEPO0vKtMup4NbeVu8nk=</DigestValue>
          </DigestMethod>
        </Reference>
      </SignedInfo>
      <SignatureValue>MC0CFFrVLtRlk=</SignatureValue>
    </Signature>
  </DoctorCheckUp>
 </Visit>
</Patient>
```

The data signed, which in our case is the `<Observations>` element, is identified by the URI attribute of the `<Reference>` element. Since it is a local reference, we use the `Id` attribute of the `<Observations>` element to identify the original object. Since our original data object is an XML element, we use a canonicalization transform algorithm as indicated by the `<Transform>` element to transform the original element before calculating the digest.

Example: Enveloping Signature

In this example, we use XML Signature to sign the `<Xray>` element of our patient visit workflow example. This element includes external references to the x-ray images and to the radiologist comments. Note that it is not sufficient just to sign the `<Xray>` element, as such a signature would not cover any changes to the referred images, compromising the radiologist's observations. In order to protect the integrity of her observations, the radiologist signature must cover both the contents of the `<Xray>` element and the referred images.

In XML Signature, this can be achieved by the following steps:

❑ Create a `<Reference>` element for each of the images resulting in two separate `<Reference>` elements. These elements contain the digest of each of the images.

❑ Create a `<Reference>` element for the `<Xray>` element separately. This `<Reference>` element contains the digest of the contents of the `<Xray>` element.

❑ Collect all these three `<Reference>` elements under the `<SignedInfo>` element.

❑ The rest of the process is similar to the previous example and to all other signature applications. This typically involves canonicalizing the `<SignedInfo>` element, calculating the digest of the `<SignedInfo>` element, and then signing the digest.

The completed signature appears below. We use the enveloping signature in this example where the `<Signature>` element envelops the original data object. The original data, which in our case is the `<Xray>` element, is contained by the `<Object>` element. When the `<Object>` element is used to enclose the original data, one can either use just the digest of the original object contained under the `<Object>` element or use the digest of the `<Object>` element itself directly. While both choices do not affect the signature or the data signed, care must be taken to set the URI attribute of the `<Reference>` element appropriately. In our example, we sign the whole `<Object>` element:

```
<Patient name="John Gartner" id="548-61-3456">
...
  <Visit date="10/10/2002" id="TenthOctoberPhysical">
    <DoctorCheckUp>...</DoctorCheckUp>
      <Signature Id="TenthOctoberKneeX-RayAnalysis"
             xmlns="http://www.w3.org/2000/09/xmldsig#">
        <SignedInfo>
          <CanonicalizationMethod
                  Algorithm="http://www.w3.org/TR/2001/REC-xml-c14n-
                  20010315"/>
          <SignatureMethod
                  Algorithm="http://www.w3.org/2000/09/xmldsig#dsa-sha1"/>
          <Reference
             URI="http://www.xlab.com/jgartner/12/10/2002/kneefront.jpeg">
             <DigestMethod Algorithm="http://www.w3.org/2000/09/xmldsig#sha1"/>
               <DigestValue>j6lwx3rvEPOup4NbeVu8nk=</DigestValue>
             </DigestMethod>
          </Reference>
          <Reference
             URI="http://www.xlab.com/jgartner/12/10/2002/kneeback.jpeg">
             <DigestMethod Algorithm="http://www.w3.org/2000/09/xmldsig#sha1"/>
               <DigestValue>j6lwx3rvEPO=</DigestValue>
             </DigestMethod>
          </Reference>
          <Reference URI="TenthOctoberJGartnerXRay"
                  type=http://www.w3.org/2000/09/xmldsig#Object>
             <Transforms>
               <Transform
                   Algorithm="http://www.w3.org/TR/2001/REC-xml-c14n-
                   20010315"/>
             </Transforms>
             <DigestMethod Algorithm="http://www.w3.org/2000/09/xmldsig#sha1"/>
               <DigestValue>KtMup4NbeVu8nk=</DigestValue>
             </DigestMethod>
          </Reference>
        </SignedInfo>
        <SignatureValue>MC0CFFrVLtRlk=...</SignatureValue>
        <Object id="TenthOctoberJGartnerXRay">
          <Xray date="12/10/2002" TechnicianName="Robert Weldon"
                  id="TenthOctoberKneeXRay">
             <Image type="RightKneeCapFront"
                    ref="http://www.xlab.com/jgartner/12/10/2002/kneefront.jpeg"/>
             <Image type="RightKneecapBack"
                    ref="http://www.xlab.com/jgartner/12/10/2002/kneeback.jpeg"/>
             <Radiologist name="Lush Murali" id="768-940-234">
               <Comments>Nothing abnormal noticed</Comments>
             </Radiologist>
          </Xray>
        </Object>
        <KeyInfo>
         <KeyValue>
```

```
            <RSAKeyValue>
              ...
            </RSAKeyValue>
          </KeyValue >
        </KeyInfo>
      </Signature>
    </DoctorCheckUp>
  </Visit>
</Patient>
```

The first two `<Reference>` elements in the above examples refer to the digest of the images. As no transform is applied to these images, the `<Reference>` element does not contain a `<Transforms>` element. The last `<Reference>` element points to the `<Object>` element that exists as part of the `<Signature>` element. We use the type attribute of the `<Reference>` element to identify the type of the referred object. In the case of the `<Object>` element, which is an XML Signature element, the specification defines a type identifier value, which we have used as the value of the type attribute of the `<Reference>` element.

In our above example, the radiologist office encloses the key information as part of the `<Signature>` element to facilitate signature validation.

Example: Enveloped Signature

The next example shows how to use XML Signature to create an enveloped signature.

Since the XML Signature is represented in XML, enveloped signature makes sense only for signing XML content. In enveloped signature, the original data element being signed contains the `<Signature>` element. If the `<Signature>` element is going to be part of the original data element, how can we calculate the digest of the original data element? Note that it is not possible to include the `<Signature>` element in the digest calculation, as the contents of `<Signature>` element undergo changes (the contents of `<SignatureValue>` for instance) as the process of signing progresses.

This is where the transforms come in handy. One needs to apply appropriate transformations to the original object to remove the `<Signature>` element from the digest calculation. There are many ways to achieve this:

❑   One could write an XPath filtering transformation to remove the `<Signature>` element. Such an XPath transform would appear as:

```
<Transform Algorithm="http://www.w3.org/TR/1999/REC-xpath-19991116">
  <XPath xmlns:dsig="&dsig;"> not(ancestor-or-self::dsig:Signature) </XPath>
</Transform>
```

❑   The here() function defined in the XPointer specification can be used to remove the `<Signature>` elements. The transform using the here() function appears as:

```
<Transform Algorithm="http://www.w3.org/TR/1999/REC-xpath-19991116">
  <XPath xmlns:dsig="&dsig;">
  count(ancestor-or-self::dsig:Signature |
  here()/ancestor::dsig:Signature[1]) >
  count(ancestor-or-self::dsig:Signature)
  </XPath>
<Transform>
```

❑   The XML Signature specification defines an enveloped signature Transform algorithm specifically meant to deal with removing the enveloped <Signature> elements. If your XML Signature implementation supports such a transform, you could use that.

In our example, we use this Enveloped Signature Transform to remove the enveloped Signature element. The Enveloped Signature Transform is identified by the type identifier http://www.w3.org/2000/09/xmldsig#enveloped-signature which is defined in the specification.

Getting back to our patient visit workflow example, we use enveloped signature to sign the lab results. The signed lab result element is shown in the following code snippet (we do not show all the child elements of <Signature> elements in this example for brevity and as they are not any different for this case):

```
<Lab date="12/10/2002" id="TenthOctoberLabResult">
  <LabTechnician name="" id="789-675-234"/>
  <Blood LDL="132" HDL="45" Triglycerides="195" Total="217"/>
  <UricAcid level="8.5"/>
  <Signature Id="TenthOctoberJGartnerLabResults"
             xmlns="http://www.w3.org/2000/09/xmldsig#">
    <SignedInfo>
    ...
      <Reference URI="#TenthOctoberLabResult">
        <Transforms>
          <Transform
          Algorithm="http://www.w3.org/2000/09/xmldsig#enveloped-
          signature"/>
          </Transform>
        </Transforms>
        <DigestMethod>...</DigestMethod>
      </Reference>
    </SignedInfo>
    <SignatureValue>MC0CFFrVLtRlk=...</SignatureValue>
  </Signature>
</Lab>
```

Example: Detached Signature and External Reference

Our earlier detached signature example used the same document references. Detached signatures with external references do not differ much from detached signatures with the same document references. The only difference lies in what the URI attribute of the <Reference> element points to. Refer to the section *The Reference Processing Model* for a discussion on URI-References for same-document references and external references.

XML Signature Processing Steps

The XML Signature specification describes a set of operations to be performed during signature generation and subsequent validation. In this section, we discuss the operations to be followed by the conforming implementations and the applications that rely on such implementations to generate and validate signatures.

We already have seen some of the processing steps involved in the earlier example. This section provides a full discussion of the steps involved.

XML Signature Generation

The signature generation process starts with the identification of the resources or the data objects to be signed through a Uniform Resource Identifier as illustrated in the diagram below.

The following diagram provides a schematic representation of the process involved:

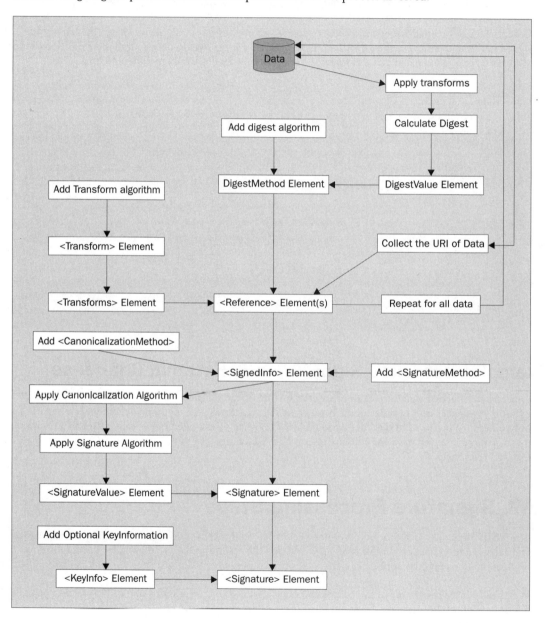

Calculate the Digest of Each Resource

The next step involves calculating the digest value for each of the data objects to be signed, and collecting the digest values under the <Reference> element. The following steps are involved in this process:

❑ Apply the transforms to the data object as specified by the application. These transforms could involve many transformation steps and each transformation step is specified under a <Transform> element, which is then collected under the <Transforms> element in the same order in which they were applied.

❑ Calculate the digest value over the transformed data object. The digest value typically is calculated by applying a message digest algorithm on the original data. The digest algorithm used must be sensitive to any changes to the data in order to preserve the integrity of the signature.

❑ Apply base64 encoding to the digest value and collect the digest value under the <DigestValue> element.

❑ Create the <Reference> element by including the <DigestValue> element and the identifier for the message digest algorithm under the <DigestMethod> element. Include the optional <Transforms> element and the optional URI identification of the original data object.

❑ Repeat the above steps for each data object.

Create the <SignedInfo> Element

The next step results in creation of the <SignedInfo> element:

❑ Create a <SignedInfo> element and collect all the <Reference> elements created in the previous step under the <SignedInfo> element.

❑ Include the <SignatureMethod> element and the <CanonicalizationMethod> element specifying the identifiers for the algorithm used for generating the signature value and for the algorithm used for canonicalization of the <SignedInfo> element.

❑ Canonicalize the <SignedInfo> element based on the algorithm specified in the <CanonicalizationMethod>. As different data streams with the same XML, the information set may have different textual representations. Canonicalization is a must to prevent inaccurate verification of the signature. Note that the signature is generated based on this canonicalized bit representation of the <SignedInfo> element.

Canonicalization may have dangerous side effects such as altering the URI information in the <SignedInfo> element. It is the application's responsibility to use appropriate canonicalization algorithms to prevent such side effects. The canonicalization algorithm required by the confirming implementations does not alter URIs.

Generate the Signature Value

This includes the following steps:

❑ Calculate the signature value of the <SignedInfo> element by using the signature algorithm specified in the <SignatureMethod> element of the <SignedInfo> element.

❑ Collect the resulting signed value under the <SignatureValue> element.

Create the <Signature> Element

Putting together the results of all the previous steps creates the <Signature> element:

❑ Create the <Signature> element and include the canonized <SignedInfo> element and the <SignatureValue> element obtained from the previous steps.

❑ Include the optional <KeyInfo> element and the <Object> element as necessary.

This <Signature> element represents the XML Signature of the data objects.

XML Signature Validation

The signature validation consists of two steps:

❑ Verification of the digest contained in each <Reference> element of the <SignedInfo> element. This is called reference validation.

❑ Verification of the cryptographic signature calculated over the <SignedInfo> element. This is called the signature validation.

For interoperability purposes, the XML Signature specification stipulates that the comparison of values in reference and signature validation be over the numeric or the decoded octet sequence of the value. This is because different XML Signature implementations may produce different encoded digest and signature values when processing the same resources due to variances in their encoding, such as accidental white space. Using numeric or octet comparison on both the stated and computed values eliminates such issues.

Reference Validation

Reference validation starts with canonicalizing the <SignedInfo> element based on the algorithm specified in the <CanonicalizationMethod> element of <SignedInfo>.

After canonicalization, verify the digest of each <Reference> element based on the following steps:

❑ Obtain the original data object to be digested and verified. The data object may be indicated by the URI attribute of the <Reference> element or provided by the application through different means.

❑ Apply the transforms on the data object as indicated by the <Transforms> element.

❑ Digest the resulting data object using the algorithm specified in the <DigestMethod> element.

❑ Compare the generated digest value against the stated digest value contained under the <DigestValue> element. Validation fails on any mismatch.

Signature Validation

Signature validation starts with obtaining the key information. The XML Signature itself may contain the key information via its <KeyInfo> element. If the <KeyInfo> element does not exist, the key information must be provided by the application through some means to the validating implementation:

❏ Use the obtained key information to calculate the encrypted digest of the canonicalized <SignedInfo> element using the algorithm specified under the <SignatureMethod> element of the <SignedInfo> element. It is a requirement to use the canonical form of the <SignatureMethod> element, as the URI may have been altered by the canonicalization of the <SignedInfo> element. As noted earlier, the canonicalization algorithm specified in this specification and required by all the confirming implementations does not alter URIs.

❏ Compare the generated signature value with the stated signature value obtained in the first step. Validation fails on mismatch.

Normal processing of XML documents, such as XML Schema validation, may introduce changes to the physical representation of the document that could result in signature invalidation. Consequently, it is the responsibility of the application to process consistently the document or refrain from using XML features such as default values or entities that could cause a change to the document during such XML validations. The section on *XML Processing Constraints* provides a detailed discussion on this topic.

Processing Instructions and Comments

Processing instructions that exist inside a <SignedInfo> element will, by default, become part of the signed content unless removed by a canonicalization algorithm during the canonicalization of the <SignedInfo> element. This means that any subsequent changes to the PI will invalidate the signature.

Similar to PIs, comments inside of the <SignedInfo> element or any other referred XML documents will become part of the signed content unless removed during canonicalization. Consequently, any changes to the comment will also invalidate the signature.

XML Processing Constraints

For digital signatures to work, both the signature creation and the validation must occur on the same bits. Validation will fail if the information content remains the same but the physical representation of the content changes. For example, even for simple ASCII text, there are three different end-of-line sequences. If the line ending sequence of the signed text changes from one convention to another, the validation would fail. Two messages that contain essentially the same content may nonetheless look quite different, having different spacing between elements and attributes, and perhaps even having attributes in different orders. If one message is embedded in another, namespace indicators may be introduced that without application of a suitable canonicalization scheme would change the digital signature.

Changes to the physical representation format are common in XML, as the XML core specifications such as XML 1.0 and XML Namespaces define multiple syntactic methods for expressing the same information that are liberally taken advantage of in XML processing tools and applications. The purpose of canonicalization is to avoid such changes to the physical representation by serializing to a standard form so that the verifier also can use the same standard form for verification. The action of canonicalization involves establishing consistent policies for the exact formatting and ordering of attributes and that will be considered authoritative, or "canonical," and applying these policies to XML documents before computing digital signatures. This way, documents that are logically equivalent can have the same digital signature values.

There are four categories of XML processing that could change the physical representation of an XML document:

❑ Basic XML processing
❑ DOM and SAX processing
❑ XML Namespace processing
❑ Character encoding

In the following sections, we'll discuss the constraints imposed by the above XML processing operations and the possible steps one can take to mitigate them.

Basic XML Processing

XML 1.0 requires XML processors to normalize the input XML document to simplify application processing. Some of the changes that might be carried out by a confirming XML processor due to such required normalizations are listed below:

1. End of line normalization. All carriage-return (#xD) characters followed by the line-feed character (#xA) and single #xD characters are replaced with #xA characters.

2. Character references are replaced with the corresponding character.

3. Missing attributes with declared default values are provided to the application as if the value existed in the document.

4. Entity references are replaced with the corresponding declared entity.

5. Attribute values are normalized by replacing the character and the entity references and by replacing all the white space characters (#xD, #xA, #x9, #x20) and the sequence #xD #xA with the space character #x20. If the attribute type is not of CDATA, then the values are further normalized by removing all the leading and the trailing spaces and by replacing the sequences of the interior spaces with a single space #x20 character.

Some of the normalizations such as those listed as items 3, 4, 5 can occur only in the presence of a DTD or XML Schema that carries such default values and type information. As the <Signature> element type is specified to be only laxly-schema-valid, one is not guaranteed to have a schema and hence those items that depend on XML Schema may not be present.

Therefore, in order to ensure that XML documents containing such content are verifiable at the recipient's end, some constraints are to be observed when generating the XML Signature over an XML document:

❑ Applications must ensure that the default attribute values are explicitly present in the document instance.

❑ All the entity references must be expanded. Exception applies to the entire standard XML 1.0 declared entities such as amp, lt, gt, apos, quot, and to those entities that cannot be represented in the chosen encoding.

❑ Normalization of attributes and white spaces as per XML 1.0 requirements.

DOM and SAX Processing

The DOM (Document Object Model) maps XML into an in-memory tree structure of nodes. The SAX (Simple API for XML) converts XML into a series of events. In both these cases, information such as attribute ordering and insignificant white spaces between one end tag and another start tag are lost. Also, in some cases the prefix information may be lost as namespace declarations are applied to the nodes.

If a DOM or SAX processor is used either to produce or verify an XML Signature, a canonicalization method must be used to serialize the relevant part of the DOM tree or SAX events. The verification must use the same canonicalization method to re-serialize the DOM/SAX input to verify the signature.

XML Namespace Processing

In the XPath data model and in the data model of the canonicalization algorithm Canonical XML defined in the specification, an element's namespace consists of the namespace declarations present in that element, namespace declarations from the ancestors that are not overridden, and the non-empty default namespaces. In addition, the Canonical XML algorithm imports all XML namespace attributes such as `xml:base` and `xml:lang` from the nearest ancestors.

Due to this inheritance behavior, a `<Signature>` element or signed XML data that is a child of elements using these data models may contain namespace declarations from its ancestors when serialized. This creates a problem when a signature that is created in the context of one XML document is expected to be valid in the context of another document.

Applications can avoid this problem by using a canonicalization algorithm that does not include ancestor context or by letting the recipient properly differentiate the signed data or the `<Signature>` element from the surrounding context before validation.

Character Encoding

Changing a character representation from one encoding to another encoding may change the bit patterns. If an XML document containing a `<Signature>` element is changed to a different encoding or the encoding of the signed data object changes, the signature may become invalid.

XML Signature Syntax

The overview and the example sections, so far, provided a glimpse of the XML Signature syntax. In this section, we focus on the formal syntax of the specification, the major elements, their purpose, and the other features supported by the specification.

In the February 2002 release of the specification, all the XML Signature elements are defined under the target namespace http://www.w3.org/2000/09/xmldsig#. To provide compact and readable examples, we make use of the prefix ds, which is mapped to the above namespace.

The XML Signature syntax is divided into a core and an optional section.

Core Syntax

The elements and the features described under this core section are mandatory and are required to be supported by the confirming implementations.

The *<Signature>* Element

The <Signature> element is the core element of XML Signature. As seen in the examples, the XML Signature is represented by the <Signature> element. It can exist as a standalone document, can envelop the data object that it signs, or can be enveloped by the data object.

The following table lists the child elements of <Signature> element in the order in which they appear:

Child Elements	Required	Max Occurrences
ds:SignedInfo	Yes	1
ds:SignatureValue	Yes	1
ds:KeyInfo	No	1
ds:Object	No	unbounded

Here is an attribute table for <Signature> element that lists all attributes:

Attribute Name	Type	Required
Id	xsd:ID	no

The Id attribute is used to associate an identifier for the <Signature> element so that it can be referenced from other elements. For instance, one of the patient examples in the earlier section represents the <Signature> element as:

```
<Signature Id="TenthOctoberDoctorobservation"
           xmlns="http://www.w3.org/2000/09/xmldsig#">
```

Since there are many <Signature> elements in the <Patient> document, one may choose to collect all the <Signature> elements under a common element for easy retrieval and processing of all signatures in the document. The patient's record would then appear as:

```
<Patient name="John Gartner" id="548-61-3456">
  <AllSignatures>
    <TenthVisitObservation ref=" TenthOctoberDoctorobservation"/>
    ...
  </AllSignatures>
</Patient>
```

The *<SignatureValue>* Element

The <SignatureValue> contains the actual value of the digital signature. The signature value is always base64 encoded. The <SignatureValue> element is a simple extension of base64Binary type defined in XML Schema and it does not have any child elements. Similar to <Signature> element, it has one Id attribute serving the similar purpose:

Attribute Name	Type	Required
Id	xsd:ID	no

The <SignedInfo> Element

As seen in the earlier examples, the <SignedInfo> element contains references to the original data objects and includes the canonicalization and signature algorithms. The encrypted digest of the canonical form of the <SignedInfo> element represents the value of the XML Signature. Here is the child element table of <SignedInfo>:

Child Elements	Required	Max Occurrences
ds:CanonicalizationMethod	Yes	1
ds: SignatureMethod	Yes	1
ds: Reference	Yes	unbounded

Similar to the <Signature> element, it has one Id attribute that can be used to refer to a <SignedInfo> element from other signatures:

Attribute Name	Type	Required
Id	xsd:ID	no

The <CanonicalizationMethod> Element

The required <CanonicalizationMethod> element specifies the canonicalization algorithm applied to the <SignedInfo> element. This element is required because the <SignedInfo> element must be canonicalized before signing using this canonicalization algorithm. The algorithm used is identified by the Algorithm attribute.

One child element is permitted for the <CanonicalizationMethod> element:

Child Elements	Required	Max Occurrences
Any element from any namespace	no	unbounded

The child element can be any element from other namespaces. The basic motivation behind this element is to enable representation of any algorithm-specific details. For instance, let us say you have a user-specified canonicalization algorithm that can control what gets canonicalized through parameters. One can specify that using the child element as shown. Here, we control whether comments are included or excluded in the canonicalization:

```
<CanonicalizationMethod
Algorithm="http//www.rwav.com/MyOwnCanonicalizationAlgorithm">
    <MyApp:Comments included="NO"/>
</ CanonicalizationMethod>
```

The XML Signature specification recommends the use of XML-based canonicalization algorithms as opposed to text-based algorithms. The specification stipulates that the `<SignedInfo>` element is presented as a set of nodes per the XPath node-set definition to the XML-based canonicalization algorithms instead of a stream of octets.

The attribute table consists of one required attribute to specify the algorithm used:

Attribute Name	Type	Required
Algorithm	xsd:anyURI	Yes

The `<SignatureMethod>` Element

The `<SignatureMethod>` element specifies the algorithm used for signature generation. This algorithm identifies all cryptographic functions involved in the signature generation:

Child Elements	Required	Max Occurrences
ds: HMACOutputLength	no	1
Any from any namespace	no	unbounded

The `<HMACOutputLength>` element is used when the HMAC (Hash-based Message Authentication Code) algorithm defined in this specification is used as a signature-generation algorithm and contains the truncation length parameter for that algorithm.

The `<HMACOutputLengthType>` is a simple restriction on integer and is defined as follows:

```
<simpleType name="HMACOutputLengthType">
  <restriction base="integer"/>
</simpleType>
```

Here is an example of an HMAC `<SignatureMethod>` element:

```
<SignatureMethod Algorithm="http://www.w3.org/2000/09/xmldsig#hmac-sha1">
  <HMACOutputLength>128</HMACOutputLength>
</SignatureMethod>
```

The `<Any>` element serves the similar purpose as in the case of `<CanonicalizationMethod>`. The attribute table consists of one required attribute that is used for specifying the algorithm used:

Attribute Name	Type	Required
Algorithm	xsd:anyURI	Yes

The `<Reference>` Element

The `<Reference>` element carries the digest value of the data object and optionally references to the original data objects. It may also include a `<Transforms>` element that specifies all the transformations that need to be applied to the data objects prior to calculating the digest.

The table below lists all the child elements of `<Reference>`:

Child Elements	Required	Max Occurrences
ds: Transforms	No	1
ds: DigestMethod	Yes	1
ds: DigestValue	Yes	1

The `<Reference>` element includes three attributes as listed in the table below:

Attribute Name	Type	Required
Id	Xsd:ID	No
URI	Xsd:anyURI	No
Type	Xsd:anyURI	No

The `Id` attribute permits the `<Reference>` element to be referenced from elsewhere.

The `Type` attribute is used to identify the type of object being signed. The `Type` attribute is purely advisory, and the specification does not require the implementations to validate the referred objects. The Enveloping Signature example makes use of this `Type` attribute that indicates that the type of the object being referred is the `<Object>` element. The code snippet is repeated below:

```
<Reference URI="TenthOctoberJGartnerXRay"
                type=http://www.w3.org/2000/09/xmldsig#Object>
```

The URI attribute is used to reference the data object. If the URI attribute is omitted altogether, the receiving application is expected to know the identity of the object. For instance, let us again look at the patient's record of detached signature example without the URI attribute of the `<Reference>` element:

```
<Patient name="John Gartner" id="548-61-3456">
   ...
   <Observations DoctorName="Arul Murali" id="TenthOctoberObservation">
   ...
   </Observations >
     <Signature Id="TenthOctoberDoctorobservation"
               xmlns="http://www.w3.org/2000/09/xmldsig#">
       <Reference>
          ...
       </Reference>
     </Signature>
</Patient>
```

The `<Signature>` element is no longer self-contained. Unless the application knows that the `<Signature>` element with the `Id` value of `"TenthOctoberDoctorobservation"` is a signature of the `<Observations>` element with an `Id` value of `"TenthOctoberObservation,"` this signature cannot be validated.

As shown in the enveloping signature example, the `<Reference>` element can occur one or more times. If it occurs more than once, the URI attributed can be omitted only once in order to support unambiguous identification of the data objects. In the case of a single `<Reference>` element, we could use some heuristics as shown in the above example to connect the signature with the original object. In case of more `<Reference>` elements, it is impossible to make any connection to the original object unless the `<Reference>` element carries an `Id` attribute. Since `Id` is optional, the URI attribute has been made mandatory in case of multiple `<Reference>` elements.

The specification allows the same set of characters for the URI attribute as XML 1.0 with a few exceptions. All non-ASCII characters and excluded characters listed in RFC 2396 are not allowed. However, this specification permits the number sign (#), the percent sign (%), and the square brackets per RFC 2732.

The disallowed characters can be used in URI references by escaping them per the following steps:

❑ Convert the disallowed characters to UTF-8 octets.

❑ Escape the octets with the URI escaping mechanism. This means converts the octets to their hexadecimal representation and prepends a percent sign resulting in %HH, where HH is the hexadecimal equivalent of the octets.

The Reference Processing Model

The XML Signature specification defines a processing model for de-referencing URIs of the `<Reference>` element and applying transforms. We cover those details in this section.

The `<Reference>` processing model recommends the use of an XPath data model to process XML. The XML Signature implementations do not need to conform to XPath in order to claim conformance to XML Signature. However, the processing is explained using XPath definitions and if the implementations do not follow Xpath, they are required to provide an equivalent functionality that corresponds to such data definitions. For instance, the term node-set used here corresponds to an XPath node-set and if XPath is not used by the implementations, the node-set referred here must be replaced with a data model equivalent to that of the XPath node-set.

All confirming implementations are required to support de-referencing of URIs, and this is recommended to follow the HTTP scheme. Except for the same document references, the result of de-referencing the URI-Reference must result in an octet stream. Specifically, an XML document identified by the URI is not parsed unless the URI is a same-document reference or unless a transform requires such parsing. The de-referencing of a same-document reference is required to result in an XPath node-set. The process of obtaining an XPath node-set from a same-document reference is detailed in the next section.

The specification does not recommend using URI-References for identifying XML fragments in external resources and instead recommends using XPath transforms for such requirements. This is because the meaning of external XML fragments is defined by the resource's MIME type, and reference validation may fail if the fragment is not processed in the same way.

Support for NULL URIs and bare name XPointers is required for same-document references. Specification also recommends support for the same-document XPointers '#xpointer (/)' and '#xpointer (id ('ID'))' if a comment-preserving canonicalization is expected to be used.

The following examples illustrate the definition of some URI-references:

❑ URI="http://www.wrox.com/wssecurity.xml"
This URI identifies the octets that represent the external resource.

❑ URI="http://www.wrox.com/wssecurity.xml/#chapter6"
This URI identifies an XML fragment with the ID attribute value of chapter6, in the external resource http://www.wrox.com/wssecurity.xml. As stated earlier, this kind of URI reference to external XML fragments is not recommended by the specification. The recommended method is to use an XPath transform to get chapter6.

❑ URI=""
This identifies the node-set of the resource containing the signature. It does not include comment nodes.

❑ URI="#chapter6"
This identifies a node-set containing the element with an ID attribute value of chapter6 in the same XML document containing the signature.

In addition to URI de-referencing, the <Reference> processing involves applying transforms as specified by the <Transforms> element. The input format required by a transform or the output produced by a transform may be an octet stream or an XPath node-set.

By default, the confirming implementations are required to convert the data objects or the result of URI de-referencing to the input format required by the transform. If a transformation then involves multiple transforms again by default, the implementations are required to convert the output of one transform to the input format required by the following transform. The XML Signature applications may specify alternative transforms to override this default behavior, and in such instances the implementations are required to use the user-specified transforms for converting an output to the input format.

In cases where a default conversion involves converting a node-set to an octet stream, the conversion must be based on using the canonicalization algorithm Canonical XML defined in the specification (refer to the *Algorithms* section for more details on Canonical XML).

The final output of URI de-referencing and transforms must be converted to an octet stream that contains the data octets that needs to be secured. The digest algorithm specified by <DigestMethod> is applied to these data octets to get the digest value to be placed under the <DigestValue> element.

The <Transforms> Element

The optional <Transforms> element contains an ordered list of <Transform> elements that describe the steps involved in obtaining the data object that was digested. Note that when transforms are used in a signature, the digest value does not indicate the digest of the original data object but of the transformed object.

The transformations are to be applied when the output of the previous transform becomes the input of the next. As noted earlier, proper conversion must be performed to the output to match the input requirements. The input of the first transformation is the result of de-referencing the URI of the <Reference> element. The output of the last <Transform> is the input for the digest method. The <Transforms> element just contains one <Transform> child element that can occur many times:

Child Elements	Required	Max Occurrences
ds: Transform	Yes	unbounded

The <Transform> Element

The <Transform> element, which specifies the transform algorithm, is also structured as the CanonicalizationMethod and SignatureMethod elements:

Child Elements	Required	Max Occurrences
Either <Any> element from any namespace or <XPath> element of type xsd:string	No	unbounded

The attribute table consists of one required attribute that is used for specifying the algorithm used:

Attribute Name	Type	Required
Algorithm	xsd:anyURI	Yes

The <DigestMethod> Element

The <DigestMethod> element specifies the digest algorithm to be used for the original (or transformed if any <Transforms> exists) data object. Its structure is identical to <CanonicalizationMethod> and hence is not repeated here.

The <DigestValue> Element

The <DigestValue> element contains the base64-encoded value of the digest and it is a simple extension of xsd:base64Binary type.

The <KeyInfo> Element

The <KeyInfo> element is an optional element that enables key information to be packaged along with the XML Signature. The <KeyInfo> element can contain keys, key names, certificates, and other public key management information.

The following table lists all the child elements of <KeyInfo>:

Child Element Name	Required	Occurrences	Purpose
ds:KeyName	No	1	Carries a direct or indirect string reference, such as a name, to identify the key
ds:KeyValue	No	1	Carries the actual public key value of the key used for signature generation

Child Element Name	Required	Occurrences	Purpose
ds:RetrievalMethod	No	1	Carries location information that points to the key used
ds:X509Data	No	1	Carries X509 certificates or some X509 identifier keys
ds:PGPData	No	1	Carries information on PGP public key pairs
ds:SPKIData	No	1	Carries SPKI certificates, SPKI public key pairs or some SPKI data
ds:MgmtData	No	1	Carrier in band key agreement data. Not recommended for use as XML Encryption defines a better mechanism
<any> element from any namespace	No	1	Carries any key information as desired by the application

Example usage of <KeyInfo> is shown in the enveloped signature example. Any of the child elements of <KeyInfo> can be used to carry the key information. Not all XML Signature implementations can be expected to support all the ways of carrying key information. For interoperability, the specification requires support of <KeyValue> from all conforming implementations. In addition, specification also recommends support for <RetrievalMethod>. Using any of these two elements may increase the chance of interoperability.

Applications are not restricted to using only the elements and types defined here to carry key information. The <any> element is meant specifically for this purpose. If interoperability is your goal, depending on proprietary extensions is not a good idea.

A single Id attribute has been defined for <KeyInfo> to facilitate references from other elements:

Attribute Name	Type	Required
Id	xsd:ID	No

The <Object> Element

The <Object> element is an optional child element of <Signature>. The example on enveloping signature shows an example usage of the <Object> element. As shown in the example, the <Object> element typically is used for enveloping signatures where the data object being signed is included in the <Signature> element. The digest of the data object in such cases includes the entire <Object> element along with the data object. If the <Object> tags are to be excluded from the digest, then the <Reference> element must identify the data object, or a transform must be used to remove the <Object> tags. In the example, we include the <Object> element as part of the signed content.

The <Object> element permits any element from any namespace:

Child Elements	Required	Max Occurrences
<any> from any namespace	no	unbounded

The attribute table consists of three attributes:

Attribute Name	Type	Required
Id	xsd:ID	No
MimeType	xsd:string	No
Encoding	xsd:anyURI	No

The encoding attribute is provided to identify the method by which the object is encoded. The MimeType plays an advisory role to describe the data within the <Object> element.

A Type identifier is defined for the <Object> element to identify the type of object being referred from the <Reference> element. The value is:

```
"http://www.w3.org/2000/09/xmldsig#Object"
```

Optional Signature Syntax

The XML Signature specification defines two more elements to carry more information that is not already possible by the core <Signature> elements. These elements are optional to implement and hence do not form part of the core syntax. Both these elements can appear only as a child of the <Object> element. We discuss these two elements in this section.

The <Manifest> Element

The <Manifest> element provides a structure to carry a list of <Reference> elements similar to that provided by the <SignedInfo> element. The difference between the two lists is that in the case of <Manifest>, the processing model of the contained <Reference> element is defined by the application. Applications may specify whether the digest should be compared against the referenced objects and what to do if the comparison fails. You may note that in the case of the <Reference> element contained in <SignedInfo>, the processing model is defined by the specification.

If you are wondering why anyone would ever want to control a <Reference> processing model, the following discussions may provide some insight:

❑ By controlling the processing of <Reference> elements, we can control the reference validation part of signature validation. You may recollect that a signature validation consists of two parts, one of which is the reference validation. Any change to the original data fails the reference validation. In cases where many <Reference> elements are involved, applications may wish to consider the reference validation as successful as long as the <Reference> element or elements they are interested in is valid. Such a control can be exercised through <Manifest> elements.

❑   The other advantage of the `<Manifest>` element has to do with efficiency. If you have a need to sign the same set of `<Reference>` elements multiple times using different keys, one way to do it would be to repeat `<Reference>` elements inside the `<SignedInfo>` element, as has been shown in all the examples in this chapter. This is wasteful and redundant. In such cases, one could put all such `<Reference>` elements inside of the `<Manifest>` element and refer to it from the `<SignedInfo>` element. An example is shown below:

```
<Signature Id="SignatureUsingManifestElement"

  <SignedInfo Id="UsesRSAKeys">
    ...

    <Reference URI="#MyFirstManifest"
                    Type="http://www.w3.org/2000/09/xmldsig#Manifest">
      <DigestMethod Algorithm="http://www.w3.org/2000/09/xmldsig#sha1"/>
          <DigestValue>345x3rvEPO0vKtMup4NbeVu8nk=</DigestValue>
    </Reference>

    <Object>
      <Manifest Id="MyFirstManifest">
        <Reference>
        </Reference>
        <Reference>
        </Reference>
      </Manifest>
    </Object>
  </SignedInfo>
  ...
</Signature>
```

The `<Reference>` inside of `<SignedInfo>` refers to the `<Manifest>` element. Note the use of the `Type` attribute, which indicates that the type of object being referred is `<Manifest>`. A type identifier is defined in the specification to facilitate that. The value is:

```
"http://www.w3.org/2000/09/xmldsig#Manifest"
```

The `<Manifest>` element supports one or many instances of `<ds:Reference>` elements and has one Id attribute, the use of which is shown in the above example.

The `<SignatureProperties>` Element

The `<SignatureProperties>` element provides a way to carry additional information about the signature. For example, one could carry information such as a date/time stamp or the serial number of the cryptographic hardware used or any such assertions about the signature. The meaning of such assertions is application-defined.

Here is an example use of this element. This example adds date/timestamp properties to the detached signature example:

```
<Signature Id="TenthOctoberDoctorobservation"
              xmlns="http://www.w3.org/2000/09/xmldsig#">
  <SignedInfo>
    ...

    <Reference URI="#TimeStampProperty"
```

```
                    Type="http://www.w3.org/2000/09/xmldsig#SignatureProperties">
    ...
  </Reference>
  <Reference URI="#TenthOctoberObservation">
    ...
  </Reference>
  </SignedInfo>
    <SignatureValue>MC0CFFrVLtRlk=...</SignatureValue>
  <Object>
    <SignatureProperties>
      <SignatureProperty Id="TimeStampProperty"
                         Target="#TenthOctoberDoctorobservation">
      <app:timestamp xmlns=app="http://www.wrox.com">
        <app:date>19990908</app:date>
        <app:time>14:34:34:34</app:time>
      </app:timestamp>
    </SignatureProperty>
  </SignatureProperties>
  </Signature>
```

The `<SignatureProperties>` element contains one or more `<SignatureProperty>` element. The `<SignatureProperty>` element is used to specify the assertions. The `<SignatureProperty>` can contain any number of application-defined elements.

The `<SignatureProperty>` element defines two attributes:

Attribute Name	Type	Required
Id	xsd:ID	No
Target	xsd:anyURI	Yes

The `Target` attribute references the `<Signature>` element to which the property applies. A `Type` identifier is defined for the `<SignatureProperties>` element to enable references from a `<Reference>` element to identify the referent's type, as shown in the example. The value is:

```
"http://www.w3.org/2000/09/xmldsig#SignatureProperties"
```

Processing Instructions and Comments

Processing Instructions (PI) that exist inside a `<SignedInfo>` element will by default become part of the signed content unless removed by a canonicalization algorithm during the canonicalization of the `<SignedInfo>` element. This means that any subsequent changes to the PI will invalidate the signature.

Similar to PIs, comments inside of the `<SignedInfo>` element or any other referred XML documents will become part of the signed content unless removed during canonicalization. Consequently, any changes to the comment will invalidate the signature.

Algorithms

The XML Signature specification defines a standard usage model that includes syntax, identifiers, and requirements for a set of algorithms that can be used with the specification. The specification requires that some of these algorithms be supported by the confirming implementations. Applications are not restricted to use only the algorithms discussed in this specification. Applications can use any algorithm of their choice, and implementations can also extend on these specified algorithms. Since the specification requires that all the conforming implementations support a subset of these algorithms, applications are assured support of some of these algorithms.

All of the algorithms discussed in the specification are associated with an identifier. This identifier is to be used as the value of the `Algorithm` attribute of the `<DigestMethod>`, the `<Transform>`, the `<SignatureMethod>`, and the `<CanonicalizationMethod>` elements defined in this specification. Most of the algorithms discussed here take implicit parameters such as the key information for `<SignatureMethod>`. Some algorithms may require explicit parameters. Such explicit parameters appear as elements with descriptive names and are algorithm-specific. The details of such explicit parameters are specified in the description of the algorithm.

It is not in the scope of this chapter to explore in detail all the algorithms discussed in the specification. Instead, we provide a brief introduction to each category of algorithms and list the algorithms specified under each category.

Message Digest

Message digest algorithms are used for computing a condensed representation of a message or any arbitrary data. The condensed representation usually is called the message digest or simply digest. It also can be considered equivalent to calculating a hash value, a more common term used in programming.

In XML Signature, message digest algorithms are used for calculating the digest of the original data object. The `<DigestValue>` element, which exists as a child of the `<DigestMethod>` element, holds the digest of the original data object.

There are several advantages to signing a digest of the data rather than the data itself. First and foremost, the digest of a data usually is much smaller than the data itself. The signing or the encryption process is time-consuming, and working with the smaller size digest greatly improves the efficiency of the signing process. In addition, a smaller size digest is much easier to transport, handle, and persist, which results in improved performance and efficiency.

Since the success of a digital signature depends greatly on the digest algorithm, it is critical that the digest algorithm used must truly reflect changes to the original data. In other words, the digest algorithm used must be such that it should be infeasible to produce the same digest for differing messages. Also, the digest algorithm must produce the same digest for the same message.

Some of the important algorithms in this area are SHA-1 and MD5.

SHA-1

SHA-1 stands for **Secure Hash Algorithm**. SHA-1 is published by the Federal Information Processing Standards Publications (FIPS). The maintenance agency for this standard is the US Department of Commerce, National Institute of Standards and Technology.

SHA-1 is a technical revision of SHA, or SHA-0 as it is sometimes called. SHA-1 is considered highly secure, as it is computationally infeasible to find a message or data that corresponds to a given digest or to find two different messages or data that produce the same digest value. SHA-1 produces a 160 bit-long digest for any message of length 2^{64} bits. More details on SHA-1 can be found at http://csrc.nist.gov/publications/fips/fips180-1/fip180-1.txt.

The XML Signature specification requires the implementation to support the SHA-1 algorithm. It is the only algorithm defined in the specification. The specification defines an identifier for this algorithm, and the value of that identifier is:

```
ID: http://www.w3.org/2000/09/xmldsig#sha1.
```

This identifier is used as the value of the algorithm attribute of <DigestMethod> element as below:

```
<DigestMethod Algorithm="http://www.w3.org/2000/09/xmldsig#sha1"/>
```

MD5

MD5 is another well-known message digest algorithm. It is the result of combined efforts by MIT Computer Science Labs and RSA Data Security, Inc. The precursors of MD5 are MD4 and MD2.

MD5 produces a 128 bit-long digest. MD5 recently has been shown to be vulnerable to some attacks, casting doubt on its strength. Hence, the XML Signature specification does not recommend MD5.

For more details on MD5 refer to http://www.ietf.org/rfc/rfc1321.txt.

Message Authentication Codes

The purpose of the **Message Authentication Code** or MAC is to authenticate the source of a message and its integrity. The MAC is an authentication tag or a checksum computed by applying a MAC algorithm together with a secret key on a message or data. Though commonly MAC algorithms are not considered as algorithms for creating digital signatures due to the shared secret key aspect, the XML Signature specification recognizes that MAC also can be used for signing a message, and defines a MAC-based algorithm for the <SignatureMethod> element.

The MAC algorithm is characterized by its use of a secret key and that is the main differentiating feature from other mainstream signature algorithms used for creating digital signatures. Since a secret key is used for computing MACs, the recipients holding the shared secret key can verify only digital signatures created using MAC.

There are four types of MACs:

- ❑ Unconditionally secure
- ❑ Hash function-based
- ❑ Stream cipher-based
- ❑ Block cipher-based.

The XML Signature specification defines one MAC algorithm that is based on a hash function. It is called HMAC, which stands for Hash function-based MAC. HMACs use a key or keys in conjunction with a hash function, such as the SHA-1 message digest algorithm discussed earlier, to produce the checksum.

The HMAC is required to be supported by the confirming implementations per the specification. An identifier is defined as the value for the `Algorithm` attribute of the `<SignatureMethod>` element. The value of the identifier is:

```
ID: http://www.w3.org/2000/09/xmldsig#hmac-sha1
```

For more details on HMAC refer to http://www.ietf.org/rfc/rfc2104.txt.

Signature Algorithms

Signature algorithms are meant for creating a digital signature for given data. They typically are a combination of a digest algorithm and a PKI-based key dependent algorithm. In terms of core functionality they are similar to MAC algorithms, but signature algorithms are based on public key cryptography. Because of the private/public key combination, they can be counted on for non-repudiation support. The shared nature of the secret key in MAC algorithms compromises non-repudiation.

The XML Signature specification defines two signature algorithms, out of which one is required and the other is recommended:

❑ Name: DSA – Required (http://www.ietf.org/rfc/rfc2437.txt)
  ID: `http://www.w3.org/2000/09/xmldsig#dsa-sha1`

❑ Name: PKCS1 (RSA_SHA1) – Recommended (http://www.ietf.org/rfc/rfc2437.txt)
  ID: `http://www.w3.org/2000/09/xmldsig#rsa-sha1`

The RSA algorithm refers to the RSASSA_PKCS1-V1_5 algorithm defined in RFC 2437. Both these algorithms do not take any explicit parameters. Both are used in the `<SignatureMethod>` element to create the signature value of the canonicalized `<SignedInfo>` element.

Canonicalization Algorithms

As discussed earlier in this chapter, XML documents need to be canonicalized prior to taking a digest in order to ensure identical physical representation format for logically equivalent XML documents. Signature validation might fail if XML documents are not canonicalized, as the same document may end up with a different textual representation in another context. Canonicalization is always used in XML Signature, since the `<SignedInfo>` element is the one that finally gets signed.

Canonicalization is the process of applying consistent policies to produce an identical textual representation format for a given XML document under any application context. Such policies are applied to the aspects of XML that can have a varying physical form without an impact on the logical form.

The XML Signature specification defines two canonicalization algorithms. The name and identifier details of those two algorithms are given below:

❑ Name: Canonical XML (no comments) – Required
  ID: `http://www.w3.org/TR/20001/REC-xml-c14n-20010315`

❑ Name: Canonical XML with comments – Recommended
  ID: `http://www.w3.org/TR/20001/REC-xml-c14n-20010315#WithComments`

Confirming implementations are required to support the Canonical XML algorithm that does not include comments in the canonized form. Both these algorithms also are called inclusive canonicalization algorithms, as these include the entire name scope context from ancestor elements. There is another form of canonicalization called exclusive canonicalization that only includes the minimum necessary namespace context from ancestors. However, it can be used as needed by the applications.

Transform Algorithms

We already have seen some uses of transform algorithms in the example sections. For instance, the example on enveloped signature showed how an XPath filtering transform or an enveloped signature transform algorithm could be used to remove the `<Signature>` element from the digest calculation of the `<Lab>` element. One of the most common uses of transform algorithms is the canonicalization applied to XML documents prior to calculating the digest. Any XML document that needs to be signed has to have undergone some form of canonicalization transformation.

Transform can be defined as an act of getting the data object ready for the signature or accessing at the right data to be signed. By providing support for transforms, the XML Signature specification acknowledges the fact that in some cases data needs to be prepared before it is ready for the signature (as in the XML case), or the referred data may need to be filtered to access the right data that actually need to be signed.

Enveloped signature can never be supported if a concept like transform does not exist.

As seen in the examples, transform algorithms are applied to the data objects referred to in the `<Reference>` elements. A data object can undergo many transforms with output of one transform forming the input for the subsequent transform. The specification defines five algorithms and recommends implementation to support all the five algorithms:

1. Canonicalization – Typically used for XML documents. Any canonicalization algorithm can be used.

2. Name: Base64 – Recommended
   ID: `http://www.w3.org/2000/09/xmlsdig#base64`

3. Name: XPath Filtering – Recommended
   ID: `http://www.w3.org/TR/1999/REC-xpath-19991116`

4. Name: XSLT Transform – Recommended
   ID: `http://www.w3.org/TR/1999/REC-xslt-19991116`

5. Name: Enveloped Signature Transform – Required
   ID: `http://www.w3.org/2000/09/xmlsdig#enveloped-signature`

User-Specified Algorithms

As mentioned earlier, the XML Signature specification does not restrict the user to the algorithms defined in the specification. Applications are free to use any algorithm of their choice.

The basic motivation for the XML Signature specification to define algorithms is to provide a common way to represent the algorithms so that the applications can understand the algorithms in use without any special intervention. Such a standard representation enables separately developed applications to interoperate with one another. Since the specification has made it a requirement for the implementations to support some algorithms, applications can expect some level of guaranteed support. By working within the scope of the required algorithms, applications can be reasonably confident of interoperability across partner applications.

So unless there is a real need, dependence on user-defined algorithms must be avoided. If you do have a real need ,how do you go about using one and what factors need to be considred? We will discuss this in the following section.

Defining a User-Specified Algorithm

The XML Signature specification does not define or require any specific steps or process to be followed to define and use a user-specific algorithm. However, from a usage point you may need to ensure the availability of the following for successful operation:

❑   Define a unique identifier for the algorithm. This is essential both for your application and for the partner application to understand the algorithm in use.

❑   Provide an implementation for the algorithm and ensure the availability of that implementation to all partner applications.

Security Considerations

The XML Signature specification provides a flexible mechanism for signing XML documents and other arbitrary digital contents. Care must be taken in using some of these mechanisms, the lack of which may compromise the strength of a signature. In this section, we focus on the factors that require special consideration from confirming implementations and XML Signature applications.

Transform Considerations

There are possibilities of introducing cryptographic vulnerabilities through the `<Transforms>` mechanism required by this specification for signature generation. The specification identifies three such areas where caution is required. We now will discuss those three considerations.

Only What is Signed is Secure

Signature over transformed data secures only the transformed data and not the source data on which the transform was applied. Only what is signed is secure. The original data may keep changing after the signature, and the signature may still be valid. For instance, the transformed and signed data may just represent a portion of the original data; therefore changes to the other portions of the original data that are not part of the transform would not invalidate the signature. Hence, applications should not assume that the validation of the signature ensures the integrity of the original data. It just ensures the integrity of the transformed data.

Also, the same XML document containing the `<Signature>` element may undergo further changes – for example, get encrypted for transport. The XML Signature does not secure the new encrypted form but just the plain text that was originally signed.

Only What is Seen Should be Signed

The transformed data resulting from the application of <Transforms> may differ considerably from the original data. As the XML Signature secures the transformed data and not the original data, the signer should see the end result of the transform and not sign based on the original data. The transformed data should be represented to the signer through some media.

If the signature conveys a judgment of some sort, or consent of the signer, then it is necessary to secure all the information presented to the signer as exactly as practical. In some cases this may involve literally signing what was presented, such as signing an image rendered to the signer. If this results in difficulties for further software processing, then one can sign the data along with all the other information necessary to reproduce the content that originally was seen by the signer.

When a resource used for transform resides external to the signed document, then it is recommended that the external resource required for the transform be signed, as well, along with the original data. Otherwise, any changes to that resource will invalidate the signature. For instance, imagine that an external XSL style sheet is used to transform an XML document. It is recommended that this style sheet be signed along with the data for proper validation.

See What is Signed

As in the case of the signer who is expected to sign only what is seen, the verification logic should operate over the transformed data and not the original data. Applications that work with directly the original data should exercise extreme caution, as security could be compromised. Working directly with the original data may not result in behavior originally intended by the signer, though the signature may hold well.

For example, consider a canonicalization transform in which the canonicalization algorithm normalizes the case of the characters in the document from lower to upper. Any changes introduced to the original document that result only in case change of the characters in the document will not invalidate the signature, as the canonicalization transform would in any case change the case of the characters. Though this case change to the original document has not invalidated the signature, that change could affect the intended meaning or the behavior of the original document. For example, a case change could change the result of an XPath selection. Due to such issues the specification makes the following requirements and recommendations:

❑ All documents operated upon and generated by the XML Signature applications must be in Unicode Normalization Form as defined in http://www.unicode.org/unicode/reports/tr15/tr15-18.html and in http://www.unicode.org/unicode/uni2errata/Normalization_Corigendum.html.

❑ It is recommended that encoding normalizations should not be done as part of a signature transform.

Security Model Considerations

The XML Signature specification supports different security models. For instance, the specification uses public key signatures and keyed hash authentication codes, both of which have different security models. Also, the specification allows user-specified algorithms that may have their own security model.

In the case of public key signatures, the public key may be published fairly widely so many parties can hold this key. The number of agents holding the private key should be minimized, preferably just to one. The interpretation of how the agents and their keys are to be trusted is managed by trust authority systems.

Keyed hash authentication codes based on secret keys are much more efficient computationally but they require that all the parties involved have possession of the same key as signer. This need to share the secret key may lead to forged signatures.

Other Considerations

The generation of an XML Signature involves many processing steps and many algorithms. As such, the strength of a signature depends on the least strong among the chain of these processing steps, such as the strength of the signature itself, the digest algorithms used, the strength of the key used and the strength of the authentication, and the distribution mechanisms used.

Applications must exercise care in the processing of any executable content such as XSLT transforms that might be provided to the algorithms used for signature generation. There are possibilities of introducing unintended behavior of algorithms, such as excessive memory requirements, by passing wrong parameters. Hence, applications must exercise care in executing the various algorithms defined in the specification. More care may be necessary in user-defined algorithms.

Implementations

While it is important to know the details of the specification, as a user of XML Signature you may more often work with the XML Signature implementations than with the syntax of the specification directly. You can expect vendor-provided implementations to insulate most of the syntactic details of the XML Signature.

The available XML Signature implementations can be classified into two main groups:

❑ One that provides toolkits, APIs, and SDKs to create and verify signatures

❑ Web services that help to create and verify signatures

The following section provides a brief insight into these two different groups.

XML Signature Web Services

Implementations in this group offer web services to process digital signatures. Such web services may provide functionality to create XML Signatures and to verify XML Signatures. OASIS started a digital signature services initiative in the month of October 2002 to support the processing of digital signatures. This initiative targets production and verification of digital signatures. Though this initiative is in its infancy stages, one can expect vendors to offer web services to process digital signatures soon.

There already is one known web service implementation that offers XML Signature verification service. Infomosaic Corporation provides this service and the interface for this service is defined in http://www.securexml.net/SecureXML/SecureXML.wsdl.

XML Signature Toolkits

Implementations in this group provide a programmatic API to create and verify XML Signatures. There are already many such toolkits available. The W3C page at http://www.w3.org/Signature/ provides full details. The same list is reproduced one of the following page for quick reference:

- ❑ Microsoft .Net framework

- ❑ IBM XML Security Suite (http://www.alphaworks.ibm.com/tech/xmlsecuritysuite)

- ❑ Verisign (http://www.xmltrustcenter.org/xmlsig/developer/verisign/index.htm)

- ❑ RSA BSAFE Cert-J (http://www.rsasecurity.com/products/bsafe/certj.html)

- ❑ Phaos (http://phaos.com/products/category/xml.html)

- ❑ Baltimore (http://www.baltimore.com/keytools/xml/)

- ❑ Entrust/Toolkit for Java (http://www.entrust.com/authority/java/index.htm)

- ❑ IAIK XML Signature Library:IXSIL (http://jce.iaik.tugraz.at/products/ixsil/index.php)

- ❑ NEC XMLDSIG (http://www.sw.nec.co.jp/soft/xml_s/appform_e.html)

- ❑ Ubisecure (http://www.ubisecure.com/index.php?page=ubisignature)

- ❑ Wedgetail (http://www.wedgetail.com/jcsi/xmldsig/)

The following section provides code snippets that show the usage of .NET Framework API to create and verify XML Signatures.

Example: Create XML Signature Using .Net Framework

In this example we use the .Net framework API to create the same enveloping signature showcased by the enveloping signature patient example earlier in the chapter:

```csharp
// The code is in C#

// Include the necessary packages
using System;
using System.IO;
using System.Xml;
using System.Security.Cryptography.Xml;
using System.Security.Cryptography;

// Load the Patient record XML document.
// Assume that the whole <Patient> document is represented in the "patientRecord"
string.
XmlDocument document = new XmlDocument();
document.LoadXml(patientRecord);

// Create the SignedXml message.
SignedXml signedXml = new SignedXml();
RSA key = RSA.Create();
signedXml.SigningKey = key;

// Create a data object to hold the data to sign.
DataObject dataObject = new DataObject();
dataObject.Data = document.ChildNodes;
dataObject.Id = "TenthOctoberKneeXRay"; //Identfies the Xray element
```

```
// Add the data object to the signature.
signedXml.AddObject(dataObject);

// Create a reference to the front knee Xray
Reference fronKneeReference = new Reference();
fronKneeReference.Uri = "http://www.xlab.com/jgartner/12/10/2002/kneefront.jpeg";

// Set the digest algorithm and add the reference
fronKneeReference.DigestMethod = new SHA1();
signedXml.AddReference(fronKneeReference);

// Create a reference to the back knee Xray
Reference backKneeReference = new Reference();
backKneeReference.Uri = http://www.xlab.com/jgartner/12/10/2002/kneeback.jpeg";

// Set the digest algorithm and add the reference
backKneeReference.DigestMethod = new SHA1();
signedXml.AddReference(backKneeReference);

// Finally Create the reference to the <Xray element identified by
Id="TenthOctoberKneeXRay"
Reference xrayElement = new Reference();
xrayElement.Uri = "#TenthOctoberKneeXRay ";

// set the type and indicate it as Object
xrayElement.Type = "http://www.w3.org/2000/09/xmldsig#Object";

// Set the canonicalization transform
xrayElement.AddTransform(new XmlDsigC14Ntransform());

// Set the digest algorithm and add the reference
xrayElement.DigestMethod = new SHA1();
signedXml.AddReference(xrayElement);

// Set the canonicalization algorithm ID
signedXml.SignedInfo.CanonicalizationMethod
    = "http://www.w3.org/TR/2001/REC-xml-c14n-20010315";

// Set the signature algorithm ID
signedXml.SignedInfo.SignatureMethod = "http://www.w3.org/2000/09/xmldsig#dsa-
sha1";

// Add a KeyInfo.
KeyInfo keyInfo = new KeyInfo();
keyInfo.AddClause(new RSAKeyValue(key));
signedXml.KeyInfo = keyInfo;

// Compute the signature.
signedXml.ComputeSignature();

signedXml.Signature.ID = "TenthOctoberKneeX-RayAnalysis";

// Get the XML representation of the signature and write it out
XmlElement xmlSignature = signedXml.GetXml();
Console.WriteLine(xmlSignature.OuterXml);
```

Example: Verify XML Signature Using .Net Framework

This code snippet verifies the signature created in the previous example:

```
using System;
using System.Security.Cryptography;
using System.Security.Cryptography.Xml;
using System.IO; using System.Xml;

// Load the Patient record XML document.
// Assume that the whole <Patient> document is represented in the "patientRecord"
string.
XmlDocument document = new XmlDocument();
document.LoadXml(patientRecord);

SignedXml signedXml = new SignedXml(document);

// Get the required signature element using the ID attribute
XMLElement signatureElement
  = xmlDocument.GetElementsById ("TenthOctoberKneeX-RayAnalysis");

signedXml.LoadXml(signatureElement);

// Write to console the results
if (signedXml.CheckSignature()) {
  Console.WriteLine("Signature check OK"); }
else {
  Console.WriteLine("Signature check FAILED");
}
```

Limitations

XML Signature provides a standard format for representing digital signatures in XML along with the other artifacts used for generating that signature. Such a standard representation format enables interoperability by facilitating exchange of signed documents and signatures across applications. While XML Signature solves many problems not already solved by existing digital signature solutions as discussed earlier in the chapter, it does not solve all the problems. In this section, we try to identify areas where problems with digital signatures still exist.

An XML Signature does not offer a standard programming API or a web service model for processing signatures. This makes the application code rely on proprietary vendor APIs, reducing the portability of applications.

XML Signature has not directly addressed the complex nature of PKI. The PKI programming is still considered as a "black art" known only to the few who have conquered its formidable layers of complexity. Though one can expect toolkits and web services such as XKMS trust services to provide that insulation from PKI complexities, it is still not addressed directly by the specification.

ID collisions are a possibility when XML signatures generated in one context are dropped in another context.

Though detached signatures and remote references are an advantage, there is no way to tell from the reference that the same is signed. This could lead to the data object being changed, inadvertently breaking the signature.

As discussed in the security considerations, it is possible to introduce security loopholes through transforms, compromising the validity of the signature.

Some of the legal issues that generally exist in digital signatures continue in XML Signature as well. For instance, a digital signature can only prove a specific private key was used to generate the signature. Binding the owner of the private key to the signature generated by the private key has unresolved legal issues.

Summary

In this chapter, we have seen what XML digital signature specification is all about and how it can be used to sign any digital content, including XML documents. Specifically, we first discussed the problem XML Signature was designed to solve. Then we looked at the process of generating an XML Signature using the specification and we took a detailed look at the formal syntax of the specification. We also looked briefly at the algorithms defined in the specification. Finally, we went over the limitations of XML Signature and other security vulnerabilities one needs to watch out for when using the same.

One key to enable acceptance of web services for running business transactions is ensuring the integrity and authenticity of the origin of business documents. By specifying a standard XML-based representation format for digital signatures and defining a standard processing model for signing any digital content, the XML digital signature specification provides an interoperable foundation for trusted exchange of data among XML-based web services.

7

XML Encryption

The last chapter provided an in-depth overview of the XML Digital Signature initiative of the W3C and the IETF. In accordance with its stated goals, the signature initiative did not define any standard mechanism for encrypting XML entities, which is another important security piece to promote the trusted use of web applications. Realizing the need for XML-based encryption, in January 2001 W3C initiated a working group to develop a process for encrypting and decrypting digital content and to represent the encrypted content in XML. In October 2002, this working group delivered a set of documents that specified a process for encrypting any arbitrary content and then representing the result in XML. As of October 2002, XML Encryption is not yet an *approved* specification, but it is close to becoming one.

In this chapter, we take a detailed look at the XML Encryption specification along with the related *Decrypt Transform* specification published by the W3C XML Encryption working group. We hope to provide enough perspective to understand all the details related to XML Encryption and to start using it in your applications. While we do provide in-depth coverage of the XML Encryption specification, this chapter is not intended to be a reference document for the specification.

On reading this chapter, you will learn:

- ❑ The motivation behind XML Encryption and the problem space XML Encryption tries to address
- ❑ A detailed overview of XML Encryption through examples and usage scenarios
- ❑ XML encryption preparation guidelines for XML documents
- ❑ XML encryption algorithms

❑ Relationship to XML Signature and the issues involved in combining encryption and signing

❑ Features and limitations of the Decrypt Transform specification

❑ Security considerations and other limitations of XML Encryption and Decrypt Transform specifications.

Why XML Encryption?

An XML document, like any other document, can be encrypted using existing encryption technologies and can be sent to one or more recipients. For instance, as discussed in Chapter 5, you could use the functionality provided by Secure Sockets Layer (SSL) to achieve encryption. Then why have XML Encryption? Does it add any new mechanism to cryptography? What added security mechanisms does it bring to web services?

Encrypting Parts of a Document

The existing encryption technologies can be used to encrypt a whole XML document. However, no standard mechanisms exist to encrypt parts of a document. Encryption is a time-consuming process. So, unless the data is considered sensitive and could compromise security, it is beneficial to leave the data unencrypted from the performance perspective. Imagine the standard purchase order document that contains details such as the customer name, address, credit information, items ordered, and a detailed description of the item, among other things. While one may not wish to reveal credit information to unknown parties, in the majority of cases the other information can safely be exposed. In such cases, having to encrypt the entire order will be an unnecessary restriction.

Performance is not the only issue here. In some cases, we do want parts of the data to be left unencrypted, while others to be protected. Going back to the same purchase order example, it is important for the shipping agent to read the address information of the buyer, while the credit information is irrelevant at the shipping stage and is better left encrypted. Enabling such limited viewing of a document is essential in a workflow environment that cannot be addressed without the ability to encrypt parts of a document.

One of the main goals of XML Encryption is to enable encryption of specific parts of a document.

Multiple Encryptions

Very closely associated with encrypting parts of a document is the ability to apply multiple encryption treatments to different parts of the same document. To illustrate the need for multiple encryption treatments, let us take a modified version of the *Patient Visit Workflow* example used in Chapter 6. In this example, we restrict our workflow process to one that occurs internally within the clinic and to the external insurance and credit card transactions.

The following diagram shows the workflow process that occurs when a patient visits for a physical check-up. As the patient comes for a check-up, the receptionist pulls out the patient record and sends it to the doctor's office. The doctor's office adds the medical observations to the patient's record and sends it to the accounts department for billing. The accounts department processes insurance claims and charges the co-pay to the patient's credit card account:

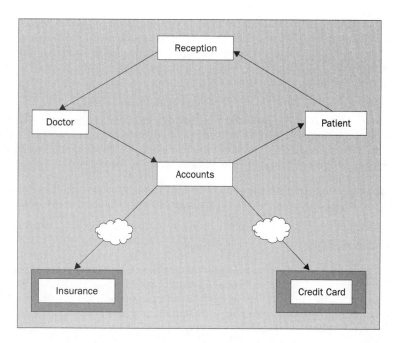

Let us assume the clinic maintains the patient record as a single document and that document contains administrative details such as insurance and credit information in addition to the medical diagnosis and visit details. The patient record appears as below:

```
<Patient name="John Gartner" id="548-61-3456">
  <Address>…</Address>
  <PreviousVisits >…</PreviousVisits>
  <Visit date="10/10/2002" id="TenthOctoberPhysical">
    <DoctorCheckUp>
      <Observation DoctorName="Vignesh Murali" id="TenthOctoberObservation">
        <BloodPressure>…</BloodPressure>
        <PatientComplaint>Right Knee pain</PatientComplaint>
        <Comments>
          Seems normal. Recommend Blood test and Kneecap x-ray
        </Comments>
      </Observation>
    </DoctorCheckUp>
  </Visit>
  <Insurance company="Cigna Health Care">
    <GroupPolicy>34567</GroupPolicy>
    <CoPay>10</CoPay>
    <Type>HMO</Type>
  </Insurance>
  <Creditcard type="Visa">
    <Number>1234 5678 9012 2345</Number>
    <Expiry>04-05</Expiry>
    <IssuedBy>MBNA</IssuedBy>
  </CreditCard>
</Patient>
```

While the accounts department needs the `Insurance` and `CreditCard` information of the patient to process insurance claims and co-pay, it is not necessary to expose the medical details of the patient to the accounts department. Similarly, the credit information need not be exposed to the doctor office. Though the workflow occurs internally, exposing all the details to all the processing points compromises security. It also pays to maintain such separation inorder to facilitate any future changes. For instance, it is not hard to imagine a situation where the clinic decides to outsource claims processing activities to a third party.

One way we could meet the above requirement is by splitting the `<Patient>` document into the medical part that has diagnostic information, and the administrative part that contains credit and insurance details. But is that a good solution? Imagine the problems it would cause in splitting them, putting them together when needed, tracking the related pieces, archiving, and retrieving those pieces.

Wouldn't it be nice if we could keep the whole document intact, and have the ability to enable different parties to view different portions of the document? The XML Encryption specification tries to achieve just that.

Persistent Storage

Encryption is not just a transport-level issue. Important details such as credit information are better left encrypted even in the back-end databases. Stories of security breaches into back-end data stores are quite common. The interactions shown in the above medical example are typically preserved for long periods of time. The ability to encrypt and archive data in place at different granularities and decrypt them as needed during retrieval is as important as transport-level encryption.

Web Services and XML Encryption

Web services impose their own set of requirements that cannot be efficiently addressed by the existing encryption solutions. These requirements are similar to those discussed in Chapter 6.

XML Representation

First and foremost, web services that are based on standard protocols such as SOAP and WSDL are characterized by their use of XML as a standard data representation and message format. It is not unreasonable to imagine web services implementations in which only XML tools exist. If encrypted messages are to exist as part of the message being communicated, it is essential and convenient to represent this encrypted content in a standard XML-based format. We would not want to tie up web services implementations that are based on open, standard protocols to any proprietary format for processing encrypted contents.

The existing encryption technologies do not provide a standard mechanism to represent the encrypted content in XML. By making it a goal to use XML syntax for representing the encrypted content, the XML Encryption initiative integrates encryption fully with the XML environment, forming a strong foundation for development of secured web services.

Multiple Parties

As explained in Chapter 6 in the section on *Multiple Parties*, applications crossing organizational boundaries and multi-party involvement are commonplace in web services. This makes it all the more important to support the various features discussed earlier, such as the ability to encrypt parts of a document, multiple encryption treatments to different parts of the same document, and the ability to persist the encrypted content without ad-hoc mechanisms.

XML Encryption Overview

Now that we are aware of the advantages of XML Encryption, let us take a closer look at the important aspects of the specification. In this section, we provide a higher-level overview of the basic syntax and core features supported by XML Encryption.

XML Encryption supports encryption of any arbitrary digital content including XML documents. In the case of XML documents, one could encrypt the entire document or an element or just the contents of an element.

In XML Encryption, the encrypted data is represented in XML format and is identified either by an <EncryptedData> element or by an <EncryptedKey> element. The <EncryptedData> element is used to represent any encrypted content other than the encryption key. If the encrypted data is an encryption key, it is represented using the <EncryptedKey> element. Both the <EncryptedData> and the <EncryptedKey> elements are stand-alone elements and can exist as a stand-alone XML document as well.

In addition to representing the encrypted content, XML Encryption enables one to represent other encryption details, such as the encryption *algorithm* used or the encryption key used along with the encrypted *content,* as part of the <EncryptedData> or <EncryptedKey> elements. Such ready availability of encryption details not only simplifies decryption processing, but also greatly simplifies applications from having to maintain any ad-hoc mechanisms to keep track of the algorithms and the keys used for every encryption.

XML Encryption does not define any new encryption algorithm for encrypting XML documents, but rather builds on existing algorithms and provides a standard representation format and processing model for encryption and decryption, enabling interoperable implementations.

Basic XML Encryption Structure

The <EncryptedData> and <EncryptedKey> are the core elements of XML Encryption. The basic structure of both the elements is the same except that the <EncryptedKey> adds a couple of *optional* elements. The structure of both these elements is shown below. In the following definition * denotes zero or more occurrences and | denotes a choice.

EncryptedData

```
<EncryptedData ID="" Type="anyURI">
  (<EncryptionMethod Algorithm="anyURI" />)*
  (<ds:KeyInfo/>)*
  <CipherData>]
    (<CipherValue> | <CipherReference>)
  </CipherData>
  (<EncryptionProperties/>)|
</EncryptedData>
```

The <CipherData> element is the only *required* element and it contains the encrypted content. XML Encryption permits the encrypted content to be carried in two ways. If the encrypted content is carried in place, it is carried as content of the <CipherValue> element, which exists as a child of the <CipherData> element.

XML Encryption permits the encrypted content to be stored at an external location and to be referred from a child element of `<CipherData>`. In such cases, the reference is carried under the `<CipherReference>` element. Ability to carry reference to the encrypted content is an important and useful feature. For instance, in our patient record example, the medical diagnosis of the patient may involve X-Ray and sonar images. Instead of cluttering the patient record with all these images, it makes perfect sense to encrypt and store these images separately and to refer to their encrypted form from the patient record.

The `<EncryptionMethod>` element is used to specify the *algorithm* used for encryption. The `<EncryptionProperties>` element is used for specifying any encryption-related detail that the application may want to convey to the recipient. For example, one could add the date and time information or details of the encryption hardware used using `<EncryptionProperties>`.

XML Encryption uses the `<ds:KeyInfo>` element defined in the XML Signature specification to carry the key information. Use of `<ds:KeyInfo>` is recommended only for transporting public key information. Note that the `<ds:KeyInfo>` element of `<EncryptedData>` is not encrypted, and unless you do not mind compromising security you would not want to transport any private or shared secret keys as part of the `<ds:KeyInfo>` element. In cases in which you need to send the key information but maintain secrecy, you can encrypt the key and send it as a stand-alone `<EncryptedKey>` element.

EncryptedKey

This is very similar to the `<EncryptedData>` element. The only difference is that the encrypted data is always the key value:

```
<EncryptedKey ID="" Type="anyURI">
  (<EncryptionMethod Algorithm="anyURI" />)*
  (<ds:KeyInfo/>)*
  <CipherData>
    (<CipherValue> | <CipherReference>)
  </CipherData>
  (<EncryptionProperties/>)*

  (<ReferenceList>
    (<DataReference> | <KeyReference>)
  </ReferenceList>)*

  (<CarriedKeyName/>*
</EncryptedKey>
```

The `<ReferenceList>` element provides a convenient mechanism for associating a list of data or keys encrypted using the key represented by the instance of the `<EncryptedKey>` element. The `<CarriedKeyName>` element is used to associate a user-readable name for the key value.

XML Encryption Examples

Now that we have got some basic idea about XML Encryption, let us use XML Encryption to encrypt some parts of our `<Patient>` element discussed in the patient visit workflow example.

Encrypting the Entire XML Element

In this example, we encrypt the entire `<Observation>` element of the `<Patient>` element, since we would not want the medical diagnosis of the patient to be available for everyone working in the clinic. We follow the process defined by the XML Encryption specification to achieve our goal. In most cases, you would probably use an XML Encryption implementation to do the job, but following the process manually gives a better understanding of the specification and the process involved.

The first thing we need to do is to select the encryption algorithm and the encryption key. The specification does not have any say in this and it is up to the application to make an appropriate choice. However, the XML Encryption specification defines a set of encryption algorithms and makes it a requirement for the confirming implementations to support some of them. If you are communicating with a third party it pays to stick with one of the required algorithms, because you can expect some guaranteed support irrespective of which XML Encryption implementation the other party uses.

In this example, we assume the clinic policy is to use one of the required block encryption algorithms called **Tripledes** and to use a shared-secret-key for encrypting the medical diagnosis.

The next step involves preparing the XML element to be encrypted. XML Encryption stipulates that XML content must be serialized into **UTF-8**-encoded octets before applying encryption. Non-XML contents need not be encoded in UTF-8 format though they must also be serialized into **octets**. In other words, any data that needs to be encrypted must be serialized into an eight-bit stream, and for XML data the eight-bit stream must be encoded in UTF-8 format.

In our case, we are serializing the XML element and hence we serialize the `<Observation>` element into a UTF-8 format. You can achieve this serialization using most of the commonly-available XML parsers.

The next step involves deciding on whether we want to include the key information and if so, whether we need to use an encrypted form of the key or just use it straight. Again, only for public keys does it makes sense to directly represent the key value. For all other keys, if they need to be transported they should be encrypted.

In our case, we use a shared-secret-key and the clinic policy is not to encode the key information as part of the encrypted content. This makes sense here because the clinic uses the same key for medical diagnosis and it is much simpler to store it safely somewhere else.

Now, we are ready to encrypt the `<Observation>` element. We typically need an encryption implementation here that will take the octets, the key, and the algorithm details and give us back the encrypted content. Let us assume such an implementation exists and the encrypted form of the `<Observation>` element with all its contents comes out to be something like ab*&%$x56dfeghrlksj.

The next step is to represent this encrypted content using the XML Encryption structure and to replace the original `<Observation>` element with the now created `<EncryptedData>` element.

The clinic represents the encrypted content of `<Observation>` in place and so we put it under the `<CipherValue>` element. Per XML Encryption, all encrypted content placed under `<CipherValue>` must be **base64**-encoded which results in the following:

```
<CipherValue>abjklekm=</CipherValue>
```

Adding the other required XML Encryption elements, we get:

```
<EncryptedData xmlns="http://www.w3.org/2001/04/xmlenc#">
  <CipherData>
    <CipherValue>abjklekm=</CipherValue>
  </CipherData>
</EncryptedData>
```

The above code snippet represents the encrypted form of the `<Observation>` element. This is the minimum required information per the specification. Looking at this, you cannot figure out much other than knowing that something is being encrypted using the XML Encryption specification.

The above information is probably enough if your application or organization follows the same encryption algorithm and/or you already know the data encrypted is an XML element or you use some ad-hoc mechanisms to store such information. Otherwise, you would typically want to make the `<EncryptedData>` self-contained as much as possible in order to facilitate decryption and further use of the decrypted content.

In this example, let us say we would like to indicate the type of the encrypted data and the algorithm used. Adding these details in XML Encryption results in the following:

```
<EncryptedData xmlns="http://www.w3.org/2001/04/xmlenc#"
               Type="http://www.w3.org/2001/04/xmlenc#Element">
  <EncryptionMethod
            Algorithm=http://www.w3.org/2001/04/xmlenc#tripledes-cbc"/>
  <CipherData>
    <CipherValue>abjklekm=</CipherValue>
  </CipherData>
</EncryptedData>
```

The `Type` attribute of `<EncryptedData>` indicates the type of the encrypted content. In the above example, the value of the `Type` attribute indicates that the encrypted content is of type XML element. XML Encryption defines some default values for all types of XML data.

Finally, we replace the `<Observation>` element with the `<EncryptedData>` element and get the following:

```
<Patient name="John Gartner" id="548-61-3456">
  <Address>...</Address>
  <PreviousVisits >...</PreviousVisits>
  <Visit date="10/10/2002" id="TenthOctoberPhysical">
    <DoctorCheckUp>
      <EncryptedData xmlns="http://www.w3.org/2001/04/xmlenc#"
                     Type="http://www.w3.org/2001/04/xmlenc#Element">
        <EncryptionMethod
            Algorithm="http://www.w3.org/2001/04/xmlenc#tripledes-cbc"/>
        <CipherData>
          <CipherValue>abjklekm=</CipherValue>
        </CipherData>
      </EncryptedData>
    </DoctorCheckUp>
  </Visit>
  <Insurance>...</Insurance>
  <Creditcard>...</CreditCard>
</Patient>
```

The complete details of the `<Patient>` element are not shown for the sake of brevity.

Encrypting the XML Element's Content

In the above example, we looked at encrypting the whole `<Observation>` element. It may make sense to keep the `<Observation>` element readable and just encrypt the content of the `<Observation>` element so that the accounts department may know and communicate to the insurance company the name of the doctor who attended the patient.

So, what do we need to change to make that possible? Essentially the encryption process remains the same with the exception that we serialize the contents of the `<Observation>` element instead of the whole `<Observation>` element. The representation also remains the same with the exception that we set the `Type` attribute of `<EncryptedData>` to indicate that we encrypted element content rather than the element itself.

Here is the changed `<Patient>` element in which we have just encrypted the contents of the `<Observation>` element. Note the change to the value of the `Type` attribute:

```
<Patient name="John Gartner" id="548-61-3456">
  <Address>…</Address>
  <PreviousVisits >…</PreviousVisits>
  <Visit date="10/10/2002" id="TenthOctoberPhysical">
    <DoctorCheckUp>
      <Observation DoctorName="Vignesh Murali" id="TenthOctoberObservation">
        <EncryptedData xmlns="http://www.w3.org/2001/04/xmlenc#"
                       Type="http://www.w3.org/2001/04/xmlenc#Content">
          <EncryptionMethod
               Algorithm="http://www.w3.org/2001/04/xmlenc#tripledes-cbc"/>
          <CipherData>
            <CipherValue>
              jklekm=
            </CipherValue>
          </CipherData>
        </EncryptedData>
      </Observation>
    </DoctorCheckUp>
  </Visit>
  <Insurance>…</Insurance>
  <Creditcard>…</CreditCard>
</Patient>
```

Encrypting XML Character Content

In the previous example, the `<Observation>` element is a complex element and has child elements. What if the content was just character data with no elements in it as the `<Comments>` element?

```
<Comments>
    Seems normal. Recommend Blood test and Kneecap x-ray
</Comments>
```

If we are to encrypt only the `<Comments>` element does the process change? Does the representation change?

Everything remains the same with the only exception that when the comments are replaced with the <EncryptedData> element, the <Comments> element is no longer a *simple* element as it now contains another element in it.

```
<Comments>
  <EncryptedData xmlns="http://www.w3.org/2001/04/xmlenc#"
                 Type="http://www.w3.org/2001/04/xmlenc#Content">
  </EncryptedData>
</Comments>
```

Encrypting the XML Document

If we choose to encrypt the entire <Patient> element we could do so using XML Encryption. The process still remains the same and so does the representation, with the exception of the Type attribute. XML Encryption does not define any special Type attribute value for XML documents. In this case, we use the optional MimeType attribute of <EncryptedData> to indicate the type of the encrypted content.

Here is what we get on encrypting the entire <Patient> element:

```
<?xml version="1.0"?>
<EncryptedData  xmlns="http://www.w3.org/2001/04/xmlenc#"
                MimeType="text/xml">
  <CipherData>
    <CipherValue>CB67AB56</CipherValue >
  </CipherData >
</EncryptedData>
```

Note that when the entire document is encrypted, the <EncryptedData> element becomes the root node of the new document. We use the text/xml MIME media type (RFC 2046) value to indicate that the encrypted content is an XML document.

Encrypting Arbitrary Content

XML Encryption is not restricted to encrypting only XML documents. Any arbitrary digital content, such as a JPEG image, can be encrypted using XML Encryption. The resulting XML structure of that encryption will be no different than the previous cases we have seen so far.

There are instances in which an XML element may refer to some arbitrary content or may contain arbitrary contents such as a JPEG image. Application of XML Encryption to such instances leads to some interesting possibilities showing both the strengths and weaknesses of XML Encryption. In the following discussions we show how XML Encryption could be applied to cases where an XML element refers to a binary JPEG image.

Let us assume that the <Patient> element contains some X-Ray images. It makes sense to store the images separately and refer to them from the <Patient> element. For the instance, original non-encrypted X-Ray image may be referred from the <Patient> element as below. Note the addition of <Xray> element to the <Patient> element:

```
<Patient>
...
  <Visit date="10/10/2002" Id="TenthOctoberPhysical">
    <DoctorCheckUp> ...</DoctorCheckUp>
```

```
        <Xray date="12/10/2002" TechnicianName="Robert Weldon"
              Id="TenthOctoberKneeXRay">
          <Image type="RightKneeCapFront"
                 ref="http://www.xlab.com/jgartner/12/10/2002/kneefront.jpeg"/>
        </Xray>
      </Visit>
    ...
  </Patient>
```

Since `<Xray>` is also part of the medical diagnosis, the clinic would like to keep it encrypted and refer to the encrypted image from the `<Patient>` element. There are a few ways of achieving this using XML Encryption. But before looking at XML Encryption options, let us see a way of referring to the encrypted image without using XML Encryption.

Option 1: Not using XML Encryption

We could choose to encrypt the `kneefront.jpeg` image using our own encryption algorithm, store it in a file named `EncryptedKneeFront.jpeg.enc` and refer to it from the `<Patient>` element:

```
<Image type="RightKneeCapFront"
 ref="http://www.xlab.com/jgartner/12/10/2002/EncryptedKneeFront.jpeg.enc"/>
```

The disadvantage with this approach is that we have to use some ad-hoc mechanisms to capture the fact that the `<Image>` element is referring to an encrypted image so we can appropriately decrypt it and use it. Also, since it is not based on a standard processing model such as XML Encryption you have to write most of the code yourself to de-reference, decrypt, and use the image. By using XML Encryption, you could rely on the XML Encryption implementations to do most of the job.

The advantage of this approach is that we have not made any alterations to the `<Image>` element.

Option 2: Encrypt the Element Containing the Reference

Your case may be such that the image at the location `http://www.xlab.com/jgartner/12/10/2002/kneefront.jpeg` itself is safe; so it does not need to be encrypted and all you care about is hiding that reference from the `<Patient>` element, preventing access to the image.

In that case, we could follow one of the above strategies of encrypting the XML elements and encrypt the whole `<Image>` element or encrypt the whole `<Xray>` element. The `<Image>` or the `<Xray>` element would then be replaced with the `<EncryptedData>` element and only when decrypted will one have access to the image. The following snippet shows encryption of the `<Xray>` element:

```
<Patient>
...
  <Visit date="10/10/2002" Id="TenthOctoberPhysical">
    <DoctorCheckUp> ...</DoctorCheckUp>
    <EncryptedData>
      ...
    </EncryptedData>
  </Visit>
...
</Patient>
```

Now you may wonder, if all we wanted is to encrypt the `ref` attribute of `<Image>` element why did we have to encrypt the whole `<Image>` or the `<Xray>` element? Note that XML Encryption does not allow you to encrypt just an attribute of an element and replace it with the `<EncryptedData>` element, since that would result in invalid XML.

Option 3: Use <CipherReference> of XML Encryption

The second option may not work in all cases because the image itself is not encrypted and hence can be accessed by someone. As a third option, we could follow part of the process followed in the first option, but use XML Encryption referencing features to refer to the encrypted image.

So as in the first option let us say the image is encrypted using the Tripeldes encryption algorithm and the encrypted form of the image is available at `http://www.xlab.com/jgartner/12/10/2002/EncryptedKneeFront.jpeg.enc`.

Using XML Encryption, we could represent this reference in XML Encryption format as below:

```
<EncryptedData xmlns="http://www.w3.org/2001/04/xmlenc#"
               MimeType="image/jpeg"
               Id="JgartnerTenthOctober2002KneeFrontImage">
  <EncryptionMethod
              Algorithm="http://www.w3.org/2001/04/xmlenc#tripledes-cbc"/>
  <CipherData>
    <CipherReference
URI="http://www.xlab.com/jgartner/12/10/2002/EncryptedKneeFront.jpeg.enc">
    </CipherReference>
  </CipherData>
</EncryptedData>
```

We use the `URI` attribute of `<CipherReference>` to refer to the remotely-kept encrypted data. Otherwise the representation of `<EncryptedData>` is similar except that we have added a `MimeType` to indicate the original datatype and have added a new `Id` attribute to associate an identifier to the `<EncryptedData>` element.

Now that we have provided a reference to the encrypted image using XML Encryption, how do we refer to this from the `<Image>` element?

There are at least two ways we could connect the above `<EncryptedData>` that represents the encrypted image to the `<Image>` element.

Add it as a Child of the Image Element

One way of adding the above XML Encryption of the encrypted image would be to add it as a child element of the `<Image>` element:

```
<Patient>
...
  <Visit date="10/10/2002" Id="TenthOctoberPhysical">
    <DoctorCheckUp> ...</DoctorCheckUp>
    <Xray date="12/10/2002" TechnicianName="Robert Weldon"
         Id="TenthOctoberKneeXRay">
      <Image type="RightKneeCapFront">
        <EncryptedData xmlns="http://www.w3.org/2001/04/xmlenc#"
                   MimeType="image/jpeg"
                   Id="JgartnerTenthOctober2002KneeFrontImage">
```

```
          <EncryptionMethod
              Algorithm="http://www.w3.org/2001/04/xmlenc#tripledes-cbc"/>
          <CipherData>
            <CipherReference
  URI="http://www.xlab.com/jgartner/12/10/2002/EncryptedKneeFront.jpeg.enc">
            </CipherReference>
          </CipherData>
        </EncryptedData>
      </Image>
    </Xray>
  </Visit>
  ...
</Patient>
```

This requires changing the *content model* of the <Image> element, which involves removing the ref attribute and adding a new child element.

Now you may begin to wonder whether you have to do all this manually or you could rely on an XML Encryption implementation to do the whole job for you. The following discussion is based on what is stipulated in the specification rather than what a specific implementation may support.

You may be able to expect the XML Encryption implementations to encrypt the arbitrary image and to provide an <EncryptedData> representation containing a <CipherReference> to the encrypted image. You may also expect the implementations to process the <Image> element that contains an <EncryptedData> with a <CipherReference> in it. All conforming XML Encryption implementations are expected to provide that support. However, altering the content model of the <Image> element will need to be done manually.

Note that if it were an XML element or an element content that is getting replaced with the <EncryptedData> element (as shown in *Encrypting XML Element* or *Encrypting the XML Element's Content* section), then you can expect the implementations to do that replacement job for you.

If the image existed as a content of the <Image> element as shown below, you could expect the whole process to be taken care of by some XML Encryption implementations:

```
<Image type="RightKneeCapFront">
   0x1235abced1234567abcdddddddccccaaaaafffffffeeeecccccccccccccccc
</Image>
```

But in our original example, the image is referred using a ref attribute and replacing that would require some manual coding.

Refer from the Image Element

While adding the <EncryptedData> representation of the encrypted image as a child of the <Image> element is one option, we also could keep the <EncryptedData> element in a separate document or as part of <Patient> and refer to it from the <Image> element using the same ref attribute.

In the following code snippet we keep all the <EncryptedData> representations of the encrypted images in one place under <EncryptedXRayImages> that exists as a child of <Patient>, and refer to the relevant image from the <Image> element:

```
<Patient>
   ...
<EncryptedXRayImages>
   <EncryptedData xmlns="http://www.w3.org/2001/04/xmlenc#"
                  MimeType="image/jpeg"
                  Id="JgartnerTenthOctober2002KneeFrontImage">
   ...
   </EncryptedData>
...
   <Visit date="10/10/2002" Id="TenthOctoberPhysical">
      <DoctorCheckUp> ...</DoctorCheckUp>
      <Xray date="12/10/2002" TechnicianName="Robert Weldon"
            Id="TenthOctoberKneeXRay">
         <Image type="RightKneeCapFront"
                ref="JgartnerTenthOctober2002KneeFrontImage">
         </Image>
      </Xray>
   </Visit>
   ...
</Patient>
```

The Id attribute of <EncryptedData> is used to connect the relevant image from the
<Image> element.

Encrypting EncryptedData Element

As XML Encryption permits different encryption treatments for different parts of the same XML
document, the XML document may end up containing more than one EncryptedData element. For
instance, the <Patient> element contains at least four <EncryptedData> elements when the
<Observation> element, the <Xray> element, the <Insurance> element, and the <CreditCard>
elements are encrypted.

In addition to encrypting specific parts for limited viewing, the clinic may decide to encrypt the entire
<Patient> element for enhanced security. Encryption of the <Patient> element may also be required
when the clinic needs to share and ship the <Patient> element to its partner clinics as the patient travels.
Can XML Encryption be used to encrypt content that already contains some encrypted contents?

Though XML Encryption does not permit the EncryptedData element to be a child or a parent of another
EncryptedData element, the actual data encrypted can be anything, including EncryptedData elements.
Encrypting contents that contain an <EncryptedData> or <EncryptedKey> element is called
super-encryption and during super-encryption, one must encrypt the entire EncryptedData element.
Encrypting only the content of the EncryptedData elements or selected child element is **not** allowed.

We already have seen an instance of super-encryption in the example on encrypting the
XML document.

Adding Key Information

This section provides an example of carrying key information along with the encrypted data.

Let us assume that the accounts department is processing the bills for the patient's visit and files a claim with the insurance company. The claim appears as below:

```
<Claim date="10-10-2002" clinicName="Vignesh Family Medicine">
  <Patient name="John Gartner" id="548-61-3456">
    <Address>…</Address>
    <Services>
      <Physical DoctorName="Vignesh Murali">
    </Services>
    <Charges>105.00</Charges>
    <GroupPolicy>34567</GroupPolicy>
  </Patient>
</Claim>
```

Since the claim is filed online, the clinic encrypts the `<Patient>` data and sends it as a SOAP message. The clinic uses the public key of the insurance company to do the encryption so that the insurance company can use its private key, known only to itself, to decrypt the data. To facilitate decryption, the clinic adds the information of the key it used. Here is the `<EncryptedData>` element along with the key information:

```
<Claim date="10-10-2002" clinicName="Vignesh Family Medicine">
  <EncryptedData xmlns="http://www.w3.org/2001/04/xmlenc#"
                 Type="http://www.w3.org/2001/04/xmlenc#Element"
                 Id="JgartnerTenthOctober2002VisitClaim">
    <EncryptionMethod
            Algorithm="http://www.w3.org/2001/04/xmlenc#tripledes-cbc"/>
    <ds:KeyInfo xmlns:ds="http://www.w3.org/2000/09/xmldsig#">
      <ds:KeyValue>
        <ds:RSAKeyValue>   ... </ds:RSAKeyValue >
      </ds:KeyValue >
    </ds:KeyInfo>
    <CipherData>
      <CipherValue>jklekm=</CipherValue>
    </CipherData>
  </EncryptedData>
</Claim>
```

Since we use a public key, it does not compromise security to send the key information unencrypted. Hence, the clinic uses the `<ds:KeyInfo>` element and directly encodes the key value to the `<EncryptedData>` element. The `<ds:KeyInfo>` element is defined in the XML Digital Signature specification. Refer to Chapter 6 for a discussion of `<ds:KeyInfo>`. The `<ds:KeyInfo>` element supports many ways of carrying the key information and in this example, the clinic uses the `<ds:KeyValue>` element to directly represent the key value.

Encrypting the Encryption Key

In the previous case, the key was a public key and hence it did not hurt to include the unencrypted key information as part of `<EncryptedData>`. If it is a shared key or a private key, we cannot directly encode the key information as in the previous case. As discussed earlier, XML Encryption can be used to encrypt key content as well, which results in the `<EncryptedKey>` element. In this section we look at an example of encrypting the key content.

Let's us say the clinic and the insurance company use some shared-secret keys to exchange data. To represent the information, the key is first encrypted. Here is an example of the encrypted key:

```
<EncryptedKey xmlns="http://www.w3.org/2001/04/xmlenc#">
  <EncryptionMethod
          Algorithm="http://www.w3.org/2001/04/xmlenc#tripledes-cbc"/>
  <ds:KeyInfo xmlns:ds="http://www.w3.org/2000/09/xmldsig#">
    <ds:KeyName>HMO Medical Claim Second Tier Key</ds:KeyName>
  </ds:KeyInfo>
  <CipherData>
    <CipherValue>jklekm=</CipherValue>
  </CipherData>
  <ReferenceList>
    <DataReference URI="#JgartnerTenthOctober2002VisitClaim"/>
  </ReferenceList>
  <CarriedKeyName>CIGNA-VIGNESH-FAMILY_MEDICINE-KEY</CarriedKeyName>
</EncryptedKey>
```

The process of encrypting the key is similar to that of encrypting any data content. The only difference is that in the case of <EncryptedKey> some additional information can be added.

In this example, we have added a <ReferenceList> element indicating the reference to the data encrypted by this key. The reference to the data is indicated by the <DataReference> element and the <EncryptedData> is identified by the <URI> attribute of <DataReference>. The <CarriedKeyName> is used to associate a label to this <EncryptedKey> so that it can be referred from the <EncryptedData> or <EncryptedKey> elements using the <ds:KeyName> element.

As you may note, the <EncryptedKey> element in this example also contains a <ds:KeyInfo> element. The information contained under <ds:KeyInfo> specifies the information of the key used to encrypt the key represented by the <EncryptedKey> element. Encryption of the key is a recursive process and the recursion stops either by using a public-private key pair or by communicating the key information through some other means.

XML Encryption Grammar

The examples in the last section provided an overview of XML Encryption and its associated syntax. In this section, we provide additional details on the major elements and cover other features supported by XML Encryption.

In the October release of the proposed recommendation of the specification, all the XML Encryption elements are defined under the http://www.w3.org/2001/04/xmlenc# namespace. The XML Encryption specification makes use of the XML Signature http://www.w3.org/2000/09/xmldsig# namespace and schema definitions.

To provide compact and readable examples, we make use of prefixes xenc and ds. The xenc prefix is mapped to the XML Encryption namespace, and the ds prefix is mapped to the XML Signature namespace as shown here:

```
xmlns:xenc="http://www.w3.org/2001/04/xmlenc#"
xmlns:ds=http://www.w3.org/2000/09/xmldsig#
```

The EncryptedData Element

As seen in the examples, the `<EncryptedData>` element replaces the encrypted content with the exception of encrypted key content. The following table lists all the allowed elements of `<EncryptedData>` in the order in which they appear:

Child Elements	Required	Max Occurrences
EncryptionMethod	No	1
ds:KeyInfo	No	1
CipherData	Yes	1
EncryptionProperties	No	1

Here is the attribute list of `<EncryptedData>`:

Attribute Name	Type	Required
Id	xsd:ID	No
Type	xsd:anyURI	No
MimeType	xsd:string	No
Encoding	xsd:anyURI	No

As seen earlier, the `Type` attribute is used to provide a hint to the decrypting application about the plain text form of the encrypted content. Though this attribute is optional, it is strongly recommended to define this attribute when the encrypted data is of type `Element` or `Content`. Note that without this information, the decrypting application will not be able to automatically restore the XML document to its original plain text form.

The identifiers for `Element` and `Content` are defined as:

Name	Attribute value
Element	http://www.w3.org/2001/04/xmlenc#Element
Content	http://www.w3.org/2001/04/xmlenc#Content

The example on *Use <CipherReference> of XML Encryption* shows the use of `MimeType`. The `MimeType` attribute is purely advisory and the implementations are not required to validate the values.

The `Encoding` attribute is used to specify the transfer encoding of the encrypted data. For instance, in the example on *Use <CipherReference> of XML Encryption*, if the encrypted X-ray image is base64-encoded, we can use the `Encoding` attribute to specify that information. The modified code snippet would appear as:

```
<EncryptedData xmlns="http://www.w3.org/2001/04/xmlenc#"
               MimeType="image/jpeg"
               Id="JgartnerTenthOctober2002KneeFrontImage">
```

```
                    Encoding="http://www.w3.org/2000/09/xmldsig#base64">
    <EncryptionMethod
               Algorithm="http://www.w3.org/2001/04/xmlenc#tripledes-cbc"/>
    <CipherData>
      <CipherReference
 URI="http://www.xlab.com/jgartner/12/10/2002/EncryptedKneeFront.jpeg.enc">
      </CipherReference>
    </CipherData>
  </EncryptedData>
```

The EncryptedKey Element

If your encryption is based on PKI or asymmetric keys, then there is no need to use <EncryptedKey> since there is no need to encrypt public keys. The <EncryptedKey> element exists for conveying **symmetric** keys that are shared among communicating parties.

The content model is similar to <EncryptedData> except that <EncryptedKey> contains two additional child elements and one additional attribute. Here is the table of <EncryptedKey> that shows the additional two elements:

Child Elements	Required	Max Occurrences
ReferenceList	No	1
CarriedKeyName	No	1

Here is a table showing the additional attributes of the <EncryptedKey> element:

Attribute Name	Type	Required
Recipient	xsd:string	No

The section on *Encrypting the Encryption Key* provides an example usage of the <EncryptedKey> element. As shown in that example, the <ReferenceList> element is used to associate the data or keys encrypted using the key from the <EncryptedKey> element. The <CarriedKeyName> element is used to associate a user-readable name for the key value. This is the name one would use to refer to a key from the <ds:KeyName> element, a child of the <ds:KeyInfo> element.

The reason for using a CarriedKeyName label as an identifier instead of using the standard XML ID type is to enable multiple occurrences of the same CarriedKeyName label within the same XML document, which is not possible with the ID attribute. However, note that within a single XML document, the value of the key associated with the same CarriedKeyName label must be the same. The real benefit of this lies in the ability to encrypt the same key value in different ways for different recipients.

The optional Recipient attribute is intended to provide a hint as to which recipient the <EncryptedKey> instance is intended for. This is useful where you encrypt the same key using different encryption standards targeting each <EncryptedKey> instance to a specific recipient. Refer to the later section on *Via ds:RetrievalMethod Element* for more discussion on the related topic.

The CipherReference Element

As seen in the examples, the `<CipherReference>` element is used if the encrypted data is at an external location. The location can be within the same document or at a remote location. The `<CipherReference>` element contains a URI attribute that points to the location of the encrypted data. In addition to this attribute, the `<CipherReference>` element can also contain an *optional* `<Transforms>` element that can be used to enumerate the steps the decrypting application needs to perform to obtain the cipher value.

Let us take another look at the example on *Use <CipherReference> of XML Encryption*. In that example, we referred directly to the cipher value of the image through `<CipherReference>`. Supposing the encrypted image at http://www.xlab.com/jgartner/12/10/2002/EncryptedKneeFront.jpeg.enc was base64-encoded after encryption, we would then need to base64-decode the image to get the cipher value. The `<Transforms>` element can be used to specify such transformations. Here is the modified `<EncryptedData>` with the `<Transforms>` element included:

```
<EncryptedData xmlns="http://www.w3.org/2001/04/xmlenc#"
               MimeType="image/jpeg"
               Id="JgartnerTenthOctober2002KneeFrontImage"
               Encoding=" http://www.w3.org/2000/09/xmldsig#base64">
  <EncryptionMethod
               Algorithm="http://www.w3.org/2001/04/xmlenc#tripledes-cbc"/>
  <CipherData>
    <CipherReference
URI="http://www.xlab.com/jgartner/12/10/2002/EncryptedKneeFront.jpeg.enc">
      <Transforms>
        <ds:Transform Algorithm="http://www.w3.org/2000/09/xmldsig#base64"/>
      </Transforms>
    </CipherReference>
  </CipherData>
</EncryptedData>
```

The `<Transforms>` element permits any number of transformations with each of the transformations specified by a unique `<ds:Transform>` element. It could be used to specify an XPath expression to identify the encrypted data in the remote XML document followed by a base64 decoding to obtain the cipher value. The `<ds:Transform>` element is borrowed from the XML Signature specification and follows the same syntax and rules defined in it. Refer to Chapter 6 for more details on `<ds:Transform>`.

The EncryptionProperties Element

The `<EncryptionProperties>` element is used to hold any additional details concerning the generation of `<EncryptedData>` or `<EncryptedKey>` elements. For example, it can be used to hold details like the date and time of the encryption or the details of the hardware used for the encryption or any other detail one may want to record about the encryption.

In the following example, we add `<EncryptionProperties>` to the `<EncryptedData>` structure we obtained in the *Encrypting the Entire XML Element* section:

```
<EncryptedData xmlns="http://www.w3.org/2001/04/xmlenc#"
               Type="http://www.w3.org/2001/04/xmlenc#Element"
               Id="XMLElementEncryption">
  <EncryptionMethod
```

```
                 Algorithm="http://www.w3.org/2001/04/xmlenc#tripledes-cbc"/>
    <CipherData>
      <CipherValue>abjklekm=</CipherValue>
    </CipherData>
    <EncryptionProperties Id="FirstExampleOfEncryptionProperties">
      <EncryptionProperty Target="XMLElementEncryption">
        <app:DateOfEncryption xmlns:app="I am an Application Defined Element">
          10-10-2002
        </app:DateOfEncryption>
        <app:EncryptionImplementation>
          IBM Security Suite
        </app:EncryptionImplementation>
      </EncryptionProperty>
    </EncryptionProperties>
  </EncryptedData>
```

The <EncryptionProperties> element contains one or more <EncryptionProperty> element. The <EncryptionProperty> element can contain any *user-defined* elements. The <app:DateOfEncryption> element and <app:EncryptionImplementation> element are defined in the application namespace.

Here is the attribute table for <EncryptionProperty>:

Attribute Name	Type	Required
Target	xsd:anyURI	No
Id	xsd:ID	No
anyAttribute	Any	No

As shown in the example, the Target attribute is used to identify the <EncryptedData> or the <EncryptedKey> element that is being described. The anyAttribute permits the inclusion of XML namespace attributes xml:lang, xml:base, and xml:space.

Carrying Key Information

As seen in the examples, XML Encryption makes it *optional* to carry the key information as part of <EncryptedData> or <EncryptedKey> elements. If you wish to send the key information along with the encrypted data, there are two ways of achieving it in XML Encryption:

❑ The key information can be specified via the <ds:KeyInfo> element, which exists as a child of the <EncryptedData> or the <EncryptedKey> element.

❑ The key information can also be specified indirectly by a stand-alone <EncryptedKey> element, which points to all the encrypted data that depends on it for decryption.

Let's look at each of these scenarios.

Using ds:KeyInfo to Carry Key information

As its namespace suggests, the <ds:KeyInfo> element is defined in the XML Signature specification. Refer to Chapter 6 or http://www.w3.org/TR/2001/PR-xmldsig-core-20010820/ for the details on XML Signature. XML Encryption uses the same <ds:KeyInfo> element to carry key information.

The <ds:KeyInfo> element provides many ways of carrying the key information. The XML Encryption specs recommend the use of ds:KeyValue, ds:KeyName, and ds:RetrievalMethod in all the available options.

The section on *Adding Key Information* provides an example of using ds:KeyInfo. As shown in the example, the ds:KeyValue is used to carry public key values.

Via ds:KeyName Element

The <ds:KeyName> element provides an indirect reference to the key. If you are using the <ds:KeyName> to refer to an <EncryptedKey> element, it is recommended that you use the value of the <CarriedKeyName> element of the <EncryptedKey> element as the value of <ds:KeyName>. Here is an example.

Let's say we have the following <EncryptedKey> already created:

```
<EncryptedKey xmlns="http://www.w3.org/2001/04/xmlenc#"
              Id="MyFirstEncryptedKey">
   <CipherData>
     <CipherValue>jklekm=</CipherValue>
   </CipherData>
   <CarriedKeyName>CIGNA-VIGNESH-FAMILY_MEDICINE-KEY</CarriedKeyName>
</EncryptedKey>
```

If we use this key to create the following <EncryptedData>, then <EncryptedData> can refer to this key through the <ds:KeyName> element as below:

```
<Claim date="10-10-2002" clinicName="Vignesh Family Medicine">
   <EncryptedData xmlns="http://www.w3.org/2001/04/xmlenc#"
                  Type="http://www.w3.org/2001/04/xmlenc#Element"
                  Id="JgartnerTenthOctober2002VisitClaim">
     <ds:KeyInfo xmlns:ds="http://www.w3.org/2000/09/xmldsig#">
       <ds:KeyName>CIGNA-VIGNESH-FAMILY_MEDICINE-KEY</ds:KeyName>
     </ds:KeyInfo>
     <CipherData>
       <CipherValue>jklekm=</CipherValue>
     </CipherData>
   </EncryptedData>
```

Via ds:RetrievalMethod Element

The <ds:RetrievalMethod> element provides an alternative way of referring to the key information. When the <ds:RetrievalMethod> element is used we refer to the key by its location using the URI attribute of <ds:RetrievalMethod>. Following is an example of using <ds:RetrievalMethod>.

Let us use the same <EncryptedKey> and the <EncryptedData> used in the previous example, but this time we'll use <ds:RetrievalMethod> to connect both the <EncryptedKey> and the <EncryptedData> elements:

```
<Claim date="10-10-2002" clinicName="Vignesh Family Medicine">
  <EncryptedData xmlns=http://www.w3.org/2001/04/xmlenc#
                 Type=http://www.w3.org/2001/04/xmlenc#Element
                 Id="JgartnerTenthOctober2002VisitClaim">
    <ds:KeyInfo xmlns:ds="http://www.w3.org/2000/09/xmldsig#">
      <ds:RetrievalMethod URI="MyFirstEncryptedKey"
              Type="http://www.w3.org/2001/04/xmlenc#EncryptedKey">
      </ds:RetrievalMethod >
    </ds:KeyInfo>
    <CipherData>
      <CipherValue>jklekm=</CipherValue>
    </CipherData>
  </EncryptedData>
```

Note the use of the Type attribute in the <ds:RetrievalMethod> element. When the URI attribute points to an <EncryptedKey>, the Type attribute must be set to the EncryptedKey identifier which is defined to be http://www.w3.org/2001/04/xmlenc#EncryptedKey.

The <ds:RetrievalMethod> can occur multiple times inside of the <ds:KeyInfo> element. In such multiple occurrences, all the referred EncryptedKey objects must contain the same key value. You may wonder about the use of this feature. It is possible that the same encrypted data is being sent to various parties.

For instance, in our case the clinic may file the same claim with the patient's primary and secondary insurance companies. When you deal with multiple parties not all parties may use the same encryption algorithms or the same encryption standards. In such cases, you can encrypt the same key using different encryption standards and create multiple instances of the <EncryptedKey> element and use multiple instances of the <ds:RetrievalMethod> element to refer to the different instances of <EncryptedKey> that all contain the same key value. The Recipient attribute of <EncryptedKey> comes in handy in such instances to specify the recipient name for each instance of <EncryptedKey> intended.

Via Additional Elements of ds:KeyInfo

In addition to the above three ways of relating the key information to <EncryptedData> or <EncryptedType> elements using <ds:KeyInfo>, XML Encryption provides two additional options by extending the content model of the <ds:KeyInfo> element.

Specifically, XML Encryption adds the following two elements to <ds:KeyInfo>:

❑   EncryptedKey

❑   AgreementMethod

Instead of indirectly referring to the <EncryptedKey> elements through <ds:KeyName> or <ds:RetrievalMethod> elements, the addition of the <EncryptedKey> element to <ds:KeyInfo> lets you embed <EncryptedKey> directly to <ds:KeyInfo> and thus to the parent <EncryptedData> or <EncryptedKey> elements.

Let us modify the previous <ds:RetrievalMethod> to use <EncryptedKey> directly:

```
<Claim date="10-10-2002" clinicName="Vignesh Family Medicine">
  <EncryptedData xmlns="http://www.w3.org/2001/04/xmlenc#"
                 Type="http://www.w3.org/2001/04/xmlenc#Element"
                 Id="JgartnerTenthOctober2002VisitClaim">
```

```
<ds:KeyInfo xmlns:ds="http://www.w3.org/2000/09/xmldsig#">
  <EncryptedKey xmlns="http://www.w3.org/2001/04/xmlenc#"
        Id="MyFirstEncryptedKey">
   <CipherData>
     <CipherValue>jklekm=</CipherValue>
   </CipherData>
   <CarriedKeyName>CIGNA-VIGNESH-FAMILY_MEDICINE-KEY</CarriedKeyName>
  </EncryptedKey>
</ds:KeyInfo>
<CipherData>
  <CipherValue>jklekm=</CipherValue>
</CipherData>
</EncryptedData>
```

The `<AgreementMethod>` element provides a way of deriving the shared-secret key information using the values contained under it. In other words, the `<AgreementMethod>` element does not carry the key values directly, but carries values that can be used to compute the shared-secret key value. The concept is based on a key agreement algorithm that enables derivation of shared secret key values based on a shared secret computed from certain types of compatible public keys from both the sender and the recipient.

Using EncryptedKey to Carry Key Information

In the previous section, we discussed the various ways of carrying key information using the `<ds:KeyInfo>` element, some of which also included using the `<EncryptedKey>` element. The `<ds:KeyInfo>` element is not the only way to attach the `<EncryptedKey>` element to the `<EncryptedData>` or `<EncryptedKey>` elements.

You may recollect that the `<EncryptedKey>` element contains a `<ReferenceList>` element. As discussed earlier, this `<ReferenceList>` element can be used to connect the `<EncryptedKey>` to all the `<EncryptedData>` and `<EncryptedKey>` elements encrypted by it. The section on *Encrypting the Encryption Key* shows an example of using the `<ReferenceList>` element of the `<EncryptedKey>` to link the key with the data encrypted by the key. Though that example shows a link to just one `<EncryptedData>` instance, note that you could have many references to both the `<EncryptedData>` and `<EncryptedKey>` elements.

Which Option to Use?

As you have realized by now, XML Encryption provides many ways of relating the key to the data encrypted by the key. Given the various options, which option would you use?

Some options serve a singular purpose. For instance:

❑ If you have the public key value, you use `<ds:KeyValue>` directly.

❑ If you have an indirect reference, such as a name of the public key, you use `<ds:KeyName>` or if you know the location of the public key you use `<ds:RetrievalMethod>`.

Some of the other influencing factors are that the `<ds:KeyValue>` provides the key value readily, while the `<ds:RetrievalMethod>` requires de-referencing the URI. On the other hand `<ds:RetrievalMethod>` enables you to keep the key value in one central place, thereby avoiding redundancy and giving you more control. The `<ds:KeyName>` reduces the bandwidth of the information carried, but requires a look-up. The support provided by the encryption implementation you use or the implementation used by the partner you communicate with would also matter here. For instance, not all implementations may support `<ds:RetrievalMethod>` for remote references.

When an `<EncryptedKey>` is used, one has the option of linking the encrypted data from the `<EncryptedKey>` element or linking the `<EncryptedKey>` element from the encrypted data. Also, note that nothing stops you from linking both ways. If the same key is used for many encryptions, collecting all the references to the encrypted data and/or the encrypted key under the `<EncryptedKey>` element provides central management and co-ordination. However, it does add some overhead since one need to maintain and update the reference information for each encryption. Also, decryption requires following the indirect references, which adds to the overhead. Linking the data to the `<EncryptedKey>` makes the key readily available for decryption, but may lead to some redundancy if the same key is used multiple times.

There are advantages and disadvantages to both the approaches, and a decision depends on your usage and the support provided by the implementation you use. Initiatives such as XML Key Management Services (Chapter 8 or http://www.w3.org/TR/2002/WD-xkms2-20020318) reduce the application complexity of managing encryption keys.

Encryption Guidelines for XML Documents

While XML Encryption makes it easy to encrypt XML documents at different granularities, working with XML documents requires some special care. More care is required in cases where an encrypted text is inserted into another document context. In this section, we focus on issues that are specific to using XML Encryption for XML documents.

Serialization Guidelines for XML Fragments

When an encrypted XML fragment is inserted into another XML document, it may not retain its original context on decryption if sufficient attention has not been paid to serialization prior to encryption. This section looks at the issues involved and proposes some serialization guidelines to preserve the original context.

Let us start with an example of the issue involved. Consider the element:

```
<foo>My name is Arul Murali</foo>
```

The `<foo>` element here exists in the empty default namespace in its original context. Imagine that the `<foo>` element gets encrypted and inserted as a child of another element:

```
<Bar xmlns="http://www.wrox.com/bar" />
```

When subsequently decrypted and parsed, `<foo>` will be parsed in the context of `<Bar>` resulting in:

```
<Bar xmlns="http//www.wrox.com/bar">
    <foo>My name is Arul Murali</foo>
</Bar>
```

What is wrong here? The `foo` element is now in the default namespace of `Bar` `xmlns="http://www.wrox.com/bar"` which is different from `foo`'s original empty default namespace `xmlns=""`.

This issue is common with empty namespaces because normal XML serialization mechanisms do not take any special care, assuming that the serialized data will be parsed in the same context where there is no default namespace. Realizing this, the XML Encryption specification proposes that serialization mechanisms add `xmlns=""` wherever appropriate when serializing XML fragments.

Based on this proposal, the serialization of `foo` appear as:

```
<foo xmlns="">My name is Arul Murali</foo>
```

When parsed in the context of `Bar`, we get:

```
<Bar xmlns="http//www.wrox.com/bar">
    <foo xmlns="">My name is Arul Murali</foo>
</Bar>
```

This maintains the original context of `foo`.

Similar issues can arise with `xml:base`, `xml:lang`, and `xml:space` attributes when an XML fragment is inserted into a new context. The suggestion made to the `xmlns` attribute does not apply to these attributes since empty value for these attributes is undefined or the context value may override empty declarations. Consequently, it is the responsibility of the applications to ensure serialized XML fragments end up valid in the parsed context by associating appropriate values for these attributes during serialization.

Encryption Guidelines for Arbitrary Data

Though XML Encryption works as well for arbitrary data as it does for XML documents, you must note that you can't expect confirming *implementations* to work with any arbitrary type of data. For example, you cannot pass an instance of your class from your favorite language to an XML Encryption implementation and expect it to encrypt that and give you an encrypted text in XML. Encryption and decryption operations are transforms on octets. Hence, it is the responsibility of the application to ensure that the data can be serialized into an octet sequence, encrypted, decrypted, and be of use to the recipient.

The only guaranteed support for types an application can expect from an encryption implementation (conforming to XML Encryption) is support for `Element` and `Content` types. For any *other* types, it is the application's responsibility to marshal the data into XML or into an appropriate octet sequence and provide hints to the recipient via the mechanisms provided by the `<EncryptedData>` or `<EncryptedKey>` elements. This way the data can be reconstructed at the recipient's end after decryption. Some of the XML Encryption mechanisms that can be used to provide such hints are `Type`, `MimeType`, and `Encoding` attributes of `<EncryptedData>` and `<EncryptedKey>` elements. The section on *Encrypting Arbitrary Content* provides usage example of these attributes.

Algorithms

The XML Encryption specification defines a standard usage model that includes syntax, identifiers, and requirements for a set of encryption and decryption algorithms that can be used with the specification. XML Encryption requires that some of these algorithms be supported by the XML Encryption implementations. Applications relying on XML Encryption for encryption are **not** restricted to use the algorithms defined in XML Encryption. Applications can use any algorithm of their choice and implementations can also extend on these specified algorithms. Since the specification requires that all the conforming implementations support a subset of these algorithms, applications are assured of guaranteed support of some of these algorithms.

All of the algorithms discussed in the specification are associated with an identifier. This identifier is to be used as the value of the `Algorithm` attribute of the `<EncryptionMethod>` element, as shown in earlier examples. All of the algorithms discussed here take *implicit* parameters, such as the data to be encrypted or decrypted, the keying material, and the direction of encryption (that is, encryption or decryption). Some algorithms may require *explicit* parameters. Such explicit parameters appear as elements with descriptive names and are algorithm-specific. The details of such explicit parameters are specified in the description of the algorithm.

It is not in the scope of this book to discuss the details of all the algorithms discussed in the specification. Instead, we provide a brief introduction to each category of algorithm and list the algorithms specified under each category.

Block Encryption

Block encryption algorithms work on chunks of fixed-size data with a key that results in blocks of encrypted text. One of the early encryption algorithms created in this category was the **Data Encryption Standard** (DES) block cipher. Later on, **Triple DES** was created, which was a minor variation on the original DES. Triple DES was a bit slower, but much more secure. Some of the other commonly used block encryption algorithms are IDEA, RC2, RC5, CAST, and Skipjack.

XML Encryption defines four algorithms in this category, out of which three are required to be implemented. The name, ID, and implementation requirements are provided below:

Name	Required	ID
TRIPLEDES	Yes	http://www.w3.org/2001/04/xmlenc#tripledes-cbc
AES-128	Yes	http://www.w3.org/2001/04/xmlenc#aes128-cbc
AES-256	Yes	http://www.w3.org/2001/04/xmlenc#aes256-cbc
AES-192	No	http://www.w3.org/2001/04/xmlenc#aes192-cbc

Key Transport

Key transport algorithms are public key encryption algorithms and are specified for encrypting and decrypting keys. Key transport algorithms can also be used for encrypting data, but they are not efficient for the transport of a large amount of data significantly larger than symmetric keys.

Their identifiers appear as the value of the `Algorithm` attribute of the `<EncryptionMethod>` element that is a sub-element of `<EncryptedKey>`, which is in turn the child of a `<ds:KeyInfo>` element.

Two algorithms are specified in this category, and both are required to be implemented:

Name	Required	ID
RSA-v 1.5	Yes	http://www.w3.org/2001/04/xmlenc#rsa-1_5
Name: RSA-OAEP	Yes	http://www.w3.org/2001/04/xmlenc#rsa-oaep-mgf1p

Key Agreement

Key agreement algorithms are used to derive shared secret key information from certain types of compatible public keys, from both the sender and the recipient. XML Encryption defines an `<AgreementMethod>` element to carry the information necessary to compute that shared secret key. As discussed earlier, the `<AgreementMethod>` exists as a child of the `<ds:KeyInfo>` element.

XML Encryption defines one algorithm under this category. Algorithms in this category require key **size** information. If the `Algorithm` attribute of `<EncryptionMethod>` does not contain that information, then the key size information must be supplied as a parameter:

Name	Required	ID
Diffie-Hellman	No	http://www.w3.org/2001/04/xmlenc#dh

Symmetric Key Wrap

Symmetric key wrap algorithms are shared secret key encryption algorithms specified for encrypting and decrypting symmetric keys. Their identifiers appear as `Algorithm` attribute values of the `<EncryptionMethod>` element that is a child of the `<EncryptedKey>` element.

Four algorithms are defined in this category, out of which three are required to be implemented:

Name	Required	ID
TRIPLEDES KeyWrap	Yes	http://www.w3.org/2001/04/xmlenc#kw-tripledes
AES-128 KeyWrap	Yes	http://www.w3.org/2001/04/xmlenc#kw-aes128
AES-256 KeyWrap	Yes	http://www.w3.org/2001/04/xmlenc#kw-aes256
AES-192 KeyWrap	No	http://www.w3.org/2001/04/xmlenc#kw-aes192

Message Digest

Message digest algorithms are used for computing a condensed representation of a message or any *arbitrary* data. The condensed representation is usually called the *message digest* or simply the *digest*. It also can be considered equivalent to calculating a **hash** value, a more common term used in programming.

These algorithms can be used in the `AgreementMethod` as part of the key derivation. They can also be used in the key transport RSA-OAEP algorithm as a hash function. The *HMAC* message authentication code defined in the XML Signature specification also uses this algorithm.

The specification defines four algorithms, out of which one is required and another is recommended for implementation. The required algorithm is **SHA1** and it is also the same one required by XML Digital Signature:

Name	Required	ID
SHA1	Yes	http://www.w3.org/2000/09/xmldsig#sha1
SHA256	Recommended	http://www.w3.org/2001/04/xmlenc#sha256
SHA512	No	http://www.w3.org/2001/04/xmlenc#sha512
RIPEMD-160	No	http://www.w3.org/2001/04/xmlenc#ripemd160

Message Authentication

This defines one XML Digital Signature-based algorithm for message authentication. It is optional for XML Encryption implementations. Refer to Chapter 6 for details on *Message Authentication* codes:

Name	Recommended	ID
XML Digital Signature	Yes	http://www.w3.org/2000/09/xmldsig#

Canonicalization

Canonicalization is the process of applying consistent *policies* to produce an identical textual representation format for a given XML document under any application context. Such policies are applied to the aspects of XML that can have a varying physical form without an impact on the logical form.

There are two kinds of canonicalization:

❑ Inclusive

❑ Exclusive

Inclusive Canonicalization

In inclusive canonicalization, the serialized XML includes both the in-scope namespace and the XML namespace attribute context from ancestors.

Two algorithms are specified under this category, which are mostly the same except that one includes comments and the other excludes them. If XML is to be encrypted and then later decrypted in a different context, and if it is necessary to preserve the original context for the decrypted XML, then the comments version of the algorithm should be used for serialization.

The details of the two algorithms are:

Name	Required	ID
Canonical XML without comments	No	http://www.w3.org/TR/2001/REC-xml-c14n-20010315
Canonical XML with comments	No	http://www.w3.org/TR/2001/REC-xml-c14n-20010315#WithComments

Exclusive Canonicalization

Exclusive canonicalization serializes XML in such a way that it includes only the minimum extent practical, the namespace details, and the XML namespace attribute context inherited from ancestors.

Similar to inclusive canonicalization, two algorithms are specified with one including comments and the other excluding comments.

The details of the two algorithms are:

Name	Required	ID
Exclusive XML Canonicalization without comments	No	http://www.w3.org/2001/10/xml-exc-c14n#WithComments
Exclusive XML Canonicalization with comments	No	http://www.w3.org/2001/10/xml-exc-c14n#WithComments

Exclusive canonicalization is the recommended method to be used where the outer context of a signed and encrypted fragment may be changed. Otherwise, the validation of the signature over the fragment may fail, as the canonicalization by signature validation would include unnecessary namespaces that may no longer exist, since the outer context of the signed fragment stands changed.

Encoding

One base64-encoding algorithm is specified for which the normative specification is MIME. The XML encryption specification only defines the ID for base64 encoding, which is the same as that of the base64 ID defined by the XML Signature specification.

In XML Encryption, the encrypted data carried as the content of the `<CipherValue>` element is base64-encoded and hence providing base64-encoding support is a requirement for the implementations:

Name	Required	ID
base64	Yes	http://www.w3.org/2000/09/xmldsig#base64

Relationship with the XML Signature

It is quite common in workflow scenarios to come across situations where encryption and signing operations may need to be performed on the same document. This combination could occur in any order and can be repeated for the same document. For example, some portions of a document could be encrypted first, then signed, and later the signed document could be subjected to further encryption even involving the previously encrypted portions.

To properly validate the signature, the recipient needs to decrypt only the portions that have been encrypted after signing; otherwise the validation would fail. To identify the signed-then-encrypted portions in a standardized way, the XML Encryption working group has proposed a **decrypt transform** mechanism. The main purpose of the decrypt transform is to propose a resolution to the decryption/verification ordering issue within signed resources, signed using the XML Signature specification.

This decrypt transform specification has been published as a separate document under a separate namespace URI: `xmlns:dcrpt="http://www.w3.org/2002/07/decrypt#"`.

This decrypt transform specification depends on the XML Encryption specification and the XML Signature specification. In this section, we look at this mechanism in detail.

Decryption Transform

The decryption transform is based on a simple concept. The specification defines a new `<dcrpt:Except>` element as a child element of the `<ds:Transform>` element defined in the XML Signature specification. The `<dcrpt:Except>` element contains a list of URIs of all the `<EncryptedData>` elements that have been encrypted prior to signing. The signature validation engine makes use of this list of URIs contained under the `<dcrpt:Except>` element in order to decipher which `<EncryptedData>` elements need to be decrypted and which are to be left as-is before commencing signature validation.

The `<dcrpt:Except>` element does not contain any child elements, but has two attributes. Here is the attributes table for `<dcrpt:Except>`:

Attribute Name	Type	Required
Id	xsd:ID	No
URI	xsd:anyURI	No

The URI attribute value must map to a non-empty document URI reference and identify `<EncryptedData>` elements. Note that the use of the `<dcrpt:Except>` element requires that the `<EncryptedData>` elements be identified by a corresponding Id attribute.

The next section provides an example of a document prepared for signing using the `dcrpt:Except` element.

Example use of the dcrpt:Except Element

Let's take the example we used in the *Adding Key Information* section. In this example, the clinic is filing a claim with the insurance company for the services provided to the patient.

Here is the claim filed by the clinic. Note that except for the `<Claim>` element, all the other data has already been encrypted:

```xml
<Claim date="10-10-2002" clinicName="Vignesh Family Medicine"
       id="JgartnerSignedClaim">
  <EncryptedData xmlns="http://www.w3.org/2001/04/xmlenc#"
                 Type="http://www.w3.org/2001/04/xmlenc#Element"
                 Id="JgartnerTenthOctober2002VisitClaim">
    <EncryptionMethod
           Algorithm="http://www.w3.org/2001/04/xmlenc#tripledes-cbc"/>
    <ds:KeyInfo xmlns:ds="http://www.w3.org/2000/09/xmldsig#">
      <ds:KeyValue>
        <ds:RSAKeyValue>
          ...
        </ds:RSAKeyValue>
      </ds:KeyValue>
    </ds:KeyInfo>
    <CipherData>
      <CipherValue>jklekm=</CipherValue>
    </CipherData>
  </EncryptedData>
</Claim>
```

For the sake of data integrity, authenticity, and non-repudiation the clinic decides to sign the claim before sending it to the insurance company. The clinic uses XML Signature for the signing and makes use of the `<dcrpt:Except>` element to identify the data that has been encrypted prior to signing.

Here is the signed claim that also includes the `<dcrpt:Except>` element:

```xml
<Claim date="10-10-2002" clinicName="Vignesh Family Medicine"
       id="JgartnerSignedClaim">
  <EncryptedData xmlns="http://www.w3.org/2001/04/xmlenc#"
                 Type="http://www.w3.org/2001/04/xmlenc#Element"
                 Id="JgartnerTenthOctober2002VisitClaim">
    <EncryptionMethod
           Algorithm="http://www.w3.org/2001/04/xmlenc#tripledes-cbc"/>
    <ds:KeyInfo xmlns:ds="http://www.w3.org/2000/09/xmldsig#">
      <ds:KeyValue>
        <ds:RSAKeyValue>
          ...
        </ds:RSAKeyValue >
      </ds:KeyValue >
    </ds:KeyInfo>
    <CipherData>
      <CipherValue>jklekm=</CipherValue>
    </CipherData>
  </EncryptedData>
  <ds:Signature xmlns:ds="http://www.w3.org/2000/09/xmldsig#"
                xmlns:dcrpt="http://www.w3.org/2002/07/decrypt#">
    ...
    <ds:Reference URI="#JgartnerSignedClaim">
      <ds:Transforms>
        <ds:Transform
         Algorithm="http://www.w3.org/2000/09/xmldsig#enveloped-signature"/>
        </ds:Transform>
        <ds:Transform Algorithm="http://www.w3.org/2002/07/decrypt">
          <dcrpt:Except URI="#JgartnerTenthOctober2002VisitClaim"/>
```

```
            </ds:Transform>
          </ds:Transforms>
        </ds:Reference>
        ...
      </ds:Signature>
   </Claim>
```

Note the presence of two `<ds:Transform>` elements inside of the `<ds:Signature>` element. Since this is an enveloped signature where the `<Signature>` element exists as part of the original data (`<Claim>` element), the first transform is used to identify and extract the data that has originally been signed.

The point of interest to us is the second transform where we identify the data that has already been encrypted using the `<dcrpt:Except>` element. Any more encryption that comes after this will not find a place inside of the `<dcrpt:Except>` element. The decrypt transform-enabled XML Signature implementation validating the signature can make use of the `<dcrpt:Except>` information to decide whether to decrypt the data before validating, or to leave it as it is. In our example, the message contains only one `<EncryptedData>` element which is being duly identified by the `<dcrpt:Except>` element. Using this information, the signature validation engine can skip the decryption part before validation.

Modes of Operation

The decryption transform supports two modes of operation:

- ❏ XML mode
- ❏ Binary mode

In the XML mode, the input data is an encrypted XML and the result of decryption is a node-set. The decryptions transform processed in the XML mode consists of two major steps.

In the first step all of the `<EncryptedData>` nodes that are not identified by the `<dcrpt:Except>` elements are decrypted. The decryption process will fail if the `Type` attribute of the `<EncryptedData>` elements is not `Element` or `Content`, or if it is absent or not known to the decryptor.

The second step involves canonicalization and replacement of the node-set decrypted in the first step. This canonicalization follows the guidelines (listed in the earlier section *Serialisation Guidelines for XML fragments*), ensuring proper inheritance of XML namespace attributes. After replacement, the entire document is parsed and a node-set is returned. In XML mode, the canonicalization and parsing occurs even if there are no decrypted `<EncryptedData>` elements.

In binary mode both the input and the result are in *octet* sequence. The binary mode of operation is intended for use when a signed binary data is to be encrypted before transmission to recipient. The processing steps of the decrypt transform in binary mode consist of decrypting all the `<EncryptedData>` elements that are not identified by the `<dcrpt:Except>` elements, child of `<ds:Transform>`. The decryption process decrypts the `<EncryptedData>` elements into an octet sequence without regard to their `Type` attribute value. The resulting octet stream will be of zero length if the document does not contain any elements of type `<EncryptedData>` that are not identified by the `<dcrpt:Except>` elements.

Restrictions and Limitations of the XML Mode of Operation

The XML mode of operation and its decryption transform processing imposes some restrictions and limitations.

First, care must be exercised when encrypting signed elements with respect to inheriting XML namespace attributes. If the serialization of the XML element to be encrypted does not include inherited namespace attributes on decryption, the same element may not exist in its original context. The signature validation will fail if the original context is not maintained during decryption and the replacement of signed elements as the signature was applied based on the original context.

For example, consider the following code segment:

```
<Document xmlns="www.vig.com">
  <SignedElement> ... </SignedElement>
</Document>
```

Assume that the signed element is later encrypted without inheriting the ancestral namespace, resulting in the following:

```
<Document xmlns="www.vig.com">
  <EncryptedData Id="ContainsSignedElement">... </ EncryptedData >
</Document>
```

On decryption we will get:

```
<Document xmlns="www.vig.com">
  <SignedElement xmlns="">... </SignedElement>
</Document>
```

The `<SignedElement>` no longer exists in the original context and hence the signature validation would fail. To rectify this, the canonicalization step of the decrypt transform is augmented to inherit XML namespace attributes from the parent context during replacement of decrypted text.

Care should be taken when assigning a URI reference value for the URI attribute of the `<dcrpt:Except>` element, as further encryption may cause structural changes to the document invalidating the URI reference. For instance, consider the following XML fragment:

```
<Document>
  <SignedElement>
    <Data1></Data1>
    <Data2></Data2>
    <EncryptedData Id="AlreadyEncrypted">...</EncryptedData>
  </SignedElement>
  <ds:Signature xmlns:ds="http://www.w3.org/2000/09/xmldsig#"
                xmlns:dcrpt="http://www.w3.org/2002/07/decrypt#">
    ...
    <ds:Transform Algorithm="http://www.w3.org/2002/07/decrypt">
        <dcrpt:Except URI="#pointer(/SignedElement/*[3]"/>
    </ds:Transform>
    ...
  </ds:Signature>
</ds:Document>
```

If the `<Data1>` element and `<Data2>` element of the `<SignedElement>` are encrypted together, we would get the following structure:

```
<Document>
  <SignedElement>
  <EncryptedData Id="Data1AndData2">... </EncryptedData>
  <EncryptedData Id="AlreadyEncrypted">... </EncryptedData>
  </SignedElement>
  <ds:Signature xmlns:ds=http://www.w3.org/2000/09/xmldsig#
                xmlns:dcrpt="http://www.w3.org/2002/07/decrypt#">
    ...
    <ds:Transform Algorithm="http://www.w3.org/2002/07/decrypt">
        <dcrpt:Except URI="#pointer(/SignedElement/*[3]"/>
    </ds:Transform>
    ...
  </ds:Signature>
</ds:Document>
```

The URI of the `<dcrpt:Except>` element will no longer resolve, as there is no third element inside of the `<SignedElement>`.

Super-encryption may cause problems if a super-encrypted `<EncryptedData>` element uses same-document references, or if a super-encrypted `<EncryptedData>` element is referenced by a non-bare name XPointer URI. Super-encryption of signed data under these conditions is not recommended.

The XML signature reference-processing model allows transforms to remove parts of a node-set undergoing transformation. The decrypt transform recommends that any such transforms appear before the decryption transform. Otherwise, encrypted data that is to be removed and cannot be processed by the recipient will cause the decryption transform to fail.

XML Encryption recommends that the `<EncryptedKey>` elements appear always as child of the `<ds:KeyInfo>` element, which in turn exists as a child of `<EncryptedData>`, when they fall in the scope of an XML Signature. This is because the decrypt transform considers only `<EncryptedData>` elements to be matched with `<dcrpt:Except>` URIs and decrypted, and does not include `<EncryptedKey>` elements in its scope. Hence stand-alone `<EncryptedKey>` elements are processed as any other data and are left in the document wherein `<EncryptedKey>` elements appearing within `<EncryptedData>` are decrypted and thrown away, leaving the original content intact.

Security Considerations

There are possibilities of introducing cryptographic vulnerabilities when combining encryption and digital signatures. In this section, we look at the security issues that could arise when encryption and signature are combined, and other security issues relevant to XML Encryption.

Plain Text Guessing Attacks

When a signed document is encrypted, the *digest* value of the signed resource still appears in clear text in a `<ds:Reference>` child of the `<ds:Signature>` element. It has been noted that such a signature may reveal information over encrypted data, increasing the encryption's vulnerability to **plain-text-guessing** attacks.

One way to overcome this problem is to encrypt the signature over the data in addition to encrypting the data. Though this solution works, in some cases the signature may be detached or already encrypted, and hence may not be able to be encrypted along with the data.

Sign What You See

Signing a previously-encrypted document is allowed and is considered as a legitimate process. However, one must not infer that a signature over the encrypted text is the same as a signature over its corresponding plain text form, or that the meaning of the signature over the encrypted data also applies to the plain text.

This principle of *Sign What you see* is important for the understanding and use of encryption and signature together, and it is similar to the XML digital signature principle of *Only What is Seen Should be Signed* (refer to Chapter 6).

Symmetric Key

When a symmetric key is shared among multiple recipients, that symmetric key should only be used for the data intended for all the recipients. One must bear in mind that even if the information is sent exclusively for a specific recipient, using the same-shared symmetric key may result in the information being discovered after decrypting it.

Application designers need to be careful not to reveal any information in parameters or algorithm identifiers that could possibly weaken the encryption.

Initialization Vector

Most of the encryption algorithms create the same cipher text for a given key and data. This invites attacks and can be mitigated by including non-repeating arbitrary data along with the plain text before encryption. In encryption chaining modes, this data is the first to be encrypted and consequently is called the *initialization value* or vector, IV for short.

Different algorithms and modes have further requirements on the characteristic of this information that affects their resistance to attack.

Denial of Service

By its design, the XML Encryption specification permits recursive processing. For example, an `EncryptedKey` may depend on another `EncryptedKey`, which in turn may depend on another `EncryptedKey`, and this may spiral into an endless loop. It is possible that an attacker might submit a document for decryption that requires constant redirection or that the decryption might require references to network resources that are very large. Consequently, it is left to the *implementations* to safeguard themselves by limiting the depth of recursion or by limiting the resources a request may consume.

Limitations

XML Encryption provides a standard processing model for encrypting and decrypting XML documents with other arbitrary contents and representing the result in XML. Such a standard representation format and processing model enables *interoperability,* facilitating easy exchange of encrypted documents. While XML Encryption addresses many problems in encryption and makes it easier to use in web services, it does have some limitations. In this section, we try to identify the limitations of XML Encryption.

The syntax and the processing model of XML encryption is complex enough that applications will find it hard to work with XML Encryption without a proper implementation support.

XML Encryption does not offer a standard programming API or a web service model for encryption and decryption. This could cause portability problems for applications that are cross-platform in nature, since the application code is dependent on proprietary vendor APIs.

Insertion of encrypted XML fragments in another context requires careful preparation of the XML document that may be missed by applications if proper implementation support does not exist. ID collisions are a possibility when encrypted contents generated in one context are dropped in another context.

Though the decrypt transform addresses the problem of mixing XML Signature and XML Encryption effectively, it comes with some restrictions that add to the complexity.

As seen in the example on *Encrypting Arbitrary Content*, in some cases the applications may have to make changes to their content model to work with XML Encryption.

Future Directions

XML Encryption is not yet a recommended specification. As of October 2002, it is in a proposed recommendation stage. Though the specification has been stable for some time it is still a work in progress, and if problems are seen one could see changes to the basic syntax and/or processing rules of the specification.

Given the fact that the specification is closer to being approved, the challenge now lies with the industry to provide interoperable implementations and user-friendly APIs that insulate the application from the complexities of working with XML Encryption. Initiatives such as XKMS already are focused on removing the ds:KeyInfo and the related PKI processing complexities out of applications. Not having to deal with PKI infrastructure will greatly simplify the use of XML Encryption, making it easier to roll out XML Encryption-enabled applications.

In addition to standard toolkits that provide an API and an implementation to work with, we may also see web services that provide encryption and decryption services. Availability of such web services is essential to promote lightweight plug-and-play web service applications. Such services also would facilitate development of encryption-enabled applications for memory-constrained devices.

Implementations

As a user of XML Encryption, you may more often work with an XML Encryption implementation rather than with the syntax of the specification directly. Though the implementations can be expected to insulate most of the syntactic details of the specification, it pays to know the details of the specification for effective use of XML Encryption.

Though XML Encryption has not yet reached a final recommendation stage as of October 2002, many XML Encryption implementations are already available.

XML Encryption Toolkits

Implementation in this group provides a programmatic API and algorithmic support to encrypt and decrypt XML and arbitrary content. Here is a list some of the encryption toolkits:

- ❏ IBM XML Security Suite (http://www.alphaworks.ibm.com/tech/xmlsecuritysuite)
- ❏ XML Security Library (http://www.aleksey.com/xmlsec/)
- ❏ Phaos XML toolkit (http://phaos.com/products/category/xml.html)
- ❏ Baltimore (http://www.baltimore.com/keytools/xml/)

Refer to Appendix A for a more elaborate list of toolkits.

Summary

In this chapter, we have seen what XML Encryption specification is all about and how it can be used to encrypt XML documents as well as any other digital content.

Encryption is a vital tool to support the security aspect of secrecy, as it provides tools that, when properly used, obscure the data so that those who are not authorized cannot easily read it. It can also support the aspect of integrity if message digests are used to provide a mechanism to detect attempts to tamper with message contents. This, along with XML Signatures, provides a crucial foundation for the secure exchange of data between web services systems.

8

XKMS

The XML Signature specification and the XML Encryption specification made it simple and easy to sign and encrypt XML documents, facilitating the use of XML-based web services for mission-critical applications. Processing digital signatures and encrypted documents involves working with Public Key Infrastructure (PKI) and its various formats. To simplify the integration of PKI and digital certificates with XML applications and web services that use them, Microsoft, VeriSign, and WebMethods jointly developed an open specification called **XML Key Management Specification (XKMS)**.

Later, this was submitted to the W3C, which started an XML Key working group to develop this further with other interested participants. This working group published a working draft of the 2.0 version of the specification on March 18, 2002, and it is available at http://www.w3.org/TR/2002/WD-xkms2-2002318/. This effort is still an ongoing one with a possibility of further changes.

In this chapter, we take a detailed look at the March working draft of the XKMS specification published by the W3C working group and the related **X-BULK** specification. We hope to provide enough perspective to help you understand all of the details related to this technology in order to use it in your applications.

In this chapter, we will cover these topics:

- ❑ Overview of XKMS and the problem space XKMS tries to address
- ❑ Detailed overview of XML Key Information Service Specification (XKISS)
- ❑ XKISS message specification
- ❑ Detailed overview of XML Key Registration Service Specification (XKRSS)
- ❑ XKRSS message specification
- ❑ X-BULK specification
- ❑ Security considerations and other limitations of XKMS

Key Management Issues

Having read Chapters 6 and 7, both XML Encryption and XML Signature involve the use of cryptographic keys. Though XML Signature allows symmetric keys, the concept of digital signing is generally based on asymmetric PKI and symmetric keys are rarely used. Though symmetric keys are prevalent in encryption, when the communication crosses organizational boundaries asymmetric PKI is the one that is used. Working with PKI is not for the faint of heart. In the following section we try to identify issues with PKI from the perspective of putting together a web service that supports XML Encryption and Signature.

PKI Complexities

Let us take a brief look at working with PKI for encryption and digital signatures. As discussed in the earlier chapters, PKI is based on public-private key pairs, where an organization owning the pair keeps the private key and distributes the public key to its partners. Partners wishing to communicate with an organization in a secured manner use the public key of the organization with which they wish to communicate to encrypt the message and send it through some transport mechanism. The target organization receives the message and decrypts it using its private key to get the plain text of the message.

In the case of digital signatures, the organization sending the document signs the message using its private key and then sends the message to its partners. The partners use the public key of the organization that sent the message to verify and validate the signature.

In short, this is how PKI works for encryption and digital signatures. This looks simple, right? Let us take a closer look to understand whether it really is simple or not. Since this book is about the security of web services, we use a web service example to discuss the issues involved.

Example: MyTravels.com

Let us assume we are tasked with developing a travel reservation web service such as Expedia.com. Let us call it MyTravels.com. As a travel reservation site, MyTravels.com deals with many partners that include airlines, hotels, car rental companies, and various package tour companies. The following shows a simple workflow that occurs between a few of the partners:

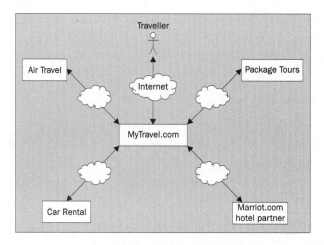

All of the reservation requests and reservation confirmation messages between the travel site and its partners are signed and encrypted. Here is one such SOAP message exchanged between the travel site MyTravels.com and its hotel partner Marriott.com:

```xml
<SOAP:Envelope xmlns:SOAP="http://www.w3.org/2000/09/"
               xmlns:Travel="http://www.myTravels.com">
  <SOAP:Header>
    <Travel:Request Type="Reservation" TransactionID="36ab70de"
                    Id="HeaderArulVigReservationRequestNov2002"
                    From="MyTravels.com"/>
  <SOAP:Header>
  <SOAP:Body>
    <EncryptedData xmlns="http://www.w3.org/2001/04/xmlenc#"
                   Type="http://www.w3.org/2001/04/xmlenc#Element"
                   Id="ArulVigReservationRequestNov2002">
      <EncryptionMethod
          Algorithm="http://www.w3.org/2001/04/xmlenc#tripledes-cbc"/>
      <CipherData>
        <CipherValue>jklekm=</CipherValue>
      </CipherData>
    </EncryptedData>
    <Signature Id="SignedArulVigReservationRequestNov2002"
               xmlns="http://www.w3.org/2000/09/xmldsig#">
      <SignedInfo>
        <CanonicalizationMethod
            Algorithm="http://www.w3.org/TR/2001/REC-xml-c14n-20010315"/>
        <SignatureMethod
              Algorithm="http://www.w3.org/2000/09/xmldsig#dsa-sha1"/>
        <Reference URI="#ArulVigReservationRequestNov2002">
          <Transforms>
            <Transform
              Algorithm="http://www.w3.org/TR/2001/REC-xml-c14n-20010315"/>
            </Transform>
            <ds:Transform Algorithm="http://www.w3.org/2002/07/decrypt"
                          xmlns:dcrpt="http://www.w3.org/2002/07/decrypt#">
              <dcrpt:Except URI="#ArulVigReservationRequestNov2002"/>
            </ds:Transform>
          </Transforms>
          <DigestMethod Algorithm="http://www.w3.org/2000/09/xmldsig#sha1"/>
            <DigestValue>j6lwx3rvEPO0vKtMup4NbeVu8nk=</DigestValue>
          </DigestMethod>
        </Reference>
        <Reference URI="#HeaderArulVigReservationRequestNov2002">
          <Transforms>
            <Transform
              Algorithm="http://www.w3.org/TR/2001/REC-xml-c14n-20010315"/>
            </Transform>
          </Transforms>
          <DigestMethod Algorithm="http://www.w3.org/2000/09/xmldsig#sha1"/>
            <DigestValue>EPO0vKtuyMup4Nbe=</DigestValue>
          </DigestMethod>
        </Reference>
      </SignedInfo>
      <SignatureValue>MC0CFFrVLtRlk=</SignatureValue>
```

```
      <KeyInfo>
        <ds:KeyName>
          http://www.mytravels.com/key?company=MyTravels.com&amp;department
          =HotelReservation&amp;CN=MyTravels HotelGroup&amp;
          issuer_serial=8e8934bcf3e469924936b42671bb9
        </ds:KeyName>
      </KeyInfo>
    </Signature>
  </SOAP:Body>
</SOAP:Envelope>
```

The body of the message is first encrypted using XML Encryption and then is signed using XML Signature. This fact is identified by the `<dcrpt:Except>` element, which is based on the decrypt transform specification defined in http://www.w3.org/2002/07/decrypt#. The signature is applied to both the `<EncryptedData>` element and the `<Travel:Request>` header element as indicated by the URI of the two `<Reference>` elements.

Let us take a look at the key processing activities that occur on both sides during this message exchange.

The sender MyTavels.com has to get the public key of Marriott.com from somewhere in order to encrypt the message and use its private key to sign the message. From where will MyTravels.com get the key of Marriott.com? It can be hard-coded into the application or come from a database. Hard coding is a **bad choice**. Database works, but MyTravels.com might need to check the validity of the key since it might have been revoked. To ensure it is keeping a valid key, MyTravels.com will need to constantly validate and update the database. Given the fact that a site such as MyTravels.com will be dealing with thousands of partners; does a database to maintain the key information sound like a good solution?

On receipt of the message, Marriott.com has to validate the authenticity and integrity of the sender. To do this, Marriott.com has to verify that the key sent via `<KeyName>` does in fact belong to MyTravels.com and is still valid. It'll probably need the help of a trust authority to do this verification. After authenticating, Marriott.com has to get the actual public key of MyTravels.com from somewhere to perform the signature validation. On successful validation, Marriott.com can decrypt the message and act on it.

A simple message exchange involves key information of the partners, management of the obtained key information, and trust authorities for key verification. Because all the partners are not going to use the same PKI implementation, to expand its reach, MyTravels.com has to work with most of the available PKI implementations, each having different syntax and semantics. Working with trust authorities involves dealing with their message exchange and communication mechanisms that may not be XML-based. This means MyTravels.com web service cannot be only based on SOAP, but must support various other protocols and data formats as well.

In addition, XML Encryption and XML Signature permit many ways of associating the key information along with the encrypted and signed data, and MyTravels.com would probably need to support all of these options.

Management of keys is no longer a small problem for MyTravels.com. It forms a bulk part of the implementation, requires PKI expertise, is no longer pure XML based, and leads to a big footprint application.

Implementation of MyTravels.com web service will be much simpler if MyTravels.com can delegate the key processing activities to a third-party. It will be even easier if such a service is based on the web services protocol, and is aware of XML Signature and XML Encryption syntax and their key processing semantics. With such a service, MyTravels.com can just hand over the `<ds:KeyInfo>` element and have the key value retrieved and validated, enabling MyTravels.com to focus on its business logic.

XKMS is designed to make such services a reality.

XKMS Overview

As stated earlier, XKMS is an initiative by the W3C (http://www.w3.org/TR/2002/WD-xkms2-2002318/) with the original input coming from an effort by Microsoft, Verisign, and WebMethods. The key objective behind the XKMS initiative is to enable development of XML-based **trust web services** for the processing and management of PKI-based cryptographic keys. By enabling the creation of such web services, XKMS hopes to remove the complexity of working with PKI, making it easier for web services (such as MyTravels.com) to incorporate security mechanisms into their applications. Applications can simply delegate all the PKI processing tasks to a third-party trust service instead of coding complex PKI functions themselves, and hence focus on their business logic. Delegation to third-party services reduces the *size* of the application, which enables the application to be used on memory-constrained devices.

To create such trust services, the XKMS specifies a protocol for registering, distributing, and processing public keys suitable for use in conjunction with the XML Signature specification and the XML Encryption specification. At a high level, the protocol consists of a set of pre-defined services, a standard set of message formats for each of those services, communication protocol bindings, processing rules, error models, and responsibilities.

XKMS provides direct support for XML Encryption and XML Signature. Applications such as MyTravels.com can simply pass the `<ds:KeyInfo>` element to an XKMS service to locate and get the key value referred by this element or to verify and validate the key. Though XKMS is closely tied to only processing the `<ds:KeyInfo>` element, the XKMS services are not. These services may be used for processing other key formats as well.

XKMS is designed to be implemented using standard XML tools. The message format of XKMS is in XML and is designed to allow use of SOAP for communication between the XKMS client and the XKMS service. An XKMS request from the client or an XKMS response from the server typically is embedded in the SOAP body. The XKMS services can be described using WSDL.

XKMS Services

XKMS-specification supports three major services:

❑ **Register Service**
The Register service is used for registering key pairs for escrow services. Once the keys are registered, the XKMS service manages the revocation, re-issue, and recovery of registered keys. The registration service supports generation of public-private key pairs. Alternatively, client-generated key pairs also can be registered. A key-pair needs to be registered before a user can locate or validate keys.

❑ **Locate Service**

The Locate service is used to retrieve a public key registered with the XKMS service. Location services accept `<ds:KeyInfo>` as their input and provide the client with the required information. The recovered public key may be used for further processing, such as signature verification or encryption.

❑ **Validate Service**

The Validate service provides all the functionality provided by the Locate service and in addition supports key validation. Applications can ensure that the public key registered with the XKMS service is valid and is not expired or revoked. The validation service also can assert the validity of the binding between different public key attributes.

Example using XKMS Services

Now that we understand XKMS at a high level, let us add XKMS services to the MyTravel.com example to understand the message flow and the interaction model of associating XKMS to an application.

In this diagram, we show the interactions that take place when MyTravel.com sends the encrypted and signed message, discussed earlier, to Marriott.com:

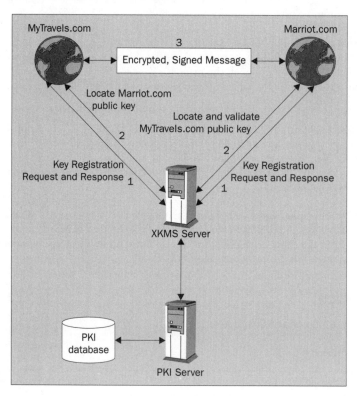

MyTravels.com no longer manages any key information and instead consults the XKMS service for key processing activities.

The process starts by both MyTravels.com and Marriott.com registering their key-pairs with the XKMS trust service using the Register service. After registering the keys, to encrypt the message to be sent to Marriot.com, MyTravels.com issues a Locate request to the XKMS server seeking the public key of Marriott.com. The XKMS server responds back with the key since Marriott.com already has registered its key with the service. MyTravels.com uses this public key to encrypt the message, uses its own private key to sign the message, and sends it to Marriott.com.

On receipt of the message, Marriott.com passes the `<ds:KeyInfo>` contained in the signed message to the XKMS service for validation. The XKMS service validates the key information and sends the status back along with the public key details of MyTravels.com. Marriott.com also uses the MyTravels.com public key to validate the signature.

The diagram below provides an architectural representation of the MyTravels.com application before and after using the XKMS services:

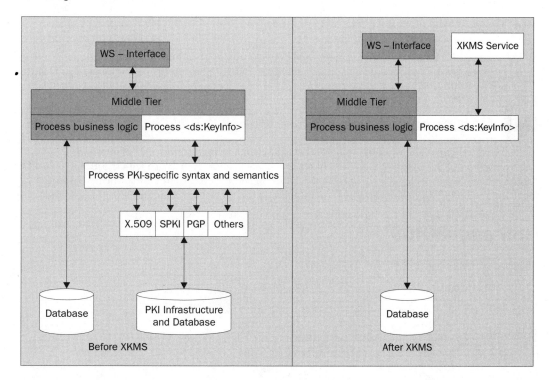

Adding XKMS services to the MyTavels.com application simplifies the implementation, making it possible to delegate the PKI processing to the XKMS service.

XKMS Benefits

The XKMS initiative provides several benefits. Some of the most important benefits are:

❑ XKMS *simplifies usage* of XML Signatures and XML Encryption mechanisms in XML applications.

❑ XKMS provides a simple, XML standards-based protocol for processing key information. This reduces the *learning curve* of understanding PKI semantics and eliminates the need to work directly with various, complex PKI syntax and semantics, enabling rapid development of trust features in XML applications and XML web services.

❑ By moving the complexity of managing PKI out to the infrastructure level, individual applications become smaller and simpler and with their security easier to verify as a result. The use of common PKI infrastructure will make it easier to attain *interoperability*.

❑ Use of XML vocabulary for representing PKI and support for WSDL and SOAP messages makes XKMS services to be platform, vendor, and transport-*protocol neutral*. XKMS fits into the developing web services environment smoothly.

❑ Since much of the processing takes place on the server side, XKMS may make PKI more usable on *small footprint devices*.

❑ Since XKMS builds a *layer of abstraction* between the application and PKI solutions, it makes it easier for the applications to support multiple PKI solutions and/or switch between different PKI solutions.

XKMS Namespaces

In the March release of the working draft, the XKMS schema is defined under the namespace http://www.w3.org/2002/03/xkms. In this chapter, we associate this namespace with the prefix xkms. The XKMS schema uses the elements defined in the XML Signature specification under the namespace http://www.w3.org/2000/09/xmldsig#. We use the prefix ds to associate with this XML Signature namespace.

XKISS and XKRSS

The XKMS is comprised of two parts:

❑ The XML Key Information Service Specification called XKISS

❑ The XML Key Registration Service Specification called XKRSS

The XKISS protocol deals with public key processing and validation, and the XKRSS protocol deals with key pair registration. We cover both of these specifications in the following sections.

XML Key Information Specification

The XKISS part of the XKMS specification deals with the processing of cryptographic key information associated with XML Signature, XML Encryption, or other public key usage in any XML-aware applications.

The XKISS protocol provides direct processing support for the ds:KeyInfo elements used by both the XML Signature and the XML Encryption applications. A client of XKISS can delegate all or part of the tasks required to process ds:KeyInfo to a XKISS trust service. By becoming a client of the trust service, the application is relieved of the complexity and syntax of the underlying public key infrastructure, which may be based on specifications such as X.509, SPKI, or PGP.

As seen in Chapter 6, the XML Signature specification does not restrict users to any specific trust policy. The ds:KeyInfo element, if present, may specify the key information through various means. For instance, it can contain either the key itself, just the key name, an X.509 certificate, a PGP key identifier, or a link to a location that contains the complete details of the key. The information provided in the ds:KeyInfo element may not be sufficient to perform signature validation, or the information may not be in a form the signature implementation can parse. The design of XKISS takes such constraints into consideration and provides a trust service that shields the client from all the complexities of processing the ds:KeyInfo element.

XKISS Services

A XKISS-compliant service supports two major operations:

❑ **Locate Service**
The Locate service provides the ability to locate and retrieve registered public keys based on identifier information. Specifically, the Locate service can resolve the ds:KeyInfo element and provide the client with the required public key information.

❑ **Validate Service**
The Validate service performs all of the operations performed by the Locate service. In addition, the Validate service can validate the binding of keys to identifier information.

The Locate service is defined as a Tier-1 service and the Validate service is defined as a Tier-2 service. XKMS also defines a Tier-0 service where the client itself locates and validates the key without the help of the XKMS service. This tier-0 service is similar to what MyTravels.com will need to do in the absence of an XKMS service.

XKMS has divided the service into multiple tiers, as not all applications may need all the services at all times. For instance, in our travel reservation example, when MyTravels.com needs to encrypt the message to be sent to Marriott.com, MyTravels.com only requires the public key of Marriott.com. No validation needs to be performed at that time. On the other hand, when Marriott.com receives the message from MyTravels.com, Marriott.com needs to verify the authenticity of the message. It is possible that some impostor claiming to be MyTravels.com could have sent that message. It is also possible that MyTravels.com originally sent the message but the message arrived late and the validity of the key has already expired. Hence, validation of the key information from the perspective of Marriott.com is important.

Another factor to be considered here is that the third parties offering these XKMS services may offer different rates for different services. Validation is likely to cost much more than merely locating the key information. That is another incentive not to combine both the services into one service and not to do validation when it is not necessary.

If you are wondering why validate service combines Locate service, note that the act of validation requires retrieving all the key information from the database and hence it makes sense to combine Locate service as part of validate requests. Also, it is more likely the key value will be needed after validation.

A client can expect the following processing from both the Locate and the Validate services:

❑   Handling of complex syntax and semantics, such as working with X.509 certificates

❑   Retrieval of information from directory and data repository infrastructure

❑   Revocation status verification

❑   Construction and processing of trust chains

Locate Service

The Locate service simplifies retrieval of cryptographic key information associated with signed and/or encrypted documents that are compliant with the XML Signature and/or the XML Encryption specifications. In specific, the Locate service resolves the ds:KeyInfo element of the XML Signature specification and provides the client with the information sought by the client. The information sought can be the key value, the key name, the X.509 certificate, or any such attributes bound to the key.

The ds:KeyInfo element may contain keys, key names, certificates, and other public key management information such as in-band key distribution or key agreement data. The ds:KeyInfo element does not restrict users to any specific PKI and so the information contained under the ds:KeyInfo element can be based on any PKI such as X.509, SPKI, or PGP. Moreover, the simple types defined for carrying key information in XML Signature may not cover all cases, leading to the possibility of applications developing their own identification and exchange semantics.

Providing for all possibilities of processing the ds:KeyInfo element for various PKI adds considerable complexity to an application that uses XML Signature or XML Encryption. Instead, the application can send such a ds:KeyInfo element to the Locate service and ask the service to return the required key value. The Locate service takes up parsing of the information contained in the ds:KeyInfo element and returns the client with the required information.

The Locate service limits itself to retrieval and does not validate the key. The service may resolve ds:KeyInfo using local data or may relay the request to other servers. For instance, the service might resolve a ds:RetrievalMethod element or act as a gateway to an underlying PKI based on a non-XML syntax.

Here is an example of a Locate service request and response message.

Locate Service Example

Let's say MyTravels.com has switched over to using the XKMS services. MyTravels.com checks the available trust services offered by various third parties and selects the trust service offered by, say, xkms.verisign.com. Refer to the implementation section on available XKMS toolkits and services.

To encrypt the message to be sent to Marriott.com, MyTravels.com constructs a request based on XKMS Locate request format and sends it to xkms.verisign.com. For this example, we assume that MyTravels.com uses a key name it obtained from Marriott.com through other means. As the public key is needed for encryption, MyTravels.com seeks the public key value of Marriott.com.

Though MyTravels.com uses SOAP as the message format, we do not show the SOAP message details here for the sake of simplicity. When SOAP is used, the messages shown here will exist as an entry in the SOAP:Body element. Also, the messages may contain SOAP headers detailing transaction information and such, and in some cases, the trust services may require the messages to be signed by the requesting parties.

In the following examples, line breaks have been added to ds:KeyName and ds:KeyValue for readability.

Locate Request

The LocateRequest element indicates the type of service requested. The details of the key to be located are contained in the KeyInfoQuery element. The Respond element contains the key information. The XKISS protocol defines identifiers such as KeyName that can be used to specify the key information required by the client. This example uses two such identifiers – KeyName and KeyValue – that exist as the children of the Respond element. The service is expected to return the requested key information. The service may return more information than that sought by the client:

```
<LocateRequest xmlns="http://www.w3.org/TR/2002/WD-xkms-2-20020318">
  <KeyInfoQuery>
    <ds:KeyName xmlns:ds="http://www.w3.org/2000/09/xmldsig#">
      http://marriott.com/key?company=Marriott&amp;department
      =OnLineReservation&amp;CN=MarriottCourtyardGroup&amp;
      issuer_serial=8eacea767bcf3e469924936b42671bb9
    <ds:KeyName>
  </KeyInfoQuery>
  <Respond>KeyName</Respond>
  <Respond>KeyValue</Respond>
</LocateRequest>
```

The Locate service obtains the key details associated with the given key name and sends a response back to the client with the information.

Locate Response

The following snippet shows the response sent back by the server:

```
<LocateResult Id="refId_0"
              xmlns="http://www.w3.org/TR/2002/WD-xkms-2-20020318"
              xmlns:ds="http://www.w3.org/2000/09/xmldsig#"
              xmlns:xkms="http://www.w3.org/TR/2002/WD-xkms-2-20020318">
  <Result>Success</Result>
  <Answer>
    <ds:KeyInfo xmlns:ds="http://www.w3.org/2000/09/xmldsig#">
      <ds:KeyName>
        http://marriott.com/key?company=Marriott&amp;department
        =OnLineReservation&amp;CN=MarriottCourtyardGroup&amp;
        issuer_serial=8eacea767bcf3e469924936b42671bb9
      <ds:KeyName>
      <ds:KeyValue>
        <ds:RSAKeyValue>
          <ds:Modulus>AMhGrU+nd5Qjx64IIDpfTBGfhLucJyEkuuz84GpTO3hEzV/o
              VTahCE3llS9PuxUuzRueRSET0S6fP/cypEtyX3M=
```

```
            </ds:Modulus>
            <ds:Exponent>AQAB</ds:Exponent>
          </ds:RSAKeyValue>
        </ds:KeyValue>
      </ds:KeyInfo>
    </Answer>
  </LocateResult>
```

The `LocateResult` element indicates that this is a response for the `LocateRequest`. The `Result` element provides a result code that indicates the outcome of the locate request. In this example, the success of the request is indicated by the `Success` result code. The key value requested by MyTravels.com is returned as a child of the `<ds:KeyInfo>` element. MyTravels.com can use this key value to encrypt the reservation request message to be sent to Marriott.com.

In this example, we got back only the information we asked for. The XKMS service also can send more information than that specifically requested by the clients.

The following diagram shows a representation of the message flow between the parties involved:

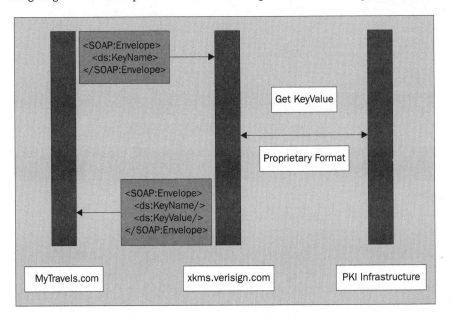

Validate Service

The Validate service provides all of the functionality provided by the Locate service and in addition performs key validation. The client can obtain an assertion from the service that specifies the status of the binding between the public key and other data such as the name. Furthermore, the Validate service asserts that the status of all the data returned to the client is valid and that they are all bound to the same public key.

Let's look at an example of an XKMS Validate service request and response formats.

Validate Service Example

We continue with the same example in which Marriott.com has received the encrypted and signed message from MyTravels.com. To validate the key, Marriott.com sends a validate request seeking validation of the key name binding and the validity status of the key value in order to ensure the key is still valid and not revoked.

Validate Request

Here is the code snippet of the validate request sent by Marriott.com. This request typically goes as a SOAP message, but the SOAP part is not shown here for brevity. Also, most trust services may require the validate requests to be signed:

```
<ValidateRequest xmlns=" http://www.w3.org/TR/2002/WD-xkms-2-20020318">
   <KeyBindingQuery>
        <TransactionID>
          b2c992f0-fb18-11d6-9031-d30cee2ed848
        </k:TransactionID>
      <Status>Indeterminate</Status>
      <ds:KeyInfo xmlns:ds="http://www.w3.org/2000/09/xmldsig#">
        <ds:KeyName>
          http://www.mytravels.com/key?company=MyTravels.com&amp;department
          =HotelReservation&amp;CN=MyTravels HotelGroup&amp;
          issuer_serial=8e8934bcf3e469924936b42671bb9
        </ds:KeyName>
      </ds:KeyInfo>
   </KeyBindingQuery >
   <Respond>KeyName</Respond>
   <Respond>KeyValue</Respond>
   <Respond>ValidityInterval</Respond>
   <Respond>KeyUsage</Respond>
   <Respond>Status</Respond>
</ValidateRequest>
```

The ValidateRequest element identifies that this is a request message seeking validation. The information to be validated is contained in the KeyBindingQuery element. This element allows for various other pieces of information to be carried along with ds:KeyInfo; enabling the client to specify the prototype of the assertion requested. In our case, Marriott.com attaches the <ds:KeyInfo> element it obtained from the message sent by MyTravels.com. Marriott.com uses the <TransactionID> element to associate a transaction number for this request for message co-relation. <TransactionID> helps to keep track of the messages, as Marriott.com may be dealing with the trust service making many such requests. In addition, Marriott.com adds a <Status> element seeking validity and specifying that the current known status is indeterminate.

In addition to seeking validation, Marriott.com seeks more information from the trust services via the <Respond> element. We already have seen the use of KeyValue in the <Respond> element. The ValidityInterval tag is used to seek the validity period of the key.

The KeyUsage field is used to seek the purposes for which the key can be used. Marriott.com will certainly respond to MyTravels.com with a confirmation message and will probably encrypt that confirmation message. If the KeyUsage field specifies that the same key can be used for encryption and if the validity interval is in range, Marriott.com can avoid another Locate request to the trust service to do the encryption.

Note that in this example, Marriott.com is seeking validity of the key before verifying the signature, since it does not have the key. If the message received from MyTravels.com already contained the public key value, it would probably be efficient to verify the signature before validating the key with the XKMS service because Marriott.com can save the key validation if the signature verification fails.

Validate Response

The XKMS service sends the following response for the validate request:

```
<ValidateResult xmlns="http://www.w3.org/TR/2002/WD-xkms-2-20020318">
  <Result>Success</Result>
  <Answer>
   <KeyBinding>
    <TransactionID>
      b2c992f0-fb18-11d6-9031-d30cee2ed848
    </k:TransactionID>
    <Status>Valid</Status>
    <ds:KeyInfo xmlns:ds="http://www.w3.org/2000/09/xmldsig#">
      <ds:KeyName>
        http://www.mytravels.com/key?company=MyTravels.com&amp;department
        =HotelReservation&amp;CN=MyTravels HotelGroup&amp;
        issuer_serial=8e8934bcf3e469924936b42671bb9
      </ds:KeyName>
      <ds:KeyValue>
        <ds:RSAKeyValue>
          <ds:Modulus>GfhLucJyEkuuz84GpTO3hEzVAMhGrU+nd5Qjx64IIDpfTB/o
              SET0S6fP/cypEtyX3MVTahCE3llS9PuxUuzRueR=
          </ds:Modulus>
          <ds:Exponent>ZDEF</ds:Exponent>
        </ds:RSAKeyValue>
      </ds:KeyValue>
    </ds:KeyInfo>
    <ValidityInterval>
      <NotBefore>2000-09-20T12:00:00</NotBefore>
      <NotAfter>2000-10-20T12:00:00</NotAfter>
    </ValidityInterval>
    <KeyUsage>Signature</KeyUsage>
    <KeyUsage>Encryption</KeyUsage>
    <KeyUsage>Exchange</KeyUsage>
   </KeyBinding>
  </Answer>
</ValidateResult>
```

The <ValidateResult> element indicates that this is a response for the <ValidateRequest>. The type of the KeyBinding element is the same as that of the KeyBindingQuery element in the request message. The KeyBinding element contains the details sought by the prototype KeyBindingQuery element. The KeyBinding element also contains the details sought by the Respond element in the request. The trust service returns back with the same TransactionID, making it possible for Marriott.com to do message co-relation.

The <ValidityInterval> element specifies time limits on the validity of the assertion. The time instances are interpreted as UTC time, unless time zone is explicitly specified. The <KeyUsage> elements indicate that the key can be used for signature, encryption, and key exchange.

Ensuring the Validity of XKISS Service Response

While the XKISS trust services validate the key information contained in the ds:KeyInfo element, the clients need to ensure and satisfy themselves that they are communicating with a genuine trust service, and that the response message has not been tampered with. The communication between the client and the trust service carries the same security vulnerabilities that exist in any network-based communication between two parties. In this section, we look at the issues involved and the XKISS ways of dealing with such issues.

The security issues involved are similar to any message exchange between two parties. Some of the possible issues are:

❑   **Authenticity**
    The response message received by the client is really issued by a trusted XKISS trust service

❑   **Integrity**
    The received response message has not been tampered with

❑   **Correspondence**
    The response received from the XKISS trust service corresponds to the request issued by the client

The XKISS specification does not mandate any specific security measures to deal with these vulnerabilities, though it does recommend one of the following options:

❑   Digital Signatures. Authenticating the response message using the XML Signature specification. The request message may also be signed if so required by the client.

❑   Transport layer security using protocols such as SSL, TLS, or WTLS.

❑   Packet layer security using protocols such as IPSEC.

In case digital signatures are used for validating the response, verifying the trustworthiness of the signing key is left to the application.

XKISS Message Specification

The Locate and Validate service examples already provided a glimpse of the XKISS syntax. In this section we discuss some of the major elements in the XKISS message set. As seen in the examples, the XKISS protocol consists of a pair of messages: the request message sent by the client to the trust service and the response message sent back by the service. The XKISS message set consists of a limited set of message elements defined under the xkms namespace. In the following definitions, the xkms prefix is mapped to the namespace URI http://www.w3.org/TR/2002/WD-xkms2-20020318.

The prefix xsd used in the schema definitions is associated with the XML Schema namespace http://www.w3.org/2001/XMLSchema. The XKMS specification makes use of elements from XML Signature. These XML Signature elements are associated with the prefix ds, which is mapped to the namespace URI http://www.w3.org/2000/09/xmldsig#.

Locate Request Message

As seen in the `LocateRequest` example, the request message for the Locate service is identified by the `LocateRequest` root element. The `LocateRequest` consists of the following child elements:

Child Elements	Required	Max Occurrences
xkms:TransactionID	No	1
ds:KeyInfoQuery	Yes	1
xkms:Respond	No	Unbounded

The `TransactionID` element is of type `xsd:string` and provides the ability to add an identifier to the request message. This could be used for message correlation at the client side.

The `ds:KeyInfoQuery` type is defined in XML Signature and its purpose is to enable inclusion of the `ds:KeyInfo` element, which is of the same type as `ds:KeyInfoQuery`.

The attribute table of `LocateRequest` consists of two attributes, which are used to specify the major and minor version numbers of the XKMS protocol:

Attribute Name	Type	Required
MajorVersion	xsd:integer	Yes
MinorVersion	xsd:integer	Yes

Locate Response Message

The Locate response message is identified by the `LocateResult` element. The `LocateResponse` consists of the following child elements:

Child Elements	Required	Max Occurrences
xkms:TransactionID	No	1
ds:KeyInfo	No	Unbounded
xkms:Result	Yes	1

The `<TransactionID>` serves the same purpose as in the case of `LocateRequest`. The `ds:KeyInfo` contains key details specified by the many instances of the `<Respond>` elements in the `<LocateRequest>` that correspond to the key referred by `ds:KeyInfoQuery` element in `<LocateRequest>`.

The attribute table of `LocateResponse` is similar to that of `LocateRequest` with the same semantics.

Validate Request Message

The Validate request message is identified by the `ValidateRequest` element. The child element of `<ValidateRequest>` is as follows:

Child Elements	Required	Max Occurrences
ds:KeyBindingQuery	Yes	1
xkms:Respond	No	Unbounded

The KeyBindingQuery element is used by the client to specify a prototype of the assertion required. The content model of <KeyBindingQuery> is same as that of the <KeyBinding> element discussed earlier. The <Respond> elements serve a similar purpose as in the case of <LocateRequest>.

The attribute table of <ValidateRequest> is similar to that of LocateRequest with the same semantics

Validate Response Message

The Validate response message is identified by the ValidateResult element. The child element table of <ValidateResult> appears below:

Child Elements	Required	Max Occurrences
xkms:KeyBinding	No	Unbounded
xkms:Result	Yes	1

The <KeyBinding> element contains the details of the assertion along with the information sought by the client via the <Respond> element. The Validate service returns a success result even if the KeyBinding assertion was found to be Invalid or Indeterminate. This is because the result code under the Result element indicates the success or failure of the *request* and not the status of the information returned for that result.

<ValidateResult> contains the same attributes as that of LocateResult with the same semantics.

Respond Element

The Respond element is part of the request message sent by the client to the service and it is used to specify the key information sought by the client. A single request may contain any number of Respond elements. The Respond element is of type xsd:string.

The XKISS protocol defines a list of identifiers corresponding to the children of the ds:KeyInfo element. The Respond element can contain one or more of these identifiers specifying the type of key information required by the client. The following table taken from the XKMS working draft dated March 18, 2002 lists all the identifiers that can be used as contents of the Respond element:

Identifier	Corresponding ds:KeyInfo element	Description
KeyName	ds:KeyName	Name of the key
KeyValue	ds:KeyValue	Public key parameters
X509Cert	ds:X509Data	X509 Certificate v3 that authenticates the specified key
X509Chain	ds:X509Data	X509 Certificate v3 chain that the specified key authenticates
X509CRL	ds:X509Data	X509 Certificate Revocation List v2
OCSP	ds:X509Data	PKIX OCSP token that validates an X509v3 certificate that authenticates the key
RetrievalMethod	ds:RetrievalMethod	Retrieval Method data
MgmtData	ds:MgmtData	Management Data
PGP	ds:PGPData	PGP key signing data
PGPWeb	ds:PGPData	Collection of PGP key signing data
SPKI	ds:SPKIData	SPKI key signing
Multiple		Specifies that the Trust Service *Should* return multiple answers to the client if more than one valid answer is available.
Private		Requests that the encrypted private key be returned in the response (Used in the X-KRSS protocol)

Result Element

The Result element is used by the response message to indicate the operational status of the request messages. This element is of enumerated type and the allowed values are as follows:

Value	Meaning
Success	Request completed successfully.
NoMatch	Service could not find a match for the search prototype given by the client.
NotFound	The given key is not registered with the service.
InComplete	Service could provide only part of the information requested.
Failure	The request operation failed.
Refused	The requested operation was refused by the service.
Pending	The request has been queued up for later processing.

KeyBinding Element

The `KeyBinding` element is used by the Validate service and the XKRSS Register service to assert a binding between the data elements that relate to a public key. This element is also used by both the Validate service and the Register service clients to specify the prototype for the assertion requested.

The element table of `KeyBinding` is given below:

Child Elements	Required	Max Occurrences
xkms:TransactionID	No	1
xkms:Status	Yes	1
xkms:KeyID	No	1
ds:KeyInfo	No	1
xkms:PassPhrase	No	1
xkms:ProcessInfo	No	1
xkms:ValidityInterval	No	1
xkms:KeyUsage	No	Unbounded

The `Status` element carries the assertion status and its value can be one of `Valid`, `Invalid`, or `Indeterminate`. The `KeyID` element specifies the URI identifier for the key and it is of type `xsd:anyURI`. The `KeyID` element is distinct from the `<ds:KeyName>` element, as `<ds:KeyName>` is not required to be a URI.

The `PassPhrase` element contains limited-use shared secret data generally established through out-of-band communication between the service and the client. The data contained in the `PassPhrase` element is a **Message Authentication Code (MAC)** output value encoded as a base64 string. The `PassPhrase` element is defined to be of type `xsd:string`.

The `ProcessInfo` element is used to specify the processing information associated with a key binding. The client should treat the data contained in `ProcessInfo` as opaque data.

As discussed in the Validate response example, the `ValidityInterval` element is used to specify time limits on the validity of the assertion. The `NotBefore` attribute specifies the time instant at which the validity interval begins. The `NotOnOrAfter` attribute indicates the time instant at which the validity interval ends. Omission of the `NotBefore` attribute indicates that the assertion is valid from any date up to the expiry date specified by the `NotOnOrAfter` attribute. If `NotOnOrAfter` is omitted, the assertion has no expiry. Omission of both the attributes indicates that the assertions are valid at any time. All time instances are considered to be in UTC unless specified.

The `KeyUsage` element is used to specify one or more intended uses of the key. The `KeyUsage` element is of *enumerated* type and the allowed values are `Encryption`, `Signature`, and `Exchange`. The `Encryption` value indicates that the key pair may be used for encryption and decryption. The `Signature` value indicates that the key may be used for signature and verification. The `Exchange` value indicates that the key pair may be used for key exchange. Omission of the `KeyUsage` element indicates that all key uses are permitted.

The `<KeyBinding>` element contains one `Id` attribute of type `xsd:ID` that is used to associate an identifier to `<KeyBinding>`.

XML Key Registration Specification

The XKRSS part of the XKMS specification defines a set of services that provide *support* for registration and further management of the public key information. The goal of the XKRSS specification is to respond to the need for a complete XML-based key life cycle management protocol. The existing *certificate management protocols* such as PKIX either focus on support of a single part of the certificate life cycle, such as certificate issuance, or are considered too complex for the lightweight XML-based applications.

The XKRSS specification supports the entire certificate life cycle by providing support for the following four operations in a single compact specification:

❑ **Register**
  The Register service binds information to a public key pair through a key binding. The information bound may be a name or an identifier or extended attributes defined by the XKRSS implementation.

❑ **Reissue**
  The Reissue service reissues a previously-registered key binding.

❑ **Revoke**
  The Revoke service revokes previously-registered key binding.

❑ **Recover**
  The Recover service recovers the private key associated with a key binding.

Key Registration

Registration is an act of binding information to a public key pair. In the registration phase, an XML application key pair holder registers its public key with the trusted infrastructure via a registration server. The XKRSS protocol defines a registration service and a set of request-response message formats to facilitate registration. To register, an XML application holding the key pair typically sends a signed request using the XKRSS request format to the XKRSS-compliant registration service. The registration service responds with an XKRSS response format confirming the status of the registration if successful, a confirmation is sent that has the name and attribute information registered with the public key. Note that sending a signed request is not the only way to authenticate the request. Request authentication is covered in more detail later in the *Request Authentication* section.

The public key pair that is being registered may be generated by the client or by the service. The protocol provides a proof-of-possession (POP) of the private key in cases where the client generated the key pair. When registering a digital signature key pair, using the corresponding private key to digitally sign the registration request acts as a proof-of-possession. However, with other types of key pairs, a separate proof-of-possession may be needed. When the key pair is generated by the service, the protocol communicates the private key to the client.

The registration request message consists of a prototype of the requested assertion. The registration service may seek more information from the client to authenticate the request. In the case of a client-generated key pair, the service may require proof-of-possession of the key. On receipt of a registration request, the registration service verifies the authentication and POP information provided. The registration service generates an assertion once the request is accepted. This assertion may include none, some, or all of the information provided by the prototype assertion of the client and may include additional information. The registration service may return part or all of the registered assertion to the client.

Let's look at an example of a register service.

Example: Client-Generated Key Pair

This example shows registration of a client-generated key pair building on the same travel reservation example used for Locate and Validate requests. For MyTravels.com to successfully locate the public key of Marriott.com in the xkms.verisign.com trust service, Marriott.com must successfully registered its public key pair with the xkms.verisign.com service. Similarly, MyTravels.com must have the same registration prior to Marriott.com's validate request.

In this example we show both the request message sent by Mytravels.com to register its key-pair, and the response message sent back by the server.

Registration Request

For this request, we assume that MyTravels.com has already been authenticated through different means and is using a key given by the trust service to authenticate the request.

The following snippet shows the XKRSS Register service request message:

```
<RegisterRequest xmlns="http://www.w3.org/TR/2002/WD-xkms-2-20020318"
                 xmlns:ds="http://www.w3.org/2000/09/xmldsig#">
  <Prototype Id="MyTravelskeybinding">
    <TransactionID>
      46156c70-fb21-11d6-98bd-ad2b2ae62770
    </TransactionID>
    <Status>Valid</Status>
    <ds:KeyInfo >
     <ds:KeyName>
       http://www.mytravels.com/key?company=MyTravels.com&amp;department
       =HotelReservation&amp;CN=MyTravels HotelGroup&amp;
     </ds:KeyName>
     <ds:KeyValue>
       <ds:RSAKeyValue>
         <ds:Modulus>GfhLucJyEkuuz84GpTO3hEzVAMhGrU+nd5Qjx64IIDpfTB/o
             SET0S6fP/cypEtyX3MVTahCE3llS9PuxUuzRueR=
         </ds:Modulus>
         <ds:Exponent>ZDEF</ds:Exponent>
       </ds:RSAKeyValue>
     </ds:KeyValue>
    </ds:KeyInfo>
    <PassPhrase>5WlbatFFQ/8s4gaBqEEFfULVFYc=</PassPhrase>
    <KeyUsage>Signature</KeyUsage>
    <KeyUsage>Encryption</KeyUsage>
    <KeyUsage>Exchange</KeyUsage>
  </Prototype>
  <AuthInfo>
```

```
        <AuthUserInfo>
          <ProofOfPossession>
            <ds:Signature>
              ...
              <ds:Reference URI="MyTravelsjeybinding">...</ds:Reference>
              ...
            </ds:Signature>
          </ProofOfPossession>
          <KeyBindingAuth>
            <ds:Signature>
              ....
              <ds:Reference URI="MyTravelsjeybinding">...</ds:Reference>
              ....
            </ds:Signature>
          </KeyBindingAuth>
        </AuthUserInfo>
      </AuthInfo>
      <Respond>KeyName</Respond>
      <Respond>KeyValue<Respond>
      <Respond>RetrievalMethod</Respond>
    </RegisterRequest >
```

The registration request is identified by the `RegisterRequest` element. Since this request is registering a client-generated key pair, it includes the full details of the key that exists as part of the `ds:KeyInfo` element. The contents of the `PassPhrase` element can be used to re-authenticate the client for any further key management operations, such as revocation of the key. In the example, the `PassPhrase` contains encrypted content.

When registering key-pairs, clients need to authenticate themselves to the trust service. The `<AuthInfo>` element contains the authentication information. The `<AuthUserInfo>` element contains user-specific authentication information. As stated earlier, MyTravels.com uses a key previously established with the trust service to authenticate the request. MyTravels.com uses this key and signs the `<Protototype>` element and represents the resulting `<Signature>` under the `<KeyBindingAuth>` element. We do not show the complete `<Signature>` element for brevity.

Since this request is for registering a client-generated key pair, the trust services may require the proof-of-possession of the private key. In this example, proof-of-possession is provided by MyTravels.com signing the `<Prototype>` element using its private key. Trust services accept digital signatures using the private key of the public key being registered as proof-of-possession.

The registration request also specifies the type of usage allowed for the key being registered through the `<KeyUsage>` element. The other elements, such as `<Respond>` and `<TransactionID>`, serve the same purpose as in the case of Locate requests.

Registration Response

The trust service responds back with a successful response. Here is the response message sent back by the server:

```
<RegisterResult xmlns="http://www.w3.org/TR/2002/WD-xkms-2-20020318">
  <Result>Success</Result>
  <Answer>
    <KeyBinding>
      <TransactionID>
        46156c70-fb21-11d6-98bd-ad2b2ae62770
```

```
          </TransactionID>
          <Status>Valid</Status>
          <KeyID>http://www.MyTravels.com/key?company=MyTravels.com&amp;
            department=HotelReservation&amp;CN=MyTravels HotelGroup&amp;
            issuer_serial=8e8934bcf3e469924936b42671bb9
          </KeyID>
          <ds:KeyInfo xmlns:ds="http://www.w3.org/2000/09/xmldsig#">
            <ds:KeyName>
              http://www.mytravels.com/key?company=MyTravels.com&amp;department
              =HotelReservation&amp;CN=MyTravels HotelGroup&amp;
              issuer_serial=8e8934bcf3e469924936b42671bb9
            </ds:KeyName>
            <ds:RetrievalMethod
                      Type="http://www.w3.org/2000/09/xmldsig#RSAKeyValue"
             URI="http://xkms.verisign.com/MyTravels.com&CN=MyTravelsHotelGorup
             &issuer_serial="8e8934bcf3e469924936b42671bb9"/>
            <ds:KeyValue>
              <ds:RSAKeyValue>
                <ds:Modulus>GfhLucJyEkuuz84GpTO3hEzVAMhGrU+nd5Qjx64IIDpfTB/o
                    SET0S6fP/cypEtyX3MVTahCE3llS9PuxUuzRueR=
                </ds:Modulus>
                <ds:Exponent>ZDEF</ds:Exponent>
              </ds:RSAKeyValue>
            </ds:KeyValue>
          </ds:KeyInfo>
          <KeyUsage>Signature</KeyUsage>
          <KeyUsage>Encryption</KeyUsage>
          <KeyUsage>Exchange</KeyUsage>
        </KeyBinding>
      </Answer>
    </RegisterResult>
```

The response for the register request is identified by the `RegisterResult` element. The `KeyBinding` element contains the details sought by the request. The service adds some more information than that asked by the client.

The trust service has associated a `<KeyID>` element with the key. A `<KeyID>` element is an alternative way to refer to the key and in most respects is similar to the `<ds:KeyName>`. The difference is that `<KeyID>` is required to be a URI wherein `<ds:KeyName>` can be any string. In our example, we use the value of the `<ds:KeyName>` as `<KeyID>`. The `<ds:RetrievalMethod>` points to the location of the key and specifies the type of the data being pointed at.

The other elements in the message carry the same semantics as in the previous cases.

Service-Generated Key Pair

The previous example used a *client-generated* key pair. As discussed earlier, trust services can also generate the key pair and return the pair to the requester. In the case of a service-generated key pair, the format of the registration request and the response remains the *same*, though the data exchanged differs. The request does not include any public key values though the requester may specify values for `KeyId` and `KeyName` elements. Proof-of-possession is also *not* required. The response would typically contain an encrypted form of the generated private key. The client can also specifically ask for the private key information using the `<Respond>Private</Respond>` element. The service would return the private key in an encrypted form for safety.

In the case of *server-generated* key pairs, instead of using the `<AuthUserInfo>` element to authenticate the user, one should use the `<AuthServerInfo>` element. Both `AuthUserInfo` and `AuthServerInfo` are similar except that `<AuthServerInfo>` does not require `<ProofOfPossession>` since the client does not yet possess the key.

We do not show an example message here because the format remains the same except for the above-discussed points.

Key Reissue

A registration service may permit clients to reissue previously issued assertions. A reissue request follows the similar procedure used for initial registration. The principal reason for reissue is to cause the registration service to create new credentials in the underlying PKI.

Key Revocation

The revocation service is also part of the registration service, and it permits clients to revoke previously issued assertions. A revocation request is similar to that of the registration request except that the status of `KeyBinding` and `KeyAssertion` prototype is specified `Invalid` in the client request. The client can use any of the elements of `<ds:KeyInfo>` or the `<KeyID>` element to identify the key to be revoked.

As in the case of registration, revocation service requires authentication of the client. Clients can authenticate using the `PassPhrase` established during registration or by signing the `<Prototype>` element using the private key being revoked. Note that in the case of registration, we used a key established in an out-of-bound manner to sign and authenticate the request. That is because one cannot use the private-key for authentication before the key is registered.

The revoke request is identified by a `<RevokeRequest>` element and the revoke response is identified by a `<RevokeResponse>` element.

If the registration service does not contain a record of the assertion, it returns with a `NotFound` status. We only show an example of the revoke request message here, as the revoke response message is similar to the register response message with the exception that the revoke response is identified by the `<RevokeResponse>` element.

Revoke Request

The following shows a revoke request message and builds on the previous MyTravels.com example. MyTravels.com decides to revoke the key and sends a revoke request to the trust service. MyTravels.com uses the `<KeyID>` element to identify the key to be revoked and uses the pass phrase established during registration to authenticate itself:

```
<RevokeRequest xmlns="http://www.xkms.org/schema/xkms-2001-01-20">
  <Prototype Id="RevokeRequestMyTravels.com">
    <TransactionID>bd36fae0-fb2f-11d6-b377-3138050d15cc</TransactionID>
      <Status>Invalid</Status>
      <KeyID>http://www.MyTravels.com/key?company=MyTravels.com&amp;
        department=HotelReservation&amp;CN=MyTravels HotelGroup&amp;
```

```
              issuer_serial=8e8934bcf3e469924936b42671bb9
         </KeyID>
       </Prototype>
       <AuthInfo>
         <AuthUserInfo>
           <PassPhrase>uN0eyMxT50hl76acpRFPvw3UKyY=</PassPhrase>
         </AuthUserInfo>
       </AuthInfo>
       <Respond>KeyName</Respond>
       <Respond>KeyValue</Respond>
     </RevokeRequest  >
```

Note the presence of a `<PassPhrase>` element inside the `<AuthInfo>` element, indicating that a pass phrase is being used for authentication.

Key Recovery

Key recovery is another operation supported by the Registration service. Similar to revocation, clients can use any of the elements of `<ds:KeyInfo>` or the `<KeyID>` element to identify the key to be recovered. As in the case of registration, authentication of the client is required. Clients can authenticate using the pass phrase established during registration or by obtaining a pass phrase through out-of-bounds communication.

The recover request is identified by a `<RecoverRequest>` element and the recover response is identified by a `<RecoverResponse>` element. Since the request and response formats are structured similar to that of the registration request, we do not show an example of `<RecoverRequest>` message or `<RecoverResponse>` message here.

If the service does not find a record of the assertion it returns with a `NotFound` status. The key recovery process may take time, and in such cases the service may return a `pending` status. Whenever a key recovery is performed, the registration service policy is to revoke the private key.

Request Authentication

Registration services need to ensure the validity of the requests by ensuring the authenticity of the requesting party and by verifying the integrity of the data sent in the request. Private key cannot be used for authentication until the corresponding public key has been registered. In the registration example, we used a key established through an out-of-band communication to sign and authenticate the sender. The revocation example showed the use of `PassPhrase` for authentication.

The XKRSS specification does not mandate any specific authentication policy to authenticate the registration requests, and the authentication is left to the trust service provider. Limited use shared secret data is the one most commonly used for this purpose. Use of shared data is also desirable for encrypting the private key generated or recovered by the service prior to returning it to the client. Limited use shared data can simply be a password or a passphrase, or may be randomly generated and can be exchanged between the two parties through human users.

XKRSS Message Specification

The register and revoke service examples already provided a glimpse of the XKRSS syntax. In this section we discuss some of the major elements in the XKRSS message set. As seen in the examples, the XKRSS protocol consists of a pair of messages: the request message sent by the client to the trust service and the response message sent back by the service.

In the following definitions, the prefix xsd used in the schema definitions is associated with the XML Schema namespace http://www.w3.org/2001/XMLSchema. The XKMS specification makes use of elements from XML Signature.

Prototype Element

As seen in the examples, the Prototype element is used by the clients to provide a prototype for the key binding to be registered. This element is of the same type as the <KeyBinding> element defined in the XKISS message set. Refer to <KeyBinding> for more details on <Prototype>.

AuthInfo Element

The AuthInfo element, as seen in the examples, contains data that authenticates the request. The form of authentication data may vary depending on the means of authentication used, the public key algorithm used, and whether the client has generated the key pair.

The AuthInfo element has two child elements: AuthUserInfo and AuthServerInfo. The AuthUserInfo element is used for authenticating the users when client-generated key pair are registered. The AuthServerInfo element is used for authenticating the users when the request is for registering the server-generated key pair.

AuthUserInfo Element

As discussed earlier, the AuthUserInfo element is used for authenticating requests when the *user-generated* key is used. Registration service may require proof-of-possession of the private key from the requesting party. The registration policy may also ensure that the requesting party is authorised to assert the binding to the public key.

The child elements of AuthUserInfo are given below:

Child Elements	Required	Max Occurrences
xkms:ProofOfPossession	No	1
xkms:KeyBindingAuth	No	1
xkms:PassPhraseAuth	No	1

The PassPhraseAuth element is of type xsd:string and contains a plaintext limited-use shared secret data that is obtained out-of-band from the trust service provider. The shared data is used to authenticate the request.

The `ProofOfPossession` element and the `KeyBindingAuth` element contain an XML Signature (`<ds:Signature>`) element. The scope of the signature for both the elements is the `<Prototype>` element. For `<ProofOfPossession>`, the signature is generated using the private key of the key pair being registered. For `<KeyBindingAuth>` the key to generate the signature must be established through some other means.

AuthServerInfo Element

The `AuthServerInfo` element is used to authenticate requests when the key pair is to be generated by the service. The schema of the `AuthServerInfo` element is similar to that of the `AuthUserInfo` element except that proof-of-possession is not needed for service-generated keys:

The child element table of `AuthServerInfo` is given below:

Child Elements	Required	Max Occurrences
xkms:KeyBindingAuth	No	1
xkms:PassPhraseAuth	No	1

Register Request Message

The register request message is used to register either a client-generated key pair or a service-generated key pair. As seen in the *Register Request* example, the register request message is identified by the `<RegisterRequest>` element. The `<RegisterRequest>` element consists of the following child elements:

Child Elements	Required	Max Occurrences
xkms:ProtoType	No	1
xkms:AuthInfo	Yes	1
xkms:Respond	No	Unbounded

We have already discussed the `ProtoType` and `AuthInfo` elements. The `Respond` element is discussed as part of the XKISS message set.

The attribute table of `<RegisterRequest>` consists of two attributes that are used to specify the major and minor version numbers of XKMS protocol:

Attribute Name	Type	Required
MajorVersion	xsd:integer	Yes
MinorVersion	xsd:integer	Yes

Reissue, Revoke, and Recover Request Messages

The content model of the other three requests (Reissue request, Revoke request, and Recover request) is similar to the `RegisterRequest` element. The only difference is in the naming of their root elements, which corresponds to the type of the operation as shown in the examples. Due to their similarity to `RegisterRequest`, their contents are not discussed here.

Register Response Message

The response message from the registration service is identified by the `<RegisterResult>` element. The `<RegisterResult>` element consists of the following child elements:

Child Elements	Required	Max Occurrences
xkms:KeyBinding	No	Unbounded
xkms:Private	No	1
xkms:Result	Yes	1

The `KeyBinding` element specifies information about the key that was registered by the service. The `Private` element provides the private key values when the key pair is generated by the Registration service. The `Private` element is also of the same type as the `<KeyBinding>` element. The `Result` element provides the status of the request call. Refer to the *XKISS Message Set* for more details on the `<Result>` element.

The attribute table of `<RegisterResult>` is similar to that of the `<RegisterRequest>` element.

Reissue, Revoke and Recover Response Messages

The response message of the recover operation is exactly similar to that of the register response message. The reissue and the revoke response messages are also similar to that of the register response message except that they do not contain the `Private` element, since the private key details are not sent by the server for the reissue and revoke requests.

SOAP Binding

When the XKMS messages are exchanged using the SOAP protocol, both the request and the response messages are encoded as an entry in the SOAP `Body` element. Here is an example of a SOAP-encoded XKMS-request message:

```
<env:Envelope xmlns:env="http://www.w3.org/2002/06/soap-envelope"
              xmlns:xkms="http://www.w3.org/2002/03/xkms"
              xmlns:ds="http://www.w3.org/2000/09/xmldsig#">
  <env:Body>
    <LocateRequest xmlns="http://www.w3.org/TR/2002/WD-xkms-2-20020318">
      <KeyInfoQuery>
        <ds:KeyName xmlns:ds="http://www.w3.org/2000/09/xmldsig#">
          http://marriott.com/key?company=Marriott&amp;department
          =OnLineReservation&amp;CN=MarriottCourtyardGroup&amp;
```

```
        issuer_serial=8eacea767bcf3e469924936b42671bb9
      <ds:KeyName>
    </KeyInfoQuery>
    <Respond>KeyName<Respond>
    <Respond>KeyValue</Respond>
  </LocateRequest>
 </env:Body>
</env:Envelope>
```

When SOAP binding is used, all `ResultCode` values other than `Success`, `Incomplete`, and `NoMatch` are expressed using the SOAP `Fault` element, with the SOAP `faultcode` element set to `env:Server` where env maps to the SOAP namespace as shown in the above snippet.

This is because the `Success`, `Incomplete`, and `NoMatch` result codes indicate the status of the information returned for the request, and do not indicate that the server has failed to serve the request.

Bulk Operations

The XKRSS protocol currently provides for one-by-one registration of key pairs. Recognizing the need for bulk registrations, the W3C XML Key working group has released a companion specification called **X-BULK** to support bulk registration of key pairs. In this section, we take a brief look at the X-BULK specification. The X-BULK specification is also in working draft stages and this section is based on the working draft dated March 18, 2002. The March working draft of the X-BULK specification is available at http://www.w3.org/TR/2002/WD-xkms2-xbulk-20020318.

Bulk Registrations Uses

The following use cases have been identified as potential targets for bulk registrations:

- ❑ Smart card factories that target enterprise, wireless, and cable-modem applications.

- ❑ Device factories in general. Examples include TPM from Trusted Computing Platform Alliance (TCPA).

- ❑ To handle functionality analogous to separated RAs and CAs from the X.509 world.

X-BULK Specification

While the XKRSS specification defines registration of a single key-pair at a time, X-BULK specification provides for bulk registration of key pairs using a single request message. The specification defines a batch element that contains either multiple registration requests or multiple server responses. The basic idea is to enable a single batch to contain a number of independently referenceable requests and responses. Both the clients and the services can produce batches. Services accept an entire batch for processing in a single call and respond with a single batch of responses.

The basic mode of operation is that the client submits a batch of registration requests to the X-BULK service. The service processes the batch and produces a response batch that contains one response for each request in the batch sent by the client. In addition to registration requests, X-BULK provides for batching multiple status requests that can be used by the requestor to track the progress of batch processing. A status request is a request to determine the status of processing of a specific batch. The service responds with the status of each individual request in that batch.

The individual requests and responses in a batch follow XKMS message formats. Also, an X-BULK service support all the four operations (Register, Reissue, Revoke, and Recover) supported by the XKRSS service. Similar to the XKRSS Register service, the X-BULK Register service supports client-generated and service-generated key pairs.

X-BULK requires that the batches be authenticated and digitally signed using RSA algorithms. Implementations are required to include a ds:X509Data element in the ds:Signature element, which is used along with an X-BULK BatchId element to ensure batch uniqueness.

The X-BULK specification is defined under the namespace http://www.w3.org/2002/03/xkms-xbulk. We use the prefix xbulk to refer to this namespace. The X-BULK specification uses elements from the XKMS specification and from the XML Digital Signature specification.

Let's look at a sample X-BULK request.

X-BULK Request

This request is to register a batch of key pairs. The elements that are not qualified are defined in the xbulk namespace. Elements from other namespaces are appropriately qualified:

```
<BulkRegister>
  <SignedPart Id="id-0">
    <BatchHeader>
      <BatchID>batch-0</BatchID>
      <BatchTime>1999-05-31T13:20:00-05:00</BatchTime>
      <NumberOfRequests>2</NumberOfRequests>
    </BatchHeader>
    <xkms:Respond>X509Cert</xkms:Respond>
    <Requests number="2">
      <Request>
        <xkms:KeyID >mailto:bar@MyTravels.com</xkms:KeyID>
          <ds:KeyInfo xmlns:ds="http://www.w3.org/2000/09/xmldsig#">
            <ds:KeyName>
          http://www.mytravels.com/key?company=MyTravels.com&amp;department
            =HotelReservation&amp;CN=MyTravels HotelGroup&amp;
          </ds:KeyName>
        <ds:KeyValue>
          <ds:RSAKeyValue>
            <ds:Modulus>GfhLucJyEkuuz84GpTO3hEzVAMhGrU+nd5Qjx64IIDpfTB/o
              SET0S6fP/cypEtyX3MVTahCE3llS9PuxUuzRueR=
            </ds:Modulus>
            <ds:Exponent>ZDEF</ds:Exponent>
          </ds:RSAKeyValue>
        </ds:KeyValue>
      </ds:KeyInfo>
```

```
                <ClientInfo>
                  <application:EmployeeID xmlns:application="urn:foo">
                  6
                  </application:EmployeeID>
                </ClientInfo>
            </Request>
            <Request>
              <xkms:KeyID>mailto:baz@foo.com</xkms:KeyID>
              <ds:KeyInfo >
                <!--Contains the Public Key Details To Be Registered -->

              </ds:KeyInfo>
              <ClientInfo>
                <application:EmployeeID xmlns:application="urn:foo">
                007
                </application:EmployeeID>
              </ClientInfo>
            </Request>
          </Requests>
        </SignedPart>
        <ds:Signature>
        ...
          <ds:Reference URI="id-0">
            ...
          </ds:Reference>
        ...
        </ds:Signature>
      </BulkRegister>
```

The `BatchHeader` element provides meta information about the batch. The `Requests` element can contain an unbounded number of `Request` elements. This element contains the actual request. Each request is required to have an `xkms:KeyID` element and it must be unique within the batch. The `ClientInfo` element is designed to carry bookkeeping data for the client. The server is required to return the contents of `ClientInfo` intact. Signing of the requests is a must per X-BULK specification, and the `ds:Signature` element represents the signature of the original `SignedPart` element that contains the batch request message.

X-BULK Response

Following is the response from the server for the above request:

```
<BulkRegisterResult >
  <SignedPart Id="id-0">
    <BatchHeader>
     <BatchID>batch-0</BatchID>
     <BatchTime>1999-05-31T13:20:00-05:00</BatchTime>
     <NumberOfRequests>2</NumberOfRequests>
    </BatchHeader>
    <RegisterResults number="2">
      <xkms:RegisterResult >
        <xkms:Result>Success</xkms:Result>
        <xkms:KeyBinding>
          <xkms:Status>Valid</xkms:Status>
          <xkms:KeyID>mailto:bar@MyTravels.com</xkms:KeyID>
          <ds:KeyInfo xmlns:ds="http://www.w3.org/2000/09/xmldsig#">
            <ds:X509Data>
```

```
            <ds:X509Certificate>
                MIIDnTCCAwagAwIBAgIQIgulbZZhm1cviRALwT......
                ...+6K7tcGxSNaVMZqE9vfttKzE
            </ds:X509Certificate>
          </ds:X509Data>
        </ds:KeyInfo>
      </xkms:KeyBinding>
    </xkms:RegisterResult>
    <xkms:RegisterResult >
      <xkms:Result>Success</xkms:Result>
      <xkms:KeyBinding >
        <xkms:Status>Valid</xkms:Status>
        <xkms:KeyID>mailto:baz@foo.com</xkms:KeyID>
        <ds:KeyInfo>
          <ds:X509Data>
            <ds:X509Certificate>...</ds:X509Certificate>
          </ds:X509Data>
        </ds:KeyInfo>
      </xkms:KeyBinding >
    </xkms:RegisterResult>
  </RegisterResults>
</SignedPart>
<ds:Signature >
... URI="#id-0" ...
</ds:Signature>
</BulkRegisterResult>
```

Similar to the requests, the response is signed and is contained under the `SignedPart` element. The `RegisterResults` element contains a collection of the `RegisterResult` element, which represents a response from the server for each corresponding request in the same order.

Security Considerations

In this section we look at some of the security issues that could compromise the security of an XKMS implementation.

Replay Attacks

Replay of a previously-sent XKMS response is one such security problem that an XKMS server implementation needs to avoid. An intruder could store the messages sent by the XKMS server to play the messages back later and effectively impersonate the XKMS service. The XKMS specification does not mandate any specific mechanism to mitigate such replay attacks. However, XKMS recommends prevention of such attacks and leaves it to the server implementations to use a mechanism of their choice. A common way of preventing replay attacks is to embed a token in each message to demonstrate to the recipient that the message is fresh. The token may need to be signed to guarantee integrity of the token and the message.

Here are some "freshness" tokens that can be used for preventing replay attacks:

❏ A timestamp specifying the message origination time

❏ A nonce, which is a random piece of data previously issued by the user

❏ A message serial number could be added

Such tokens may be encoded as XML Signature properties within the message.

Denial of Service

XKMS implementations need to take measures to prevent or mitigate DoS attacks. Operations such as URL resolution, Signature verification, and Key exchange are some examples of resource-intensive operations. XKMS implementations should avoid performing an unlimited number of resource-intensive operations prior to source authentication.

Recovery Policy

A key recovery operation may involve an unacceptable loss of confidence in the security of a private key component. This could lead to the possibility of repudiation of a signed document or of accountability of an encrypted document.

The XKMS specification does not mandate any specific recovery policy. XKMS implementations should exercise care in assessing the vulnerability of the recovery operations and accordingly apply sufficient controls, including revocation of the underlying key binding.

Limited Use Shared Data

If a limited use shared data is used, care must be taken to ensure that the secret data is not revealed to an attacker. Encrypting the shared secret alone is not sufficient, as the `PassPhraseAuth` element is not cryptographically bound to the message. Any means employed must provide for both encryption and integrity, such as SSL.

Future of XKMS

XKMS is an ongoing effort. The code snippets and the schema definitions used in this chapter are based on the published working draft dated March 18, 2002. This March draft does not yet meet all the XKMS requirements and contains points that are still under discussion. This draft also contains examples that do not match the corresponding schema definitions. The draft can be expected to go through few more revisions before it becomes a specification.

Going by the current thinking of the working group indicated by the editor's copy of the specification, it appears that there is agreement on the high-level goals and the basic concepts behind XKMS. The three different services (Register, Locate, and Validate) offered by XKMS will continue to remain the same. Most of the changes are expected to be in the areas of XKISS and XKRSS message syntax.

There are proposals to augment the request and response messages to carry more information. New elements are being added to the message set to represent additional information. Support for asynchronous processing of requests is being proposed. This will result in the addition of new elements to facilitate notification of asynchronous call completion and to enable clients to query the server to check the status of pending operations.

The working group is also focused on addressing some of the security considerations mentioned in this chapter. This is expected to result in a new security protocol binding for XKMS messages. For instance, two-phase request-response is being proposed to deal with request replay attacks and DoS attacks. A standard message correlation model is being proposed to deal with response replay and request substitution attacks. One may also expect to see proposals to provide binding to some new security initiatives such as the WS-Security specification.

XKMS was to become a W3C recommendation by November 2002, but unfortunately, development of XKMS fell behind schedule, pointing towards approval in 2003. XKMS implementations have already started to appear based on the preliminary specifications, which will doubtless help demonstrate what changes will be needed to allow XKMS to mature.

The future of XKMS is dictated by its evolution as the standard, and its adoption pertinent to the industry. While XKMS has made an attempt to abstract away the complexities of working with PKI, it is up to the industry to offer portable and interoperable implementations with an easy-to-use API for widespread adoption and success.

Implementations

Working with XKMS requires trust service implementations that support both the XKISS and the XKRSS protocols. Though XKMS is still in the working draft stages, trust service implementations have started to appear. Some of these implementations come with client side toolkits that provide a set of libraries and APIs to create XKMS request messages, send them to the XKMS server, and work with the server response and error messages.

In this section, we take a look at the upcoming implementations. Before exploring the implementations let us try and understand the options available to us both on the client side and the server side of XKMS.

Client Side Technologies and Options

Since the majority of the users of XKMS will be XKMS clients, we start our discussions with a focus on the technology options available to develop XKMS clients.

XKMS is based on XML and the trust services are designed as web services supporting SOAP and WSDL specifications. Though XKMS has not made it a requirement, it is reasonable to expect most server implementations to require digital signing of some request messages based on XML Signature. It is also not unreasonable to expect HTTP to be used as a transport protocol for SOAP messages.

Putting this all together, an XKMS client would need, at the minimum, support for the following technologies:

❑   XML Parser

❑   SOAP

❑   XML Signature

If you are working with XML you must be already using some XML parser. Support for SOAP is strong and many interoperable implementations in many languages are readily available. Since XKMS requires a basic level of SOAP support, you could work with many of the SOAP implementations without detailed knowledge on SOAP. Support for XML Signature implementation is not widespread, but stable implementations in Java and .NET environments do exist. Use of these signature implementations may require some XML Signature knowledge.

Using these technologies and toolkits it is possible to hand-code XKMS clients, since at the basic level we are only talking about creating and sending a SOAP message confirming to XKMS schema. However, you must note that such an approach does require detailed knowledge of XKMS syntax and grammar and would tie your application tightly to XKMS unless you take the time to design it appropriately. If you are building production applications with XKMS support based on the direct hand-coding approach, it makes sense to build the XKMS support as a layer on top to provide some insulation to your application from possible changes to XKMS.

An alternative approach to hand-coding XKMS clients is to use the WSDL document published by the XKMS service implementations and generate clients using WSDL code generators. WSDL code generators are available in Java, .NET, C++, and various other platforms. Success on this approach requires proper WSDL documents from service providers and good WSDL code generators. There is some learning curve here, as you need to understand the API of the generated code to link it to your applications. Also, it is unlikely that these WSDL code generators support XML Signature and you would mostly need to do XML Signature code yourself using some XML Signature implementation.

The third option is to use the client-side toolkits provided by the XKMS service implementers and other third-party library providers. These toolkits are based on proprietary API and they provide some level of insulation from XKMS syntax and semantics. It makes perfect sense to use the XKMS implementer toolkit if you are already using the vendor XKMS server implementation and are hosting your own XKMS services. If that is not the case, note that though these toolkits do provide some insulation from XKMS syntax, these are proprietary APIs, and an XKMS application developed with one vendor's toolkit is not guaranteed to work with an XKMS service offered by another vendor.

The last option is based on the fact that XKMS is not limited to a SOAP and WSDL based model. Other communication and transport protocols are possible. Though not all XKMS implementations will offer other forms of support, this option is still a possibility.

Server Side Options

There are two options for working with XKMS server implementations. One option is to run your own XKMS service implementation. The other option is to subscribe to an online XKMS service implementation run by a trusted third party.

Running your own XKMS implementations provides you with more control and flexibility, but comes with very high costs. A service such as an XKMS service needs to be very highly secured, highly available, highly scalable, and also requires military grade security with natural disaster prevention mechanisms. Running a 7*24-hour service with such security is a high-cost operation requiring highly skilled technical and legal resources. Also, your partners need to buy into your closed solution. With your own service implementation you may be limited to offering support only for a restricted set of underlying PKI implementations. If you are already running a closed PKI network or really need absolute control over your PKI operations, this option would be attractive. For others, subscription may appeal as a good alternative. Ultimately it is a business decision that needs to be based on the factors that are important to you.

Subscribing to a third party-run XKMS service makes it easy to add PKI support to your applications. Here are some of the factors that you may need to consider in selecting the right service provider:

❑ Support for open protocols, openness of the client API, adherence to XKMS standards, and underlying PKI support

❑ Availability and scalability of the service

❑ Security infrastructure, including disaster recovery support

❑ Flexibility and control of operation provided to the users

❑ Financial and legal liability of the partnership

❑ Pricing

Commercial XKMS implementations are available that support both the run-your-own option and the subscription option. Alternatively, if you would like to build your own XKMS implementation, the following article gives some guidance on building an XKMS service using ASP.NET.

http://www.xmltrustcenter.org/xkms/dotnet/articles/service/index.htm

XKMS Implementations

As of November 2002, there are at least three XKMS service implementations available in the market:

❑ Entrust (http://xkms.entrust.com/xkms/index.htm)

❑ Phaos XKMS Java Toolkit (http://www.phaos.com/)

❑ Verisign XKMS Toolkit (http://www.verisign.com/developer/xml/xkms.html) (http://www.xmltrustcenter.org/developer/verisign/tsik/download.htm)

The Entrust implementation does not offer a client side toolkit, but provides an XKMS server implementation supporting all the three XKMS services. The Entrust implementation is offered as a reference implementation for online *testing* purposes only. One can use direct HTTP POST messages to communicate with the Entrust service. Here is a sample of an Entrust HTTP POST message as specified in http://xkms.entrust.com/xkms/help/samplepost.htm:

```
POST /xkms/portal HTTP/1.0
Content-Type: text/xml
Host: xkms.entrust.com
Content-Length: 1234
Connection: Close
Cache-Control: no-cache

--- XML text goes here ---
```

Phaos provides a client and a server side toolkit in Java that can be used to build your own XKMS implementation. Phaos does not provide an online XKMS service that to which can subscribe.

The Verisign XKMS implementation is available for production purposes, and the next section takes a closer look at the Verisign implementation.

Additional XKMS toolkits are also starting to appear in the market. You can find more details by following the links given below:

❑   XKMS & .Net:
http://www.xmltrustcenter.org/xkms/dotnet/articles/client/1.htm
http://www.xmltrustcenter.org/xkms/dotnet/index.htm

❑   General Information on XKMS:
http://www.xmltrustcenter.org/xkms/index.htm

Verisign Implementation

Verisign offers a complete XKMS implementation along with a client side toolkit in Java. The Verisign service implementation offers three different levels of service support:

❑   Interoperability service

❑   Pilot service

❑   Production service

The interoperability service is a *free* service where one can enroll for testing the service without becoming a customer. This is an ideal service to become familiar with XKMS and test some trial applications.

The pilot service is a *paid* service where one can enroll for testing the service. The difference between interoperability and pilot service is that in pilot service users have more control, such as assigning a pass code to generate keys.

The production service provides more privileges. As a production service customer you can use the online trust service provided by Verisign, or you can purchase the XKMS implementation and use it as a stand-alone product.

Verisign Client Toolkit

The Verisign client-side toolkit is a Java implementation. Using the API, you can create XKMS messages, sign them, send them over to the server, and deal with the server responses and errors.

In this section, we show an example of using the Verisign API to register a key pair and another example that locates the registered key pair.

Both the examples require the following include list:

```
import com.verisign.resource.ResourceFactory;
import com.verisign.resource.XMLResource;
import com.verisign.messaging.AbstractTransport;
import com.verisign.messaging.XmlTransportSOAP;
import com.verisign.xkms.client.XKMSAuthInfo;
import com.verisign.xkms.client.XKMSException;
import com.verisign.xkms.client.XKMSKeyData;
import com.verisign.xkms.client.XKMSKeyName;
import com.verisign.xkms.client.XKMSLocate;
import com.verisign.xkms.client.XKMSLocateResponse;
import com.verisign.xkms.client.XKMSRegister;
```

```
import com.verisign.xkms.client.XKMSRegisterResponse;
import com.verisign.xkms.client.XKMSKeyInfo;
import com.verisign.xmlsig.tools.KeyConverter;
import com.verisign.xpath.XPath;
import java.io.File;
import java.io.FileInputStream;
import java.io.FileOutputStream;
import java.io.IOException;
import java.net.URL;
import java.security.KeyPair;
import java.security.KeyPairGenerator;
import java.security.KeyStore;
import java.security.PrivateKey;
import java.security.PublicKey;
import java.security.cert.X509Certificate;
import java.util.List;
import org.w3c.dom.Document;
```

Register a Client Generated Keypair

This example uses Verisign's API to register a client-generated key pair. The Versign 1.1 XKMS implementation does not support registration of server-generated key pair.

The global variables raCert and raKey are the certificate and key obtained from a Trust service using out-of-band communication for authenticating the sender. We assume that values for these globals are set at some place prior to invoking the registerClientGeneratedKeyPair() method:

```
public class XKMSRegisterExample {

    X509Certificate raCert;
    PrivateKey raKey;

    //Name of the key to be registered
    String keyName = new
            String("http://www.mytravels.com/key?company=MyTravels.com&amp;
                department=HotelReservation&amp;CN=MyTravels HotelGroup&amp;");

    //URL of the trust service
    String url = new String("http://interop-
                                    xkms.verisign.com/xkms/Acceptor.nano");
```

Here the passPhrase in plain text is used by the client for later revocation or recovery operations. This is sent as part of the <RegisterRequest> element:

```
    String passPhrase = new String("MyFirstXKMSExample");
```

The certificate and the key used by the sender to sign the entire SOAP message:

```
    X509Certificate msgSigningCert;
    PrivateKey msgSigningKey;
```

The main function for registering the client generated key pair:

```
    void registerClientGeneratedKeyPair() {

    try {
```

We create the authorization data for authenticating the user. This is equivalent to creating a `<KeyBindingAuth>` element and a `<PassPhrase>` element. XKMS will encrypt the `passPhrase` using the `raKey`:

```
XKMSAuthInfo authInfo = new XKMSAuthInfo(passPhrase, raCert, raKey);
```

We generate the key pair to be registered, which is expected to be available. Here we generate a 512 bit RSA key pair using Java security mechanisms:

```
KeyPairGenerator gen = KeyPairGenerator.getInstance("RSA");
gen.initialize(512);
KeyPair keyPair = gen.generateKeyPair();
```

Now we collect the register parameters that contain the value and the name of the key to be registered:

```
XKMSKeyData keyData
    = new XKMSKeyData(keyPair, new XKMSKeyName(keyName));
```

Create a registration request using the key data and the authentication information created earlier:

```
XKMSRegister request = new XKMSRegister(keyData, authInfo);

  //Create a SOAP transport to send the request
AbstractTransport transport = new XmlTransportSOAP(new URL(url));

  //This is to sign the whole transported message being sent for integrity.
transport.setSigningPrivateKey(msgSigningKey);
transport.setSigningCertificate(msgSigningCert);

  //You can access the key information from the response returned
XKMSRegisterResponse response = request.sendRequest(transport);
}catch (XKMSException e) {
    if (e.getErrorCode() != null) {
        System.out.println("Code: " + e.getErrorCode());
        }
    }catch(Exception ignoreOtherExceptions) {
    }

  }//registerClientGeneratedKeyPair

}// XKMSRegisterExample
```

Locate a Key using KeyName

In this code snippet we locate a key using a key name:

```
public class LocateKeyUsingKeyName {

  //This code snippet assumes that values for the following globals are set
  //at some place prior to invoking the locateKey() method

  //URL of the trust service
  String url = new String("http://interop-
                          xkms.verisign.com/xkms/Acceptor.nano");
```

```
        //Certificate and key used by sender to sign the whole SOAP message
        X509Certificate msgSigningCert;
        PrivateKey msgSigningKey;

        void locateKey(String keyName)
        {

            try{

            //Set the details of the key to be returned via the <Respond> element
                String respondWith[] = {XKMSLocate.KeyName, XKMSLocate.KeyValue};

            //Create a locate request giving keyName and respond details
                XKMSLocate request = new XKMSLocate(keyName, respondWith);

            //Create a SOAP transport to send the request
                AbstractTransport transport = new XmlTransportSOAP(new URL(url));

        //This is to sign the whole transported message being sent for integrity.
                transport.setSigningPrivateKey(signingKey);
                transport.setSigningCertificate(signingCert);

                //Send the request
                XKMSLocateResponse response = request.sendRequest(transport);

                //This walks through the response and prints out the keyname
                List list = response.getXKMSKeyInfos();
                System.out.println("Number of matches returned: " + list.size());
                for (int i = 0; i < list.size(); i += 1) {
                    XKMSKeyInfo info = (XKMSKeyInfo) list.get(i);
                    System.out.println("KeyName "+(i+1)+" is "+info.getKeyName());
                }

            }catch(Exception e) {
            }

        }//locateKey()
    }//class
```

Summary

In this chapter, we have seen what XML Key Management specification is all about and how it simplifies the process of working with PKI. Specifically, we first discussed the motivation behind the XKMS specification and the major benefits provided by XKMS.

Our XKISS coverage included an overview of XKISS, examples of XKISS messages, and finally a detailed discussion of the XKISS message set. We then moved on to the XKRSS part of the XKMS specification and went through an overview of XKRSS, an example of XKRSS messages, and a detailed analysis of the XKRSS message set. We also looked at the closely related X-BULK specification that deals with bulk registration of key pairs. Finally, we reviewed the limitations of XKMS and other security vulnerabilities one needs to watch for when using XKMS.

XKMS provides a sound framework for XML-based trust services. The challenge lies with the industry to make coding away the PKI complexity a reality by providing portable and inter-operable implementations that require minimum client effort.

9

SAML

By the time you read this, the Organization for the Advancement of Structured Information Standards (OASIS) will have approved this specification and it will officially become a standard. In less than two years, all major security vendors are expected not only to have only supported the standard but also to have implemented it already in their products. Liberty Alliance (the alternative to the Microsoft Passport service) already uses SAML as the basis of its specification.

This chapter is divided into three sections. The first section defines the SAML specification. The second section covers the products and toolkits that are currently available. We will also see one of these toolkits. The third section describes how applications can use SAML. Finally, we will look at the Liberty Alliance specification and the Microsoft Passport service.

What is SAML

SAML (**Security Assertion Markup Language**) is an XML-based security standard for exchanging authentication and authorization credentials across different security domains over the Internet. This entitlement information is expressed through assertions (declarations on facts about subjects).

SAML is a security standard for exchanging information. SAML is useful for transporting authentication and authorization credentials across different security domains. A security domain is an area that manages and controls resources governed by a specific access control policy. Subjects within a security domain request resources from another security domain. Either the subject should be defined within this security domain, or the second security domain must trust the security domain to which the subject belongs. This is known as single sign-on.

Within a security domain, organizations usually use third-party products to manage resource access, and to provide single sign-on capability. Therefore SAML will enable products from different vendors to exchange this type of information, and will enable single sign-on across organizational boundaries.

Who's Behind SAML

Securant and Netegrity were working on separate specifications to address the same problem: that of sharing entitlement information between access management systems from different organizations.

Netegrity, VeriSign, and a number of industry partners introduced the **Security Services Markup Language** (S2ML) in November 2000. The standard was compatible with the XML Key Management Specification (XKMS), which VeriSign had just introduced the same day. S2ML enabled interoperability between security systems that needed to communicate authentication, authorization, and profile information.

A few weeks later, Securant and a number of industry partners introduced their Authentication and Authorization in XML (**AuthXML**) in December 2000. Additionally, the Working Group was finalizing its preparations on the AuthXML specification that was to be submitted to the World Wide Web Consortium (W3C) and to the Organization for the Advancement of Structured Information Standards (OASIS).

In early 2001, both specifications were submitted to the OASIS Security Services Technical Committee (SSTC), which in a few months resulted in what we now know as SAML. Originally designed to address the product interoperability problem, it quickly grew to encompass much more as we will see in this chapter.

SAML started its life in January 2001 as a combination of two efforts: Securant's AuthXML and Netegrity's S2ML. The consolidation of the various specifications into SAML means that system implementers only have one standard they need to support, which should reduce the production of interoperable systems.

Why SAML is needed

The biggest challenges for web services, in the area of gaining long-term success, are related to security. The most important security challenge is that of user authentication, and single sign-on across a number of federated systems. Single Sign-on (SSO) provides the ability to use multiple web services, or a single web service made up of multiple web services, based on a single authentication. SAML provides for distributed authorization, federated identity management as proposed by the Liberty Alliance, multi-vendor portals, and the development of Web Services Access Controls.

SAML does not impose a centralized, decentralized, or federated infrastructure or solution, but instead facilitates the communication of authentication, authorization, and attribute information. It does not introduce any new form or method of authentication, is not an alternative to other security standards like WS-Security, and is not limited to legacy applications or Web Browser applications.

Let's look at a simple example to better understand how SAML is used in a Single Sign-on environment. Let's say a subscriber visits a travel agency portal to purchase airline tickets. The travel agency portal is offering a number of special deals with affiliated partner sites on hotel stays, on car rentals, and on flight insurance. The subscriber would like to initiate transactions with some of these affiliated partners. In order to conduct business with each of those partner sites, the subscriber would have to sign in separately to each site, using different user names, passwords, and authentication information, all of which needs to be remembered individually.

With SAML, the subscriber would have to sign in only to the travel agency portal to be authenticated via SAML at the affiliated sites. The Use Case section of this chapter will show how this entitlement information is shared between federated sites and how SAML facilitates this exchange.

The SAML Specification

The SAML specifications depict four main components of SAML. They are:

- ❑ Assertions
- ❑ Request and response protocols
- ❑ Binding
- ❑ Profiles

Assertions

Assertions can convey information about authentication acts performed by subjects, attributes of subjects, and authorization decisions about whether subjects are allowed to access certain resources. They are represented as XML constructs and have a nested structure. A single assertion might contain several different internal statements about authentication, authorization, and attributes.

Assertions are issued by SAML authorities, namely authentication authorities, attribute authorities, and Policy Decision Points (PDP). SAML defines a protocol by which clients can request assertions from SAML authorities and get a response from them. This protocol consists of XML-based request and response message formats, and can be bound to many different underlying communications and transport protocols. SAML authorities can use various sources of information, such as external policy stores and assertions that were received as input in requests, in creating their responses. Thus, while clients always consume assertions, SAML authorities can both be producers and consumers of assertions.

SAML provides the following three kinds of assertions:

- ❑ **Authentication assertions** in which the subject's identity has already been proven. The authentication information is described in the authentication assertion.
- ❑ **Attribute assertions** contain specific information about the subject, such as his credit limit, his access level, his credit rating, or any other qualifying statement.
- ❑ **Authorization decision assertions** identify what the subject can or is authorized to do. For example, it can identify whether he is authorized to conduct a specific transaction.

Protocols

A protocol defines an agreed way of asking for and receiving information, and in this case the assertion. As we have seen, we have authentication, attribute, and authorization assertions. But how do we compose a request and what should we expect in terms of response? How will these assertions be packaged?

SAML defines a request and response protocol. The request protocol defines messages that can be sent to request a response? The requests are SubjectQuery, AuthenticationQuery, AttributeQuery, and AuthorizationDecisionQuery. SAML has only one response format regardless of the type of request. It includes a response as the answer, which in this case would be assertions that match the type of request received, and errors if any.

Bindings

Bindings define how SAML messages are communicated over standard transport and messaging protocols. For example, an SAML SOAP binding describes how SAML request and response message exchanges are mapped into SOAP message exchanges. The following figure illustrates what that means and where the SAML protocol fits in the SOAP message:

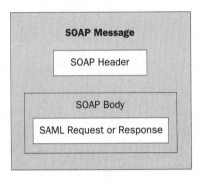

The following figure illustrates this relationship:

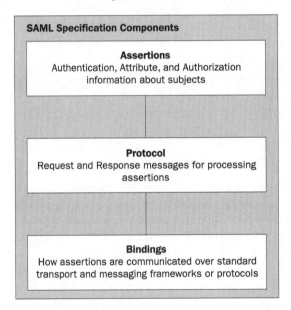

The next diagram illustrates the relationship between all the pieces that we have seen in the last figure:

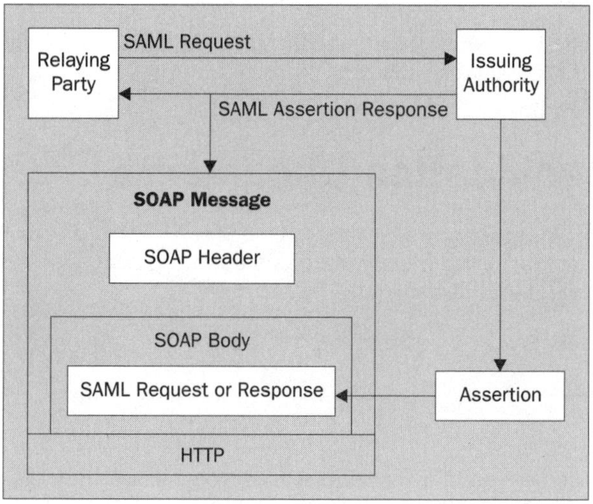

The Relying Party is the requester who sends an SAML request for assertion to an Issuing Authority. This Issuing Authority then generates a response, which is bound to the body of a SOAP Message, and is sent back to the Relying Party using HTTP.

Profiles

Profiles are the rules for embedding, extracting, and integrating. If you look at our previous diagram, you can see that the SOAP bindings do not tell us anything about how SAML errors are reflected in SOAP messages. This is the job of the SOAP profile of SAML.

The specification defines SAML's profiles as a set of rules describing how to insert SAML assertions into other message.

A profile describes how SAML assertions are embedded in or combined with other objects, and are processed from a Web source to a Web destination. For instance, the SOAP profile for SAML describes how SAML assertions are added to SOAP messages, how SOAP headers are affected by SAML assertions, and how SAML-related errors should be reflected in SOAP messages. These provide integration rules for other standards to integrate and work with SAML.

Three profiles have currently been defined: two for Web browser single sign-on, and one as a SOAP profile of SAML. The committee is currently developing a procedure for registering profile specifications openly.

Benefits of SAML

❑   Enables disparate security services systems to interoperate.

❑   Provides a single sign-on authentication facility. This can greatly reduce the need for duplication of security and authentication information across sites.

❑   Is independent of any system with which it interacts. Each system can establish its own policies for user authentication and authorization.

❑ Provides a decentralized authorization environment. This provides a scalable security model, which eliminates the need for a point-to-point solution.

❑ Provides attribute-based authorization, which goes significantly beyond current authentication based upon anXML digital signature.

The SAML Specification Documents

The SAML Specification Set is currently at level 1.0. As of May 31, 2002, the specification was at revision 01. All of these documents are available at http://www.oasis-open.org/committees/security/. The current specification set is made up of the following documents:

❑ Assertions and Protocol

   ❑ Assertion Schema

   ❑ Protocol Schema

   These define Assertions and the request response protocol, and form the core of the specification.

❑ Bindings and Profiles

   These define the SOAP Binding and the two-browser profiles of SAML.

❑ Security and Privacy Considerations

   These outline the security risks to which SAML systems are subject, and which are still not addressed in the current specification. Recommendations for counter measures are also included.

❑ Conformance Program Specification

   For implementers this document describes the program and technical requirements for the SAML conformance system. This is to ensure compatibility and interoperability of software products.

❑ Glossary

   This document defines the important terms used throughout the specification.

The remainder of this section will provide a summary of the information found within these documents. At the end of this section, readers should have enough information to use in applications of their own. We will also cover documents that are not part of the current 1.0 specification and are currently in draft mode.

Use Cases

This section is based on the Consensus Draft 1, dated May 30th, 2001. It is worth looking at the requirements, use cases, and sequence diagrams described in this document. This should provide you with a clear explanation of how SAML could be integrated within your environment. Later in this chapter we will look at products and toolkits that are currently available to support your efforts.

Authentication is described as a time-based event with an associated authentication protocol. It is important to understand that authentication statements or assertions describe the type of authentication that has already occurred, and provide information on the protocol that was used for authentication.

Authorization is described as follows: attributes that are used to make authorization decisions and a format or structure to capture these decisions.

Again the primary goal of SAML is a protocol for cross-domain authentication and authorization information exchange, and not for the underlying authentication or authorization mechanisms that generate this information.

Requirements

The document describes a number of requirements that the specification must handle, namely:

❑ User sessions, which handle login, logout, timein and timeout. This was not included in the 1.0 specification, but is an important concept in relation to specific SAML implementations.

❑ Anonymous users, and users with assumed identifications, as well as the ability to push or pull assertions (models that we will look at next) from an authoritative source or Web Source. An authoritative source could be a trusted third party, a Certificate Authority, a bank, an association, or any party that can provide assertions on a given subject.

❑ Confidentiality, and optional signing and encryption. This touches on a number of other specifications that are managed by W3C and OASIS.

❑ Bindings to standard Internet protocols like HTTP, MIME, and SOAP.

Single Sign-on Use Case

A Web Source or subject requests information and content, and a Web Destination provides them. Post-authentication, the subject (web, mobile, or other) uses secured resources at a Web Destination. With this basic picture in mind, let us understand the Pull and Push scenarios.

Pull Scenario

A token is an SAMl artifact that is 8 bytes long, and is drawn from a random sequence. The pull scenario is defined where a subject receives a token from the Web Source, which the Web Destination uses to pull the SAML Authentication. This could provide more security, as the SAML Authentication assertion does not travel with the subject, but instead must be retrieved by the Web Destination through another channel. The below figure illustrates the pull scenario:

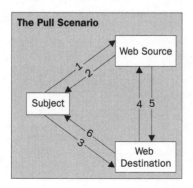

The following steps are the actions numbered in the previous diagram above:

1. Authenticate and request link

2. Redirect using SAML authentication token

3. Request secured resource using token

4. Request SAML authentication assertion using token

5. Provide SAML authentication assertion

6. Provide secured resource

In the pull scenario, the authentication token is generated by the Web Source, and only is retrieved by the Web Destination when and if the subject is re-directed. The Web Source must manage the life cycle of the token.

Push Scenario

The push scenario takes place in the following steps:

1. The SAML Authentication is sent from the Web Source to the Web Destination.

2. The Web Destination returns an SAML authorization decision token to the Web Source.

3. The Web Destination keeps this generated SAML token perhaps in a session or in some persistent repository.

4. The subject is then redirected with this token from the Web Source to the Web Destination.

The following figure illustrates the push scenario:

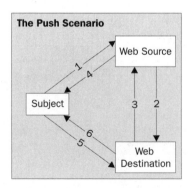

The following steps are the actions numbered in the previous diagram:

1. Authenticate, request link

2. Request SAML authorization token

3. Provide SAML authorization token

4. Redirect using SAML authorization token

5. Request secured resource using token

6. Provide secured resource

In the push scenario, the Web Destination generates the authorization token that the Web Source uses to redirect the subject.

> *It is important to understand that depending on the model, we have used a different type of assertion. In the pull scenario the Web Source authenticates the subject and issues a token for the Web Destination to use. In the push scenario the Web Source requests a token from the Web Destination and it passes an authorization token since this is required when the subject comes to the Web Destination. Both models are acceptable, and the choice will come down to the preferred deployment model.*

You will need to determine which of these two models is a better fit within your environment. If you have a Web Source which acts as a portal with hundreds of Web Destinations, then a push model might be better. In this scenario, the portal would not have to manage the tokens it generates, or the assertions associated with them, until the Web Destination retrieves them later.

Third-Party Scenario

A third scenario is introduced wherein a third-party security service authenticates the subject, which in turn accesses a number of Web Destinations using a pull model for the first Web Destination, and using a push model for the second Web Destination. This model is preferred over the previous one if the organizations rely on an external security service like that offered by Microsoft Passport.

If the organizations use the Liberty Alliance and create a central service as opposed to having one of its members host the service, this may also be a feasible solution, since the Web Source and Web Destination may not be able to handle the extra load of managing all these tokens. A central dedicated service would then make more sense.

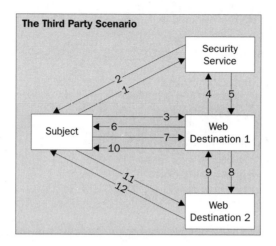

1. Authenticate

2. Redirect using SAML authentication token

3. Request secured resource using token

4. Request SAML authentication assertion using token

5. Receive SAML authentication assertion

6. Provide secured resource

7. Request secured resource for Web Destination

8. Request authorization using SAML authentication from security service

9. Provide SAML authorization token

10. Send SAML authorization token

11. Request secured resource using SAML authorization token

12. Provide secured resource

Authorization Use Case

This use case explores the authorization decision and enforcement point once a subject tries to access a secured resource. The Policy Enforcement Point (PEP) checks permissions with the Policy Decision Point (PDP) before making a decision and releasing the secured resource to the subject. This is what happens behind the scenes, and a Privileged Management Infrastructure (PMI) product could manage much of this.

If you look at our previous scenarios for the Single Sign-on use case, this would happen between the Request Secured Resource step and the Provide Secured Resource step. Depending on the deployment, these components would be deployed in different security domains. In the following chapter on XACML we will see that this specification will give us this flexibility. Traditionally these components are implemented by ACLs (Access Control List) and usually are implemented in a proprietary way within a vendor product. The following figure illustrates this behind-the-scenes process:

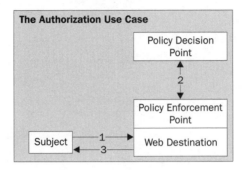

1. Request secured resource

2. Check permissions

3. Provide secured resource

Back-Office Transaction Use Case

This use case deals with two subjects: a buyer subject and a seller subject. This use case has the following three scenarios:

❑ The Back-office transaction scenario

❑ The third party security service scenario

❑ Intermediary add service scenario

The Back-Office Transaction Scenario

In the first scenario subjects are authenticated with respect to the authentication system within their security domain, to confirm their identity. The buyer requests authorization assertions, and then exchanges these authentication and authorization assertions with the seller. The seller does the same with its authentication assertion. The seller then validates the authentication and authorization assertions. Once this is done, and both parties are satisfied with the information that is exchanged, the transaction is executed. As mentioned earlier, the SAML specification does not deal with the trust negotiation that occurs out-of-band between the buyer and the seller organizations. This scenario is illustrated in the following figure:

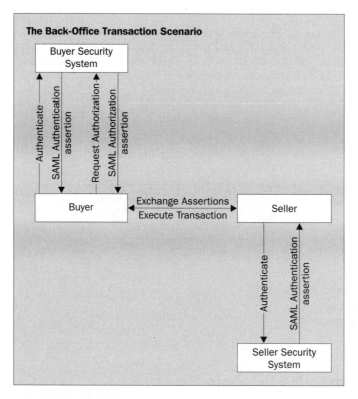

The Third-Party Security Service Scenario

In the second scenario a third-party security service authenticates subjects and provides them with SAML authentication assertions that are exchanged as part of the transaction.

This should be familiar to most of you, since the vertical portals such as Chemdex.com, SciQuest, and VerticalNet use this model. For example, SciQuest (www.SciQuest.com) is a portal for pharmaceutical and biotechnology companies that help scientists find and acquire chemicals, biological compounds, laboratory supplies, and equipment from a variety of suppliers. The vertical marketplaces not only acts as a trusted third-party service, handling and managing the trust relation and collecting fees for matching buyers and sellers, but also provides security services in the form of authentication, and possibly authorization.

SAML would be ideal if, for example, we wanted to open up all the vertical portals by providing them some means to exchange authentication and authorization information. A buyer could register with a specific vertical portal (probably the one where the bulk of his purchase is made), but could make a purchase at another vertical portal using a push or a pull model without having to register at each and every vertical portal with which he conclucts business.

This scenario clearly illustrates the possible use and implementation of SAML. It also applies to third-party security services like Microsoft Passport, and to specifications like the Liberty Alliance. We will look at both of these services later in this chapter.

The following figure illustrates this scenario:

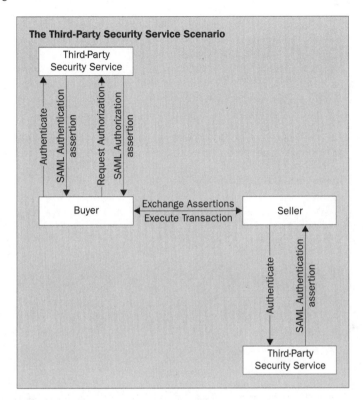

Intermediary Add Service Scenario

The third scenario is that of intermediaries adding authentication and authorization assertions as the transaction goes through the system.

A simple example would be a vertical portal buyer who wishes to purchase goods from a seller and who uses a credit card for payment. The vertical portal would add its authentication and authorization assertions to the transaction. This transaction would also be sent to the credit card service, which would also add its own authentication and authorization assertions. The seller would process the transaction based on the assertions provided by both the parties. In this type of transaction the optional signing and encryption feature would be required by the seller to trust the assertions made by the vertical portal and the credit card service. What is interesting in this scenario is that the seller can make a decision based on the assertions that he trusts the most. We will discuss this in detail later.

This could be important, for example, if we add a third service: a credit rating service that added an assertion regarding the overall credit worthiness of the buyer. This could be different from that provided by the credit card service, which only has one type of relation with the buyer. This scenario is illustrated in the following figure:

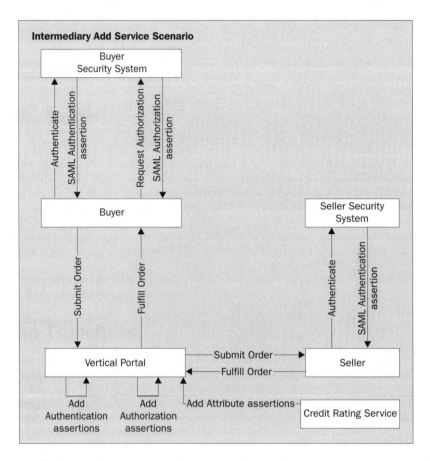

User Session Use Case

User session explores the use of a user session that is maintained as the subject goes to a number of different Web Destinations. The user session must be able to manage logins, timeouts, and logouts. We will look at this use case in more detail in the next section under Session Management. As indicated earlier, Session Management is not part of the 1.0 specification, but it is important to understand to implement SAML within your organization.

Session Management

This concept might be integrated in future versions of the specification. The session management document is currently only a working draft. We will look at the basic requirements, use cases, and scenarios for session management.

Requirements

Session management must support the following requirements:

❑   Session information should easily map to the concept of a web session.

❑   The implementation must be robust and must handle errors such as communication and notification errors.

❑   Session management must support different types of clients (like web and wireless).

❑   Session handling for timeouts must be handled in a consistent manner between authority web sites and Web Destinations.

❑   Offline support is not required.

Session Management also makes the following assumptions:

❑   Subjects interact frequently with a single Web Destination and infrequently across multiple Web Destinations. This means that the number of outstanding sessions should be low and that the need to communicate or notify should be small. If not, the session manager will need to notify all the interested parties that are listening for a particular session, which could create lots of network traffic and the possibility of performance problems.

❑   The Trust relationship between authority and Web Destination is pre-established.

❑   The Content of the session, or what the session is made up of is defined separately.

❑   A Web Destination will only have to deal with one logical session authority for a given subject for a given session.

❑   Authorization information exchange is not required. Session is only concerned from the time a subject is authenticated untill the time that he timeouts or logouts. These are the events that define the scope of a session.

The following use cases have been identified:

Single Sign-on Use Case

A subject authenticates with an authority web site. The login creates a session. The subject requests access to a secured resource at a Web Destination. The subject is then redirected with a token to the Web Destination. The Web Destination uses the token to get session information from the Authority web site via a getSession message. The authorization to the resources is controlled by the session recipient, or in this case the Web Destination. This is centralized authentication and delegated (or distributed) authorization.

This is the same single sign-on use case that we saw earlier using the pull model (refer to the figure in the Pull Scenario section above). The token given out is a pointer to a session object that also manages the associated assertions. In addition, the protocol used between authority web site and Web Destination can be seen. Notably, this is not part of the specification at this time.

Time-out Use Case

Let's say the subject is not active on the authority web site. The authority web site will query each Web Destination web site that requested session information of the subject to inquire if the subject has been active. If the subject is not on any Web Destination, then the authority web site will instruct all Web Destinations to delete the session associated with the subject.

You can see why it was assumed that a subject would interact frequently with a single Web Destination and infrequently across multiple Web Destinations. This notification process could become a bottleneck. Depending on your deployment, you might discover that alternative solutions would better fit your requirements.

Logout Use Case

As the subject logs out of the authority web site, the authority web site will instruct all Web Destinations to delete the session associated with the subject.

Let's look at some of the interactions between the authority web site and the Web Destinations:

❑ A session is created at the authority web site after a subject has logged in.

❑ A local session also is created at the Web Destination for the same subject upon access.

❑ A `getSession` message is sent from the Web Destination to the authority web site.

❑ The authority web site adds the Web Destination to its list of active session recipients for this subject.

❑ An addSession response is sent back. This is the process that initially creates a session and adds listeners. These listeners will then be informed of a logout with a `DeleteSession` message.

This process is shown in the diagram below:

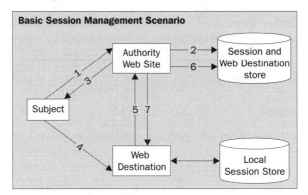

1. Log in and request secured resource

2. Create a session

3. Redirect with SAML token

4. Request secured resource using SAML token

5. GetSession(token)

6. Associate Web Destination to session for subject

7. AddSession(session)

This is the basic starting scenario. After this, a number of possible interactions and outcomes can be explored:

The subject accesses a Web Destination, which manages a local session. There is no interaction with the authority web site session. Local activity is handled locally and communicating back to the authority web site is not required.

The authority web site, on timeout, checks all the active session recipients that are attached to the subject session. The authority web site then sends a `getSession` message to every Web Destination recipient to determine if the subject has an active session at this time. If there are no active sessions or if the subject has logged out, the authority web site deletes the session and notifies every active Web Destination session recipient about the subject, via a `deleteSession` message. This could cause excessive network traffic, with a large number of Web Destinations possibly associated with that subject's session.

When the subject's session times out of the Web Destination site, then there is no interaction with the authority web site session. If the subject requests access to the same Web Destination web site, it can create another session (local) by itself, since it has all the required information and does not need to communicate back to the authority web site.

It is quite clear that there are many synchronization issues to be dealt with while implementing Session Management timeouts.

The document presents six possible options for synchronization:

1. The authority web site pulls state information whenever it needs it. This is the design selected for timeout.

2. The authority web site pulls a state at periodic intervals.

3. The Web Destination pushes the state to the authority web site whenever a change occurs.

4. The Web Destination pushes the state at periodic intervals.

5. The Web Destination pulls the state from the authority web site whenever a potential change could occur, like a timeout.

6. The Web Destination pulls the state at periodic intervals.

An initial handshake negotiation is desired between the authority web site and the destination web site regarding who informs whom and at what intervals. This could be based on a number of parameters that depend on the capabilities of each site in handling and managing session information. This is the same idea as is used in an SSL session, where there is an initial handshake when a number of parameters are negotiated before the communication begins.

Session Management Messages

The number of XML messages, as part of Session Web Services and as defined within the WSDL, is quite small. So are the error messages. This could well expand when Session Management is integrated within the specification.

Initiator	Message	Explanation
Authority website		
	GetSession(SessionID)	Retrieves a session
	DeleteSession(SessionID)	Makes a subject session inactive
Web Destination		
	GetSession(UserID)	Retrieves a session
	DeleteSession(SessionID)	Makes a subject session inactive
Errors		
	InvalidSessionID	
	InvalidSessionInfo	
	InvalidCompanyID	
	InvalidUserID	

The information in the above table gives an idea of the messages initiated by the Authorithy web site, the Web Destination, and the errors that need to be handled. Since this is only a draft document and not part of the specification at this time, the final document may be substantially different.

The Core Specification

The core specification is made up of two documents that cover assertions and protocols in one document and bindings and profiles in the other. The goal of this section is not to go through every aspect of these two documents and their associated schemas, but to cover the core parts with the use of XML examples. Here, we will discuss assertions, protocols, bindings, and profiles with their syntactic details. The specification may also be read from
http://www.oasis-open.org/committees/security/docs/cs-sstc-core-01.pdf.

As most people will be using toolkits or products, which would be hidden through the vendor API, it is important to understand the general constructs that tie in what we have seen so far, in terms of use cases and scenarios. This will help us as we look at a particular vendor toolkit.

Assertions

An assertion is a package of individual statements made by a certain authority. The purpose of assertions is to verify as true the statements that are generated by a specific authority. SAML provides three kinds of assertions, namely Authentication, Attribute, and Authorization. An assertion can also carry the following additional information: issuer and issuance timestamp, assertion ID, subject, conditions under which an assertion is valid, and advice. Once we have an agreement at this level, and have packaged all our statements within an assertion, then we exchange these using the SAML protocol and supporting bindings.

SAML has been designed to be extensible, as good standards are. However, the others are often proprietary, which defeat the purpose of having an interoperable open standard.

In order to trust the authorities that create assertions, we make use of the digital signature. Assertions can also be digitally signed using the XML Signature standard, which is covered in this book.

Assertions are the core of SAML, which is the standard exchange of security information. They are represented using XML, which can have a nested structure. It is comprised of an envelope assertion element, which is common to all assertions, followed by a series of inner elements representing a series of statements.

Let us look at our example followed by a description of each of these elements. The example illustrates a subscriber who has logged into a content portal, and is being redirected to an affiliated syndicate web site. Information is being sent in the form of an SAML statement to the syndicated web site that indicates who the subject is and what rights or attributes have been established at the portal.

Before our example is a summary of what an assertion contains. Below is the pared-down example simplifying the bigger example. We see that an assertion contains a version number, an assertion ID that uniquely identifies it, an issuer (which is the authority) and the time when this was made. Lastly, the assertion can contain a number of authentication, attribute, or authorization statements.

```
<saml:Assertion
        xmlns:saml
        MajorVersion
        MinorVersion
        AssertionID
        Issuer
        IssueInstant >
    <saml:Conditions/>
    <saml:AuthenticationStatement/>
    <saml:AttributeStatement/>
    <saml:AuthorizationDecisionStatement/>
</saml:Assertion>
```

And now, the unabridged version:

```
<saml:Assertion
        xmlns:saml="http://www.oasis-open.org/committees/security/docs/draft-
                    sstc-schema-assertion-16.xsd"
        MajorVersion="1"
        MinorVersion="0"
        AssertionID="250.192.2.150.1003876543098"
        Issuer="Content Portal"
        IssueInstant="2002-11-03T16:28:22-05:00" >

    <saml:Conditions
        NotBefore="2002-11-03T16:28:22-05:00"
        NotOnOrAfter="2002-11-03T16:38:22-05:00">

    <saml:AbstractCondition
        xsi:type="AudienceRestrictionConditionType"
```

```
            xmlns:xsi="http://www.w3.org/2001/XMLSchema-instance">
      <saml:Audience>
            "http://www.contentportal.com/PartnerAgreementAugust2000""
      </saml:Audience>
    </saml:AbstractCondition>
  </saml:Conditions>

  <saml:AuthenticationStatement
      AuthenticationMethod="Password" AuthenticationInstant="2002-11-
                        03T16:28:22-05:00" >
    <saml:Subject>
      <saml:NameIdentifier
            SecurityDomain="www.contentportal.com"
            Name="contentPortal" />
    </saml:Subject>
    <saml:AuthenticationLocality
          IPAddress="250.192.2.150"
          DNSAddress="secure_server" />
  </saml:AuthenticationStatement>

  <saml:AttributeStatement>
    <saml:Subject>
      <saml:NameIdentifier
            SecurityDomain="www.contentPortal.com"
            Name="subscriber" />
    </saml:Subject>

    <saml:Attribute
      AttributeName="PartnerAttribute"
      AttributeNamespace="http://www.contentportal.com/syndicated/namespace" >
      <saml:AttributeValue>
        <Partner>
          <Company>Content Portal</Company>
          <SubscriptionCategory>Silver</SubscriptionCategory>
          <AccessLevel>10</AccessLevel>
        </Partner>
      </saml:AttributeValue>
    </saml:Attribute>

  </saml:AttributeStatement>

  <saml:AuthorizationDecisionStatement
      Decision="Permit"
      Resource=" http://www.contentportal.com/latestnews.jsp">
    <saml:actions />
    <saml:Subject>
      <saml:NameIdentifier
            SecurityDomain="www.contentportal.com"
            Name="contentPortal" />
    </saml:Subject>

  </saml:AuthorizationDecisionStatement>

</saml:Assertion>
```

The <Assertion> Element

The Assertion element can be split into outer and inner elements. The outer elements, common to all assertions, consist of an envelope of information, while the inner elements deal with the specific type of assertion. This determines how an assertion is processed. You will want to validate the envelope information first before opening the body, which requires much more processing.

This element may include the following outer elements and attributes:

Attribute	Required	Type	Description
MajorVersion	Yes	Integer	Currently defined as 1.
MinorVersion	Yes	Integer	Currently defined as 0.
AssertionID	Yes	IDType	The identifier for this assertion. In the example this was derived from an IP address.
Issuer	Yes	String	The issuer of the assertion contains a URI reference, which is context-independent.
IssueInstant	Yes	dateTime	The time of issue in UTC (Universal Coordinated Time).

Subelement	Required	Type	Description
Conditions	Optional	complexType	Conditions that must be taken into account in assessing the validity of the assertion, or the conditions under which the assertion is valid. Examples include assertion validity period, and audience and target restrictions.
Advice	Optional	complexType	Additional information related to the assertion that assists processing. Could provide information on how the assertion was constructed.
ds:Signature	Optional	complexType	An XML Digital Signature that can be associated to an assertion. This element is comes from another name namespace, namely ds for Digital Signature, which is covered in this book.

This is the list of inner elements, all of which are optional:

Subelement	Description
AttributeStatement	The AttributeStatement provides us with additional information that is associated with the Subject, like his AccessLevel and SubscriptionCategory.
SubjectStatement	It contains a Subject element that allows an issuer to describe a subject.
AuthenticationStatement	The AuthenticationStatement element supplies a statement by the issuer that its subject was authenticated by a particular means at a particular time. As indicated earlier, the authentication statements only describe acts of authentication that have already occurred. In our example we have a basic password authentication that occurred. Additional information is given regarding the security domain and IP address within that security domain documenting that this authentication took place.
AuthorizationDecisionStatement	The AuthorizationDecisionStatement element provides us with a decision statement made by the issuer or the authority, with regard to a specified secured resource which is identified by means of a URI reference.

The <Conditions> Element

The Conditions Element tells us many things. It tells us the range of time that this assertion is valid. It also tells us the audience to which this assertion is applicable. This is probably the most important element within the assertion. This tells us by whom, and the general rules under which, this assertion is governed. For example, when two parties sign an agreement to conduct business with each other, then this agreement could be a URL pointing to the agreement, which usually has a start and an end date.

```
<saml:Conditions NotBefore NotOnOrAfter>
  <saml:AbstractCondition xsi:type xmlns:xsi>
    <saml:Audience>        </saml:Audience>
  </saml:AbstractCondition>
</saml:Conditions>
```

The `<Conditions>` element may contain the following attributes:

Attribute	Required	Type	Description
NotBefore	Optional	dateTime	Specifies the earliest time instant at which the assertion is valid. The time value is encoded in UTC.
NotOnOrAfter	Optional	dateTime	Specifies the time instant at which the assertion has expired. The time value is encoded in UTC.

The following table shows the sub-elements of the `<Conditions>` element:

Subelement	Required	Description
`<Condition>`	0 or more	Provides an extension point allowing extension schemas to define new conditions.
`<AudienceRestrictionCondition>`	0 or more	Specifies that the assertion be addressed to a particular audience.

If any assertion contains a condition element, the following rules must be used to determine the overall validity of the assertion:

- ❑ If no sub-elements or attributes are supplied in the `Conditions` element, then the assertion is considered valid.

- ❑ If any sub-element or attribute of the `condition` element is determined to be invalid, then the assertion is invalid.

- ❑ If any sub-element or attribute of the `conditions` element cannot be evaluated, then the validity of the assertion cannot be determined and is indeterminate.

- ❑ If all sub-elements and attributes of the `condition` element are determined to be valid, then the assertion is considered valid.

The `<Subject>` Element

The `Subject` element specifies the principal that is the subject of the statement. It contains either or both of the following elements:

Element/ Attribute	Type	Description
NameIdentifier		An identification of a subject by its name and security domain
NameQualifier	string	The security domain that qualifies the name of the subject
Format	anyURI	The format value must be a URI reference. The following URI references are defined by this specification, where only the fragment identifier portion is shown, assuming a base URI of the SAML assertion namespace name:
		#emailAddress
		#X509SubjectName (part of a PKI certificate)
SubjectConfirmation		Information that allows the subject to be authenticated
SubjectConfirmationData	anyType	
ConfirmationMethod	anyURI	
KeyInfo	Digital Signature	

Note, all the attributes/elements shown above are optional. Also, this element is described here because it is reused in other elements within the assertion.

The <AuthenticationStatement> Element

The authentication statement describes our subject in order to ensure that he is not confused with others. Any confusion could cause us apply an assertion to the wrong person. A subject can have a name and be associated to a specific security domain with a specific IP and DNS address. As we also saw in the previous section, we can further qualify our subject with a name that is in the form of an e-mail address or that belongs to an X.509 certificate that is probably stored in a corporate directory.

```
<saml:AuthenticationStatement AuthenticationMethod AuthenticationInstant>
  <saml:Subject>
    <saml:NameIdentifier SecurityDomain Name/>
  </saml:Subject>
  <saml:AuthenticationLocality IPAddress DNSAddress />
</saml:AuthenticationStatement>
```

Attribute/Element	Required	Type	Description
AuthenticationMethod	Required	anyURI	A URI reference that specifies the type of authentication that took place. In our example this was a basic authentication of userid and password.
AuthenticationInstant	Required	dateTime	Specifies the time at which the authentication took place.

Attribute/Element	Required	Type	Description
SubjectLocality	Optional		Specifies the DNS domain name and IP address for the system entity from which the Subject was authenticated.
IPAddress	Optional	string	IPAddress of Authorithy.
DNSAddress	Optional	string	DNSaddress of Authorithy.

Attribute/Element	Required	Type	Description
<AuthorityBinding>	0 or more		Indicates that additional information about the subject may be available other than what was requested.
Location	Required	anyURI	This gives information on how to communicate with the Authority if we want additional information.
Binding	Required	anyURI	The binding that should be used when communicating with the Authority.
AuthorityKind	Required	Qname	This specifies the type of SAML protocol queries to which the Authority will respond.

The <AttributeStatement> Element

Element	Required	Type	Description
Attribute	1 or more		Specifies an attribute of the subject
AttributeValue	Any Number	anyType	Specifies the time instant at which the assertion has expired. The time value is encoded in UTC.

In our example the attribute statements illustrate that the subject has an access level of 10 and is a registered subscriber at the Silver level. These attribute statements mostly would be used to give access to content located at syndicated web sites.

The <AuthorizationDecisionStatement> Element

The AuthorizationDecisionStatement is a statement indicating the result of a decision made regarding to the access of a resource made by the Subject. The URL of the resource that the Subject wanted to access is provided as well as the decision, along with what the can Subject do against this resource. Evidence is also itself an assertion (it also can be an ID that references the evidence) that was used in comment up with the specific decision.

Attribute	Required	Type	Description
Resource	Required	anyURI	
Decision	Required	DecisionType	Takes values: Permit, Deny, Indeterminate
Action	One or more		The set of actions authorized to be performed on the specified secured resource.
Evidence	Optional		A set of assertions that the issuer relied on in making this decision.

Protocol Request and Response

SAML defines a protocol by which clients can request assertions from SAML authorities and get a response from them. This protocol consists of XML request and response messages. These requests can be bound to different communication and transport protocols. SAML currently has one binding, that of SOAP over HTTP. All types of SAML requests are met with one common SAML response. The specification currently defines the following types of requests:

- ❑ SubjectQuery
- ❑ AuthenticationQuery
- ❑ AttributeQuery
- ❑ AuthorizationDecisionQuery
- ❑ AssertionIDReference
- ❑ AssertionArtifact

Request

We will describe what each type of query can be used for and also will show an example of what an attribute query looks like.

The following example illustrates a typical request showing how a request for a financial rating attribute is initiated. An affiliated syndicate partner that requires additional information from the content portal could use this request.

```
<samlp:Request
        MajorVersion="1"
        MinorVersion="0"
        RequestID="250.192.2.150.1003876543098"
        xmlns:samlp="http://www.oasis-open.org/committees/security/docs/draft
```

```
                    -sstc-schema-protocol-16.xsd">

   <samlp:AttributeQuery CompletenessSpecifier="Partial">

     <saml:Subject
        xmlns:saml="http://www.oasis-open.org/committees/security/docs/
                             draft-sstc-schema-assertion-16.xsd">
          <saml:NameIdentifier
               Name="contentPortal"
               SecurityDomain="www.contentPortal.com"/>
     </saml:Subject>

     <saml:AttributeDesignator
          AttributeName="FinancialRating"
          AttributeNamespace="http://www.moodys.com/financial_rating.xsd"
          xmlns:saml="http://www.oasis-open.org/committees/
                      security/docs/draft-sstc-schema-assertion-16.xsd"/>

   </samlp:AttributeQuery>
</samlp:Request>
```

Let's explain what we have just seen. We have a request for attribute information (`AttributeQuery`). The envelope information tells us that this request uses the SAML protocol with a major version of 1 and a minor version of 0. The requester has given a request ID that means something to it and that should be unique for this requester. In the body of the request, we see that the subject has been provided. This indicates that the name of the subject is our content portal organization, and belongs to this Security Domain.

RequestAbstractType

All SAML requests are of types that are derived from the abstract `RequestAbstractType` complex type. This type defines common attributes and elements that are associated with all SAML requests. This is very similar to the assertion's common elements.

Attribute	Required	Type	Description
RequestID	Yes	IDType	An identifier for the request.
MajorVersion	Yes	integer	Currently set at 1.
MinorVersion	Yes	integer	Currently set at 0.
IssueInstant	Yes	dateTime	The time instant of issue of the request.
RespondWith		Any Number	Each `RespondWith` element specifies a type of response that is acceptable to the requester. For example the requester wants only to receive an attribute statement.
ds:Signature	Optional		An XML Digital Signature that authenticates the request.

The <Request> Element

As mentioned earlier we will provide a description for each type of request. The goal is for you to understand which type of query you need to issue to get the required response. The <Request> element provides either a query or a request for a specific assertion identified by AssertionIDReference.

Attribute	Type	Description
SubjectQuery	Choice	An extension point that allows schemas to define new types of queries that specify a single SAML subject. This probably is a query you won't issue very often since we are usually looking for information on a given subject.
AuthenticationQuery	Choice	Makes a query for authentication information in regards to the subject. The response should return authentication assertions for the matching subject. The requester and responder must ensure that they are talking about the same subject. We need to provide as much information as possible on the subject to ensure that we get the correct assertions back.
AttributeQuery	Choice	Makes a query for attribute information. The response should return information on the listed attributes for this subject. The requester may want information on a number of attributes but will only receive information that he is entitled to see. In our example we wanted information on the financial rating of the subject based on the Moody's organization.
AuthorizationDecisionQuery	Choice	Makes a query for an authorization decision. It answers the questions: Is this subject authorized to access this secured resource in this manner given this evidence?
AssertionIDReference	1 or more	Requests assertions by reference to its assertion identifier.
AssertionArtifact	1 or more	Requests assertions by supplying an assertion artifact that represents it.

Response

As mentioned earlier, all responses are the same regardless of the type of request. However, in the envelope information we also will get a Status Code that will let us see the result of our request. We can use this to determine if we want to go any further and process the rest of the response. In the body of the response we will get back an assertion based on the type of request we have made. As you recall from the Assertion section a number of elements can be returned such as attribute statements, authentication statements, authorization decision statements, and conditions.

The following example illustrates a typical response to an assertion request:

```
<samlp:Response
        InResponseTo="250.192.2.150.1003876543098"
        MajorVersion="1"
        MinorVersion="0"
        ResponseID="250.192.2.150.1003876543098"
        StatusCode="Success"
        xmlns:samlp="http://www.oasis-open.org/committees/security/docs/
                        draft-sstc-schema-protocol-16.xsd">

   <saml:Assertion
        AssertionID="251.192.2.150.1003876543098"
        IssueInstant="2002-11-03T16:28:22-05:00"
        Issuer="Moodys Inc."
        MajorVersion="1"
        MinorVersion="0"
        xmlns:saml="http://www.oasis-open.org/committees/
                        security/docs/draft-sstc-schema-assertion-16.xsd">

    <saml:Conditions
           NotBefore="2002-11-03T16:28:22-05:00"
           NotOnOrAfter="2002-11-03T16:38:22-05:00">

     <saml:AbstractCondition
            xmlns:xsi="http://www.w3.org/2001/XMLSchema-instance"
            xsi:type="AudienceRestrictionConditionType">
        <saml:Audience>
          http://www.moodys.com/disclaimer.xml
        </saml:Audience>
     </saml:AbstractCondition>
    </saml:Conditions>

    <saml:AttributeStatement>
      <saml:Subject>
        <saml:NameIdentifier
              Name="contentPortal"
              SecurityDomain="www.contentPortal.com"/>
      </saml:Subject>

      <saml:Attribute AttributeName="FinancialRating"
            AttributeNamespace="http://www.moodys.com/financial_rating.xsd">
        <saml:AttributeValue>
          <FinancialRating Rating="AAA"/>
        </saml:AttributeValue>
      </saml:Attribute>
    </saml:AttributeStatement>

   </saml:Assertion>

</samlp:Response>
```

Notice that it is the assertion issued by Moody's on a specific date, and that it included a Conditions statement that indicates that this assertion is valid for a period of about 10 minutes with an associated disclaimer. It also has an attribute statement that describes the subject that was originally sent, and provides the important piece of information that we wanted – the fianancial rating attribute that has a value of AAA.

This type defines common attributes and elements that are associated with all SAML responses:

Attribute/Element	Required	Type	Description
ResponseID	Yes	IDType	An identifier for the response.
InResponseTo	No	IDReferenceType	A reference to the identifier of the request to which the response corresponds.
MajorVersion	Yes	integer	The major version of this response. The identifier for the version of SAML defined in this specification is 1.
MinorVersion	Yes	integer	The minor version of this response. The identifier for the version of SAML defined in this specification is 0.
IssueInstant	Yes	datetime	The time instant of issue of the response.
Recipient	No	anyURI	The intended recipient of this response. This is useful to prevent malicious forwarding of responses to unintended recipients, a protection that is required by some use profiles.
<ds:Signature>	No		An XML Digital Signature that authenticates the response.

The <Response> Element

The <Response> element specifies the status of the associated SAML request and specifies a list of zero or more assertions that answer the request. Again this response is applicable to all request types.

The <status> element of the response has three sub-elements as given below:

Attribute	Required	Type	Description
StatusCode	Yes	QName	The StatusCode element specifies one or more nested codes representing the status of the corresponding request.
StatusMessage	Optional	String	A message which may be returned to an operator.
StatusDetail	Optional		Specifies additional information concerning an error condition.

The `StatusCode` element has a value attribute that takes the following values:

Value	Description
Success	The request succeeded.
VersionMismatch	The receiver could not process the request because the version was incorrect.
Requester	The request could not be performed due to an error on the part of the requester.
Responder	The request could not be performed due to an error on the part of the responder.
RequestVersionTooHigh*	The protocol version specified in the request is a major upgrade from the highest protocol version supported by the responder.
RequestVersionTooLow*	The responder cannot respond to the particular request using the SAML version specified in the request because the version is too low.
RequestVersionDeprecated*	The responder does not respond to any requests with the protocol version specified in the request.
TooManyResponses*	The response would contain more elements than the responder will return.
RequestDenied*	The responder is able to process the request but has chosen not to respond. This may be used when the responder is concerned about the security context of the request or the sequence of requests received from a particular client.
ResourceNotRecognized*	The responder does not wish to support resource-specific attribute queries, or the resource value provided is invalid or unrecognized.

In the table above, * indicates second-level status codes that are referenced at various places in the specification. Additional sub-codes may be defined in future versions of the SAML specification.

XML Digital Signature

SAML Assertions, Requests, and Response messages may be digitally signed, which gives the following additional benefits:

❑ An assertion signed by the asserting party (AP) strengthens the assertion by adding:

   ❑ Message integrity.

   ❑ Authentication of the asserting party to a relying party (RP).

   ❑ If the signature is based on the asserting party's public-private key pair, then it also provides for non-repudiation of origin.

❑   An SAML request or an SAML response message signed by the message originator strengthens the message by adding the following:

   ❑   Message integrity.

   ❑   Authentication of message origin to a destination.

   ❑   If the signature is based on the originator's public-private key pair, then it also provides for non-repudiation of origin.

We will look at an example in the following section on Bindings.

Bindings

So far we have looked at the Assertion and Protocol documents of the standard. These are probably the most important parts to understand. The rest tend to be hidden from most developers using products and toolkits.

SAML assertions may use a variety of existing protocols for transportation. At this time the currently available bindings for SAML are SAML HyperText Transport Protocol (HTTP) Binding and SAML Simple Object Access Protocol (SOAP). The SAML SOAP binding defines how SOAP is used to send and receive SAML requests and responses. You may have noticed that we said "SOAP binding" and not "SOAP binding using HTTP". HTTP is mandatory but could easily use other protocols like FTP or SMTP. SAML is really independent of the underlying transport protocol associated with binding.

A typical SOAP message consists of the following three parts:

   ❑   An envelope part

   ❑   A header data part

   ❑   A message body part

Here are a few facts and restrictions imposed by this binding:

   ❑   SAML requests and responses elements must be enclosed within the SOAP message body.

   ❑   An SAML request cannot include more than one request per SOAP message.

   ❑   The response must return a response element within the body of the SOAP message. If an error occurs, then it returns a SOAP fault code. An SAML response cannot include more than one response per SOAP message.

The binding does not add additional SOAP headers, and requesters should not process any additional headers. Much of the security in terms of authentication, message integrity, and message confidentiality relies on the use of SSL or TLS.

Here is an example of a request that asks for an assertion containing an authentication statement:

```
POST /SamlContentPortal HTTP/1.1
Host: www.syndicated.com
Content-Type: text/xml
Content-Length: nnn

SOAPAction: http://www.oasis-open.org/committees/security
```

```
<SOAP-ENV:Envelope
xmlns:SOAP-ENV="http://schemas.xmlsoap.org/soap/envelope/">
  <SOAP-ENV:Body>
    <samlp:Request xmlns:samlp="…" xmlns:saml="…" xmlns:ds="…">
      <ds:Signature>
…
      </ds:Signature>
      <samlp:AuthenticationQuery>
        …
      </samlp:AuthenticationQuery>
    </samlp:Request>
  </SOAP-ENV:Body>
</SOAP-ENV:Envelope>
```

Here is the corresponding response, which supplies an assertion and contains an authentication statement as requested:

```
HTTP/1.1 200 OK
Content-Type: text/xml
Content-Length: nnnn

<SOAP-ENV:Envelope
xmlns:SOAP-ENV="http://schemas.xmlsoap.org/soap/envelope/">
  <SOAP-ENV:Body>
    <samlp:Response xmlns:samlp""="…" xmlns:saml""="…" xmlns:ds="…">
      <Status>
        <StatusCodevalue=""samlp:Success""/>
      </Status>
      <ds:Signature>
        . . .
      </ds:Signature>
      <saml:Assertion>
        <saml:AuthenticationStatement>
          …
        </saml:AuthenticationStatement>
      </saml:Assertion>
    </samlp:Response>
  </SOAP-ENV:Body>
</SOAP-ENV:Envelope>
```

Profiles

The specification has also defined profiles of SAML as sets of rules describing how to insert and extract SAML assertions from a message framework.

For example, a SOAP profile of SAML describes how SAML assertions can be added to SOAP messages and how SOAP headers are affected by SAML assertions, as well as how SAML-related errors should be reflected in SOAP messages. This is not the same as the SOAP binding. The SOAP binding only defines how to use SOAP to send and receive SAML requests and responses, which are located in the SOAP body. Think of profiles as the rules for embedding, extracting, and integrating.

Next is an overview of profiles.

Push or Browser Post Profile

One lets a Web Source push authentication data to a Web Destination. If you look back at our push use cases we never really said how the information travels. SAML assertions are uploaded to the browser and conveyed to the Web Destination as part of an HTTP POST payload.

Cookies are not employed in any profile, as cookies impose the limitation that both the Web Source and the Web destination site must belong to the same cookie domain.

The specification also outlines security measures in the generation and handling of the SAML response, to prevent possible forged or stolen responses as well as attacks or malicious Web Destinations.

Pull or Browser Artifact Profile

This lets the Web Destination pull the authentication data from the Web source. A SAML artifact or SAML token as we have seen, is carried as part of a URL query string such that, when the token is conveyed to the Web Source, the SAML token references a particular assertion. The SAML token is conveyed via redirection to the Web Destination. This technique is used in the browser/artifact profile of SAML. If you look back at our pull use cases we never really said how the information travels.

The committee is developing a procedure for openly registering profile specifications in order to promote availability and reuse. A WS-Security profile is in the works as well as others.

If we go back to our SAML protocol, we can see that for a request we have the ability to send a AssertionArtifact request to retrieve the assertion that was created by the Web Source. This is a one-time request. Once the Web Destination has retrieved the assertion using the SAML token, it cannot do so again.

The specification also outlines security measures in the generation and handling of the SAML artefact to prevent possible forged or stolen artifacts as well as attacks or malicious Web Destinations.

Key Standards and Specifications Related to SAML

The XML security space is starting to fill up quickly with various industry specifications and standards. It's sometimes hard to keep track as new specs often come on board, and old ones are merged or removed. The current SAML 1.0 Specification has not spend much time to integrate other security specifications; it does cover XML Digital Signatures and XML Encryption. We expect other versions of the specification to address this area in more detail. Below a list of the most important specifications that SAML is associated with. Most of these can be found in the book.

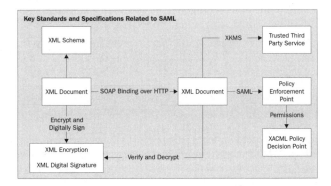

This application-independent framework was developed by W3C. It provides integrity, message authentication, and signer authentication services for data of any type, whether located within the XML that includes the signature or elsewhere. The SAML specification has a working draft on the role of Digital Signatures and SAML.

SAML Assertions, Request, and Response messages may be digitally signed. If an issuer signs on an assertion then this would support message integrity, authentication of the issuer, and non-repudiation of origin. If an SAML request or response is digitally signed then it would also provide the same benefits of a digitally-signed assertion.

XKMS (XML Key Management Specification): It establishes a standard for XML applications to use Public Key Infrastructure (PKI) when handling digitally-signed or encrypted XML documents. It provides on previous line the ability to obtain key information. It is currently being developed through the W3C. SAML is not tied to XKMS for trust services, and remains agnostic to the various security mechanisms used to register, validate, and revoke cryptographic material.

XML Encryption: A companion to XML Digital Signature, it addresses the encryption and decryption of XML documents and portions of those documents. It is currently being developed through the W3C. This could be used if assertions that are involved in privacy, such as communication between a hospital web site and a physician.

XML messaging services (SOAP, ebXML, BEEP, XML-P): SOAP allows objects or code of any kind, on any platform, to communicate across a decentralized, distributed environment. Now, SOAP over HTTP is the only messaging service implemented. Refer to SAML Bindings and Profiles earlier in this chapter.

XACML (XML Access Control Markup Language): This defines a standard that helps define schemas for expressing policies for information access over the Internet. XACML is expected to address fine-grained control of authorized activities based on access requester characteristics, the protocol over which the request is made, and the authentication mechanism used. It is currently being developed through OASIS. At this time the SAML 1.0 specification does not address this topic. XACML was designed to integrate with SAML and with XML Digital Signature. We will look in more detail at XACML in the following chapter.

Earlier in the chapter, we looked at the Authorization Use Case, in which the Policy Decision Point (PDP) would grant access to a secure resource. Now it would consult policies encoded in XACML to determine whether access would be granted to a secured resource.

The following is a small sample of an XACML policy rule, which says that citizens are allowed to read their own tax records. This example illustrates the connection between SAML and XACML. We will look in detail at XACML in the following chapter.

SPML (Service Provisioning Markup Language): This allows for exchanging user resource and service provisioning information. It currently is being developed through OASIS as part of the OASIS Provisioning Services TC. This is an interesting specification because so much service provisioning information is involved in setting up a subject in a new domain. One of the benefits of SAML is the fact that the SAML assertions do not have to be duplicated, but are just consumed by Web Destinations.

WS-Security (Web Services Security): WS-Security describes enhancements to SOAP messaging that address message integrity, message confidentiality, and single message authentication. These enhancements can be used to accommodate a wide variety of security models and encryption technologies. WS-Security also provides a general-purpose mechanism for associating security tokens with messages. No specific type of security token is required by WS-Security. It is designed to be extensible. This is where SAML would be integrated with WS-Security by being just another type of Security Token format. It is possible that someone would develop a WS-Security profile of SAML.

In addition, the WS-Security road map has proposed a set of specifications yet to come that address a variety of other security, policy, messaging, and trust issues associated with Web Services security. They include WS-Policy, WS-Trust, WS-Privacy, WS-Secure Conversation, WS-Federation, and WS-Authorization. We will have to see how SAML will work with these specifications.

Products and Toolkits

Since its inception SAML has gained rapid acceptance within the security community. A number of products and toolkits are already available with more to follow. Here is a partial list of some of these products and toolkits. Most of these organizations recently showcased their products and issued press releases at the first public demonstration at the OASIS SAML Interoperability Event, which was held at the Burton Catalyst Conference on July 15, 2002 in San Francisco:

Organization	URL	Product Details
Baltimore Technologies	http://www.baltimore.com/	Baltimore Technologies recently announced the integration of SAML into its SelectAccess 5.0 product. Commercial Product.
BEA Systems	http://www.bea.com/	BEA Systems will be integrating SAML into its product line in the future. Commercial Product.
CrossLogix	http://www.crosslogix.com/	CrossLogix delivers e-business entitlement software. It recently announced the integration of SAML into its CrossLogix3 entitlement authorization platform. Commercial Product.

Organization	URL	Product Details
Entegrity Solutions	http://www.entegrity.com/	Entegrity Solutions is a provider of Application Security for Java-based web, portal, and web services applications. Entegrity Solutions recently has announced the integration of SAML into its AssureAccess access management software. Commercial Product.
Entrust	http://www.entrust.com/	Entrust delivers enhanced Internet security services that provide identification, entitlements, verification, privacy, and security management capabilities. Entrust offers a product called GetAccess which incorporates SAML as part of a Privilege Management Infrastructure (PMI). Commercial Product.
IBM	http://www.ibm.com/	IBM is integrating SAML into its Tivoli product line. Tivoli technology management software gives IT departments the ability to manage e-business infrastructure. Commercial Product.
Internet2	http://www.internet2.edu/	Internet2 is a consortium led by over 190 universities working in partnership with industry and government to develop and deploy advanced network applications and technologies. It offers a set of open source Java and C++ libraries under the name OpenSAML that are fully consistent with the SAML 1.0 specification. Open Source.
Netegrity	http://www.netegrity.com/	Netegrity is a provider of solutions for securely managing e-business relationships. Netegrity offers a product called AffiliateMinder and an associated service, Affiliate Service, to enable secure e-business networks based on SAML. Netegrity also offers a toolkit based on Java called JSAML which is available for download. We will look at this toolkit later in this section. Commercial Product.
Novell	http://www.novell.com/	Novell recently unveiled project Destiny, the company's roadmap for the next generation of directory services. The roadmap consists of several key directory releases over the next 18 months that incorporate SAML as part of its Federated Trust Infrastructure. Commercial Product.

Table continued on following page

Organization	URL	Product details
Oblix	http://www.oblix.com/	Oblix enables companies to secure and manage e-business with the use of enterprise identity management and web access control solution. Oblix has recently announced the integration of SAML into its NetPoint 6 identity-based solution. Commercial Product.
OpenNetwork	http://www.opennetwork.com/	OpenNetwork is a developer of web access management software. OpenNetwork has recently announced the integration of SAML into its DirectorySmart Web identity and access management security solution. OpenNetwork also demonstrated the interoperability of its SAML product with Microsoft Passport. SAML could be the integration technology between the Microsoft Passport service and the Liberty Alliance specification. We will look at this topic later in this chapter. Commercial Product.
Phaos Technology Corporation	http://www.phaos.com/	Phaos Technology Corporation provides Java developers with security products and services. Phaos has developed a Java product called Phaos SAML as part of its XML security suite. Phaos also has developed an SDK that implements the Liberty Alliance 1.0 specification. Commercial Product.
Quadrasis	http://www.quadrasis.com/	Quadrasis products and services are provided by the Software Solutions Division of Hitachi Computer Products (America), Inc. Quadrasis, a business unit of Hitachi, introduced a developer tool called EASI Security Unifier which is based on SAML for enterprise application security integration. Commercial Product.
RSA Security	http://www.rsa.com/	RSA announced earlier this year that it would grant non-exclusive royalty-free license use of two of its patents to companies deploying applications that make use of the SAML specification. RSA Security has recently announced the integration of SAML into its RSA ClearTrust web access management solution. Commercial Product.
Sigaba	http://www.Sigaba.com/	Sigaba is an e-mail security company, providing enterprise-class, secure messaging solutions. Sigaba has recently announced the integration of SAML into its product line. Commercial Product.

Organization	URL	Product details
SUN	http://www.sun.com/	Sun has announced support for SAML and the new Liberty Alliance specification as part of its Sun ONE Identity Server 6.0 software. Commercial Product.
Vordel	http://www.vordel.com/	Vordel is a Web Services security company. Vordel recently has announced the integration of SAML into its VordelSecure product. Commercial Product.

Netegrity's JSAML Toolkit

Netegrity has made available to developers an easy-to-use toolkit with lots of documentation and sample applications for Java developers who want to develop SAML-aware applications.

The toolkit includes support for the following features:

❑   Components for constructing and reading SAML assertions

❑   Components for interpreting SAML requests and responses

❑   Wrappers for PKI and XML Digital Signature implementations

❑   Security libraries for validating SAML

The Java implementation is included in a single JAR file (JSAML), which has the following packages structure:

❑   `com.netegrity.jsaml.assertion`

  Components for reading and constructing SAML assertions

❑   `com.netegrity.jsaml.protocol`

  Components for reading and building SAML requests and responses

❑   `com.netegrity.jsaml.sign`

  Components for signing assertions and verifying digital signatures

JSAML's API

Here are some of the main classes in each of these packages, grouped according to their functionality. The names would be familiar since they have kept the same names as the specification. The API is small and quite easy to use:

Assertion Classes

SAML_AbstractAssertion
SAML_Assertion
SAML_Conditions
SAML_Advice
SAML_Statement
SAML_AttributeStatement

SAML_AuthenticationStatement
SAML_AuthorizationStatement
SAML_SubjectStatement
SAML_Attribute
SAML_Subject
SAML_NameIdentifier

Protocol Classes

SAML_AbstractRequest
SAML_Request
SAML_AbstractResponse
SAML_Response
SAML_Query
SAML_AttributeQuery
SAML_AuthenticationQuery
SAML_AuthorizationQuery
SAML_SubjectQuery

Digital Signature Classes

SAML_SignedAssertion
SAML_SignedAssertionList
SAML_SignedRequest
SAML_SignedResponse

The Content Portal Example using JSAML

The purpose of the following example is to demonstrate the following:

❑ The typical interaction found in an SAML application. This will validate some of the use cases we have seen previously.

❑ The messages that are sent back and forth between our web services.

❑ The use of JSAML in accomplishing this task. We are only concerned with the specific API that is required to accomplish this. There is almost no Java code, and you should easily be able to take any toolkit that is available for your environment, assuming that toolkit has the same API.

What you will learn is that it is very easy to develop and deploy an application and that working at the API level is a lot easier than having to understand and deal with every aspect of the specification. This is another way of saying that if you are not already a fan of specification, then going though this example will give you the equivalent knowledge.

The example is taken from personal experience while working at InfoSpace inc, a private label portal that aggregates its own and third-party content and applications for delivery over broadband, the web, and wireless. We did not use SAML so this example will be new.

We will look at a subscriber-based content portal in which content has been aggregated from many syndicated partners. The content portal has established agreements to syndicate the content in return for a fee. Subscribers pay a fee to the content portal and benefit from all the available content. The following outlines the sequence of events (some events to not require or use SAML, and we will not explore those further) that needs to occur. We will then look at which API from the JSAML toolkit is required. Again, there is a direct one-to-one mapping between the API and the specification, and you can easily refer to earlier sections of this chapter to see what the toolkit is doing behind the scenes.

1. A subscriber must log on to the content portal. This is accomplished by presenting a login page typically generated by a JSP or ASP application. The subscriber submits this login page containing his subscriber identification and password. This login information is passed to an authentication web service that authenticates the subscriber.

2. The subscriber is then directed to the portal content web service, which will be used to generate the dynamic content as the subscriber navigates or searches inside the portal. At this point, there is no use of SAML; the subscriber has just logged on to the portal and is looking at pages and links aggregated by the portal and tailored for each subscriber at run time.

3. As the subscriber moves around the portal content, the Web Service serves up the content pages in the form of links to its aggregated content that it has assembled through its network of affiliated partners. It only gets interesting when the subscriber clicks on a link that belongs to an affiliated partner. We will begin to see the exchange of SAML messages.

4. The request is intercepted by the redirect web service (this is our Web Source from our earlier use cases). The SAML redirect web service creates the SAML assertion, generates an SAML token for that assertion, and forwards or re-directs the subscriber to the syndicated resource site.

5. The syndicated web service at the syndicated site calls back (this is our pull scenario use case) using the SAML token. This also is our Web Destination from this same pull scenario use case.

6. Once the syndicated web service gets the SAML assertion back then it processes or consumes the SAML assertion and displays the requested content to the subscriber.

We will look at these two web services (redirect and syndicated) with the goal of showing the correct SAML API to use and to get a better understanding of how it matches with the SAML specification we just covered. A small note: anything in bold within the web service indicates that this is coming from the JSAML toolkit.

Redirect Web Service

The Redirect Web Service generates an SAML token, creates the SAML assertion, and stores it with the generated SAML token. It then re-directs the subscriber to the syndicated site with the SAML token.

The content portal maintains a repository of all its subscribers. When a subscriber registers with the portal a number of pricing plans and categories are made available (bronze, silver, and gold memberships, for example). The following is a list of attributes that we will associate with a given subscriber: Username, Category, accessLevel, and spendingLimit.

In addition, the portal maintains a repository of all its syndicated content partners as well as all the negotiated agreements. The following is a list of attributes that we will associate with a given syndicated partner: siteID, partnerID, Name, Audience (an Audience defines the terms of the agreement under which this partnership is operating), and Target (a Target URL of where the Syndicated Web Service is located).

With this information, we have enough to build our assertion.

```
SAML_AbstractAssertion generateAssertion(String Username, String Audience)
  STEP 1: CREATE THE CONDITION
    String[] permissions = {"Display"}
      String[] audiences = {Audience}

SAML_Conditions Conditions = new
SAML_Conditions(NotBeforeStartDate,NotAfterEndDate,audiences)
```

Cliched as it may be, it is important always to keep the audience in mind. This is to ensure that when the syndicated portal receives this assertion, it knows that it must evaluate the condition and ensure that it is meant for it before processing the rest of the assertion. In addition, the partnership could be operating under multiple agreements, and both parties may need to know what agreement is governing this transaction for billing purposes.

```
STEP 2: CREATE THE SUBJECT
    String SecurityDomain = "www.contentportal.com"

    SAML_NameIdentifier[] NameIdentifier =
    {new SAML_NameIdentifier(SecurityDomain, Username}

    SAML_Subject Subject = new SAML_Subject(NameIdentifier)


STEP 3: CREATE THE AUTHENTICATION STATEMENT USING OUR SUBJECT
    SAML_AuthenticationStatement AuthenticationStatement = null

    String IPAddress = InetAddress.getLocalHost().getHostAddress()
    String DNSAddress = InetAddress.getLocalHost().getHostName()

SAML_AuthenticationLocality AuthenticationLocality = new
SAML_AuthenticationLocality(IPAddress, DNSAddress)
```

This illustrates that the subscriber is a known subscriber at this IPAddress and DNSAddress.

```
    AuthenticationStatement = new SAML_AuthenticationStatement("Password", new
Date(), AuthenticationLocality, Subject)
```

This statement says that the subscriber was authenticated on a particular date using a password for authentication. We have thus defined to which subscriber this authentication statement applies.

```
STEP 4: CREATE AN ATTRIBUTE STATEMENT

    SAML_AttributeStatement AttributeStatement = null

    SAML_Attribute[] Attributes = new SAML_Attribute("PartnerAttribute",
"http://www.contentportal.com/syndicated/namespace", Username)
```

This shows how an attribute statement is created. It requires a name that we refer to as a names space and the attribute value. A number of additional attribute statements would be created based on what needs to be exchanged such as Category, spendingLimit, and accessLevel.

```
AttributeStatement = new SAML_AttributeStatement(Attributes, Subject)

STEP 5: CREATE THE SAML STATEMENT

SAML_Statement[] Statements = (AuthenticationStatement, AttributeStatement)
```

Next, create the SAML statement. Use our previously created Authentication and Attribute statements.

```
STEP 6: PUT IT ALL TOGETHER: ISSUER + CONDITIONS + SAML STATEMENT

String Issuer = "Content Portal"
SAML_AssertionList AssertionList = new SAML_AssertionList(uniqueID, Issuer,
Conditions, Statements)

return AssertionList
```

Write the Assertion to a repository and return an SAML token that will later be used to retrieve the Assertion. These Assertions also need to be managed and removed if they are not claimed within a predefined amount of time, similar to garbage collection.

```
SAMLToken storeAssertion(Assertion)
```

This web service will receive the from the portal content web service the subscriber information, the siteID where the actual content resides, and the content which the subscriber has requested. The siteID will be used to retrieve the particulars of the syndicated site such as the terms of agreement, which is reflected as part of the Condition.

```
Generate the Assertion
SAML_AbstractAssertion Assertion = generateAssertion(username, audience)
This method is the one that goes thought steps 1 to 6.
```

Redirect the Subscriber off to the Syndicated site, pointing them to the location of the Syndicated Web Service at that site with an SAML Token that will be used by that web service to retrieve and consume the Assertion.

Syndicated Web Service

If you recall the session use case, the SAML token was a unique pointer to a session object. It contained the assertion that was probably stored in some repository. Once we have a valid (one that has not expired) matching token, we can return the associated assertion.

This would be accomplished with the following method where `AssertionList` is of type `SAML_abstractAssertion`, which is an abstract class provided by JSAML.

```
SAML_AssertionList retrieveAssertion(SAMLToken)
```

This method would make a network call to another web service provided at the content portal, which would return SAML assertions using valid SAML Tokens. The Syndicate Web Service processes the SAML assertion and then returns the requested content to the subscriber. The syndicated web site also maintains a repository of portals with which it has made agreements. It also has the same kinds of attributes such as partnerID, Company, Audience, and tokenURL (where it returns the subscriber).

The incoming assertion will have attributes regarding the subscriber that the syndicated site will use namely Company, Username, Category, and accessLevel that will determine if the subscriber is allowed to view the content.

```
    AttributeCollection AC = new AttributeCollection()

STEP 1 RETRIEVE ASSERTION USING SAML TOKEN
    SAML_AssertionList AssertionList = retrieveAssertion(SAMLToken)
```

Here, the AssertionList is parsed in an XML DOM structure that can easily be manipulated and searched.

```
STEP 2 TEST THE VALIDITY OF THE ASSERTION
    testValidity(PartnerID, AssertionList)
```

Here, PartnertID was passed along with the AssertionList. Within this XML DOM structure we need to navigate and find the PartnerAttribute. We can then use this node to find all the attributes and populate our AC AttributeCollection.

```
STEP 3 GET THE ATTRIBUTES OF THE ASSERTION
    getAttributes(AssertionList, AC)

STEP 4 CHECK THE SUBSCRIBER ACCESS LEVEL
    Assertion is valid at this point, check the access level
    accessLevelCheck(AC, Article)

STEP 5 IF EVERYTHING IS TRUE THEN REDIRECT SUBSCRIBER TO CONTENT
```

Let's cover the most important steps in more detail.

```
STEP 2 IN MORE DETAIL
    testValidity(PartnerID, AssertionList)

    Issuer = AssertionList.getIssuer()
Look up the partner's entry and compare the expected name on the Assertion's
issuer. We want to make sure that this is a known partner. Issuer should have a
value of "Content Portal."

    Check Date, making sure that it is valid today.
    SAML_Conditions Conditions = AssertionList.getConditions()
    Conditions.checkDateValidity(new Date())

    Check Audience validity
    String Audience = getAudience(partnerID) Stored in repository
    Conditions.checkAudience(Audience)
```

```
STEP 3 IN MORE DETAIL
    getAttributes(SAML_AssertionList AssertionList, AttributeCollection AC)

    Iterator StatementIterator = AssertionList.getStatements()

    Perform the following until no more statements are found
SAML_Statement Statement =(SAML_Statement)StatementIterator.next()

    if (Statement.getStatementType() == SAML_Statement.ATTRIBUTE_STATEMENT)

We are only looking for Attribute statements. We ignore the rest and continue
through the iterator until we are done. Once we have found an attribute statement
we can process its attributes.

    SAML_AttributeStatement AttrStatement = (SAML_AttributeStatement) Statement

Perform the following until no more attributes are found.
```

Now that we have found an attribute statement, we need to make sure that it is the one we expect, which is our PartnerAttribute.

```
    Iterator AttributeIterator = AttributeStatement.getAttributes()
    SAML_Attribute Attribute = (SAML_Attribute)AttributeIterator.next()
    If (Attribute.getAttributeName().compareTo("PartnerAttribute")==0)

Since we found what we were looking for, now check this PartnerAttribute Attribute
and get the attributes that are needed.

    processPartnerAttribute(Attribute.getAttributeValue(), AC)

    Populate username from the Subject
    SAML_Subject Subject = AttributeStatement.getSubject()
    Iterator SubjectIterator = Subject.getNameIdentifiers()

    if (SubjectIterator.hasNext())
      SAML_NameIdentifier NameIdentifier =
      (SAML_NameIdentifier)SubjectIterator.next ()
    AC.setUsername(NameIdentifier.getName))
    processPartnerBlock(Element Element, AttributeCollection AC)
```

This is where the actual XML parsing and populating AC from the incoming assertion is done. It also is where the DOM structure is parsed and the following element values are retrieved and set in the attribute collection: Company, subscriptionCategory, and accessLevel.

```
    AC.setCompany(parsed Company element)
    AC.setCategory(parsed Category element)
    AC.setLevel(parsed accessLevel element)
STEP 4 IN MORE DETAIL
Determines if a user has a high enough access level to get the based on the Access
level of the resource itself. Each ResourceEntry represents a specific URL for
which a different minimum access level has been assigned.
```

```
accessLevelCheck(AttributeCollection AC, String URL)

int UserAccessLevel = AC.getLevel()
int ResourceMinAccessLevel = ResourceEntry.getMinAccessLevel(URL)

return UserAccessLevel > ResourceMinAccessLevel
```

Liberty Alliance, Microsoft Passport, and SAML

Enterprises have always been challenged with the concept of user identity and its use in authenticating consumers. This has become much more complex with the introduction of the web and with the emergence of the issue of authentication required across multiple or federated enterprises. Microsoft Passport, Liberty Alliance, and AOL's Magic Carpet all represent efforts to create a standard federated identity infrastructure for consumer-based authentication, enabling applications to gain access across multiple, federated enterprises.

At its core, the Liberty Alliance specification and the Microsoft Passport service have the same goal: to manage web-based identification and authentication. Both will let subscribers have a single web identity that provides single sign-on functionality to those web sites that have implemented either specification.

However, there are differences. Microsoft Passport is a service and not an open specification. It makes use of its underlying authentication system of the Microsoft Hotmail and the Microsoft MSN Network.

The Liberty Alliance is a specification that is implemented by vendors and enterprises. Thus, the identity data is stored by enterprises, and not by a single organization or service. The Microsoft Passport service certainly raises issues that must be addressed in terms of privacy, trust, overall performance, and service availability. These issues will begin to surface as the number of accounts and demands for stronger authentication increases.

Microsoft has announced that it would support the SAML specification, but may not support all of it. Microsoft is concentrating its efforts on the WS-Security specification, which would provide support for SAML as one of several security models or tokens, including, amongst others, Kerberos (a trusted third-party authentication protocol)and X.509 certificates.

On the other hand the Liberty specification builds on SAML. It provides the ability for a subscriber to link accounts held by different service providers. Once a subscriber's accounts are linked, she can authenticate across these accounts, communicate information between accounts, and even log-out across all sites.

SAML could well be the bridge that brings Microsoft Passport and Liberty Alliance together, or at least brings interoperability between the two competing standards. We will look at the Liberty Alliance specification because of its heavy reliance on SAML.

Liberty Alliance Overview

The Liberty Alliance began in September 2001. Sun and 32 other partners announced their alliance with the goal of providing an open solution for network identity. This essentially was a response to the Microsoft Passport service. The 1.0 specification was released last July, which focused on interoperability between systems and single sign-on functionality. At this time the number of members has grown to about 100.

The primary purpose of the Liberty Alliance is to facilitate commerce between consumers and enterprises without compromising the privacy and security of these consumers. The Liberty Alliance specification provides a framework for exchanging authentication information between enterprises while specific details about the consumer's identity are not necessarily shared. The Liberty Alliance refers to this as Federated Network Identity.

The specification also allows consumers to choose which accounts they want to link together, and thus maintain separate identities in different locations while still benefiting from a seamless single sign-on experience. Some of the features and benefits of the Liberty Alliance specifications that consumers will enjoy include the following:

❑ **B2B applications**

This promotes interoperability and integration between different applications.

❑ **B2C applications**

This will allow consumers to choose their identity provider or providers (as opposed to the Microsoft Passport service), and also specify what they want to share.

❑ **B2E (Business to Employee) applications**

This will allow all enterprises to consolidate identities within their own extended enterprise, enabling employees to move seamlessly from one service or application to another without having to re-establish their identity or re-authenticate.

❑ **Privacy**

The current specification defines information-sharing or disclosure, with permission controls for federated network identity and authentication sharing. Future releases of the specification will enable enterprises to share certain consumer information according to the permissions and preferences granted by the consumer. Also, the specification plans to include the concept of circle-of-trust between selected enterprises.

Liberty Alliance Objectives

The key objectives of the Liberty Alliance are:

❑ To enable consumers to protect the privacy and security of their network identity information (network identities are the preferences that a consumer sets up when using a particular service). For example, when using Amazon.com all the preferences associated with this service provider make up the network identity of the consumer.

❑ To enable businesses to maintain and manage their customer relationships without third party participation.

❏   To provide an open single sign-on standard that includes decentralized authentication and open authorization from multiple providers. In other words, a federation of service providers and identity providers that have established business and operational agreements.

❏   To create a network identity infrastructure that supports all current and emerging network access devices.

We have to remember that the Liberty Alliance builds and extends much of what has been done by SAML. This basically is an implementation or extension of the SAML specification. SAML is concerned with providing a standard way of exchanging this information rather than how the consumer links his network identities, the circle of trust, or the implementation site of a federated infrastructure.

Functional Requirements

The functional requirements of the Liberty Alliance are listed below:

Identity Federation

This covers the management of the identity as it goes through its life cycle, by the following delegations:

1. Service providers and identity providers have to provide the ability for consumers to view their federated identities.

2. Service providers must notify consumers upon identity federation and de-federation.

3. Identity providers have to notify the service providers whenever consumers terminate their accounts.

4. Service providers and identity providers must notify each other about consumer identity de-federation.

Pseudonyms

These provide the ability to support the use of pseudonyms. These pseudonyms will be unique within the boundary of the federation.

Global Logout

This supports the notification of service providers when a consumer logs out. This should be included in the next version of the SAML specification.

Authentication

This primarily requires supporting all methods of navigation between identity providers and service providers. This is because the consumer may have a number of ways to navigate within the federation, like bookmarks and URL address. Also, support for a range of authentication methods and mechanisms is essential.

Secondly, identity providers must authenticate themselves first. This ensures that consumers know who they are dealing with before identifying themselves and potentially having identity information that could fall into the wrong hands.

Lastly, authentication also involves maintaining the confidentiality, integrity, and authenticity of information exchanged between identity providers and service providers.

Liberty Alliance Specification Documents

The specification defines a set of protocols that provide a solution for identity federation management, cross-domain authentication, and session management.

The Liberty architecture contains three actors: Principal (consumer), identity provider (SAML Asserting Party or Authentication Authority), and service provider (SAML Relying party). A Principal is an entity that has an identity provided by an identity provider. A service provider provides services to the Principal.

Once the Principal is authenticated to the identity provider, the identity provider can provide an authentication assertion (SAML) to the Principal, who can then present the assertion to the service provider. An identity federation is said to exist between an identity provider and a service provider when the service provider accepts authentication assertions regarding a particular Principal from the identity provider. SAML covers this with its AudienceRestrictionCondition, which can point to a partner agreement, where assertions are only valid if the parties belonged to this agreement.

This specification also defines a protocol where the identity of the Principal can be federated between the identity provider and the service provider.

Because the Liberty protocols are extensions of the SAML protocol, and a SOAP protocol binding for SAML has been defined, the SOAP binding for Liberty must adhere to the processing rules for "SOAP binding for SAML." Naturally just like SAML, the SOAP binding for Liberty uses HTTP as the transport mechanism.

Overview of the Specification Documents

To cover all the specification documents would take a chapter of its own. We are just providing a description of what each document covers. However, with the knowledge acquired in this chapter and the knowledge that the specifcation is built using SAML, this will certainly ease the understanding of any reader who wishes to explore the specification further.

Liberty Architecture Overview

This document presents an overview of the Liberty Version 1.0 architecture, which offers a solution for implementing single sign-on with federated identities based on current deployed technologies.

Liberty Bindings and Profiles Specification

This document defines the bindings and profiles of the Liberty protocols and messages. The specification relies on the SAML framework and makes use of SAML profiles. A separate specification is used to define the Liberty protocols and messages used within these profiles.

Liberty Protocols and Schemas Specification

This document defines the abstract Liberty protocols for identity federation, single sign-on, name registration, federation termination, and single logout.

Liberty Authentication Context Specification

Authentication context is defined as the additional information associated with the authentication assertion that the service provider may require before it makes any entitlements or authorization decisions. The purpose of this is to allow the service provider to know in greater detail which technologies, protocols, and processes were followed and used to generate the authentication assertion. Much of this could be added to the next version of the SAML specification.

Liberty Architecture Implementation Guidelines

This document defines the recommended implementation guidelines and checklists for Liberty architecture, focusing on deployments for service providers, identity providers, and Liberty-enabled clients or proxies (LECPs).

It is a credit to the SAML specification team that so much of it is reflected in the Liberty Alliance specification. If you understand the SAML specification then you understand the Liberty Alliance specification. This is just a particular implementation or deployment or solution using the SAML specification as its basis.

Recent Developments

At the time of writing this chapter, the 1.0 specification had just come out and a number of other developments followed, which raise more questions about how all these specifications work with each other.

Companies like RSA, Entrust, Novell, NeuStar, and Sun announced in July 2002 that they would introduce products that support the 1.0 specification. We should see these products sometime in late 2002 to mid-2003. Sun has recently released an open-source software development tool for testing and building online identification. This will run on Sun's Identity Server 6.0. Phaos has been one of the first to release a Java toolkit, with the commercial version having been released recently. They also have an SAML toolkit.

What is the Liberty Alliance planning for version 2 now that version 1 is out? It wants to include features for permission-based attribute sharing, and more on the concept of the circle of trust, to which enterprises would be able to link and extend their service offerings.

The Future of SAML

The OASIS committee chose to keep SAML 1.0's functionality relatively narrow in the hope of getting early vendor and product adoption. The large number of SAML implementations that have emerged over about 18 months seem to bear out this strategy.

The two areas that the committee omitted from the specification were session management and policy language. Session management was covered in this chapter because of its importance and the likeliness of it being in the next version of the specification. We did not cover policy language, as it is the topic of our next chapter, which deals with XACML. These two specifications will likely ultimately be merged, much as several other specifications have already been consolidated to generate SAML. Another area where we should see a lot of activity is profiles. A number of additional profiles should be defined, such as a WS-Security Profile and an XML Encryption Profile.

The future seems bright for SAML due to the rapid adoption of the standard, as well as the variety of products and toolkits that are on the market today. It is also highly significant that the Liberty Alliance uses and builds on SAML in its specification. It is likely that SAML will represent an integration solution between Microsoft Passport and the Liberty Alliance, perhaps through standards emerging from WS-Security efforts. It will also be interesting to see how WS-Security and all its sub-parts unfold in relation to SAML, XACML, and the Liberty Alliance. Stay tuned; unfortunately we may be in for some reconciliation down the road.

SAML is a specification that will be crucial to the use of Web Services for e-commerce applications. This justifies paying close attention to how it progresses over the next few years.

Summary

We started with an overview of SAML, seeing how it came to life, and knowing the purpose it serves. We then reviewed the most important documents within the specification, namely the requirements, use cases, session, assertions and protocols, and the bindings and profiles. We briefly saw various vendors with their toolkits and products that currently support the 1.0 specification. We looked at one of these toolkits in detail. SAML is not a standalone specification, but belongs to the general family of security specifications primarily managed by W3C and OASIS. We highlighted the role of SAML in the Liberty Alliance specification and its relationship to the Microsoft Passport service.

In the following chapter we will look at the XACML (eXtensible Access Control Markup Language) specification, which defines a language (XML) for expressing authorization policies for information access. This was purposely left out of SAML to keep it simple and to enable rapid acceptance and adoption from the vendor community.

10

XACML

Access control, which is often called *rights management* or *entitlement management*, determines who has access to view something, what they can do with it, and the type of device with which they can view it. **eXtensible Access Control Markup Language** or XACML is an XML-based security standard for expressing rules and policies for controlling access to information. These rules and policies are associated with a target resource in the context of an overall access control and privacy strategy.

This chapter is divided into three sections. In the first section we will look at ACLs, their use, and functionality. We will also look at SAML and roles database. This will provide us with an historical perspective of what traditionally has been provided by computer systems for access control.

In the second section we will cover selected documents within the XACML specification. The goal of the remainder of this section is to provide a summary of the information found within these documents. By the end of this section, the reader should have a good understanding of the specification and should have enough information to be able to use it in building applications.

In the third section we will look at a typical application and show three XML documents that will demonstrate a typical request and response. Then we will see the XACML document that will be used to evaluate the request and to provide an authorization response. The context of the application is a citizen who wishes to access (read) his personal tax record.

Who's behind XACML?

XACML is an XML specification that is being directed by OASIS. It began in the summer of 2001 with the goal of consolidating the efforts of various parties and their work, principally those of IBM and the University of Milan.

IBM has already come up with its version of XACML, which it calls **XML Access Control Language,** or XACL. Originally this language was going to be a component within their XML Security Suite. Its purpose earlier was to be a fine-grained access control language targeted at XML documents and XML documents fragments. These were the considerations taken into account while making XACML.

A number of organizations such as Affinitex, Crosslogix, Entegrity, Entrust, Hitachi, IBM, Overxeer, Sterling Commerce, Sun, and Xtradyne are an active part of the working group for XACML.

The current XML specification still has a number of missing pieces that you would expect to see, and all of the documents are still only in working draft. In addition, at the time of this writing no products or toolkits are available. These might become available in early 2003, most likely by vendors such as IBM and Entrust (http://www.oasis-open.org/committees/xacml/).

The Need for XACML

The majority of current access control and authorization systems implement a proprietary and simplistic model, which usually follows a pattern:

❑   First, a subject in a particular context makes a request to a system

❑   Next the system checks a *repository* and either authorizes or denies the request

The repository contains information about the target resource, the subject, groups that the subject may belong to, and permission given or associated with the subject or group. All these elements are stored in the repository and are called **Access Control Lists (ACL)**. We will discuss ACLs in depth in the following section.

ACLs that first came in the 70s are still being used, and these over time have led to various solutions being implemented in an ad-hoc manner, which have turned out as proprietary solutions. In addition, due to security sometimes being an afterthought, inadequate and simplistic solution result. Often we see new software products being released with little or no security being implemented. These problems have generated the need for a new technology, and XACML shows some promising features.

XACML provides a framework with the following advantages:

❑   First, XACML provides a portable and unified way of describing these access control elements.

❑   Second, XACML provides a standard format to allow security control information to be exchanged between various systems. This can even facilitate security information transfer between legacy systems.

❑   Third, this standardized format of XACML also allows us to tie together and provide a consolidated or federated view of what were formerly islands of ACLs. This will allow organizations to manage, control, monitor their assets, and comply with regulating bodies in the proper use of these assets in a better way. This will reduce the risk of privacy or other regulatory violations.

❑   Last, this will allow non-IT resources to have the ability to create these policies for their area. These might include the human resources, finance, and legal department to have the capability to articulate the policies surrounding the use of enterprise resources.

We also need to provide a much finer-grained access control model than one that simply grants or denies access. Additionally, we need the ability to specify **provisional actions** that the subject must either agree to (like a user agreement) or perform (like digitally sign) before ultimately receiving access to the target resource. For example, provisional actions might include:

❑   Having to digitally sign a terms and conditions statement

❑   Having to digitally sign a privacy or non-disclosure agreement

❑   Having to be at a certain location (physical or web), or during a period of time or at a specific date

❑   Having to use a specific protocol like HTTPS

❑   Having to authenticate using a specific authentication method like PKI

Access Control Lists

An access control list is a data structure that guards access to resources. It might be a list or database indicating what access privileges are to be granted on system objects to various subjects or principals that use the system. Traditionally, these *objects* have consisted of files and directories, *subjects* include users and identifiable groups of users, and *privileges* include actions such as reading to or from a file, deleting a file, or executing the file as a program.

ACLs date back to the 1970s, when many concepts were pioneered on the Multics operating system. Some of these concepts were carried forward to Unix, VMS, and to more recent derivative systems such as Linux and Windows NT. In some of the modern systems, ACLs can be associated with additional system resources such as devices, queues, and such; there may also be additional sorts of privileges. In web services, the logical extension is to have SOAP methods to be objects on which access controls may be defined, and for *subjects* to access those methods that are permitted.

Unfortunately, there has been no portable, unified way of describing these access controls, and many different proprietary approaches have been used. As security controls have since been applied to relational databases, web servers, application servers, and to individual custom applications, the proliferation of *private* ACL schemes has continued. Each system has its own unique security model, its own unique *language* for representing access controls, and its own *user interface* for configuring those controls. Worse still, systems that have cosmetically similar ACL schemes may have different semantics. This is where XACML comes to provide a portable and unified way of describing these access controls with a much richer vocabulary.

For those who have not had to work with ACLs before, we will briefly look at one of Sun's Java packages that provides us with an implementation. As part of Sun's **Java Security package** (available in JDK 1.1 and above) a number of interfaces and classes have been defined that allow users to create and manipulate ACLs. The java.security.acl package provides the interfaces to the ACL and related structures such as ACL entries, groups, and permissions, and the sun.security.acl classes provide a default implementation of these interfaces. We will briefly look at three of the interfaces.

AclEntry Interface

This package (java.security.acl.AclEntry) is the interface used to represent each entry in an ACL.

Each ACL contains a set of permissions associated with a particular principal or subject. Each ACL is specified either as being positive or negative to the associated principal. If positive, the permissions are to be granted. If negative (or both positive and negative), the permissions are to be denied.

A few relevant methods from this interface are shown below:

Method	Meaning
`boolean setPrincipal (Principal user)`	Specifies the subject/principal (individual user or group) for which permissions are granted or denied by this ACL
`boolean addPermission (Permission permission)`	Adds the specified permission to the ACL
`boolean removePermission (Permission permission)`	Removes the specified permission from this ACL
`boolean isNegative()`	Returns `true` if this is a negative (denied) ACL
`Enumeration permissions()`	Returns an enumeration of the permissions in this ACL

ACL Interface

An `ACL` is made up of multiple ACL entries. An `ACL` can be thought of as a data structure with multiple ACL entry objects that uses the `AclEntry` interface.

A few methods from this interface (`java.security.acl.Acl`) are as follows:

Method	Meaning
`boolean addEntry(Principal caller, AclEntry entry)`	Adds an `AclEntry` to this ACL
`boolean removeEntry(Principal caller, AclEntry entry)`	Removes an `AclEntry` from this ACL
`Enumeration entries()`	Returns an enumeration of the entries in this ACL
`Enumeration getPermissions(Principal user)`	Returns an enumeration for the set of allowed permissions for the specified subject
`boolean checkPermission(Principal authenticUser, Permission permission)`	Checks whether or not the specified subject has the specified permission

Method	Meaning
`void setName(Principal caller, String name)`	Sets the name of this ACL
`String getName()`	Returns the name of this ACL

Group Interface

This interface (`java.security.acl.Group`) is used to represent a group of principals. The group interface also extends the principal interface (`java.security.Principal`), which means that either a `Group` or a `Principal` object can be passed as an argument. As you can imagine, it is much easier to manage a limited number of groups where principals belong to a group as opposed to managing each individual member. What tends to happen is that permissions will be added or removed not to one principal but to a group. This makes it easier if these principals are already in the same group.

A few methods from this interface are as follows:

Method	Meaning
`boolean addMember(Principal user)`	Adds the specified subject to the group
`boolean isMember(Principal member)`	Returns true if the passed subject is a member of the group
`Enumeration members()`	Returns an enumeration of the subject is in the group
`boolean removeMember(Principal user)`	Removes the specified subject from the group

To learn more about these interfaces go to http://java.sun.com/products/jdk/1.1/docs/api/Package-java.security.acl.html.

SAML and Roles Database

Before we dive into the XACML specification, we will briefly look at the relationship of XACML to SAML and the use of roles database. A **roles database** is a repository that maintains people's authorizations for various computer-based systems in order to make this maintenance easier, less time-consuming, and less error-prone or more consistent. Those who would like more information on this and the software that is currently available can follow the link http://web.mit.edu/rolesdb/.

If you recall from Chapter 9, *SAML*, a similar figure as the following one, was used to illustrate the SAML *authorization* use case. This use case shows the work behind the scenes that needs to take place to generate an **SAML Authorization Assertion** based on an SAML request. This use case introduced a number of new terms that really belonged more to XACML. In Chapter 9, not much was said on the content of the authorization assertion and how it was generated. It even seemed odd to have this particular use case, as it went beyond what was required of SAML. This was a prelude to XACML and also clearly shows the integration point between the two specifications:

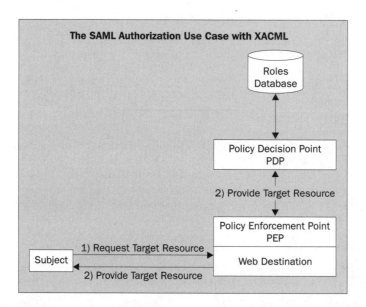

In this use case a request is received to access a target resource from a web destination. The **Policy Enforcement Point (PEP)** checks permissions with a **Policy Decision Point (PDP)** before making a decision and releasing the target resource to the subject. In this use case, XACML would be used to store and exchange policy decisions generated by the PDP and enforced by the PEP. In this chapter we will specifically look at the PDP, the PEP, and the messages that are exchanged between them.

The XACML message is generated based on what has been captured in a roles database. The roles database is used to determine a subject's fine-grained access to data and applications. Ideally, a roles database should be hosted centrally and should provide distributed services to applications that need it.

The following figure shows the major entities (which would be represented by tables in a database or by an object class in a directory) and their relationship (the arrows in the diagram would become foreign keys in a database) that would belong to a roles database schema. The schema could be implemented using a variety of technologies such as databases or directories. X500 or LDAP is one particular technology that is expected to be used for this purpose:

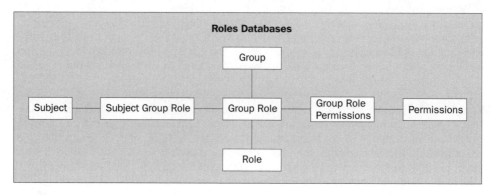

XACML combines all these concepts of subject, group, role, and permission into authorization attributes. Authorization attributes then become *authorization assertions* that SAML can then use and transport. Permissions then become what the subject can do to which target resource.

XACML would look at this in terms of the following: the policy around the relationship of object (target) to subject to action (grant or deny) to condition (provisional actions).

Ideally, this roles database is in an XACML format or in a format that can be transformed easily into an XACML format. This means that a compliant PDP may choose an entirely different representation for its internal evaluation and decision-making processes. The result is that XACML becomes an interchange format that conveys policy information.

We will provide you with an example of an XACML message (an object rule in this case) in response to an SAML `AuthorizationDecisionQuery` for access (action) from a citizen (subject) to view personal tax records (target). We will briefly explain the sample XML, but in case you don't understand, this will make more sense once we go through the specification and once we look at an XACML example that re-uses this example.

It is also recommend that all the XML examples from this chapter be downloaded and viewed with **XMLSpy** or other similar products, and Internet Explorer or any browser that can parse XML. It will be much easier to understand, and you will be able to quickly view and play with the structure (as the examples get more complicated it will help to see them visually). This is especially true with some of the other examples.

So what are we looking at below? We are looking at the definition of a rule (permission). The rule is divided into three main sections: the *target*, the *condition*, and the *effect*. A `subject`, a `resource`, and an `action` define the target of this rule. At a high level this tells us that this rule applies to subjects that are trying to *read* (actions) a tax record (resource). The `condition` tells us that the subject name must match the citizen name that is attached to the tax record the subject is trying to read. This means that you should be able to read your own tax records. If the condition is **true** then the *effect* will be `Permit`, which means that you will be allowed to read this resource:

```
<?xml version="1.0" ?>
<rule>
  <target>
    <subject>
      samlp:AuthorizationDecisionQuery/Subject/NameIdentifier/Name
    </subject>
    <resource>
      <patternMatch>
        <attributeRef>
          samlp:AuthorizationDecisionQuery/Resource
        </attributeRef>
        <attibuteValue>tax.com/record.*</attibuteValue>
      </patternMatch>
    </resource>
    <actions>
      <saml:Actions xmlns:saml="urn:oasis:names:tc:SAML:1.0:assertion">
        <saml:Action>read</saml:Action>
      </saml:Actions>
    </actions>
  </target>
```

```
<condition>
    <equal>
      <attributeRef>
        samlp:AuthorizationDecisionQuery/Subject/NameIdentifier/Name
      </attributeRef>
      <attributeRef>
        //tax.com/records/citizen/citizenName
      </attributeRef>
    </equal>
  </condition>

  <effect>Permit</effect>
</rule>
```

The XACML Specification Documents

The XACML Specification set is comprised of the following documents. They are all available for public viewing at http://www.oasis-open.org/committees/xacml/:

❑ **Committee Working Draft**
   This covers the core specification and probably is the most important document at this time.

   ❑ Policy Schema (XSD Schema)

   ❑ Context Schema (XSD Schema)

❑ **Conformance Test Cases**
   Test case used to verify that an XACML implementation is successful or compliant using the 1.0 Specification.

❑ **Use Case**
   This is a list of approximately a dozen scenarios that highlight different aspects of XACML.

❑ **Requirements**
   This document provides a summary of the Use Case document.

   Remember that all these documents are still in working draft as of this writing, and may change substantially.

The goal of this section is to provide you with a summary of the information found within these documents. At the end of this chapter, the reader should have a good understanding of the current specification and should have enough information to be able to use it in architecting and begin mapping the sets of subjects, roles, resources, and actions onto XACML policies. We will concentrate our efforts on the following documents: Use Case and the Committee Working Draft.

The following acronyms are used frequently within the specification and are also part of the glossary:

❑ **Policy Administration Point (PAP)**
   The component that creates a policy or a policy set

❑ **Policy Decision Point (PDP)**
   The component that evaluates applicable policy and returns an authorization decision

❑ **Policy Enforcement Point (PEP)**
The component that performs access control by enforcing authorization decisions

❑ **Policy Information Point (PIP)**
The component that acts as a source of attribute values

❑ **Policy Retrieval Point (PRP)**
The component that locates and retrieves applicable policy information for a particular decision request

Application Use Cases

The current XACML specification Use Case document (issued September 2001) provides a dozen or so examples of how XACML would work within a specific application context. We will be looking at a sample of these use cases, which highlight different aspects in the use of XACML. Some of the examples have been changed to provide a theme consistent with the rest of the chapter. All of the use cases presented are variations of the SAML Authorization Use Case with XACML presented earlier in this chapter. The goal is to provide you with a better understanding of where and how XACML will be used.

Use Case 1: Online Access Control

This is the simplest of all the use cases is which a subject makes a request via an application that is hosted by an application server. A **Policy Decision Point (PDP)** evaluates a policy associated with this request to determine if access should be granted.

Elements within the application or the application server act as a **Policy Enforcement Point (PEP)**, either granting or denying access. As mentioned earlier in the chapter, ACLs and the elements (either as custom software or provided by the vendor product) that make use of them effectively act as PDP and PEP. The goal of XACML is to provide an access control representation that is sufficiently expressive to describe access controls used in proprietary systems that are already in use. As such, it can provide a single unified representation to operate with both legacy and new systems.

The following diagram illustrates this use case:

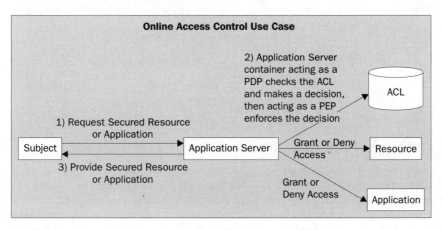

This use case can also be enhanced from just a simple grant or deny action. We can extend our PDP and allow it to evaluate the request based on a number of provisional actions such as:

❑ Subject is an employee of the organization – attribute

❑ Subject is an employee and a member of the finance group – attribute

❑ Request is made during normal business hours – time

❑ Request is made during the normal work week – day of week

❑ Subject IP Address or DNS name is of known value – attribute

❑ Subject has been authenticated using specified method (UserID and Password or PKI) – authentication protocol

❑ Connection is protected using SSL – connection protocol

In our original use case, this could be accomplished by creating an application that manages all of this additional information and works in conjunction with the application server. This application would be an additional PDP node, and a specific code within the application server would need to invoke this application after checking its own ACL, but before the PEP enforced the decision. In this use case you could say that the ACL acts a coarse-grained access control while the provisional actions act as a fine-grained access control. The following diagram shows our enhanced use case:

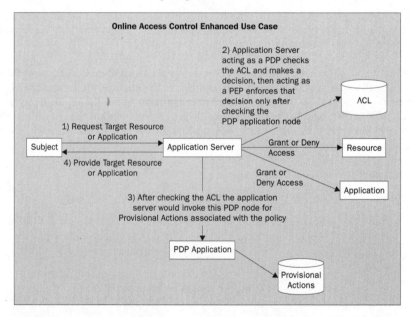

Use Case 2: Policy Provisioning

This use case presents the situation where a previously created or modified policy is transferred from a **Policy Retrieval Point (PRP)** to a **Policy Decision Point** (PDP). The PDP is the initiator and uses a pull model on all the PRPs that it knows. This pull can be initiated based on time and notification from the PRP or some other mechanism. The protocol of communication and the policy interchange standard between the PDP and PRP has not been specified by XACML. This will not be tackled by the 1.0 specification and might be addressed in future versions.

This use case also implies that the PDP has processes that are able to manage this environment. This is very similar to the *SAML User Session* use case that we saw in Chapter 9, which also used a Pull or a Push model. The following diagram illustrates this use case:

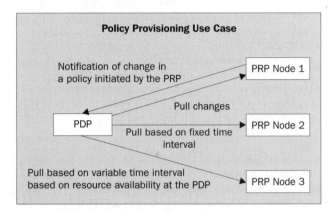

This use case also highlights the different implementation strategies that will have to be used to integrate and communicate with other PRPs to exchange these policies. Do not expect vendors to offer the same implementation or solution, but expect a number of solutions that best match the type of PRP and the particular requirement of the application, like performance and manageability.

Use Case 3: SAML Authorization Decision Request

This use case presents a scenario where the PEP creates a SAML request for an **Authorization Decision Request** by specifying the policy inputs that apply. A PDP replies with an authorization assertion that specifies the policy inputs that it used to make the decision.

This is a good example of the integration between SAML and XACML. There is a possibility that both the specifications will merge in the future. The following diagram illustrates this use case:

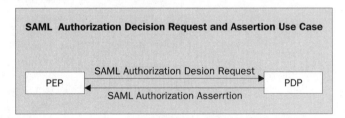

We will refer to this use case again when we look at the XACML context, which will provide a more detailed view of the exchanges of messages between PEP and PDP.

Use Case 4: Attribute-Dependent Access Control on XML Resources

This is an interesting use case that is augmented in the specifications. The context of this use case is as follows.

A *news portal* that aggregates content from a number of syndicated sources then re-sells that content to its subscribers. These news articles are associated with specific access policies. These policies are written based on the subscription level of the subscriber or the group to which the subscriber belongs. In addition, the date on which the news article was written is also added to the policy. The date of access would work as follows: Any premium news article that was written seven or more days ago would then become available to normal subscribers. The premium value of that article has disappeared. In addition, if the news article was older than a month then it would go in the archive, and anyone wishing to search the archive would need to have a premium membership.

This use case presents a target resource that has an attribute-dependent access control policy, as well as provisional actions in the form of a date of access. The access control policy is represented as a set of 4-tuple (object, subject, action, and condition). Conditions are represented in the form of XACML statements.

Here, subjects can subscribe to one of the two groups (a group here represents a subscriber category that is defined by the content portal usually tied to a pricing plan): the *normal level* group or the *premium level* group. Some target resources are available to both types of subscriptions, while others are available only to those subjects that have subscribed to the premium level group.

The following diagram illustrates this use case:

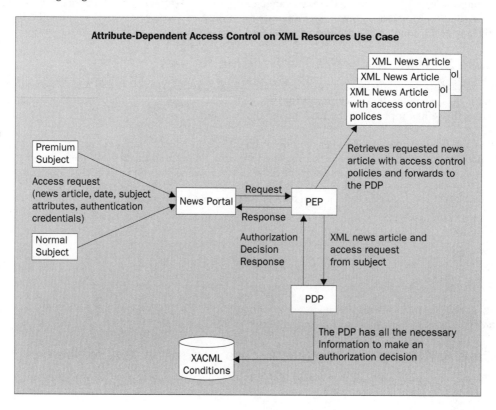

Use Case 5: Requester-Dependent Access Control on XML Resources

In this case, an author submits a specification document to the system. The chairperson receives the specification and assigns one or more reviewers to review and comment on the submission. Comments are sent back to the author. Once the chairperson is satisfied with the document, it is then made available to voting and non-voting members for final discussion and approval. The following figure illustrates this use case where a member wishes to review a specification document.

This use case presents a target resource that has an attribute-dependent access control. The access control policy is represented as a set of 4-tuple (object, subject, action, and condition). Conditions are represented in the form of XACML statements. Subjects wishing to access a target resource belong to a specific group depending on their position within a working committee. The five positions are *chair*, *reviewer*, *author*, *voting member*, and *non-voting member*. Target resources are available to members based on their position, role, and responsibility. In addition, each position provides certain privileges on the target resource such as read, write, or both.

The following diagram illustrates this use case:

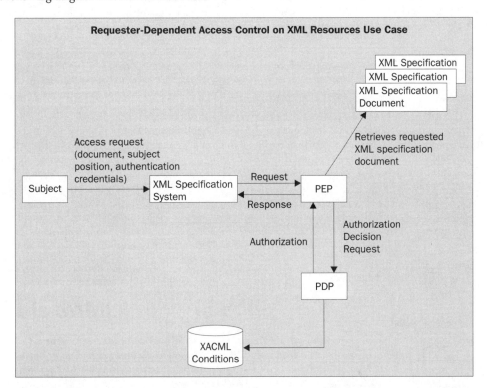

Use Cases 4 and 5 are very similar, and the difference is that in Use Case 4, a number of attributes and provisional actions have been defined for the target resource, whereas in Use Case 5, the access decision is driven by the attributes of the requester. These use cases could be unified together into a somewhat more complex scenario. This illustrates the flexibility provided by XACML and shows the need to go beyond what most traditional ACL systems have been able to express.

Use Case 6: Provisional Access Control on XML Resources

This use case is a variation on our first use case. It shows how provisional actions, such as the use of digital signature, can be used in an online transaction between two trading partners that belong to the same trading group or that belong to the same vertical portal.

Here, a buyer has a key pair used for digital signature with a certificate issued by the vertical portal. The buyer has the capability of digitally signing any purchase request that provides the equivalent of a real signature. With organizations that have already established a trust relationship, a purchase order number would provide the equivalent, but for the purposes of this use case we assume that a digital signature is required. This will be determined if provisional actions are associated with a target resource that requires digital signatures.

The access control policy is represented as a set of 4-tuple (object, subject, action, and condition). Conditions are represented in the form of XACML statements. In this use case the PDP grants access to the purchase order on condition that a digital signature be attached with the purchase order. The PEP relays this information to the buyer who submits the purchase order with an attached digital signature. The PEP then checks the validity of the digital signature before accepting the purchase order on behalf of the buyer. The following figure illustrates this use case:

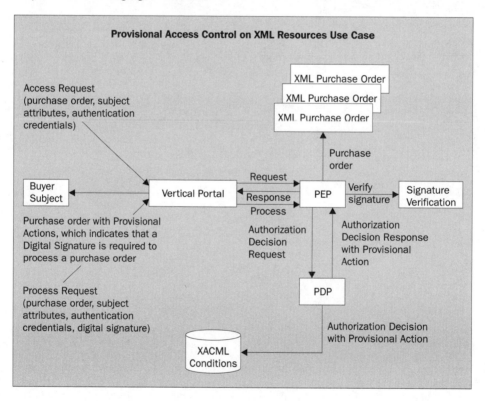

The process flow is as follows:

First, a buyer sends a purchase request to the Vertical Portal. The PEP then sends an **Authorization Decision Request** to the PDP. The PDP gathers its information and evaluates all the rules associated with this request. All this is captured in XACML. It returns its response to the PEP with a **Provisional Action** that basically says that it cannot accept/process a purchase order unless it has been digitally signed by the buyer. The PEP enforces this decision and since no digital signature was attached to the purchase order, it returns, a message to the buyer informing him of this fact. The buyer then digitally signs the request and submits it. This time the request passes the PEP (it is never mentioned if an authorization decision request is sent again to the PDP or the PEP uses a cached version), which forwards it to a signature verification component for verification before sending it to the seller.

Use Case 7: Provision User for Third-Party Service

Portals and **service aggregators** provide a facility through which subjects can subscribe to and access an array of individual services. This use case presents the scenario whereby a subject is provisioned by a third-party service. What comes to mind based on our last chapter on SAML is the Microsoft Passport central service or organizations that implement the Liberty Alliance specification with the purpose of creating a federated network with their affiliated partners. These provide the ability for subscribers to create an account or profile, and to manage their authorization policies. These policies will be used later when authorization queries are received from known service providers.

A subject creates his own account with a third-party authentication and authorization service such as Microsoft Passport. The subject has also created an account with the portal. The subject accesses the portal for the purposes of using a service. Before the portal can grant access to the service, it queries the third-party service for the list of relevant attributes.

The portal can also have its own PEP and PDP. In this case the portal's PDP would return an *authorization decision* with *provisional actions* regarding the attributes with the third-party service. This would trigger the PEP to submit an *Authorization Decision Request* to the third-party service. The third-party service then would return a list of *attribute assertions*, which would be used by the portal's PEP to validate the provisional actions. Once validated, access to the service would be granted. The following diagram illustrates this use case:

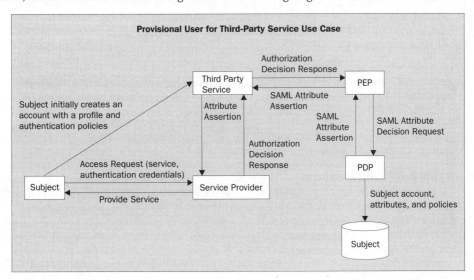

369

The basic process flow is as follows:

A subject initially creates an account with a third-party service like the Microsoft Passport service with his authentication credentials and profile information. This information in turn is stored and XACML rules are generated. The subject then makes a request to a service provider to access a service. The service provider sends an *authorization decision* request to the **third-party** service. The third-party service sends an authorization decision request to the **PEP**, which generates an SAML authorization decision request to the **PDP**. The PDP evaluates the request based on its XACML rules and returns an *SAML attribute assertion*, which is returned all the way to the service provider, who grants or denies the subject access to the requested service.

Committee Working Draft

The goal of this section is to provide the reader with an understanding of the key elements of the specifications and their use. The reader should be able to go back to the use cases we have covered and understand the role of the PDP, as well as understand the structure of the XACML conditions to which we kept referring to.

Requirements

The XACML specification defines a number of requirements that the policy language should fulfil. The following key requirements of the XACML policy language will be covered:

❏ **Combine rules**
To provide a method for combining individual rules and policies elements into a single policy statement set that applies to a given action. This means that different policy writers can write policies that affect the same resource. All these policies should belong to the same policy set and need to be evaluated by the PDP. XACML defines three elements to meet this requirement, namely: *Rule*, *Policy*, and *PolicySet*.

❏ **Define algorithms**
To provide a flexible method for the definition of algorithms by which, rules and policies elements are combined. XACML defines the following two attributes to meet this requirement, namely: `RuleCombiningAlgId` (part of the `Rule` element which combines rules to policies) and `PolicyCombiningAlgId` (part of the `Policy` element which combines policy to `PolicySet`).

❏ **Decision element**
To provide a method for determining an authorization policy decision based on attributes of the subject and resource. This means basing the decision not on the identity, but on attributes such as role, responsibility, and security level. XACML uses the `SubjectAttributeDesignator` and `ResourceAttributeDesignator` elements to represent subject and resource attributes. These elements will be used within a `SubjectMatch` or `ResourceMatch` element. The main purpose is to ensure that the correct target is being evaluated.

❏ **Apply functions to elements**
To provide a set of logical and mathematical operators on attributes of the subject, resource, and environment. This means that some computation may need to occur on the attributes before an authorization decision can be rendered. XACML borrows from **MathML** to accomplish much of this requirement. XACML includes a number of built-in functions and a method of adding non-standard functions. XACML uses the `Apply` element with an attribute called `FunctionId` that identifies the function to be applied to the contents of the element.

❑ **Distribute policies**
To provide a method for distribution of policy statements to the resources to which they apply. For the PDP to be able to accomplish this, XACML defines the `Target` element. PDPs should examine this element and ensure that the correct policy is being used.

❑ **Identify policies for actions**
To provide a method for identifying the policy statement that applies to a given action, based either on the identity or attributes of either the subject or the resource. This means that multiple policy statements may exist independently and would need to be retrieved. The concept of policy indexing facilitated by the `Target` element is used to meet this requirement.

❑ **Implementation independency**
To provide an abstraction-layer that insulates the policy-writer from the details of the application environment. This means that different PEPs should operate in a consistent fashion regardless of PEP implementation. This requirement is met by defining a canonical form of the request and response handled by an XACML PDP. This canonical form is called the XACML **Context**. Many technologies could be used to meet this requirement, such as XPath and XSLT.

❑ **Actions for policy enforcement**
To provide a method for specifying a set of actions that must be performed in conjunction with policy enforcement. XACML uses the `Obligations` element to specify actions that must be performed. PEPs that conform to the 1.0 XACML specification are required to deny access unless they understand all of the `Obligations` elements associated with the applicable policy.

XACML Context

The XACML Context plays a pivotal role by insulating the XACML core language from the application environment and vice versa. As the following diagram shows, the XACML context provides the input and outputs to the PDP from the application environment. This means that applications must convert to an XACML Context from their representation or environment, whether it is SAML, .NET, or Corba. You may have noticed in some of the use cases diagrams that while communicating with the PDP we sometimes had an XACML message and sometimes an SAML message. The assumption in these use cases is that a transformation had occurred before reaching the PDP. The transformation of an SAML message into an XACML message can be as simple as running an XSLT transformation as shown in the following diagram:

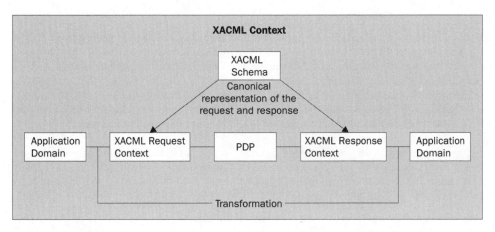

The *Application Domain* will typically be PEP. PEPs can come in many flavors such as a web server, a mail server, or a custom application. The XACML Context basically insulates the policy writer from having the specifics of the environment and allows one format to be used across the enterprise.

Policy Language Model

The following diagram shows the main elements from the policy language model and their relationships:

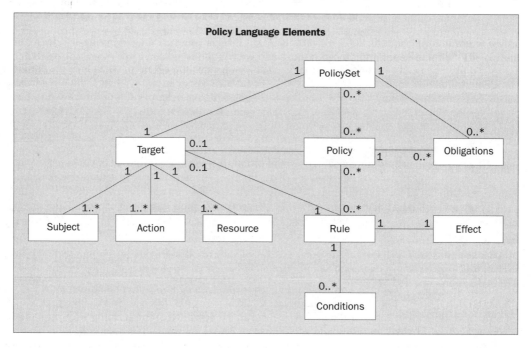

The following section is probably the most important in this chapter. We will explain the top-level elements of XACML and how they interact with each other.

Policy

A policy is a *collection of rules*. Different groups within an organization may need to create separate rules that apply to the same target. These rules are then combined to make up a policy. A policy is the basic unit of work that a PDP performs and it forms the basis for an authorization decision.

The rules within a policy need to be evaluated before an authorization decision can be rendered. These individual rules are combined based on a *rule combining algorithm*, which provides an algorithm for combining the results obtained from evaluating the individual rules within a policy.

Policies can also be distributed throughout the organization. XACML does not define any ways for the distribution, retrieval, or association of policies by PDPs. But how do we know which policy to apply when a request is received? This is the purpose of the `Target` element. You can almost say that the `Target` acts like a *primary key* in a database, so when a request is received we retrieve all the policies that have a matching target.

PolicySet

A PolicySet is a collection of policies. The policies within a policy set need to be evaluated before an authorization decision can be rendered. These individual policies are combined based on a *policy combining algorithm*, which provides an algorithm for combining the results obtained from evaluating the individual policies within a PolicySet. This provides added flexibility, whereby you can regroup your rules within a single policy that can be evaluated or you can regroup your rules within a number of policies, which are then regrouped within a policy set.

Target

A Target is an aggregation of the following elements: Subject, Resource, and Action. At a minimum a Target must be composed of at least one of each of these elements. These elements can only be associated to one Target. The Subject can contain information regarding identity, role, or any other attribute. The same applies to a Resource in that it can contain information regarding its identity or any other attribute. Both of these elements can use a URL or an XPath expression to identify their location and value. A good example for a Subject is a URL that points to an attribute stored in an LDAP directory.

A Target can be associated to a PolicySet, a Policy, or an individual Rule.

The Target element defines the applicability of the PolicySet to the authorization decision request. If there is a match between the Target element within the PolicySet and the authorization decision request, then the PolicySet element may be used by the PDP in making its authorization decision.

Rule

A Rule element has an effect, which means once evaluated it provides a decision on a particular Target object. A Rule is not meant to provide an authorization decision on its own; this is left to the Policy. A Rule may be associated with multiple policies. Rules can also be distributed throughout the organization. XACML does not define any methods for this distribution.

These are the four top-level elements of the Policy Language Model. We now will look at a couple of second-level elements that will complete the picture.

Obligations

The Obligations element is a set of obligations that must be fulfilled by the PEP in conjunction with the authorization decision from the PDP. If the PEP does not understand the obligation (or any obligations, if more than one is provided), then it must deny the authorization. This is what we earlier referred to as, *provisional* (or conditional) actions. You may have noticed that an Obligation can be associated with a Policy or PolicySet, but not with a Rule. This is why we said earlier that a rule is not meant to be used by a PDP to return an authorization decision since it lacks a relationship with the Obligations element. Not all Obligations will be returned to the PEP, but only the ones that match the authorization decision.

Effect

The positive (evaluated to be True) outcome of a Rule will be assigned the value of the Effect, which has one of the two values of Permit or Deny. This is a one-to-one relationship.

This essentially is XACML in a nutshell. Before looking at the Policy Language Model syntax, we will see the typical dataflow using some of our top-level elements – the XACML context and the main actors that participate in the exchange of messages:

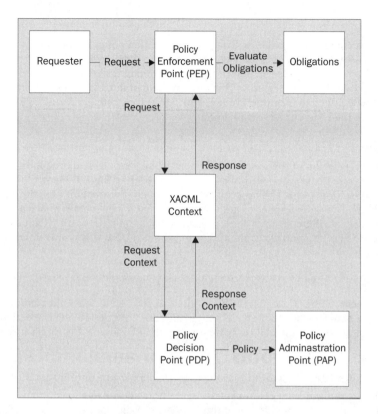

A request arrives at a PEP, which is then transformed into an independent context that the PDP can understand and work with. The PDP evaluates the matching `Policy` or `PolicySet`, which has been created by a policy writer and is managed by the PAP. The results are returned in a response context, which is then translated back to the PEP. The PEP with the authorization decision then uses any `Obligations` associated with the authorization decision to enforce the decision.

The following section will look at the syntax of the top-level elements of the Policy Language Model with the use of an example to show how these elements typically would be used.

Policy Language Model Syntax

The following example will be used to cover the majority of the Policy Language Model syntax. This example will be continued in the next section when we look at our application example. This example represents (in XML) a *policy system* for determining whether a citizen has access to a particular record. The purpose of this is to show and explain as many elements as possible:

```
<?xml version="1.0" encoding="utf-8"?>
<Policy xmlns="urn:oasis:names:tc:xacml:0.16f:policy"
        xmlns:function="urn:oasis:names:tc:xacml:0.16f:function"
        xmlns:xsi="http://www.w3.org/2001/XMLSchema-instance"
        xsi:schemaLocation="urn:oasis:names:tc:xacml:0.16f:policy draft-
                        xacml-schema-policy-16f.xsd"
```

```
         xmlns:ctx="urn:oasis:names:tc:xacml:0.16f:context"
         xmlns:tax="http:www.tax.com/schemas/taxrecord.xsd"
         PolicyId="urn:oasis:names:tc:xacml:example:TaxPolicy"
         RuleCombiningAlgId="urn:oasis:names:tc:xacml:1.0:rule-combining-
                       algorithm:deny- overrides">

<Description>Policy for all tax records</Description>

<Target>
  <Subjects>
    <AnySubject />
  </Subjects>

  <Resources>
    <Resource>
      <ResourceMatch MatchId="function:string-match">
        <ResourceAttributeDesignator
          AttributeId="urn:oasis:names:tc:xacml:resource:target-namespace"
          DataType="xsi:string" />
        <AttributeValue DataType="xsi:string">
          http://www.tax.com/schemas/taxrecord.xsd
        </AttributeValue>
      </ResourceMatch>

      <ResourceMatch MatchId="function:node-match">
        <ResourceAttributeDesignator
          AttributeId="urn:oasis:names:tc:xacml:resource:xpath"
          DataType="xsi:string" />
        <AttributeValue DataType="xsi:string">/tax:record</AttributeValue>
      </ResourceMatch>
    </Resource>
  </Resources>

  <Actions>
    <ActionMatch MatchId="function:string-equal">
      <ActionAttributeDesignator
        AttributeId="urn:oasis:names:tc:xacml:action"
        DataType="xsi:string" />
      <AttributeValue DataType="xsi:string">read</AttributeValue>
    </ActionMatch>
  </Actions>
</Target>

<Rule RuleId="urn:oasis:names:tc:xacml:example:TaxRule" Effect="Permit">
  <Description>A citizen may read any record defined by the
  http//:www.tax.com/schemas/taxrecord.xsd namespace for which he
  is a designated tax payer</Description>

  <Target>
    <Subjects>
      <AnySubject />
    </Subjects>

    <Resources>
```

```
              <Resource>
                <ResourceMatch MatchId="function:string-match">
                  <ResourceAttributeDesignator
                  AttributeId="urn:oasis:names:tc:xacml:resource:target-namespace"
                   DataType="xsi:string" />

                  <AttributeValue DataType="xsi:string">
                  http://www.tax.com/schemas/taxrecord.xsd</AttributeValue>
                </ResourceMatch>

                <ResourceMatch MatchId="function:node-match">
                  <ResourceAttributeDesignator
                  AttributeId="urn:oasis:names:tc:xacml:resource:xpath"
                  DataType="xsi:string" />

                  <AttributeValue DataType="xsi:string">
                  /tax:record</AttributeValue>
                </ResourceMatch>
              </Resource>
            </Resources>

            <Actions>
              <Action>
                <ActionMatch MatchId="function:string-equal">
                  <ActionAttributeDesignator
                    AttributeId="urn:oasis:names:tc:xacml:action"
                    DataType="xsi:string" />
                  <AttributeValue DataType="xsi:string">read</AttributeValue>
                </ActionMatch>
              </Action>
            </Actions>
          </Target>

        <Condition FunctionId="function:string-equal">
          <SubjectAttributeDesignatorWhere
             AttributeId="urn:oasis:names:tc:xacml:example:attribute:taxreturn-
                          number"
             DataType="xsi:string" />

          <AttributeSelector  RequestContextPath="/ctx:Request/ctx:Resource
                 /ctx:ResourceContent/tax:record/tax:citizen/tax:TaxReturnNumber"
             DataType="xsi:string" />
        </Condition>
      </Rule>

  <Obligations>
    <Obligation ObligationId="urn:oasis:names:tc:xacml:example:obligation
                              :termsAgreement"
      FulfilOn="Permit">
      <AttributeAssignment
        AttributeId="urn:oasis:names:tc:xacml:examples:attribute:agreement"
        DataType="xs:string">
        <AttributeSelector
          RequestContextPath="/ctx:Request//ctx:ResourceContent/tax:/
```

```
                       record/tax:citizen/tax:citizenAgreement/tax:agreement"
          DataType="xs:string" />
      </AttributeAssignment>

      <AttributeAssignment
        AttributeId="urn:oasis:names:tc:xacml:example:attribute:text"
        DataType="xs:string">
        <AttributeValue DataType="xs:string">
          Your tax record has been accessed by:
        </AttributeValue>
      </AttributeAssignment>

      <AttributeAssignment
        AttributeId="urn:oasis:names:tc:xacml:examples:attribute:text"
        DataType="xs:string">
        <SubjectAttributeDesignator
          AttributeId="urn:osasis:names:tc:xacml:subject:subject-id"
          DataType="xs:string" />
      </AttributeAssignment>
    </Obligation>
  </Obligations>
</Policy>
```

If you look at our example we have a `Subjects` element with a wild card match of `AnySubject`, and an `Actions` element that basically says we are looking for a string match of `"Read."` This will be important if there are any `Obligations` elements that have a `FulfilOn="Read"` attribute. We also have a `Resources` element that specifies that this `Target` applies to the tax record resources defined by a matching tax record schema.

PolicySet Element

The `PolicySet` element is an aggregation of `Policy` elements or other `PolicySet` elements. A `PolicySetIdReference` or `PolicyIdReference` element may be used to reference a `PolicySet` or a `Policy`. If a `PolicySet` is composed of `Policy` elements, then a `PolicyCombiningAlgorithm` element must be present in order to determine the evaluation procedure once the results from the individual policies are known.

In our example, we have chosen not to show a `PolicySet` element, but to show an individual `Policy`:

Element	Required	Type	Description
PolicySetId	Yes	anyURI	Should be unique and could use a URN or URI scheme.
PolicyCombiningAlgId	Yes	anyURI	Must match a predefined algorithm. This indicates how policies are to be combined, if there is more than one. A number of pre-defined algorithms have been specified by the specification.
Description	No	string	Free-form description of the `PolicySet`.

Table continued on following page

Element	Required	Type	Description
Target	Yes		This is used to ensure that the correct (correct means that there is a match between the context request and the `Target` in regards to the `Subject`, `Resource`, and `Action` elements) `PolicySet` is being used by the PEP to make an authorization decision request. Can contain: PolicySet, Policy, PolicySetIdReference, or PolicyIdReference.
Obligations	No		A collection of `Obligation` elements that are also part of the decision that the PEP must understand. If it does not understand any `Obligation` element then it must deny the authorization. It is important to understand that each `Obligation` element must have a trigger attached with it. This trigger is in the form of an attribute, the `FulfilOn` attribute. For example if the result of the evaluation by the PDP is a decision to `permit`, then it will look to see if there are any `Obligations` that have `FulfilOn="Permit"`. If it does find any then it will include those as part of the response to the PEP.

Target Element

As the name implies, it is the target of a `PolicySet`, `Policy`, or `Rule`. It is composed of the `Subjects`, `Resources`, and `Actions` elements. All these elements must match the request context before a PDP evaluates a `Rule`, `Policy`, or `PolicySet`. Each element provides for a wild card match with the following elements: `AnySubject`, `AnyResource`, and `AnyAction`.

The snippet below shows the sub-elements of the `Target` element. Note, here * indicates zero or more occurrences, | indicates choice between the adjacent elements, ? indicates zero or one occurrence, and otherwise the elements are required:

```
<Target>
  <Subjects>
    (<AnySubject> | <Subject> |
      (<SubjectMatch>
        <MatchId>
          (<SubjectAttributeDesignator/> | <AttributeSelector/>)
        </MatchId>
        (<AttributeValue/>)?
      </SubjectMatch>)*
    )
  </Subjects>
```

```
<Resources>
  (<AnyResource> | <Resource> |
    (<ResourceMatch>
       <MatchId>
         (<ResourceAttributeDesignator/> | <AttributeSelector/>)
       </MatchId>
       (<AttributeValue>)?
     </ResourceMatch>)*
   )
</Resources>

<Actions>
  (<AnyAction> | <Action> |
    (<ResourceMatch>
       <MatchId>
         (<ActionAttributeDesignator/> | <AttributeSelector/>)
       </MatchId>
       (<AttributeValue>)?
     </ResourceMatch>)*
   )
</Actions>
</Target>
```

Policy Element

Policy is the smallest unit of work that a PDP can perform. We will describe each element in the following table:

Element	Required	Type	Description
PolicyId	Yes	anyURI	Should be unique and could use a URN or URI scheme
RuleCombiningAlgId	Yes	anyURI	Must match a predefined algorithm
Rule	Any number		The Rule elements will be combined based on the RuleCombiningAlgID, and will be evaluated only if they have a matching Target element

The following are some of the algorithms used with the RuleCombiningAlgID:

❑ **Deny-overrides Algorithm**

If any rule evaluates to Deny, then the result is Deny. If all the rules evaluate to Permit, then the result is Permit. If all the rules evaluate to NotApplicable, then the result is Deny. If some of the rules evaluate to Permit and some evaluate to NotApplicable, then the result is Permit.

❑ **Permit-overrides Algorithm**

This is the opposite of the previous rule. Here Permit overrides.

❑ **First-applicable Algorithm**

Each Rule is evaluated in the order it is listed in the Policy. If the Target matches and the conditions evaluate to True, then processing stops and we use the Effect (Permit or Deny) for this rule. If not, we move on to the next Rule.

Looking back at our example, we have the following:

- ❑ PolicyId of TaxPolicy.
- ❑ RuleCombiningAlgId of deny-overrides.
- ❑ RuleID of TaxRule with an effect of Permit.
- ❑ A Target element that we have already looked at.
- ❑ An Obligations element, which has its FulfilOn attribute set to Permit.

The Obligations indicate that the Subject, a citizen or a taxpayer, has to agree to a tax agreement before viewing the record. This is very similar to the act of downloading software in which the vendor makes you click the "read agreement" button before allowing you to download the software.

Rule Element

The Rule element defines the rules that are part of a policy. The following are the sub-elements of the Rule element:

Element	Required	Type	Description
RuleId	Yes	anyURI	Should be unique and could use a URN or URI scheme.
Effect	Yes	Effect	Values: Permit or Deny.
Description	No	string	Free from description of the Rule.
Target	No		This is used to ensure that the correct (correct means that there is a match between the context request and the target in regards to the Subject, Resource, and Action elements) PolicySet is being used by the PEP to make an authorization decision request.
Condition	No		A predicate that must be satisfied before a rule can be executed and assigned an Effect value.

If you look at our example we have the following:

- ❑ We have a RuleID of TaxRule with an effect of Permit.
- ❑ We have a Target element, at which we have already looked.
- ❑ We have a Condition element, which basically stipulates that before we evaluate the rule we have to be sure that we have the right citizen or taxpayer. We accomplish this by ensuring that we have a matching tax-return-number value. It is important to understand that prior authentication of the taxpayer has already been accomplished by other means. Here we are interested only in the authorization aspect and the access to a particular resource.

Obligation Element

The Obligation element contains an identifier for the obligation and a set of attributes that form arguments of the action defined by the obligation. The FulfilOn attribute indicates the decision value for which this Obligation must be fulfilled:

Element	Required	Type	Description
ObligationId	Yes	anyURI	Should be unique and **could** use a URN or URI scheme
FulfilOn	Yes	Effect	Values: Permit or Deny
AttributeAssignment	One or more		

XACML Access Control XML Example

In the last section we covered the `Policy` element and its syntax, which was written to control access to a taxpayer's record. In this section we see the target resource that is our tax record in XML format. We then look at the XACML **request** initiated by the PEP and processed by a PDP (using our `TaxPolicy`). We finish by looking at the XACML **response** generated by the PDP that is sent back to the PEP for enforcement.

Tax Record

The following is our XML record that is probably generated from data extracted from a database and is presented in this format. The tax record provides us with a citizen's tombstone information and his tax return information:

```xml
<?xml version="1.0" encoding="UTF-8"?>
<record xmlns="tax.gov/taxrecords.xsd"
xmlns:xsi="http://www.w3.org/2001/XMLSchema-instance"
xsi:schemaLocation="tax.gov/taxrecords.xsd
http://www.tax.gov/schema/taxrecord.xsd">
  <citizen>
    <citizenName>
      <first>John</first>
      <last>Public</last>
    </citizenName>
    <Contact>
      <street>1631 Main Street</street>
      <city>Ottawa</city>
      <province>ON</province>
      <zip>k1a2a5</zip>
      <phone>6135551212</phone>
    </Contact>
    <citizenDoB xsi:type="date">1962-01-21</citizenDoB>
    <TaxReturnNumber xsi:type="string">248544532</TaxReturnNumber>
  </citizen>

  <taxReturn>
    <statement>
      <dateofReturn>2002-05-01</dateofReturn>
      <yearofReturn>2001</yearofReturn>
      <grossIncome>
        <line150value>45000.00</line150value>
      </grossIncome>
      <expenses>
```

```
          <line350value>4500.00</line350value>
        </expenses>
        <taxesOwed>
          <line450value>12425.32</line450value>
        </taxesOwed>
        <taxesDeductedEmployer>
          <line550value>13000.00</line550value>
        </taxesDeductedEmployer>
      </statement>
    </taxReturn>
  </record>
```

XACML Request

The following is an XACML request example that is initiated by PEP and then processed by a PDP:

```
<?xml version="1.0" encoding="UTF-8"?>
<Request xmlns="urn:oasis:names:tc:xacml:0.16f:context"
  xmlns:identifier="urn:oasis:names:tc:xacml:identifier"
  xmlns:xacml="urn:oasis:names:tc:xacml:0.16f:policy"
  xmlns:xsi="http://www.w3.org/2001/XMLSchema-instance"
  xsi:schemaLocation="urn:oasis:names:tc:xacml:0.16f:context draft-xacml-
    schema-context-16f.xsd">
```

We have the `Subject` element that has five `Attribute` elements that qualify the subject. The subject is qualified if it has a `subject-category` of `access-subject`, a `subject-id` of "John Public" – which is in the format of an X500 name – has a role of `citizen`, and has a `TaxReturnNumber` attribute with a value of `248544532`:

```
<Subject>
  <Attribute
    AttributeId="urn:oasis:names:tc:xacml:1.0:subject:subject-category"
    Issuer="www.tax.gov" IssueInstant="2002-10-01T08:40:40-06:00">
    <AttributeValue>
      urn:oasis:names:tc:xacml:1.0:subjectcategory:access-subject
    </AttributeValue>
  </Attribute>
  <Attribute
    AttributeId="urn:oasis:names:tc:xacml:1.0:subject:subject-id"
    Issuer="www.tax.gov"
    IssueInstant="2002-10-01T08:40:40-06:00">
    <AttributeValue>John Public</AttributeValue>
  </Attribute>
  <Attribute
    AttributeId="urn:oasis:names:tc:xacml:1.0:subject:name-format"
    Issuer="www.tax.gov"
    IssueInstant="2002-10-01T08:40:40-06:00">
    <AttributeValue>
      urn:oasis:names:tc:xacml:1.0:datatype:x500name
    </AttributeValue>
  </Attribute>
  <Attribute
```

```
        AttributeId="urn:oasis:names:tc:xacml:1.0:example:attribute:role"
        Issuer="www.tax.gov"
        IssueInstant="2002-10-01T08:40:40-06:00">
        <AttributeValue>citizen</AttributeValue>
      </Attribute>
      <Attribute
        AttributeId="urn:oasis:names:tc:xacml:1.0:example:
                        attribute:TaxReturnNumber" Issuer="www.tax.gov"
        IssueInstant="2002-10-01T08:40:40-06:00">
        <AttributeValue>248544532</AttributeValue>
      </Attribute>
    </Subject>
```

We have a `Resource` element with three attributes, which basically indicates that we are interested in a tax record resource that belongs to a `John Public` who has a `citizenDOB` of `1962-01-21`:

```
    <Resource>
      <ResourceContent>
        <tax:taxrecord xmlns:tax="http:www.tax.gov/shemas/taxrecord.xsd">
          <tax:citizen>
            <tax:citizenDoB >1962-01-21</tax:citizenDoB >
          </tax:citizen>
        </tax:taxrecord>
      </ResourceContent>

      <Attribute
        AttributeId="urn:oasis:names:tc:xacml:1.0:resource:resource-uri">
          <AttributeValue>
//tax.gov/records/john-public.xml#xmlns(tax=http:www.tax.gov/schemas/
taxrecord.xsd)xpointer(/tax:taxrecord/tax:citizen/tax:citizenDOB)
          </AttributeValue>
      </Attribute>

      <Attribute AttributeId="urn:oasis:names:tc:xacml:1.0:resource:xpath">
          <AttributeValue>
xmlns(tax=http:www.tax.gov/schemas/taxrecord.xsd)xpointer(/tax:taxrecord/tax:citiz
en/tax:citizenDoB)
          </AttributeValue>
      </Attribute>
    </Resource>
```

You can easily see that any of the `Attribute` elements can be added, all of which must be understood by the PEP.

Next we have an `Action` element with an attribute value `read`:

```
    <Action>
      <Attribute AttributeId="urn:oasis:names:tc:xacml:1.0:action">
        <AttributeValue>read</AttributeValue>
      </Attribute>
    </Action>
  </Request>
```

Let's look at the elements that make up a request.

Request Element

Any application system (most likely the PEP) communicating with a compliant PDP must transform its proprietary input into an XACML *context* request:

Element	Required	Description
Subject	One or more	
Resource	Yes	This details the resource on which we wish to receive an authorization decision. It could include a `ResourceContent` element, but must contain a number of predefined `Attribute` elements.
Action	Yes	This identifies the request action on the `Resource`.

Attribute Element

The `Attribute` element acts as a meta-data structure that is used throughout the request context. This provides the necessary flexibility in building a request:

Element	Required	Type	Description
AttributeId	Yes		A number of identifiers have been reserved by XACML to denote commonly used attributes
Issuer	No	string	This could also be a URI that points to something that binds to some identity proving information that can be used like a public key
IssueInstant	No	dateTime	The date and time of the issue in UTC time
AttributeValue		anyType	

As mentioned previously the main purpose of the request is to match a corresponding `Target` element. This is used to retrieve the appropriate `PolicySet`, `Policy`, and `Rules` that will be used to evaluate the authorization request and to return a corresponding authorization response.

XACML Response

Consider the message, submitted earlier, requesting taxpayer data. The PDP would evaluate the request against the XACML policy, and would return a message similar to the following, indicating its authorization decision:

```xml
<?xml version="1.0" encoding="UTF-8"?>
<Response
    xmlns:xsi="urn:oasis:names:tc:xacml:1.0:context"
    xsi:schemaLocation="urn:oasis:names:tc:xacml:1.0:context http://www.oasis-
        open.org/tc/xacml/1.0/sc-xacml-schema-context-01.xsd">
    <Result>
```

The decision was to `Permit` the access request. The PEP would then have a green light to proceed to release the taxpayer information. It would then likely bundle the "tax record" we saw into a SOAP request, and pass that back to the requestor:

```
<Decision>Permit</Decision>
```

We have a collection of `Obligations`, which basically indicates that the `Subject`, the citizen, has to agree to a tax agreement before viewing the record. If you recall, when we wrote our `Policy` in the previous section we used the same `Obligations` element. The PEP evaluated the request and used the `Policy`, which gave it a decision of `Permit`. It then looked at the `Obligations` element with a `FulfilOn` attribute set to `Permit` and just passed it along to the PEP. The PDP did not do anything with the `Obligations` element except return the ones that match with the decision to the PEP:

```
    <Obligations>
      <Obligation
        ObligationId="urn:oasis:names:tc:xacml:example:
                          obligation:termsAgreement"
        FulfilOn="Permit">

      <AttributeAssignment
        AttributeId="urn:oasis:names:tc:xacml:examples:attribute:agreement"
        DataType="xs:string">
        <AttributeSelector
          RequestContextPath="/ctx:Request//ctx:ResourceContent/tax:
                    /record/tax:citizen/tax:citizenAgreement/tax:agreement"
          DataType="xs:string"/>
      </AttributeAssignment>

      <AttributeAssignment
        AttributeId="urn:oasis:names:tc:xacml:example:attribute:text"
        DataType="xs:string">
        <AttributeValue DataType="xs:string">
         Your tax record has been accessed by:
        </AttributeValue>
      </AttributeAssignment>

      <AttributeAssignment
          AttributeId="urn:oasis:names:tc:xacml:examples:attribute:text"
          DataType="xs:string">
          <SubjectAttributeDesignator
            AttributeId="urn:osasis:names:tc:xacml:subject:subject-id"
            DataType="xs:string"/>
      </AttributeAssignment>
    </Obligation>
  </Obligations>
  </Result>
</Response>
```

Let's look at the elements that make up a response.

Response Element

The `Response` element encapsulates the authorization decision returned by the PDP to the PEP:

Element	Required	Type	Description
Result	One or more		The Result element represents an authorization decision result for the requested resource. If it includes a set of Obligations, then the PEP must be able to evaluate all of them. If it cannot, then it must deny access to the requested resource.
ResourceURI	No	anyURI	The URI for the requested resource.
Decision	Yes		The authorization decision for this request. This can be Permit, Deny, Indeterminate, or NotApplicable.
Obligations	No		A collection of Obligations elements that become part of the decision that must understood by the PEP. If it does not understand any Obligations element then it must deny the authorization.
Status	No		This represents the status of the authorization decision.

The following are the sub-elements/attributes of the Status element:

Element	Required	Type	Description
StatusCode	Yes		The StatusCode element contains a major status code value and an optional sequence of minor status codes. A list of values has already been defined.
StatusMessage	No	string	This describes the StatusCode.
StatusDetail	No		Provides additional status information.

Decision Flow

It is worth looking at the decisions that are made as the request goes through, and at the elements that affect the response.

PDP

The first thing that happens when a PDP receives a request is that it finds a Target that matches the request context. We can see this in our following table, where we have the "target" column with values of Match, No-Match, and Indeterminate (underlying error has occurred):

Target	Condition	Rule Value
Match	True	Effect
Match	False	Not-Applicable
Match	Indeterminate	Indeterminate
Match	Not-Applicable	Not-Applicable
No-match	Don't care	Not-Applicable
Indeterminate	Don't care	Indeterminate

If we have a `No-match`, the PDP will return a response with a `Status` of `OK` and a `Decision` of `NotApplicable`, which will cause the PEP to permit access to the resource.

If we have an `Indeterminate`, the PDP will return a response with a `Status` of either `Missing-Attribute`, `Processing-Error`, or `Syntax-Error` depending on the actual error, and a `Decision` of `Indeterminate`, which will cause the PEP to **deny** access to the resource.

Lastly if we have a `Match`, then the PDP will need to evaluate a `PolicySet`, `Policy`, and `Rules`. The result is that the PDP will need to evaluate rules. These are our conditions, which will either evaluate to `Indeterminate`, `True`, or `False` (rules return a Boolean value unless some error occurs, in which case the `RuleValue` is `Indeterminate` or `NotApplicable`). If the condition is `False`, then the `RuleValue` is `NotApplicable`. If it is `True`, then we must assign the value of the `Effect` element, which will either be `Permit` or `Deny`. Naturally these individual rules may belong to a policy, to a policy set, or to a policy that in turns belongs to a policy set. Either way we cannot make our ultimate decision until these individual rules decisions are somehow combined. This is accomplished in our next two figures depending if we are referring to a policy set or to a policy; basically, both behave the same.

Policy and PolicySet

At this point, we have a `Match` and one of the four rule values for each rule that we have evaluated, which is either `True`, `False`, `NotApplicable`, or `Indeterminate`. We need to know how to combine these individual results. This is the task of these two figures (Policy and PolicySet) and their associated **Policy-Combining-Algorithm** and **Rule-Combining-Algorithm**.

The table shows that if none are applicable then the PDP will return a response with a `Status` of `OK` and a `Decision` of `Permit`, which will cause the PEP to permit access to the resource:

Target	Policies	Policy Value	PolicySet Value
Match	Some applicable	Rule-combining Algorithm	Policy-combining Algorithm
Match	None applicable	Not-Applicable	Not-Applicable
Match	Indeterminate	Rule-combining Algorithm	Policy-combining Algorithm

All the other combinations must rely on the following *combining algorithm*, which when executed will return a decision:

❑ **Deny-Override**

If any rule returns a `Deny`, then deny is the final decision.

❑ **Permit-Override**

If any rule returns a `Permit`, then permit is the final decision.

❑ **First-Applicable**

Returns the first decision obtained, except if it is `NotApplicable`, it then continues to the next one.

❑ **First-Applicable-Policy**

Same as *First-Applicable*, but for policy.

❑ **Only-One-Applicable-Policy**

If none are applicable, then returns a decision of `NotApplicable`, causing the PEP to return a response with a status of `OK`, and a decision of `NotApplicable`, which will permit access to the resource. If more than one is evaluated, then returns a decision of `Indeterminate`, causing the PEP to return a response with a status of `Processing-Error` and a decision of `Indeterminate`, which will deny access to the resource.

In the end if we have a final decision of `Permit` or `Deny`, then the PDP will set the `Status` of the response to `OK` with the matching `Decision`, and return to the PEP with all `Obligations`.

PEP

As mention in the previous paragraph, if we have a decision of `Permit` or `Deny` then the PEP must enforce the matching obligations. If the PEP cannot understand any one of the obligations, then it must deny access even if the decision from the PDP was to permit:

Status	Decision	Enforcement
OK	Permit	`Obligations FulfilOn="Permit"`
OK	Deny	`Obligations FulfilOn="Deny"`
OK	Not-Applicable	Permit
Missing-Attribute	Indeterminate	Deny
Processing-Error	Indeterminate	Deny
Syntax-Error	Indeterminate	Deny

In addition, if any of the obligations is not fulfilled, then the PEP must deny access to the resource until all obligations have been met. It is less restrictive when we already have a decision of `Deny` in which case the PEP will fulfil all the obligations it can, but no matter what happens, access to the resource will be denied.

You might ask why or under what circumstance you would have obligations if the decision was `Deny`. One example would be that the PEP would need to log all information for auditing purposes.

The Future of XACML

XACML has not yet received the attention that its cousin specification SAML has received. In about the same amount of time, SAML has managed to merge two competing specifications and have more than 20 vendors support the specifications and release compliant versions of their products. In addition, the Liberty Alliance Specification is built on top of SAML. It also has broad vendor support, and products already are being released that conform to its 1.0 specification.

A lot of good work has gone into XACML by its working group. The problem domain that it tackles is more complex than that of the SAML specification. The XACML specification could have a greater impact than SAML due to this reason.

The good news is that many of the vendors that support SAML are also supporting XACML. As well, the same vendors that have released products supporting SAML will ultimately be the same vendors that will be incorporate XACML into these same products.

As indicated in the beginning of the chapter, there is a critical need in current corporate environments to better manage, control, monitor their assets, and comply with regulating bodies in the proper use of these assets. The risk of privacy or other regulatory violations is too high to ignore.

It is also believed that we will see, in the near future, the merger or the incorporation of the XACML specification into the SAML specification. This will happen when XACML-compliant products start emerging. IBM Security Suite, which has an XACL implementation, has promised an XACML implementation in its next release.

At the time of writing, the XACML committee indicated that it expected the standard to be finalized in October 2002 and for products to be released at that time. This has been delayed until January of 2003. On the horizon it appears that Xerox has three patents granted that might apply to the protocols of XACML. We will have to wait and see how this unfolds in the coming months, and the resulting impact on vendors that are developing XACML-compliant products.

Summary

This chapter started by providing an overview of XACML, how it came into existence, and the purposes it serves. We briefly reviewed the nature of ACLs, since many products currently manage the granting of security access through these mechanisms. We looked at roles database and the schema that they use to capture access control information and even serve as a repository source for a PDP. We reviewed some of the anticipated use cases, which helps describe the role of XACML, and reviewed the current committee working draft. Both of these artifacts will change when we see a firmer specification.

We defined an XACML policy, which highlighted the majority of XACML elements. We finished the chapter by taking this XACML policy and developing an XACML request and response around this policy. This simulates what the PEP would send to the PDP and what it would receive and process to enforce an authorization decision.

11

WS-Security

We have thusfar covered the subjects of web services, Security, Security in the XML Context, various XML specifications that contribute to various aspects of security in an XML document like Digital Signature, XML Encryption, and XML Key Management and various subsets of XML Key Management Specifications. In this chapter, we will be taking a detailed look at the WS-Security Specifications, which bind all the topics covered earlier to the Web Services Context.

The software giants – Microsoft, IBM, and VeriSign-submitted a group of web services security specifications, named WS-Security, to a standards body called the Organization for the Advancement of Structured Information Standards (OASIS). These specifications can be seen at http:// www.verisign.com/wss/wss.pdf.

Later, Sun Microsystems's Liberty Alliance Technology Group also announced that it would focus development work on WS-Security, and would cooperate to improve the specification through the OASIS group. Thus, WS-Security is emerging as the *de facto* standard for enforcing certain elements of security in web service transactions.

In a nutshell, the WS-Security specification is a leading web services standards effort to support, integrate, and unify multiple security models, mechanisms, and technologies, allowing a variety of systems to interoperate in a platform- and language-neutral manner.

What is WS-Security?

SOAP Web Services today face a major challenge in security considerations they will have to address, while keeping all the implementation structures open. The inherent contradiction between security and openness has prompted the definition of limits and proportions to which they can go in implementing security.

WS-Security specifies a SOAP-aware mechanism for signing and sealing parts of a SOAP message. It also can be described as a standard set of SOAP extensions that can be used when building secure web services to implement message integrity and confidentiality.

WS Specifications are a collection of the existing XML specifications, bunched together in the context of a SOAP message. None of the protocols supported by the existing SOAP specifications is dropped or left unsupported. SOAP messages that implement WS Specifications can continue to rely on these existing protocols.

With the objective of understanding the rationale behind the WS-Security Specifications, and viewing its grammar and processing rules, this chapter is structured as follows:

❑ Design considerations taken into account by the creators of the WS Specifications. They would enable us to appreciate the specs in a proper perspective.

❑ Individual aspects of security the specifications seek to address.

❑ The three major elements covered by the specifications – message integrity, security token propagation, and message confidentiality. We will use the example of an imaginary online shoe store, through which customers can place orders through web services.

An Umbrella of Security for Web Services

The WS-Security specifications cover almost all aspects of security in relation to web service transactions, while at the same time providing enough extensibility to the users to cover all contingencies. We first will take a brief look at the design principles upon which these specifications have been formulated.

Design Principles

WS-Security has been built by its creators on a set of shared design principals acting as its guidelines and influencing its design and application.

Decentralization

The fact that two parties have to agree on the semantics and syntax of a message is the most unique feature of the XML web service. These parties may differ in the programming language, operating system, runtime virtual machine, or databases used, but they should be in agreement about the syntax of the messages to be exchanged. WS-Security uses the hierarchical nature of a URI mechanism to decentralize these two entities, leveraging the existing namespace system of XML and the Internet.

As an example, you may like to offer a web service that guards against leakage of sensitive information using the X509 Certificate-based security. There may be a user who depends on the Public Key Infrastructure (PKI) for accessing the service. To enable the user to avail of the web service, there has to be a uniform mechanism for communicating to him the security mechanism used in the web service. This would include the nature of the key usage, the cryptography algorithm used, the location of the key, and whether the key is encrypted or not.

The following is a sample illustration representing a portion of a SOAP message:

```
1   <EncryptedData xmlns="http://www.w3.org/2001/04/xmlenc#"
2   Type="http://www.w3.org/2001/04/xmlenc#Content">
3     <EncryptionMethod Algorithm=
4     "http://www.w3.org/2001/04/xmlenc#tipledes-cbc"/>
5       <ds:KeyInfo xmlns:ds="http://www.w3.org/2000/09/xmldsig#">
6       <ds:RetrievalMethod URI="#SessKey"
7       Type="http://www.w3.org/2001/04/xmlenc#EncryptedKey"/>
8       </ds:KeyInfo>
9       <CipherData>
10         <CipherValue>2hD9okcTVK2AT+HHg</CipherValue>
11      </CipherData>
12  </EncryptedData>
13  <EncryptedKey Id="SessKey"
14  xmlns="http://www.w3.org/2001/04/xmlenc#">
15    <EncryptionMethod Algorithm=
16    "http://www.w3.org/2001/04/xmlenc#rsa-1_5"/>
17    <ds:KeyInfo xmlns:ds="http://www.w3.org/2000/09/xmldsig#">
18      <ds:KeyName>
19        XYZ Shoe Company Company's Public/Private   Key
20      </ds:KeyName>
21    </ds:KeyInfo>
22    <CipherData>
23      <CipherValue>YPCBCoBADwPCwVR0</CipherValue>
24    </CipherData>
25    <ReferenceList>
26      <DataReference URI="#SessKey"/>
27    </ReferenceList>
28  </EncryptedKey>
```

The line numbers have been added above for the sake of explanation. The above block of XML code means the following:

❑ Lines 3 – 6 tell the SOAP parser that the message has been encrypted using the Triple DES algorithm using a session key.

❑ Line 10 gives out the cipher value, which is the encrypted value of the message.

❑ Lines 17 – 28 contain information about the key used for this encryption.

❑ Lines 13 – 16 mention that the key has been encrypted using the RSA algorithm.

❑ Lines 17 – 21 identify the RSA Key used in the key encryption as "XYZ Shoe Company's Public / Private Key," where "XYZ Shoe Company" is the recipient of the message.

❑ Line 23 gives out the cipher value of the encrypted session key.

The above portion of the SOAP message leverages PKI for message encryption. Another part of the same message may read as follows:

```
<wssec:credentials xmlns:wssec = "http://schemas .xmlsoap.org/
ws/2001/10/security">
  <wsse:BinarySecurityToken xmlns:wsse = "http://schemas.xmlsoap.org/
  ws/2002/04/secext"
  Id="myToken"
  ValueType="wsse:X509v3"
  EncodingType="wsse:Base64Binary">
    MIIEZzCCA9CgAwIBAgIQEmtJZc0...
  </wsse:BinarySecurityToken>
  <KeyInfo>
    <X509Data>
    <X509Certificate>Br+gAIH1zCCwIBAMI</X509Certificate>
    </X509Data>
  </KeyInfo>
</wssec:credentials>
```

Here, the same message relies on an X 509 Certificate infrastructure to present the credentials of the user of the service. Note the similarity of the presentation style used in these code snippets. `KeyInfo` is a common node to both. Here, within the `KeyInfo` element, the X 509 Certificate is presented as an `X509Data` element, whereas in the earlier code section, the RSA public key is presented by its identifying name.

Modularity

The success of SOAP is largely due to its modularity. SOAP is really a simple modular element that can carry itself through any of the protocols - TCP, HTTP, or SMTP. WS-Security promotes modularity through extended metadata, which express the capabilities and requirements of a web service or its policies, as they may be called. This allows for late binding by applications to a web service.

A SOAP message may carry a set of parameters required for a method invocation on the server. We will see this in the following illustration:

```
<?xml version="1.0" encoding="utf-8"?>
<SOAP:Envelope xmlns:SOAP="http://schemas.xmlsoap.org/soap/envelope/"
               xmlns:xsd="http://www.w3.org/2001/XMLSchema"
               xmlns:xsi="http://www.w3.org/2001/XMLSchema-instance">
  <pp:shoeOrder xmlns:pp="http://XYZshoes.com/shoeOrders">
    <pp:shoeType>Large Moccassins</pp:shoeType>
    <pp:qty>100</pp:qty>
  </pp:shoeOrder>
</SOAP:Envelope>
```

The above message carries some parameters for invoking a method called `shoeOrder` on the server. These parameters are carried in an envelope, which shows the SOAP action required.

WS-Security extends the modular structure of the SOAP message by adding to it a security header at the top of the real SOAP message. This carries the attributes of the SOAP message that are concerned with the security in sharing the information carried within the SOAP message.

In the above bare SOAP message, we can add meta data on the sender, as follows:

```
<?xml version="1.0" encoding="utf-8"?>
<SOAP:Envelope xmlns:SOAP="http://schemas.xmlsoap.org/soap/envelope/"
               xmlns:xsd="http://www.w3.org/2001/XMLSchema"
               xmlns:xsi="http://www.w3.org/2001/XMLSchema-instance">
  <SOAP:header>
    <UsernameToken Id="...">
      <Username>...</Username>
      <Password Type="...">...</Password>
    </UsernameToken>
  </SOAP:header>
  <SOAP:Body>
    <pp:shoeOrder xmlns:pp="http://XYZshoes.com/shoeOrders">
      <pp:shoeType>Large Moccassins</pp:shoeType>
      <pp:qty>100</pp:qty>
    </pp:shoeOrder>
  </SOAP:Body>
</SOAP:Envelope>
```

Thus the message has been enhanced by placing some meta data on top of it in the form of a header. This is similar to meta data placed on top of a class or a method declaration, as it's done by using an attribute in modern languages like C#.

It is pertinent to ask why the extra information can't be carried as two extra parameters to the method. Placing the UsernameToken on top of the method call, instead of within the body of the SOAP message, we are enabling the SOAP processor to tackle the user name token verification as a separate and distinct activity on the server, which may be processed either concurrently with the processing of the SOAP message or at a stage prior to it.

For example, a HTTP module which processes the web request prior to passing it on to the web service request processor may deal with the information in the SOAP header on its own and if the credentials are not acceptable, throw an exception at that stage itself, thus saving valuable processing time of the web service request processor.

The WS Specifications therefor make security verification a versatile capability in a web service.

Transport Neutrality

WS-Security Specifications act at the SOAP message-level communications, without requiring an RPC style request/reply message pattern. The required security information is carried as out-of-band control information. This is to be carried either as part of the application-level message exchange, or via independent channels established by infrastructure components like the authentication servers. Therefore, the WS Specification protocol is designed to function at the message level independent of the underlying transport.

For example, when the SOAP message uses HTTP as the transport protocol, it does not rely upon the HTTP syntax or semantics for its own structure. The SOAP message structure is capable of being sent over any other protocol like SMTP.

Thus, WS-Security Specifications do not rely on the syntax or semantics of any protocol like HTTP for carrying the security-related information. They provide an alternative approach. Please consider the following HTTP header:

```
REQUEST:  POST
http://localhost/wroxbank/memberservice/SimpleAuthenticationService.asmx?op=GetAcc
ountBalance HTTP/1.0
DATE: 30-Sep-02 3:04:07 PM GMT


Accept: image/gif, image/x-xbitmap, image/jpeg, image/pjpeg, application/vnd.ms-
excel, application/vnd.ms-powerpoint, application/msword, */*
Accept-Language: hi
Authorization: Basic VXNlck5hbWU6cGFzc3dvcmQ=
User-Agent: Mozilla/4.0 (compatible; MSIE 6.0; Windows NT 5.0; .NET CLR 1.0.3705)
Host: localhost
Proxy-Connection: Keep-Alive
```

The above is the header information sent in an HTTP request carrying a SOAP message. Here the security token is carried in the line beginning with the word Authorization. The word Basic here signifies that the authentication mode attempted is the HTTP basic authentication, as opposed to digest authentication in which the security token is carried in its digest form. The group of letters following the word Basic are the base64-encoded security token. It is in the form of the base64-encoded octet stream of the login name and the password, separated by a colon mark. This format will work only when the transport protocol for the message submission is HTTP. Other transport protocols like SMTP or Jabber have their own different ways of sending such security token information.

On the other hand, the same authentication credentials can be sent as follows:

```
POST /wroxbank/services/SimpleSoapHeaderService.asmx HTTP/1.1
Host: localhost
Content-Type: text/xml; charset=utf-8
Content-Length: length
SOAPAction: "http://tempuri.org/GetAccountBalance"

<?xml version="1.0" encoding="utf-8"?>
<soap:Envelope xmlns:xsi="http://www.w3.org/2001/XMLSchema-instance"
xmlns:xsd="http://www.w3.org/2001/XMLSchema"
xmlns:soap="http://schemas.xmlsoap.org/soap/envelope/">
  <soap:Header>
    <Credentials xmlns="http://tempuri.org/">
      <UserName>string</UserName>
      <PassWord>string</PassWord>
    </Credentials>
  </soap:Header>
  <soap:Body>
    <GetAccountBalance xmlns="http://tempuri.org/">
      <AccountID>string</AccountID>
    </GetAccountBalance>
  </soap:Body>
</soap:Envelope>
```

Here also, the transport protocol used is HTTP. However, the credentials are not transported in the HTTP header, but they are re-sent over the SOAP header. The whole SOAP message including the header can be sent over any other transport protocol without any change in its form or structure.

Application Domain Neutrality

WS-Security Specifications are designed to be domain-neutral general-purpose solutions to broad security problems across application domains, while at the same time providing for a consistent and well-defined extensibility mechanism. This allows the WS-Security protocol to be used as a baseline that provides the majority of what is needed while still allowing domain-specific specialization.

Securing a piece of information, identifying users, and establishing who has sent a message, all are matters of personal discretion. For example, one application may be interested only in learning what your role is when accessing a web service. Another application may require knowing who you are before allowing you access to any confidential information dispensed by a web service. On the other hand, there can be an application which would like to know who the user is as well as the role in which he is asking for information from a web service.

Therefore, it is very difficult to generalise the security needs of a web service. In the midst of this seemingly insurmountable difficulty, WS Specifications attempt to provide a general framework which encompasses as many of these requirements as possible.

These specifications try to identify the least common factor among these diverse requirements and place them within a standard format or syntax. By doing so, the WS Specifications achieve the status of a baseline upon which the individual requirements may build according to individual needs.

Different Aspects of Security

Broadly, the WS Specifications provide three main mechanisms: security token propagation, message integrity, and message confidentiality. All of these are encompassed within a broad main element called `Security`.

Brief Explanation of the WS-Security Schema

Interestingly, the WS-Security Specifications by themselves define just four main elements, which are:

- ❑   licenseLocation
- ❑   Integrity
- ❑   Confidentiality
- ❑   Credentials

The following diagram presents an overview of the WS-Security Specifications:

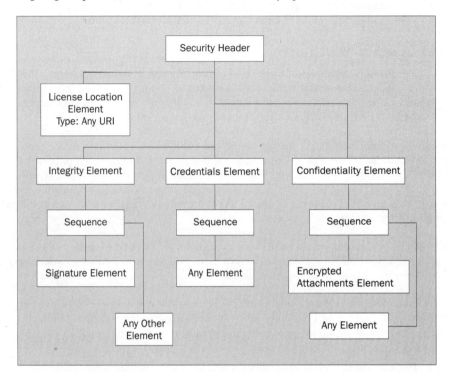

A more detailed discussion of these main elements will follow later in this chapter. A brief introduction to these elements is given in the following paragraphs. In the remaining part of this chapter, the namespace references given indicate the following URIs:

Prefix Namespaces:

S	http://www.w3.org/2001/12/soap-envelope
Ds	http://www.w3.org/2000/09/xmldsig
Xenc	http://www.w3.org/2001/04/xmlenc
M	http://schemas.xmlsoap.org/rp/
Wsse	http://schemas.xmlsoap.org/ws/2002/07/secext
Wsu	http://schemas.xmlsoap.org/ws/2002/07/utility
Xsd	http://www.w3.org/2001/XMLSchema

The licenseLocation Element

The licenseLocation element is of the XML Schema Definition of the W3C (XSD) type. AnyURI means that the node may contain any element. The business rules of the web service may define that it will deliver its services according to a prior license granted to a user in order to use it. In such a scenario, the web service needs to know the particulars of the license before allowing access to the service. The licenseLocation element is intended for this purpose. The element is included to be used within an XML Signature KeyInfo tag, in order to provide a URI that points to an assertion/license that may be useful in determining the trust associated with an XML Signature. The schema for this element is stated in the specification below:

```
<xsd:element name="licenseLocation" type="xsd:anyURI">
</xsd:element>
```

The Credentials Element

The credentials element can contain only one sub-element. This, in turn, is a sequence of limitless elements, in which the users can add as many elements as they want of any type.

The schema for this element reads as follows:

```
<xsd:element name="credentials">
  <xsd:complexType>
    <xsd:sequence>
      <xsd:any namespace="##other" processContents="lax" minOccurs="0"
        maxOccurs="unbounded" />
    </xsd:sequence>
    <xsd:anyAttribute namespace="##other" processContents="lax" />
  </xsd:complexType>
</xsd:element>
```

A more detailed explanation of what this element can possibly contain follows in a latter portion of this chapter.

The Integrity and Confidentiality Elements

The contents of the integrity and confidentiality elements are based on the W3C working drafts for XML Digital Signature and XML Encryption Syntax and Processing. For example the encryptedAttachment element, which can be a child element of the confidentiality element, is of the type EncryptedDataType, which has been defined in the XML encryption syntax and processing specifications of W3C. Similarly, the integrity element has a child element called Signature, which is defined in the XML digital signature specifications.

Although the integrity and confidentiality elements have been tagged on to other XML schema specifications like XML Encryption and XML Signature, the WS Specifications add extensibility. Users can add as many child elements as they like to these two elements.
The schema definition for these two elements is given later in this chapter.

Because the WS-Security document depends on the recommendations of the W3C in respect to the bulk of the operative portions of its specifications, our discussion in this book naturally leads to the W3C Working Drafts as they relate to the XML Digital Signatures and XML Encryption Syntax and Processing.

The Security Element

Every SOAP message has a receiver functioning to receive the message, and to process and prospectively respond to it. The specifications call the receiver an actor. Therefore, every SOAP message has at least one actor – the person who is acting based on the SOAP message. A message can have more than one actor when it passes through a series of intermediaries, as is envisaged in the WS routing specifications.

The `security` header element provides a mechanism for attaching security-related information, targeted at a specific receiver, and specified by the `actor` attribute, to this element.

Consider a case in which a SOAP message is sent to an online store by a customer giving away his credit card payment information. This message is routed through the bank, which processes the credit card payment information. If the information is found tobe valid, the portion of the message containing the credit card Information is removed, and a token of acceptance is put in its place, before the SOAP message is passed on to the store. In such a scenario, the most efficient way of encoding the message would be to encrypt the two parts of the message, one containing the credit card information and the other containing the purchase order, separately, so that each part of the information may be processed independent of the other.

Consequently, this `security` header element can be present multiple times in a SOAP message. One or more new headers may be added for unspecified additional targets.

Message security information targeted at different receivers must appear in different `security` header elements. The `actor` attribute in each of these `security` headers identifies whom that information is targeted. The security header element, without a specified actor attribute, can be consumed by anyone, but it should not be removed prior to the final destination.

The `security` header element represents the signing and encryption steps the sender took to create the message. It should be prepended to ensure that the receiving application may process sub-elements in the order they appear in the `security` header element, because there will be no forward dependency among the sub-elements. However, the WS-Security specification does not impose any specific order of processing the sub-elements. The receiving application can use whatever policy is needed.

Similarly, when a sub-element refers to a key carried in another sub-element (for example, a signature sub-element that refers to a binary security token sub-element that contains the X.509 certificate used for the signature), it must be ensured that the key material appears before the key.

Consider the following example:

```
<soap:header>
  <security actor = "http://wroxbank.com">
    <credentials>
      <binarySecurityToken ID="MyToken" ValueType="X509V3"
      EncodingType="Base64Binary">
      </binarySecurityToken>
      <KeyInfo>
        <X509Data> … </X509Data>
```

```
        </KeyInfo>
      </credentials>
    </security>
    <security actor="XYZ Shoe Shop">
      <Signature xmlns="http://www.w3.org/2000/09/xmldsig#">
        <SignedInfo>
          <CanonicalizationMethod
          Algorithm="http://www.w3.org/2001/10/xml-exc-c14n#" />
          <SignatureMethod Algorithm="http://www.w3.org/2000/09
          /xmldsig#rsa-sha1" />
          <Reference URI="Some URI">
            <Transforms>
              <Transform Algorithm="
              http://www.w3.org/2001/10/xml-exc-c14n#" />
            </Transforms>
            <DigestMethod Algorithm=
            "http://www.w3.org/2000/09/xmldsig#sha1" />
            <DigestValue>  ...   </DigestValue>
          </Reference>
        </SignedInfo>
      <SignatureValue>  ...     </SignatureValue>
        <KeyInfo>
          < SecurityTokenReference>
            < Reference URI="MyToken" />
          </ SecurityTokenReference>
        </KeyInfo>
      </Signature>
   </ Security>
</soap:header>
```

In the above example, there are two `<security>` headers, one marked with an `actor` attribute of Wroxbank, and the other with an `actor` attribute with the value XYZ Shoe Shop. The `<KeyInfo>` node within the first `<security>` header contains the actual value of the X.509 certificate of the sender, and is identified as `MyToken`.

However, when the `<KeyInfo>` of the second `<security>` header is given, it merely identifies the key location as `MyToken`.

According to the processing rules of the system, if the prepended message is processed first and the `<Security>` header meant for that actor, WroxBank, is deleted, then there will be no way for the processor of the second security header, XYZ Shoe Shop, to get the actual value of the sender's X 509 Certificate. In such a scenario, it is the responsibility of the sender to see that the key information is prepended subsequently.

According to the schema of the WS-Security specification, the `security header` element should have three main child elements:

❑   Message integrity

❑   Message confidentiality

❑   Credentials

Message Integrity

The `Integrity` element provides a security token for the message that assures that the message has originated from the specified sender, and that it has not been tampered with during its transmission. In accordance to the specifications, this element should have one `Signature` child node besides any number of child nodes or attributes of any type.

The schema of this element reads as follows:

```
<xsd:element name="integrity">
  <xsd:annotation>
    <xsd:documentation>
        This element defines the WS-Security integrity header.
        Its purpose is to encapsulate the XML digital signatures
        of the SOAP message that contains this header.  This header
        is designed to allow all valid SOAP attributes as well
        as other namespace-qualified attributes that are appropriate
        in the context within which this is being used.
    </xsd:documentation>
  </xsd:annotation>
  <xsd:complexType>
    <xsd:sequence>
      <xsd:element ref="ds:Signature" minOccurs="0" maxOccurs="unbounded">
        <xsd:annotation>
          <xsd:documentation>
              This element defines a reference to the XML Digital
              Signature element which is the top level element for
              defining digital signatures of portions of an XML document.
          </xsd:documentation>
        </xsd:annotation>
      </xsd:element>
      <xsd:any namespace="##other" processContents="lax" minOccurs="0"
        maxOccurs="unbounded">
        <xsd:annotation>
          <xsd:documentation>
            This free-form extension may include additional
            namespace-qualified XML.
          </xsd:documentation>
        </xsd:annotation>
      </xsd:any>
    </xsd:sequence>
    <xsd:anyAttribute namespace="##other" processContents="lax"/>
  </xsd:complexType>
</xsd:element>
```

The namespace qualified as `ds:` in the above schema refers to the XML Digital Signature specification namespace of http://www.w3.org/2000/09/xmldsig#. It is found in the schema available at http://www.w3.org/TR/2001/PR-xmldsig-core-20010820/xmldsig-core-schema.xsd. The above schema can better be appreciated in the following SOAP header illustration:

```
<se:Security xmlns:wsse="http://schemas.xmlsoap.org/ws/2002/04/secext">
  <wsse:UsernameToken Id="MyID">
    <wsse:Username>XYZ</wsse:Username>
  </wsse:UsernameToken>
  <ds:Signature>
    <ds:SignedInfo>
```

```
              <ds:CanonicalizationMethod Algorithm =
              http://www.w3.org/2001/10/xml-exc-c14n#"/>
              <ds:SignatureMethod Algorithm =
              "http://www.w3.org/2000/09/xmldsig#hmac-sha1"/>
              <ds:Reference URI="#MsgBody">
                <ds:DigestMethod Algorithm =
                "http://www.w3.org/2000/09/xmldsig#sha1"/>
                <ds:DigestValue>LyLsF0Pi4wPU</ds:DigestValue>
              </ds:Reference>
            </ds:SignedInfo>
            <ds:SignatureValue>DJbchm5gK</ds:SignatureValue>
            <ds:KeyInfo>
               <se:SecurityTokenReference>
                 <se:Reference URI="#MyID"/>
               </se:SecurityTokenReference>
            </ds:KeyInfo>
          </ds:Signature>
       </se:Security>
```

The specifications of the elements called `Signature`, `SignedInfo`, and `KeyInfo` all have been defined in the XML-Signature syntax and processing Specification recommendations of the W3C found in http://www.w3.org/TR/2002/REC-xmldsig-core-20020212/ and http://www.ietf.org/ rfc/ rfc3275.txt. This leads us to a discussion of the XML signatures.

XML Signatures

To understand the use of XML signatures in the context of a SOAP message, let us examine the following case study in which a SOAP document for a purchase order from XYZ Shoe Company is shown below:

```
<pp:shoeOrder xmlns:pp="http://XYZshoes.com/shoeOrders">
  <pp:shoeType>Large Moccassins</pp:shoeType>
  <pp:qty>100</pp:qty>
</pp:shoeOrder>
```

ABC's Shoe Mart, a customer, has sent this order to XYZ Shoe Company. How would XYZ Shoe Company know that it came from ABC's Shoe Mart?

Here comes the use of the W3C XML-signature syntax. A possible solution is to have ABC's Shoe Mart digitally sign the above XML document. Using the W3C XML-signature syntax, the above document signed by ABC's Shoe Mart might look like this:

```
1.   <pp:secureShoeOrder xmlns:pp="http://XYZShoes.com/shoeOrders">
2.     <Signature xmlns="http://www.w3.org/2000/09/xmldsig#">
3.       <SignedInfo>
4.         <CanonicalizationMethod Algorithm="http://www.w3.org/TR/2001/REC-
           xml-c14n-20010315"/>
5.         <SignatureMethod
           Algorithm="http://www.w3.org/2000/09/xmldsig#rsa-sha1"/>
6.         <Reference URI="">
7.           <Transforms>
8.             <Transform Algorithm="http://www.w3.org/2000/09/
```

```
                   xmldsig#enveloped-signature"/>
9.                 </Transforms>
10.                <DigestMethod Algorithm="http://www.w3.org/
                   2000/09/xmldsig#sha1"/>
11.                <DigestValue>up4NbeVj6lwx3rvu8nk=EPO0vKtM</DigestValue>
12.              </Reference>
13.            </SignedInfo>
14.            <SignatureValue>eWajXup5xNqK2PizJaaiYECAvQaRw</SignatureValue>
15.            <KeyInfo>
16.              <X509Data>
17.                <X509Certificate>Br+gAIH1zCCwIBAMI</X509Certificate>
18.              </X509Data>
19.            </KeyInfo>
20.          </Signature>
21.          <pp:shoeOrder>
22.            <pp:OrderID>E7E1AED1-8F64-4FA06-4E8A-D91B41D7CEA</pp:OrderID>
23.            <pp:shoeType> Large Moccasins </pp:shoeType>
24.            <pp:quantity>100</pp:quantity>
25.          </pp:shoeOrder>
26.        </pp:secureShoeOrder>
```

The original shoeOrder element, which is contained in the last six lines of the above XML, is now a child element of the root secureShoeOrder element. The secureShoeOrder element now has another child, the Signature element. The line numbers have been added to the original XML for ease of explanation.

Line numbers 21 to 26 contain the original purchase order SOAP message, on top of which the <Signatrue> element has been added. Line number 11 contains the digest value of the purchase order, which has been calculated using the SHA1 algorithm as specified by the <DigestMethod> element in line number 11. Line numbers 3 to 13 contain the <SignedInfo> element, upon which the digital signature is applied. You may note that the digital signing is not done upon the purchase order as such and it is done only upon the message digest and certain other pieces of information on how the digest was prepared.

Line number 14 gives out the signature value, which was calculated using the RSA – SHA1 algorithm as specified in line number 6. It may also be noted that line number 6, which gives out the method of signing, is also kept within the signed information block, so that no one can substitute the signature with a weaker algorithm, where doing so will affect the signature value.

Line numbers 15 to 19 give out the key information regarding the RSA key used in signing the document. This information is given in the form of the Signer's X.509 certificate, which contains his RSA public key as well.

The Signature Element

This is the element that holds the digital signature information. Included in the Signature element is information about canonicalizing the data, any transforms performed on the data, the digest algorithm, and the signature algorithm. The signature information also contains the Reference element, which indicates the data to be validated. In the above example the URI of the data to be validated is given a "", or a null value, indicating that the entire XML document containing the Signature element should be signed. The URI attribute also could have included an XPointer reference to indicate a specific portion of this document for which to compute the signature. In this case, a signature for the whole document is being created. This is indicated by the "" or null XPointer specified in line 6 above. However, the addendum specifications of WS-Security recommend that an ID attribute of the type specified in the XML utility specifications of http://schemas.xmlsoap.org/ws/2002/07/utility be used instead of the XPointer.

Transforms

A question that may arise is how we can sign the entire document which envelopes this signature, since it changes when we place the actual signature value into the `SignatureValue` node. Also, can the `DigestValue` be computed by the signing process if the data for computing the digest changes when the digest is included? To answer this, we refer to the "Transform" part of the process, which is used to remove the entire signature element from the data to be digested and signed.

The `Transforms` element is used to perform transform. This example uses the transform, indicated by the http://www.w3.org/2000/09/xmldsig#enveloped-signature. An XPath transform removes the `Signature` element.

Using explicit transforms with the transform code listed in a `Transform` node is always recommended. This helps in explicitly indicating the precise data to be signed, instead of relying on exclusion rules to cut out particular nodes. If a message is being passed around to different applications, new nodes could be added that would break an exclusive approach to defining the integrity area. Therefore, an inclusive approach is suggested to tackle this problem.

Algorithm for Digital Signature

To start with creating a digital signature, get the data indicated by the `Reference` element, and pass it through the specified canonicalization algorithm. Then pass it through any transforms specified, and calculate the digest based on the results. The digest of the reference information is stored in the `DigestValue` element inside the `SignedInfo` element. As tampering with the information would invalidate the signature, the data in the `SignedInfo` element is digested and encrypted with the appropriate key to create the final signature, which is placed in the `SignedValue` element. The `DigestValue` of the reference is also within the `SignedInfo` node. So, the `SignedValue` not only verifies that no one has tampered with the algorithm selections, but it also verifies that the data indicated by the `Reference` has not been tampered with.

The KeyInfo Element

There is another optional element within the `Signature` element. This is the `KeyInfo` element. This is simply a container for holding the key information required to validate the signature. In this case, it would hold an X.509 certificate that carries the public key for ABC's Shoe Mart. Thus, XYZ Shoe Company can easily verify that the order did in fact come from ABC, and that it has not been tampered with along the way.

Although the certificate information reveals only if the identity of the sender is correct and nothing more, in this case there also is a special purpose. The digital certificate carried within the `<X509Certificate>` element in base 64-encoded form also contains the public key of the sender. This public key is used by the verification mechanism to decode the signature value, to arrive at the digest value which was signed and to compare it with the digest value kept inside the `<SignedInfo>` element.

Preventing Replay Attacks using the <Timestamp> Element

It is important to note that the initial `shoeOrder` node has one new child element, the `OrderID` element.

A primary vulnerability of message protocols that rely on digital signatures is the susceptibility to replay attacks. A malicious programmer conceivably could empty ABC's bank balance by resending ABC's signed message repeatedly to XYZ Shoe Company.

This can be overcome by ABC including an identifier, which could take the form of a timestamp. The XYZ SOAP message handler could detect whether it already has processed ABC's order, and if it has, it could throw out any additional copies it might receive. Similarly, if SOAP messages are being routed through various paths, through no malicious action whatsoever can multiple copies of the same order arrive at XYZ SHOE COMPANY. Again, the OrderID would allow XYZ to realize it had a duplicate, and it could reject any such requests after the initial order was processed.

Precisely to cover such a scenario, the addendum to the WS-Security Specifications issued in August 2002 has included a <Timestamp> element in the WS-Security Specifications. This element is to be included under the SOAP header as a stand-alone element.

Please consider the following SOAP message:

```
<S:Envelope xmlns:S="http://www.w3.org/2001/12/soap-envelope"
            xmlns:wsu="http://schemas.xmlsoap.org/ws/2002/07/utility">
  <S:Header>
    <wsu:Timestamp>
        <wsu:Created>2001-09-13T08:42:00Z</wsu:Created>
        <wsu:Expires>2001-10-13T09:00:00Z</wsu:Expires>
        <wsu:Received Actor="http://x.com/" Delay="60000">
                2001-09-13T08:44:00Z</wsu:Received>
    </wsu:Timestamp>
    . . .
  </S:Header>
  <S:Body>
    . . .
  </S:Body>
</S:Envelope>
```

The <Timestamp> element has three child elements. The first child element states the time at which the message was created. This child is placed by the sender of the message. The WS specifications merely recommend that the UTC Time be used and assumes that the receiver has a mechanism to synchronize time.

The <Expires> element, which is optional, enables the sender to indicate a time frame within which the message can be acted upon by the receiver, after which it should be ignored.

The <Received> element is for the intermediary nodes through which the message passes. The WS-Security Specifications, in conjunction with the WS routing specifications, have included this element so that the ultimate receiver of the message can judge whether to accept the delay period of the message or reject it. The Actor attribute of this element indicates the identity of the intermediate node that processed the message. A message can have more than one <Received> element with one for each of the intermediate nodes.

To preserve the overall integrity of each Timestamp header, it is recommended by the specifications that each actor create or update the appropriate Timestamp header destined to the particular actor. It is also recommended that each actor sign its elements by referencing the ID. The Timestamp header is not to be signed, as the header is mutable, but it may be modified by a subsequent intermediary node.

Security Token Propagation

From the digital signatures and message digests, we now move on to the area of claim assertions in the form of security tokens. Although this topic comes under the `Credential` element of the WS-Security schema, which is explained later in this chapter, we take it up at this point for the sake of continuity of the discussion.

A security token represents a collection of claims. It can be a `UserNameToken` or a `BinarySecurityToken`.

To understand the need for a security token, let us look at a real-world scenario. In everyday life we do a lot of things that require us to prove our identity inorder to authorize what we seek to do. For example, when we go to a shop to buy a car, when it comes to making a payment we flaunt our credit card.

This credit card is a security token. It tells the car dealer that the owner of the credit card is so-and-so and has enough credit in his bank to pay for the car. This information is encoded into the card; our identity is encoded into the card in the form of our signature. The car dealer can verify this information by asking us to sign on the charge slip. If the signatures match, it proves that the card is ours.

In the world of web services, security token performs a similar function as our credit card. It informs the service provider of who requires the service. Whenever the service provider wants an independent authority to corroborate to him this information, the X.509 certificate appears. The government seal on the driving license is substituted by the digital signature of the certificate authority on the X.509 certificate.

In the WS Specifications, there are two types of recognized security tokens, while the specifications allow other unknown types through the extensibility mechanism.

Username Token

The `UserNameToken` is a way of providing a username and optional password information. The simple syntax of this element is illustrated below:

```
<UsernameToken Id="...">
    <Username>...</Username>
    <Password Type="...">...</Password>
</UsernameToken>
```

The sub-elements `UserName` and `Password` both are optional. The message can have any element in their place. The `Password` element can have one more optional sub-element named `Type`, which can have a value indicating the nature of the password. The possible values can be the following predefined types:

```
wsse:PasswordText (default)  - The actual password for the username.
wsse:PasswordDigest  - The digest of the password for the username. The value is a
base64-encoded SHA1 hash value of the UTF8-encoded password.
```

While the `PaswordText` element is quite straightforward and represents the password in clear text, the `PasswordDigest` element has been defined as the base64-encoded SHA1 hash value of the UTF-8-encoded password. However, even this offers no real protection when it is sent over an open channel, since anyone could reverse the base64-encoding or use replay attacks.

Therefore, the addendum to the WS-Security Specifications has recommended two new optional elements, `<wsse:Nonce>` and `<wsu:Created>`, as sub-elements of the `PasswordDigest` element. It also suggests an alternative to these two elements in the form of a password digest that concatenates the nonce value, the creation time, and the actual password. They will look as follows:

```
Password_digest = SHA1 ( nonce + created + password )
```

The nonce is a randomly-generated value sent by the server when it asks the client to log in. The created value represents the time at which the password is encrypted.

Although the concept of nonce has been advanced in the addendum to the WS Specifications, since a nonce is a value generated by a server, it provides no indication of how this value is to be communicated to the client. If the client were to first call the server to collect the nonce, it would defeat the very basis of the WS-Security Specifications, which is modularity, since that would amount to an additional round trip to the server.

According to the specifications, nonce is hashed using the octet sequence of its decoded value, while the timestamp is hashed using the octet sequence of its UTF8 encoding, as specified in the contents of the element.

Binary Security Token

Any XML-based security token can be specified in the `Security` header. However, binary formats (for example, X.509 certificates and Kerberos tickets) and other non-XML formats require a special encoding format for inclusion. The BinarySecurityToken element serves this purpose.

A binary security token has two attributes that are used to interpret it. The `ValueType` attribute indicates what the security token is (for example, a Kerberos ticket). The `EncodingType` tells how the security token is encoded (for example `Base64Binary`).

The `BinarySecurityToken` element defines a security token that is binary encoded. The encoding is specified using the `EncodingType` attribute, and the value type and space are specified using the `ValueType` attribute.

The `EncodingType` attribute can have any of the two predefined values, namely `Base64Binary` (which refers to XML Schema base64 encoding), or `HexBinary` (which is XML Schema hex encoding).

The `SecurityToken` element's schema provides for any attribute. The `ValueType` attribute has the following predefined values:

```
wsse:X509v3 :  X.509 v3 certificate
wsse:Kerberosv5TGT  :  Kerberos v5 ticket as defined in Section 5.3.1 of Kerberos.
This ValueType is used when the ticket is a ticket-granting ticket (TGT)
wsse:Kerberosv5ST  :     Kerberos v5 ticket as defined in Section 5.3.1 of
Kerberos. This ValueType is used when the ticket is a service ticket (ST).
```

The following example illustrates the `BinarySecurityToken` element:

```
<wsse:BinarySecurityToken
xmlns:wsse="http://schemas.xmlsoap.org/ws/2002/04/secext"
          Id="myToken"
          ValueType="wsse:X509v3"
          EncodingType="wsse:Base64Binary">
          MIIEZzCCA9CgAwIBAgIQEmtJZc0...
       </wsse:BinarySecurityToken>
```

In the addendum to the specifications, two new elements have been included to the existing list of three security token types suggested by it (X509V3, Kerberosv5TGT and Kerberosv5ST), as mentioned above. These are <PKCS7> and <PKIPath>, the name spaces being wsse.

The <PKCS7> element can contain a PKCS#7 SignedData object, with the only significant field being certificates. In particular, the signature and the contents are ignored. If no certificates are present, a zero-length CertPath is assumed. The fuller details of a PKCS7 SignedData object can be found on the Internet at http://www.rsasecurity.com/rsalabs/pkcs/pkcs-7/index.html.

The <PKIPath> element can contain an ASN.1 DER-encoded sequence of certificates. Within the sequence, the order of certificates is such that the subject of the first certificate is the issuer of the second certificate. Each certificate in PkiPath should be unique. No certificate may appear more than once in a value of a certificate in PkiPath.

Security Token Reference Element

A security token conveys a set of claims. Sometimes these claims reside somewhere else and need to be tagged to the tokens by the receiving application. The SecurityTokenReference element provides an extensible mechanism for referencing security tokens. The following illustrates the syntax of this element:

```
<SecurityTokenReference Id="...">
    <Reference URI="..."/>
</SecurityTokenReference>
```

The URI attribute specifies a URI for where to find a security token. Just like all other elements in the WS-Security Specifications, this element also has a mechanism for extensibility by way of schema defined "any" element and "any" attribute. The following is an example of the SecurityTokenReference element when used to refer to an X 509 certificate, to be found at a different URI:

```
<wsse:SecurityTokenReference
xmlns:wsse="http://schemas.xmlsoap.org/ws/2002/04/secext">
    <wsse:Reference
       URI="http://www.XYZShoes.com/tokens/XYZ#X509token"/>
</wsse:SecurityTokenReference>
```

Message Confidentiality

The following is the schema of the confidentiality element, as provided in the WS-Security Specifications:

```
<xsd:element name="confidentiality">
  <xsd:annotation>
    <xsd:documentation>
            This element defines the WS-Security confidentiality header.
            Its purpose is to identify encrypted Attachments. This header
            is designed to allow all valid SOAP attributes as well
            as other namespace-qualified attributes that are appropriate
            in the context within which this is being used.
    </xsd:documentation>
```

```
        </xsd:annotation>
        <xsd:complexType>
          <xsd:sequence>
            <xsd:element ref="encryptedAttachment" minOccurs="0"
                maxOccurs="unbounded">
              <xsd:annotation>
                <xsd:documentation>
                            The encryptedAttachment element provides
                            a reference and encryption
                            metadata for message attachments.
                </xsd:documentation>
              </xsd:annotation>
            </xsd:element>
            <xsd:any namespace="##other" processContents="lax" minOccurs="0"
                maxOccurs="unbounded">
              <xsd:annotation>
                <xsd:documentation>
                                This free-form extension may include additional
                                Namespace-qualified XML.
                </xsd:documentation>
              </xsd:annotation>
            </xsd:any>
          </xsd:sequence>
          <xsd:anyAttribute namespace="##other" processContents="lax"/>
        </xsd:complexType>
      </xsd:element>
```

The above schema tell us that the `confidentiality` top level element can contain a sequence of sub-elements either of the type `EncryptedAttachment`, which has been defined in the XML encoding specifications, or of any other type.

However, this can better be understood if we turn our attention to the hypothetical case of XYZ Shoe Company, discussed earlier.

In the transaction previously discussed, the circumstances may warrant the inclusion of payment information with the order, such as a credit card number or a purchase order number, so that XYZ Shoe Company can charge the account. However, ABC's Shoe Mart will not want the payment information to be open to the public. Therefore, it will be advisable to encrypt the payment information so that only XYZ Shoe Company can read it. Let's look at how this might be done.

We first will look at an XML document before encryption or signatures are applied:

```
<pp:ShoeOrder xmlns:pp="http://XYZShoes.com/ShoeOrders">
  <pp:ShoeType>Large Moccassins</pp:ShoeType>
  <pp:quantity>100</pp:quantity>
  <bank:paymentInfo xmlns:bank="http://www.MyBank.com/payspec/1.0">
    <bank:PaymentAmount>$1999.95</bank:PaymentAmount>
    <bank:CreditCardNumber>1239123912391239</bank:CreditCardNumber>
  </bank:paymentInfo>
</pp:ShoeOrder>
```

Here we find that a payment amount and a credit card number are included with the order. ABC woud not want its credit card number to be available to anyone accessing this document. Therefore, it would have to be encrypted. Using W3C's XML encryption syntax and processing working draft as a guideline, an encrypted version of this XML document might look like this:

```
<pp:ShoeOrder xmlns:pp="http://XYZShoes.com/ShoeOrders">
  <pp:OrderID> E7E1AED1-8F64-4FA06-4E8A-D91B41D7CEA </pp:OrderID>
  <pp:ShoeType>Large Moccassins</pp:ShoeType>
  <pp:quantity>100</pp:quantity>
  <bank:paymentInfo xmlns:bank="http://www.MyBank.com/payspecs/1.0">
    <EncryptedData xmlns="http://www.w3.org/2001/04/xmlenc#"
                   Type="http://www.w3.org/2001/04/xmlenc#Content">
      <EncryptionMethod
              Algorithm="http://www.w3.org/2001/04/xmlenc#tipledes-cbc"/>
      <ds:KeyInfo xmlns:ds="http://www.w3.org/2000/09/xmldsig#">
          <ds:RetrievalMethod URI="#SessKey"
                  Type="http://www.w3.org/2001/04/xmlenc#EncryptedKey"/>
      </ds:KeyInfo>
      <CipherData>
        <CipherValue>2hD9okcTVK2AT+HHg</CipherValue>
      </CipherData>
    </EncryptedData>
    <EncryptedKey Id="SessKey" xmlns="http://www.w3.org/2001/04/xmlenc#">
      <EncryptionMethod Algorithm="http://www.w3.org/2001/04/xmlenc#rsa-1_5"/>
      <ds:KeyInfo xmlns:ds="http://www.w3.org/2000/09/xmldsig#">
          <ds:KeyName>XYZ Shoe Company Company's Public/Private Key</ds:KeyName>
      </ds:KeyInfo>
      <CipherData>
        <CipherValue>YPCBCoBADwPCwVR0</CipherValue>
      </CipherData>
      <ReferenceList>
        <DataReference URI="#SessKey"/>
      </ReferenceList>
    </EncryptedKey>
  </bank:paymentInfo>
</pp:ShoeOrder>
```

Here you find that neither the credit card number nor the payment amount has been displayed, since each has been replaced with an `EncryptedData` node.

The above code illustrates that:

❑ The encrypted data is stored in the `CipherValue` subelement (it has been truncated here for readability).

❑ The data was encrypted with a symmetric triple-DES algorithm.

❑ The session key used for encrypting and decrypting the payment data also is included in the document under the `EncryptedKey` node.

❑ The `EncryptedKey` node has a copy of the session key encrypted with a public key for XYZ Shoe Company.

❑ XYZ should first use the corresponding private key to decrypt the session key, and once it has the session key, it can decrypt the rest of the payment data.

It should be noted that using asymmetric encryption algorithms to encode data is computationally expensive, so usually asymmetric methods only are used to encrypt a symmetric key, which is then used to encrypt the majority of the data. Symmetric and asymmetric encryptions were dealt with earlier in Chapter 7.

You may also note that there is a `KeyInfo` element, which is used to describe the Private/ Public keys used to encrypt the session key. In this case, it will take the private key to decrypt the information. Therefore, there is no need for ABC to send a certificate to XYZ Shoe Company. XYZ just has to know how to identify the public key that might have been used. This is why the name associated with the key pair is used.

ABC would digitally sign the message, to ensure the confidentiality of the message, and to confirm that it originated from ABC itself.

Credentials Transfer

The schema of the `credentials` element of the WS-Security schema reads as follows:

```
<xsd:element name="credentials">
    <xsd:annotation>
      <xsd:documentation>
            This element defines the WS-Security credentials header.
            Its purpose is to encapsulate credentials that
            are agreed to between the SOAP producer and consumer. Credentials
            have additional properties which are defined in the WS-Security
            specification located at:
            http://msdn.microsoft.com/ws/2001/10/Security/.  This header
            is designed to allow all valid SOAP attributes as well
            as other namespace-qualified attributes that are appropriate
            in the context within which this is being used.
      </xsd:documentation>
    </xsd:annotation>
    <xsd:complexType>
      <xsd:sequence>
        <xsd:any namespace="##other" processContents="lax" minOccurs="0"
          maxOccurs="unbounded">
          <xsd:annotation>
            <xsd:documentation>
              This element is a placeholder that indicates where the
              credential(s) contained in the WS-Security credentials tag
              belong.
            </xsd:documentation>
          </xsd:annotation>
        </xsd:any>
      </xsd:sequence>
      <xsd:anyAttribute namespace="##other" processContents="lax"/>
    </xsd:complexType>
</xsd:element>
```

The `credentials` header can accommodate as many sub elements of such types as the user may require.

The need to identify the person who is sending a SOAP message is a key part of any sort of security solution. The mechanism for passing credentials in a web service is different from the regular HTTP's basic authentication. Merely sending a username and password with a request does not provide sufficient security for normal needs. Therefore, we think of sending a certificate, or a Kerberos ticket, as the mechanism for identifying an individual.

The web services security language draft defines a `credentials` element that would be passed in the SOAP headers with a SOAP request. The `credentials` element, like SOAP in general, is very flexible and can hold almost any sort of information. It will often be used to carry X.509 certificates and Kerberos tickets.

It must be remembered that that the credentials header can hold any number of credentials, and they may be used for any number of reasons beyond just authenticating the sender of the message. For instance, as mentioned earlier, the credentials may include the certificate that holds the public key used to encrypt a session key. Additional certificates may be included to identify the certificate authority chain for a particular certificate. A certificate may be forwarded even if it is not used for performing any encryption, but the most common reason for this being done is to identify the sender of the message. The SOAP message with credentials will look like this:

```xml
<?xml version="1.0" encoding="utf-8"?>
<SOAP:Envelope xmlns:SOAP="http://schemas.xmlsoap.org/soap/envelope/"
               xmlns:xsd="http://www.w3.org/2001/XMLSchema"
               xmlns:xsi="http://www.w3.org/2001/XMLSchema-instance">
  <SOAP:Header>
    <wssec:credentials xmlns:wssec = "http://schemas .xmlsoap.org/
    ws/2001/10/security">
    <KeyInfo>
      <X509Data>
       <X509Certificate>Br+gAIH1zCCwIBAMI</X509Certificate>
      </X509Data>
    </KeyInfo>
    </wssec:credentials>
  </SOAP:Header>
  <SOAP:Body>
<pp:ShoeOrder xmlns:pp="http://XYZShoes.com/ShoeOrders">
  <pp:ShoeType>Large Moccassins</pp:ShoeType>
  <pp:quantity>100</pp:quantity>
  <bank:paymentInfo xmlns:bank="http://www.MyBank.com/payspec/1.0">
    <bank:PaymentAmount>$1999.95</bank:PaymentAmount>
    <bank:CreditCardNumber>1239123912391239</bank:CreditCardNumber>
  </bank:paymentInfo>
</pp:ShoeOrder>
  </SOAP:Body>
</SOAP:Envelope>
```

In the above example, the `credentials` node holds an X.509 certificate. The `KeyInfo` element, defined by the XML signature syntax discussed earlier, also is used. The web services security language draft allows for a lot of flexibility in the format of credential information, but it accepts the XML Signature `KeyInfo` schema for passing certificates or other key data. It also defines a number of its own mechanisms for passing certificates that are equivalent to the `KeyInfo` approach. Microsoft recommends using the licensing schemas defined in the web service license language draft, since they are more flexible and can be strongly typed, consequently providing for better schema validation.

Putting it All Together

We have so far covered the significant aspects of the five principal elements specified in WS-Security, of which the most relevant three are:

- Integrity
- Confidentiality
- Credentials

When these elements are added appropriately to a SOAP message, the message will look as follow:

```
1.<?xml version="1.0" encoding="utf-8"?>
2.  <SOAP:Envelope xmlns:SOAP="http://schemas.xmlsoap.org/soap/envelope/"
              xmlns:xsd="http://www.w3.org/2001/XMLSchema"
              xmlns:xsi="http://www.w3.org/2001/XMLSchema-instance">
3.    <SOAP:Header>
4.      <wssec:credentials
          xmlns:wssec="http://schemas.xmlsoap.org/ws/2001/10/security">
5.      <ds:KeyInfo xmlns:ds="http://www.w3.org/2000/09/xmldsig#"
          Id="SigningCertificate">
6.        <ds:X509Data>
7.          <ds:X509Certificate>MIIH1zCCBr+gAwIBA...</ds:X509Certificate>
8.        </ds:X509Data>
9.      </ds:KeyInfo>
10.     </wssec:credentials>
11.     <wssec:integrity
          xmlns:wssec="http://schemas.xmlsoap.org/ws/2001/10/security">
12.       <ds:Signature xmlns:ds="http://www.w3.org/2000/09/xmldsig#">
13.         <ds:SignedInfo>
14.           <ds:CanonicalizationMethod
                Algorithm="http://www.w3.org/TR/2001/xml-exc-c14n#"/>
15.           <ds:SignatureMethod Algorithm="http://www.w3.org/
                2000/09/xmldsig#rsa-sha1"/>
16.           <ds:Reference URI=""/>
17.             <ds:Transforms>
18.               <ds:Transform Algorithm="http://schemas.xmlsoap.org/
                    2001/10/security#RoutingSignatureTransform"/>
19.               <ds:Transform Algorithm="http://www.w3.org/TR/2001/REC-
                    xml-c14n-20010315"/>
20.             </ds:Transforms>
21.             <ds:DigestMethod Algorithm="http://www.w3.org/2000/
                  09/xmldsig#sha1"/>
22.             <ds:DigestValue>j6lwx3rvEPO0vKtMup4NbeVu8nk=</ds:DigestValue>
23.           </ds:Reference>
24.         </ds:SignedInfo>
25.         <ds:SignatureValue> ...</ds:SignatureValue>
26.         <ds:KeyInfo>
27.           <wssec:licenseLocation="#SigningCertificate"/>
28.         </ds:KeyInfo>
29.       </ds:Signature>
30.     </wssec:integrity>
31.   </SOAP:Header>
```

```
32.    <SOAP:Body>
33.      <pp:ShoeOrder xmlns:pp="http://XYZShoes.com/ShoeOrders">
34.        <pp:OrderID> E7E1AED1-8F64-4FA06-4E8A-D91B41D7CEA </pp:OrderID>
35.        <pp:ShoeType>Large Moccassins</pp:ShoeType>
36.        <pp:quantity>100</pp:quantity>
37.        <bank:paymentInfo
           xmlns:bank="http://www.MyBank.com/payspecs/1.0">
38.        <EncryptedData xmlns="http://www.w3.org/2001/04/xmlenc#"
           Type="http://www.w3.org/2001/04/xmlenc#Content">
39.          <EncryptionMethod
             Algorithm="http://www.w3.org/2001/04/xmlenc#tipledes-cbc"/>
40.          <ds:KeyInfo xmlns:ds="http://www.w3.org/2000/09/xmldsig#">
41.            <ds:RetrievalMethod URI="#SessKey"
42.             Type="http://www.w3.org/2001/04/xmlenc#EncryptedKey"/>
43.          </ds:KeyInfo>
44.          <CipherData>
45.            <CipherValue>2hD9okcTVK2AT+HHg</CipherValue>
46.          </CipherData>
47.        </EncryptedData>
48.        <EncryptedKey Id="SessKey"
           xmlns="http://www.w3.org/2001/04/xmlenc#">
49.          <EncryptionMethod
             Algorithm="http://www.w3.org/2001/04/xmlenc#rsa-1_5"/>
50.          <ds:KeyInfo xmlns:ds="http://www.w3.org/2000/09/xmldsig#">
51.            <ds:KeyName>XYZ Shoe Company Company's Public/Private Key
             </ds:KeyName>
52.          </ds:KeyInfo>
53.          <CipherData>
54.            <CipherValue>YPCBCoBADwPCwVR0</CipherValue>
55.          </CipherData>
56.          <ReferenceList>
57.            <DataReference URI="#SessKey"/>
58.          </ReferenceList>
59.        </EncryptedKey>
60.        </bank:paymentInfo>
61.      </pp:ShoeOrder>
62.    </SOAP:Body>
63.  </SOAP:Envelope>
```

The above code indicates the following ways in which the WS-Security Specifications can be implemented in a SOAP message:

Lines 4 to 10 of the message contain the `credentials` header. In this, the credentials of the sender are presented in the form of a `BinarySecurityToken` containing an X.509 V3 certificate issued to the sender. Although the WS Specifications recommend a slightly different format for presenting an X.509 certificate as a `BinarySecurityToken`, it is presented here within a `KeyInfo` element, with a dual purpose. This key is identified by an ID element as the signing certificate. The web service can verify the veracity of the certificate by validating it against its list of trusted certificates and by checking on the digital signature of the issuer in the certificate. At the same time the certificate contains the public key of the sender, which can be used to verify his signature on the message, which is contained in the `Integrity` element.

Lines 11 to 30 show the XML signature on the message. Lines 13 to 24 contain the `SingnedInfo`, where Line 16 identified that the entire message has been signed by showing a blank XPointer as the Reference URI value. Line 22 contains the `DigestValue`, which is the hashed digest value of the whole of the message, excluding the security headers, as indicated by the transforms.

Line 25 contains the digital signature value, which was computed using the signing certificate mentioned earlier, as identified by the `KeyInfo` element in Lines 26 to 28.

Leaving behind the headers, when we examine the message body, we notice that it has been encrypted, as prescribed by the WS Specifications. Line 45 contains the cipher value of the original message in its encrypted form. The `keyInfo` in Lines 40 to 43 shows that the message was encrypted using a session key which is presented in Line 54 as an encrypted key. The KeyInfo in Lines 50 & 51 shows that the session key was encrypted using an RSA algorithm, using the public key of XYZ Shoe Company – obviously for the receiver of the message, who must have the private portion of the key to do the decryption.

Advantages of WS-Security

Here is a list of the advantages of WS-Security:

- ❑ A major advantage of XML encryption, which is a part of WS-Security, is that it allows for encrypting only what needs to be encrypted. Extra processing cycles, requiring encrypting every byte sent between two applications, are avoided.

- ❑ In the vision of SOAP messaging for the future, all or part of a SOAP message may need to be processed by multiple nodes. For instance, in the case of a purchase order, part of the message may need to go to the delivery department for completing the order, and part may need to go to the finance department, and then the whole message may need to be forwarded to the company's internal audit department for historical storage. The delivery department needs to know the details of the actual quantity ordered, but does not need to know the payment details. They, however, need to verify that the message came from the specified customer. The WS-Security Specifications take care of such intricate details.

- ❑ If the entire message is encrypted, then the entire message would have to be decrypted in order for anyone to process it. This would expose redundant financial information to people who do not need to know it. Thus if we use the previous methods of providing privacy by using SSL encryption to only encrypt the underlying transport channel, then every point through which the message was routed would be able to see all of the payment details.

- ❑ The power of XML encryption even makes it possible for the payment information, plus a few additional details, to be encrypted with a bank's public key. The recipient of the SOAP message, prospectively a web-enabled supplier, would simply forward the encrypted payment information to the banking institution where it would be decrypted. Then funds would be transferred to the supplier according to the ultimate user's encrypted directions. Thus, the supplier would simply get verification that the funds transfer took place from the bank, and he would ship the order without knowing any of the user's account details.

- ❑ WS-Security is the foundation for a broader road map and additional set of proposed Web services security capabilities outlined by IBM and Microsoft today to tackle the growing need for consistent support of more secure web services. The proposed road map, titled "Security in a web services world," and authored by Microsoft and IBM, outlines additional web services security specifications the companies plan to develop along with key customers, industry partners, and standards organizations

❑ A modular approach to web services security, as is exposed by the WS-Security Specifications, is necessary because of the variety of systems that make up today's IT environments.

❑ While the Security Assertion Markup Language (SAML) provides an XML framework for exchanging authentication and authorization credentials, another spec was needed to spell out the confidentiality and integrity checks required for web services messages. The WS-Security specifications fill that gap with a comprehensive web service security model that supports, integrates, and unifies several popular security models, mechanisms, and technologies (including both symmetric and public key technologies), in a way that enables a variety of systems to securely interoperate in a platform- and language-neutral manner.

Limitations

Here is a list of limitations of WS-Security:

❑ Although the only thing WS-Security seems to buy is a consistent approach with the approach required for intermediaries, it may have its own costs at run time. For example, a rival technology, SSL, has the advantage of being able to repay the cost of establishing the session key over multiple message exchanges, via HTTP-persistent connections.

❑ At present, only IBM has an implementation of the WS-Security Specifications, while Microsoft is expected to make available soon the required assemblies for implementing these specs in its .NET framework.

Summary

In this chapter we have seen what the WS-Security Specifications are all about, and how they leverage the other XML specifications concerning security in the context of web services. WS specifications are in the evolutionary stage and have a long way to go, as shown by the release of addendum to these specifications approximately six months after the release of the original specifications.

However, the fact that some of the leading names in the software industry have wilfully associated themselves into this effort shows its importance in the future of web services.

WS-Security Specifications are to be considered as a part of the Global XML Architecture, which is fast evolving with such other specifications as WS Referral, WS Routing, and XML Information Sets. These protocols have been conceived as infrastructure protocols, composed to provide a cohesive platform for web services and applications. They provide an application-aware network layer that can be secured independent of underlying transport, with a promise to pave the way for more protocols and specifications to enhance this network. This will enable the network to support reliable message delivery, transaction coordination, and ubiquitous metadata and discovery.

12

P3P

While providing your personal information in a transaction on the Internet, how many times have you pressed the I Agree or Register button without reading the privacy agreement completely? Each time you do so, you increase your chances of getting spammed with unwanted material.

It has been observed, in the numerous privacy survey reports, that when users register at a site they hardly read the content of the privacy policy for the site, which describes how the information should be used. This is primarily because users find these verbose legal documents to be boring and difficult to read.

Web sites use cookies and other tracking mechanisms to observe visitors' navigation patterns through their sites, and to thereby build up profiles about visitors' interests. The resulting profiles may then be sold to other companies. The lack of visible information or policies about the use of such user information leads both to confusion and mistrust.

The **Platform for Privacy Preferences** (P3P) tries to address this problem by providing a standard way for web sites to encode their privacy policies in a computer-readable format that can be automatically retrieved and interpreted by user agents. P3P is a project that addresses the twin goals of meeting the data privacy expectations of consumers on the Web while assuring that the medium remains available and productive for electronic commerce. It is a **World Wide Consortium** (W3C) project, which released its P3P 1.0 recommendation in April 2002. This project enables the user to make informed decisions about when their personal information should be revealed.

P3P also becomes important in the context of web services, as they are XML/SOAP-based services residing on SOAP servers. Some of these services are wrapped around a JSP/servlet and are hosted on a web site. In this context, the web services providers can use P3P to specify their privacy policies.

This chapter delves into the P3P 1.0 specifications, and will cover the following:

- ❏ The fundamentals of privacy
- ❏ The history of P3P development
- ❏ The working of P3P and current tools
- ❏ Current tools and implementations
- ❏ Deploying P3P policies in your site
- ❏ The pros and cons of P3P and its future directions

Understanding Privacy

Privacy of personal information depends on protecting three things:

- ❏ Privacy
  When and with whom *you* share your personal information
- ❏ Confidentiality
  When and with whom *another person* or organization shares your personal information
- ❏ Security
  How well your information is *protected* from unauthorized access, alteration, or destruction

Privacy protection is defined as the right of an individual to control the collection and use of personal information by others. The US law, at a state level, has adopted this and there are many international agreements like the 1980 Organization for Economic Cooperation and Development (OECD) guidelines. These guidelines are based on the **Fair Information Practices** (http://www.privacy.ca.gov/fairinfo.htm), whose goals are transparency and fairness. Transparency refers to reporting to the user the information collected from him or her and how and where it is used. Fairness is about making sure that private information is used only for the purpose for which it was collected.

Privacy has been a concern for users on the Internet. In this section we look deeper into the major findings about these concerns. We then look at how a user provides his or her personal information unknowingly. This is followed by an examination of some of the existing privacy solutions.

Privacy Concerns

As the Internet has become more and more a part of our daily lives, online privacy concerns have increased. Numerous surveys have taken place to figure out the nature of online privacy concerns. Here we will summarize these findings:

- ❏ Data is often collected unknowingly and only a few sites offer meaningful alternatives. The Internet allows rather inexpensive ways to collect the personal profile of a user without the user's knowledge. Many of the sites do not offer enough alternatives for users who do not wish to share personal information.
- ❏ Data collected for business purpose is often used in other contexts. This data collected for business purpose may be sold to various agencies or be used in civil and criminal proceedings.

❑ Data from multiple sources may be merged. The data collected by various web sites may be merged, which may reveal a lot of a user's personal profile information.

❑ Internet users are more likely to provide information when they are anonymous.

❑ Internet users dislike automatic data transfer and unsolicited communications. There is a growing dislike for software tools that send profiling or other information to the *master* web site automatically.

❑ Only 3% of users read the online policies *carefully* and most of the time they find the policies time-consuming and difficult to understand. Users are more likely to read the privacy policy when providing sensitive information like their social security number or credit card information.

❑ 70% of users prefer to have a standard privacy policy format. A majority of users found it preferable to have standard policy format, so that it becomes easier to understand across various sites.

❑ People are comfortable at sites that have privacy policies, even if they don't read them.

The surveys we referred to were from the following organizations:

❑ Beyond Concern: Understanding Net Users' Attitudes About Online Privacy by Lorrie Faith Cranor, Joseph Reagle, and Mark S. Ackerman.
http://www.research.att.com/projects/privacystudy/

❑ Tutorial on P3P by Lorrie Faith Cranor, http://lorrie.cranor.org/

❑ Privacy Leadership Initiative
http://www.ftc.gov/bcp/workshops/glb/supporting/harris%20results.pdf

❑ Numerous surveys at http://www.privacyexchange.org/

The importance of privacy is highlighted in all the surveys, and the studies by analysts estimate the Internet retail sales lost due to privacy concerns may be as much as $18 billion.

In general, web users should ask themselves these main privacy questions:

❑ How do web sites use my information when I sign up as a member or to buy something?

❑ What information do web sites collect about me?

❑ How do I know my information is secure?

In the following section we will look at the various mechanisms by which user data is risked to exposure. Then we will look at the privacy solutions offered by the current technologies.

Web Site Surveillance Techniques

Web sites employ a variety of techniques to gather personal information. Some of the techniques described have perfectly innocent uses, with the result that it would not be acceptable to forbid them. In most cases, multiple techniques must be coordinated in order to maximize the amount of personal information collected. These techniques include server logs, cookies, web bugs, and so on. Let's look at these in detail.

Browser and Server Logs

Browsers carry user information in the form of IP address, domain name, platform, browser type, OS, referring page, and cookies, and make the information available to web servers, ISP providers, third-party advertisements, and so on.

The Internet Protocol (IP) used to transmit web pages creates a privacy risk that is not imposed by web browsers, but in the transmission of web pages through the IP. When a browser requests a page from a server, the browser's IP address is transmitted as the return address to which the requested page is to be sent.

The `Referer` part of the HTTP header identifies the URL of the page that caused the current page to be requested, which is another privacy-impacting feature. In the example below, you can notice that the `Referer` header reveals that the user has reached the current site from www.amazon.com. It also shows how the cookie information appears in the HTTP header:

```
GET /retail/searchresults.asp?qu=books HTTP/1.0
Referer: http://www.amazon.com/default.asp
User-Agent: User-Agent: Mozilla/4.0 (compatible; MSIE 6.0; Windows NT 5.0;
H010818)
Host: www.buy.com
Accept: image/gif, image/jpeg, image/pjpeg, */*
Accept-Language: en-us
Cookie: buycountry=us; dcLocName=Basket; dcCatID=6773; dcLocID=6773;
dcAd=buybasket; loc=; parentLocName=Basket; parentLoc=6773;
ShopperManager%2F=ShopperManager%2F=7766FUQULL0QBT8MMTVSC5MMNKBJFWDVH7; Store=107;
Category=0
```

Server logs can store the URL from which the request originated. This is revealing when the GET method of HTTP is used, as it sends the values in the URL as name-value pairs and are visible in clear text.

For example, such a log file can be used by the web site later to comb through the personal details of the users:

```
http://www.buy.com/cgi_bin/order?name=Ravi+Trivedi&address=somewhere+here&credit+c
ard=234876923234&PIN=987234
```

Also, using the GET method sends the complete URL in the `Referer` header for the next request, which is also revealing.

Cookies

A cookie is a unique identifier that a web server places on your computer. It is a serial number that may be used to retrieve your records from their (the web site's) database. It's usually a string of random-looking letters long enough to be unique.

Since HTTP is a stateless protocol, nothing links one HTTP request to a later HTTP request. Cookies were designed to extend the protocol to allow sites to send state information to the browser that may later be queried by the web server. Cookies RFC 2109 is present at http://www.cis.ohio-state.edu/cgi-bin/rfc/rfc2109.html.

Common *innocent* uses of cookies include:

❑ Allowing the web server to thereby establish some form of *session*, which is useful in e-commerce applications where the user browses a catalogue, periodically adding items to a *basket*. The server can, when needed, query the cookie to get the session identifier, which simplifies development of the web application.

❑ Allowing the web server to identify returning users, so that they do not need to expressly identify themselves in order to get user-oriented functionality.

On the darker side, cookies may be used to track the identity of the users without their knowledge as they navigate within a web site. Cookies can sometimes even track their navigation across multiple web sites.

Cookies were designed to keep user information on the client's (browser) machine, but their typical use has been that each user is assigned a unique visitor number (session ID) from a computer, which is stored on the client machine, and personal information is then kept on the web site server. This profiling information can later be used by the web site for its benefit.

There are typically two types of cookies – **session** and **permanent**. Session cookies are valid during a session between the browser and the site, and they expire in time. The permanent cookies, however, reside on the client machine and are more privacy-invasive (they give others an opportunity to use the machine and log in as you). Cookies are not only sent back to the site that set them, but also are sent to any host in the domain that requests them.

A **first-party cookie** either originates on or is sent to the web site you are currently viewing, or one that originates from the host domain.

A **third-party cookie** either originates on or is sent to a web site different from the one you are currently viewing, or sent from a domain other than the page on the host domain. Third-party web sites may provide some content on the web site you are viewing. For example, many sites use advertising from third-party web sites, and those third-party web sites may use cookies. A common use for this type of cookie is to track your web page use for advertising or other marketing purposes.

Unsatisfactory cookies are ones that might allow access to personally identifiable information that could be used for a secondary purpose without your consent.

The sorts of cookies that are particularly considered *objectionable* are those which store visible personal information that may be accessed by another web site without your consent. It would be a *very* bad idea, for instance, for a web site to store your credit card information in a cookie, as there is a risk of other web sites accessing this information.

For more information on the use of cookies to track private information, see http://www.junkbusters.com/ht/en/cookies.html.

Web Bugs

A web bug or web beacon is a transparent graphic on a web page or in an e-mail message designed to monitor who is reading the page or message. Web bugs are graphics on web pages for monitoring purposes. They are often invisible because they are typically only 1-by-1 pixels in size, represented as an HTML IMG tag. As they are transparent you can't see anything, yet any HTML-enabled viewer, including your browser, e-mail, news, or other clients will fetch the tiny `.gif` image from a foreign server whenever the image is displayed. If cookies are enabled then a full *cookie exchange* can transpire as well and this means loss of privacy.

Bugnosis (http://www.bugnosis.org/) is a tool that detects web bugs. When you run Bugnosis it points you at the image, which is hidden in the page and is collecting data. You can learn more about web bugs at http://www.privacyfoundation.org/resources/webbug.asp.

If cookies are not enabled, a technique called **fake dates** can still be used to track you individually by using web beacons. By uniquely and individually *faking* the last modified date of a web bug image (or of a traditional web advertisement for that matter), it is possible for you to be tracked just as deliberately and uniquely as if all cookies were being accepted. Whenever your browser already contains a web bug image in its cache, it asks the foreign server if the image has been modified since the *fake date*, which instantly and uniquely identifies you to the server since every person being tracked is given a different fake date.

Spyware

Spyware is software that uses the user's Internet connection to transfer information without their knowledge and their explicit permission. By using these, detailed user profiles may be collected, which may then be used for commercial or other purposes. A lot of such software is often hard to uninstall.

There are examples of many shareware and freeware products that contain spywares like Comet Curson, GoZilla Download Manager, and so on. You can refer to sites like http://www.spychecker.com/ that contain a listing of spyware, before installing software if you are not sure about a new product. Also, free tools like **Ad-aware** (http://www.lavasoft.de/) scan the memory, registry, and hard drive for known spyware components and let you remove them.

Privacy Solutions

In this section we will evaluate several solutions that help improve the privacy problem currently faced by Internet users.

Privacy Policies

Each web site could declare its privacy policy describing the site's privacy practices. The presence of such a policy would help users make an informed decision, and they could decide to opt in or out. According to the privacy surveys, the mere presence of such a policy increases user confidence in the site. Such policies are often expressed in natural language text (like English). Such policies suffer from drawbacks such as that they are difficult to understand, hard to find, use varying formats, contain a lot of fine print, and change without notice.

P3P provides a machine-readable and XML-based description of the privacy policy asserted by a web site. By using common, standards-based approaches to define policy, automated agents may be able to read the policies and act on the users' behalf based on their preferences.

Privacy Certification Programs

Seal programs are certifications by privacy agencies for compliance with a stated policy. Such programs have independent auditors who certify that the site is compliant with their stated privacy policies. These programs also specify a complaint process and specify how disputes can be resolved. BBBOnline, TRUSTe, and CPA Webtrust are some such seal programs. The web sites that employ these certifications contain their logos.

Such programs have the drawback that they can certify only a limited set of privacy policies. It is also hard for the seal programs to maintain compliance levels although some programs have introduced random checks. The policies certified by the seal programs are not always adequate to describe the site's policy.

These privacy policies often are published as legal documents, in what is commonly termed *legalese*. The language may be quite satisfactory for lawyers, but the rest of us find it painful to read and difficult to understand. Different organizations often will generate documents that mostly mean the same thing, but that use different wordings and formats, replete with fine print and notices that are subject to change without notice.

Privacy Laws and Organizations

Privacy laws and regulatory bodies play an important role in the privacy landscape, as they are the enforcing agencies. However, the Internet encompasses every part of the world, and the law is different in various parts of the world. The US has a lot of important laws like the **Freedom of Information Act**, **Children's Online Privacy Protection Act (COPPA)**, and so on. These laws focus on increasing the transparency and fairness in Internet transactions. COPPA requires parental consent before collecting personal information from children. The European Union has the Data Protection Directive that requires all the European countries to adopt similar laws. This directive prohibits the secondary use of data without informed consent.

Software Tools

Encryption tools are useful in preventing eavesdroppers from listening to your communication. *Anonymity* tools act as proxies for several users, thus protecting the information from being revealed. Examples of such tools are **Crowds** from AT&T (http://www.research.att.com/projects/crowds) and **Anonymizer** (http://www.anonymizer.com/).

A variety of web filter tools are available that provide ways of building rules to filter out undesirable cookies or web pages. These typically behave as a small HTTP server/web proxy on your system. For example, *Cookie Cutters* provide fine-grained cookie control, and filter ads, referrer headers, and so on.

Other tools include the following:

- ❑ GuideScope – http://internet.junkbuster.com/guidescope.html
- ❑ JunkBuster – http://internet.junkbuster.com/
- ❑ Privoxy – http://www.privoxy.org/
- ❑ AdZapper – http://www.zipcon.net/~adamf/adzapper/

History of P3P

P3P standards grew out of its earlier work at W3C called PICS (Platform for Internet Content Selection at http://www.w3.org/PICS/), and is based on RDF (Resource Description Framework at http://www.w3.org.TR/RDF) and DSIG (Digital signature Initiative at http://www.w3.org/DSig/Overview.html).

PICS pertained to web sites being rated according to their content, where the browsers restricted access to sites based on the web user's configuration. This was a useful feature, because a parent could configure the browser for his or her child's computer, avoiding unwanted exposure to objectionable content.

The work on P3P started at W3C in June 1997. Several working groups were convened by W3C for the five years until the P3P 1.0 W3C recommendation was released in April 2002. These included members from various security companies and privacy seal companies. There was also participation from privacy advocates and government bodies. A large number of W3C member organizations have been involved with P3P efforts, including: Akamai, America Online, AT&T, Center for Democracy and Technology, Citigroup, Crystaliz, Direct Marketing Association, Electronic Network, Hewlett Packard, and many more.

The initial versions of the P3P draft included the concept of multi-step negotiation, agreement, and data transfer, which was later removed. This was done because the working group felt these features would be too complex to implement in the first version and would hinder widespread deployment of the P3P standards.

As the P3P specifications evolved, several public working drafts were issued. The P3P *Harmonized Vocabulary Specification* public working draft was then made available on March 30, 1998, and the P3P 1.0 working draft (from the *Syntax and Encoding Working Group*) was publicly released on July 2, 1998. Based on these drafts and public releases various tools were developed, and several companies and organizations deployed P3P on their web sites. These included companies like Microsoft, HP, IBM, AT&T, Yahoo, and so on.

Understanding P3P

P3P can help balance the IT economy's need by providing consumers with desired services. This will help individuals have control over personal information with the help of tools to notice and make decisions based on their own preferences. The idea behind P3P design is that web sites disclose their privacy practices in a machine-readable P3P format, which is retrieved automatically by the *user agent* accessing the site. The user agent then compares the practices with the users' privacy preferences, based on which it provides controlled access.

> **The term *user agent* in the specification refers to client programs, media players, plug–ins, or web browsers that act on behalf of the users and fetch and process the P3P policies. It is also assumed that there is a complete trust between the user agents and the user.**

The P3P specification consists of the following:

❑ A set of basic data elements that can be referred to by web sites while describing their data- usage practices. This is used for declaring the kind of information collected by a web site.

❑ A standard vocabulary for describing a web site's data usage practices. This is used by a web site to describe what it does with the data.

❑ Using the underlying transport protocol for the exchange of the web site's privacy policy. Currently it is only built on the HTTP protocol even though there can be bindings with other protocols, but that is not defined in the specification as yet.

In addition to this, the specification contains recommended guidelines regarding the responsible use of P3P and the intent of P3P development.

How does P3P Work?

A **policy reference file** is an XML file with namespaces that contain links to P3P privacy statements files for a web site.

It specifies what policy (stored in a single or multiple policy files) applies to a given URI. A policy reference file may contain multiple POLICY-REF elements. Each of these elements specifies to which URIs the given policy is relevant. Here is an example of the policy reference file:

```
<META xmlns="http://www.w3.org/2002/01/P3Pv1">
 <POLICY-REFERENCES>
  <EXPIRY max-age="172800"/>
    <POLICY-REF about="http://www.hp.com/w3c/policy1.xml">
      <INCLUDE>/*</INCLUDE>
      <EXCLUDE>/catalog/*</EXCLUDE>
      <EXCLUDE>/servlet/*</EXCLUDE>
    </POLICY-REF>
    <POLICY-REF about="http://www.hp.com/w3c/policy2.xml">
      <INCLUDE>/catalog/*</INCLUDE>
      <INCLUDE>/servlet/*</INCLUDE>
    </POLICY-REF>
  </POLICY-REFERENCES>
</META>
```

The above file contains <INCLUDE> and <EXCLUDE> elements that specify all the portions of the site that are governed by a particular policy file. The about attribute in the POLICY-REF element refers to the location of the policy being referred. It is possible that a single page contains a graphics frame and may have references to multiple parts of the sites, each governed by different P3P policies. In such a case, user agents should fetch and process all the relevant files before rendering the page.

In the above example all URIs of the form catalog/* and servlet/* are governed by privacy policies as specified in http://www.hp.com/w3c/policy2.xml, whereas the rest of the site is governed by http://www.hp.com/w3c/policy1.xml.

The policy reference file can be placed in a well-known location (/w3c/p3p.xml) or in other locations. In case it is placed in other locations, the site must declare this location using a policyref HTTP header, or by using the link tag in the HTML files.

For example, consider the following request made by a user agent to access a web page. This is the first step in accessing the P3P policy:

```
GET /index.html HTTP/1.1 200 OK
Host: www.hp.com
Accept: */*
Accept-Language: de, en
User-Agent: IE 6.0
```

The server responds with the reference to location using the policyref field as shown:

```
HTTP/1.1 200 OK
P3P: policyref="http://www.hp.com/P3P/PolicyReferences.xml"
Content-Type : text/xml
Content Length : 4555
Server: Swetha/11.11.0
```

427

Alternatively, the server can have an embedded `link` tag in the HTML content as below:

```
<link rel="P3Pv1"  href="http://www.hp.com/P3P/PolicyReferences.xml">
```

Next, the user agent tries to obtain the P3P policy reference file (`PolicyReferences.xml`), the location of which was just determined (http://www.hp.com/P3P/PolicyReferences.xml).

There may be one single policy for the entire site or several different policy files referenced in the policy reference file. It is the responsibility of the user agent to fetch all the related policies, parse them, and then decide the actions to be taken on behalf of the user based on the user's preferences.

The following diagram shows a typical process of retrieving a P3P policy file, when the policy reference file exists in a non-standard location. The exact order of the flow depends on the P3P user agent. The P3P specification allows user agents to make P3P requests before, after, or in parallel with requesting the content:

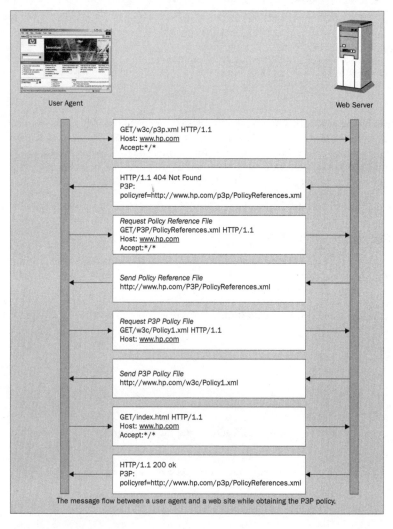

The message flow between a user agent and a web site while obtaining the P3P policy.

Understanding the Specification

The specification is the authoritative source of information on the P3P protocol and is available for download at http://www.w3c.org/TR/P3P/. The current version of the specification (1.0) is a W3C recommendation released in April 2002. There is a set of useful reference documents like FAQ and brochures present at http://www.w3.org/P3P/. This site also contains the W3C notes on how to deploy P3P on your site, in addition to a variety of other articles.

The specification refers to **safe zone** practices, which should be used by all P3P-enabled user agents and services while fetching the P3P policy and policy reference files. The safe zone policies are an example of a solution to the chicken and egg problem. We need to fetch the P3P policy and policy reference files in order to start using P3P privacy filtering, but the question is what policy should be adhered to while fetching these files? For this bootstrapping purpose a minimal policy is defined, known as the *safe zone* policy.

> **Any request for fetching a P3P policy or policy reference file should be covered by safe zone policies. These policies allow minimal data to be collected and used in a non-identifiable way.**

Example of a P3P Policy file

Let's look at the P3P policy file (`policy1.xml`) that was returned to the user agent in the previous example to understand details of what is specified in this file.

To begin with, there are two portions to a P3P policy. The first portion contains general information, like the company's details that is hosting the site (included in the `ENTITY` tag), the location of human readable policies, the dispute, and the resolution information. The second portion consists of what data is collected and what is done with it. This includes information about the consequences of providing data (`CONSEQUENCE` tag), how data will be used (`PURPOSE` tag), and with whom the data is shared (`RECEIPIENT`):

```
<?xml version="1.0" ?>
<POLICY xmlns="http://www.w3.org/2000/12/P3Pv1"
        discuri="http://www.hp.com/w3c/privacy.htm"
        opturi="http://www.hp.com/w3c/assist-general.html" name="policy1">
  <EXPIRY max-age="604800" />
  <ENTITY>
    <DATA-GROUP>
      <DATA ref="#business.name">Hewlett Packard Company</DATA>
      <DATA ref="#business.contact-info.online.email">Privacy@hp.com</DATA>
      <DATA ref="#business.contact-info.online.uri">http://www.hp.com</DATA>
      <DATA ref="#business.contact-info.telecom.telephone.number">
        650-857-4731
      </DATA>
      <DATA ref="#business.contact-info.postal.organization">
        Hewlett Packard Company
      </DATA>
      <DATA ref="#business.contact-info.postal.street">
        3000 Hanover Street
      </DATA>
      <DATA ref="#business.contact-info.postal.city">Palo Alto</DATA>
      <DATA ref="#business.contact-info.postal.stateprov">CA</DATA>
      <DATA ref="#business.contact-info.postal.postalcode">94304</DATA>
      <DATA ref="#business.contact-info.postal.country">USA</DATA>
    </DATA-GROUP>
  </ENTITY>
```

The following table describes the meaning of each of the tags used above:

Element	Meaning
POLICY	This is the *root* tag, which holds the policy document. Multiple POLICY elements can be held in POLICIES tags with each representing a separate policy. The attribute discuri specifies the location of a natural language privacy statement, whereas the opturi is the URI of the instructions that can be followed to request or decline the use of personal data (opt-in or opt-out procedures). The name attribute contains the name of the policy.
EXPIRY	The EXPIRY element states how long the policy remains valid, where the time is specified in seconds. In the example, the policy is valid for 604800 seconds, or 7 days.
ENTITY	The ENTITY element gives a description of the legal entity making the representation of the privacy practice. This contains various data elements describing the business entity and contains fields like name, contact information, e-mail address, and so on. The example shows the address and contact details of Hewlett Packard.

The P3P specification defines a set of base data sets and data structures. A data set consists of grouping of data elements, whereas a data structure contains hierarchy of a set of data elements.

These are used to describe the data collected by the site and to provide more information about the owner of the site. In the example above, business.name, dynamic.http, and business.contact-info.online.email are examples of data elements.

P3P can also carry any number of *optional* elements, including physical contact information, online contact information, unique identifiers, financial account identifiers, demographic and socio-economic data, preference data, and so on.

```
<ACCESS>
  <nonident />
</ACCESS>
```

The ACCESS element indicates if the site allows users to access their identified information. The value <nonident/> here indicates that the site does not collect identified data. The other valid values include <all/> and <none/>, which means all or no access to the identified data.

```
<DISPUTES-GROUP>
  <DISPUTES
    resolution-type="independent"
    service="http://www.bbbonline.org"
    verification="http://www.bbbonline.org/cnfm.cfm?company=03311999100448"
    short-description="BBBOnLine">
    <LONG-DESCRIPTION>BBBOnLine Privacy Seal</LONG-DESCRIPTION>
    <IMG src="http://www.bbbonline.org/images/congraphic.gif"
      alt="BBBOnLine Privacy Seal Participant Certification" />
    <REMEDIES>
      <correct />
    </REMEDIES>
  </DISPUTES>
</DISPUTES-GROUP>
```

Let's have a look at what the above elements mean:

Element	Meaning
DISPUTES-GROUP	This element contains several DISPUTES elements.
DISPUTES	Each of the DISPUTES elements describes the possible dispute resolution procedure to be followed. The above example refers to the BBBOnline seal program as a dispute-resolution body, and also indicates that the site implements policies compliant with the seal program.
REMEDIES	The REMEDIES element denotes how a policy breach would be corrected; in this case the <correct/> tag depicts that the site will ensure the correction of such wrongful actions.

```
<STATEMENT>
  <EXTENSION optional="yes">
    <GROUP-INFO
      xmlns="http://www.software.ibm.com/P3P/editor/extension-1.0.html"
      name="hp.com" />
  </EXTENSION>

  <CONSEQUENCE>
    Information is collection for navigation purposes only, contains no
    personal data, and is stored for the session only.
  </CONSEQUENCE>

  <PURPOSE>
    <admin />
    <current />
    <develop />
  </PURPOSE>

  <RECIPIENT>
    <ours />
  </RECIPIENT>

  <RETENTION>
    <no-retention />
  </RETENTION>

  <DATA-GROUP>
    <DATA ref="#dynamic.miscdata">
      <CATEGORIES>
        <navigation />
      </CATEGORIES>
    </DATA>
    <DATA ref="#dynamic.http" />
    <DATA ref="#dynamic.cookies" optional="yes">
      <CATEGORIES>
        <navigation />
        <other-category />
      </CATEGORIES>
    </DATA>
  </DATA-GROUP>
</STATEMENT>
</POLICY>
```

Let's look at all the tags and attributes used in the above policy and what they mean:

Element	Meaning
STATEMENT	This element is a container that groups together several elements, namely PURPOSE, RECIPIENT, RETENTION, DATA_GROUP, and CONSEQUENCE. All of the data referenced by the DATA-GROUP is handled according to the disclosures made in the other elements.
CONSEQUENCE	This element provides a further explanation of the site's policy, and contains a natural language-based explanation.
PURPOSE	This element specifies the purpose of the data collection. The above example mentions its usage for `<admin/>`, `<current/>`, and `<develop/>`. The `<admin/>` element specifies the information that will be used for the technical support of the web site. The `<current/>` element means that the information collected could be used to complete the transaction, as in the case of placing an order. `<develop/>` means the information may be used to enhance, evaluate, and review the site.
RECIPIENT	This element specifies the recipient of the collected data, based on the classification. In the example above, the element `<ours/>` shows that the data is collected for the company or agents acting on behalf of the company; Hewlett Packard in this case.
RETENTION	This is the kind of retention policy adapted by the site. The above example shows that Hewlett Packard follows a `<no-retention/>`, or no data is retained for more than a brief period of time necessary to make use of it in a transaction.
DATA-GROUP	Each statement element that contains an identifiable element must contain at least one DATA-GROUP element that contains one of more DATA elements. The DATA elements are used to describe the type of data a site collects. In the example above, the site collects information about the `dynamic.http`, `dynamic.cookies`, and `dynamic.miscdata` data elements that is the HTTP access information, the HTTP cookies, and miscellaneous data like web logs.
CATEGORIES	This element is inside the data elements and provides hints to the users and user agents about the intended uses of the data. For example, `<navigation/>` present in Hewlett Packard's policy file depicts that the miscellaneous data collected contains the navigation and click stream data, which includes which pages are visited by a user and how long the users stayed on each page.

Compact Policies

The P3P policies can also be specified completely in the HTTP header as "compact policy" when cookies are set using a SET_COOKIE directive. Compact policies are summarized P3P policies that provide hints to user agents to make quick decisions, and are a performance optimization. It is optional for a site to implement compact policies. Compact policies specify the site preferences related only to cookies, and do not fully express all the aspects of the policy. Configuring the web server to issue special P3P headers can do this.

Here is an example of a compact policy of the Hewlett Packard's policy:

```
P3P: CP ="NOI DSP COR CURa ADMa DEVa OUR NOR COM NAV OTC"
```

Each of the compact values has been obtained by compacting the tags into developer-readable language and most of the tags are three letter codes. For example `<nonident/>` becomes NOI, `<disputes/>` becomes DSP, and `<correct/>` becomes COR.

Each of the abbreviated policies can be interpreted as shown in the table below:

Field	Meaning	Tag in Policy
CP	This is the compact policy **header**; it indicates that what follows is a P3P compact policy	

NOI	No identifiable information is collected, so no access is possible	`<ACCESS>`
		  `<nonident />`
		`</ACCESS>`

DSP	The policy contains at least one dispute-resolution mechanism	`<DISPUTES-GROUP>`
		  `<DISPUTES resolution-type="independent"`
		    `service="http://www.bbbonline.org"`
		    `verification=" …../>`
		    `...`
		  `</DISPUTES>`
		`</DISPUTES-GROUP>`

COR	Violations of this policy will be corrected	`<REMEDIES>`
		  `<correct />`
		`</REMEDIES>`

CURa	The data is used for completion of the current activity, always	`<PURPOSE>`
		  `<current />`
		  `...`
		`</PURPOSE>`

ADMa	The data is used for site administration, always	`<PURPOSE>`
		  `...`
		  `<admin />`
		`</PURPOSE>`

Table continued on following page

Field	Meaning	Tag in Policy

DEVa	The data is used for research and development, always	`<PURPOSE>`
		`<develop />`
		...
		`</PURPOSE>`

OUR	The data is given to our agents and ourselves	`<RECIPIENT>`
		`<ours />`
		`</RECIPIENT>`

NOR	The data is not kept beyond the current transaction	`<RETENTION>`
		`<no-retention />`
		`</RETENTION>`

COM	Computer information is collected	`<CATEGORIES>`
		`<navigation />`
		`<other-category />`
		`</CATEGORIES>`

NAV	Navigation and click stream data is collected	`<CATEGORIES>`
		`<navigation />`
		`</CATEGORIES>`

OTC	Other types of information are collected	`<CATEGORIES>`
		`<navigation />`
		`<other-category />`
		`</CATEGORIES>`

Similarly, there are several other tags defined in the specification for compact policies. The compact policy does not have a way to specify the expiry time and assumes the policy is valid at least through the lifetime of the cookie to which it applies. Also there is no caching of the compact policy done by the user agents, so the server always sends this policy. In the section describing the deployment of a P3P policy, we will learn how to configure various servers to send the privacy policy.

P3P Tools

There are a number of tools that implement P3P. A good listing of such tools is available at http://www.p3ptoolbox.org/ and http://www.w3.org/P3P/implementations. Some of the important tools are:

❑ P3P User Agents/Proxies
AT&T Privacy Bird, Internet Explorer 6, and JRC P3P proxy

❑ Policy Generators/Editors/Checkers
IBM P3P Policy Editor, P3P Validator, and P3PEdit P3P Policy Generator

❑ Compact Policy Generators/Editors/Checkers
Zero-Knowledge Systems P3P Analyzer and P3P Compact Policy Translator

❑ Tools/Libraries for Developers
APPEL engine

The specification provides some directives for the user agents' functioning. The user agents act upon only those P3P policies and policy reference files that are well-formed XML files, and they do not modify these files locally to confirm to the XML schema. User agents can asynchronously fetch and evaluate the P3P policies. Until the policy is evaluated, the agent would treat the site as having no privacy policies and use the *safe zone* practices. Typically, user agents cache the privacy policies for performance reasons and fetch them again only when they expire.

Let us look at some of the tools that are P3P-compliant.

Internet Explorer 6.0

Internet Explorer 6.0 (IE 6) is a P3P-compliant user agent that allows you to specify your privacy preferences. IE 6 checks each web site's privacy policy, as expressed by the web site using the P3P protocol. Then, based on what it finds, it permits – or declines – the web site to install information-gathering cookies on the user's computer. The IE 6 implementation has a limited support of P3P. It provides various levels of cookie access as specified in the Privacy|Settings tab of IE 6, which is shown in the screenshot below:

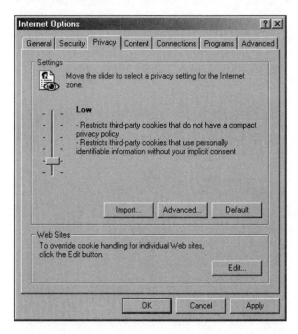

It checks P3P *compact* policies at the site that set cookies. Users can configure IE6 such that it blocks these cookies from sites that don't have such compact policies. Whenever it encounters a mismatch it blocks or restricts cookies and will display a privacy icon on the status bar as shown in the image below:

Clicking on this icon shows the site for which cookies have been blocked or restricted as shown in the screenshot below:

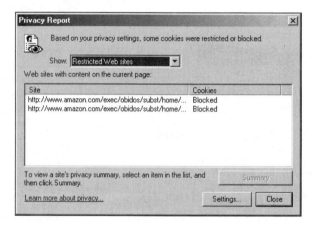

It is also possible to view the privacy summary in English (by selecting the site and the Summary button shown above), which is generated from the complete P3P policy. The following screenshot shows the privacy policy summary generated from the P3P policy by Internet Explorer 6.0:

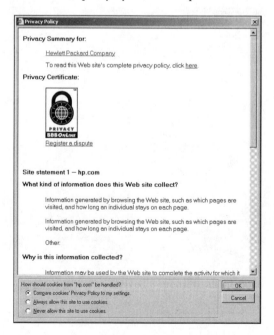

The IE 6 policies are related to the handling of personally identifiable information by cookies. IE 6 can restrict cookies so that they are returned only to the sites from which they originated. It also can delete cookies when it exits. The default policies in IE 6 for handling cookies for the *first-party* cookies and *third-party* cookies are shown in the table below:

Privacy Level	First-party cookies	Third-party cookies
Accept All Cookies	Accepts	Accepts
Low	Accepts	*Restricts* if no compact P3P policy. *Restricts* cookies that use personal information without *implicit* consent.
Medium	*Restricts* cookies that use personal information without implicit consent	*Blocks* if no compact P3P policy. *Blocks* cookies that use personal information without *implicit* consent.
Medium High	*Blocks* cookies that use personal information without implicit consent	*Blocks* if no compact P3P policy. *Blocks* cookies that use personal information without *explicit* consent.
High	*Blocks* if no compact P3P policy. *Blocks* cookies that use personal information without *explicit* consent.	*Blocks* if no compact P3P policy. *Blocks* cookies that use personal information without *explicit* consent.
Blocks All Cookies	Cookies from all web sites will be *blocked.* Existing cookies from the computer cannot be read.	Cookies from all web sites will be *blocked.* Existing cookies from the computer cannot be read.

AT&T Privacy Bird

AT&T **Privacy Bird** (http://www.privacybird.com/) is another P3P user agent that displays whether the policy at the site matches the user preference or not. It is an extension program that may be attached to the Microsoft Internet Explorer. It shows a *happy* bird icon in green when the P3P policies match with users' preferences, and a red *angry* bird when there is a mismatch. On clicking the bird icon, a summary of the site's policy can be seen. However, this tool does not control access to a site and is informational only. The following screenshot shows two different sites with a happy green bird showing policy match (look in the upper right corner of the screen):

And here we have the red bird showing a mismatch with the user's policy:

Like IE 6, various privacy levels can be set in Privacy Bird as shown below:

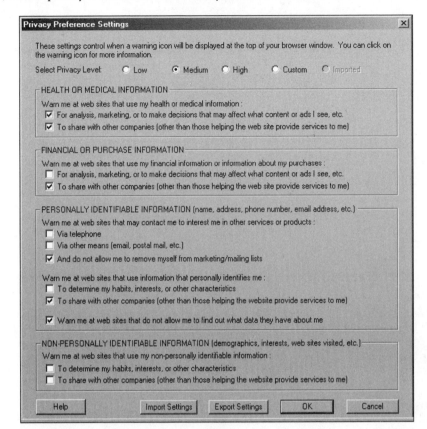

IBM P3P Policy Editor and Parser

A P3P Preference Exchange Language (APPEL) is a language for describing collections of preferences regarding P3P policies between P3P agents. Using this language, users can express their preferences in a set of preference-rules, which can then be used by their user agent to make automated or semi-automated decisions regarding the acceptability of machine-readable privacy policies from P3P-enabled web sites. The APPEL working group released a Working Draft 1.0 of this specification in April 2002.

IBM **Policy Editor** allows you to edit and create the P3P policies. This tool has a drag-and-drop interface, and comes with a good documentation and a set of templates. You can view the XML file that is created as part of adding individual data elements, as well as the compact policies. It can generate and display the policies in a human readable form. It also contains an error tab that shows the errors encountered in your policy. This tool also can be used for constructing policy reference files. There are templates available for Safe Zone Policy, Online Shopping Site, and other generic policies.

This is a recommended tool for creating a site policy, and is available for a free download from the IBM Alphaworks site at http://www.alphaworks.ibm.com/tech/p3peditor/. Below is a screenshot of the P3P Policy Editor:

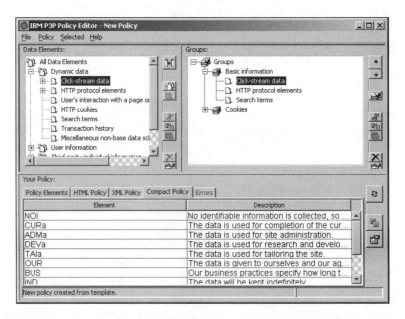

IBM's **P3P Parser** is a P3P protocol parser and constructor, written in 100% pure Java. It is available at http://www.alphaworks.ibm.com/tech/p3p/. The package (`com.ibm.p3p`) contains classes and methods for parsing, generating, manipulating, and evaluating P3P proposals and responses. It also contains a parser and an evaluator for APPEL. It works on either JDK 1.2.2 or later versions, or JRE 1.3.1, and thus runs on most of the platforms on which Java is supported.

Implementing P3P on Your Site

There are two key components to the successful implementation of P3P – the web site component and the client software component.

In the web site component, P3P enables web sites to *translate* their human-readable privacy practices into a standard, machine-readable format (XML) that can be retrieved automatically and can be interpreted easily by a user's browser.

In the client software component, P3P clients automatically fetch and parse the P3P privacy policies on web sites. A user's browser that is equipped for P3P can check a web site's privacy policy automatically and inform the user of a web site's information practices. P3P client software can be built into a web browser, or built into plug-ins, browser helper objects, proxies, or other application software.

There are several reasons why you should implement P3P on your site. By deploying P3P policies you make your privacy practices more transparent to your site customers. In this way you show them that you respect their privacy. Some of the recent web browsers, IE6 and Netscape 7.0, have P3P support and users may soon start to choose to block your cookies if you have not defined and published a P3P policy. If users choose to have their web browsers require P3P documents, the absence of them leads to *Denial of Service* vulnerability, where users cannot access the web site. Soon when web services clients supporting P3P appear, they could similarly block access to your web service.

Developing and deploying a P3P policy is the most important aspect to be learned by web site administrators. It is technically simple to do so, but involves coordination with multiple parties within an organization. This includes privacy officers, lawyers, and company executives who decide on the company's privacy policy.

Overview

P3P is designed to be deployed on existing web servers without any changes to the software, or any extra server side programs. The P3P implementation at your site can be divided into two stages: planning and development, and deployment. The following figure shows the overview of the steps involved in deploying P3P on your site:

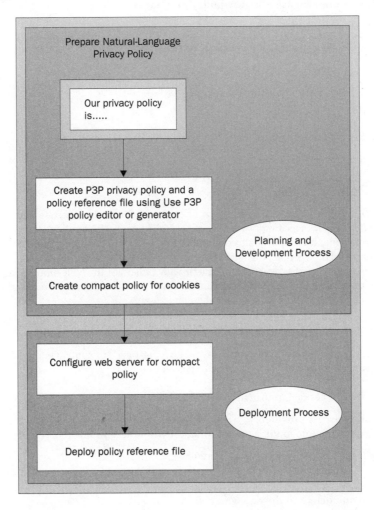

There is a W3C note on deploying P3P policies is available at
http://www.w3.org/TR/2002/NOTE-p3pdeployment-20020211.

Planning and Development

There are several important things that you should consider and do before deploying a P3P privacy policy on your web site, including the following:

- ❑ What does your policy cover?
- ❑ Create a natural language privacy policy for your company.
- ❑ How many policies for your site?
- ❑ Where will you place the policy reference file?
- ❑ Will you provide compact policies?
- ❑ Will you have policies specific to cookies?
- ❑ How will you handle policy updates?
- ❑ Create the P3P policy for your site.
- ❑ Create a policy reference file.

What does a Policy Cover?

The P3P policy file, as described earlier, consists of a description of data collection and sharing practices. It is the policy reference file that specifies to which portion of the site the P3P policy refers to. When developing a site's policy reference file, it is important to remember that you should declare practices at the point where data collection occurs. For example, the data about your name and address is collected only when the form is submitted and not when it is just displayed. So the privacy policy for the collection of data should refer to the URL where the form is loaded. This way, you can have one privacy policy for pages that only display data and another for pages where the data is collected.

Create a Natural Language Privacy Policy for your Company

The privacy policy, identified with policymakers and lawyers, needs to contain enough details to create a P3P policy. The information needed to construct the P3P policy is:

- ❑ The name and contact information for your company.
- ❑ The kind of access provided:
  Do you allow people to view the information you hold and how do you give access to that?
- ❑ Mechanisms for resolving privacy disputes.
- ❑ The privacy seal programs you participate in.
- ❑ The type and details of the data you collect.
- ❑ Information on when and how the data is shared and if there are opt-in and opt-out policies.
- ❑ The site's data retention policy.
- ❑ Any special policy to deal with children's data.

This basic information needed for P3P and the other kind of declarations describing your site's commitment to privacy form the privacy policy statement in a natural language.

How many Policies for your Site?

The specification allows several P3P policies to be specified and a site owner can choose a number of policy statements to cover the site. There are pros and cons to both the approaches. A single policy is easier to maintain. In places where there are different owners in an organization for different parts of the domain, it is better to have multiple policies per owner or organization as it keeps clean separation between various people working, and it is easier to manage as well. However, having too many policies for a site is difficult to maintain.

Since only certain parts of the web site collect data, having multiple policies allows you to have a more descriptive policy for such portions of the site. This helps users with restrictive user agent settings, who are just browsing the site and not ordering products to view the homepage and other product information.

Where will you Place the Policy Reference File?

There are typically three choices of how to place a policy reference file namely:

- ❏ Place it in a default well-known location that is `/w3c/p3p.xml`
- ❏ Add an extra `policyref` HTTP header in the response containing the location
- ❏ Place a link to the policy file in each HTML page of the site

The preferred deployment choice is the default location as it is the simplest, and does not require any change in the server configuration or the web pages. This is also easier and faster for the user agent to access, as there is no extra messaging needed to get to the policy.

However, in cases where you don't have access to the web site's main hosting location and as an individual you want to specify your privacy policies you can do that by placing a link to the policy file in each of the HTML pages.

Will you Provide Compact Policies?

The compact policy summarizes the cookies handling policies described in the P3P policy statement, and is sent out in a HTTP response header. The use of compact policies is optional for a web site, but it is recommended to implement it. IE 6 uses the compact policies to handle site's cookies, and still does not implement the `COOKIE-INCLUDE` mechanism described in the spec. Hence, if you want IE 6 to not block your cookies you should have compact policies in place. Compact policies are a performance optimization, allowing user agents to process the policies more quickly.

While compact policies are encouraged they should not be an alternative to the full P3P statements, besides there are significant restrictions on what can be expressed using the compact policies.

Will you have Policies Specific to Cookies?

Use of a cookie is disclosed using the data element `dynamic.cookies` in a statement. Since cookies are used to collect or link may types of data, this must disclose the type of data being processed by a cookie.

You can write separate P3P policies for each of the cookies and then list the cookies separately by cookie name, value, domain, and path in the policy reference file. This is useful if your site uses multiple cookies and each has different data collection practices. Here is an sample policy reference file that specifies policy at a cookies level:

```
<META xmlns="http://www.w3.org/2000/12/P3Pv1">
<POLICY-REFERENCES>
    <POLICY-REF about="http://www.hp.com/P3P/PolicyReferences.xml">
        <COOKIE-INCLUDE
            name="*"
            value="*"
            domain="*"
            path="*"/>
    </POLICY-REF>
</POLICY-REFERENCES>
</META>
```

How will you Handle Policy Updates?

Both the P3P policy and policy reference file have an expiry period mentioned. The user agents typically cache the contents of the policy and policy reference file, as this reduces the time to access a web page. User agents reload their cache once the contents expire. There is a lower limit of one day for the expiry time of the policy files.

You should find a lifetime that balances two factors:

❑ The lifetime should be long enough to allow user agents to benefit from caching

❑ The site should be able to change its policy without waiting too long

When you change the P3P policy for your site, the old policy holds good for the data collected earlier when the earlier policy was in effect. Hence you need to keep *records* of all the P3P policies and policy reference files you maintained on your web site. Whenever there is a change to your privacy policy, you must provide a notice and inform users of the change.

Create the P3P Policy for your Site

After collecting all the information, you are ready to create a P3P policy and a policy reference file. Depending upon the size and complexity of your site you can choose several ways to construct these two files. You could use another site's policy as a reference and modify the relevant sections, or you could use a tool. The earlier-mentioned editor, *Policy Editor* from IBM, is an excellent tool with which to construct your policy file. It contains several *templates* of various kinds of policies like Safe Zone policy, online purchasing, and so on that are recommended for creating your privacy preference files.

Create a Policy Reference File

You could use the same method to construct a policy reference file as you used to create the P3P policy: editing by hand or by using a tool like IBM's *P3P Editor*.

Deployment

Once the P3P privacy policy and policy reference file are ready for deployment, the following steps need to be taken for deployment:

- ❑ Place the policy files
- ❑ Configure the web server for P3P
- ❑ Test the site
- ❑ Go live with P3P
- ❑ Track and maintain the P3P policies

Place the Policy Files

Create and define the safe zone area, including the location for the P3P policy reference file, so that you perform only minimal data collection, and any data that is collected is used only in ways that would not reasonably identify an individual. See the P3P specifications for more information about the safe zone practices.

The P3P policy file and the policy reference file should be placed in the locations as decided in the planning stage. Ensure that the P3P policy file is accessible by the URL listed in the policy reference file. Also, place the human-readable policy files and the opt-out policy in the specified locations as referred by the P3P policy file.

Configure the Web Server for P3P Compact Policies

A web site may need to add custom HTTP headers for either giving the location of the policy reference file or for sending the compact P3P policies. This is done by adding an HTTP header to your web server with a name-value format pair. The header values used are CP for compact policy and policyref for the location of policy reference file. If both the headers are needed, then they are comma separated. Here is an example of how both of the policies would appear in an HTTP header:

```
HTTP/1.1 200 OK
P3P: policyref="http://www.hp.com/P3P/PolicyReferences.xml",
    CP ="NOI DSP COR CURa ADMa DEVa OUR NOR COM NAV OTC"
Content-Type: text/html
Content-Length: 8104
```

Let's look at the configuration of some of the popular web servers for P3P headers.

Apache

The Apache web server includes a headers module called mod_headers, which is used to add extra headers to the HTTP responses. This module has been available since release 1.2 of the Apache server. The headers module is an *Extension* module, which means it is not included in the source distribution by default, and so if you build your own server you will have to rebuild after including mod_headers.

Here are the steps to add the P3P headers to the Apache web server:

You should ensure that the mod_headers module is being loaded and is enabled. If it has been compiled as a dynamic shared object, then ensure that httpd.conf contains a LoadModule directive, like this:

```
LoadModule headers_module path/mod_headers.so
```

In case it is compiled as a dynamic linked library on a Windows platform, then uncomment the following line in `httpd.conf`:

```
LoadModule headers_module path/ApacheModuleHeaders.dll
```

However, you should note that recent Apache versions, 1.3.14 and beyond, use `mod_headers.so` (just like the Unix versions of Apache).

Also ensure that the `httpd.conf` contains a directive to activate the header module:

```
AddModule mod_headers.c
```

This directive is required even if `mod_headers` is compiled into the server (even if it is not dynamically loaded by a `LoadModule` directive).

Create an empty section as shown to place the P3P headers in the appropriate scope sections in the server configuration file (`httpd.conf`):

```
<Location / >
</Location>
```

Now add the P3P header. To do this, place a `Header` directive within the section created in the previous step. The / (root) in the `Location` element specifies the URL for which this action should be taken. In this case, whenever someone refers the root URL, the `policyref` header's location would be sent:

```
<Location / >
Header append P3P "policyref=\"http://www.hp.com/P3P/PolicyReferences.xml\""
</Location>
```

Microsoft Internet Information Server (IIS)

Internet Services Manager on Windows 2000 is used to manage IIS and to set custom P3P header properties to pages, virtual directories, or entire web sites. Setting the P3P header will add bytes both to the initial responses and to all requests that contains that cookie.

Here are the steps to enable P3P custom headers using Internet Services Manager to configure IIS also shown in the following diagram:

1. Start the Internet Service Manager. This can be accessed from the **Start** menu by clicking **Programs, Administrative Tools**, and then **Internet Information Services** in case of a Windows server, or from **Control Panel** in case of Windows Desktop.

2. Navigate to the web site to which you want to apply the privacy policy.

3. Select the web site and use **Action|Properties** to see the web site properties. Now select the **HTTP Headers** property page. If you want to apply the P3P headers only to specific pages, select them and right click to show properties for that page. Select the **HTTP Headers** property tab from that.

4. Select Add... The Add/Edit Custom HTTP Header dialog box appears.

5. In the Custom Header Name text box, type in P3P. In the Custom Header Value dialog box, type in the contents of the P3P header.

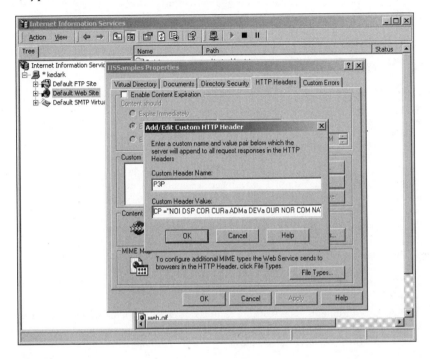

Test the Site

After setting up all the previously-mentioned items, you should use a manual check or a user agent to verify if all the files are in the correct location. The W3C **P3P Validator** tool present at http://www.w3.org/P3P/validator/ can be used to test the site, and will report back the list of problem it finds. It ensures that your policy- and policy reference file are according to the correct schema, that your files are accessible, and that your configuration is working fine. However, it *cannot* validate whether the policies stated by you, and the privacy policy practiced by you, are the same.

Now you are ready to go live with P3P.

Tracking and Maintaining P3P policies

It is equally important to maintain and keep track of the P3P policies with respect to the data practices of the organization on the web site. You should have a continued testing effort to ensure that the P3P policy files are accessible and valid.

There will be instances when you need to make changes to the P3P policy files, perhaps due to the addition of content (web pages and cookies) or perhaps due to the change in the data practices in the organization. You should update the P3P policies and keep track of all the policy practices that you had on your site earlier for legal and management reasons. You should also note the *time* when you changed the privacy policy.

The EXPIRY element of a policy- or policy reference file indicates a time period during which a user agent can safely assume that the policy- or policy reference file has not changed. The user agents do not re-fetch the P3P policy until the expiry. This can cause an overlap when the old and the new policies are valid for a site. To make a change to a P3P policy you would need to address the issue by adhering to either way of data collection during the overlap period. To overcome the overlap period you can specify an absolute time in the EXPIRY field.

P3P and Web Services

The P3P specification does not explicitly mention how it can be used in the context of web services. The specification mainly deals with privacy policies for web sites, though these web sites could be using web services at their backend for providing various services.

Similar to web sites, the web services also collect personal information during their transactions, and hence similar concerns of privacy exist for them as well. The P3P specification could be used to specify a web service privacy policy while accessing it. The web services clients would need modification in order to process a privacy policy before using the web service, similar to a user agent.

HTTP headers are used to send the P3P compact policies for cookies, as well as the location of the policy reference file. In case of a non-HTTP transport binding, an equivalent mechanism would need to be created. For example, there can be a P3P-specific header in the SOAP envelope while using web services.

The work on P3P and web services started in 2002 at the *Web Services Architecture* group at W3C, which worked on making a web services reference architecture. As a first step, this group is defining the web services architecture requirements. The working draft requirements document of October 2002 (http://www.w3.org/TR/2002/WD-wsa-reqs-20021011) lists the requirements for privacy protection in its security requirement, which we have listed below:

❑ AC020 – enables privacy protection for the consumer of a web service across multiple domains and services.

❑ AR020.1 – the Web Services Architecture (WSA) must enable privacy policy statements to be expressed about web services.

❑ AR020.2 – advertised web service privacy policies must be expressed in P3P

❑ AR020.3 – the WSA must enable a consumer to access a web service's advertised privacy policy statement

❑ AR020.5 – the WSA must enable delegation and propagation of the privacy policy

❑ AR020.6 – web services must not be precluded from supporting interactions in which one or more parties of the interaction is anonymous

As work progresses in the W3C WSA group, we will see web services clients appearing with P3P support (P3P user agent). However, the use of P3P in web services is likely to differ from its usage in web sites. Web services usually do not need to make use of mechanisms like cookies; therefore, many of the vulnerabilities that have been mentioned do not apply in the same way to web services. Some other differences are:

❑ SOAP messages that contain digital signatures contain much more specific identity and authentication information than do cookies.

❑ The components of SOAP messages are not arbitrarily executed to display their contents, with the result that the notion of a *web bug* is not likely to exist for a web service.

That being said, you may need to have the web site configured with a suitable set of P3P controls in place to give would-be users confidence that you have suitable privacy protection controls in place, and to assure them that they can download and run the web services application with the expectation that their privacy will be respected.

Challenges to P3P Deployment

P3P is an individual empowerment technology that is intended to allow web sites to express their privacy practices and to allow users to exercise preferences over those practices. P3P is a part of the privacy framework and is *not* a silver bullet for all the privacy solutions. It fits in well with other complementary technologies like seal programs, encryption tools, anonymity tools, and law and regulatory bodies.

There has been criticism of P3P by a few privacy bodies, and also there has been support from the industry of P3P. Let's look at each of the criticisms and examine the pros and cons of P3P from a balanced perspective.

Lack of Interest in Protecting Users' Privacy

The fact that so many organizations running web sites implement *surveillance systems* to collect personal information about their viewers demonstrates that there is great interest in collecting such information.

People involved in performing such surveillance will be understandably *reluctant* to voice public opposition to mechanisms like P3P. They would doubtless prefer to continue collecting information about you, remain very quiet about it, and sell the information, since this activity generates revenue for them.

The only likely way to overcome this kind of opposition is for governments to impose privacy legislation on Internet activities, which is likely to elicit opposition from a variety of sources.

Lack of Enforcement

This is one of the most often-heard criticisms of P3P. Although P3P offers a platform for specifying privacy preferences, it lacks the teeth to enforce discipline. It should be understood that P3P is one of the first attempts to standardize privacy practices in an automated manner. It needs to be implemented in conjunction with various complementary technologies, including law enforcement agencies, for it to be completely successful.

For law enforcement agencies to have any say in this, the use of P3P must be enforceable by law. Thus, for P3P to be *completely* successful, governments must first impose laws to require web sites to use P3P.

In the absence of laws and effective law enforcement mechanisms, those that benefit from doing web surveillance may find it in their interests to publish dishonest P3P documents and/or locate web sites in jurisdictions where specific national laws do not apply. For instance, some *casino* web sites are located in the Caribbean islands specifically to evade US laws on gambling.

The legal concerns about the exact ramifications of adopting P3P policies and the lack of a legal context in which they are implemented may add to practitioners' reluctance in advising users to adapt to the P3P policies.

EU Recommendation

The European Commission issued an opinion on P3P in 1998, which mentioned that P3P should be expanded to contain privacy protection for individuals. There were comments on the automatic data transfer between user agents and web sites. Based on this feedback, the P3P specification was modified to remove the automatic data transfer and included a disputes resolution section in the specification. There is still some confusion among a few users about the EU rejecting the P3P specification completely.

Expensive to Maintain and Implement

Developing a natural privacy policy and accurately documenting that is a daunting task. Converting it to a P3P policy is a relatively lighter overhead with numerous benefits. If the design decisions about the P3P policy deployment for your web site were done in a reasonable fashion, the manageability of the policies wouldn't be a problem.

Implementing a P3P policy is technically simple, involving a few changes to the site's configuration. With some user agents implementing compact P3P policies for cookies, some server configuration is needed to add the P3P header.

The Future of P3P

The Platform for Privacy Preferences project is an individual empowerment technology that is intended to allow web sites to express their privacy practices and to allow users to exercise preferences over those practices. Big companies like Microsoft, IBM, AT&T, and HP have implemented P3P at their sites. The tools and user agents that implement P3P also are appearing in the market. Despite resistance from a few privacy groups, initial feedback on P3P acceptance has been positive. Some legal concerns still exist about the exact ramifications of adopting P3P policies and the lack of a legal context in which they are implemented, which may prove to be the inhibiting factors for users in the adoption of P3P policies.

Work on the next version of the P3P specification has been kicked off, and it may contain more automated and advanced features like *negotiation*, *automatic data transfer*, and *non-repudiation of agreements*. It will be interesting to see if P3P will be widely accepted as a *de facto* standard for managing privacy preferences. It will be equally interesting to see what *de jure* standards emerge as governments consider that privacy standards they wish to impose. In the aftermath of the terror attacks of September 11, 2001, governments seem to be interested in *increasing* surveillance, which isn't a direction that would particularly point towards increased use of mechanisms like P3P.

It will be interesting to see how P3P gets used in the context of web services as reference architecture is developed by the web services architecture group at W3C.

Summary

In this chapter we have looked at P3P, a platform for privacy preferences that is a standard for specifying a web sites privacy policy using XML. It is a platform for greater transparency in privacy policies, and helps users make an informed decision about sharing their personal information. We examined the privacy concerns of the users and how their information was being compromised, which was followed up with a review of how P3P evolved in W3C.

P3P policy contains statements about a company's data collection and usage policies. User agents that act on behalf of the user while accessing a site, match the user preferences to the site's policy in order to provide a controlled access to the site, thus protecting the user's personal information. If the user chooses to share such information, only then does it become available to a site.

There are a number of P3P implementations appearing in the market, the most significant ones being Internet Explorer 6.0 and Netscape 7.0. Hence it would be wise to implement P3P for your site to avoid possible restriction by browsers.

The important thing to note is that P3P is a *framework* that enables privacy conversation in a standard way. It is **not** a silver bullet for all the solutions. It has to be implemented along with a combination of government legislation and law enforcement support, privacy seal programs, and encryption tools. Work for the next version of the P3P standard is now starting, and the next release may have more automated features like negotiation and automatic data transfer.

References:

1. Privacy, Consumers, and Costs, by Gellman, Robert, EPIC March 2002. http://www.epic.org/reports/dmfprivacy.html

2. P3P specification 1.0 – http://www.w3.org/TR/P3P

3. P3P 1.0 deployment guide – http://www.w3.org/TR/2002/NOTE-p3pdeployment-20020211

13

J2EE Web Services: Case Study

The earlier chapters of this book have talked about web services security specifications. Now let's take a look at how to implement them. To do so, we're going to conjure up a fictional bank called the WROX Bank, and create a web service for the same. The first version of the web service will be quite insecure. We will then revise it using the technologies we've reviewed previously in the book (XML Signatures, XML Encryption, and such) to secure the service.

To implement our web service and its associated client application, we'll use the Java J2EE platform. J2EE has enjoyed enterprise dominance in recent years and, together with Microsoft's new .NET platform, is one of the best tools available for the creation of web services.

Since the material in this case study is of an advanced level, we will assume that the reader is familiar with both the J2SE and J2EE platforms.

Case Study Overview

Let's say that WROX Bank has decided to give its clients the ability to check account balances and transfer money between accounts via the Internet. It will implement this functionality via web services and a Swing client.

Configuration

In the next few sections, we'll build the application as described above. Let's take a moment to discuss the components that we will need to install for our application. Note, however, that because the standards are changing rapidly, this case study is only likely to function properly with the exact versions shown here. It might work on subsequent versions or it might not. The required components are:

- ❑ JDK 1.4.1
- ❑ Apache Jakarta Tomcat 4.0.6 (as of this writing, Tomcat 4.1.2 has some glitches with Axis)
- ❑ Apache Axis 1.0
- ❑ Apache XML Security 1.0.4
- ❑ Verisign TSIK 1.5

Installation Instructions

We'll now provide some basic installation instructions to save you the trouble of looking them up for each of these packages. If you have questions, please refer to the instructions in these individual packages:

- ❑ Ensure that you have JDK 1.4.1_01 installed.
- ❑ Ensure that you have a Servlet 2.3/JSP 1.2-compliant container installed. Note that, as of this writing, the Tomcat 4.1.x branch has some minor glitches with Axis. Specifically, when we visited the Axis admin page with Tomcat 4.1.12, we received an error 500. We did not experience this problem with the 4.0.x branch.
- ❑ Download Apache Axis 1.0 from www.xml.apache.org/axis and unzip it into its own directory.
- ❑ Copy the [axisdir]/webapps/axis directory to your servlet container's web application directory (for example, jakarta-tomcat/webapps/axis).
- ❑ Download Apache XML Security 1.0.4 from www.xml.apache.org/security and unzip it into its own directory.
- ❑ Copy the JAR files in [xmlsecurity_dir]/build to [servlet_container]/webapps/axis/WEB-INF/lib.
- ❑ Download the Verisign TSIK from http://www.xmltrustcenter.org/developer/verisign/tsik/index.htm and uncompress it into its own directory.
- ❑ Copy the tsik.jar file from the [verisign]/lib directory to [servlet_container]/webapps/axis/WEB-INF/lib.

❑ Add the following elements to your CLASSPATH:

```
[axis]/lib/axis.jar;
[axis]/lib/commons-logging.jar;
[axis]/lib/commons-discovery.jar;
[axis]/lib/jaxrpc.jar;
[axis]/lib/saaj.jar;
[axis]/lib/log4j-1.2.4.jar;
[axis]/lib/xmlsec.jar;
[axis];
[tomcat]/common/lib/servlet.jar
```

❑ If you're using the Tomcat Light Edition, copy the Java Activation Framework JAR into Tomcat's shared class loader: [tomcat_home]/lib.

❑ If you haven't already overridden the Xalan parser that ships with the default JDK 1.4, copy the [xmlsecurity_dir]/libs/xalan.jar file to [jdk_home]/jre/lib/endorsed (or wherever the Endorsed Standards Override directory is on your platform).

❑ Finally, if you're using Tomcat 4.1.x, be aware that it overrides the default JDK Endorsed Standards Override directory, so you'll want to make sure either:

  ❑ That you're not using the Light Edition, or

  ❑ That you've copied the xalan.jar in the previous step to the following directory as well: [tomcat_home]/common/endorsed.

Verifying the Installation

To verify your installation, start up your servlet container and visit the URL http://127.0.0.1:8080/axis/happyaxis.jsp.

You should see that all needed components and optional components have been installed. If they are, the following statement will be displayed:

The core axis libraries are present. The optional components are present.

If this is not the case, you've done something wrong and need to go back to the instructions above or the instructions that come with the individual components. To find out more about Axis, refer to *Axis: The Next Generation of Java SOAP* from *Wrox Press (ISBN 1-861007-15-9)*.

Version 0.1

We will implement the case study application as introduced above in several iterations. The first iteration (version 0.1) will demonstrate how to create and consume web services in Axis, but will make no attempt to secure the web service. Subsequent iterations will become secure.

In other words, the first version of our application is functionally complete, but does not use web services in any secure way. We'll start out with a tour of version 0.1 and we will then show the code that we used for this version.

Application Tour

WROX Bank uses a system of accounts and sub accounts that works like this: Customers each have one unique account number which in turn is associated with multiple separate sub account numbers. Think of the account number, therefore, as a unique identifier, and the sub accounts as being the actual bank accounts, such as a savings account or checking account. Our application would look something like this:

This screen functions as a sort of login. Users enter their account number and pin, and then click on the Get Info button. The WROX Bank Application then passes the account number and pin to a web service that validates the information and returns a list of all of the sub accounts associated with the account. The returned list of sub-accounts is added to the WROX Bank Application interface, as well as a new option, as shown below:

Once users have entered their account number and pin into the application and have retrieved the sub-accounts using the Get Info button, they are now able to transfer money between those accounts. The user selects the source account in the left-most drop-down, enters the destination account in the right-most drop-down, enters the amount of the transfer, and then clicks on Transfer. When the user clicks Transfer, the application communicates with another web service that transfers the funds. Following the transfer, the application updates the display with the new balances, as shown below:

Note the new balances displayed in the Account Balances pane.

Web Services

The following three web services are involved in this application:

❑   getAccounts
    Returns a list of all of the sub accounts associated with an account

❑   getAccountBalance
    Returns the current balance of a sub account

❑   transferFunds
    Transfers funds from one sub account to another

To understand each service better, let's take a look at the actual XML being tossed around from the WROX Bank Application to the web services server.

getAccounts Web Service

When the user enters an account number and pin and then clicks on Get Info, the WROX Bank Application sends the following XML to the server:

```
<?xml version="1.0" encoding="UTF-8"?>
<soapenv:Envelope xmlns:soapenv="http://schemas.xmlsoap.org/soap/envelope/"
    xmlns:xsd="http://www.w3.org/2001/XMLSchema"
    xmlns:xsi="http://www.w3.org/2001/XMLSchema-instance">
  <soapenv:Body>
    <getAccounts
      soapenv:encodingStyle="http://schemas.xmlsoap.org/soap/encoding/">
      <arg0 xsi:type="xsd:string">12345678</arg0>
      <arg1 xsi:type="xsd:string">1234</arg1>
    </getAccounts>
  </soapenv:Body>
</soapenv:Envelope>
```

As you can see, the getAccounts web service is passed two string-type arguments, which in this case are the account number and pin number. Note that these two are being passed in plaintext for the users to see.

Upon receipt of this XML SOAP message, the `getAccounts` web service responds with this XML:

```
<?xml version="1.0" encoding="UTF-8"?>
<soapenv:Envelope xmlns:soapenv="http://schemas.xmlsoap.org/soap/envelope/"
    xmlns:xsd="http://www.w3.org/2001/XMLSchema"
    xmlns:xsi="http://www.w3.org/2001/XMLSchema-instance">
  <soapenv:Body>
    <getAccountsResponse
      soapenv:encodingStyle="http://schemas.xmlsoap.org/soap/encoding/">
      <getAccountsReturn xsi:type="soapenc:Array"
      soapenc:arrayType="xsd:string[2]"
      xmlns:soapenc="http://schemas.xmlsoap.org/soap/encoding/">
        <item>12345678-1</item>
        <item>12345678-2</item>
      </getAccountsReturn>
    </getAccountsResponse>
  </soapenv:Body>
</soapenv:Envelope>
```

As stated earlier, the web service responds with an array containing the sub accounts associated with the account, which in this case are `12345678-1` and `12345678-2`.

getAccountBalance Web Service

Upon retrieving the list of accounts from the `getAccounts` web service, the WROX Bank Application automatically calls the `getAccountBalance` for each sub account. What follows is the SOAP message from one of those calls to `getAccountBalance`:

```
<?xml version="1.0" encoding="UTF-8"?>
<soapenv:Envelope xmlns:soapenv="http://schemas.xmlsoap.org/soap/envelope/"
    xmlns:xsd="http://www.w3.org/2001/XMLSchema"
    xmlns:xsi="http://www.w3.org/2001/XMLSchema-instance">
  <soapenv:Body>
    <getAccountBalance
      soapenv:encodingStyle="http://schemas.xmlsoap.org/soap/encoding/">
      <arg0 xsi:type="xsd:string">12345678</arg0>
      <arg1 xsi:type="xsd:string">1234</arg1>
      <arg2 xsi:type="xsd:string">12345678-1</arg2>
    </getAccountBalance>
  </soapenv:Body>
</soapenv:Envelope>
```

Note that we're again passing the account number and pin to this web service, in addition to the sub account for which we want the balance. Once again, packet sniffers can learn much more about our application's user than should be allowed. The web service replies with the following:

```
<?xml version="1.0" encoding="UTF-8"?>
<soapenv:Envelope xmlns:soapenv="http://schemas.xmlsoap.org/soap/envelope/"
    xmlns:xsd="http://www.w3.org/2001/XMLSchema"
    xmlns:xsi="http://www.w3.org/2001/XMLSchema-instance">
  <soapenv:Body>
    <getAccountBalanceResponse
```

```
    soapenv:encodingStyle="http://schemas.xmlsoap.org/soap/encoding/">
    <getAccountBalanceReturn xsi:type="xsd:double">
       100.0
    </getAccountBalanceReturn>
  </getAccountBalanceResponse>
  </soapenv:Body>
</soapenv:Envelope>
```

transferFunds Web service

The final web service used by the application is `transfer`. Let's look at the SOAP message sent in the application's HTTP request:

```
<?xml version="1.0" encoding="UTF-8"?>
<soapenv:Envelope xmlns:soapenv="http://schemas.xmlsoap.org/soap/envelope/"
    xmlns:xsd="http://www.w3.org/2001/XMLSchema"
    xmlns:xsi="http://www.w3.org/2001/XMLSchema-instance">
  <soapenv:Body>
    <transferFunds
      soapenv:encodingStyle="http://schemas.xmlsoap.org/soap/encoding/">
      <arg0 xsi:type="xsd:string">12345678</arg0>
      <arg1 xsi:type="xsd:string">1234</arg1>
      <arg2 xsi:type="xsd:string">12345678-1</arg2>
      <arg3 xsi:type="xsd:string">12345678-2</arg3>
      <arg4 xsi:type="xsd:double">15.0</arg4>
    </transferFunds>
  </soapenv:Body>
</soapenv:Envelope>
```

In addition to the now-familiar account/pin pair, we pass the source sub account, the destination sub account, and the amount of money to transfer. The web service responds with:

```
<?xml version="1.0" encoding="UTF-8"?>
<soapenv:Envelope xmlns:soapenv="http://schemas.xmlsoap.org/soap/envelope/"
    xmlns:xsd="http://www.w3.org/2001/XMLSchema"
    xmlns:xsi="http://www.w3.org/2001/XMLSchema-instance">
  <soapenv:Body>
    <transferFundsResponse
      soapenv:encodingStyle="http://schemas.xmlsoap.org/soap/encoding/">
      <transferFundsReturn xsi:type="xsd:boolean">true</transferFundsReturn>
    </transferFundsResponse>
  </soapenv:Body>
</soapenv:Envelope>
```

In this case, the web service responds with a simple Boolean value indicating the success of the transfer.

Java Code

This case study application consists of seven class files and one XML file spread across two different packages. These are:

- ❑ com.wrox.client package – all files for the GUI client

  - ❑ AccountBalancesPanel.java – descendent of JPanel; draws the **Account Balances** panel in the GUI

  - ❑ BankGateway.java – container for all web services-related code

  - ❑ Client.java – entry point for the GUI client; draws the main application window

  - ❑ GetInfoActionListener.java – implements the ActionListener interface; calls all necessary web services when the **Get Info** button is clicked

  - ❑ TransferFundsListener.java – implements the ActionListener interface; calls all necessary web services when the **Transfer** button is clicked

  - ❑ TransferFundsPanel.java – descedent of JPanel; draws the **Transfer Funds** panel in the GUI

- ❑ com.wrox.service package – all files for the Apache Axis web service

  - ❑ Bank.java – contains all the methods that become web services in Axis

- ❑ deploy.wsdd – an XML file containing metadata used by Axis to deploy the compiled Bank class as a web service

We'll now provide the listing for each of these files. If you're following along, create these files in the packages named above, type them in, and when you're done, compile them. For the files to compile properly, you may need to include some or all of the JARs located in [servlet_container]/webapps/axis/WEB-INF/lib in your CLASSPATH environment variable at compile time.

AccountBalancesPanel.java

To make it easy to toggle the state of the **Account Balances** and **Transfer Funds** areas of the application, we've created objects to encapsulate them:

```
package com.wrox.client;

import javax.swing.*;
import java.util.*;
import java.awt.*;

public class AccountBalancesPanel extends JPanel {
    private Map balances;

    public AccountBalancesPanel(Map balances) {
        super();
        this.balances = balances;
        buildPanel();
    }
```

Upon creation, the `AccountBalancesPanel` populates itself with various other Swing components to create its interface. The parameter of the constructor is a `Map` with all of the user's account name/balance pairs:

```java
private void buildPanel() {
    GridBagLayout layout = new GridBagLayout();
    setLayout(layout);

    GridBagConstraints accountConstraints = new GridBagConstraints();
    accountConstraints.gridx = 0;
    accountConstraints.anchor = GridBagConstraints.EAST;
    accountConstraints.insets = new Insets(0, 0, 0, 5);

    GridBagConstraints balanceConstraints = new GridBagConstraints();
    balanceConstraints.gridx = 1;
    balanceConstraints.anchor = GridBagConstraints.WEST;
    balanceConstraints.insets = new Insets(0, 0, 0, 0);

    JLabel header = new JLabel("Account Balances");
    header.setFont(new Font("Arial", Font.BOLD, 14));
    layout.addLayoutComponent(header, new GridBagConstraints(0, 0, 2,
            1, 0, 0, GridBagConstraints.CENTER,
            GridBagConstraints.NONE, new Insets(5, 0, 5, 0), 0, 0));
    add(header);

    java.util.List accounts = new LinkedList(balances.keySet());
    Collections.sort(accounts);
    Iterator i = accounts.iterator();
    int counter = 1;
    while (i.hasNext()) {
        String key = (String) i.next();
        Double balance = (Double) balances.get(key);

        JLabel accountLabel = new JLabel(key + ":");
        accountLabel.setFont(new Font("Arial", Font.BOLD, 12));
        accountConstraints.gridy = counter;
        if (!i.hasNext()) accountConstraints.insets.bottom = 5;
        layout.addLayoutComponent(accountLabel, accountConstraints);
        add(accountLabel);

        JLabel balanceLabel = new JLabel(String.valueOf(balance));
        balanceLabel.setFont(new Font("Arial", Font.PLAIN, 12));
        balanceConstraints.gridy = counter;
        if (!i.hasNext()) balanceConstraints.insets.bottom = 5;
        layout.addLayoutComponent(balanceLabel, balanceConstraints);
        add(balanceLabel);

        counter++;
    }
}

public void refreshBalances(Map newBalances) {
    balances = newBalances;
    removeAll();
    buildPanel();
}
}
```

This control can be updated at any time by calling the refreshBalances(Map) method shown above. We've chosen to simply clear and rebuild the underlying JPanel for this implementation; more optimized redraw methods are probably not worth the maeger savings.

BankGateway.java

As mentioned above, BankGateway encapsulates all of the logic involved with calling the web services. This is, therefore, probably the class that you should examine in the greatest detail. As the program evolves, this is one of the classes that we'll be changing the most:

```java
package com.wrox.client;

import org.apache.axis.client.Call;
import org.apache.axis.client.Service;

import javax.xml.rpc.ServiceException;
import javax.xml.namespace.QName;
import java.rmi.RemoteException;

public class BankGateway {
    private static BankGateway bg = null;

    private Call call;

    private BankGateway() throws ServiceException {
        String endPoint = "http://127.0.0.1:8080/axis/services/Bank";
        Service service = new Service();
        call = (Call) service.createCall();
        call.setTargetEndpointAddress(endPoint);
    }
```

As mentioned above, we're using Apache Axis for our web service functionality. Note our approach to using the JAX-RPC (that is, Java remote procedure call via SOAP messages) API is a little different; rather than creating a Service and Call object for different web services we wish to access, we reuse a single Call object. This Call instance is created in the constructor above and is set as a private class-level instance variable.

While conceptually somewhat different than one might expect, this approach is more convenient and consistent with the examples included with Apache Axis.

Below, we have the first of many methods which encapsulate the process of retrieving data from WROX Bank's various web services:

```java
    /**
     * Retrieves an array of all sub account numbers that belong to the
     * passed account number and pin number.
     */
    public String[] getAccounts(String account, String pin) {
        String[] accounts = null;

        try {
            call.setOperationName(new QName("getAccounts"));
```

Because we didn't set the name of the web service when we obtained the `Call` object from the `Service` object (as explained above), we must set the name as shown below:

```
accounts = (String[]) call.invoke(new Object[]{account, pin});
```

Here's where the action occurs. By calling the `Call` object's `invoke()` method, we send a SOAP message to the web service. Note that we're setting the SOAP message's parameters via the `Object` array that we send to the `invoke()` method. The `invoke()` method is synchronous, so our application will block here until a response is received and parsed by our program:

```
            if ((accounts == null) || (accounts.length == 0)) {
                throw new RemoteException("No accounts found");
            }
        } catch (RemoteException re) {
            showErrorMessage(re.getMessage());
        }

        return accounts;
    }
```

The following two methods in this class act in a very similar manner as the preceding method. The only differences are the parameters that we pass to the `Call.invoke()` method and the values that the `Call.invoke()` method returns:

```
    /**
     * Retrieves the current balance of the passed sub account. Note that
     * the account number and pin must be passed for authentication.
     */
    public double getAccountBalance(String account, String pin,
                                    String subAccount) {
        Double balance = null;

        try {
            call.setOperationName(new QName("getAccountBalance"));
            balance = (Double) call.invoke(new Object[]{account, pin,
                                                        subAccount});
            if (balance.doubleValue() == -1) {
                throw new RemoteException("Couldn't get balance for " +
                    "account " + subAccount);
            }
        } catch (RemoteException re) {
            showErrorMessage(re.getMessage());
        }

        return (balance == null) ? -1 : balance.doubleValue();
    }

    public boolean transferFunds(String account, String pin,
                                 String sourceAcct, String destAcct,
                                 double amount) {
        Boolean result = null;
```

```
        try {
            if (sourceAcct.equals(destAcct)) {
                throw new RemoteException("You cannot transfer money " +
                    "from the same account.");
            }

            if (amount <= 0) {
                throw new RemoteException("You must enter a positive " +
                    "amount of money to transfer.");
            }

            call.setOperationName(new QName("transferFunds"));
            result = (Boolean) call.invoke(
                    new Object[]{account, pin, sourceAcct, destAcct,
                            new Double(amount)});
            if ((result == null) || (!result.booleanValue())) {
                throw new RemoteException("Couldn't transfer funds!");
            }
        } catch (RemoteException re) {
            showErrorMessage(re.getMessage());
        }

        return (result == null) ? false : true;
    }

    private void showErrorMessage(String message) {
        Client.showErrorMessage(message);
    }
```

The showErrorMessage() is a convenient method for displaying any errors to the user. Here we simply pass the message to a static method on the Client class, but if in the future we wished to provide some additional logic to make the error messages less cryptic, we could insert that logic in the above method and pass the friendly method to Client.showErrorMessage().

The following method is a standard idiom for implementing the *Singleton* design pattern:

```
    public synchronized static BankGateway getInstance()
            throws ServiceException {
        if (bg == null) {
            bg = new BankGateway();
        }

        return bg;
    }
}
```

Client.java

Client is the entry point for the WROX Bank Application client program. There is nothing about Client that is specific to web services; in fact, Client could just as easily be the front-end to a JDBC application.

All of the various methods on `Client` are concerned either to enable other objects to obtain information from the user interface or to modify or display the interface in some way:

```
package com.wrox.client;

import javax.swing.*;
import java.awt.event.WindowAdapter;
import java.awt.event.WindowEvent;
import java.awt.*;
import java.util.Map;

public class Client {
    private static Client client;

    private JFrame frame;
    private JTextField account = null;
    private JTextField pin = null;
    private AccountBalancesPanel accountsPanel = null;
    private TransferFundsPanel transferPanel = null;
    private JPanel pane = null;
    private GridBagLayout layout = null;
    private GridBagConstraints constraints = null;

    private String currentAccount;

    public static void main(String[] args) throws Exception {
        client = new Client();
        client.display();
    }

    public void display() {
        frame = new JFrame("Wrox Bank Application");
        frame.setSize(500, 300);
        frame.addWindowListener(
                new WindowAdapter() {
                    public void windowClosing(WindowEvent e) {
                        System.exit(0);
                    }
                }
            );

        pane = new JPanel();
        pane.setBorder(BorderFactory.createEmptyBorder(5, 5, 5, 5));
        frame.getContentPane().add(pane);

        layout = new GridBagLayout();
        constraints = new GridBagConstraints();
        constraints.insets = new Insets(5, 0, 0, 0);
        constraints.anchor = GridBagConstraints.CENTER;
        constraints.fill = GridBagConstraints.HORIZONTAL;
        constraints.weightx = 1;
        pane.setLayout(layout);

        JPanel headerPane = new JPanel();
```

```java
            JLabel label = new JLabel("Welcome to the Wrox Bank Application!");
            label.setFont(new Font("Arial", Font.BOLD, 14));
            headerPane.add(label);
            constraints.gridx = 0;
            constraints.gridy = 0;
            layout.addLayoutComponent(headerPane, constraints);
            pane.add(headerPane);

            JPanel accountPane = new JPanel();
            accountPane.setBorder(BorderFactory.createEtchedBorder());

            label = new JLabel("Account:");
            accountPane.add(label);

            account = new JTextField();
            account.setPreferredSize(new Dimension(100, 20));
            accountPane.add(account);

            label = new JLabel("Pin:");
            accountPane.add(label);

            pin = new JTextField();
            pin.setPreferredSize(new Dimension(50, 20));
            accountPane.add(pin);

            JButton getInfo = new JButton("Get Info");
            getInfo.setMargin(new Insets(0, 0, 0, 0));
            getInfo.setFont(new Font("Arial", Font.PLAIN, 10));
            getInfo.setPreferredSize(new Dimension(75, 20));
            getInfo.addActionListener(new GetInfoActionListener());
            accountPane.add(getInfo);
            constraints.gridx = 0;
            constraints.gridy = 1;
            layout.addLayoutComponent(accountPane, constraints);
            pane.add(accountPane);

            frame.show();
    }

    private String getAccount() {
        return account.getText();
    }

    private String getPin() {
        return pin.getText();
    }

    public static Client getInstance() {
        return client;
    }

    public void updateTransfer(String[] accounts) {
        if (transferPanel == null) {
            if (accounts == null) return;
```

```
                transferPanel = new TransferFundsPanel(accounts);
                transferPanel.setBorder(BorderFactory.createEtchedBorder());
                constraints.gridx = 0;
                constraints.gridy = 3;
                layout.addLayoutComponent(transferPanel, constraints);
                pane.add(transferPanel);
            } else {
                if (accounts == null) {
                    pane.remove(transferPanel);
                    transferPanel = null;
                } else {
                    transferPanel.refreshAccounts(accounts);
                    transferPanel.repaint();
                }
            }
            pane.validate();
    }

    public void updateAccounts(Map balances) {
        if (accountsPanel == null) {
            if (balances == null) return;
            accountsPanel = new AccountBalancesPanel(balances);
            accountsPanel.setBorder(BorderFactory.createEtchedBorder());
            constraints.gridx = 0;
            constraints.gridy = 2;
            layout.addLayoutComponent(accountsPanel, constraints);
            pane.add(accountsPanel);
        } else {
            if (balances == null) {
                pane.remove(accountsPanel);
                accountsPanel = null;
            } else {
                accountsPanel.refreshBalances(balances);
                accountsPanel.repaint();
            }
        }
        pane.validate();
    }

    public String[] getXferData() {
        return transferPanel.getXferData();
    }

    public void setBusy() {
        frame.setCursor(new Cursor(Cursor.WAIT_CURSOR));
    }

    public void setReady() {
        frame.setCursor(new Cursor(Cursor.DEFAULT_CURSOR));
    }

    public String getCurrentAccount() {
        return currentAccount;
```

```
        }

        public void setCurrentAccount(String currentAccount) {
            this.currentAccount = currentAccount;
        }

        public String[] getAccountAndPin() {
            String account = Client.getInstance().getAccount();
            if ((account == null) || (account.equals(""))) {
                showErrorMessage("You must enter an account number.");
                return null;
            }

            String pin = Client.getInstance().getPin();
            if ((pin == null) || (pin.equals(""))) {
                showErrorMessage("You must enter a pin.");
                return null;
            }

            return new String[]{account, pin};
        }

        public static void showErrorMessage(String message) {
            JOptionPane.showMessageDialog(null, message,
                    "Wrox Bank Application", JOptionPane.ERROR_MESSAGE);
        }
}
```

GetInfoActionListener.java

This class, along with `TransferFundsListener`, is called when the user clicks on either the **Get Info** or **Transfer** buttons, respectively. As such, both of these classes implement the `ActionListener` interface. While `ActionListeners` are often implemented as anonymous inner classes, we've chosen to create separate classes for these objects since they contain a fair amount of code, and it is easier to follow along if they are separate:

```
package com.wrox.client;

import javax.xml.rpc.ServiceException;
import java.awt.event.ActionListener;
import java.awt.event.ActionEvent;
import java.util.HashMap;
import java.util.Map;

public class GetInfoActionListener implements ActionListener {
    public void actionPerformed(ActionEvent e) {
        Map balances = null;
        String[] accounts = null;

        /* returns a two-element array: 0 = account, 1 = pin */
        String[] accountPin = Client.getInstance().getAccountAndPin();
        if (accountPin == null) return;

        /* display the "system busy" cursor */
        Client.getInstance().setBusy();
```

The first thing `GetInfoActionListener` does is obtain the information it needs from the interface using the `Client.getAccountAndPin()` method, and then instruct the interface to show that it is busy.

The next several lines of code obtain a reference to the `BankGateway` object and then pass the information from the interface to various methods of `BankGateway`, effectively calling the WROX web services:

```
BankGateway bg = null;
try {
    bg = BankGateway.getInstance();
} catch (ServiceException se) {
    Client.showErrorMessage(se.getMessage());
    Client.getInstance().setReady();
    return;
}

/* get array of subaccounts associated with this account */
accounts = bg.getAccounts(accountPin[0], accountPin[1]);
Client.getInstance().setCurrentAccount(accountPin[0]);

/* get the balances of each of the subaccounts */
balances = new HashMap();
for (int i = 0; i < accounts.length; i++) {
    double balance = bg.getAccountBalance(accountPin[0],
            accountPin[1], accounts[i]);
    if (balance != -1) balances.put(accounts[i],
            new Double(balance));
}
```

Note that there are actually multiple calls to our web services going on to accomplish this one task. First, the client application must determine which sub accounts belong to the account number, and then the client application makes a separate call for each account number to determine the balance.

Below, we can see this class instructing the interface to display the data that it just obtained:

```
/* update the interface with the data we just obtained */
Client.getInstance().updateAccounts(balances);
Client.getInstance().updateTransfer(accounts);

/* display the default cursor */
Client.getInstance().setReady();
    }
}
```

TransferFundsListener.java

`TransferFundsListener` performs the same basic tasks as `GetInfoActionListener`; it just uses different data:

```
package com.wrox.client;

import javax.xml.rpc.ServiceException;
import java.awt.event.ActionListener;
import java.awt.event.ActionEvent;
import java.util.Map;
```

```java
import java.util.HashMap;

public class TransferFundsListener implements ActionListener {
    public void actionPerformed(ActionEvent e) {
        Map balances = null;
        double amount = -1;

        String[] accountPin = Client.getInstance().getAccountAndPin();
        if (accountPin == null) return;

        /*
         * returns a three-element array: 0 - source account,
         * 1 - destination account, 2 - amount to transfer
         */
        String[] xferData = Client.getInstance().getXferData();
        if (xferData == null) return;

        try {
            if (xferData[2].equals("")) throw new Exception("");
            amount = Double.parseDouble(xferData[2]);
        } catch (Exception ex) {
            Client.showErrorMessage("You must enter a (numeric) amount " +
                    "of money to transfer.");
            return;
        }

        Client.getInstance().setBusy();

        BankGateway bg = null;
        try {
            bg = BankGateway.getInstance();
        } catch (ServiceException se) {
            Client.showErrorMessage(se.getMessage());
            Client.getInstance().setReady();
            return;
        }

        boolean result = bg.transferFunds(accountPin[0], accountPin[1],
                xferData[0], xferData[1], amount);

        if (result) {
            String[] accounts = bg.getAccounts(accountPin[0],
                    accountPin[1]);

            balances = new HashMap();
            for (int i = 0; i < accounts.length; i++) {
                double balance = bg.getAccountBalance(accountPin[0],
                        accountPin[1], accounts[i]);
                if (balance != -1) balances.put(accounts[i],
                        new Double(balance));
            }
            Client.getInstance().updateAccounts(balances);
        }

        Client.getInstance().setReady();
    }
}
```

TransferFundsPanel.java

TransferFundsPanel is quite similar to AccountBalancesPanel:

```java
package com.wrox.client;

import javax.swing.*;
import java.awt.*;

public class TransferFundsPanel extends JPanel {
    private JComboBox sourceAccount = null;
    private JComboBox destAccount = null;
    private JTextField transferAmount = null;

    public TransferFundsPanel(String[] accounts) {
        super();
        buildPanel(accounts);
    }

    public String[] getXferData() {
        return new String[]{sourceAccount.getSelectedItem().toString(),
                            destAccount.getSelectedItem().toString(),
                            transferAmount.getText()};
    }

    private void buildPanel(String[] accounts) {
        GridBagLayout layout = new GridBagLayout();
        setLayout(layout);

        GridBagConstraints constraints = new GridBagConstraints();
        constraints.gridy = 1;
        constraints.anchor = GridBagConstraints.WEST;
        constraints.insets = new Insets(0, 5, 5, 0);

        JLabel header = new JLabel("Transfer Funds");
        header.setFont(new Font("Arial", Font.BOLD, 14));
        layout.addLayoutComponent(header, new GridBagConstraints(0, 0, 4,
                1, 0, 0, GridBagConstraints.CENTER,
                GridBagConstraints.NONE, new Insets(5, 0, 5, 0), 0, 0));
        add(header);

        sourceAccount = new JComboBox(accounts);
        sourceAccount.setPreferredSize(new Dimension(100, 20));
        constraints.gridx = 0;
        layout.addLayoutComponent(sourceAccount, constraints);
        add(sourceAccount);

        destAccount = new JComboBox(accounts);
        destAccount.setPreferredSize(new Dimension(100, 20));
        constraints.gridx = 1;
        layout.addLayoutComponent(destAccount, constraints);
        add(destAccount);

        transferAmount = new JTextField();
```

```
            transferAmount.setPreferredSize(new Dimension(100, 20));
            transferAmount.setMinimumSize(new Dimension(20, 20));
            constraints.gridx = 2;
            layout.addLayoutComponent(transferAmount, constraints);
            add(transferAmount);

            JButton transfer = new JButton("Transfer");
            transfer.addActionListener(new TransferFundsListener());
            transfer.setMargin(new Insets(0, 0, 0, 0));
            transfer.setPreferredSize(new Dimension(100, 20));
            transfer.setFont(new Font("Arial", Font.PLAIN, 10));
            constraints.gridx = 3;
            constraints.insets.right = 5;
            layout.addLayoutComponent(transfer, constraints);
            add(transfer);
        }

    public void refreshAccounts(String[] accounts) {
        removeAll();
        buildPanel(accounts);
    }

}
```

Bank.java

As mentioned earlier, Bank contains the methods that will become web services. In this class, every public accessor method (that is, the getXXX methods) will be transformed into web services by Axis. As you examine this class, you'll note that the data it returns has been "hard-coded" into local variables (this was done to keep the case study focused on web services security – of course, in a real application, one would never do this):

```
package com.wrox.service;

import java.util.Map;
import java.util.HashMap;
import java.util.Iterator;
import java.rmi.RemoteException;

public class Bank {
    private Map balances;
    private Map accounts;
    private Map pins;
```

Note that in our constructor we are setting all of the values for our data model:

```
    public Bank() {
        accounts = new HashMap();
        accounts.put("12345678", new String[] { "12345678-1",
                                                 "12345678-2" });

        pins = new HashMap();
        pins.put("12345678", "1234");

        /* initialize each account with $100 */
        balances = new HashMap();
        Iterator i = accounts.keySet().iterator();
```

```
        while (i.hasNext()) {
            String key = (String) i.next();
            String[] accts = (String[]) accounts.get(key);
            for (int z = 0; z < accts.length; z++) {
                balances.put(accts[z], new Double(100));
            }
        }
    }
}
```

The public methods of Bank are two very simple JavaBean-style accessor methods and a single business logic method, transferFunds():

```
public String[] getAccounts(String account, String pin)
        throws RemoteException {
    if (!validatePin(account, pin)) {
        throw new RemoteException("Account/pin combination invalid");
    }
    return (String[]) accounts.get(account);
}

public double getAccountBalance(String account, String pin,
                                String subAccount)
        throws RemoteException {
    if (!validatePin(account, pin)) {
        throw new RemoteException("Account/pin combination invalid");
    }

    Double balance = (Double) balances.get(subAccount);
    if (balance != null) {
        return balance.doubleValue();
    } else {
        return -1;
    }
}

public synchronized boolean transferFunds(String account, String pin,
                                          String sourceAccount,
                                          String destAccount,
                                          double amount) {
    if (!validatePin(account, pin)) return false;

    Double sourceAmount = (Double) balances.get(sourceAccount);
    Double destAmount = (Double) balances.get(destAccount);
    if ((sourceAmount == null) || (destAmount == null)) {
        return false;
    }

    if (sourceAmount.doubleValue() < amount) return false;

    destAmount = new Double(destAmount.doubleValue() + amount);
    balances.put(destAccount, destAmount);

    sourceAmount = new Double(sourceAmount.doubleValue() - amount);
    balances.put(sourceAccount, sourceAmount);

    return true;
}

private boolean validatePin(String account, String pin) {
```

```
        String acctPin = (String) pins.get(account);
        if ((acctPin == null) || (pin == null) || (!acctPin.equals(pin))) {
            return false;
        } else {
            return true;
        }
    }
}
```

deploy.wsdd

Axis uses WSDD XML files to configure its web services. This is a typical WSDD file. Note that we've set the scope parameter to the application value; this indicates that a single instance of Bank will be kept in memory for all requests that Axis receives. We need to employ this option because we're using instance variables to store our application's data:

```
<deployment xmlns="http://xml.apache.org/axis/wsdd/"
            xmlns:java="http://xml.apache.org/axis/wsdd/providers/java">
    <service name="Bank" provider="java:RPC">
        <parameter name="className" value="com.wrox.service.Bank"/>
        <parameter name="allowedMethods" value="*"/>
        <parameter name="scope" value="application"/>
    </service>
</deployment>
```

Run the Application

Now that we've reviewed the code for version 0.1 of this case study, let's talk about how to execute it. First, type in the code in the files listed above if you haven't already done so. Take special care to ensure that you place the class files into the packages in which they belong.

First, unless Tomcat is already running, start it up. Next, compile all the classes, and place them into the [servlet_container]/webapps/axis/WEB-INF/classes directory. Then, copy the deploy.wsdd file into the same location as the Bank.class file. Now we're ready to deploy the web service into Axis. You can accomplish this by executing the following commands:

```
cd [servlet_container]/webapps/axis/WEB-INF/classes/com/wrox/service
java org.apache.axis.client.AdminClient deploy.wsdd
```

If you followed the instructions properly you should see the following message:

```
- Processing file deploy.wsdd
- <Admin>Done processing</Admin>
```

We can further verify that the web service is deployed properly by visiting this URL:
http://127.0.0.1:8080/axis/servlet/AxisServlet.

Upon doing so, you should see a screen like this:

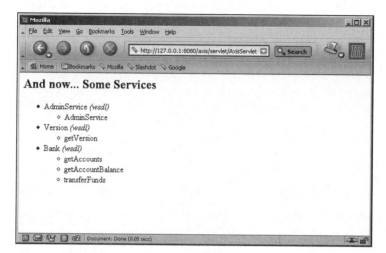

The important thing to notice is the Bank service and its three methods. If you see those, you're clear to move on to the next step. Execute the following commands:

```
cd $TOMCAT_HOME/webapps/axis/WEB-INF/classes
java com.wrox.client.Client
```

Once you do that, the application should pop up on your screen.

Version 0.2

Now that we've created the basic application, it's time to start making it secure. One of the security holes in our application is a potential "man-in-the-middle" exploit. We're doing nothing to our XML messages to authenticate that the requests are coming from an authorized user or that the responses are coming from WROX Bank. Let's take care of it right now.

XML Signatures

As we learned in Chapter 4, there is an existing technology designed to solve the problem of authenticating the source of an electronic communication: Public Key Infrastructure, or PKI. There is additionally an emerging specification for applying PKI to SOAP in a standardized way: XML Signatures, or XML-SIG (also called XML Digital Signatures or XML-DSIG).

Creating Keys and a Certificate

Before either WROX Bank or its customers can sign their XML messages with a private key and certificate using XML-SIG, we must first generate the necessary private/public keys and a X.509 certificate. The JDK comes with the just the right tool for the job: the keytool command-line utility.

Of course, in a real-world application, a bank is not likely to expect customers to generate their own keys – rather, they would generate keys and certificates for their customers, have them signed by a CA, (Certificate Authority) and then store the certificates in an XKMS-compliant key store. However, as of this writing, the XKMS specification is quite unstable, and while a handful of reference implementations have emerged, we feel that getting them working in this case study is not yet worth the effort.

Instead, we will simulate the use of some kind of key-retrieval mechanism by creating a single file-based key store and sharing that between the client and the server. This key store will contain the public and private keys for both the client and the server in our application, as well as their certificates.

To create this file, execute the following commands:

```
cd [java_home]/bin

keytool -genkey -dname "cn=John Doe, ou=Palo Alto Branch, o=Wrox Bank, c=US"
    -alias 12345678 -keypass wroxbank -keystore
    [servlet_container]/webapps/axis/WEB-INF/classes/wroxbankstore.jks
    -storepass wroxbank

keytool -genkey -dname "cn=Web Branch, ou=Wrox Bank On-line, o=Wrox Bank,
    c=US" -alias webbranch -keypass wroxbank -keystore
    [servlet_container]/webapps/axis/WEB-INF/classes/wroxbankstore.jks
    -storepass wroxbank
```

> **NOTE: All of the lines above that begin with `keytool` should be placed on the same line when you type them. They have been wrapped here due to space limitations. Also, `[java_home]` and `[servlet_container]` should be replaced by their respective home directories.**

Revising the Application

Now that we've created the key store, we need to update the application to use the appropriate keys to sign our XML messages. To the user, this change is transparent (although it does make the application quite a bit slower) so we won't review any new screenshots. We will, however, take a look at what the new-signed XML messages look like. Rather than review all three of our web services, we'll just take a look at one of them: getAccounts.

getAccounts with an XML Signature

The XML that the client sends in its request to the getAccounts web service looks like this:

```xml
<?xml version="1.0" encoding="UTF-8"?>
<soapenv:Envelope soapenv:actor="some-uri" soapenv:mustUnderstand="1"
    xmlns:SOAP-SEC="http://schemas.xmlsoap.org/soap/security/2000-12"
    xmlns:soapenv="http://schemas.xmlsoap.org/soap/envelope/"
    xmlns:xsd="http://www.w3.org/2001/XMLSchema"
    xmlns:xsi="http://www.w3.org/2001/XMLSchema-instance">
  <soapenv:Header><SOAP-SEC:Signature><ds:Signature
          xmlns:ds="http://www.w3.org/2000/09/xmldsig#">
    <ds:SignedInfo>
      <ds:CanonicalizationMethod Algorithm="http://www.w3.org/TR/2001/REC-
```

```
        xml-c14n-20010315"/>
      <ds:SignatureMethod Algorithm="http://www.w3.org/2000/09/xmldsig#dsa-
          sha1"/>
      <ds:Reference URI="#Body">
      <ds:DigestMethod Algorithm="http://www.w3.org/2000/09/xmldsig#sha1"/>
      <ds:DigestValue>2jmj7l5rSw0yVb/vlWAYkK/YBwk=</ds:DigestValue>
    </ds:Reference>
  </ds:SignedInfo>
```

The `<ds:SignatureValue>` element here contains the XML signature used to validate the contents of our message:

```
<ds:SignatureValue>
    XOzR6sgmPiOZxwP7fTtFyjPua2KE3/3cJv28qR1e4kff41UfuXxAJw==
</ds:SignatureValue>
```

And embedded within the `<ds:KeyInfo>` element are the signer's X509 certificate and public key:

```
<ds:KeyInfo>
  <ds:X509Data>
    <ds:X509Certificate>
MIIC1TCCApMCBD2mpc4wCwYHKoZIzjgEAwUAMFAxCzAJBgNVBAYTAlVLMRIwEAYDVQQKEwlXUk9Y
IEJhbmsxGjAYBgNVBAsTEUNhbGlmb3JuaWEgQnJhbmNoMREwDwYDVQQDEwhKb2huIERvZTAeFw0w
MjEwMTExMDE5NThaFw0wMzAxMDkxMDE5NThaMFAxCzAJBgNVBAYTAlVLMRIwEAYDVQQKEwlXUk9Y
IEJhbmsxGjAYBgNVBAsTEUNhbGlmb3JuaWEgQnJhbmNoMREwDwYDVQQDEwhKb2huIERvZTCCAbgw
ggEsBgcqhkjOOAQBMIIBHwKBgQD9f1OBHXUSKVLfSpwu7OTn9hG3UjzvRADDHj+AtlEmaUVdQCJR
+1k9jVj6v8X1ujD2y5tVbNeBO4AdNG/yZmC3a5lQpaSfn+gEexAiwk+7qdf+t8Yb+DtX58aophUP
BPuD9tPFHsMCNVQTWhaRMvZ1864rYdcq7/IiAxmd0UgBxwIVAJdgUI8VIwvMspK5gqLrhAvwWBz1
AoGBAPfhoIXWmz3ey7yrXDa4V7l5lK+7+jrqgvlXTAs9B4JnUVlXjrrUWU/mcQcQgYC0SRZxI+hM
KBYTt88JMozIpuE8FnqLVHyNKOCjrh4rs6Z1kW6jfwv6ITVi8ftiegEkO8yk8b6oUZCJqIPf4Vrl
nwaSi2ZegHtVJWQBTDv+z0kqA4GFAAKBgQCQGQx+ZED/oC7rXMYOG2Rd5zzmYnPJZTlJKWWuNZUs
a2xNw95r/eiZynExQylyJ8QyCKGBRaPjmSZM0Ih+LmKMNNqWhIQZQVoCsrLEhOyG6DaxE6B6Vn5t
oEjvlTmr2r3vJ4IztvTTvbFHriMNgJ/o2HQtziZA+Kpkuk8H/n4kMDALBgcqhkjOOAQDBQADLwAw
LAIURa7PE3uaRGuSFxulUKDEx1iKO8ECFFjyxGXXT5wvQeOcm5JPUwpkW+sV
    </ds:X509Certificate>
  </ds:X509Data>
  <ds:KeyValue>
    <ds:DSAKeyValue>
      <ds:P>
/X9TgR11EilS30qcLuzk5/YRt1I870QAwx4/gLZRJmlFXUAiUftZPY1Y+r/F9bow9subVWzXgTuA
HTRv8mZgt2uZUKWkn5/oBHsQIsJPu6nX/rfGG/g7V+fGqKYVDwT7g/bTxR7DAjVUE1oWkTL2dfOu
K2HXKu/yIgMZndFIAcc=
      </ds:P>
      <ds:Q>l2BQjxUjC8yykrmCouuEC/BYHPU=</ds:Q>
      <ds:G>
9+GghdabPd7LvKtcNrhXuXmUr7v6OuqC+VdMCz0HgmdRWVeOutRZT+ZxBxCBgLRJFnEj6EwoFhO3
zwkyjMim4TwWeotUfIOo4KOuHiuzpnWRbqN/C/ohNWLx+2J6ASQ7zKTxvqhRkImog9/hWuWfBpKL
Z16Ae1UlZAFMO/7PSSo=
      </ds:G>
      <ds:Y>
kBkMfmRA/6Au61zGDhtkXec85mJzyWU5SSllrjWVLGtsTcPea/3omcpxMUMpcifEMgihgUWj45km
TNCIfi5ijDTaloSEGUFaArKyxITshug2sROgelZ+baBI79U5q9q97yeCM7b0072xR64jDYCf6Nh0
```

```
Lc4mQPiqZLpPB/5+JDA=
            </ds:Y>
          </ds:DSAKeyValue>
        </ds:KeyValue>
      </ds:KeyInfo>
    </ds:Signature>
  </SOAP-SEC:Signature>
</soapenv:Header>
  <soapenv:Body>
    <getAccounts
        soapenv:encodingStyle="http://schemas.xmlsoap.org/soap/encoding/">
    <arg0 xsi:type="xsd:string">12345678</arg0>
    <arg1 xsi:type="xsd:string">1234</arg1>
    </getAccounts>
  </soapenv:Body>
</soapenv:Envelope>
```

The size of our request just much lot bigger, as you can compare with the previous SOAP message. A new header, `<SOAP-SEC:Signature>`, was added to the SOAP message envelope, which contains:

❑   The various standards and their versions used for our XML signature

❑   A signature of the SOAP message body

❑   The public key of the client

❑   The certificate of the client

Once the server receives this message, it will perform two steps:

1. Ensure that the SOAP body matches the signature contained in the envelope header

2. Ensure that the private key used to sign the SOAP body belongs to the correct individual

We will show these steps in the forthcoming Java code.

Java Code

To add this new XML Security support to our application, we're going to create a new package: `com.wrox.security`. In this package, we'll place the following new files:

❑   `com.wrox.security`

   ❑   `AddSignature` – processes a SOAP message and adds a signature header to its envelope

   ❑   `SignedSOAPEnvelope` – child of `SOAPEnvelope`; contains methods specific to creating a signature header to a SOAP envelope

   ❑   `ValidateSignature` – processes a SOAP message and validates that (a) the signature is valid for the message and (b) the signer is the correct individual

   ❑   `SecurityUtils` – container for a general-purpose static method for extracting the client's account number from a SOAP message

❑   `serverdeploy.wsdd` – metadata used by Axis to deploy `AddSignature` and `ValidateSigature`

❑   `client-config.wsdd` – metadata used by Axis to configure the web service client to use `AddSignature` and `ValidateSignature`; this file should be placed in the working directory of the WROX Bank Application (`[servlet_container]/webapps/axis/WEB-INF/classes`)

AddSignature.java

`AddSignature` is an Axis handler; this means that it can be configured to "handle" or process web service requests/responses after they are generated but before they are sent, as well as after they are received but before they are processed. This is great news for us, as it means we can add XML Signatures to our application without modifying any of the existing class files.

The API contract for Axis handlers is rather complex, but fortunately we can just override a single method in an existing implementation, `BasicHandler`, to get our desired result:

```
package com.wrox.security;

import org.apache.axis.handlers.BasicHandler;
import org.apache.axis.AxisFault;
import org.apache.axis.MessageContext;
import org.apache.axis.Message;
import org.apache.axis.message.SOAPEnvelope;

public class AddSignature extends BasicHandler {
    /*
     * Initializes the Apache XML Security library; can be safely called
     * multiple times.
     */
    static {
        org.apache.xml.security.Init.init();
    }
```

In this version of the application, we've configured Axis to call this handler, `AddSignature`, on SOAP messages before it sends them. Axis will call `AddSignature.invoke()`, passing it the SOAP message as well as other objects and attributes wrapped in a `MessageContext` object.

For more information on how Axis works with handlers, see
http://cvs.apache.org/viewcvs.cgi/~checkout~/xml-axis/java/docs/architecture-guide.html.

In this method, we need to swap out the unsigned SOAP message that Axis produces by default with a new signed SOAP message. To do this, we must perform various steps, such as determining which key we'll need to use to sign the certificate, actually signing the message, and so on.

We've encapsulated various steps of this process in several different classes, and we'll talk about more of this throughout this section:

```
public void invoke(MessageContext msgContext) throws AxisFault {
    SOAPEnvelope unsignedEnvelope;
    String type;
    try {
        /*
```

```
     * Because this Handler is used by both the client and the
     * server, we need a mechanism to determine context. This
     * mechanism is a property named "alias" in the Axis client and
     * server configuration files.
     */
    String alias = (String) getOption("alias");
    if (alias.equals("client")) {
        alias = SecurityUtils.getAccountFromMessage(
                msgContext.getRequestMessage());
        unsignedEnvelope = msgContext.getRequestMessage().
                getSOAPEnvelope();
        type = Message.REQUEST;
    } else {
        unsignedEnvelope = msgContext.getResponseMessage().
                getSOAPEnvelope();
        type = Message.RESPONSE;
    }
```

The comment in the code describes most of what's going on in the block above. For simplicity, we're going to reuse this handler on both the Axis server and our Swing client. Both tiers will need to sign the SOAP messages, after all.

This method uses a property called `alias` in the Axis configuration file to determine if it's on the server or the client. If the property's value is set to `client`, this method must determine the account number of the client in order to know which key to use from the key store to sign the message. That's where the `SecurityUtils.getAccountFromMessage()` method comes in; it parses the SOAP message to determine what the account number is.

If the `alias` property is set to any other value, this method will assume it is being run on the server.

Below, the `SignedSOAPEnvelope` class encapsulates the process of converting the unsigned SOAP message into a signed SOAP message, and it does this in the class `constructor`:

```
SignedSOAPEnvelope signedEnvelope = new SignedSOAPEnvelope(
        msgContext, unsignedEnvelope, alias, type);
msgContext.setCurrentMessage(new Message(signedEnvelope));
```

The line above, `msgContext.setCurrentMessage()`, is where we swap out the unsigned message with the new signed message:

```
    } catch (Exception e) {
        throw AxisFault.makeFault(e);
    }
    }
}
```

SecurityUtils.java

This class contains a single static method, `getAccountFromMessage()`, used to extract the client's account number from a SOAP message:

```
package com.wrox.security;

import org.apache.axis.Message;
```

```
import org.apache.axis.message.SOAPBodyElement;
import org.w3c.dom.Element;
import org.w3c.dom.NodeList;
import org.w3c.dom.Node;

import java.util.Vector;

public class SecurityUtils {
    public static String getAccountFromMessage(Message message) {
        try {
            Vector v = message.getSOAPEnvelope().getBodyElements();
            SOAPBodyElement elem = (SOAPBodyElement) v.get(0);
            Element e = elem.getAsDOM();
            NodeList nl = e.getElementsByTagName("arg0");
            Node n = nl.item(0);
            return n.getChildNodes().item(0).getNodeValue();
        } catch (Exception ex) {
            ex.printStackTrace();
        }
```

In this method we pay the price for not having typed our SOAP parameters – that's why we're searching for `arg0` (as opposed to `account`). For our case study, it's certainly fine, but it's not robust enough for a real-world production system. Changing the order of the parameters would break this method. The following snippet completes the code:

```
        return null;
    }
}
```

SignedSOAPEnvelope.java

This class performs the task of adding the signature to the SOAP envelope:

```
package com.wrox.security;

import org.apache.axis.message.SOAPEnvelope;
import org.apache.axis.message.SOAPHeaderElement;
import org.apache.axis.MessageContext;
import org.apache.axis.Constants;
import org.apache.axis.Constants;
import org.apache.axis.client.AxisClient;
import org.apache.axis.configuration.NullProvider;
import org.apache.axis.encoding.DeserializationContextImpl;
import org.apache.axis.encoding.SerializationContextImpl;
import org.apache.axis.encoding.SerializationContext;
import org.apache.axis.message.SOAPEnvelope;
import org.apache.axis.message.SOAPHeaderElement;
import org.apache.axis.utils.*;
import org.apache.xml.security.c14n.Canonicalizer;
import org.apache.xml.security.signature.XMLSignature;
import org.w3c.dom.Document;
import org.w3c.dom.Element;
import org.xml.sax.InputSource;
```

```
import java.io.*;
import java.security.KeyStore;
import java.security.PrivateKey;
import java.security.cert.X509Certificate;

public class SignedSOAPEnvelope extends SOAPEnvelope {
    static String SOAPSECNS = "http://schemas.xmlsoap.org/soap/security/" +
            "2000-12";
    static String SOAPSECprefix = "SOAP-SEC";

    static {
        org.apache.xml.security.Init.init();
    }

    public SignedSOAPEnvelope(MessageContext msgContext, SOAPEnvelope env,
                            String alias, String type) {
        init(msgContext, env, alias, type);
    }

    private void init(MessageContext msgContext, SOAPEnvelope env,
                    String alias, String type) {
        try {
            env.addMapping(new Mapping(SOAPSECNS, SOAPSECprefix));
            env.addAttribute(Constants.URI_SOAP11_ENV,"mustUnderstand","1");

            SOAPHeaderElement header =
                new SOAPHeaderElement(XMLUtils.StringToElement(SOAPSECNS,
                                                        "Signature",
                                                        ""));
            env.addHeader(header);
```

The first lines in the `try { }` block shown above add some of the necessary SOAP headers to indicate that the SOAP message is signed. These headers are the same regardless of who is signing the message. Note that we're adding the `mustUnderstand` attribute, indicating that if the web service provider doesn't understand XML signatures, it must fail.

Now we need to load in the key and certificate that will be used to sign the message:

```
Document doc = getSOAPEnvelopeAsDocument(env, msgContext);

KeyStore ks = KeyStore.getInstance(KeyStore.getDefaultType());
InputStream fis = Thread.currentThread().
        getContextClassLoader().
        getResourceAsStream("wroxbankstore.jks");
ks.load(fis, "wroxbank".toCharArray());
```

Above we are loading in the `KeyStore` that we created, making use of Java's ability to load in external resources using the `ClassLoader` system. We pass a stream handler that points the `KeyStore` to the `KeyStore.load()` method, as well as the password to the key store.

In the next line, we are obtaining the private key for either the server or the client, using the alias variable to determine which key we will load:

```
PrivateKey privateKey = (PrivateKey) ks.getKey(alias,
        "wroxbank".toCharArray());

Element soapHeaderElement = (Element) ((Element)
        doc.getFirstChild()).getElementsByTagNameNS("*",
                "Header").item(0);
Element soapSignatureElement = (Element) soapHeaderElement.
        getElementsByTagNameNS("*", "Signature").item(0);

XMLSignature sig = new XMLSignature(doc, "http://xml-security",
        XMLSignature.ALGO_ID_SIGNATURE_DSA);

soapSignatureElement.appendChild(sig.getElement());
sig.addDocument("#Body");

X509Certificate cert =
        (X509Certificate) ks.getCertificate(alias);

sig.addKeyInfo(cert);
sig.addKeyInfo(cert.getPublicKey());
sig.sign(privateKey);
```

In the lines above we're adding more information to our SOAP headers, including both the X509 Certificate and the public key used by the signer in the SOAP message. Finally, in the last line above, we sign the message, adding the signature to the header after we're done.

In the next lines, we create a new DeserializationContextImpl object, which is necessary for Axis to properly process our new message. The DeserializationContextImpl object is used by Axis to "deserialize" the parameters in the SOAP body, converting them into Java objects. Axis creates a DeserializationContextImpl object when the SOAP message is first received, but because we've materially changed the SOAP message we'll need to create a new instance of it:

```
Canonicalizer c14n = Canonicalizer.getInstance(
        Canonicalizer.ALGO_ID_C14N_WITH_COMMENTS);
byte[] canonicalMessage = c14n.canonicalizeSubtree(doc);

InputSource is = new InputSource(new
        ByteArrayInputStream(canonicalMessage));
DeserializationContextImpl dser = null;
if (msgContext == null) {
    AxisClient tmpEngine = new AxisClient(new NullProvider());
    msgContext = new MessageContext(tmpEngine);
}
dser = new DeserializationContextImpl(is, msgContext,
        type, this);

dser.parse();
} catch (Exception e) {
    e.printStackTrace();
```

```
                        throw new RuntimeException(e.toString());
                }
        }

        private Document getSOAPEnvelopeAsDocument(SOAPEnvelope env,
                                                  MessageContext msgContext)
                throws Exception {
            StringWriter writer = new StringWriter();
            SerializationContext serializeContext =
                    new SerializationContextImpl(writer, msgContext);
            env.output(serializeContext);
            writer.close();

            Reader reader = new StringReader(writer.getBuffer().toString());
            Document doc = XMLUtils.newDocument(new InputSource(reader));
            if (doc == null)
                throw new Exception(
                        Messages.getMessage("noDoc00",
                                writer.getBuffer().toString()));
            return doc;
        }
}
```

ValidateSignature.java

ValidateSignature is implemented as an Axis handler, just like AddSignature:

```
package com.wrox.security;

import org.apache.axis.handlers.BasicHandler;
import org.apache.axis.AxisFault;
import org.apache.axis.MessageContext;
import org.apache.axis.Message;
import org.apache.xml.security.utils.Constants;
import org.apache.xml.security.signature.XMLSignature;
import org.apache.xpath.CachedXPathAPI;
import org.w3c.dom.Document;
import org.w3c.dom.Element;

import java.io.InputStream;
import java.security.KeyStore;
import java.security.cert.X509Certificate;

public class ValidateSignature extends BasicHandler {
    /*
     * Initializes the Apache XML Security library; can be safely called
     * multiple times.
     */
    static {
        org.apache.xml.security.Init.init();
    }

    public void invoke(MessageContext msgContext) throws AxisFault {
        try {
```

```
String mode = (String) getOption("mode");

String alias;
Message inMsg;
if (mode.equals("client")) {
    alias = "webbranch";
    inMsg = msgContext.getResponseMessage();
} else {
    inMsg = msgContext.getRequestMessage();
    alias = SecurityUtils.getAccountFromMessage(inMsg);
}

Document doc = inMsg.getSOAPEnvelope().getAsDocument();
String BaseURI = "http://xml-security";
CachedXPathAPI xpathAPI = new CachedXPathAPI();

Element nsctx = doc.createElement("nsctx");
nsctx.setAttribute("xmlns:ds", Constants.SignatureSpecNS);

Element signatureElem = (Element) xpathAPI.selectSingleNode(
        doc, "//ds:Signature", nsctx);
```

In the lines above we get the SOAP message and select the element from it that contains the XML signature using an XPath query. We will validate that this signature is valid below:

```
/* make sure that the document claims to have been signed */
if (signatureElem == null) {
    throw new Exception("Request not signed!");
}

XMLSignature sig = new XMLSignature(signatureElem, BaseURI);

boolean verify = sig.checkSignatureValue(sig.getKeyInfo().
        getPublicKey());
if (!verify) {
    throw new Exception("Request signature not valid!");
}

InputStream is = Thread.currentThread().
        getContextClassLoader().
        getResourceAsStream("wroxbankstore.jks");
KeyStore ks = KeyStore.getInstance(KeyStore.getDefaultType());
ks.load(is, "wroxbank".toCharArray());
X509Certificate sigCert = sig.getKeyInfo().
        getX509Certificate();
X509Certificate ksCert = (X509Certificate)
        ks.getCertificate(alias);
if (!ksCert.getSerialNumber().equals(
        sigCert.getSerialNumber())) {
    String msg;
    if (mode.equals("client")) {
        msg = "Server response not signed by valid party!";
    } else {
```

485

```
                    msg = "Client request not signed by valid party!";
                }
                throw new Exception(msg);
            }
        } catch (Exception e) {
            throw AxisFault.makeFault(e);
        }
    }
}
```

serverdeploy.wsdd

This file is used to deploy the two handlers into the Axis engine. It should be placed in the com.wrox.security package:

```
<deployment xmlns="http://xml.apache.org/axis/wsdd/"
            xmlns:java="http://xml.apache.org/axis/wsdd/providers/java">
  <globalConfiguration>
    <requestFlow>
      <handler type="java:com.wrox.security.ValidateSignature">
        <parameter name-"mode" value="server"/>
      </handler>
    </requestFlow>
    <responseFlow>
      <handler type="java:com.wrox.security.AddSignature">
        <parameter name="alias" value="webbranch"/>
      </handler>
    </responseFlow>
  </globalConfiguration>
</deployment>
```

client-config.wsdd

This file controls how the WROX Bank Application generates web service requests. It is not placed in a package, and therefore resides in the [servlet-container]/WEB-INF/classes directory:

```
<?xml version="1.0" encoding="UTF-8"?>
<deployment xmlns="http://xml.apache.org/axis/wsdd/"
    xmlns:java="http://xml.apache.org/axis/wsdd/providers/java">
  <globalConfiguration>
    <parameter name="adminPassword" value="admin"/>
    <parameter name="sendXsiTypes" value="true"/>
    <parameter name="sendMultiRefs" value="true"/>
    <parameter name="sendXMLDeclaration" value="true"/>
    <requestFlow>
      <handler type="java:com.wrox.security.AddSignature">
        <parameter name="alias" value="client"/>
      </handler>
    </requestFlow>
    <responseFlow>
      <handler type="java:com.wrox.security.ValidateSignature">
        <parameter name="mode" value="client"/>
      </handler>
```

```
        </responseFlow>
    </globalConfiguration>
    <transport name="java"
               pivot="java:org.apache.axis.transport.java.JavaSender"/>
    <transport name="http"
               pivot="java:org.apache.axis.transport.http.HTTPSender"/>
    <transport name="local"
               pivot="java:org.apache.axis.transport.local.LocalSender"/>
</deployment>
```

Run the Application

If you're continuing to follow along by typing the code, or if you've downloaded it, then let's run the application. We'll need to deploy the new handlers into Axis first. Here's how we do it:

```
cd [servlet_container]/webapps/axis/WEB-INF/classes/com/wrox/security
java org.apache.axis.client.AdminClient serverdeploy.wsdd
```

You should see the following:

```
- Processing file serverdeploy.wsdd
- <Admin>Done processing</Admin>
```

Now, run the application in the same way you did before:

```
cd [servlet_container]/webapps/axis/WEB-INF/classes
java com.wrox.client.Client
```

Go ahead and play around with the application. If everything works though it's quite slow, you'll know that you've done everything correctly. If the application doesn't work, in addition to checking for typos, you'll also want to ensure that wroxbankstore.jks and client-config.wsdd are in the [servlet_container]/webapps/axis/WEB-INF/classes directory.

Version 0.3

Now that we've secured our application against "man-in-the-middle" exploits and have added secure authentication to it, we still need to do one important thing – add encryption. As we've seen before, the client's account number and pin are being passed in plaintext through the wire, so to speak, as shown in this excerpt of a SOAP message:

```
<soapenv:Body>
  <getAccounts
      soapenv:encodingStyle="http://schemas.xmlsoap.org/soap/encoding/">
   <arg0 xsi:type="xsd:string">12345678</arg0>
   <arg1 xsi:type="xsd:string">1234</arg1>
  </getAccounts>
</soapenv:Body>
```

This needs to change.

XML Encryption

Unfortunately, as of this writing, the Apache XML Security library (v.1.0.4) that we've been using doesn't support XML encryption. As a result, we'll have to look elsewhere for a library that supports the standard.

Verisign Trust Services Integration Kit

Verisign is one of a handful of vendors that currently provides support for this emerging standard. Using their Trust Services Integration Kit (TSIK), we'll be able to write Axis handlers that encrypt messages as they leave one host and decrypt them when they arrive at another.

In addition, it is also worth noting that Verisign's TSIK also supports the XML Signature API. We choose Apache implementation of XML Signature because we think that in the near future the combination of Apache's XML Security package (once it supports XML encryption) with Apache Axis will be quite popular – especially when its integration is tighter and has more supporting documentation.

Revising the Application

As with XML Signatures, our application won't change from the user's perspective at all, other than introducing increased latency. On the server-side, we will add a new encryption handler to Axis, which is called after signing a message, and we'll also introduce a decryption handler to be called before verifying the signature of a message.

Once again, we will begin by reviewing the changes made to the SOAP messages by examining one of our web services.

getAccountBalance Web Service with XML Signature and XML Encryption

Let's now take a look at the getAccountBalance SOAP message after having both the XML Encryption and XML Signature transformations applied to it:

```
<?xml version="1.0" encoding="UTF-8"?>
<soapenv:Envelope soapenv:mustUnderstand="1" xmlns:SOAP-
    SEC="http://schemas.xmlsoap.org/soap/security/2000-12"
    xmlns:soapenv="http://schemas.xmlsoap.org/soap/envelope/"
    xmlns:xsd="http://www.w3.org/2001/XMLSchema"
    xmlns:xsi="http://www.w3.org/2001/XMLSchema-instance">
  <soapenv:Header><SOAP-SEC:Signature><ds:Signature
      xmlns:ds="http://www.w3.org/2000/09/xmldsig#">
    <ds:SignedInfo>
      <ds:CanonicalizationMethod Algorithm="http://www.w3.org/TR/2001/REC-
          xml-c14n-20010315"/>
      <ds:SignatureMethod
          Algorithm="http://www.w3.org/2000/09/xmldsig#dsa-sha1"/>
      <ds:Reference URI="#Body">
        <ds:DigestMethod
            Algorithm="http://www.w3.org/2000/09/xmldsig#sha1"/>
        <ds:DigestValue>2jmj7l5rSw0yVb/vlWAYkK/YBwk=</ds:DigestValue>
      </ds:Reference>
    </ds:SignedInfo>
  <ds:SignatureValue>XmKeirsUMAVDiAwtasQYzpp9Yn1HvJsLLNy1lmAUEz+AJ7ZPrLR96g==</ds:Si
gnatureValue>
```

```
<ds:KeyInfo>
<ds:X509Data>
<ds:X509Certificate>
MIIC1jCCApQCBD3EbdQwCwYHKoZIzjgEAwUAMFExCzAJBgNVBAYTAlVTMRQwEgYDVQQKEwtXcm94
IEJyYW5jaDEZMBcGA1UECxMQUGFsbyBBbHRvIEJyYW5jaDERMA8GA1UEAxMISm9obiBEb2UwUWhcN
MDIxMTAzMDAyOTA4WhcNMDMwMjAxMDAyOTA4WjBRMQswCQYDVQQGEwJVUzEUMBIGA1UEChMLV3Jv
eCBCcmFuY2gxGTAXBgNVBAsTEFBhbG8gQWx0byBCcmFuY2gxETAPBgNVBAMTCEpvaG4gRG9lMIIB
tzCCASwGByqGSM44BAEwggEfAoGBAP1/U4EddRIpUt9KnC7s5Of2EbdSPO9EAMMeP4C2USZpRV1A
IlH7WT2NWPq/xfW6MPbLm1Vs14E7gB00b/JmYLdrmVClpJ+f6AR7ECLCT7up1/63xhv4O1fnxqim
FQ8E+4P2O8UewwI1VBNaFpEy9nXzrith1yrv8iIDGZ3RSAHHAhUAl2BQjxUjC8yykrmCouuEC/BY
HPUCgYEA9+GghdabPd7LvKtcNrhXuXmUr7v6OuqC+VdMCz0HgmdRWVeOutRZT+ZxBxCBgLRJFnEj
6EwoFhO3zwkyjMim4TwWeotUfI0o4KOuHiuzpnWRbqN/C/ohNWLx+2J6ASQ7zKTxvqhRkImog9/h
WuWfBpKLZl6Ae1UlZAFMO/7PSSoDgYQAAoGAIieUd6VrkePZm+b1Utq28892q0hxOnZltbu4F7tP
IsyQI3DP20icAdTzvqVCTaKT/ZnjsGLM0EM8GtLPWQ4U88rPM32jnm7FyMyUYIeiWRw//BDAReyY
ib2XKhD21ELiE5sBegqaqoTSPHUWNzHBVzbleFJxVIvaOA7qiBVLhqswCwYHKoZIzjgEAwUAAy8A
MCwCFDVDHDaHtrMG/lsJEqB1AOuMSFr9AhQN8br6wUaRZPwrwhiv2vaAA+LTgQ==
</ds:X509Certificate>
</ds:X509Data>
<ds:KeyValue>
<ds:DSAKeyValue>
<ds:P>
/X9TgR11EilS30qcLuzk5/YRt1I870QAwx4/gLZRJmlFXUAiUftZPY1Y+r/F9bow9subVWzXgTuA
HTRv8mZgt2uZUKWkn5/oBHsQIsJPu6nX/rfGG/g7V+fGqKYVDwT7g/bTxR7DAjVUEloWkTL2dfOu
K2HXKu/yIgMZndFIAcc=
</ds:P>
<ds:Q>l2BQjxUjC8yykrmCouuEC/BYHPU=</ds:Q>
<ds:G>
9+GghdabPd7LvKtcNrhXuXmUr7v6OuqC+VdMCz0HgmdRWVeOutRZT+ZxBxCBgLRJFnEj6EwoFhO3
zwkyjMim4TwWeotUfI0o4KOuHiuzpnWRbqN/C/ohNWLx+2J6ASQ7zKTxvqhRkImog9/hWuWfBpKL
Zl6Ae1UlZAFMO/7PSSo=
</ds:G>
<ds:Y>
IieUd6VrkePZm+b1Utq28892q0hxOnZltbu4F7tPIsyQI3DP20icAdTzvqVCTaKT/ZnjsGLM0EM8
GtLPWQ4U88rPM32jnm7FyMyUYIeiWRw//BDAReyIib2XKhD21ELiE5sBegqaqoTSPHUWNzHBVzbl
eFJxVIvaOA7qiBVLhqs=
</ds:Y>
</ds:DSAKeyValue>
</ds:KeyValue>
</ds:KeyInfo>
</ds:Signature></SOAP-SEC:Signature> </soapenv:Header>
<soapenv:Body>
    <xenc:EncryptedData Type="http://www.w3.org/2001/04/xmlenc#Element"
    xmlns:xenc="http://www.w3.org/2001/04/xmlenc#">
    <xenc:EncryptionMethod
        Algorithm="http://www.w3.org/2001/04/xmlenc#tripledes-cbc"/>
    <xenc:CipherData>
<xenc:CipherValue>p8fKlDKdZ/9M809SQNwkWbQbpClHFc7+JG6lar1fH1J0c9gd9MMnGHiy9L3nSOnr
+mda7o1x
fd3kmhefWneu80TKvl2GfXWjxw5d5y7qQ3ybLe8jAYymMc/s/XMK627bUs0f/+eItZO+p7zN
0Ivn9q/shNJPkVLZaFewx1IRealIp4tQfWuVGRBeLK7QwsnAfgs4oXtDwW3/zFGpOLM1eNj6
+hRtvaG6QUGrh96mUR3iTNMdiKST+rqlH8IY7ApwJTMDHKgw0+VUM4D0qlFmLOdbH24Aqp5I
igv7aZzRiwQL8IJ/ARBrwJz/iES+1etkSblkSE2UqQ0jXKzErpHCGTHI3ItYyK7AUh7v52d2
BynnZVfDIYedulR0P1xqknnNENAhYTPT5hArv3DZnwyj7emOQj8Y+ISLTeVjSDcm00Bc9UQz
gw2NQnxLi7eSCOEhhCgNIwwzwUzpVld/aSW3tUzdJGCRPmb9YQ3wjBW/nSxb+5dIfLD0VeqS
AHU4XyZsC1iDgDteqGEhsiGrSzZRlYcZvm7HxvAbMjBgiKwCGI+p0EiKwHHEbA==</xenc:CipherValue
>
    </xenc:CipherData>
  </xenc:EncryptedData>
</soapenv:Body>
</soapenv:Envelope>
```

489

We've encrypted the entire contents of our SOAP body. This will prevent anyone "listening in" from knowing anything about what this SOAP message contains, such as the bank customer performing the transaction, the type of transaction, the PIN number, and so forth.

Some folks might prefer encrypting the entire SOAP message. We've chosen to encrypt just the SOAP body to showcase what is possible with XML encryption as opposed to SSL encryption; we can arbitrarily encrypt parts of the SOAP message.

Java Code

To accomplish our changes, we've added two new classes to our application:

- ❑ `Encrypt.java`
  Encrypts the body of the SOAP message
- ❑ `Decrypt.java`
  Decrypts the body of the SOAP message

We will also be modifying the following files:

- ❑ `com.wrox.security.SecurityUtils`
- ❑ `client-config.wsdd` (located in `[servlet_container]/webapps/axis/WEB-INF/classes`)
- ❑ `server-config.wsdd` (located in `[servlet_container]/webapps/axis/WEB-INF`)

Let's take a look at the new classes first.

Encrypt.java

`Encrypt`, and its sister class `Decrypt`, are both similar in function to `AddSignature` and `ValidateSignature`. They act as Axis handlers, modifying the SOAP message before Axis uses it on either the client or the server tiers:

```
package com.wrox.security;

import org.apache.axis.handlers.BasicHandler;
import org.apache.axis.MessageContext;
import org.apache.axis.AxisFault;
import org.apache.axis.Message;
import org.apache.axis.message.SOAPEnvelope;
import org.w3c.dom.Document;
import org.w3c.dom.NodeList;

import java.security.Key;
import java.io.*;

import com.verisign.xmlenc.Encryptor;
import com.verisign.xmlenc.AlgorithmType;
import com.verisign.xpath.XPath;

import javax.xml.transform.Transformer;
import javax.xml.transform.TransformerFactory;
```

```
import javax.xml.transform.stream.StreamResult;
import javax.xml.transform.dom.DOMSource;

public class Encrypt extends BasicHandler {
    public void invoke(MessageContext msgContext) throws AxisFault {
        Message message;

        try {
```

First we load the secret key that we're going to generate prior to running the application:

```
        Key key = SecurityUtils.loadKey();

        message = msgContext.getCurrentMessage();
        SOAPEnvelope se = message.getSOAPEnvelope();
```

Next we set the `Encryptor` object, from the Verisign TSIK API, to encrypt the message. Note that an XPath expression is used to select the element we wish to encrypt. In this case, we're encrypting the child element of `soapenv:Body`, which will take care of encrypting the entire SOAP body:

```
        Encryptor e = new Encryptor(se.getAsDocument(), key,
                AlgorithmType.TRIPLEDES);
        Document newD = e.encrypt(
            new XPath("//*[name()='soapenv:Body']/*"));
```

Unfortunately, Apache Axis doesn't make it as easy as it might to replace the old SOAP message with our new partially encrypted SOAP message. The quickest route we found was transforming the `Document` into an array of bytes, creating a new `SOAPEnvelope` object from those bytes, and then creating a new `Message` from the `SOAPEnvelope`:

```
        Transformer t =
                TransformerFactory.newInstance().newTransformer();
        Writer w = new StringWriter();
        t.transform(new DOMSource(newD), new StreamResult(w));

        SOAPEnvelope newSe = new SOAPEnvelope(
                new ByteArrayInputStream(w.toString().getBytes()));

        msgContext.setCurrentMessage(new Message(newSe));
    } catch (Exception e) {
        e.printStackTrace();
        throw AxisFault.makeFault(e);
    }
    }
}
```

Decrypt.java

This class performs the inverse operation of encrypt. Let's take a look at its code:

```
package com.wrox.security;

import org.apache.axis.handlers.BasicHandler;
import org.apache.axis.MessageContext;
import org.apache.axis.AxisFault;
import org.apache.axis.Message;
import org.apache.axis.encoding.DeserializationContextImpl;
import org.apache.axis.message.SOAPEnvelope;
import org.w3c.dom.Document;
import org.xml.sax.InputSource;

import java.security.Key;
import java.io.*;

import com.verisign.xmlenc.Decryptor;
import com.verisign.xpath.XPath;

import javax.xml.transform.Transformer;
import javax.xml.transform.TransformerFactory;
import javax.xml.transform.stream.StreamResult;
import javax.xml.transform.dom.DOMSource;

public class Decrypt extends BasicHandler {
    public void invoke(MessageContext msgContext) throws AxisFault {
        Message message;

        try {
            Key key = SecurityUtils.loadKey();

            message = msgContext.getCurrentMessage();
            SOAPEnvelope se = message.getSOAPEnvelope();
```

`Decryptor` is the VeriSign class used to decrypt the XML. Just like Encryptor, we use an `XPath` expression to select the element that we wish to decrypt:

```
Decryptor d = new Decryptor(se.getAsDocument(), key,
        new XPath("//*[name()='xenc:EncryptedData']"));
Document newD = d.decrypt();
```

Just as we had to transform the XML in our previous example to a String and rebuild the SOAP envelope with it, we need to do it here, too. However, this works just fine here because we need the raw bytes of the XML to create a new `DeserializationContextImpl` object, as shown below:

```
Transformer t = TransformerFactory.newInstance().
        newTransformer();
Writer w = new StringWriter();
t.transform(new DOMSource(newD), new StreamResult(w));
SOAPEnvelope newSe = new SOAPEnvelope(
        new ByteArrayInputStream(w.toString().getBytes()));
```

```
            String mode = (String) getOption("mode");
            String type = (mode.equals("server")) ? Message.REQUEST
                                                   : Message.RESPONSE;
            DeserializationContextImpl dser =
                  new DeserializationContextImpl(new InputSource(
                        new ByteArrayInputStream(
                              w.toString().getBytes())),
                        msgContext, type, newSe);
            dser.parse();
```

The `DeserializationContextImpl` object is used by Axis to "deserialize" the parameters in the SOAP body, converting them into Java objects. Axis creates a `DeserializationContextImpl` object when the SOAP message is first received, but because we've materially changed the SOAP message (we've decrypted part of it) we'll need to create a new instance of it:

```
            msgContext.setCurrentMessage(new Message(newSe));
        } catch (Exception e) {
            e.printStackTrace();
            throw AxisFault.makeFault(e);
        }
    }
}
```

Now, let's take a look at the modifications that we need to make to our existing files.

SecurityUtils.java

In order to sign our messages, we had to create public/private key pairs and an X509 certificate. We did this using Sun's `keytool` application. In order to encrypt our messages, we need to generate a secret key. Unfortunately, `keytool` cannot generate these types of keys; however, the J2SE is capable of generating these keys for us.

J2SE, via its Java Cryptography Extension API, is quite capable of generating keys for a wide variety of encryption algorithms. However, VeriSign makes our selection process simple; it only supports Triple DES (referred to in Java as "DESede"). So we'll generate a secret key for use with that algorithm.

We will modify our `SecurityUtils` class to contain another static method used to create our secret key, and will create an entry point in the class for generating this key. We will also add a method for loading this secret key after we've created it:

```
package com.wrox.security;

import org.apache.axis.Message;
import org.apache.axis.message.SOAPBodyElement;
import org.w3c.dom.Element;
import org.w3c.dom.NodeList;
import org.w3c.dom.Node;

import javax.crypto.SecretKey;
import javax.crypto.KeyGenerator;
```

```
import javax.crypto.SecretKeyFactory;
import javax.crypto.spec.DESedeKeySpec;
import java.util.Vector;
import java.io.*;
import java.security.Key;
import java.security.NoSuchAlgorithmException;
import java.security.InvalidKeyException;
import java.security.spec.InvalidKeySpecException;
import java.net.URL;

public class SecurityUtils {
    public static void main(String[] args) throws Exception {
        SecurityUtils.generateKey();
    }

    public static String getAccountFromMessage(Message message) {
        ...
    }
}
```

The following method, loadKey(), is used for retrieving the secret key after we've created it. We'll rely on ClassLoader to do the heavy lifting for us, just as we did with our key store file earlier:

```
public static Key loadKey() {
    URL url = Thread.currentThread().getContextClassLoader().
            getResource("tripledes.key");
    if (url == null) return null;

    InputStream is = null;
    byte[] bytes = null;
    try {
        File file = new File(url.getFile());
        bytes = new byte[(int) file.length()];
        is = new FileInputStream(file);
        is.read(bytes);
        is.close();
    } catch (FileNotFoundException fnfe) {
        fnfe.printStackTrace();
        return null;
    } catch (IOException ie) {
        ie.printStackTrace();
        return null;
    } finally {
        try { is.close(); } catch (Exception e) { e.printStackTrace(); }
    }
```

Once we load the key, we'll need to covert it from bytes into an actual Key object. Fortunately, J2SE comes with all the necessary functionality we need to accomplish this, as shown below:

```
    Key key = null;
    try {
        SecretKeyFactory keyFactory =
                SecretKeyFactory.getInstance("DESede");
        DESedeKeySpec keyspec = new DESedeKeySpec(bytes);
        key = keyFactory.generateSecret(keyspec);
    } catch (NoSuchAlgorithmException e) {
        e.printStackTrace();
    } catch (InvalidKeyException e) {
```

```
            e.printStackTrace();
        } catch (InvalidKeySpecException e) {
            e.printStackTrace();
        }

        return key;
    }
```

And here's where we generate our random secret key:

```
    public static void generateKey() throws Exception {
        KeyGenerator keyGen = KeyGenerator.getInstance("DESede");
        SecretKey tripleDesKey = keyGen.generateKey();
        SecretKeyFactory keyFactory =
                SecretKeyFactory.getInstance("DESede");
        DESedeKeySpec keySpec = (DESedeKeySpec)
          keyFactory.getKeySpec(tripleDesKey,
                javax.crypto.spec.DESedeKeySpec.class);
        byte[] keyBytes = keySpec.getKey();

        OutputStream out = new FileOutputStream("tripledes.key");
        out.write(keyBytes);
        out.close();
    }
}
```

Run the Application

Before we run this application, we need to make a few modifications to the Axis configuration files. Edit the `<globalConfiguration>` section of `[servlet_container]/webapps/axis/WEB-INF/server-config.wsdd` so that it contains the additional lines highlighted below:

```
<globalConfiguration>
 <parameter name="adminPassword" value="admin"/>
 <parameter name="sendXsiTypes" value="true"/>
 <parameter name="sendMultiRefs" value="true"/>
 <parameter name="sendXMLDeclaration" value="true"/>
 <requestFlow>
  <handler type="java:com.wrox.security.Decrypt"/>
   <parameter name="mode" value="server"/>
  </handler>
  <handler type="java:com.wrox.security.ValidateSignature">
   <parameter name="mode" value="server"/>
  </handler>
 </requestFlow>
 <responseFlow>
     <handler type="java:com.wrox.security.AddSignature">
      <parameter name="alias" value="webbranch"/>
     </handler>
     <handler type="java:com.wrox.security.Encrypt"/>
 </responseFlow>
</globalConfiguration>
```

We've now added the `Encrypt` and `Decrypt` classes to our request-and-response chains on the web service server. Now we need to add similar entries to the `<globalConfiguration>` section of `[servlet_container]/webapps/axis/WEB-INF/classes/client-config.wsdd` for our client:

```
<globalConfiguration>
  <parameter name="adminPassword" value="admin"/>
  <parameter name="sendXsiTypes" value="true"/>
  <parameter name="sendMultiRefs" value="true"/>
  <parameter name="sendXMLDeclaration" value="true"/>
  <requestFlow>
   <handler type="java:com.wrox.security.AddSignature">
    <parameter name="alias" value="client"/>
   </handler>
   <handler type="java:com.wrox.security.Encrypt"/>
  </requestFlow>
    <responseFlow>
      <handler type="java:com.wrox.security.Decrypt"/>
          <parameter name="mode" value="client"/>
      </handler>
      <handler type="java:com.wrox.security.ValidateSignature">
          <parameter name="mode" value="client"/>
      </handler>
    </responseFlow>
  </globalConfiguration>
```

Before we run our application, however, we need to generate the secret key with our new additions to `SecurityUtils.java`. Generate the key with the following commands:

```
cd [servlet_container]/webapps/axis/WEB-INF/classes
java com.wrox.security.SecurityUtils
```

Now we're set to run the application:

```
cd $TOMCAT_HOME/webapps/axis/WEB-INF/classes
java com.wrox.client.Client
```

Summary

In this case study, we've gone from a totally insecure web service to one that is secured through the use of the XML digital signature and XML Encryption APIs. These APIs are still evolving, as are all of the other XML Security APIs, but in this case study you've been able to see how they can be applied today, and to understand their use in a real-world application.

14

.NET Web Services: Case Study

The previous chapter contained a case study on building a secure web service in Java. The case study illustrated a fictional WROX Bank and its web services, enabling a customer to log in, retrieve the balances for the various accounts maintained with the bank, and transfer funds between these accounts.

Microsoft has been promoting its .NET Framework as a new computing platform that simplifies application development in the highly distributed environment of the Internet. In this chapter, we will see how a similar application can be developed in the .NET Framework, using ASP.NET Web Services as the basic building block. You will be shown the various options open to you to secure such applications.

However, before proceeding into the case study, let us first look at the .NET Framework and its significant advantages. Those of you who are already familiar with the Framework may skip the section entitled *Web Services Architecture of the Framework*, and jump directly to *Web Services Security Architecture*.

Web Service Framework Architecture

The major advantages of the .NET Framework are:

- ❑ A managed environment
- ❑ A type safe, protected security system
- ❑ A rich library
- ❑ Easy development
- ❑ Easy deployment
- ❑ Cross-language integration

The .NET Framework provides a collection of classes, called the Base Class Library, and tools to aid in the development and consumption of XML Web Service applications. XML Web Services are built on standards such as XML (an extensible data representation language) and are implemented in the XML vocabularies of SOAP (an object-based remote procedure-call protocol) and WSDL (the Web Services Description Language). The .NET Framework implementation of web services is built on these standards to promote interoperability with non-Microsoft solutions.

If we develop and publish our own web services, the .NET Framework provides a set of classes that conform to all the underlying communication standards, such as SOAP, WSDL, and XML. Using those classes enables us to focus on the logic of our service, without concerning ourselves with the communication infrastructure required by distributed software development.

Building a simple web service using ASP.NET is relatively straightforward. Web services created using ASP.NET conform to the XML Web Service standards, and this allows clients from other platforms to interoperate with them. As long as a client can send standards-compliant SOAP messages, formatted according to a service description, that client can invoke a .NET web service method, regardless of the platform on which the client resides. When we build a web service using ASP.NET, it automatically supports all clients that communicate using SOAP, and the HTTP-GET and HTTP-POST protocols.

Developing a web service using ASP.NET starts with the following steps:

❑ Create a file in the specified format and save it with an `.asmx` file name extension

❑ Within the file, declare the XML Web Service using an attribute

❑ Define the web service methods that compose the service's functionality

Web Services Security Architecture

The authentication and authorization options for ASP.NET applications are manifold. They can be broadly classified into three categories:

❑ Windows mode authentication.

❑ Custom authentication and authorization. In the case of Web Services, this consists of SOAP header-based authentication and authorization

❑ Forms mode authentication.

Of these three, Forms mode authentication is not supported for web services. This is a system by which unauthenticated requests are redirected to an HTML form using HTTP client-side redirection. Most clients of XML Web Services will not want to provide credentials using a UI. We will have to work around this, avoiding the logon form.

Windows mode authentication can take several forms:

❑ **Windows Basic**

Non-secure identification of clients uses this, as the username and password are sent in base64-encoded strings in plain text. Usernames and passwords are encoded, but not encrypted, in this type of authentication. A determined, malicious computer users equipped with a network-monitoring tool can intercept these.

❑ **Windows Basic over SSL**

This is used for secure identification of clients in the Internet scenarios. The username and password are transmitted over the network using Secure Sockets Layer (SSL) encryption, rather than plain encoded text. This is relatively easy to configure and works for the Internet. However, using SSL degrades performance and violates one of the basic tenets of the web service security specifications – a single round trip per message, rather than multiple round trips between client and server, which occurs during SSL.

❑ **Windows Digest**

This method is used for secure identification of clients over the Internet. It uses hashing to transmit client credentials in a secure fashion so that the password never transmits over plain text. In addition, digest authentication works through proxy servers, but it is not widely supported on all platforms.

Version 1 of the Framework provides very few security features specific to web services. However, the CLI enables a developer to create an adequate security infrastructure, with a rudimentary understanding of the various classes within the framework under the `System.Security`, `System.Security.Cryptography`, and `System.Security.Cryptography.Xml` namespaces.

For the purposes of this case study, we will create our application using Visual Studio .NET as the development platform. However, it is also possible to build ASP.NET web services using a simple text editor like Notepad.

Case Study: WROX Bank

We will be creating a web service for an imaginary bank, WROX Bank. The bank's customers automatically communicate with the bank through this web service and perform such tasks as checking the balance and transferring funds from one account to another. All of these are critical activities involving enormous security considerations. The customer application that uses the service will have to be securely authenticated.

The organization of the various parts of this case study will be in accordance with the three main aspects of the web service security specifications, which are:

❑ Credentials Transfer
❑ Message Confidentiality
❑ Message Integrity

Authentication and Credentials

The first section will be a lesson in how *not* to do something. Don't use this code in any of your final projects.

We first will build a rudimentary web service, without any element of security, and will examine the security loopholes that can be plugged in order to make the service secure. We also will build a client application using the .NET Framework. The client application will be a Windows Form application that allows the user to query the bank for a balance, or transfer funds to another account.

As a second step to show how *not* to do something, we will make the web service slightly more secure by introducing the HTTP Basic Authentication. For this process, the user needs a legitimate user account on the bank's server – a condition not practicable in the case of a bank with a large client base. For the client side, we will show you how to make use of this form of authentication.

For reliable security, we will then move to SOAP security. The SOAP specifications permit the transfer of metadata about SOAP messages through its message headers. We will create a web service that accepts these SOAP headers and authenticates users and passwords using this infrastructure. However, this will be a rudimentary form of credentials transfer, since our aim at this stage will be to demonstrate the use of SOAP headers, and security will not be our primary concern. We will also show how to extend the client application to support this authenticated web service.

Message Confidentiality

Thereafter, we will take up the task of fully securing the SOAP web service. This will show how we can use cryptography and encryption to secure the authentication process. To keep our progress smooth, we also will demonstrate the Message Confidentiality aspect of web service security. The implementation of these security mechanisms will occur at the message processing level, and they will not use any underlying SOAP extension mechanism for their implementation. We will see how easy it is to use complex cryptographic algorithms like DES and RSA, which are part of the inbuilt classes of the .NET Framework.

Message Integrity

Finally, we will explore the complex world of SOAP extensions – a mechanism available to developers in the SOAP specification to extend and enhance the quality of a SOAP web service. Here, we will implement a web service that enables the users to transfer their credentials in a secure way through SOAP headers and that provides for digital signing of the message using cryptographic hashing and signing techniques. The implementation will follow the web service security specifications as closely as possible within the limitations of version 1 of the .NET Framework.

This implementation will improve on the SOAP extensions and the SOAP extension processing capabilities of the .NET Framework, to present a modular and reusable solution using attributes – a powerful feature of the .NET Framework. Similarly for the client-side implementation of the web service, we will write a custom class, with which the process of digital signing can be hidden behind a compiled assembly to help enable ease of reuse and modularity.

The OpenService Web Service

Our first web service for WROX Bank will consist of two operations, encapsulated within method calls:

❑ GetAccountBalance(), which submits an account ID and a PIN (or password) as a string value and fetches the various child accounts held under that account ID. The balance of each account is identified by the given account ID as a **DataSet** (an in-memory cache of data).

❑ TransferMoney(), which receives as parameters an account ID, a PIN, a child account, and a destination child account ID as string values, and an amount as an integer value. The server completes this operation by transferring funds from the account identified by the account ID value, a sum equivalent to the amount received in the specified bank account.

To keep things simple, we will not implement any business logic for these transactions, and the web service will return only static values upon receipt of the request over the Web. However, within a session, the server will keep track of the moving balances in an account by storing the values in a cache.

The Web Service in a Web Browser

Once compiled and opened in a browser, the service looks as follows:

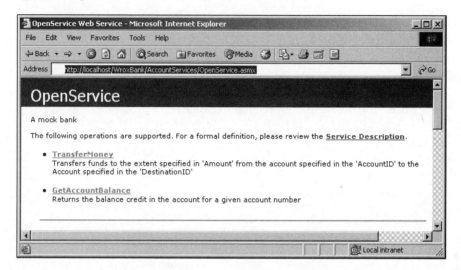

In ASP.NET, a web service is declared by placing a file with an .asmx extension in the appropriate virtual directory. This file should have the following declaration on top of the page:

```
<%@ WebService Language="C#" Class="AccountServices.OpenService"
               CodeBehind="OpenService.asmx.cs"%>
```

However, since we will be using the Visual Studio as our Integrated Development Environment (IDE), all we do is:

1. Open Visual Studio .NET

2. Select New Project

3. Click C# ASP.NET Web Service

4. Type in the name AccountServices as the name of the web service application and http://localhost/WROXBank/AccountServices as the application's virtual path. Obviously, if it isn't hosted on your local machine, then specify the URL of the machine to which to deploy it.

The IDE creates the virtual path in the local default web server and it creates a virtual subdirectory, AccountService, within the WROXBank virtual directory. It also creates a template web service class called Service1. Switch to the Code View of the web service, and you should see the various declarations, including the line shown above.

The first thing to do is to create a set of helper functions that will enable us to set up the child accounts of a customer in the WROX Bank and provide mechanisms for getting and setting the balances in these accounts.

To do that, add a new code file to the application by right-clicking the project and selecting to add a new Empty Code file item to the project. Call this file `AccountServicesHelper.cs`.

In the new file, add the following code lines:

```csharp
using System;
using System.Data; // for DataSet
using System.ComponentModel; // For Default Value Attribute

namespace AccountServices
{
  /// <summary>
  /// A helper class containing two static methods - one to create
  /// and fill a <c>DataSet</c> object with two dummy account numbers
  /// with dummy balances - another to extract a <c>DataRow</c> from
  /// a <c>DataSet</c> with given Row and Column Identifiers
  /// </summary>
  public class AccountServicesHelper
  {
    /// <summary>
    /// A static method to create and populate a <c>DataSet</c> object
    /// with a <c>DataTable</c> called "AccountInfo" containing two
    /// <c>DataColumn</c> objects called "SubAccountID" and "Balance"
    /// and two <c>DataRow</c> object containing dummy information
    /// for use in the imaginary WROXBank WebServices
    /// </summary>
    /// <returns>a <c>DataSet</c> object</returns>
```

The above lines declare the namespace and class, along with all the documentation.

```csharp
    public static DataSet CreateDataSet()
    {
      DataSet ds = new DataSet();
      DataTable dt = new DataTable("AccountInfo");

      DataColumn dc = new DataColumn("SubAccountID",typeof(string));
      dt.Columns.Add(dc);
      dc = new DataColumn("Balance",typeof(int));
      dt.Columns.Add(dc);

      DataRow dr = dt.NewRow();
      dr["SubAccountID"] = "2145B4567K-01";
      dr["Balance"] = 1500;
      dt.Rows.Add(dr);

      dr = dt.NewRow();
      dr["SubAccountID"] = "2145B4567K-02";
      dr["Balance"] = 3500;
      dt.Rows.Add(dr);

      ds.Tables.Add(dt);
      return ds;
    }
```

In the above code, the `CreateDataSet()` method creates a new `DataSet` object containing a `DataTable` called `AccountInfo`, which contains two rows of data about two sub accounts and their current balances. A DataSet is an in-memory representation of a database.

```
    /// <summary>
    /// A static method which returns a reference to a <c>DataRow</c>
    /// from a given <c>DataSet</c> and the unique identifiers of that row
    /// </summary>
    /// <param name="ds">the <c>DataSet</c> for which the <c>DataRow</c>
    /// is to be obtainied</param>
    /// <param name="TableName">Name of the <c>DataTable</c>
    /// containing the required <c>DataRow</c></param>
    /// <param name="UniqueRowID">A value with which to search for
    /// the required <c>DataRow</c> within the <c>DataTable</c></param>
    /// <param name="IDColumnName">The Name of the <c>DataColumn</c>
    /// which contains the <c>UniqueRowID</c></param>
    /// <returns>a <c>DataRow</c> containing the given
    /// parameters</returns>
    public static DataRow GetDataField(DataSet ds,
                                       string tableName,
                                       string uniqueRowID,
                                       string idColumnName)
    {
      return ds.Tables[tableName].Select(idColumnName + "='" +
          uniqueRowID + "'")[0];
    }
  }
}
```

The second method defined in the above code enables us to retrieve a particular row of data from the `DataSet` by specifying the `DataSet`, a table within it, the name of the key column, and the identifying value. It is equivalent to a `SELECT` statement in a database.

The next thing to do is rename the `Service1` object in Visual Studio .NET to `OpenService`. Add the following lines of code:

```
using System;
using System.Collections;
using System.ComponentModel;
using System.Data;
using System.Diagnostics;
using System.Web;
using System.Web.Services;

namespace AccountServices
{
  /// <summary>
  /// The First Version of the Demo <c>WebService</c>. This version has
  /// no Security
  /// in its operations.
  /// </summary>
  [WebService(Description="A mock bank")]
```

```
public class OpenService : System.Web.Services.WebService
{
  private DataSet ds;
  /// <summary>
  /// The default Constructor
  /// </summary>
  public OpenService()
  {
    //CODEGEN: This call is required by ASP.NET
    InitializeComponent();
    if (Application["2145B4567K"] == null)
    {
      ds = AccountServicesHelper.CreateDataSet();
      Application["2145B4567K"] = ds;
    }
  }
}
```

Please note that within the class definition, we have added a private field called `ds` of type `DataSet`. The default constructor of the web service has been modified. It first checks to see if the `Application` object (the `HttpApplicationState` property of the web service) contains a stored object called `2145B4567K`, which is the unique account number chosen for the client application. If such an object does not yet exist, calling the helper function shown earlier creates a new DataSet object. This `DataSet` is then stored in the `Application` object collection.

Then we add the following lines of code:

```
/// <summary>
/// Gets a <c>DataSet</c> object containing information about two
/// dummy Sub Accounts for a given Account No: 2145B4567K and PIN:
/// "4848"</summary>
[WebMethod(Description="Returns the balance credit in the " +
                      "account for a given account number")]
public DataSet GetAccountBalance(string accountID, string pin)
{
  if((accountID=="2145B4567K") && (pin=="4848"))
    return (DataSet) Application["2145B4567K"];
  else
    throw new ApplicationException("No Such Account Exists");
}
/// <summary>
/// Transfers money from one Sub Account to another
/// </summary>
[WebMethod(Description="Transfers funds to the extent specified " +
                      "in 'Amount' from the account specified in " +
                      "the 'AccountID' to the Account specified in " +
                      "the 'DestinationID'")]
public bool TransferMoney(string accountID, string pin,
                          string source, string destination,
                          int amount)
{
  if((accountID=="2145B4567K") && (pin=="4848"))
  {
    ds = (DataSet) Application["2145B4567K"];
```

```
        DataRow dr = AccountServicesHelper.GetDataField(
            ds,"AccountInfo",source,"SubAccountID");
        dr["Balance"] = (int)dr["Balance"] - amount;
        dr = AccountServicesHelper.GetDataField(
            ds,"AccountInfo",destination, "SubAccountID");
        dr["Balance"] = (int)dr["Balance"] + amount;
        return true;
      }
    else
      throw new ApplicationException("No such account exists");
    }
  }
}
```

What we see above are just two simple C# methods called `GetAccountBalance()` and `TransferMoney()`. By giving each of them an attribute called `WebMethod`, these simple class methods are transformed into web service methods. This is also because there was an attribute placed on the class declaration as follows:

```
[WebService(Description="A mock bank")]
public class OpenService : System.Web.Services.WebService
{
  ...
```

The description defines how the service should be described whenever the web service's entry point is called in a web browser. Besides the `Description` property, we may also specify some further properties within the `WebService` attribute, including the namespace URL of the web service.

The SOAP Messages for the Web Service

It is as simple as shown above to create a basic web service in the .NET Framework. If we hit the *F5* key in the Visual Studio .NET, the web service compiles into a DLL file called `AccountService.dll` and is placed in the `bin` sub directory of the virtual directory. The entry-point URL of the web service, http://localhost/WROXBank/AccountService/OpenService.asmx, opens in the browser and the page gives an introduction to the web service with the description previously added to it, and lists the two web methods. The SOAP messages necessary to call the two web methods are shown below:

```
POST /AccountServices/OpenService.asmx HTTP/1.1
Host: localhost
Content-Type: text/xml; charset=utf-8
Content-Length: length
SOAPAction: "http://tempuri.org/TransferMoney"

<?xml version="1.0" encoding="utf-8"?>
<soap:Envelope xmlns:xsi="http://www.w3.org/2001/XMLSchema-instance"
xmlns:xsd="http://www.w3.org/2001/XMLSchema"
xmlns:soap="http://schemas.xmlsoap.org/soap/envelope/">
  <soap:Body>
    <TransferMoney xmlns="http://tempuri.org/">
      <accountID>string</accountID>
      <pin>string</pin>
```

```
      <source>string</source>
      <destination>string</destination>
      <amount>int</amount>
   </TransferMoney>
  </soap:Body>
</soap:Envelope>
```

```
POST /AccountServices/OpenService.asmx HTTP/1.1
Host: localhost
Content-Type: text/xml; charset=utf-8
Content-Length: length
SOAPAction: "http://tempuri.org/GetAccountBalance"

<?xml version="1.0" encoding="utf-8"?>
<soap:Envelope xmlns:xsi="http://www.w3.org/2001/XMLSchema-instance"
               xmlns:xsd="http://www.w3.org/2001/XMLSchema"
               xmlns:soap="http://schemas.xmlsoap.org/soap/envelope/">
  <soap:Body>
    <GetAccountBalance xmlns="http://tempuri.org/">
      <accountID>string</accountID>
      <pin>string</pin>
    </GetAccountBalance>
  </soap:Body>
</soap:Envelope>
```

The web service will respond to either SOAP request in the following format. The one shown below is for the `TransferMoney()` method:

```
HTTP/1.1 200 OK
Content-Type: text/xml; charset=utf-8
Content-Length: length

<?xml version="1.0" encoding="utf-8"?>
<soap:Envelope xmlns:xsi="http://www.w3.org/2001/XMLSchema-instance"
               xmlns:xsd="http://www.w3.org/2001/XMLSchema"
               xmlns:soap="http://schemas.xmlsoap.org/soap/envelope/">
  <soap:Body>
    <TransferMoneyResponse xmlns="http://tempuri.org/">
      <TransferMoneyResult>boolean</TransferMoneyResult>
    </TransferMoneyResponse>
  </soap:Body>
</soap:Envelope>
```

We can see the headers for both methods in a web browser when we navigate to this service.

Creating a Client Application

Having created the web service, we will now turn our attention to creating a client application that enablest his web service to provide the customers of the WROX Bank with facilities such as account balance enquiry and funds transferal.

To do that in Visual Studio .NET, add a new Windows Form Application to the project and call it WROXClient. In the Form Designer window presented by the IDE, place various controls arranged as shown below, and name the form BankClientConsole:

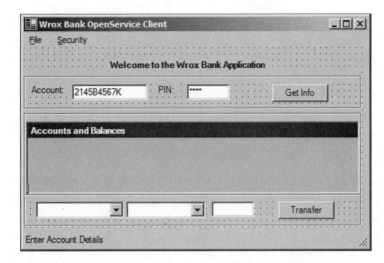

The following table lists all the components, their names, types, and other relevant properties, in the order in which they appear in their respective parent containers:

Control Type	Control Name	Other Relevant Properties
Form	WROXBankClient	Text: "WROX Bank Open Service Client" Contains MainMenu, lblCaption, grpInfo, grpDataGrid, grpTransfer, and StatusBar.
MenuItem	MainMenu	Contains mnuFile and mnuSecurity
MenuItem	mnuFile	Text: "&File" Contains mnuExit
MenuItem	mnuExit	Text: "E&xit"
MenuItem	mnuSecurity	Text: "&Security" Contains mnuNoSecurity, mnuHttpAuth, mnuSoapHeadAuth, mnuSoapEncrypt, mnuWSDKSecurity
MenuItem	mnuNoSecurity	Text: "No Security" Checked: "True"
MenuItem	mnuHttpAuth	Text: "HTTP Authentication"
MenuItem	mnuSoapHeadAuth	Text: "SOAP Header Authentication"
MenuItem	mnuSoapEncrypt	Text: "SOAP Encryption"

Table continued on following page

Control Type	Control Name	Other Relevant Properties
MenuItem	mnuWSDKSecurity	Text: "WSDK Security"
Label	lblCaption	Text: "Welcome to the WROX Bank Application"
GroupBox	grpInfo	Text: "" Contains lblAccount, txtAccount, lblPIN, txtPIN, and btnGetInfo
Label	lblAccount	Text: "Account:"
TextBox	txtAccount	Text:"2145B4567K"
Label	lblPIN	Text: "PIN:"
TextBox	txtPIN	Text:"4848" PasswordChar: "*"
Button	btnGetInfo	Text: "Get Info"
GroupBox	grpDataGrid	Text: "" Contains AccountInfoGrid
DataGrid	AccountInfoGrid	CaptionText: "Accounts and Balances" FlatMode: "True" ReadOnly: "True" BackgroundColor: "Silver" Dock: "Fill" PreferredColumnWidth: "200"
GroupBox	grpTransfer	Text: "" Visible: False Contains cmbSource, cmbDestination, txtMoney, and btnTransfer
ComboBox	cmbSource	Text: ""
ComboBox	cmbDestination	Text: ""
TextBox	txtMoney	Text: ""
Button	btnTransfer	Text: "Transfer"
StatusBar	StatusBar	Text: "Enter Account Details"

When we define the event handlers for the buttons and menu items, we will include the event handler code like this:

```
this.btnGetInfo.Click += new System.EventHandler(this.btnGetInfo_Click);
```

This is when the btnGetInfo_Click() method is defined elsewhere in the code and takes an Object and an EventArgs as parameters. You would include these handlers in the InitializeComponent() method ordinarily. Many of the menu items here won't be used until later when we develop this code further and improve its security.

Generating a Proxy for the Web Service

Now, we must write the code to expose the methods of the web service object. To do this, we must create a proxy class for the `OpenService` web service. In the Visual Studio .NET environment, right-click the **Web Reference** node in **Solution Explorer** and select **Add Web Reference**. In the **Add Web Reference** dialog box, type the URL of the web service mentioned above. The IDE will fetch the Web Service Description Language (WSDL) file of the web service and will show the various web methods available from the service. We must select to add a reference to the web service in our project. This action makes the IDE run the `wsdl.exe` .NET Framework tool and generates a file called `Reference.cs` within a newly-created `WebReferences/localhost` subdirectory. We may also manually create this file by running the following command line from within the **Project** folder:

```
> wsdl /language:cs /out:OpenService.cs http://localhost/WROXBank/Services/
  OpenService.asmx?wsdl
```

After generating the file `OpenServices.cs` manually, we must include it in the project through the **Solution Explorer** window, after selecting to **Show all files** through the **Project** menu.

This file contains the declaration of a public class object called `OpenService` under the `localhost` namespace. Obviously, you will want to alter the command line above (and perhaps the namespace in the generated `OpenService.cs` file) to match your web service.

Client Application

In the `WROXClient` class, add references to the `System.Configuration` and `System.Data` namespaces, and declare a variable called `OpenService` of `localhost.OpenService` type as follows:

```
private localhost.OpenService wsOpenService;
```

In the constructor, we also instantiate the variable as follows:

```
ServiceToUse = new localhost.OpenService();
ServiceToUse.Url = ConfigurationSettings.AppSettings["OpenService"];
```

Please note that the second line of the above code modifies the `Url` property of the proxy class generated by the WSDL tool by substituting it with a value given by the user in the configuration file of the project. The namespace of the service above may be different on your system depending on where your web service is located.

To specify this value in the configuration file, we must create one, if it does not exist. In the VS.NET environment, the configuration file for a windows application is called `app.config`. However, when using the .NET Framework SDK, the configuration file must be named with the name of the assembly file, with a `.config` extension added. For example, the configuration file for an application called `MyProgram.exe` should be called `MyProgram.exe.config`. When you work in the Visual Studio .NET environment, you must add your custom configuration values in a file called `app.config` and the IDE will generate an appropriately-named configuration file for the application. If the `app.config` file is not automatically generated by the IDE, you can create one by selecting **Add New Item** menu item in the Solution Explorer and selecting the **XML File** option. After we create our `app.config` file, we add the following lines of code to it:

```
<configuration>
  <appSettings>
    <add key="OpenService" value=
        "http://localhost/WROXBank/AccountServices/OpenService.asmx" />
  </appSettings>
</configuration>
```

In a configuration file in the .NET Framework, <appSettings> is a section where the custom configuration information can be stored as string values in name-value pairs. The syntax is shown above, and the key attribute stores the name of the configuration item, whereas the value attribute is its value. These are attributes of the <add> element. Remember also that XML is case-sensitive. The framework enables us to retrieve these values within code by using the "ConfigurationSettings" class's AppSetting static property.

We also want to define a DataSet object that will be bound to the DataGrid when we have retrieved the relevant data, so we should include this line:

```
private System.Data.DataSet ds;
```

We will also define an enumeration and a further field, which will be used later when we extend this service. The code is shown below:

```
private enum Services : int
{
    OpenService,
    HttpAuthenticationService,
    SOAPHeaderService,
    SOAPEncryptionService,
    MessageIntegrityService,
    WSDKService
}

private Services ServiceToUse;
```

The event handlers for the Click event of various UI controls on the form are declared below. The code to add the event handlers to the events is included here, although this code will normally be located in the same place the rest of the controls' properties are defined.

The Click event handler for the mnuExit menu is defined as follows:

```
#region Menu Items Click Event Handlers
this.mnuExit.Click += new System.EventHandler(this.mnuExit_Click);
private void mnuExit_Click(object sender, System.EventArgs e)
{
    Application.Exit();
}
```

The Click event handler for the nuNoSecurity menu item is:

```
this.mnuNoSecurity.Click += new EventHandler(this.mnuNoSecurity_Click);
private void mnuNoSecurity_Click(object sender, System.EventArgs e)
{
  for(int x = 0; x<mnuSecurity.MenuItems.Count; x++)
    mnuSecurity.MenuItems[x].Checked = false;
  mnuNoSecurity.Checked = true;
  this.wsOpenService = localhost.OpenService;
  this.Text = "WROX Bank OpenService Client";
}
```

The Click event handler for the btnGetInfo button is as follows:

```
this.btnGetInfo.Click += new EventHandler(this.btn_GetInfo_Click);
private void btnGetInfo_Click(object sender, System.EventArgs e)
{
  this.StatusBar.Text = "Contacting WROXBank. Please wait...";
  this.btnGetInfo.Enabled = false;

  switch (this.ServiceToUse)
  {
    case Services.OpenService:
      ds = this.GetInfo_OpenService();
      break;
    default:
      break;
  }

  if(ds == null)
  {
    this.btnGetInfo.Enabled = true;
    return;
  }

  this.statusBar1.Text = "Query Successful";
  this.AccountInfoGrid.SetDataBinding(ds,"AccountInfo");
  this.cmbSource.Items.Clear();
  this.cmbDestination.Items.Clear();

  foreach(DataRow dr in this.ds.Tables["AccountInfo"].Rows)
  {
    this.cmbSource.Items.Add(dr["SubAccountID"]);
    this.cmbDestination.Items.Add(dr["SubAccountID"]);
  }

  this.cmbSource.SelectedIndex = 0;
  this.cmbDestination.SelectedIndex = 1;
  this.grpTransfer.Visible = true;
  this.btnGetInfo.Enabled = true;
}
```

In the above code, the line containing the method call (`ds = this.GetInfo_OpenService();`) fetches a `DataSet` object. More information on this method call is shown later. The .NET Framework allows us to use data binding of controls to attach a `DataSet` to a `DataGrid` using the control's `SetDataBinding()` method, which takes the name of a `DataSet` and the name of a `DataTable` as its parameters. Besides populating the `DataGrid`, we also populate the two combo boxes by reading the `SubAccountID` of each row in the data table.

The `Click` event handler for the `btnTransfer` button is shown below:

```csharp
this.btnTransfer.Click += new EventHandler(this.btnTransfer_Click);
private void btnTransfer_Click(object sender, System.EventArgs e)
{
  int Amount = 0;
  this.btnTransfer.Enabled = false;
  try
  {
    Amount = int.Parse(this.txtMoney.Text);
  }
  catch
  {
    this.StatusBar.Text = "Please enter a numeric value "
        + "in the 'Amount' field";
    this.txtMoney.Text = String.Empty;
    this.btnTransfer.Enabled = true;
    this.txtMoney.Focus();
    return;
  }
```

In the above method, we first check to see if the user has filled in a numeric value in the **Amount** text box. This occurs by using the `Int32.Parse()` method. This method checks the user's current locale to permit them to write the number in the form consistent with their language and region (for instance, using commas or periods as thousands separators) and converts it into an integer type.

```csharp
if(this.cmbSource.SelectedItem == this.cmbDestination.SelectedItem)
{
  this.StatusBar.Text = "You cannot transfer any money "
      + "to the same Account";
  this.txtMoney.Text = String.Empty;
  this.btnTransfer.Enabled = true;
  this.cmbSource.Focus();
  return;
}

DataRow[] SelectedRows = this.ds.Tables["AccountInfo"].Select(
    "SubAccountID = '" + (string)this.cmbSource.SelectedItem + "'");
if((int)SelectedRows[0]["Balance"] < Amount)
{
  this.statusBar1.Text = "You don't have enough "
      + "funds to effect this transfer";
  this.txtMoney.Text = String.Empty;
  this.btnTransfer.Enabled = true;
  this.cmbSource.Focus();
  return;
}
```

We also check to ensure that the names of the source and destination accounts are not the same and that the current balance in the source account is higher than the amount to be transferred. We use this `DataRow` array again in the following code:

```
this.statusBar1.Text = "Contacting WROXBank. Please wait...";
bool success = false;
switch (this.ServiceToUse)
{
  case Services.OpenService:
    success = this.TransferMoney_OpenService(Amount);
    break;
  default:
    break;
}
```

After these checks, a call is made to another private method, `Transfer_OpenService()`, which returns a Boolean value indicating if the call was successful.

```
if (success)
{
  this.StatusBar.Text = "Transfer successful";
  SelectedRows = this.ds.Tables["AccountInfo"].Select(
      "SubAccountID = '" + (string)this.cmbSource.SelectedItem + "'");
  SelectedRows[0]["Balance"] = (int)SelectedRows[0]
      ["Balance"]-Amount;
  SelectedRows = this.ds.Tables["AccountInfo"].Select(
      "SubAccountID = '" +
      (string) this.cmbDestination.SelectedItem + "'");
  SelectedRows[0]["Balance"] = (int) SelectedRows[0]
      ["Balance"]+Amount;
}
else
  this.statusBar1.Text = "Transfer unsuccessful. "
      + "Please try again later";
  this.txtMoney.Text = "";
  this.txtMoney.Focus();
  this.btnTransfer.Enabled = true;
}
# endregion
```

On successful completion of the call, the status bar is set with an appropriate message and the values in the `Balance` column of the data grid are appropriately set. This is done by altering their values in the `DataSet` object, by accessing the corresponding fields, using the `Select()` method of the `DataTable` object – which was explained earlier.

Now we can see the private methods called by these event handlers. The first is shown below, `GetInfo_OpenService()`:

```
#region Get Account Info from Open Service
private DataSet GetInfo_OpenService()
{
  try
  {
    return this.wsOpenService.GetAccountBalance(this.txtAccount.Text,
                                                this.txtPIN.Text);
```

```
        }
        catch(Exception e)
        {
            MessageBox.Show(e.ToString());
            this.StatusBar.Text = e.Message;
            return null;
        }
    }
    #endregion
```

In the `return this.wsOpenService.GetAccountBalance();` line we call a method in the web service, just as we would call any other local method. Nothing needs be done regarding invoking the HTTP protocol, writing the SOAP Message, etc. All of these are taken care of by the .NET Framework. The method returns `null` if the web service failed to retrieve the required data (the .NET Framework automatically converts into a DataSet object if it succeeds).

Similarly, the code for transferring funds is as follows:

```
    #region Transfer Money with Open Service
    private bool TransferMoney_OpenService(int amount)
    {
        bool success = false;
        try
        {
            success = this.wsOpenService.TransferMoney(
                    this.txtAccount.Text, this.txtPIN.Text,
                    (string)this.cmbSource.SelectedItem,
                    (string)this.cmbDestination.SelectedItem, amount);
        }
        catch(Exception e)
        {
            MessageBox.Show(e.ToString());
            this.StatusBar.Text = e.Message;
        }
        return success;
    }
    #endregion
```

Pitfalls of our Web Service

Although this `OpenService` web service is quite easy to create and enables us produce an adequate client-side program for the user, easily overcoming all the complexities of accessing information from the web, it is a rather rudimentary web service, fraught with every known security risk. In terms of pure data validation, little data validation exists on the server, which means that someone could create a false client and perform operations that are not permitted, like transferring too much money from one account to the other. We won't worry about those yet, however.

The following are the common security risks posed by attackers, which also have a bearing on the web services:

Eavesdropping

In general, the majority of network communications occur in an unsecured or clear text format, which allows an attacker who has gained access to data paths in our network to "listen in" or interpret (read) the traffic. When an attacker is eavesdropping on our communications, it is referred to as sniffing or snooping. The ability of an eavesdropper to monitor the network is generally the biggest security problem that administrators face in an enterprise. Without strong encryption services, our data can be read by others as it traverses the network.

Data Modification

After an attacker has read our data, the next logical step is to alter it. An attacker can modify the data in the packet without the knowledge of the sender or receiver. Even if we do not require confidentiality for all communications, we do not want any of our messages to be modified in transit. For example, if we are exchanging purchase requisitions, we do not want the items, amounts, or billing information to be modified.

Identity Spoofing (IP Address Spoofing)

Most networks and operating systems use the IP address of a computer to identify a valid entity. In certain cases, it is possible for an IP address to be falsely assumed – known as identity spoofing. An attacker might also use special programs to construct IP packets that appear to originate from valid addresses inside the corporate intranet.

Man-in-the-Middle Attack

As the name indicates, a man-in-the-middle attack occurs when a third party is actively monitoring, capturing, and controlling our communication transparently. For example, the attacker can re-route a data exchange. Software may not be able to determine with whom he is exchanging data.

Man-in-the-middle attacks are like someone assuming our identity in order to read our message. The person on the other end might believe it is us because the attacker might be masquerading as us to keep the exchange going and to gain more information.

Sniffer Attack

A sniffer is an application or device that can read, monitor, and capture network data exchanges and read network packets. If the packets are not encrypted, a sniffer provides a full view of the data inside the packet. Even encapsulated (tunneled) packets can be broken open and read unless they are encrypted and the attacker does not have access to the key.

Using a sniffer, an attacker can do any of the following:

- Analyze the network and gain information to eventually cause the software to crash or to become corrupted
- Read our communications

Imagine that anyone who can understand SOAP and construct a web request in SOAP can learn your personal bank balance and even transfer money to any other account. The bank's web service does not even ask him for a user name or a password.

517

Creating and Configuring a Web Service for Basic HTTP Authentication in IIS

To know about HTTP Authentication we must first know about IIS Security.

IIS Authentication

IIS provides two main security features: filtering based on IP Address and Windows-based authentication.

IP/DNS Security

IP/DNS security means that IIS restricts or allows access to requests based upon the IP address or DNS of the requesting machine. This authentication is always the first to occur. This security can be set up for a directory or for individual files. In the IIS management console, we right click on the directory or file for which we wish to set the IP security settings. Select Properties, and on the Directory Security tab of the properties sheet, we will find a button to edit IP Address and Domain Name Restrictions. (Note that this option will only be available on server platforms; for workstations this button will be disabled.) From here, we can enter IP addresses or ranges, or domain names. We can make our list either inclusive or exclusive; that is, we can make it deny all connections except those addresses specified, or we can specifically deny addresses from a specific range.

We must keep in mind, however, that if we choose to enter domains names, IIS will have to perform a DNS lookup, a potentially expensive operation that could impact on the performance of the web service. Furthermore, if the DNS lookup fails, the client will be denied access to the site. Another point to consider is that if the clients are behind a proxy server or firewall, then only the proxy server's or firewall's IP address will be available. This will make it impossible to differentiate between these clients. One potential use for IP Security could be in a business-to-business (B2B) scenario, where we know in advance the IP addresses for the machines with which we will be interacting.

Windows Security

The next layer of security provided by IIS actually consists of several different techniques, but they are collectively referred to as Windows Authentication. These techniques are Basic, Digest, Integrated Windows, and Client Certificates. All of these methods rely on Windows User Accounts (which are stored in the Access Control List, or ACL); therefore, each user must have a valid Windows account. This requirement limits the usefulness of Windows security for sites open to the public.

These Windows security methods can be used with SSL if desired. However, the use of SSL can slow server response due to the overhead of encryption, especially if large amounts of data are returned to the client.

If we choose to open our application to users outside our immediate network, and implement a custom security solution, these Windows security options would generally not be used. However, one situation where these methods may be practical is in a B2B setting, where we are exchanging information with business partners/clients whose numbers are small enough to allow setting up accounts for these entities with limited rights, or where we can manage the use of client certificates.

Once IIS has authenticated the request, it will pass that request and an authentication token to the ASP.NET runtime. If the server is set to accept anonymous users, then the IUSR_machinename account will be passed as the authentication token; otherwise, a token for the authenticated user will be passed. Let's go on to create a new web service akin to the open service and try to secure it using the Windows mode authentication, disabling anonymous users.

Creating the Basic HTTP Authentication Service

To start with, using Windows Explorer, we will have to create a new subfolder within the WROXBank directory since we will be canceling "anonymous user" permission for this service. Then, in the Visual studio environment, using the Solution Explorer window, we must add a new web service project, specifying the newly created directory as the location of the project. This folder will be called MemberServices, implying that this service will be available only to members who have an account in the Domain's ACL. We will call the project HttpAuthenticationService.

In the HttpAuthenticationService.asmx.cs file, which is the CodeBehind file of the web service, created by the IDE, we may initially copy and paste the entire contents of OpenService.asmx.cs, taking care to change the name OpenService into HttpAuthenticationService. No further code needs be written.

After this, we will have to set up Basic IIS Security. To do this, using Windows Explorer, right-click on the MemberService folder and select the Properties | Sharing tab. Click open the Permissions dialog box, remove the Everyone permission granted by default and add permissions to selected Windows users, not forgetting to add our own account or that of another administrators group.

Then we open the IIS Console and navigate to the WROXBank/MemberServices entry in the directory tree. To set up a virtual directory to require Basic Authentication we need to:

- ❏ Go to the Properties | Directory Security | Edit Anonymous Access and Authentication control menu.
- ❏ Uncheck Anonymous Access.
- ❏ Enable Basic Authentication. We will see a warning message. Click OK to continue to use Basic Authentication.
- ❏ Click the Basic Authentication Edit button. Enter the domain name. Enter \ to use the default domain name.

That's all we need to do on the server side to set up a web service with Windows Basic Authentication. The SOAP messages sent to access this web service are similar to those of OpenService. However, on the client side we still have a few things to do.

Creating the Basic HTTP Authentication Client

You may remember that we had already created the UI components needed to extend our bank console application to be able to access the HttpAuthenticationService. We need to code the Click event for when the user clicks mnuHttpAuth:

```
    this.mnuHttpAuth.Click += new EventHandler(this.mnuHttpAuth_Click);
    private void mnuHttpAuth_Click(object sender, System.EventArgs e)
    {
      for(int i=0; i<mnuSecurity.MenuItems.Count; i++)
        mnuSecurity.MenuItems[i].Checked = false;
      mnuHttpAuth.Checked = true;
      this.ServiceToUse = Services.HttpAuthenticationService;
      this.Text = "WROX Bank HttpAuthenticationService Client";
    }
```

We now need to create a proxy object for this web service. We do this by adding a web reference in the
Solution Explorer window to the web address of the HTTP authentication service. The web service proxy
will be created under a subfolder by Visual Studio .NET. However, if we are to create the proxy ourselves,
we need to again invoke the wsdl.exe tool as explained earlier in the *Generating a Proxy for the Web Service*
section, and generate a C# source file, which should be placed within the same directory of the application
and added to the project. If you generate this file manually, give it sensible namespace, like localhost if
hosted locally, and save it. If this is generated from Visual Studio .NET, then it will be called localhost1
by default.

Next, we create a variable to represent the web service underneath that for wsOpenService:

```
    private localhost.HTTPAuthenticationService wsHttpAuthService;
```

Remember to change the namespace above if applicable for your service. We will then instantiate the web
service object within the constructor as follows:

```
    this.wsHttpAuthService = new localhost.HTTPAuthenticationService();
    wsHttpAuthService.Url =
        ConfigurationSettings.AppSettings["HttpAuthenticationService"];
```

Remember to add a new key-value pair to your configuration file, which looks as follows:

```
    <add key="HttpAuthenticationService" value=
  "http://localhost/WROXBank/MemberServices/HttpAuthenticationServices.asmx" />
```

The code for the Click event of the btnGetInfo button, which has already been written, will be
extended to handle the case where the user selects mnuHttpAuth. These lines are added to the
select block:

```
        case Services.HttpAuthenticationService:
          ds = this.GetInfo_HttpAuthenticationService();
          break;
```

Similarly, the following lines will be placed within the Click event handler of the btnTransfer button for
the transfer operation:

```
        case Services.HttpAuthenticationService:
          success = this.TransferMoney_HttpAuthenticationService(Amount);
          break;
```

The proxy object created by the WSDL tool is a class derived from the `SoapHttpClientProtocol` class in the `System.Web.Services` namespace of the .NET Framework class library. The base class contains a public property called `Credentials`, which is of the `CredentialCache` type found in the `System.Net` Namespace. This property will have to be set to inform the web service proxy to carry the Windows credentials of the user in the HTTP header of every message sent through the proxy. To do this, we will include the following lines in the `GetInfo_HttpAuthenticationService()` private method. This method will be listed in full shortly.

```
CredentialCache cc = new CredentialCache();
string domainName = System.Net.Dns.GetHostName();
NetworkCredential credential =
    new NetworkCredential(this.txtAccount.Text, this.txtPIN.Text,
                          domainName);
cc.Add(new Uri(this.wsHttpAuthService.Url),"Basic", credential);
this.wsHttpAuthService.Credentials = cc;""
```

The `CredentialCache` is a collection object that holds objects of the type `NetworkCredential`. The constructor of the `NetworkCredential` object takes three string parameters – the username, the password, and the domain. While the username and password are entered by the user in the text boxes, we will get the domain name using the static `GetHostName()` method, available in the `System.Net.Dns` class. Once we have created the `NetworkCredential` object we add it to the `CredentialCache` using its `Add()` method. To do all this, we also need to reference the `System.Net` namespace at the top of the code for the client:

```
using System.Net;
```

Having done this, the code for sending the web request will be as follows:

```
#region Get Account Info from Http Authentication Service
private DataSet GetInfo_HttpAuthenticationService()
{
   CredentialCache cc = new CredentialCache();
   string domainName = System.Net.Dns.GetHostName();
   NetworkCredential credential =
       new NetworkCredential(this.txtAccount.Text, this.txtPIN.Text,
                             domainName);
   cc.Add(new Uri(this.wsHttpAuthService.Url),"Basic", credential);
   this.wsHttpAuthService.Credentials = cc;

   try
   {
      return wsHttpAuthService.GetAccountBalance(this.txtAccount.Text
                                                 this.txtPIN.Text);
   }
   catch(Exception e)
   {
      MessageBox.Show(e.ToString());
      this.StatusBar.Text = e.Message;
      return null;
   }
}
#endregion
```

Similarly, we add the following code to transfer funds:

```
#region Transfer Money with Http Authentication
private bool TransferMoney_HttpAuthenticationService(int amount)
{
  bool success = false;
  try
  {
    success = this.wsHttpAuthService.TransferMoney(
        this.txtAccount.Text, this.txtPIN.Text
        (string)this.cmbSource.SelectedItem,
        (string)this.cmbDestination.SelectedItem,
        amount);
  }
  catch(Exception e)
  {
    MessageBox.Show(e.ToString());
    this.StatusBar.Text = e.Message;
  }
  return success;
}
#endregion
```

When the user runs the program and presses the btnGetInfo after selecting **Basic HTTP Authentication**, a SOAP message is sent to the server, which looks as follows if the authentication fails:

```
REQUEST:  POST
http://localhost/WROXBank/MemberServices/HttpAuthenticationService.asmx?op=GetAcco
untBalance HTTP/1.0
RESPONSE: HTTP/1.1 401 Access Denied
DATE: 14-Nov-02 3:04:07 PM GMT

Accept: image/gif, image/x-xbitmap, image/jpeg, image/pjpeg, application/vnd.ms-
excel, application/vnd.ms-powerpoint, application/msword, */*
Accept-Language: hi
Authorization: Basic VXNlck5hbWU6cGFzc3dvcmQ=
User-Agent: Mozilla/4.0 (compatible; MSIE 6.0; Windows NT 5.0; .NET CLR 1.0.3705)
Host: localhost
Proxy-Connection: Keep-Alive
```

The credentials are sent in the Authorization: line, and are the base64-encoded value of the login name and password, separated by a colon.

Pitfalls of Basic HTTP Authentication

Basic authentication is very insecure. The username and password are sent base64-encoded over the wire without encryption. The problem is not only that an attacker can get to a resource secured by Basic authentication, but also that the attacker gets the actual values of our user name and password and can use them to access other secure resources. However, basic authentication is a part of the HTTP 1.0 protocol and is the most widely supported authentication scheme.

Encryption is the only foolproof way of sending one's credentials over the Web. To do that in a web service scenario, we must select the custom authentication model, which requires that the credentials be sent either in the body of the SOAP message or in its headers.

We will next learn how to send SOAP headers by constructing a simple web service that accepts the username and password in clear text sent via these SOAP headers.

Creating and Configuring a Web Service for SOAP Headers

Create a new web service project and give its name as **SOAP Header Service** in the dialog box. Rename the default web service, Service1, to SOAPHeaderService. The code from the OpenService.asmx.cs is copied and pasted and ensures that all occurrences of OpenService within this file are changed to SOAPHeaderService.

In the .NET Framework library, a class object called SoapHeader is available in the System.Web.Services.Protocols namespace. This is the class used for creating any SOAP headers.

For the sake of code modularity, we will define our SOAP header in a separate file, called AccountServicesHelper.cs. The code for creating the "credentials" header object will be as follows:

```
using System;
using System.ComponentModel;
using System.Web.Services.Protocols

public class Credentials :System.Web.Services.Protocols.SoapHeader
{
  public string AccountID;
  public string PIN;
}
```

In the SOAPHeaderService.asmx.cs file, this header object is instantiated as a public global class variable as follows:

```
    public Credentials token;
```

We then modify our web methods to check for the credentials of the user as follows:

```
    [WebMethod(Description="Returns the balance credit in the account "
        + "for a given account number")]
    [SoapHeader("token", Direction = SoapHeaderDirection.In)]
    public DataSet GetAccountBalance()
    {
      if ((token.AccountID == "2145B4567K")&&(token.PIN=="4848"))
        return (DataSet) Application["2145B4567K"];
      else
        throw new ApplicationException("Authentication Failed");
    }

    [WebMethod(Description = "Transfers funds to the extent specified "
        + "in 'Amount' from the account specified in the 'AccountID' to "
        + "the Account specified in the 'DestinationID'")]
```

523

```
    [SoapHeader("token", Direction = SoapHeaderDirection.In)]
    public bool TransferMoney(string Source, string Destination, int Amount)
    {
      if((token.AccountID == "2145B4567K")&&(token.PIN =="4848"))
      {
        ds = (DataSet)Application["2145B4567K"];
        DataRow dr = AccountServicesHelper.GetDataField(
            ds,"AccountInfo",Source,"SubAccountID");
        dr["Balance"] = (int)dr["Balance"] - Amount;
        dr = AccountServicesHelper.GetDataField(
            ds,"AccountInfo",Destination,"SubAccountID");
        dr["Balance"] = (int)dr["Balance"] + Amount;
        return true;
      }
      else
        throw new Exception("Authentication Failed");
    }
```

For the sake of simplicity, we still make the service accept only one account ID one PIN. We have placed a special attribute below the standard WebMethod attribute explained earlier:

```
[SoapHeader("token", Direction=SoapHeaderDirection.In)]
```

This attribute is the SOAP header attribute and tells the WSDL generator of the web service that the web service contract should include a clause that users of the service are expected to send a SOAP header to the service of the Credentials type, to which the variable token belongs. The second property added in the SOAP header attribute is the direction of the header. The direction is provided through the System.Web.Services.Protocols.SoapHeaderDirection enumeration. The SoapHeaderDirection can be one of In (for inward messages), Out (for outward messages), or InOut (for both).

The SOAP message format for the inward message for the GetAccountBalance() operation should be as follows, if placed within a Services virtual web folder:

```
POST /WROXBank/Services/SOAPHeaderService.asmx HTTP/1.1
Host: localhost
Content-Type: text/xml; charset=utf-8
Content-Length: length
SOAPAction: "http://tempuri.org/GetAccountBalance"

<?xml version="1.0" encoding="utf-8"?>
<soap:Envelope xmlns:xsi="http://www.w3.org/2001/XMLSchema-instance"
               xmlns:xsd="http://www.w3.org/2001/XMLSchema"
               xmlns:soap="http://schemas.xmlsoap.org/soap/envelope/">
  <soap:Header>
    <Credentials xmlns="http://tempuri.org/">
      <AccountID>string</AccountID>
      <PIN>string</PIN>
    </Credentials>
  </soap:Header>
  <soap:Body>
    <GetAccountBalance xmlns="http://tempuri.org/" />
  </soap:Body>
</soap:Envelope>
```

The format for the return value will be as follows:

```
HTTP/1.1 200 OK
Content-Type: text/xml; charset=utf-8
Content-Length: length

<?xml version="1.0" encoding="utf-8"?>
<soap:Envelope xmlns:xsi="http://www.w3.org/2001/XMLSchema-instance"
               xmlns:xsd="http://www.w3.org/2001/XMLSchema"
               xmlns:soap="http://schemas.xmlsoap.org/soap/envelope/">
  <soap:Body>
    <GetAccountBalanceResponse xmlns="http://tempuri.org/">
      <GetAccountBalanceResult>
        <xsd:schema>schema</xsd:schema>
        xml
      </GetAccountBalanceResult>
    </GetAccountBalanceResponse>
  </soap:Body>
</soap:Envelope>
```

The messages for the `TransferMoney()` operation will look like this:

```
POST /WROXbank/services/SOAPHeaderService.asmx HTTP/1.1
Host: localhost
Content-Type: text/xml; charset=utf-8
Content-Length: length
SOAPAction: "http://tempuri.org/TransferMoney"

<?xml version="1.0" encoding="utf-8"?>
<soap:Envelope xmlns:xsi="http://www.w3.org/2001/XMLSchema-instance"
               xmlns:xsd="http://www.w3.org/2001/XMLSchema"
               xmlns:soap="http://schemas.xmlsoap.org/soap/envelope/">
  <soap:Header>
    <Credentials xmlns="http://tempuri.org/">
      <AccountID>string</AccountID>
      <PIN>string</PIN>
    </Credentials>
  </soap:Header>
  <soap:Body>
    <TransferMoney xmlns="http://tempuri.org/">
      <Source>string</Source>
      <Destination>string</Destination>
      <Amount>int</Amount>
    </TransferMoney>
  </soap:Body>
</soap:Envelope>
HTTP/1.1 200 OK
Content-Type: text/xml; charset=utf-8
Content-Length: length
```

```
<?xml version="1.0" encoding="utf-8"?>
<soap:Envelope xmlns:xsi="http://www.w3.org/2001/XMLSchema-instance"
               xmlns:xsd="http://www.w3.org/2001/XMLSchema"
               xmlns:soap="http://schemas.xmlsoap.org/soap/envelope/">
  <soap:Body>
    <TransferMoneyResponse xmlns="http://tempuri.org/">
      <TransferMoneyResult>boolean</TransferMoneyResult>
    </TransferMoneyResponse>
  </soap:Body>
</soap:Envelope>
```

Creating the Client for the SOAPHeaderService

On the client side, a proxy class is added to the project in the usual manner. This class is declared within the WROXClient class as follows:

```
private localhost.SOAPHeaderService wsSoapheaderService;
```

Then it is instantiated in the constructor with the following code:

```
this.wsSoapheaderService = new localhost.SOAPHeaderService();
wsSoapheaderService.Url =
    ConfigurationSettings.AppSettings["SOAPHeaderService"];
```

However, this time there is a difference in the proxy class file generated by the WSD1.exe tool. If you open the file containing the proxy class, you will see the following difference. Besides the usual class for the proxy object containing the name of the web service itself, there is a new class declaration for the Credentials class, the one created in the server, as explained a few paragraphs previously.

The WSDL tool created this code, since it found the following additional lines of XML in the WSDL file generated by the server for this web service:

```
<types>
  <s:element name="Credentials" type= "s0:Credentials" />
    <s:complexType name="Credentials">
      <s:sequence>
        <s:element minOccurs="0" maxOccurs="1" name="AccountID"
                   type="s:string" />
        <s:element minOccurs="0" maxOccurs="1" name="PIN"
                   type="s:string" />
      </s:sequence>
    </s:complexType>
  <s:element name="Credentials" type="s0:Credentials" />
</types>
```

This is how the WSDL file generated by ASP.NET conveys the structure of the class declared in the server code, by the process of XML serialization.

The code for accessing the web service, after creating and populating the SOAP header, is as follows:

```
#region Get Account Info from SOAP Header Service
private DataSet GetInfo_SOAPHeaderService()
{
  localhost.Credentials token = new localhost.Credentials();
  token.AccountID = this.txtAccount.Text;
  token.PIN = this.txtPIN.Text;
  wsSoapheaderService.CredentialsValue = token;
  try
  {
    return wsSoapheaderService.GetAccountBalance();
  }
  catch (Exception e)
  {
    MessageBox.Show(e.ToString());
    this.StatusBar.Text = e.Message;
    return null;
  }
}
#endregion
```

Here, we first instantiate an instance of the `Credentials` class and populate it with the `AccountID` and `PIN` entered by the user. This object is then added to the proxy class by assigning it to the `CredentialsValue` property. The naming of this property occurs automatically through the WSDL tool by combining the word "Value" to its assigned type name – `Credentials`.

All that's left to do are the other usual changes for the `Click` handlers and for the `TransferMoney_SoapHeaderAuthenticationService()`. These are predictable and so little has been added here. There are a few differences in the transfer method, as shown below:

```
bool success = false;
try
{
    success = this.wsSoapHeaderService.TransferMoney(
        (string)this.cmbSource.SelectedItem,
        {string{this.cmbDestination.SelectedItem,
        amount);
}
```

As the credentials are already part of the `wsSoapHeaderService` object, we don't need to explicitly add them again. The other changes are straightforward and are included in the code download from this chapter

Cryptography and Web Services

All this while, we have been getting to know how to create a web service, how to use HTTP mode authentication for a web service, and how to create and use SOAP headers in the .NET Framework. Now, we move on to the more serious business of securing our web services in a foolproof way using cryptography.

The .NET Framework comes with numerous cryptography-related classes in the following namespaces:

- ❑ `System.Security.Cryptography`
- ❑ `System.Security.Cryptography.X509Certificate`
- ❑ `System.Security.Cryptography.Xml`

Cryptographic Algorithms in .NET

There are basically three types of cryptographic algorithms, as you have read in this book. These are symmetric cryptography algorithms, asymmetric cryptography algorithms, and hash algorithms. The .NET Framework defines an abstract base class for each of these three algorithms, to enable further development of specific implementations of the cryptographic systems. The Framework also emphasizes stream-oriented encryption, decryption, and hashing, by providing an `ICryptoStream` interface. All these abstract classes and interfaces are defined in the `System.Security.Cryptography` namespace. You will need to familiarize yourself with these concepts of the Framework to use cryptography for encrypting and decrypting SOAP messages. The following paragraphs discuss the basic design of cryptography in the Framework.

Stream Oriented Design

The CLR uses a stream-oriented design for implementing symmetric and hash algorithms for cryptography. The core of this design is `CryptoStream`, a class that derives from the `Stream` class. Stream-based cryptographic objects all support a single standard interface (`ICryptoStream`) for handling the data transfer portion of the object. Because all of the objects are built on a standard interface, we can chain together multiple objects (such as a hash object followed by an encryption object), and we can perform multiple operations on the data without needing any intermediate storage for it. The streaming model also allows us to build objects from smaller objects. For example, a combined encryption and hash algorithm is seen as a single stream object, even though this object could be constructed from several stream objects.

Symmetric Algorithms

Typically, private-key algorithms, called block ciphers, are used to encrypt one block of data at a time. If we want to encrypt or decrypt a sequence of bytes, we have to do it block by block. Because the size of n is small ($n = 8$ bytes for RC2, DES, and TripleDES, or $n = 32$ bytes for Rijndael), values larger than n have to be encrypted one block at a time.

The block cipher or symmetric algorithm classes provided in the base class library use a chaining mode called **Cipher Block Chaining** (**CBC**), which uses a key and an Initialization Vector (**IV**) to perform cryptographic transformations on data. For a given private key, a simple block cipher that does not use an initialization vector will encrypt the same input block of plaintext into the same output block of cipher text. To combat this problem, information from the previous block is mixed into the process of encrypting the next block. Thus, the output of two identical plaintext blocks is different. Because this technique uses the previous block to encrypt the next block, an IV is used to encrypt the first block of data. Using this system, common message headers that might be known to an unauthorized user cannot be used to deduce a key.

Use of a symmetric algorithm requires that the sender and the receiver only know the secret key and the IV. In the .NET Framework, `DESCryptoServiceProvider`, `RC2CryptoServiceProvider`, and `TripleDESCryptoServiceProvider` are implementations of symmetric algorithms.

Asymmetric Algorithms

Over the Web, where the customer and shop owners are complete strangers, there is no way of having a common secret key. The .NET Framework provides the following classes to implement public key encryption algorithms:

- ❑ `DSACryptoServiceProvider` – for digital signing

- ❑ `RSACryptoServiceProvider` – for encryption as well as for signing

In the .NET Framework, numerous abstract classes define cryptographic services. Apart from these abstract classes, the Framework also provides limited implementation of these abstract classes. A cryptographic service is always associated with a particular algorithm or type, and it provides cryptographic operations (like those for digital signatures or message digests), generates them, or supplies the cryptographic material (keys or parameters) required for cryptographic operations.

Hashing Algorithms

Hashing algorithms map data of any length to a fixed-length and unique byte sequence. Therefore, when class objects or other kind of type data is serialized into bytes, they can be made to represent themselves in cryptographic hashes to identify their uniqueness. **Message Authentication Code** (**MAC**) hash functions are commonly used with digital signatures to sign data, while **Message Detection Code** (**MDC**) hash functions are used for data integrity.

The .NET Framework provides the following classes that implement hashing algorithms:

- ❑ `HMACSHA1`

- ❑ `MACTripleDES`

- ❑ `MD5CryptoServiceProvider`

- ❑ `SHA1`

- ❑ `SHA256`

- ❑ `SHA384`

- ❑ `SHA512`

Using Cryptography in Message Encryption

Since cryptography is a costly operation, encrypting the whole of a SOAP message could become a very expensive operation. Therefore, the proponents of WS-Security specify encryption of the important data alone. In addition, since web services are available over the Internet, and exchange of information takes place mostly between two unrelated and unseen parties, there can be no common acceptable key shared between them. Therefore, as mentioned earlier, we use asymmetric cryptography, at least to exchange the common key for any symmetric algorithm used. Since the asymmetric cryptography is several times more resource-intensive than its symmetric sibling, it will be prudent to do the bulk of encryption and decryption using a symmetric algorithm and only use the asymmetric algorithm for the encryption of the shared key.

Finally, it will be our objective to ensure each operation has only one round trip between the server and the client. We will also try to keep the cryptographic information as metadata rather than making it primary data for the operation, so that the processing of the metadata is segregated from the core implementation of the operation. However, for the sake of simplicity, in this first model we will not modularize the processing of the cryptographic data from the core processing operation, and this topic is discussed in the next section of this chapter.

Creating the SOAP Encryption Web Service

Create the web service in the usual manner and call it SoapEncryptionService and rename the .asmx file to SoapEncryptionService. Initially, we just copy and paste the contents of the SoapHeaderService.asmx.cs into the SoapEncryptionService.asmx.cs file, taking care to change the name of the class and the constructor definition from SOAPHeaderService to SOAPEncryptionService.

Extending the Credentials Object

Earlier in this chapter, we created a class object called Credentials derived from the base class SoapHeader. That object contained just two public fields – AccountID and PIN. To enable the cryptographic key exchange and other data relevant for encryption, we will extend the class definition by adding a few more lines of code as follows:

```
using System;
using System.ComponentModel;

public class Credentials :System.Web.Services.Protocols.SoapHeader
{
  public string AccountID;
  public string PIN;
  public bool IsPINEncrypted;
  public bool AreParametersEncrypted;
  public string[] EncryptedParameterNames;
  public bool RequireEncryptedResponse;
  public string EncryptionMethod;
  public KeyInformation KeyInfo;

  public Credentials()
  {
    KeyInfo = new KeyInformation();
  }
}
```

These fields will form part of the SOAP header sent by the client application to the server to enable to process the encrypted tokens and parameters. Before we see what the KeyInformation type represents, we need to generate a key pair for the server's permanent use. Look at the following simple application:

```
// Compile using: csc /r:System.dll,System.Security.dll InitializeRSA.cs
using System;
using System.Security.Cryptography;
using System.IO;

class InitializeRSA
{
  [STAThread]
```

```
static void Main(string[] args)
{
  if(args.Length==0)
    Create("MyKey.xml", "MyPublicKey.xml");
  else
  {
    if(args.Length != 2)
    {
      string assemblyLocation = typeof(InitializeRSA).Assembly.Location;
      int substringPosition = assemblyLocation.LastIndexOf('\\');
      Console.WriteLine("Usage: {0} <secretkeyfile> <publickeyfile>",
          assemblyLocation.Substring(substringPosition + 1);
    }
    else
      Create(args[0], args[1]);
  }
}

static void Create(string keyPairFileName, string publicKeyFileName)
{
  try
  {
    RSACryptoServiceProvider rsa = new RSACryptoServiceProvider();
    string keypair = rsa.ToXmlString(true);
    StreamWriter sw = new StreamWriter(keyPairFileName);
    sw.Write(keypair);
    sw.Flush();
    sw.Close();
    sw = new StreamWriter(publicKeyFileName);
    string publickey = rsa.ToXmlString(false);
    sw.Write(publickey);
    sw.Flush();
    sw.Close();
  }
  catch(Exception e)
  {
    Console.WriteLine(e.ToString());
  }
}
```

What we see above is a simple console program that generates two XML files called `MyKey.xml` and `MyPublicKey.xml`, if no arguments are used. The code first initializes an instance of the `RSACryptoServiceProvider` class. It then extracts its public key and the public-private key pair using the method `ToXmlString()` available in the `RSACryptoServiceProvider` class. The Boolean parameter of the `ToXmlString()` method specifies if the output key contains the private portion of the key as well.

This will be our web service's permanent encryption key pair and we will use these keys within our code. There should be no need to stress the importance of keeping the generated XML files away from prying eyes. Once the program is completed and the web service is put into production, we must destroy or lock away the key pair file, since the full key pair value will then be hard coded into the web service's class file.

The public key will be embedded into the WSDL file and since the secret key is kept secret, only the server hosting the web service can decrypt any encoded message.

Passing the Public Key to the Client Application

Having created a permanent key pair for our server using the command line utility InitializeRSA, we need to pass on the public portion of the key to the WSDL contract of the web service. Therefore, we create a KeyInformation class object as follows:

```
public class KeyInformation
{
  public string EncryptedKey;

  [DefaultValue("<RSAKeyValue><Modulus>rsegppYiztg+sUuiXIxlec3h5gzQyvXZiX+vI
ejTxctNVzDht82U4fzknOfRrDdLuFxmqdp63P9waJHR8Ur7jzMLDecYq9QEBJVMjHrd3CrrUUgyLySbrsu
py1YMwMAppw1CUOpjM3qwQ1Xag+I8w0JxRPQthFmN249LHeLqYjc=</Modulus><Exponent>AQAB</Exp
onent></RSAKeyValue>")]
  public string EncryptionPublicKey;
}
```

It is just a simple object containing two string fields – EncryptedKey for the client to pass on the encrypted, symmetric session key with which the data will be encrypted, and EncryptionPublicKey for passing the public key to the client. This occurs by setting a DefaultValue attribute on the field declaration, and the public key's XML string form is hardcoded as the default value. You will enter the public key generated when you ran the InitializeRSA tool here.

The KeyInfo class appears in the SOAP header declared as Credentials. Its public field KeyInfo is of the KeyInformation type. See what occurs when you look at the WSDL generated:

```
<types>
  <s:schema elementFormDefault="qualified"
           targetNamespace="http://tempuri.org/">
    <s:element name="Credentials" type="s0:Credentials" />
      <s:complexType name="Credentials">
        <s:sequence>
          ...
            <s:element minOccurs="0" maxOccurs="1" name="KeyInfo"
                    type="s0:KeyInformation" />
        </s:sequence>
      </s:complexType>
    ...
    <s:complexType name="KeyInformation">
      <s:sequence>
        <s:element minOccurs="0" maxOccurs="1" name="EncryptedKey"
        type="s:string" />
        <s:element minOccurs="0" maxOccurs="1"
        default="<RSAKeyValue><Modulus>rsegppYiztg+sUuiX
        Ixlec3h5gzQyvXZiX+vIejTxctNVzDht82U4fzknOfRrDdLuFxmqdp63P
        9waJHR8Ur7jzMLDecYq9QEBJVMjHrd3CrrUUgyLySbrsupy1YMwMAppw1
        CUOpjM3qwQ1Xag+I8w0JxRPQthFmN249LHeLqYjc=</Modulus><Exponent>
        AQAB</Exponent></RSAKeyValue>" name="EncryptionPublicKey"
        type="s:string" />
      </s:sequence>
    </s:complexType>
  </s:schema>
</types>
```

When we generate the proxy class file using the WSDL tool, the code for the proxy class definition (in the file `Reference.cs`) incorporates the default value and so the public key is incorporated into the client code:

```
[System.Xml.Serialization.XmlTypeAttribute(Namespace=
    "http://tempuri.org/")]
public class KeyInformation
{
    public string EncryptedKey;

    public string SigningKey;

    [System.ComponentModel.DefaultValueAttribute("<RSAKeyValue><Modulus>r
segppYiztg+sUuiXIxlec3h5gzQyvXZiX+vIejTxctNVzDht82U4fzknOfRrDdLuFxmqdp63P9waJHR8Ur
7jzMLDecYq9QEBJVMjHrd3CrrUUgyLySbrsupy1YMwMAppw1CUOpjM3qwQ1Xag+I8w0JxRPQthFmN249Lh
eLqYjc=</Modulus><Exponent>AQAB</Exponent></RSAKeyValue>")]
    public string EncryptionPublicKey = <RSAKeyValue><Modulus>rsegppYiztg+
sUuiXIxlec3h5gzQyvXZiX+vIejTxctNVzDht82U4fzknOfRrDdLuFxmqdp63P9waJHR8Ur7jzMLDecYq9
QEBJVMjHrd3CrrUUgyLySbrsupy1YMwMAppw1CUOpjM3q"wQ1Xag+I8w0JxRPQthFmN249LHeLqYjc=</M
odulus><Exponent>AQAB</Exponent>";
}
```

Thus, we successfully transmit the public key information of the server to every client using the web service. You'll see this in action when we create the client code

Creating the GetAccountBalance() Method

In the `SoapEncryptionService` web service, opening the `SoapEncryptionService.asmx.cs` file, we modify the `GetAccountBalance()` method as follows:

```
[WebMethod(Description="Returns the balance credit in the account for "
    + "a given account number") ]
[SoapHeader("token", Direction=SoapHeaderDirection.In, Required=false)]
public DataSet GetAccountBalance()
{
    this.CheckCredentials();
    ds = (DataSet)Application["2145B4567K"];
    DataSet retVal = ds.Copy();
    if (token.RequireEncryptedResponse)
    {
        this.EncryptReturnValues(retVal);
    }
    return retVal;
}
```

The method first calls the `CheckCredentials()` method, which can call the `DecryptString()` method. If an encrypted response is required, it then calls the `EncryptReturnValues()` method on the return value before returning it. This method is shown shortly. The code for `CheckCredentials()` and `DecryptString()` is shown below:

```
private void CheckCredentials()
{
    if(this.token.AccountID != "2145B4567K")
        throw new ApplicationException("Authentication Failed");
    if(this.token.IsPINEncrypted)
        this.token.PIN = DecryptString(token.PIN);
```

```
    if(token.PIN != "4848")
        throw new ApplicationException ("Authentication Failed");
}

DESCryptoServiceProvider des;
private string DecryptString(string input)
{
    if(this.des==null)
    {
        System.Security.Cryptography.CspParameters param =
            new CspParameters();
        param.Flags = CspProviderFlags.UseMachineKeyStore;
        RSACryptoServiceProvider rsa =
            new RSACryptoServiceProvider(param);
        rsa.FromXmlString("<RSAKeyValue> ... </RSAKeyValue>");
```

The code is straightforward; CheckCredentials() just ensures that the credentials are fine, throwing an exception if not. If des is not defined yet, then a CspParameters object is created here. This is because under the security settings of ASP.NET, we cannot create a new crypto object from the private key; the RsaCryptoServiceProvider will prevent the restricted ASP.NET user from doing so. We work around this by creating a new CspParameter object, setting it to use the machine store, and then passing this parameter to the RSACryptoServiceProvider object on construction. Without this, a CryptographicException would be thrown on construction.

The last line of code has to be coded differently for every system. You need to copy and paste the value contained in the XML public-private key pair, between and including the <RSAKeyValue> tags, and enter it here. This ties the service to a specific key pair.

```
        byte[] _SessionKey = Convert.FromBase64String(
            token.KeyInfo.EncryptedKey);
        byte[] SessionKey = rsa.Decrypt(_SessionKey, false);
        des = new DESCryptoServiceProvider();
        des.Key = SessionKey;
        des.IV = new byte[]{ 0, 0, 0, 0, 0, 0, 0, 0 };
    }
    ICryptoTransform cc = des.CreateDecryptor();
    byte[] _input = Convert.FromBase64String(input);
    byte[] retVal = cc.TransformFinalBlock(_input,0,_input.Length);
    System.Text.UnicodeEncoding encoder = new UnicodeEncoding();
    return encoder.GetString(retVal);
}
```

The code above creates a byte array of the public-key encrypted, base64-encoded session key, which will be the key used to encrypt the data in the SOAP message. This array is decrypted via the RSACryptoServiceProvider object, and is then stored in a new byte array. A new DESCryptoServiceProvider object is created and is stored in the des field. Its Key property is set to the newly-decrypted key, and its IV property is set to the zero-valued byte array shown above, since the key is unique enough in this case.

Then, once des is instantiated, a new ICryptoTransform object is created that decrypts the value entered as a parameter. This is converted back into a Unicode string and is then returned to the calling method.

Below we will recap how the decryption process occurs.

- ❑ Initially, an instance of the `RSACryptoServiceProvider` class is created. Doing this in a web scenario generates a few problems. The ASP.NET engine, which processes the ASP.NET web applications, does so using a special Windows domain identity called `ASPNET`. This identity does not have the power to access the default key store of any other user, while it does not have a key store of its own. Hence, it cannot obtain a crypto service provider when required.

  Therefore, we must force it to use the machine key store available in the documents and settings folder for all users under: `Application Data/Microsoft/Crypto/RSA/MachineKeys`. We must first make this folder a shared folder in the usual way. We must also allow the ASP.NET user full privileges to the folder. In our code, we must also create an instance of a `CspParameters` class and set its `Flags` property to `CspProviderFlags.UseMachineKeys`. Using the `RSACryptoServiceProvider`'s overloaded constructer, which takes the `CspParameter` as a parameter, creates the object. Unless we perform these operations, the default constructor of the `RSACryptoServiceProvider` will throw a cryptographic exception that it was unable to acquire the required crypto service provider for this instance.

  The RSA object is then formed using the private key pair of the server, which is hardcoded (truncated in the above code listing for the sake of clarity). Be warned that storing the private key in the source code is not a perfect solution, since the source code files are often targets of attack and can be stolen, leaving the web service vulnerable.

- ❑ The `KeyInfo.EncryptedKey` variable sent by the client is first converted into a byte array using the `FromBase64String()` static method of the `Convert` class and the byte array is passed into the RSA object through the `Decrypt()` method, whose second parameter is set to `false`. This parameter can only be set as true if both the client and the server computers have the high encryption pack installed, and we cannot be certain that this will be the case.

- ❑ A des crypto object is also created and populated with the decrypted session key returned from the RSA object, as well as the IV value of eight zeros. The `ICryptoStream` is obtained using the `CreateDecryptor()` method.

- ❑ The string value received from the client is converted into a byte array, using the `Convert.FromBase64String()` method, and this value is passed into the `ICryptoTransform` object to get the decrypted value of the string as a byte array.

- ❑ For converting this byte array back into a string, we use the UnicodeEncoding class. All strings are Unicode in the .NET Framework, so this will allow users in various locales to perhaps use a different alphabet for their data.

Let's return to the `GetAccountBalance()` method. If the response should be encrypted, the `GetAccountBalance()` method calls an `EncryptReturnValues()` method and passes to it a copy of the DataSet ds. As the name of the method suggests, this method encrypts the values of the `SubAccountID` column in the data set. Instead of passing the data set ds directly into this method, a copy of it is made. This is because encrypting the values within the DataSet will permanently alter the in-memory DataSet, which is not required, as only the client requires this. The code for the `EncryptReturnValues()` method is as follows:

```
private DataSet EncryptReturnValues(DataSet retVal)
{
    ICryptoTransform cc = des.CreateEncryptor();
    System.Text.UnicodeEncoding encoder = new UnicodeEncoding();
    foreach(DataRow dr in retVal.Tables["AccountInfo"].Rows)
```

```
    {
        byte[] _input = encoder.GetBytes((string)dr["SubAccountID"]);
        dr["SubAccountID"] = Convert.ToBase64String(
            cc.TransformFinalBlock(_input, 0, _input.Length));
    }
    return retVal;
}
```

Here you will find that we access the string values within the SubAccountID column of the data table and pass that value to the ICryptoTransform object cc to get the encoded values, which are then converted into a base64-encoded string and are placed inside the DataSet.

Creating the TransferMoney() Method

In this section, we will see how the second operation of the web service, TransferMoney(), is coded. For this method, there will be a few additional parameters encrypted. Change the method as follows:

```
[WebMethod(Description = "Transfers funds to the extent specified in "
    + "'Amount' from the account specified in the 'AccountID' to "
    + "the Account specified in the 'DestinationID'")]
[SoapHeader("token", Direction=SoapHeaderDirection.In, Required=false)]
public bool TransferMoney(string sourceID, string destinationID,
                          int amount)
{
    this.CheckCredentials();
    if (this.token.AreParametersEncrypted)
    {
        foreach(string name in this.token.EncryptedParameterNames)
        {
            if(name.Equals("SourceID"))
                sourceID = this.DecryptString(sourceID);
            if(name.Equals("DestinationID"))
                destinationID = this.DecryptString(destinationID);
        }
    }
    ds = (DataSet)Application["2145B4567K"];
    DataRow dr = AccountServicesHelper.GetDataField(
        ds,"AccountInfo",sourceID,"SubAccountID");
    dr["Balance"] = (int)dr["Balance"] - amount;
    dr = AccountServicesHelper.GetDataField(
        ds,"AccountInfo",destinationID,"SubAccountID");
    dr["Balance"] = (int)dr["Balance"] + amount;
    return true;
}
```

The above method takes the source and destination account numbers and the amount to be transferred between them as parameters. It checks the credentials of the user, as usual, and if the parameters are encrypted it then decrypts them first using the DecryptString() method we coded earlier. As with the TransferMoney() methods seen earlier, it then retrieves the DataSet from the Application object and amends its values accordingly, returning true on success. An exception will be thrown if it fails.

Now that the service is created, we can move on to creating the client side code.

Creating the SOAP Encryption Client Code

Add the event handlers for the `mnuSOAPEncrypt` item, as for the other items, only setting `this.ServiceToUse` to `Services.SOAPEncryptionService`, and `this.Text` to "WROX Bank SOAP Header Encryption Client." In the `btnGetInfo_Click()` method, add the following statement:

```
case Services.SOAPEncryptionService:
  ds = this.GetInfo_SOAPEncryptionService();
  break;
```

Run the `wsdl.exe` tool and output the contents to `SOAPEncryptService.cs`. Again, add a sensible namespace to this code, say `SOAPEncrypt`, and add it to your project. Add the following lines to the top of your class, and to the constructor, respectively:

```
private SOAPEncrypt.SOAPHeaderService wsSoapEncryptionService
...
  wsSOAPEncryptionService = new SOAPEncrypt.SoapEncryptionService();
  wsSOAPEncryptionService.Url =
      ConfigurationSettings.AppSettings["SoapEncryptionService"];
```

Add the relevant key-value pair to the config file for this application as seen in the earlier sections. Also, add statements for `System.Text` and `System.Security.Cryptography`.

Coding of Client Side Encryption

When the user presses the button on the form, if `mnuSoapEncrypt` is selected, control passes to the following function:

```
#region Get Account Info from SOAP Encryption Service
private DataSet GetInfo_SOAPEncryptionService()
{
  SOAPEncrypt.Credentials token = new SOAPEncrypt.Credentials();
  token.KeyInfo = new SOAPEncrypt.KeyInformation();
  token.AccountID = this.txtAccount.Text;
  token.PIN = this.txtPIN.Text;
  token.IsPINEncrypted = true;
  token.AreParametersEncrypted = false;
  token.RequireEncryptedResponse = true;
  EncryptHeaderInformation(token, null);
  this.wsSOAPEncryptionService.CredentialsValue = token;
  try
  {
    return DecryptReturnValues(
        wsSOAPEncryptionService.GetAccountBalance());
  }
  catch(Exception e)
  {
    MessageBox.Show(e.ToString());
    this.StatusBar.Text = e.Message;
    return null;
  }
}
```

We initially create an instance of the SOAPEncrypt.Credentials object. This token variable is then passed as parameters of a EncryptHeaderInformation() method, together with a second parameter set as null, indicating that we don't, at present, require any of the parameters of this service to be encrypted, since there are no parameters for the CheckBalance() method. The token becomes the CredentialsValue of the wsSOAPEncryptionService object. The method then attempts to return the unencrypted DataSet returned by the web service.

The decryption of the DataSet takes place through the DecryptReturnValues() method:

```
private DataSet DecryptReturnValues(DataSet retVal)
{
  if(this.SessionKey != null)
  {
    DESCryptoServiceProvider des = new DESCryptoServiceProvider();
    des.Key = this.SessionKey;
    des.IV = new byte[]{ 0, 0, 0, 0, 0, 0, 0, 0 };
    ICryptoTransform cc = des.CreateDecryptor();
    System.Text.UnicodeEncoding encoder = new UnicodeEncoding();
    foreach(DataRow dr in retVal.Tables["AccountInfo"].Rows)
    {
      byte[] _input = Convert.FromBase64String(
          (string)dr["SubAccountID"]);
      dr["SubAccountID"] = encoder.GetString(
          cc.TransformFinalBlock(_input, 0, _input.Length));
    }
  }
  return retVal;
}
```

The SessionKey field is a byte array and is set during the EncryptHeaderInformation() method, shown next. If it is defined, we create a new DESCryptoServiceProvider object and set the IV to a byte array filled with zeroes, as in the web service code. The key used is that stored in the SessionKey field. The rest of the code is similar to that used in the EncryptReturnValues() method in the web service. The difference is we create an ICryptoTransform decryptor object, rather than an encryptor object.

The EncryptHeaderInformation() Method

In this section, we will see the code of the EncryptHeaderInformation() method, which encrypts the PIN and parameter values. As the code is lengthy, it is split into smaller sections and explanation is offered for each section:

```
private byte[] SessionKey;

private string[] EncryptHeaderInformation(SOAPEncrypt.Credentials token,
                                          string[] paramValues)
{
  token.EncryptionMethod = "DES";
  System.Security.Cryptography.CspParameters param =
      new CspParameters();
  param.Flags = CspProviderFlags.UseMachineKeyStore;
  RSACryptoServiceProvider rsa = new RSACryptoServiceProvider(param);
  rsa.FromXmlString(token.KeyInfo.EncryptionPublicKey);
```

In the above lines, an instance of the `RSACryptoServiceProvider` class is instantiated in the method explained earlier. This RSA object is given the value of the server's public key. The value of the server's public key is collected from the instance of the `token` field by reading the default value of its `KeyInfo.EncryptionPublicKey` field.

```
DESCryptoServiceProvider des = new DESCryptoServiceProvider();
des.IV = new Byte[]{ 0, 0, 0, 0, 0, 0, 0, 0 };
des.GenerateKey();
SessionKey = des.Key;
```

Here, an instance of the `DESCryptoServiceProvider` is created using the default constructor and its `IV` property with a byte array containing eight zeros, as used in all the code so far. The `des` object thus created contains a randomly generated key, which we are going to use as the session key. We extract its key value into a byte array called `SessionKey`, defined at class level.

```
System.Text.UnicodeEncoding converter = new UnicodeEncoding();
byte[] InputBytes = converter.GetBytes(token.PIN);
ICryptoTransform cc = des.CreateEncryptor();
byte[] OutputBytes = cc.TransformFinalBlock(InputBytes, 0,
                                        InputBytes.GetLength(0));
```

Next, we convert the PIN value entered by the user into a byte array, using the `UnicodeEncoding` class described earlier. At this stage, we extract an instance of `ICryptoStream` from the `des` object, invoking its `CreateEncryptor()` method. When we pass a byte array into this stream, we get an encrypted byte array as its output.

```
token.PIN = Convert.ToBase64String(OutputBytes);
```

The byte array containing the cipher value of the PIN is converted into a base64-encoded string. The following lines are required to repeat the process if the user wants to encrypt any of the parameters passed to the web service.

```
if(token.AreParametersEncrypted)
{
  for (int x=0; x<paramValues.Length; x++)
  {
    InputBytes = converter.GetBytes(paramValues[x]);
    OutputBytes = cc.TransformFinalBlock(InputBytes, 0,
        InputBytes.GetLength(0));
    paramValues[x] = Convert.ToBase64String(OutputBytes);
  }
}
```

Now we need to encrypt the `SessionKey` using the RSA crypto object. The following lines of code do that:

```
byte[] EncodedSessionKey = rsa.Encrypt(SessionKey, false);
token.KeyInfo.EncryptedKey =
    Convert.ToBase64String(EncodedSessionKey);
```

539

Here the `SessionKey` is passed into the RSA object and its encrypted double is collected using the RSA object's `Encrypt()` method. The result of this encryption is converted into a string using Base64 encoding and is stored in the `KeyInformation` object's `EncryptedKey` value.

```
    return paramValues;
}
```

The process is identical in respect to the other web method, `TransferMoney()`, except that in this case, there are two parameters for encryption and the `RequireEncryptedResponse` value is set to `false`, since this method returns only a Boolean value.

Pitfalls to be Wary Of and Precautions to be Taken

Although the above service uses strong key encryption, which is very difficult to crack, we must focus our attention on a few pitfalls.

First of all, mere encryption does not guard against **Play Back** attacks, in which a malicious attacker snoops on the client server communications, records the SOAP message, and replays it over and over again – especially the "`TransferMoney()`" method – using IP address spoofing, thus draining the account of its entire balance.

Adding a timestamp and attaching it to the session key can prevent this. To do that, we must convert the session key into a string form before its encryption, attach the time stamp as a fixed number of characters at the end of the string, and convert it back into a byte array for encryption. The server performs the opposite of this process; it first decrypts the session key into a string and strips the specified number of characters from the end and reads these values into a time value.

The remaining part of the session key is then converted into a byte array to create the decryptor. The time stamp and the session key are stored in its internal data storage, which may be a database backend, and are compared with an earlier request received from the same client. If the client sends the same time stamp and session key pair twice, this means that it is a Play Back; therefore, we must also write code that writes this to a security audit log and informs the administrators that hackers are attempting a Play Back attack.

The SOAP message sent by the client is not tamper-proof. A Man-in-the-Middle attacker will be able to send his own messages, masquerading as a genuine client message, since the public key of the web service is publicly available through the WSDL of the service. Therefore, it needs digital signing to ensure that the message is tamper-proof.

The Man-in-the-Middle can obviously interrupt the WSDL-transmitted public key and send another key to the client. Since the key is not digitally signed, the client doesn't know that the key received is the one the server sent. This allows a malicious individual to snoop on the transmitted message and send a new message, pretending to be the original client, and so also tamper with the return message from the server.

Digitally Signing SOAP Messages

XML Signature is a standard recommended by the W3C and was discussed in detail in Chapter 7. The WS-Security specifications also embed this standard in its recommendations for SOAP messages, which were discussed in Chapter 11.

In the .NET Framework, the `System.Security.Cryptography.Xml` namespace contains various options for digitally signing an XML document. Therefore, it is quite an easy task to digitally sign an XML document and then verify the signature using the `SignedXml` class found in the said namespace. However, over the Web there is no provision in the `SignedXml` class to generate an asymmetric signing key, since the base class uses a 40 byte SHA1 session key and cannot take a user-generated `RSACryptoServiceProvider` value at the decryption end. Therefore, there have been few models available for digitally signing a SOAP message for a web service operation.

This restriction would require us to write our own implementation of a digital signature of SOAP messages, using the cryptographic classes found in the Framework. However, if we used this mechanism, we would still have no guarantee that the public key transmitted from the server is the one received by the client. It would require far more work than has been done so far to achieve this still-insecure mechanism.

In light of this, we will not discuss the process involved in coding an XML Signature principle here. It requires much tinkering with a class that derives from the `SoapExtensionAttribute`, and requires much code at the client and the server end to deal with this while achieving no further levels of security. If you implemented the timestamp discussed in the previous section, and somehow securely transmitted the public key to the client, the system discussed in the previous section would be secure.

We can do better than this, however, by looking at a tool provided by Microsoft. This is a pre-release version of the **Web Services Development Kit** (**WSDK**). The managed classes provided in this package contain the required support to access and manage certificates and certificate stores.

A WSDK Service

For the WSDK service we are about to create to work, you must have the following:

❑ The WSDK

You may download, free of charge, the pre-release from Microsoft's web site. Either search in MSDN downloads, or navigate to this link:
http://msdn.microsoft.com/downloads/default.asp?URL=/downloads/sample.asp?url=/MSDN-FILES/027/001/997/msdncompositedoc.xml.

❑ A valid X509Certificate issued by a trusted certificate authority

This is capable of being used for digitally signing an e-mail message and has a private key associated with it within your computer. You may obtain the certificate from a public certificate authority like Verisign and follow the instructions to install it. If your server machine is installed with a certificate server, you may obtain a digital certificate by accessing the http://<yourserver>/certserv web page on your browser and applying for a certificate through the web pages presented.

For installing the WSDK, please follow the instructions given in the supplied `Readme.txt` file very carefully, since according to reports posted in various lists, not many people have succeeded in successfully installing and testing the WSDK, especially the security-related samples. The WSDK should be installed at both the server and client machine.

You can verify if the certificates are properly installed for use with this sample by going through the following steps:

- ❏ Open the Microsoft Management Console by typing MMC in the Run dialog.
- ❏ In MMC, select the Console | Add/Remove Snap in... menu item.
- ❏ Select "Add" from the dialog that appears, and choose the Certificates item.
- ❏ In the wizard that follows, select the "My user account" option and click Finish.
- ❏ Again press Add and select Certificates. This time select the "Computer account" option.

At the end of this, you will be presented with a console that contains two certificate stores with subfolders. If you expand the "Personal" node in the "Certificates - Current User" root node, you will find the name of the right-hand side pane.

Since your own machine's certificate server has issued the certificate, it is issued by a "Trusted" source. To ensure that the server can verify the certificate, you must export the certificate using the context menu in the MMC and choosing the Export option. When exporting the certificate, export the private key also. In that case, you will be asked for a password so that the file isn't saved in an openly viewable form.

Configuration of the Certificate Store on the Server

The next step is to import the certificate into the "Personal" node of your server's local computer store. To do that, you must first copy the exported certificate file to the server machine. Because this file is password-protected and encrypted using strong key encryption, it can safely be sent over the wire.

In the server machine, which hosts the web service, create an MMC snap in the same manner as specified above. This time select the "Personal" node of the "local computer" root node. Using the context menu, select the "Import" option and give the address of the saved certificate file when asked. At the end of this step, you will find that the certificate's name appears in the "personal" node of the "local Computer" root node in the MMC snap-in.

Setting up the Web Service

Just as you did before, add a new web service item to the project called WSDKService and add a reference to the AccountServices project. If you have correctly installed the WSDK, Microsoft.WSDK.dll will also be an available assembly to reference. Select this item.

In the WSDKService.asmx.cs code behind the file, add the following using statements:

```
using Microsoft.WSDK;
using Microsoft.WSDK.Security;
using Microsoft.WSDK.Security.Cryptography;
using Microsoft.WSDK.Security.Cryptography.X509Certificates;
using Microsoft.WSDK.Timestamp;
using System.Configuration;
```

Now open the `web.config` file and add the following lines to this configuration file under the `System.Web` node:

```
<httpModules>
  <add name="WSDK" type="Microsoft.WSDK.HttpModule, Microsoft.WSDK,
    Version=1.0.0.0, Culture=neutral, PublicKeyToken=31bf3856ad364e35" />
</httpModules>
```

The above code specifies that the `ASP.NET` processor should handle the `Microsoft.WSDK.WSDKModule object`, which is derived from the `System.Web.HttpModule` base class whenever a web request is received for any file within the virtual subdirectory. The **WSDK** does most of its processing at the module level.

The code for declaring the `DataSet` variable and initializing it in the constructor is as in the earlier versions. However, the code for the two web methods is different and is shown below:

```
/// <summary>
/// Gets a <c>DataSet</c> object containing information about two dummy
/// Sub Accounts for a given Account No: 2145B4567K and PIN: "4848"
/// </summary>
    [WebMethod(Description="Returns the balance credit in the account "
        + "for a given account number")]
    public DataSet GetAccountBalance(string AccountID, string PIN)
    {
      ds = (DataSet)Application["2145B4567K"];
      SoapContext requestContext = HttpSoapContext.RequestContext;
      if (requestContext == null)
        throw new ApplicationException("Only SOAP requests are permitted.");

      // Make sure the security information is acceptable
      if ( !IsValid(requestContext) )
      {
        throw new SoapException("The security information supplied " +
            "was not valid.", new System.Xml.XmlQualifiedName(
            "Bad.Security", "http://microsoft.com/gxatk/samples/SumService")
        );
      }
      // Retrieve the response's SOAP context
      SoapContext responseContext = HttpSoapContext.ResponseContext;
      // Set the expiration on the response to 1 minute
      responseContext.Timestamp.Ttl = 60000;
      if ((AccountID == "2145B4567K")&&(PIN=="4848"))
        return (DataSet) Application["2145B4567K"];
      else
        throw new Exception("No Such Account Exists");
    }
```

The **WSDK**'s `HttpContext` object has a static property called `RequestContext` that obtains the context of the present web method call. This `SoapContext` allows us to read all the security-related information passed by the client. Therefore, if we get an empty context, or a null value, we reject the method call.

The context is then passed into a private method, `IsValid()`, shown below:

```
private bool IsValid(SoapContext context)
{
  // No tokens means that the message can be rejected quickly
  if ( context.Security.Tokens.Count == 0 )
    return false;
  bool valid = false;
  // Checks for a Signature that signed the SOAP body and uses a token
  // that we accept.
  for(int i = 0; valid == false && i < context.Security.Elements.Count;
      i++ )
  {
    Signature signature = context.Security.Elements[i] as Signature;
    // We only care about signatures that signed the soap Body
    if(signature != null && signature.IncludesSoapBody)
    {
      X509SecurityToken x509token =
          signature.SecurityToken as X509SecurityToken;

      if (x509token != null)
      {
        // This is where a typical web service would actually perform
        // authorization given the certificate. In this sample we let
        // everybody through
        valid = true;
      }
    }
  }
  return valid;
}
```

This method just checks to see if the request context has a `Signature` element, and an `X509Certificate` within it. If the request passes both these tests, the request is permitted.

Although this may look very simple, all the security checks take place at the `HttpModule` level. Decryption of the client message also takes place there. For the purpose of message decryption, we need not do anything within the web service class. If the `WSDKModule` sees an `<EncryptedData>` element within the SOAP message, it is automatically decrypted.

The second web method is similar:

```
[WebMethod(Description="Transfers funds to the extent specified in "
    + "'Amount' from the account specified in the 'AccountID' to "
    + "the Account specified in the 'DestinationID'")]
public bool TransferMoney(string accountID, string pin, string source,
                     string destination, int amount)
{
  SoapContext requestContext = HttpSoapContext.RequestContext;
  if (requestContext == null)
    throw new ApplicationException("Only SOAP requests are permitted");

  // Make sure the security information is acceptable
```

```
            if(!IsValid(requestContext))
            {
              throw new SoapException("The security information supplied was "
                 + "not valid.", new System.Xml.XmlQualifiedName(
                 "Bad.Security",
                 "http://microsoft.com/gxatk/samples/SumService"));
            }

            // Retrieve the response's SOAP context
            SoapContext responseContext = HttpSoapContext.ResponseContext;

            // Set the expiration on the response to 1 minute
            responseContext.Timestamp.Ttl = 60000;
            if((accountID == "2145B4567K")&&(pin=="4848"))
            {
              ds = (DataSet)Application["2145B4567K"];
              DataRow dr = AccountServicesHelper.GetDataField(
                 ds,"AccountInfo",Source,"SubAccountID");
              dr["Balance"] = (int)dr["Balance"] - Amount;
              dr = AccountServicesHelper.GetDataField(
                 ds,"AccountInfo",Destination,"SubAccountID");
              dr["Balance"] = (int)dr["Balance"] + Amount;
              return true;
            }
            else
              throw new ApplicationException("No Such Account Exists");
      }
```

Setting up the WSDK Client

In this section we are going to add a new code file to the WROXClient project. To use the WSDK Service in the WROXClient project, we need to add a new dialog box contained in a code file called X509CertificateStoreDialog.cs. Instead of creating a new dialog box ourselves, we choose to add this file from the samples provided by Microsoft in the WSDK. You will find this file in the <WSDK installation Directory>\samples\quickstart\ folder. Copy this file into your project and add it to the project using the solution explorer, using the Add New Item | Existing File context menu option.

The code contains the definition for two classes, StoreDialog and SelectCertificateDialog. The latter is a Form. The StoreDialog class's constructor accepts a user-supplied X509CertificateStore object. This class has a SelectCertificate() public method. When called, this method first checks if the computer's operating system is Windows XP. If the machine is run under Windows XP, it uses Win XP's built-in "Certificate Dialog" SDK method and retrieves the certificate selected by the user, through an interop mechanism. If the machine is not run on Windows XP, an instance of the SelectCertificateDialog is created. This is a simple dialog box with a DataList containing the names of the X509Certificates available in the user's certificate store. When the user selects a certificate it is returned to the calling code.

A more detailed explanation of the code is available in the WSDK documentation.

Adding a Proxy Object to the WSDK Web Service

In this section we will see how a proxy class for the WSDK web service is generated and how it is modified and added to the project.

At this stage, we must create the proxy class object for the `WSDKService` web service, using `wsdl.exe`.

Once generated, and Now, we open this `Reference.cs` file and make the following modifications in it:

❑ Add a reference to the `Microsoft.WSDK` namespace

❑ Modify the class declaration so it derives from `Microsoft.WSDK.WSDKClientProtocol`, instead of `System.Web.Services.Protocols.SoapHttpClientProtocol`

❑ Give the class a sensible namespace, like `localhost` or `WSDKService`

The relevant lines of code read as follows:

```
namespace WROXClient.localhost4 {
    using System.Diagnostics;
    using System.Xml.Serialization;
    using System;
    using System.Web.Services.Protocols;
    using System.ComponentModel;
    using System.Web.Services;


    /// <remarks/>
    [System.Diagnostics.DebuggerStepThroughAttribute()]
    [System.ComponentModel.DesignerCategoryAttribute("code")]
    [System.Web.Services.WebServiceBindingAttribute(Name=
     "MessageIntegrityServiceSoap", Namespace="http://tempuri.org/")]
    public class MessageIntegrityService :
    System.Web.Services.Protocols.SoapHttpClientProtocol {

        public PublicKeyHeader PublicKeyHeaderValue;
```

The GetInfo_WSDKService() Method

Add an event handler for `mnuWSDKSecurity` in the same way we did for the other menu options, and add the following lines to the class file above and inside the constructor:

```
    private WSDKService.MessageIntegrityService wsWSDKService;
    ...
      wsWSDKService = new WSDKService.MessageIntegrityService();
      wsWSDKService.Url =
          ConfigurationSettings.AppSettings["WSDKService"];
```

Now add another case statement in the `btnGetInfo` event handler so that if `ServiceToUse` is set to `Services.WSDKService`, it calls the `GetInfo_WSDKService()` method. The code for this function is as follows:

```
    #region Get Account Info from WSDK Service
    X509Certificate cert;
    private DataSet GetInfo_WSDKService()
    {
      SoapContext requestContext = wsWSDKService.RequestSoapContext;
      X509SecurityToken token;
    // X509Certificate cert;
      try
      {
```

```
            if(cert==null)
              cert =GetCertificate();
            // Generate the Asymmetric key
            token = GetToken(true);
            if(token == null)
              throw new ApplicationException("No security token provided");
            // Adds the X.509 certificate to the header.
            requestContext.Security.Tokens.Add(token);
            // Specifies that the SOAP message is signed using this X.509
            // certificate
            requestContext.Security.Elements.Add(new Signature(token));
            // Adds an EncryptedData element to the security collection
            // to encrypt the request.
            token = GetToken(false);
            // Adds the X.509 certificate to the header.
            requestContext.Security.Tokens.Add(token);
            // Specifies that the SOAP message is encrypted using
            // this X.509 certificate
            requestContext.Security.Elements.Add(new EncryptedData(token));
            return wsWSDKService.GetAccountBalance(this.txtAccount.Text,
                                        this.txtPIN.Text);
          }
        catch(Exception e)
        {
          MessageBox.Show(e.ToString());
          this.StatusBar.Text = e.Message;
          return null;
        }
      }
      #endregion
```

Just as we had done on the server, here the code first obtains the `SoapContext` object using the static `HttpContext.RequestSoapContext` property. It then calls the private `GetCertificate()` method if `cert` hasn't yet been defined. The code for this is given in the next section. This method returns an X509 Certificate selected by the user to use in the web service operation. This certificate is stored in the global variable, `cert`.

The following tasks are performed at this stage:

❑ The code calls a `GetToken()` method, which returns a valid `X509SecurityToken` object. The `true` parameter passed to it tells it to return a token capable of digital signature.

❑ It adds the token to the `Security.Tokens` collection. This action instructs the WSDK to include the `KeyInfo` XML element necessary for the digital signature

❑ It then adds a new `Signature` object to the `Security.Elements` collection. This action tells the WSDK to add the element to the SOAP message, and to digitally sign the message. In the current pre-release version of the WSDK, there is no provision to specify which part of the SOAP message to be signed. It signs the entire message, excluding the `Signature` element.

❑ It then calls the `GetToken()` method with `false` passed as its parameter. This parameter value tells the method to return a token capable of encryption. This is added to the `Security.Tokens` collection.

❑ Finally it adds a new `EncryptedData` element to the `Security.Elements` collection.

The GetCertificate() Method

In the previous section we saw that a private method called GetCertificate() is called to obtain the X509 certificate chosen by the user. The code for the GetCertificate() method is as follows:

```
public X509Certificate GetCertificate()
{
  //
  // The certificate for the target receiver should have been imported
  // into the "My" certificate store. This store is listed as "Personal"
  // in the Certificate Manager
  //
  X509CertificateStore store = X509CertificateStore.CurrentUserStore(
      X509CertificateStore.MyStore);
  bool open = store.OpenRead();
  try
  {
    //
    // Open a dialog to allow user to select the certificate to use
    //
    StoreDialog dialog = new StoreDialog(store);
    X509Certificate cert = dialog.SelectCertificate(IntPtr.Zero,
        "Select Certificate",
        "Choose a Certificate below for encryption.");
    if(cert==null)
      throw new ApplicationException("You chose not to select an "
          + "X509 certificate for encrypting your messages.");
    return cert;
  }
  finally
  {
    if(store!=null)
      store.Close();
  }
}
```

The code sets the certificate store to be used for a valid X509Certificate. Since we are selecting a user certificate for a client machine, the current user store is chosen for the purpose, and the certificate within the Current User Store is selected. The code then creates an instance of the StoreDialog object, passing the Store selected in the previous step at construction, and using the SelectCertificate() method. Finally the code checks that the certificate returned is not null before returning it.

The GetToken() Method

The code for the GetToken() method is as follows:

```
public X509SecurityToken GetToken(bool IsTokenForSigning)
{
  X509SecurityToken token = null;
  if((IsTokenForSigning) &&
      (!cert.SupportsDigitalSignature || !cert.PrivateKeyAvailable))
  {
    throw new ApplicationException("The certificate must support "
```

```
                + "digital signatures and have a private key available.");
        }
        else if((!IsTokenForSigning) &&
            !(cert.SupportsDataEncryption || cert.SupportsKeyEncipherment))
        {
            throw new ApplicationException("The certificate must support key "
                + "encipherment.");
        }
        else
            token = new X509SecurityToken(cert);
        return token;
    }
```

The X509Certificate object contains public methods to check if the certificate has a private key associated with it and if it supports encipherment. The above code first checks these properties, depending upon whether the parameter is true or false. If the parameter is true, it checks the later option, otherwise it checks for the former option.

After these tests, the method creates a new X509SecurityToken, passing the X509Certificate as the parameter for the constructer of the object. The X509SecurityToken is nothing but an encapsulation of the RSACryptoService provider in the WSDK. This object has internal methods to sign or encrypt messages. All we need to do is add a security token to the Security Collection of the message to use these capabilities.

The TransferMoney_WSDKCertificate() method

The code for the TransferMoney_WSDKService() method is shown below:

```
#region Transfer Money using WSDK service Service
private bool TransferMoney_WSDKService(int Amount)
{
    bool success = false;
    // return true;
    SoapContext requestContext = wsWSDKService.RequestSoapContext;
    X509SecurityToken token;
    // X509Certificate cert;
    try
    {
        if (cert== null)
            cert = GetCertificate();
        // Generate the Asymmetric key
        token = GetToken(true);
        if (token == null)
            throw new ApplicationException("No security token provided.");
        requestContext.Security.Tokens.Add(token);
        requestContext.Security.Elements.Add(new Signature(token));
        token = GetToken(false);
        requestContext.Security.Tokens.Add(token);
        // Specifies that the SOAP message is encrypted using
        // this X.509 certificate
        requestContext.Security.Elements.Add(new EncryptedData(token));
        success = this.wsWSDKService.TransferMoney(this.txAccount.Text,
```

```
            this.txPIN.Text, (string)this.cmbSource.SelectedItem,
            (string)cmbDestination.SelectedItem, Amount);
     }
     catch (Exception e)
     {
       MessageBox.Show(e.ToString());
       this.StatusBar.Text = e.Message;
       return false;
     }
     return success;
   }
   #endregion
```

Advantages and Pitfalls of the WSDKService

The WSDK provides us with a near-perfect mechanism for securing the SOAP messages. Since it uses X509 Certificates, the key management is taken care of by the inherent security mechanisms provided by the operating system, and neither the programmer nor the user is required to do anything for the safe custody of the keys.

The WSDK also automatically provides the time stamp specifications of the WS-Security, without the user having to do anything. However, in the server, we need to include a mechanism to log the time stamps and check if there is a Play Back attack on the server. The WSDK, besides supporting the WS Security protocol, also supports other web service protocols like WS Routing.

However, the WSDK is very difficult to configure, since the WSDK gives very little debugging information to the developer when an exception occurs. Because the entire security-related processing takes place at the HttpModule level, we are not able to see the actual SOAP message sent or received.

The present version of the WSDK has no provision for using a SmartCard certificate, so one has to rely on the e-mail protection X509 Certificate only. The present version of the WSDK does not support signing of parts of a SOAP message. However, Microsoft has indicated that these pitfalls will disappear in the final release of the WSDK.

Summary

In this chapter, we took a comprehensive look at how we can implement a secure web service, in a step-by-step incremental approach. We also examined the various problems arising in each of the implementations and how we can solve them, thus giving us a real-world perspective of the web services security scenario.

Toolkits

Toolkits provide some specific benefits to developers, such as:

- Providing additional documentation and training material for a particular application or language
- Shortening the learning curve required to implement with the given language
- Providing additional tools that were not available with the original software package
- Providing examples for use of the toolkit or SDK that act as template code
- Providing a means to enhance or extend the original application or language

We'll look at some of the toolkits available in the market today and a chart that shows all the standards implemented by these toolkits.

Resources

The web site URLs for the toolkits available are as follows:

Toolkit	Description	URL
Netegrity	Federated Identity, SAML	http://www.netegrity.com/
Oblix NetPoint 6	(Identity, SAML)	http://www.oblix.com/

Table continued on following page

Toolkit	Description	URL
Quadrasis	Enterprise Application Security Integration (EASI) platform	http://www.quadrasis.com/
Infomosaic Corporation SecureXML	XML digital signature	http://www.infomosaic.net/
IAIK JCE Toolkit	Java Cryptography Extension (JCE)	http://jce.iaik.tugraz.at/products/01_jce/index.php
NEC XML Digital Signature Library	W3C XML signature syntax and processing	http://www.sw.nec.co.jp/soft/xml_s/appform_e.html
Wedgetail JCSI XMLDsig	Java Crypto Security Implementation (JCSI) of W3C XML signature syntax and processing	http://www.wedgetail.com/jcsi/xmldsig/
Baltimore Keytools	W3C XML signature syntax and processing	http://www.Baltimore.com/keytools/xml/
Phaos	Phaos XML, Phaos SAML, Phaos XKMS, Phaos Liberty	http://www.phaos.com/products/category/xml.html
Ubisecure	Ubisignature, Ubilogin, Ubikey, Cryptobox	http://www.ubisecure.com/
RSA Bsafe		http://www.rsasecurity.com/products/bsafe/
Entrust Toolkits		http://www.entrust.com/products/index.htm
Verisign	XML Signature SDK	http://www.xmltrustcenter.org/xmlsig/developer/verisign/index.htm
IBM XML Security Suite		http://www.alphaworks.ibm.com/tech/xmlsecuritysuite/
Microsoft Visual Studio		http://www.microsoft.com/

Standards Chart

The information from the chart below reflects the study as published on the W3C web site. The chart reflects support for the standard with a *blank*, and lack of support with an *N*. Entrust and Verisign are not reflected in the W3C evaluation. The reference chart for W3C can be found at http://www.w3.org/Signature/2001/04/05-xmldsig-interop.html:

Standard	Baltimore	HP	IAIK	IBM	Infomosaic	Microsoft	NEC	Phaos	RSA	Ubisecure	Wedgetail
Detached Signature											
Enveloping Signature											
Enveloped Signature											
Signature Value generation and validation											
Manifest Digest Value generation and validation					N	N					N
Xpointer support									N		
Xpath support									N	N	N
DSig Xpath for enveloped signatures						N				N	N
XSLT					N				N	N	N
Retrieval Method				N		N				N	N
Digest Algorithm											
Encoding Algorithm											
MAC Algorithm											
Signature Algorithm											
Canonicalization Algorithm											
Signature Transform											

Tomcat/Axis Installation

We will begin by showing the installation on Windows, which is very simple for the 4.x branch of Tomcat. We will illustrate both of the most common options, starting with the installer.

For each of the following steps – for Windows, Linux, and Unix systems – you can get the distributions from the same folder on the Jakarta web site. Navigating to ttp://jakarta.apache.org/builds/ will present a list of the Jakarta projects. Choose the Tomcat version of your choice, which for the purpose of this chapter is Tomcat 4.0.4 (though later versions shouldn't change much from the process we will describe). At the time of writing, it can be found in http://jakarta.apache.org/builds/jakarta-tomcat-4.0/release/v4.0.4/bin/.

In the unlikely event that the files have been moved (the main Tomcat project page can be found at http://jakarta.apache.org/tomcat/ if you encounter trouble), it should not prove difficult to navigate to the files by following convention as above.

Navigating to the specific project will present you with a possibility of downloading archives, nightly builds (very likely to be unstable), test builds, and release builds (which is the type we want). As stated previously, we will be using the 4.0.4 version and we will begin with the binary distributions.

A final note before we begin: the available distributions of Tomcat are split into J2SDK 1.4 and JDK 1.3 versions. As discussed previously, J2SDK 1.4 includes an XML parser, which Tomcat requires. To save you 1.2 Mb of download, there is a Tomcat Light Edition available that does not include xerces.jar – the XML parser usually bundled with Tomcat. If you already have xerces.jar downloaded, then you can also download this edition.

The operative point is that, regardless of the JDK type you have installed and the JARs you have on your system, the full download will work; therefore we will show the installation of Tomcat from the full download. In addition, the JDK version you have does not change the way the server is installed at this time.

The Linux installation notes will be self-contained. If you are planning to deploy Tomcat on Linux, you should skip the next section.

Tomcat Windows Installer

Within the bin folder (on the page http://jakarta.apache.org/builds/jakarta-tomcat-4.0/release/v4.0.4/), you will find at least six distributions. The one we want is called `jakarta-tomcat-4.0.4.exe`. Save this file at a convenient location on your machine, and double-click the file to begin installation. You must agree with the general Apache license to continue.

.The next window allows you to install the following options:

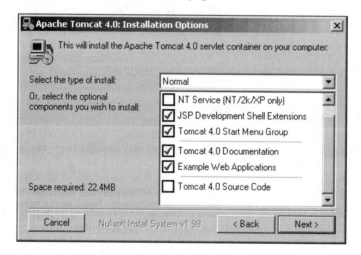

NT Service

Selecting the NT Service option allows you to start, stop, and restart Tomcat in the same way as any other NT service. This option is recommended if you are accustomed to managing your system services in this way.

It is only available for Windows NT, 2000, and XP, since Windows 98 is not a server OS. Tomcat will start as soon as the computer is switched on (and therefore will survive reboots of the machine) and will run in the background even when there is no user logged in. This clearly is the better deployment option, but it is probably not what you want for development.

> A bug in JDK 1.3 causes the termination of Java services when the user logs off – this
> has been fixed in JDK 1.4 and so you may wish to choose this as your JDK, as
> mentioned above.

This option is not available to Windows 98 users, who will be required to manually start and stop the server.

JSP Development Shell Extensions

In brief, this is a very useful scripting tool and it is recommended that you install the extensions.

Start Menu Group

This option adds shortcuts to the Start menu for starting, stopping, and uninstalling the server, as well as shortcuts to the key configuration files, the installation directory, and the documentation.

Tomcat Documentation

The Tomcat documentation is improving with time and is certainly worth installing.

Example Web Applications

The example web applications may be useful as a reference; however if they are installed and are operational, they represent a certain security risk since they provide a documented and known path into your server that may be used for DoS attack attempts. Choose to install them for now, since we will use them to check that the installation is working correctly.

> The latest information, including security issues with Tomcat, is available at
> http://jakarta.apache.org/tomcat/news.html.

Source Code

Finally, if you are keen to have the latest source code or want to ensure that Tomcat will compile from source, it is available.

Setting Environment Variables

In most cases, the various scripts provided with Tomcat will be able to determine the setup of your machine in such a way that no further intervention is strictly necessary. However, it is wise to add the following environment variables.

%CATALINA_HOME%

%CATALINA_HOME% is the directory where Tomcat is installed. Tomcat needs to know this information to find the resources that are referenced as relative paths to this folder. If you chose the default directory while installing, this will be C:\Program Files\Apache Tomcat 4.0.

Catalina is the codename of the Tomcat 4 project.

To add the environment variable, navigate to Start | Settings | Control Panel and choose System. Now choose the Advanced tab and select the Environment Variables... button. Now select the New button in the system variables (lower half) section and enter the following values, substituting the path to your installation if it is different from the one shown:

Windows 9x-and ME-Specific Issues

In Windows 9x, setting the environment variables is done by editing the file c:\autoexec.bat. Open the file and add the following line:

```
set CATALINA_HOME=c:\jakarta-tomcat-4.0.4
```

Notice that because of file length and spaces in the path issues, it is safer to install Tomcat directly onto c:\ rather than under Program Files. You will also need to increase the default environment space to Tomcat by opening a DOS prompt window, right-clicking on it, choosing Properties, selecting the Memory tab, and setting the initial environment to 4096 bytes (4Kb):

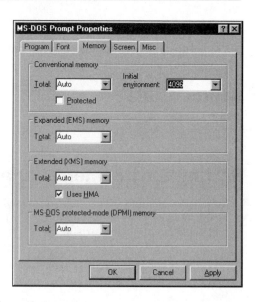

It also is possible to set another variable, called %CATALINA_BASE%, that allows multiple instances of the same distribution to be configured independently of each other. This is particularly relevant to hosting providers or in other situations in which multiple users have access to the same server.

Installing Tomcat On Windows Using the ZIP File

Installing Tomcat using the ZIP file is not much different from the process described above. The ZIP file is provided for those concerned with the security implications of downloading and running an executable over the Internet. The ZIP file is significantly bigger than the executable installer but has the same contents.

To install Tomcat using the ZIP, simply unpack the contents of the file, normally to C:\Program Files\Jakarta Tomcat 4.0.

Now add the %CATALINA_HOME% environment variable as above. To check your installation, you will need to follow slightly different instructions than before. Because the shortcuts for the server will not be created automatically, you will need to call a couple of batch files provided in the %CATALINA_HOME%\bin directory for this purpose.

To start the server, navigate to %CATALINA_HOME%\bin within the command prompt and type:

```
> cd %CATALINA_HOME%\bin
> startup.bat
```

Alternatively, you can start the server from the command prompt from any directory by adding the path C:\Program Files\Jakarta Tomcat 4.0 to the Path variable before calling the startup file as follows:

```
> set path=%path%;c:\Program Files\Jakarta Tomcat 4.0
> startup
```

A new window will open, just as in the previous installation method, showing that the server has started. To shut down Tomcat type shutdown.

Installing Tomcat On Linux

Installing Tomcat on Linux or Unix is easy. Many of the problems that existed with the other branch of Tomcat development, the 3.2.x line, do not exist for Tomcat 4. Download either the ZIP file or gzipped tar file if you have GNU gzip. The files can be found at http://jakarta.apache.org/builds/jakarta-tomcat-4.0/release/v4.0.4/bin/. If you have any problem finding it, try navigating to it from the Tomcat project site, http://jakarta.apache.org/tomcat/.

The Light Edition, available as jakarta-tomcat-4.0.4-LE-jdk14.zip and jakarta-tomcat-4.0.4-LE-jdk14.tar.gz, does not contain Xerces, an XML parser required by Tomcat, and is therefore 1.2Mb lighter in download size. This edition is aimed at installations on top of the 1.4 JDK, which has an XML parser included. In addition, the Light Edition does not provide support for JNDI or JavaMail, the JDBC 2 Extensions, or Tyrex (security, transactions, and resource pooling).

If you are using JDK 1.3, then download either `jakarta-tomcat-4.0.4.tar.gz` or `jakarta-tomcat-4.0.4.zip`. Also, if you have any stability issues with Tomcat 4 on JDK 1.4 it may be worth installing the complete binary before going to the trouble of installing 1.3 JDK. Since the 1.4 JDK itself is very stable, it is likely that it is Tomcat that is the problem.

RPMs are available for installation in the `rpms` folder if you prefer. Alternatively, the ZIP file has exactly the same contents, and you can then simply unzip the file without compatibility issues.

> **Opera 6.0 occasionally crashes, presumably because it does not recognize the `tar` MIME type. If you have these problems, try another browser or use the ZIP file.**

Unzip (and untar if necessary) the file onto your hard drive to a path such as `/usr/java/jakarta-tomcat-4.0.4`.

Installing the RPM for the full version 4.0.4 is done as follows:

```
# rpm -iv tomcat4-4.0.4-full.2jpp.noarch.rpm
```

`noarch` signifies the package is suitable for all architectures.

You should now export the `$CATALINA_HOME` variable, using the following command (in bash):

```
# CATALINA_HOME=/usr/java/jakarta-tomcat-4.04
# export CATALINA_HOME
```

Alternatively, add these commands to `~/.bashrc` or `/etc/profile` as we did for the JDK installation, or create a shell file, `tomcat.sh`, and place it in `/etc/profile.d`. It will be run automatically by `/etc/profile` at boot time to make the variable available to all users.

Catalina is the codename of the Tomcat 4 project.

You can now start Tomcat by running the following shell command:

```
# $CATALINA_HOME/bin/startup.sh
```

You can shut down Tomcat using `shutdown.sh`. If you want a script for restarting the server, copy and rename `shutdown.sh` as `restart.sh` and add the following line to the end:

```
exec "$PRGDIR"/"$EXECUTABLE" start "$@"
```

Alternately, you can simply write a script that calls shutdown followed by startup.

Viewing the Default Installation

To check that Tomcat is running, point your browser to http://localhost:8080/. You should see the following screenshot:

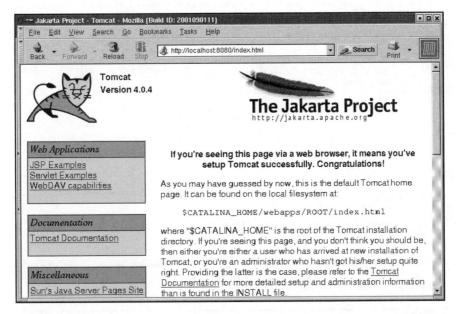

Choose the JSP Examples link from the left-hand side menu and select some of the examples to run. Check that they run without error messages. Do the same for the Servlet Examples to test this functionality.

Installing Axis

The Axis installation file may be downloaded from http://xml.apache.org/axis/. Extract the gzipped file to the desired folder. After extracting the files, we will need to configure Axis with Tomcat. Copy the newly created AXIS_HOME/webapps/axis folder to the CATALINA_HOME/webapps folder. We will configure our web applications in this folder. Now, to configure the web application folder under Tomcat, add the following line under the <Host> element in the CATALINA_HOME/conf/server.xml file:

```
<Context path="/axis" docBase="axis" debug="0" reloadable="true"/>
```

Next, we need to add the .jar files in AXIS_HOME/lib directory to the CLASSPATH. Also, we need to add the XML parser (xerces.jar) file in the CLASSPATH. This is done using the following command:

```
export CLASSPATH=$CLASSPATH:$CATALINA_HOME/common/lib/xerces.jar:
<AxisInstallation>/lib/axis.jar:<AxisInstallation>/lib/clutil.jar: <AxisInstallation>/lib/jaxrpc.jar:
<AxisInstallation>/lib/log4j-core.jar: <AxisInstallation>/lib/commons-logging.jar:
<AxisInstallation>/lib/tt-bytecode.jar: <AxisInstallation>/lib/wsdl4j.jar
```

Before running the above command, replace `<AxisInstallation>` with the appropriate directory name of the Axis installation.

To test the installation, start Tomcat and browse to http://localhost:8080/axis/. If the installation is correct, you will see the Axis home page in the browser as shown below:

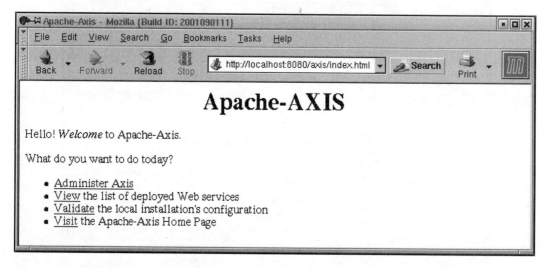

Now, follow the View link on this page, and you will get the following page:

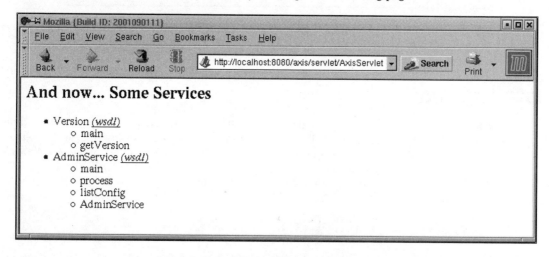

Tomcat SSL Configuration

To start with, we will have to acquire JSSE, if we are not running Java 2 SDK 1.4, since JSSE comes bundled with Java 2 SDK 1.4. **JSSE (Java Secure Socket Extension)** is collection of Java packages used to provide secured communication between the server and the client.

There might be some restrictions for SSL-based software depending upon the country you are in. Visit http://java.sun.com/products/jsse/ for further details and download the bundle accordingly.

Now extract the downloaded .jar file to any directory. Proceed with copying the jsse.jar, jcert.jar, and jnet.jar files in your %JAVA_HOME%/jre/lib/ext folder. We then add the following line in the java.security file located in the %JAVA_HOME%/jre/lib/security/ folder:

```
security.provider.3=com.sun.net.ssl.internal.ssl.Provider
```

Let's now have a look at how to configure Tomcat for SSL.

Generating Keystores and Certificates

First, we will start by generating keystore and the certificate, using the keytool tool bundled with Java 2 SDK 1.4. Make sure that %JAVA_HOME%\bin is in the path:

```
keytool -genkey -alias myservice -dname "CN=localhost, OU=X, O=Y, L=Z, S=XY, C=YZ"
 -keyalg RSA -keypass mypassword -storepass mypassword -keystore server.keystore
```

Now let's export it to the server.cer file:

```
keytool -export -alias myservice -storepass mypassword -file server.cer -keystore
server.keystore
```

The server's certificate is ready to be imported in the client's `keystore`:

```
keytool -import -v -trustcacerts -alias myservice -file server.cer -keystore
client.keystore -keypass mypassword -storepass mypassword
```

Tomcat Configuration

Uncomment the lines related to SSL in the `server.xml` file. Change the values of `keystoreFile` and `keystorePass` attributes. You could change the default port value of 8443:

```
<!-- Define an SSL HTTP/1.1 Connector on port 8443 -->
<Connector className="org.apache.catalina.connector.http.HttpConnector"
  port="8443" minProcessors="5" maxProcessors="75"
  enableLookups="true"
  acceptCount="10" debug="0" scheme="https" secure="true"<
  <Factory className="org.apache.catalina.net.SSLServerSocketFactory"
    keystoreFile="c:\path\name\to\your\server.keystore"
    keystorePass="mypassword"
    clientAuth="false" protocol="TLS"/<
  </Connector>
```

Restart the server and point your browser to https://localhost:8443/ in order to test it.

Deployment of Secure Web Service

It is easy to deploy the web service you have already created. Just create a deployment descriptor like:

```
<deployment xmlns="http://xml.apache.org/axis/wsdd/"
            xmlns:java="http://xml.apache.org/axis/wsdd/providers/java">

  <service name="YourSecureWebService" provider="java:RPC">
    <parameter name="className" value="YourSecureServer"/>
    <parameter name="methodName" value="*"/>
  </service>
</deployment>
```

And deploy:

```
java -Djava.protocol.handler.pkgs=com.sun.net.ssl.internal.www.protocol
-Djavax.net.ssl.trustStore= <path/to/your/client.keystore>
org.apache.axis.client.AdminClient
-lhttps://localhost:8443/axis/services/AdminService
<path/to/your/YourSecureWebService.wsdd>
```

Notice the use of `com.sun.net.ssl.internal.www.protocol` as the system property `java.protocol.handler.pkgs`, which is a URL handler for the `https` URL protocol type. The system property `javax.net.ssl.trustStore` is initialized to the client's `keystore` to make sure the certificate is furnished.

Index

A Guide to the Index

The index is arranged hierarchically, in alphabetical order, with symbols preceding the letter A. Most second-level entries and many third-level entries also occur as first-level entries. This is to ensure that users will find the information they require however they choose to search for it.

D

W

p2p.wrox.com
The programmer's resource centre

A unique free service from Wrox Press
With the aim of helping programmers to help each other

Wrox Press aims to provide timely and practical information to today's programmer. P2P is a list server offering a host of targeted mailing lists where you can share knowledge with your fellow programmers and find solutions to your problems. Whatever the level of your programming knowledge, and whatever technology you use, P2P can provide you with the information you need.

ASP — Support for beginners and professionals, including a resource page with hundreds of links, and a popular ASP.NET mailing list.

DATABASES — For database programmers, offering support on SQL Server, mySQL, and Oracle.

MOBILE — Software development for the mobile market is growing rapidly. We provide lists for the several current standards, including WAP, Windows CE, and Symbian.

JAVA — A complete set of Java lists, covering beginners, professionals, and server-side programmers (including JSP, servlets, and EJBs)

.NET — Microsoft's new OS platform, covering topics such as ASP.NET, C#, and general .NET discussion.

VISUAL BASIC — Covers all aspects of VB programming, from programming Office macros to creating components for the .NET platform.

WEB DESIGN — As web page requirements become more complex, programmer's are taking a more important role in creating web sites. For these programmers, we offer lists covering technologies such as Flash, Coldfusion, and JavaScript.

XML — Covering all aspects of XML, including XSLT and schemas.

OPEN SOURCE — Many Open Source topics covered including PHP, Apache, Perl, Linux, Python, and more.

FOREIGN LANGUAGE — Several lists dedicated to Spanish and German speaking programmers; categories include: NET, Java, XML, PHP and XML.

How to subscribe:
Simply visit the P2P site, at http://p2p.wrox.com/

wrox

Programmer to Programmer™

Registration Code : 76553T4Q9X007CK01

Wrox writes books for you. Any suggestions, or ideas about how you want information given in your ideal book will be studied by our team. Your comments are always valued at Wrox.

Free phone in USA 800-USE-WROX
Fax (312) 893 8001

UK Tel.: (0121) 687 4100   Fax: (0121) 687 4101

Professional Web Services Security – Registration Card

Name _____

Address _____

_____

_____

City _____ State/Region _____

Country _____ Postcode/Zip_____

E-Mail _____

Occupation _____

How did you hear about this book?

❏ Book review (name) _____

❏ Advertisement (name) _____

❏ Recommendation _____

❏ Catalog _____

❏ Other _____

Where did you buy this book?

❏ Bookstore (name) _____ City_____

❏ Computer store (name) _____

❏ Mail order_____

❏ Other _____

What influenced you in the purchase of this book?

❏ Cover Design ❏ Contents ❏ Other (please specify):

_____

How did you rate the overall content of this book?

❏ Excellent   ❏ Good   ❏ Average   ❏ Poor

What did you find most useful about this book? _____

_____

_____

What did you find least useful about this book? _____

_____

Please add any additional comments. _____

_____

_____

What other subjects will you buy a computer book on soon?

_____

What is the best computer book you have used this year?

_____

Note: This information will only be used to keep you updated about new Wrox Press titles and will not be used for any other purpose or passed to any other third party.

7655   Check here if you DO NOT want to receive support for this book ■   7655

wrox

Programmer to Programmer™

Note: If you post the bounce back card below in the UK, please send it to:

Wrox Press Limited, Arden House, 1102 Warwick Road,
Acocks Green, Birmingham B27 6HB. UK.

Computer Book Publishers